YO-BDI-804

IoT Fundamentals: Networking Technologies, Protocols, and Use Cases for the Internet of Things

David Hanes, CCIE No. 3491

Gonzalo Salgueiro, CCIE No. 4541

Patrick Grossetete

Robert Barton, CCIE No. 6660, CCDE No. 2013:6

Jerome Henry, CCIE No. 24750

Cisco Press

800 East 96th Street

Indianapolis, Indiana 46240 USA

IoT Fundamentals: Networking Technologies, Protocols, and Use Cases for the Internet of Things

David Hanes, CCIE No. 3491
Gonzalo Salgueiro, CCIE No. 4541
Patrick Grossetete
Robert Barton, CCIE No. 6660, CCDE No. 2013:6
Jerome Henry, CCIE No. 24750

Copyright© 2017 Cisco Systems, Inc.

Published by:
Cisco Press
800 East 96th Street
Indianapolis, IN 46240 USA

Printed in the United States of America

1   17

Library of Congress Control Number: 2017937632

ISBN-13: 978-1-58714-456-1

ISBN-10: 1-58714-456-5

Warning and Disclaimer

This book is designed to provide information about the core technologies that make up the Internet of Things, IoT. Every effort has been made to make this book as complete and as accurate as possible, but no warranty or fitness is implied.

The information is provided on an "as is" basis. The authors, Cisco Press, and Cisco Systems, Inc. shall have neither liability nor responsibility to any person or entity with respect to any loss or damages arising from the information contained in this book or from the use of the discs or programs that may accompany it.

The opinions expressed in this book belong to the author and are not necessarily those of Cisco Systems, Inc.

Trademark Acknowledgments

All terms mentioned in this book that are known to be trademarks or service marks have been appropriately capitalized. Cisco Press or Cisco Systems, Inc., cannot attest to the accuracy of this information. Use of a term in this book should not be regarded as affecting the validity of any trademark or service mark.

Special Sales

For information about buying this title in bulk quantities, or for special sales opportunities (which may include electronic versions; custom cover designs; and content particular to your business, training goals, marketing focus, or branding interests), please contact our corporate sales department at corpsales@pearsoned.com or (800) 382-3419.

For government sales inquiries, please contact governmentsales@pearsoned.com.

For questions about sales outside the U.S., please contact intlcs@pearson.com.

Feedback Information

At Cisco Press, our goal is to create in-depth technical books of the highest quality and value. Each book is crafted with care and precision, undergoing rigorous development that involves the unique expertise of members from the professional technical community.

Readers' feedback is a natural continuation of this process. If you have any comments regarding how we could improve the quality of this book, or otherwise alter it to better suit your needs, you can contact us through email at feedback@ciscopress.com. Please make sure to include the book title and ISBN in your message.

We greatly appreciate your assistance.

Editor-in-Chief: Mark Taub

Product Line Manager: Brett Bartow

Business Operation Manager, Cisco Press: Ronald Fligge

Executive Editor: Mary Beth Ray

Managing Editor: Sandra Schroeder

Development Editor: Eleanor Bru

Project Editor: Mandie Frank

Copy Editor: Kitty Wilson

Technical Editors: Robb Henshaw, Samuel Pasquier

Editorial Assistant: Vanessa Evans

Cover Designer: Chuti Prasertsith

Composition: codeMantra

Indexer: Cheryl Lenser

Proofreader: Sasirekha Durairajan

Americas Headquarters
Cisco Systems, Inc.
San Jose, CA

Asia Pacific Headquarters
Cisco Systems (USA) Pte. Ltd.
Singapore

Europe Headquarters
Cisco Systems International BV Amsterdam,
The Netherlands

Cisco has more than 200 offices worldwide. Addresses, phone numbers, and fax numbers are listed on the Cisco Website at **www.cisco.com/go/offices**.

Cisco and the Cisco logo are trademarks or registered trademarks of Cisco and/or its affiliates in the U.S. and other countries. To view a list of Cisco trademarks, go to this URL: www.cisco.com/go/trademarks. Third party trademarks mentioned are the property of their respective owners. The use of the word partner does not imply a partnership relationship between Cisco and any other company. (1110R)

About the Authors

David Hanes, CCIE No. 3491, is a Technical Leader specializing in IoT and working in Cisco Technical Services as part of the Cloud Support Technical Assistance Center (TAC). With experience in the incubation of new technologies, he is currently leading the TAC support effort for Cisco's IoT cloud solutions. He also has technical expertise in the areas of collaboration and cognitive computing.

David has multiple patents issued and pending in the areas of IoT and collaboration. He is an active participant in the SIP Forum and in the IETF as an RFC contributor and author. David has written and contributed to various industry publications and white papers and is a coauthor of the Cisco Press book *Fax, Modem, and Text for IP Telephony*. He has spoken at industry and technical conferences worldwide and has been honored as a Hall of Fame speaker by Cisco Live.

Since joining Cisco in 1997, David has worked as a TAC engineer for the WAN, WAN Switching, and Multiservice Voice teams; as a team lead for the Multiservice Voice team; as an escalation engineer covering a variety of VoIP technologies; and as a field trial support engineer. Prior to working at Cisco, David was a systems engineer for Sprint, where he gained his first computer networking experience working on the Frame Relay and X.25 protocols. He holds a degree in electrical engineering from North Carolina State University.

Gonzalo Salgueiro, CCIE No. 4541, is a Principal Engineer in Technical Services, working on several emerging technologies and the services opportunities they offer. Gonzalo has spent more than 20 years at Cisco, establishing himself as a subject matter expert, innovator, and industry thought leader in various technologies, including Collaboration, ML/AI, Cloud, and IoT.

Gonzalo is an established member of numerous industry organizations and is a regular presenter and distinguished speaker at a variety of technical industry conferences and Cisco events around the world. He currently holds various industry leadership roles, including serving as a member of the Board of Directors of the SIP Forum, co-chair of the INSIPID and SIPBRANDY IETF working groups, member of the IoT Directorate in the IETF, and co-chair of the WebRTC Task Group, IPv6 Task Group, and FoIP Task Group in the SIP Forum. He is an active contributor to various industry organizations and standardization activities.

Gonzalo co-authored the Cisco Press book *Fax, Modem, and Text for IP Telephony*. He has also co-authored 24 IETF RFCs, 4 IEEE papers, 4 ITU contributions, and numerous industry and academic research papers on a variety of different technical topics. He is also coinventor of 65+ patents (issued and pending) and has contributed to various interop and open source development efforts. Gonzalo received a master's degree in physics from the University of Miami.

Patrick Grossetete is a Distinguished Engineer, Technical Marketing, working on field communication architecture and design (IEEE 802.15.4g/e RF, IEEE 1901.2a PLC, LoRaWAN, IPv6, 6LoWPAN, RPL, …) in the Cisco Internet of Things Connected Group.

He joined Cisco through its acquisition of Arch Rock, where he was Director of Product Management and Customer Solutions, focusing on IPv6-based wireless sensor network technology for smart grid, energy, and environmental optimization applications.

Previously, Patrick led a product management team at Cisco, responsible for a suite of Cisco IOS software technologies, including IPv6 and IP Mobility. Patrick regularly speaks at conferences and industry events, including the IPv6 Forum, which he joined in 1999 as a Cisco representative. Patrick also acts as reviewer on European Commission–sponsored projects, including GEANT and ENVIROFI.

Patrick is coauthor of the books *Global IPv6 Strategies* and *Deploying IPv6 Networks*, published by Cisco Press, as well as several white papers, such as *Unified Field Area Network Architecture for Distribution Automation* (2014) and *IPv6 Architecture for Field Area Networks* (2012). In June 2003, he received the IPv6 Forum Internet Pioneer Award at the San Diego Summit, and he is an IPv6 Forum Fellow. Before his days at Cisco and Arch Rock, he worked at Digital Equipment Corporation as a consulting engineer and was involved with network design and deployment. He received a degree in computer science from the Control Data Institute, Paris, France.

Rob Barton, CCIE No. 6660 (R&S and Security), CCDE No. 2013:6, is a Principal Systems Engineer working in Cisco's Digital Transformation and Innovation organization. Rob is a registered professional engineer (P.Eng) and has worked in the IT industry for more than 20 years, the last 17 of which have been at Cisco. Rob graduated from the University of British Columbia with a degree in engineering physics, where he specialized in computer and radio communications. Rob's areas of interest include wireless communications, IPv6, IoT, and industrial control systems. Rob coauthored the Cisco Press book *End-to-End QoS,* 2nd edition. He resides in Vancouver, Canada, with his wife and two children.

Jerome Henry, CCIE No. 24750, is a Principal Engineer in the Enterprise Infrastructure and Solutions Group at Cisco systems. Jerome has more than 15 years' experience teaching technical Cisco courses in more than 15 countries and 4 languages, to audiences ranging from bachelor's degree students to networking professionals and Cisco internal system engineers. Focusing on his wireless and networking experience, Jerome joined Cisco in 2012. Before that time, he was consulted and taught heterogeneous networks and wireless integration with the European Airespace team, which was later acquired by Cisco to become their main wireless solution. He then spent several years with a Cisco Learning partner, developing networking courses and working on training materials for emerging technologies.

Jerome is a certified wireless networking expert (CWNE No. 45) and has developed multiple Cisco courses and authored several wireless books and video courses. Jerome is also a member of the IEEE, where he was elevated to Senior Member in 2013, and also participates with Wi-Fi Alliance working groups, with a strong focus on IoT and low power. With more than 10,000 hours in the classroom, Jerome was awarded the IT Training Award Best Instructor silver medal. He is based in Research Triangle Park, North Carolina.

Chapter Contributors

The authors would like to thank the following people for their content contributions and industry expertise in the following chapters:

Security (Chapter 7):

Robert Albach, Senior Product Manager, Cisco Industrial Security Portfolio

Rik Irons-McLean, Energy Solutions Architecture Lead, Cisco

Data Analytics (Chapter 8):

Brian Sak, CCIE No. 14441, Technical Solutions Architect, Big Data Analytics, Cisco

Kapil Bakshi, Distinguished Systems Engineer, Big Data and Cloud Computing, US Public Sector

Manufacturing (Chapter 9):

Brandon Lackey, Technology Entrepreneur and Co-Founder, DronePilots Network

Ted Grevers, Engineering Manager, Cisco IoT Vertical Solutions

Oil and Gas (Chapter 10):

Willy Fotso Guifo, Senior Manager IoT Services, Global Business Lead for the Oil and Gas Vertical, Cisco

Dimitrios Tasidis, Solutions Architect, IoT Services Technical Lead for the Oil and Gas Vertical, Cisco

Smart and Connected Cities (Chapter 12):

Munish Khetrapal, Director of Business Development, Smart + Connected Cities group, Cisco

Prachi Goel, Program Analyst, Smart + Connected Cities Solutions Management, Cisco

Mining (Chapter 14):

Lyle Tanner, Customer Solutions Architect, Cisco

Public Safety (Chapter 15):

Kevin Holcomb, Technical Marketing Engineer, IoT Vertical Solutions, Cisco

Kevin McFadden, Vertical Solutions Architect, Cisco

About the Technical Reviewers

Robb Henshaw is the head of Global Communications, IoT Cloud, at Cisco Jasper. Robb was previously the senior director of Global Communications for Jasper, a global IoT platform leader that was acquired by Cisco in March 2016. Prior to working at Jasper, Rob spent 15 years establishing and running global communications programs for mobile and wireless companies, including Airespace (acquired by Cisco), Proxim Wireless, and SugarSync (acquired by J2 Global).

Samuel Pasquier is head of Product Management for the IoT Connectivity portfolio in the Enterprise Networking Group (ENG) at Cisco. Based in San Jose, California, he is responsible for working closely with both the sales team and the engineering team to develop and execute the product strategy and roadmap for the entire IoT Connectivity portfolio, as well as the Cisco fog computing software solution (IOx).

Samuel has been with Cisco Systems since 2004. He spent six years on the Catalyst 6500 engineering team as a software technical leader. He designed, implemented, and sustained several key infrastructure features on the platform. Thanks to that previous experience, Samuel has a very deep understanding of software development and architecture. He was the product line manager for the Catalyst 6500/6800 and led the team of product managers that completed a full refresh of the Catalyst 6500 Portfolio with the launch of Catalyst 6800.

Prior to his current role, Samuel was leading the team of product managers defining the roadmap for the Catalyst Fixed Access Switches Portfolio (Catalyst 2960-X, 3750, 3650, and 3850).

Samuel holds a master's degree in computer science from *Ecole pour l'informatique et les techniques avancees* (EPITA) in France. He is a regular speaker at network industry events.

Dedications

From David Hanes:

To my loving wife, Holly, my best friend, inspiration, and biggest fan, whose unconditional love, support, and selflessness are the foundation for all the successes and achievements in my life, and to my amazing children, Haley, Hannah, and Kyle, who are true joys and blessings and ensure that my life never has a dull moment.

I would also like to dedicate this book to my wonderful parents—to my Dad for instilling in me a love of learning and always challenging me to push to new heights, and to my Mom for providing the encouragement and confidence to reach those heights.

From Gonzalo Salgueiro:

This book is dedicated to my family. First and foremost, to my loving wife and best friend, Becky, who is my inspiration and makes every day a dream come true. It's always been you—then, now, and forever. To our four amazing children: Alejandro, Sofia, Gabriela, and Mateo. They fill my life with immeasurable joy, wonder, and purpose. I love you all.

I also dedicate this book to my parents, Alberto and Elena, who are my inspiration and to whom I owe everything for all that I am today. I simply don't have the words to express my eternal gratitude for all you have sacrificed and given on my behalf.

Finally, I dedicate this book to my grandmother, Nelida, whom we tragically lost this past year. Only recently have I realized the extent to which my life is filled with the fingerprints of her kindness and grace.

From Patrick Grossetete:

To Mya and all new generations that will live with the Internet of Things.

From Rob Barton:

First, I would like to dedicate this book to my beautiful wife, Loretta. You have been my biggest supporter and cheerleader and have taught me so much over the past 20 years. Without your unending encouragement (not to mention your extreme patience and willingness to share my time with another book project), this undertaking would never have happened. Thanks to your loving support, I find myself in a position where I can pass on what I have learned to the next generation of Internet engineers. 너무 사랑해요.

I also want to dedicate this book to my parents, Richard and Peggy. It's thanks to mom and dad that I began to develop my interest in science and engineering, beginning with my first Lego set when I was four years old, down to the many hours Dad and I spent discussing physics and calculus and watching *The Mechanical Universe* together when I was a teenager.

I love you all so much!

From Jerome Henry:

This book is dedicated to my children, Ines and Hermes. Your curious minds stimulate my research every day.

Acknowledgments

We would like to acknowledge the following people, who helped us complete this project.

Michael Boland: Michael, your suggestions and industry expertise in mining were an incredible asset in the development of this book. We truly appreciate your time, thoughtfulness, and clear suggestions!

Maik Seewald: Maik, you are a true Internet engineer! Your assistance and suggestions helped clarify the utilities industry's direction on standards and protocols, helping make our book as up-to-date as possible.

Rick Geiger: Rick, you are one of the top utility experts in the world. Thanks for your help and suggestions on the utilities chapter.

Ken Batke: Thanks for your contribution and guidance of the utilities section. Your feedback was much appreciated.

Mahyar Khosravi: Mahyar, thanks for lending us your expertise in the oil and gas industry and all the feedback and suggestions to the oil and gas chapter.

Dave Cronberger: Huge thanks go out to Dave for his excellent guidance and feedback on the book. Dave, you're never shy to tell someone the straightforward advice they need and bring them back on track. Your reviews and feedback on the manufacturing section were invaluable!

Kyle Connor and Barb Rigel: Thanks, Kyle and Barb, for your very thorough reviews and feedback on the transportation section. Your guidance and insights on the state of this quickly transforming industry were an incredible help to our team.

Eleanor Bru: Ellie was our development editor on this project, and it was an absolute pleasure working with her. Thanks for your dedication and patience and for making the review process go so well.

Mary Beth Ray: We'd also like to send out a big thanks to Mary Beth for keeping us on track and supporting us all the way through this challenging project and ensuring that we had everything we needed to bring the book to completion.

Mandie Frank: As our project editor, Mandie tied up all the loose ends and helped us put the finishing touches on this book. Thanks, Mandie, for all your help in guiding us to the finish line!

Kitty Wilson: As our copyeditor, we thank you for the long hours you contributed in making the final edits to our text. Your meticulous attention to detail is greatly appreciated.

We would also like to acknowledge our management teams for their unwavering support and understanding as we worked long hours to meet the many deadlines associated with a publication such as this.

David would like to give a special thanks to Marty Martinez, Rob Taylor, Jitendra Lal, and Shane Kirby, for their guidance and support.

Gonzalo would like to thank the TS leadership team, especially Marc Holloman, Marty Martinez, and Tom Berghoff. This book wouldn't have been possible without their unwavering encouragement, belief, and support.

Patrick thanks the product management and engineering team from the IoT Connected Business Unit for their support and tireless efforts in making IoT products real.

Jerome would like to give a special thanks to Matt MacPherson, for sharing his wisdom and vision on the convergence of enterprise, 5G, and IoT.

Rob would also like to express his thanks to his leadership team, including Dr. Rick Huijbregts and Bernadette Wightman, for their strong support and backing during this project. Your focus on innovation is at the heart of the digital transformation revolution and has inspired much of the wisdom woven throughout the pages of this book.

Contents at a Glance

Contents

Reader Services

Register your copy at www.ciscopress.com/title/ISBN for convenient access to downloads, updates, and corrections as they become available. To start the registration process, go to www.ciscopress.com/register and log in or create an account.* Enter the product ISBN 9781587144561 and click Submit. Once the process is complete, you will find any available bonus content under Registered Products.

* Be sure to check the box saying that you would like to hear from us to receive exclusive discounts on future editions of this product.

Icons Used in This Book

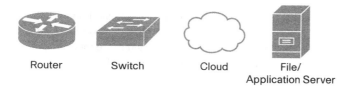

Router   Switch   Cloud   File/
Application Server

Command Syntax Conventions

The conventions used to present command syntax in this book are the same conventions used in the IOS Command Reference. The Command Reference describes these conventions as follows:

- **Boldface** indicates commands and keywords that are entered literally as shown. In actual configuration examples and output (not general command syntax), boldface indicates commands that are manually input by the user (such as a **show** command).

- *Italic* indicates arguments for which you supply actual values.

- Vertical bars (|) separate alternative, mutually exclusive elements.

- Square brackets ([ ]) indicate an optional element.

- Braces ({ }) indicate a required choice.

- Braces within brackets ([{ }]) indicate a required choice within an optional element.

Foreword

Greetings from the past. I am writing this foreword in what is for you the bygone techno-logical era of February 2017. Back then (or now, to me), most cars still had human drivers. We still needed traffic lights, and most of those lights ran on timers, completely blind to the traffic on the streets. As I write this, most residential utility meters are mechanical, and utility workers have to walk from house to house to get readings. The vast majority of toasters can't tweet.

I joined Cisco in 2013 and became the company's Internet of Things leader in 2015. The scope and velocity of the technological change my team sees is immense—so much so that book forewords can have a short shelf life.

But we can prepare for the changes and opportunities that are coming at us. We will have to use different tools from the ones we used to build the current Internet. We need a rock-solid understanding of the fundamentals of the Internet of Things: Where we are today, the challenges we face, and where those opportunities lie. Cisco's most knowledge-able engineers and top technical talent wrote this book so we could build toward this future together.

Where Things Are

I expect this book to be a useful tool for you, even if you don't pick it up until 2020, when the number of "Internet of Things" (if we still call it that) devices might have reached 50 billion, from a paltry 6.4 billion in 2016. Manufacturing plants will be smarter and more efficient than they've ever been, thanks to their capabilities to process, share, and react to sensor information and other data. Complex machines like cars will be comprehensively metered, down to the component level, with their massive data streams fanning out into vast analytics systems that serve life-safety, ecological, and financial ser-vices—and even the manufacturing plants that made them—in real time. The things will become so smart—tractors, teacups, tape measures—that the product companies will be transformed into services companies.

It will have been the biggest technology transition the world has ever seen.

Currently, the networking protocols to collect and collate and analyze and transmit that data are still evolving—fast. We have a robust and stable Internet, but it was built to con-nect people and general-purpose computers, not billions of highly specialized devices sending out constant streams of machine data.

Our global network is designed to mimic point-to-point connectivity, and it is, for the most part, neutral to the devices that connect to it and to the types of data they are designed to send and receive. Currently, several companies, including Cisco, are coming up with ways to add a layer of mediation between the billions of devices coming online and the data and analytical warehouses that will be the repositories of their data for busi-ness and other applications. (We call this layer "the edge," for now.)

Since a lot of the data and telemetry that devices create will need to be sent wirelessly, we're also doing what we can to improve the reliability and speed of data transfer, as well as to lower its latency and the power it takes to send each bit. There are several emerging wireless standards in this race. And in a few years, there will still be several—because different types of devices and applications will need different things from their wireless systems. Currently, the mobile carriers are the big players that are being joined by the largest consumers of data services, like the energy and transportation companies. The next few years are going to see a lot of competition and innovation as old and new companies compete to be the transporters of all this information.

We're also working to make sure that IoT devices themselves can strengthen the security of the networks they use. Right now (in your past), the network itself has very limited knowledge of what types of data it should be sending and what it should not be. Devices can get hijacked to attack other devices—or the network itself. By the time you read this, I am confident that this security problem along with other IoT challenges, such as scalability and interoperability issues, will be closer to getting solved. This book will help us get there. It is an educational resource that captures the fundamentals of IoT in a coherent and comprehensive manner. IoT is poised to change our world, and this book provides the necessary foundation for understanding and navigating the shifting IoT landscape.

The Adoption Curve

From my vantage point in 2017, it's clear we have a lot of work ahead of us to make the Internet of Things into a fabric that all businesses can easily connect to. I'm sure it's going to get done, though. And soon. I know this because we're building the tools ourselves here at Cisco and because I talk all the time to business leaders and entrepreneurs who are betting their companies on IoT-powered processes.

Building IoT solutions, keeping them safe, making them inexpensive and maintainable, and processing and profiting from the data they generate are all enormous opportunities. My team's job is to make all these jobs easier for you, and it all starts with education—ours and yours.

— **Rowan Trollope**, SVP and GM of IoT and Applications Groups, Cisco

Introduction

A major technology shift is happening in our world, and it is centered around the Internet of Things (IoT). The IoT is all about connecting the unconnected. Most of the objects in our current world are not connected to a computer network, but that paradigm is rapidly changing. Previously unconnected objects that are all around us are being provided with the ability to communicate with other objects and people, which in turn drives new services and efficiencies in our daily lives. This is the basic premise behind IoT and illustrates why some theorize that it will be as transformative as the Industrial Revolution.

We, the authors of this book, have decades of computer networking experience, much of it focused on IoT and related technologies. Our combined experience with IoT ranges from early product deployments and testing, to network design, to implementation, training, and troubleshooting. This experience allowed us to take a pragmatic approach to writing on this subject and distill the essential elements that form the foundation or fundamentals for this topic. This book embodies principal elements that you need for understanding IoT from both a technical perspective and an industry point of view.

This book leverages a three-part approach for teaching the fundamentals of IoT. Part I provides a high-level overview of IoT and what you need to know from a design perspective. Part II takes you through the technical building blocks of IoT, including the pertinent technologies and protocols. Finally, Part III steps you through common industry use cases so you can see how IoT is applied in the real world.

To successfully work in the IoT area, you must have a fundamental understanding of IoT principles and use cases. This book provides this knowledge in a logical format that makes it not only a great general resource for learning about IoT now but also a handy reference for more specific IoT questions you may have in the future.

Who Should Read This Book?

This book was written for networking professionals looking for an authoritative and comprehensive introduction to the topic of IoT. It is focused on readers who have networking experience and are looking to master the essential concepts and technologies behind IoT and how they are applied, resulting in basic proficiency. Therefore, readers should have a basic understanding of computer networking concepts and be familiar with basic networking terminology. Readers may be advanced-level networking students or hold titles or positions such as network operator, administrator, and manager; network designer or architect; network engineer; network technician; network analyst or consultant; and network database administrator.

How This Book Is Organized

Part I, "Introduction to IoT"

Part 1 helps you make sense of the IoT word. This word has often been misused and can cover multiple realities. This first part of the book helps you understand what exactly IoT is and provides an overview of the landscape of smart objects, from those that control telescope mirrors with hundreds of actions per seconds, to those that send rust information once a month. This part also shows you how IoT networks are designed and constructed.

Chapter 1, "What Is IoT?"

This chapter provides an overview of the history and beginnings of IoT. This chapter also examines the convergence of operational technology (OT) and informational technology (IT) and provides a reference model to position IoT in the general network landscape.

Chapter 2, "IoT Network Architecture and Design"

Multiple standards and industry organizations have defined specific architectures for IoT, including ETSI/oneM2M and the IoT World Forum. This chapter compares those architectures and suggests a simplified model that can help you articulate the key functions of IoT without the need for vertical-specific elements. This chapter also guides you through the core IoT functional stack and the data infrastructure stack.

Part II, "Engineering IoT Networks"

Once you understand the IoT landscape and the general principles of IoT networks, Part II takes a deep dive into IoT network engineering, from smart objects and the network that connects them to applications, data analytics, and security. This part covers in detail each layer of an IoT network and examines for each layer the protocols in place (those that have been there for a long time and new protocols that are gaining traction), use cases, and the different architectures that define an efficient IoT solution.

Chapter 3, "Smart Objects: The 'Things' in IoT"

Smart objects can be of many types, from things you wear to things you install in walls, windows, bridges, trains, cars, or streetlights. This chapter guides you through the different types of smart objects, from those that simply record information to those that are programmed to perform actions in response to changes.

Chapter 4, "Connecting Smart Objects"

Once you deploy smart objects, they need to connect to the network. This chapter guides you through the different elements you need to understand to build a network for IoT: connection technologies, such as 802.15.4, 802.15g, 802.15e 1901.2a, 802.11ah, LoRaWAN, NB-IoT, and other LTE variations; wireless bands and ranges; power considerations; and topologies.

Chapter 5, "IP as the IoT Network Layer"

Early IoT protocols did not rely on an OSI network layer. This chapter shows you how, as IoT networks now include millions of sensors, IP has become the protocol of choice for network connectivity. This chapter also details how IP was optimized, with enhancements like 6LoWPAN, 6TiSCH, and RPL, to adapt to the low-power and lossy networks (LLNs) where IoT usually operates.

Chapter 6, "Application Protocols for IoT"

Smart objects need to communicate over the network with applications to report on environmental readings or receive information, configurations, and instructions. This chapter guides you through the different common application protocols, from MQTT, CoAP, and SCADA to generic and web-based protocols. This chapter also provides architecture recommendations to optimize your IoT network application and communication efficiency.

Chapter 7, "Data and Analytics for IoT"

Somewhere in a data center or in the cloud, data coming from millions of sensors is analyzed and correlated with data coming from millions of others. *Big data* and *machine learning* are keywords in this world. This chapter details what big data is and how machine learning works, and it explains the tools used to make intelligence of large amount of data and to analyze in real time network flows and streams.

Chapter 8, "Securing IoT"

Hacking an IoT smart object can provide very deep access into your network and data. This chapter explains the security practices for IT and OT and details how security is applied to an IoT environment. This chapter also describes tools to conduct a formal risk analysis on an IoT infrastructure.

Part III, "IoT in Industry"

Once you know how to architect an IoT network, Part III helps you apply that knowledge to key industries that IoT is revolutionizing. For each of the seven verticals covered in this part, you will learn how IoT can be used and what IoT architecture is recommended to increase safety, operational efficiency, and user experience.

Chapter 9, "Manufacturing"

Any gain in productivity can have a large impact on manufacturing, and IoT has introduced a very disruptive change in this world. This chapter explains connected manufacturing and data processing for this environment, and it details the architecture and components of a converged factory, including IACS and CPwE. This chapter also examines the process automation protocols, including EtherNet/IP, PROFINET, and Modbus/TCP.

Chapter 10, "Oil and Gas"

Oil and gas are among the most critical resources used by modern society. This chapter shows how IoT is massively leveraged in this vertical to improve operational efficiency. This chapter also addresses the sensitive topic of OT security and provides architectural recommendations for IoT in the oil and gas world.

Chapter 11, "Utilities"

Utility companies provide the services that run our cities, businesses, and entire economy. IoT in this vertical, and the ability to visualize and control energy consumption, is critical for the utility companies and also for end users. This chapter guides you through the GridBlocks reference model, the substation and control systems, and the FAN GridBlocks, to help you understand the smart grid and how IoT is used in this vertical.

Chapter 12, "Smart and Connected Cities"

Smart and connected cities include street lighting, smart parking, traffic optimization, waste collection and management, and smart environment. These various use cases are more and more being combined into organized citywide IoT solutions where data and smart objects serve multiple purposes. This chapter discusses the various IoT solutions for smart and connected cities.

Chapter 13, "Transportation"

This chapter talks about roadways, rail, mass transit, and fleet management. You will learn how IoT is used to allow for communication between vehicles and the infrastructure through protocols like DSRC and WAVE and how IoT increases the efficiency and safety of the transportation infrastructure.

Chapter 14, "Mining"

The mining industry is often described as "gigantic vehicles moving gigantic volumes of material." IoT is becoming a key component in this world to maintain competiveness while ensuring safety. From self-driving haulers to radar-guided 350-metric-ton shovels, this chapter shows you the various use cases of IoT in mining. This chapter also suggests an architectural IoT strategy for deploying smart objects in an ever-changing and often extreme environment.

Chapter 15, "Public Safety"

The primary objective of public safety organizations is to keep citizens, communities, and public spaces safe. These organizations have long been at the forefront of new technology adoption, and IoT has become a key component of their operations. This chapter describes the emergency response IoT architecture and details how public safety operators leverage IoT to better exchange information and leverage big data to respond more quickly and efficiently to emergencies.

Introduction to IoT

Chapter 1

What Is IoT?

Imagine a world where just about anything you can think of is online and communicating to other things and people in order to enable new services that enhance our lives. From self-driving drones delivering your grocery order to sensors in your clothing monitoring your health, the world you know is set to undergo a major technological shift forward. This shift is known collectively as the Internet of Things (IoT).

The basic premise and goal of IoT is to "connect the unconnected." This means that objects that are not currently joined to a computer network, namely the Internet, will be connected so that they can communicate and interact with people and other objects. IoT is a technology transition in which devices will allow us to sense and control the physical world by making objects smarter and connecting them through an intelligent network.[1]

When objects and machines can be sensed and controlled remotely across a network, a tighter integration between the physical world and computers is enabled. This allows for improvements in the areas of efficiency, accuracy, automation, and the enablement of advanced applications.

The world of IoT is broad and multifaceted, and you may even find it somewhat complicated at first due to the plethora of components and protocols that it encompasses. Instead of viewing IoT as a single technology domain, it is good to view it as an umbrella of various concepts, protocols, and technologies, all of which are at times somewhat dependent on a particular industry. While the wide array of IoT elements is designed to create numerous benefits in the areas of productivity and automation, at the same time it introduces new challenges, such as scaling the vast numbers of devices and amounts of data that need to be processed.

This chapter seeks to further define IoT and its various elements at a high level. Having this information will prepare you to tackle more in-depth IoT subjects in the following chapters. Specifically, this chapter explores the following topics:

- **Genesis of IoT:** This section highlights IoT's place in the evolution and development of the Internet.

- **IoT and Digitization:** This section details the differences between IoT and digitization and defines a framework for better understanding their relationship.

- **IoT Impact:** This section shares a few high-level scenarios and examples to demonstrate the influence IoT will have on our world.

- **Convergence of IT and OT:** This section explores how IoT is bringing together information technology (IT) and operational technology (OT).

- **IoT Challenges:** This section provides a brief overview of the difficulties involved in transitioning to an IoT-enabled world.

Genesis of IoT

The age of IoT is often said to have started between the years 2008 and 2009. During this time period, the number of devices connected to the Internet eclipsed the world's population. With more "things" connected to the Internet than people in the world, a new age was upon us, and the Internet of Things was born.

The person credited with the creation of the term "Internet of Things" is Kevin Ashton. While working for Procter & Gamble in 1999, Kevin used this phrase to explain a new idea related to linking the company's supply chain to the Internet.

Kevin has subsequently explained that IoT now involves the addition of senses to computers. He was quoted as saying: "In the twentieth century, computers were brains without senses—they only knew what we told them." Computers depended on humans to input data and knowledge through typing, bar codes, and so on. IoT is changing this paradigm; in the twenty-first century, computers are sensing things for themselves.[2]

It is widely accepted that IoT is a major technology shift, but what is its scale and importance? Where does it fit in the evolution of the Internet?

As shown in Figure 1-1, the evolution of the Internet can be categorized into four phases. Each of these phases has had a profound impact on our society and our lives. These four phases are further defined in Table 1-1.

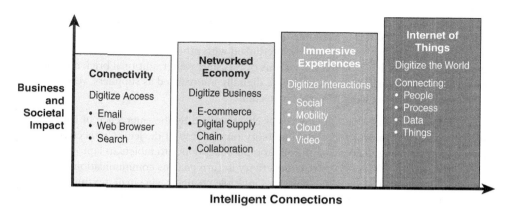

Figure 1-1   *Evolutionary Phases of the Internet*

Table 1-1   *Evolutionary Phases of the Internet*

Internet Phase	Definition
Connectivity (Digitize access)	This phase connected people to email, web services, and search so that information is easily accessed.
Networked Economy (Digitize business)	This phase enabled e-commerce and supply chain enhancements along with collaborative engagement to drive increased efficiency in business processes.
Immersive Experiences (Digitize interactions)	This phase extended the Internet experience to encompass widespread video and social media while always being connected through mobility. More and more applications are moved into the cloud.
Internet of Things (Digitize the world)	This phase is adding connectivity to objects and machines in the world around us to enable new services and experiences. It is connecting the unconnected.

Each of these evolutionary phases builds on the previous one. With each subsequent phase, more value becomes available for businesses, governments, and society in general.

The first phase, Connectivity, began in the mid-1990s. Though it may be hard to remember, or even imagine if you are younger, the world was not always connected as it is today. In the beginning, email and getting on the Internet were luxuries for universities and corporations. Getting the average person online involved dial-up modems, and even basic connectivity often seemed like a small miracle.

Even though connectivity and its speed continued to improve, a saturation point was reached where connectivity was no longer the major challenge. The focus was now on leveraging connectivity for efficiency and profit. This inflection point marked the beginning of the second phase of the Internet evolution, called the Networked Economy.

With the Networked Economy, e-commerce and digitally connected supply chains became the rage, and this caused one of the major disruptions of the past 100 years. Vendors and suppliers became closely interlinked with producers, and online shopping experienced incredible growth. The victims of this shift were traditional brick-and-mortar retailers. The economy itself became more digitally intertwined as suppliers, vendors, and consumers all became more directly connected.

The third phase, Immersive Experiences, is characterized by the emergence of social media, collaboration, and widespread mobility on a variety of devices. Connectivity is now pervasive, using multiple platforms from mobile phones to tablets to laptops and desktop computers. This pervasive connectivity in turn enables communication and collaboration as well as social media across multiple channels, via email, texting, voice, and video. In essence, person-to-person interactions have become digitized.

The latest phase is the Internet of Things. Despite all the talk and media coverage of IoT, in many ways we are just at the beginning of this phase. When you think about the fact that 99% of "things" are still unconnected, you can better understand what this evolutionary phase is all about. Machines and objects in this phase connect with other machines and objects, along with humans. Business and society have already started down this path and are experiencing huge increases in data and knowledge. In turn, this is now leading to previously unrecognized insights, along with increased automation and new process efficiencies. IoT is poised to change our world in new and exciting ways, just as the past Internet phases already have.

IoT and Digitization

IoT and *digitization* are terms that are often used interchangeably. In most contexts, this duality is fine, but there are key differences to be aware of.

At a high level, IoT focuses on connecting "things," such as objects and machines, to a computer network, such as the Internet. IoT is a well-understood term used across the industry as a whole. On the other hand, digitization can mean different things to different people but generally encompasses the connection of "things" with the data they generate and the business insights that result.

For example, in a shopping mall where Wi-Fi location tracking has been deployed, the "things" are the Wi-Fi devices. Wi-Fi location tracking is simply the capability of knowing where a consumer is in a retail environment through his or her smart phone's connection to the retailer's Wi-Fi network. While the value of connecting Wi-Fi devices or "things" to the Internet is obvious and appreciated by shoppers, tracking real-time location of Wi-Fi clients provides a specific business benefit to the mall and shop owners. In this case, it helps the business understand where shoppers tend to congregate and how much time they spend in different parts of a mall or store. Analysis of this data can lead to significant changes to the locations of product displays and advertising, where to place certain types of shops, how much rent to charge, and even where to station security guards.

Note   For several years the term *Internet of Everything*, or *IoE*, was used extensively. Over time, the term IoE has been replaced by the term *digitization*. Although technical terms tend to evolve over time, the words *IoE* and *digitization* have roughly the same definition. IoT has always been a part of both, but it is important to note that IoT is a subset of both IoE and digitization.

Digitization, as defined in its simplest form, is the conversion of information into a digital format. Digitization has been happening in one form or another for several decades. For example, the whole photography industry has been digitized. Pretty much everyone has digital cameras these days, either standalone devices or built into their mobile phones. Almost no one buys film and takes it to a retailer to get it developed. The digitization of photography has completely changed our experience when it comes to capturing images.

Other examples of digitization include the video rental industry and transportation. In the past, people went to a store to rent or purchase videotapes or DVDs of movies. With digitization, just about everyone is streaming video content or purchasing movies as downloadable files.

The transportation industry is currently undergoing digitization in the area of taxi services. Businesses such as Uber and Lyft use digital technologies to allow people to get a ride using a mobile phone app. This app identifies the car, the driver, and the fare. The rider then pays the fare by using the app. This digitization is a major disruptive force to companies providing traditional taxi services.

In the context of IoT, digitization brings together things, data, and business process to make networked connections more relevant and valuable. A good example of this that many people can relate to is in the area of home automation with popular products, such as Nest. With Nest, sensors determine your desired climate settings and also tie in other smart objects, such as smoke alarms, video cameras, and various third-party devices. In the past, these devices and the functions they perform were managed and controlled separately and could not provide the holistic experience that is now possible. Nest is just one example of digitization and IoT increasing the relevancy and value of networked, intelligent connections and making a positive impact on our lives.

Companies today look at digitization as a differentiator for their businesses, and IoT is a prime enabler of digitization. Smart objects and increased connectivity drive digitization, and this is one of the main reasons that many companies, countries, and governments are embracing this growing trend.

IoT Impact

Projections on the potential impact of IoT are impressive. About 14 billion, or just 0.06%, of "things" are connected to the Internet today. Cisco Systems predicts that by 2020, this number will reach 50 billion. A UK government report speculates that this number could be even higher, in the range of 100 billion objects connected. Cisco further estimates that these new connections will lead to $19 trillion in profits and cost savings.[3] Figure 1-2 provides a graphical look at the growth in the number of devices being connected.

What these numbers mean is that IoT will fundamentally shift the way people and businesses interact with their surroundings. Managing and monitoring smart objects using real-time connectivity enables a whole new level of data-driven decision making. This in turn results in the optimization of systems and processes and delivers new services that save time for both people and businesses while improving the overall quality of life.

The following examples illustrate some of the benefits of IoT and their impact. These examples will provide you with a high-level view of practical IoT use cases to clearly illustrate how IoT will affect everyday life. For more in-depth use cases, please refer to the chapters in Part III, "IoT in Industry."

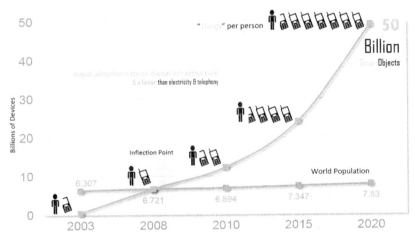

Figure 1-2   *The Rapid Growth in the Number of Devices Connected to the Internet*

Connected Roadways

People have been fantasizing about the self-driving car, or autonomous vehicle, in literature and film for decades. While this fantasy is now becoming a reality with well-known projects like Google's self-driving car, IoT is also a necessary component for implementing a fully connected transportation infrastructure.

IoT is going to allow self-driving vehicles to better interact with the transportation system around them through bidirectional data exchanges while also providing important data to the riders. Self-driving vehicles need always-on, reliable communications and data from other transportation-related sensors to reach their full potential. *Connected roadways* is the term associated with both the driver and driverless cars fully integrating with the surrounding transportation infrastructure. Figure 1-3 shows a self-driving car designed by Google.

Figure 1-3 *Google's Self-Driving Car*

Basic sensors reside in cars already. They monitor oil pressure, tire pressure, temperature, and other operating conditions, and provide data around the core car functions. From behind the steering wheel, the driver can access this data while also controlling the car using equipment such as a steering wheel, pedals, and so on. The need for all this sensory information and control is obvious. The driver must be able to understand, handle, and make critical decisions while concentrating on driving safely. The Internet of Things is replicating this concept on a much larger scale.

Today, we are seeing automobiles produced with thousands of sensors, to measure everything from fuel consumption to location to the entertainment your family is watching during the ride. As automobile manufacturers strive to reinvent the driving experience, these sensors are becoming IP-enabled to allow easy communication with other systems both inside and outside the car. In addition, new sensors and communication technologies are being developed to allow vehicles to "talk" to other vehicles, traffic signals, school zones, and other elements of the transportation infrastructure. We are now starting to realize a truly connected transportation solution.

Most connected roadways solutions focus on resolving today's transportation challenges. These challenges can be classified into the three categories highlighted in Table 1-2.

Table 1-2 *Current Challenges Being Addressed by Connected Roadways*

Challenge	Supporting Data
Safety	According to the US Department of Transportation, 5.6 million crashes were reported in 2012 alone, resulting in more than 33,000 fatalities. IoT and the enablement of connected vehicle technologies will empower drivers with the tools they need to anticipate potential crashes and significantly reduce the number of lives lost each year.

Challenge	Supporting Data
Mobility	More than a billion cars are on the roads worldwide. Connected vehicle mobility applications can enable system operators and drivers to make more informed decisions, which can, in turn, reduce travel delays. Congestion causes 5.5 billion hours of travel delay per year, and reducing travel delays is more critical than ever before. In addition, communication between mass transit, emergency response vehicles, and traffic management infrastructures help optimize the routing of vehicles, further reducing potential delays.
Environment	According to the American Public Transportation Association, each year transit systems can collectively reduce carbon dioxide (CO_2) emissions by 16.2 million metric tons by reducing private vehicle miles. Connected vehicle environmental applications will give all travelers the real-time information they need to make "green" transportation choices.

Sources: Traffic Safety Facts, 2010; National Highway Traffic Safety Administration, June 2012; and WHO Global Status Report on Road Safety, 2013.

By addressing the challenges in Table 1-2, connected roadways will bring many benefits to society. These benefits include reduced traffic jams and urban congestion, decreased casualties and fatalities, increased response time for emergency vehicles, and reduced vehicle emissions.

For example, with IoT-connected roadways, a concept known as Intersection Movement Assist (IMA) is possible. This application warns a driver (or triggers the appropriate response in a self-driving car) when it is not safe to enter an intersection due to a high probability of a collision—perhaps because another car has run a stop sign or strayed into the wrong lane. Thanks to the communications system between the vehicles and the infrastructure, this sort of scenario can be handled quickly and safely. See Figure 1-4 for a graphical representation of IMA.

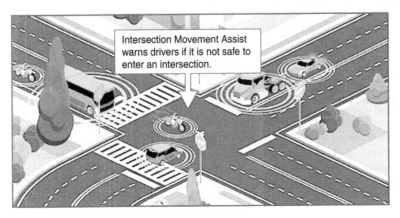

Figure 1-4   *Application of Intersection Movement Assist*

IMA is one of many possible roadway solutions that emerge when we start to integrate IoT with both traditional and self-driving vehicles. Other solutions include automated vehicle tracking, cargo management, and road weather communications.

With automated vehicle tracking, a vehicle's location is used for notification of arrival times, theft prevention, or highway assistance. Cargo management provides precise positioning of cargo as it is en route so that notification alerts can be sent to a dispatcher and routes can be optimized for congestion and weather. Road weather communications use sensors and data from satellites, roads, and bridges to warn vehicles of dangerous conditions or inclement weather on the current route.

Today's typical road car utilizes more than a million lines of code—and this only scratches the surface of the data potential. As cars continue to become more connected and capable of generating continuous data streams related to location, performance, driver behavior, and much more, the data generation potential of a single car is staggering. It is estimated that a fully connected car will generate more than 25 gigabytes of data per hour, much of which will be sent to the cloud. To put this in perspective, that's equivalent to a dozen HD movies sent to the cloud every hour—by your car! Multiply that by the number of hours a car is driven per year and again by the number of cars on the road, and you see that the amount of connected car data generated, transmitted, and stored in the cloud will be in the zettabytes range per year (more than a billion petabytes per year). Figure 1-5 provides an overview of the sort of sensors and connectivity that you will find in a connected car.

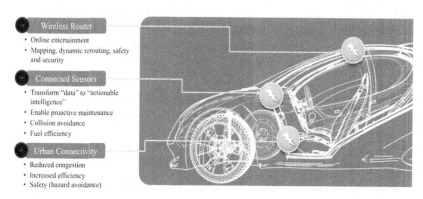

Figure 1-5   *The Connected Car*

Another area where connected roadways are undergoing massive disruption is in how the data generated by a car will be used by third parties. Clearly, the data generated by your car needs to be handled in a secure and reliable way, which means the network needs to be secure, it must provide authentication and verification of the driver and car, and it needs to be highly available. But who will use all this data? Automobile data is extremely useful to a wide range of interested parties. For example, tire companies can collect data related to use and durability of their products in a range of environments in real time. Automobile manufacturers can collect information from sensors to better understand how the cars are being driven, when parts are starting to fail, or whether the car has broken down—details that will help them build better cars in the future. This becomes especially true as autonomous vehicles are introduced, which are sure to be driven in a completely different way than the traditional family car.

In the future, car sensors will be able to interact with third-party applications, such as GPS/maps, to enable dynamic rerouting to avoid traffic, accidents, and other hazards. Similarly, Internet-based entertainment, including music, movies, and other streamings or downloads, can be personalized and customized to optimize a road trip.

This data will also be used for targeted advertising. As GPS navigation systems become more integrated with sensors and wayfinding applications, it will become possible for personalized routing suggestions to be made. For example, if it is known that you prefer a certain coffee shop, through the use of a cloud-based data connector, the navigation system will be able to provide routing suggestions that have you drive your car past the right coffee shop.

All these data opportunities bring into play a new technology: the IoT data broker. Imagine the many different types of data generated by an automobile and the plethora of different parties interested in this data. This poses a significant business opportunity. In a very real sense, the data generated by the car and driver becomes a valuable commodity that can be bought and sold. While the data transmitted from the car will likely go to one initial location in the cloud, from there the data can be separated and sold selectively by the data broker. For example, tire companies will pay for information from sensors related to your tires, but they won't get anything else. While information brokers have been around a long time, the technology used to aggregate and separate the data from connected cars in a secure and governed manner is rapidly developing and will continue to be a major focus of the IoT industry for years to come.

Connected roadways are likely to be one of the biggest growth areas for innovation. Automobiles and the roads they use have seen incredible change over the past century, but the changes ahead of us are going to be just as astonishing. In the past few years alone, we have seen highway systems around the world adopt sophisticated sensors systems that can detect seismic vibrations, car accidents, severe weather conditions, traffic congestion, and more. Recent advancements in roadway fiber-optic sensing technology is now able to record not only how many cars are passing but their speed and type. Due to the many reasons already discussed, connected cars and roadways are early adopters of IoT technology. For a more in-depth discussion of IoT use cases and architectures in the transportation industry, see Chapter 13, "Transportation."

Connected Factory

For years, traditional factories have been operating at a disadvantage, impeded by production environments that are "disconnected" or, at the very least, "strictly gated" to corporate business systems, supply chains, and customers and partners. Managers of these traditional factories are essentially "flying blind" and lack visibility into their operations. These operations are composed of plant floors, front offices, and suppliers operating in independent silos. Consequently, rectifying downtime issues, quality problems, and the root causes of various manufacturing inefficiencies is often difficult.

The main challenges facing manufacturing in a factory environment today include the following:

- Accelerating new product and service introductions to meet customer and market opportunities

- Increasing plant production, quality, and uptime while decreasing cost

- Mitigating unplanned downtime (which wastes, on average, at least 5% of production)

- Securing factories from cyber threats

- Decreasing high cabling and re-cabling costs (up to 60% of deployment costs)

- Improving worker productivity and safety[4]

Adding another level of complication to these challenges is the fact that they often need to be addressed at various levels of the manufacturing business. For example, executive management is looking for new ways to manufacture in a more cost-effective manner while balancing the rising energy and material costs. Product development has time to market as the top priority. Plant managers are entirely focused on gains in plant efficiency and operational agility. The controls and automation department looks after the plant networks, controls, and applications and therefore requires complete visibility into all these systems.

Industrial enterprises around the world are retooling their factories with advanced technologies and architectures to resolve these problems and boost manufacturing flexibility and speed. These improvements help them achieve new levels of overall equipment effectiveness, supply chain responsiveness, and customer satisfaction. A convergence of factory-based operational technologies and architectures with global IT networks is starting to occur, and this is referred to as the *connected factory*.

As with the IoT solutions for the connected roadways previously discussed, there are already large numbers of basic sensors on factory floors. However, with IoT, these sensors not only become more advanced but also attain a new level of connectivity. They are smarter and gain the ability to communicate, mainly using the Internet Protocol (IP) over an Ethernet infrastructure.

In addition to sensors, the devices on the plant floor are becoming smarter in their ability to transmit and receive large quantities of real-time informational and diagnostic data. Ethernet connectivity is becoming pervasive and spreading beyond just the main controllers in a factory to devices such as the robots on the plant floor. In addition, more IP-enabled devices, including video cameras, diagnostic smart objects, and even personal mobile devices, are being added to the manufacturing environment.

For example, a smelting facility extracts metals from their ores. The facility uses both heat and chemicals to decompose the ore, leaving behind the base metal. This is a multistage process, and the data and controls are all accessed via various control rooms in a facility. Operators must go to a control room that is often hundreds of meters away for data and production changes. Hours of operator time are often lost to the multiple trips to the control room needed during a shift. With IoT and a connected factory solution, true "machine-to-people" connections are implemented to bring sensor data directly to operators on the floor via mobile devices. Time is no longer wasted moving back and forth between the control rooms and the plant floor. In addition, because the operators now receive data in real time, decisions can be made immediately to improve production and fix any quality problems.

Another example of a connected factory solution involves a real-time location system (RTLS). An RTLS utilizes small and easily deployed Wi-Fi RFID tags that attach to virtually any material and provide real-time location and status. These tags enable a facility to track production as it happens. These IoT sensors allow components and materials on an assembly line to "talk" to the network. If each assembly line's output is tracked in real time, decisions can be made to speed up or slow production to meet targets, and it is easy to determine how quickly employees are completing the various stages of production. Bottlenecks at any point in production and quality problems are also quickly identified.

While we tend to look at IoT as an evolution of the Internet, it is also sparking an evolution of industry. In 2016 the World Economic Forum referred to the evolution of the Internet and the impact of IoT as the "fourth Industrial Revolution."[5] The first Industrial Revolution occurred in Europe in the late eighteenth century, with the application of steam and water to mechanical production. The second Industrial Revolution, which took place between the early 1870s and the early twentieth century, saw the introduction of the electrical grid and mass production. The third revolution came in the late 1960s/ early 1970s, as computers and electronics began to make their mark on manufacturing and other industrial systems. The fourth Industrial Revolution is happening now, and the Internet of Things is driving it. Figure 1-6 summarizes these four Industrial Revolutions as Industry 1.0 through Industry 4.0.

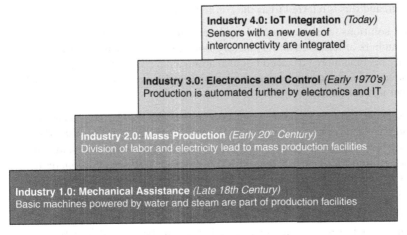

Industry 4.0: IoT Integration *(Today)*
Sensors with a new level of interconnectivity are integrated

Industry 3.0: Electronics and Control *(Early 1970's)*
Production is automated further by electronics and IT

Industry 2.0: Mass Production *(Early 20th Century)*
Division of labor and electricity lead to mass production facilities

Industry 1.0: Mechanical Assistance *(Late 18th Century)*
Basic machines powered by water and steam are part of production facilities

Figure 1-6   *The Four Industrial Revolutions*

The IoT wave of Industry 4.0 takes manufacturing from a purely automated assembly line model of production to a model where the machines are intelligent and communicate with one another. IoT in manufacturing brings with it the opportunity for inserting intelligence into factories. This starts with creating smart objects, which involves embedding sensors, actuators, and controllers into just about everything related to production. Connections tie it all together so that people and machines work together to analyze the data and make intelligent decisions. Eventually this leads to machines predicting failures and self-healing and points to a world where human monitoring and intervention are no longer necessary.

Smart Connected Buildings

Another place IoT is making a disruptive impact is in the smart connected buildings space. In the past several decades, buildings have become increasingly complex, with systems overlaid one upon another, resulting in complex intersections of structural, mechanical, electrical, and IT components. Over time, these operational networks that support the building environment have matured into sophisticated systems; however, for the most part, they are deployed and managed as separate systems that have little to no interaction with each other.

The function of a building is to provide a work environment that keeps the workers comfortable, efficient, and safe. Work areas need to be well lit and kept at a comfortable temperature. To keep workers safe, the fire alarm and suppression system needs to be carefully managed, as do the door and physical security alarm systems. While intelligent systems for modern buildings are being deployed and improved for each of these functions, most of these systems currently run independently of each other—and they rarely take into account where the occupants of the building actually are and how many of them are present in different parts of the building. However, many buildings are beginning to deploy sensors throughout the building to detect occupancy. These tend to be motion sensors or sensors tied to video cameras. Motion detection occupancy sensors work great if everyone is moving around in a crowded room and can automatically shut the lights off when everyone has left, but what if a person in the room is out of sight of the sensor? It is a frustrating matter to be at the mercy of an unintelligent sensor on the wall that wants to turn off the lights on you.

Similarly, sensors are often used to control the heating, ventilation, and air-conditioning (HVAC) system. Temperature sensors are spread throughout the building and are used to influence the building management system's (BMS's) control of air flow into a room.

Another interesting aspect of the smart building is that it makes them easier and cheaper to manage. Considering the massive costs involved in operating such complex structures, not to mention how many people spend their working lives inside a building, managers have become increasingly interested in ways to make buildings more efficient and cheaper to manage. Have you ever heard people complain that they had too little working space in their office, or that the office space wasn't being used efficiently? When people go to their managers and ask for a change to the floor plan, such as asking for an increase in the amount of space they work in, they are often asked to prove their case. But workplace floor efficiency and usage evidence tends to be anecdotal at best. When smart building sensors and occupancy detection are combined with the power of data analytics (discussed in Chapter 7, "Data and Analytics for IoT"), it becomes easy to demonstrate floor plan usage and prove your case. Alternatively, the building manager can use a similar approach to see where the floor is not being used efficiently and use this information to optimize the available space. This has brought about the age of building automation, empowered by IoT.

While many technical solutions exist for looking after building systems, until recently they have all required separate overlay networks, each responsible for its assigned task. In an attempt to connect these systems into a single framework, the building automation system (BAS) has been developed to provide a single management system for the HVAC, lighting, fire alarm, and detection systems, as well as access control. All these systems may support different types of sensors and connections to the BAS. How do you connect them together so the building can be managed in a coherent way? This highlights one of the biggest challenges in IoT, which is discussed throughout this book: the heterogeneity of IoT systems.

Before you can bring together heterogeneous systems, they need to converge at the network layer and support a common services layer that allows application integration. The value of converged networks is well documented. For example, in the early 2000s, Cisco and several other companies championed the convergence of voice and video onto single IP networks that were shared with other IT applications. The economies of scale and operational efficiencies gained were so massive that VoIP and collaboration technologies are now the norm. However, the convergence to IP and a common services framework for buildings has been slower.

For example, the de facto communication protocol responsible for building automation is known as BACnet (Building Automation and Control Network). In a nutshell, the BACnet protocol defines a set of services that allow Ethernet-based communication between building devices such as HVAC, lighting, access control, and fire detection systems. The same building Ethernet switches used for IT may also be used for BACnet. This standardization also makes possible an intersection point to the IP network (which is run by the IT department) through the use of a gateway device. In addition, BACnet/IP has been defined to allow the "things" in the building network to communicate over IP, thus allowing closer consolidation of the building management system on a single network. Figure 1-7 illustrates the conversion of building protocols to IP over time.

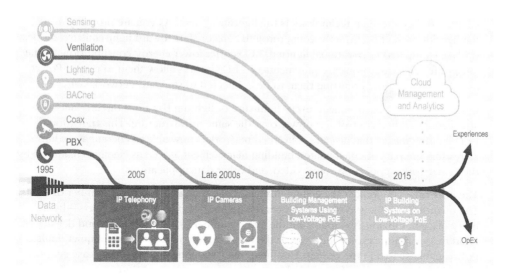

Figure 1-7 *Convergence of Building Technologies to IP*

Another promising IoT technology in the smart connected building, and one that is seeing widespread adoption, is the "digital ceiling." The digital ceiling is more than just a lighting control system. This technology encompasses several of the building's different networks—including lighting, HVAC, blinds, CCTV (closed-circuit television), and security systems—and combines them into a single IP network. Figure 1-8 provides a framework for the digital ceiling.

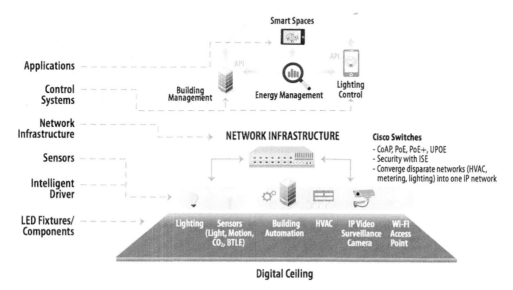

Figure 1-8 *A Framework for the Digital Ceiling*

Central to digital ceiling technology is the lighting system. As you are probably aware, the lighting market is currently going through a major shift toward light-emitting diodes (LEDs). Compared to traditional lighting, LEDs offer lower energy consumption and far longer life. The lower power requirements of LED fixtures allow them to run on Power over Ethernet (PoE), permitting them to be connected to standard network switches.

In a digital ceiling environment, every luminaire or lighting fixture is directly network-attached, providing control and power over the same infrastructure. This transition to LED lighting means that a single converged network is now able to encompasses luminaires that are part of consolidated building management as well as elements managed by the IT network, supporting voice, video, and other data applications.

The next time you look at the ceiling in your office building, count the number of lights. The quantity of lights easily outnumbers the number of physical wired ports—by a hefty margin. Obviously, supporting the larger number of Ethernet ports and density of IP addresses requires some redesign of the network, and it also requires a quiet, fanless PoE-capable switch in the ceiling. That being said, the long-term business case supporting reduced energy costs from LED luminaries versus traditional fluorescent or halogen lights is so significant that the added initial investment in the network is almost inconsequential. The business case for the digital ceiling becomes even stronger when a building is being renovated or a new structure is being built. In these cases, the cost benefit of running CAT 6/5e cables in the ceiling versus plenum-rated electrical wiring to every light is substantial.

The energy savings value of PoE-enabled LED lighting in the ceiling is clear. However, having an IP-enabled sensor device in the ceiling at every point people may be present opens up an entirely new set of possibilities. For example, most modern LED ceiling fixtures support occupancy sensors. These sensors provide high-resolution occupancy data collection, which can be used to turn the lights on and off, and this same data can be combined with advanced analytics to control other systems, such as HVAC and security. Unlike traditional sensors that use rudimentary motion detection, modern lighting sensors integrate a variety of occupancy-sensing technologies, including Bluetooth low energy (BLE) and Wi-Fi. The science here is simple: Because almost every person these days carries a smart device that supports BLE and Wi-Fi, all the sensor has to do is detect BLE or Wi-Fi beacons from a nearby device. When someone walks near a light, the person's location is detected, and the wireless system can send information to control the air flow from the HVAC system into that zone in real time, maximizing the comfort of the office worker. Figure 1-9 shows an example of an occupancy sensor in a digital ceiling light.

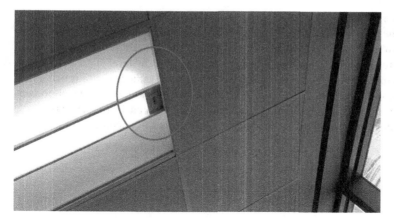

Figure 1-9 *An LED Digital Ceiling Light with Occupancy Sensor*
(Photo by Bill MacGowan)

You can begin to imagine the possibilities that IoT smart lighting brings to a workplace setting. Not only does it provide for optimized levels of lighting based on actual occupancy and building usage, it allows granular control of temperature, management of smoke and fire detection, video cameras, and building access control. IoT allows all this to run through a single network, requiring less installation time and a lower total cost of system ownership.

Smart Creatures

When you think about IoT, you probably picture only inanimate objects and machines being connected. However, IoT also provides the ability to connect living things to the Internet. Sensors can be placed on animals and even insects just as easily as on machines, and the benefits can be just as impressive.

One of the most well-known applications of IoT with respect to animals focuses on what is often referred to as the "connected cow." Sparked, a Dutch company, developed a sensor that is placed in a cow's ear. The sensor monitors various health aspects of the cow as well as its location and transmits the data wirelessly for analysis by the farmer.

The data from each of these sensors is approximately 200 MB per year, and you obviously need a network infrastructure to make the connection with the sensors and store the information. Once the data is being collected, however, you get a complete view of the herd, with statistics on every cow. You can learn how environmental factors may be affecting the herd as a whole and about changes in diet. This enables early detection of disease as cows tend to eat less days before they show symptoms. These sensors even allow the detection of pregnancy in cows.

Another application of IoT to organisms involves the placement of sensors on roaches. While the topic of roaches is a little unsettling to many folks, the potential benefits of IoT-enabled roaches could make a life-saving difference in disaster situations.

Researchers at North Carolina State University are working with Madagascar hissing cockroaches in the hopes of helping emergency personnel rescue survivors after a disaster. As shown in Figure 1-10, an electronic backpack attaches to a roach. This backpack communicates with the roach through parts of its body. Low-level electrical pulses to an antenna on one side makes the roach turn to the opposite side because it believes it is encountering an obstacle. The cerci of the roach are sensory organs on the abdomen that detect danger through changing air currents. When the backpack stimulates the cerci, the roach moves forward because it thinks a predator is approaching.

Figure 1-10   *IoT-Enabled Roach Can Assist in Finding Survivors After a Disaster (Photo courtesy of Alper Bozkurt, NC State University)*

The electronic backpack uses wireless communication to a controller and can be "driven" remotely. Imagine a fleet of these roaches being used in a disaster scenario, such as searching for survivors in a collapsed building after an earthquake. The roaches are naturally designed to efficiently move around objects in confined spaces. Technology has also been tested to keep the roaches in the disaster area; it is similar to the invisible fencing that is often used to keep dogs in a yard. The use of roaches in this manner allows for the mapping of spaces that rescue personnel cannot access, which helps search for survivors.

To help with finding a person trapped in the rubble of a collapsed building, the electronic backpack is equipped with directional microphones that allow for the detection of certain sounds and the direction from which they are coming. Software can analyze the sounds to ensure that they are from a person rather than from, say, a leaking pipe. Roaches can then be steered toward the sounds that may indicate people who are trapped. In addition, the microphones provide the ability for rescue personnel to listen in on whatever sounds are detected.

These examples show that IoT often goes beyond just adding sensors and more intelligence to nonliving "things." Living "things" can also be connected to the Internet and this connection can provide important results.

Convergence of IT and OT

Until recently, information technology (IT) and operational technology (OT) have for the most part lived in separate worlds. IT supports connections to the Internet along with related data and technology systems and is focused on the secure flow of data across an organization. OT monitors and controls devices and processes on physical operational systems. These systems include assembly lines, utility distribution networks, production facilities, roadway systems, and many more. Typically, IT did not get involved with the production and logistics of OT environments.

Specifically, the IT organization is responsible for the information systems of a business, such as email, file and print services, databases, and so on. In comparison, OT is responsible for the devices and processes acting on industrial equipment, such as factory machines, meters, actuators, electrical distribution automation devices, SCADA (supervisory control and data acquisition) systems, and so on. Traditionally, OT has used dedicated networks with specialized communications protocols to connect these devices, and these networks have run completely separately from the IT networks.

Management of OT is tied to the lifeblood of a company. For example, if the network connecting the machines in a factory fails, the machines cannot function, and production may come to a standstill, negatively impacting business on the order of millions of dollars. On the other hand, if the email server (run by the IT department) fails for a few hours, it may irritate people, but it is unlikely to impact business at anywhere near the same level. Table 1-3 highlights some of the differences between IT and OT networks and their various challenges.

Table 1-3 *Comparing Operational Technology (OT) and Information Technology (IT)*

Criterion	Industrial OT Network	Enterprise IT Network
Operational focus	Keep the business operating 24x7	Manage the computers, data, and employee communication system in a secure way
Priorities	1. Availability 2. Integrity 3. Security	1. Security 2. Integrity 3. Availability
Types of data	Monitoring, control, and supervisory data	Voice, video, transactional, and bulk data
Security	Controlled physical access to devices	Devices and users authenticated to the network
Implication of failure	OT network disruption directly impacts business	Can be business impacting, depending on industry, but workarounds may be possible

Criterion	Industrial OT Network	Enterprise IT Network
Network upgrades (software or hardware)	Only during operational mainte- nance windows	Often requires an outage window when workers are not onsite; impact can be mitigated
Security vulnerability	Low: OT networks are isolated and often use proprietary protocols	High: continual patching of hosts is required, and the network is connected to Internet and requires vigilant protection

Source: Maciej Kranz, *IT Is from Venus, OT Is from Mars*, blogs.cisco.com/digital/it-is-from-venus-ot-is-from-mars, July 14, 2015.

With the rise of IoT and standards-based protocols, such as IPv6, the IT and OT worlds are converging or, more accurately, OT is beginning to adopt the network protocols, technology, transport, and methods of the IT organization, and the IT organization is beginning to support the operational requirements used by OT. When IT and OT begin using the same networks, protocols, and processes, there are clear economies of scale. Not only does convergence reduce the amount of capital infrastructure needed but networks become easier to operate, and the flexibility of open standards allows faster growth and adaptability to new technologies.

However, as you can see from Table 1-3, the convergence of IT and OT to a single consolidated network poses several challenges. There are fundamental cultural and priority differences between these two organizations. IoT is forcing these groups to work together, when in the past they have operated rather autonomously. For example, the OT organization is baffled when IT schedules a weekend shutdown to update software without regard to production requirements. On the other hand, the IT group does not understand the prevalence of proprietary or specialized systems and solutions deployed by OT.

Take the case of deploying quality of service (QoS) in a network. When the IT team deploys QoS, voice and video traffic are almost universally treated with the highest level of service. However, when the OT system shares the same network, a very strong argu- ment can be made that the real-time OT traffic should be given a higher priority than even voice because any disruption in the OT network could impact the business.

With the merging of OT and IT, improvements are being made to both systems. OT is looking more toward IT technologies with open standards, such as Ethernet and IP. At the same time, IT is becoming more of a business partner with OT by better understanding business outcomes and operational requirements.

The overall benefit of IT and OT working together is a more efficient and profitable business due to reduced downtime, lower costs through economy of scale, reduced inventory, and improved delivery times. When IT/OT convergence is managed correctly, IoT becomes fully supported by both groups. This provides a "best of both worlds" scenario, where solid industrial control systems reside on an open, integrated, and secure technology foundation.[6]

IoT Challenges

While an IoT-enabled future paints an impressive picture, it does not come without significant challenges. Many parts of IoT have become reality, but certain obstacles need to be overcome for IoT to become ubiquitous throughout industry and our everyday life. Table 1-4 highlights a few of the most significant challenges and problems that IoT is currently facing.

Table 1-4 *IoT Challenges*

Challenge	Description
Scale	While the scale of IT networks can be large, the scale of OT can be several orders of magnitude larger. For example, one large electrical utility in Asia recently began deploying IPv6-based smart meters on its electrical grid. While this utility company has tens of thousands of employees (which can be considered IP nodes in the network), the number of meters in the service area is tens of millions. This means the scale of the network the utility is managing has increased by more than 1,000-fold! Chapter 5, "IP as the IoT Network Layer," explores how new design approaches are being developed to scale IPv6 networks into the millions of devices.
Security	With more "things" becoming connected with other "things" and people, security is an increasingly complex issue for IoT. Your threat surface is now greatly expanded, and if a device gets hacked, its connectivity is a major concern. A compromised device can serve as a launching point to attack other devices and systems. IoT security is also pervasive across just about every facet of IoT. For more information on IoT security, see Chapter 8, "Securing IoT."
Privacy	As sensors become more prolific in our everyday lives, much of the data they gather will be specific to individuals and their activities. This data can range from health information to shopping patterns and transactions at a retail establishment. For businesses, this data has monetary value. Organizations are now discussing who owns this data and how individuals can control whether it is shared and with whom.
Big data and data analytics	IoT and its large number of sensors is going to trigger a deluge of data that must be handled. This data will provide critical information and insights if it can be processed in an efficient manner. The challenge, however, is evaluating massive amounts of data arriving from different sources in various forms and doing so in a timely manner. See Chapter 7 for more information on IoT and the challenges it faces from a big data perspective.

Challenge	Description
Interoperability	As with any other nascent technology, various protocols and architectures are jockeying for market share and standardization within IoT. Some of these protocols and architectures are based on proprietary elements, and others are open. Recent IoT standards are helping minimize this problem, but there are often various protocols and implementations available for IoT networks. The prominent protocols and architectures—especially open, standards-based implementations—are the subject of this book. For more information on IoT architectures, see Chapter 2, "IoT Network Architecture and Design." Chapter 4, "Connecting Smart Objects," Chapter 5, "IP as the IoT Network Layer," and Chapter 6, "Application Protocols for IoT," take a more in-depth look at the protocols that make up IoT.

Summary

This chapter provides an introductory look at the Internet of Things and answers the question "What is IoT?" IoT is about connecting the unconnected, enabling smart objects to communicate with other objects, systems, and people. The end result is an intelligent network that allows more control of the physical world and the enablement of advanced applications.

This chapter also provides a historical look at IoT, along with a current view of IoT as the next evolutionary phase of the Internet. This chapter details a few high-level use cases to show the impact of IoT and some of the ways it will be changing our world.

A number of IoT concepts and terms are defined throughout this chapter. The differences between IoT and digitization are discussed, as well as the convergence between IT and OT. The last section details the challenges faced by IoT.

This chapter should leave you with a clearer understanding of what IoT is all about. In addition, this chapter serves as the foundational block from which you can dive further into IoT in the following chapters.

References

1. Lindsay Hiebert, Public Safety Blog Series-Connecting the Unconnected in Public Safety Response, https://blogs.cisco.com/government/connecting-the-unconnected-in-public-safety-response, October 25, 2013.

2. Arik Gabbai, "Kevin Ashton describes the Internet of Things," *Smithsonian Magazine*, January 2015, www.smithsonianmag.com/innovation/kevin-ashton-describes-the-internet-of-things-180953749/.

3. UK Government Chief Scientific Adviser, *The Internet of Things: Making the Most of the Second Digital Revolution*, Accessed December 2016, www.gov.uk/government/uploads/system/uploads/attachment_data/file/389315/14-1230-internet-of-things-review.pdf.

4. Cisco, *The Cisco Connected Factory: Powering a Renaissance in Manufacturing* (white paper), Accessed December 2016, www.cisco.com/c/dam/m/es_la/| internet-of-everything-ioe/industrial/assets/pdfs/cisco-connected-factory.pdf.

5. Klaus Schwab, *The Fourth Industrial Revolution: What It Means, How to Respond*, https://www.weforum.org/agenda/2016/01/ the-fourth-industrial-revolution-what-it-means-and-how-to-respond/

6. Adapted from Rockwell/Cisco presentation, https://salesconnect.cisco.com/#/ content-detail/a5c09760-7260-4870-9019-0fb6a4a98af0 (Login required).

Chapter 2

IoT Network Architecture and Design

Imagine that one day you decide to build a house. You drive over to the local construction supply store and try to figure out what materials you will need. You buy the lumber, nails and screws, cement mix for the foundation, roofing materials, and so on. A truck comes by and drops off all the materials at the site of your future home. You stare at the piles of materials sitting on what you hope will one day become your front lawn and realize you have no idea where to start. Something important is missing: You don't have architectural plans for the new house! Unfortunately, your plans to build a beautiful new home will have to wait until you get the help of an architect.

As most home builders know, even the simplest construction projects require careful planning and an architecture that adheres to certain standards. When projects become more complex, detailed architectural plans are not only a good idea, they are, in most places, required by law.

To successfully complete a construction project, time and effort are required to design each phase, from the foundation to the roof. Your plans must include detailed designs for the electrical, plumbing, heating, and security systems. Strong architectural blueprints (and the required engineering to support them) are necessary in all construction projects, from the simple to the very complex. In the same vein, a computer network should never be built without careful planning, thorough security policies, and adherence to well-understood design practices. Failure to carefully architect a network according to sound design principles will likely result in something that is difficult to scale, manage, adapt to organizational changes, and, worst of all, troubleshoot when things go wrong.

Most CIOs and CTOs understand that the network runs the business. If the network fails, company operations can be seriously impaired. Just as a house must be designed with the strength to withstand potential natural disasters, such as seismic events and hurricanes, information technology (IT) systems need to be designed to withstand "network earthquakes," such as distributed denial of service (DDoS) attacks, future growth requirements, network outages, and even human error. To address these challenges, the art of network architecture has gained tremendous influence in IT organizations over the past two decades. In fact, for many companies, the responsibility of overseeing network architecture is often seen as one of the most senior positions in the IT and operational technology (OT) organizations. For example, the title chief enterprise architect (CEA) has gained so much traction in recent years that the position is often equated to the responsibilities of a CTO, and in many instances, the CEA reports directly to the CEO.

Enterprise IT network architecture has matured significantly over the past two decades and is generally well understood; however, the discipline of IoT network architecture is new and requires a fresh perspective. It is important to note that while some similarities between IT and IoT architectures do exist, for the most part, the challenges and requirements of IoT systems are radically different from those of traditional IT networks. The terminology is also different to the point where IoT networks are often under the umbrella of OT, which is responsible for the management and state of operational systems. In contrast, IT networks are primarily concerned with the infrastructure that transports flows of data, regardless of the data type.

This chapter examines some of the unique challenges posed by IoT networks and how these challenges have driven new architectural models. This chapter explores the following areas:

- **Drivers Behind New Network Architectures:** OT networks drive core industrial business operations. They have unique characteristics and constraints that are not easily supported by traditional IT network architectures.

- **Comparing IoT Architectures:** Several architectures have been published for IoT, including those by ETSI and the IoT World Forum. This section discusses and compares these architectures.

- **A Simplified IoT Architecture:** While several IoT architectures exist, a simplified model is presented in this section to lay a foundation for rest of the material discussed in this book.

- **The Core IoT Functional Stack:** The IoT network must be designed to support its unique requirements and constraints. This section provides an overview of the full networking stack, from sensors all the way to the applications layer.

- **IoT Data Management and Compute Stack:** This section introduces data management, including storage and compute resource models for IoT, and involves edge, fog, and cloud computing.

Drivers Behind New Network Architectures

This chapter begins by comparing how using an architectural blueprint to construct a house is similar to the approach we take when designing a network. Now, imagine an experienced architect who has built residential houses for his whole career. He is an expert in this field and knows exactly what it takes to not only make a house architecturally attractive but also to be functional and livable and meet the construction codes mandated by local government. One day, this architect is asked to take on a new project: Construct a massive stadium that will be a showpiece for the city and which will support a variety of sporting teams, concerts, and community events, and which has a seating capacity of 60,000+.

While the architect has extensive experience in designing homes, those skills will clearly not be enough to meet the demands of this new project. The scale of the stadium is several magnitudes larger, the use is completely different, and the wear and tear will be at a completely different level. The architect needs a new architectural approach that meets the requirements for building the stadium.

The difference between IT and IoT networks is much like the difference between residential architecture and stadium architecture. While traditional network architectures for IT have served us well for many years, they are not well suited to the complex requirements of IoT. Chapter 1, "What Is IoT?" introduces some of the differences between IT and OT, as well as some of the inherent challenges posed by IoT. These differences and challenges are driving fundamentally new architectures for IoT systems.

The key difference between IT and IoT is the data. While IT systems are mostly concerned with reliable and continuous support of business applications such as email, web, databases, CRM systems, and so on, IoT is all about the data generated by sensors and how that data is used. The essence of IoT architectures thus involves how the data is transported, collected, analyzed, and ultimately acted upon.

Table 2-1 takes a closer look at some of the differences between IT and IoT networks, with a focus on the IoT requirements that are driving new network architectures, and considers what adjustments are needed.

Table 2-1 *IoT Architectural Drivers*

Challenge	Description	IoT Architectural Change Required
Scale	The massive scale of IoT endpoints (sensors) is far beyond that of typical IT networks.	The IPv4 address space has reached exhaustion and is unable to meet IoT's scalability requirements. Scale can be met only by using IPv6. IT networks continue to use IPv4 through features like Network Address Translation (NAT).
Security	IoT devices, especially those on wireless sensor networks (WSNs), are often physically exposed to the world.	Security is required at every level of the IoT network. Every IoT endpoint node on the network must be part of the overall security strategy and must support device-level authentication and link encryption. It must also be easy to deploy with some type of a zero-touch deployment model.

Challenge	Description	IoT Architectural Change Required
Devices and networks constrained by power, CPU, memory, and link speed	Due to the massive scale and longer distances, the networks are often constrained, lossy, and capable of supporting only minimal data rates (tens of bps to hundreds of Kbps).	New last-mile wireless technologies are needed to support constrained IoT devices over long distances. The network is also constrained, meaning modifications need to be made to traditional network-layer transport mechanisms.
The massive volume of data generated	The sensors generate a massive amount of data on a daily basis, causing network bottlenecks and slow analytics in the cloud.	Data analytics capabilities need to be distributed throughout the IoT network, from the edge to the cloud. In traditional IT networks, analytics and applications typically run only in the cloud.
Support for legacy devices	An IoT network often comprises a collection of modern, IP-capable endpoints as well as legacy, non-IP devices that rely on serial or proprietary protocols.	Digital transformation is a long process that may take many years, and IoT networks need to support protocol translation and/or tunneling mechanisms to support legacy protocols over standards-based protocols, such as Ethernet and IP.
The need for data to be analyzed in real time	Whereas traditional IT networks perform scheduled batch processing of data, IoT data needs to be analyzed and responded to in real-time.	Analytics software needs to be positioned closer to the edge and should support real-time streaming analytics. Traditional IT analytics software (such as relational databases or even Hadoop), are better suited to batch-level analytics that occur after the fact.

The following sections expand on the requirements driving specific architectural changes for IoT.

Scale

The scale of a typical IT network is on the order of several thousand devices—typically printers, mobile wireless devices, laptops, servers, and so on. The traditional three-layer campus networking model, supporting access, distribution, and core (with subarchitectures for WAN, Wi-Fi, data center, etc.), is well understood. But now consider what happens when the scale of a network goes from a few thousand endpoints to a few million. How many IT engineers have ever designed a network that is intended to support millions of routable IP endpoints? This kind of scale has only previously been seen by the Tier 1 service providers. IoT introduces a model where an average-sized utility, factory, transportation system, or city could easily be asked to support a network of this scale. Based on scale requirements of this order, IPv6 is the natural foundation for the IoT network layer.

Security

It has often been said that if World War III breaks out, it will be fought in cyberspace. We have already seen evidence of targeted malicious attacks using vulnerabilities in networked machines, such as the outbreak of the Stuxnet worm, which specifically affected Siemens programmable logic controller (PLC) systems.

The frequency and impact of cyber attacks in recent years has increased dramatically. Protecting corporate data from intrusion and theft is one of the main functions of the IT department. IT departments go to great lengths to protect servers, applications, and the network, setting up defense-in-depth models with layers of security designed to protect the cyber crown jewels of the corporation. However, despite all the efforts mustered to protect networks and data, hackers still find ways to penetrate trusted networks. In IT networks, the first line of defense is often the perimeter firewall. It would be unthinkable to position critical IT endpoints outside the firewall, visible to anyone who cared to look. However, IoT endpoints are often located in wireless sensor networks that use unlicensed spectrum and are not only visible to the world through a spectrum analyzer but often physically accessible and widely distributed in the field.

As more OT systems become connected to IP networks, their capabilities increase, but so does their potential vulnerability. For example, at 3:30 p.m. on December 23, 2015, the Ukrainian power grid experienced an unprecedented cyber attack that affected approximately 225,000 customers. This attack wasn't simply carried out by a group of opportunistic thieves; it was a sophisticated, well-planned assault on the Ukrainian power grid that targeted the SCADA (supervisory control and data acquisition) system, which governs communication to grid automation devices.

Traditional models of IT security are simply not designed for the new attack vectors introduced by highly dispersed IoT systems. IoT systems require consistent mechanisms of authentication, encryption, and intrusion prevention techniques that understand the behavior of industrial protocols and can respond to attacks on critical infrastructure. For optimum security, IoT systems must:

- Be able to identify and authenticate all entities involved in the IoT service (that is, gateways, endpoint devices, home networks, roaming networks, service platforms)

- Ensure that all user data shared between the endpoint device and back-end applications is encrypted

- Comply with local data protection legislation so that all data is protected and stored correctly

- Utilize an IoT connectivity management platform and establish rules-based security policies so immediate action can be taken if anomalous behavior is detected from connected devices

- Take a holistic, network-level approach to security

See Chapter 8, "Securing IoT," for more information on IoT security.

Constrained Devices and Networks

Most IoT sensors are designed for a single job, and they are typically small and inexpensive. This means they often have limited power, CPU, and memory, and they transmit only when there is something important. Because of the massive scale of these devices and the large, uncontrolled environments where they are usually deployed, the networks that provide connectivity also tend to be very lossy and support very low data rates. This is a completely different situation from IT networks, which enjoy multi-gigabit connection speeds and endpoints with powerful CPUs. If an IT network has performance constraints, the solution is simple: Upgrade to a faster network. If too many devices are on one VLAN and are impacting performance, you can simply carve out a new VLAN and continue to scale as much as you need. However, this approach cannot meet the constrained nature of IoT systems. IoT requires a new breed of connectivity technologies that meet both the scale and constraint limitations. For more detailed information on constrained devices and networks, see Chapter 5, "IP as the IoT Network Layer."

Data

IoT devices generate a mountain of data. In general, most IT shops don't really care much about the unstructured chatty data generated by devices on the network. However, in IoT the data is like gold, as it is what enables businesses to deliver new IoT services that enhance the customer experience, reduce cost, and deliver new revenue opportunities. Although most IoT-generated data is unstructured, the insights it provides through analytics can revolutionize processes and create new business models. Imagine a smart city with a few hundred thousand smart streetlights, all connected through an IoT network. Although most of the information communicated between the lighting network modules and the control center is of little interest to anyone, patterns in this data can yield extremely useful insights that can help predict when lights need to be replaced or whether they can be turned on or off at certain times, thus saving operational expense. However, when all this data is combined, it can become difficult to manage and analyze effectively. Therefore, unlike IT networks, IoT systems are designed to stagger data consumption throughout the architecture, both to filter and reduce unnecessary data going upstream and to provide the fastest possible response to devices when necessary.

Legacy Device Support

Supporting legacy devices in an IT organization is not usually a big problem. If someone's computer or operating system is outdated, she simply upgrades. If someone is using a mobile device with an outdated Wi-Fi standard, such as 802.11b or 802.11g, you can simply deny him access to the wireless network, and he will be forced to upgrade. In OT systems, end devices are likely to be on the network for a very long time—sometimes decades. As IoT networks are deployed, they need to support the older devices already present on the network, as well as devices with new capabilities. In many cases, legacy devices are so old that they don't even support IP. For example, a factory may replace machines only once every 20 years—or perhaps even longer! It does not want to upgrade multi-million-dollar machines just so it can connect them to a network for better visibility and control. However, many of these legacy machines might support older protocols, such as serial interfaces, and use RS-232. In this case, the IoT network must either be capable of some type of protocol translation or use a gateway device to connect these legacy endpoints to the IoT network. Chapter 6, "Application Protocols for IoT," takes a closer look at the transport of legacy IoT protocols.

Comparing IoT Architectures

The aforementioned challenges and requirements of IoT systems have driven a whole new discipline of network architecture. In the past several years, architectural standards and frameworks have emerged to address the challenge of designing massive-scale IoT networks.

The foundational concept in all these architectures is supporting data, process, and the functions that endpoint devices perform. Two of the best-known architectures are those supported by oneM2M and the IoT World Forum (IoTWF), discussed in the following sections.

The oneM2M IoT Standardized Architecture

In an effort to standardize the rapidly growing field of machine-to-machine (M2M) communications, the European Telecommunications Standards Institute (ETSI) created the M2M Technical Committee in 2008. The goal of this committee was to create a common architecture that would help accelerate the adoption of M2M applications and devices. Over time, the scope has expanded to include the Internet of Things.

Other related bodies also began to create similar M2M architectures, and a common standard for M2M became necessary. Recognizing this need, in 2012 ETSI and 13 other founding members launched oneM2M as a global initiative designed to promote efficient M2M communication systems and IoT. The goal of oneM2M is to create a common services layer, which can be readily embedded in field devices to allow communication with application servers.[1] oneM2M's framework focuses on IoT services, applications, and platforms. These include smart metering applications, smart grid, smart city automation, e-health, and connected vehicles.

One of the greatest challenges in designing an IoT architecture is dealing with the heterogeneity of devices, software, and access methods. By developing a horizontal platform architecture, oneM2M is developing standards that allow interoperability at all levels of the IoT stack. For example, you might want to automate your HVAC system by connecting it with wireless temperature sensors spread throughout your office. You decide to deploy sensors that use LoRaWAN technology (discussed in Chapter 4, "Connecting Smart Objects"). The problem is that the LoRaWAN network and the BACnet system that your HVAC and BMS run on are completely different systems and have no natural connection point. This is where the oneM2M common services architecture comes in. oneM2M's horizontal framework and RESTful APIs allow the LoRaWAN system to interface with the building management system over an IoT network, thus promoting end-to-end IoT communications in a consistent way, no matter how heterogeneous the networks.

Figure 2-1 illustrates the oneM2M IoT architecture.

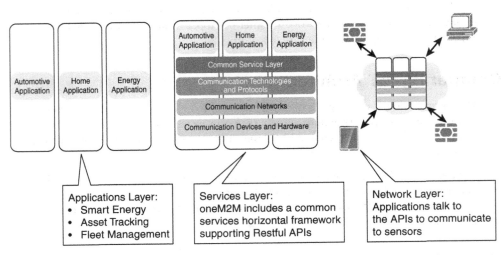

Figure 2-1   *The Main Elements of the oneM2M IoT Architecture*

The oneM2M architecture divides IoT functions into three major domains: the application layer, the services layer, and the network layer. While this architecture may seem simple and somewhat generic at first glance, it is very rich and promotes interoperability through IT-friendly APIs and supports a wide range of IoT technologies. Let's examine each of these domains in turn:

■ **Applications layer:** The oneM2M architecture gives major attention to connectivity between devices and their applications. This domain includes the application-layer protocols and attempts to standardize northbound API definitions for interaction with business intelligence (BI) systems. Applications tend to be industry-specific and have their own sets of data models, and thus they are shown as vertical entities.

■ **Services layer:** This layer is shown as a horizontal framework across the vertical industry applications. At this layer, horizontal modules include the physical network that the IoT applications run on, the underlying management protocols, and the hardware. Examples include backhaul communications via cellular, MPLS networks, VPNs, and so on. Riding on top is the common services layer. This conceptual layer adds APIs and middleware supporting third-party services and applications. One of the stated goals of oneM2M is to "develop technical specifications which address the need for a common M2M Service Layer that can be readily embedded within various hardware and software nodes, and rely upon connecting the myriad of devices in the field area network to M2M application servers, which typically reside in a cloud or data center." A critical objective of oneM2M is to attract and actively involve organizations from M2M-related business domains, including telematics and intelligent transportation, healthcare, utility, industrial automation, and smart home applications, to name just a few.[2]

■ **Network layer:** This is the communication domain for the IoT devices and end-points. It includes the devices themselves and the communications network that links them. Embodiments of this communications infrastructure include wireless mesh technologies, such as IEEE 802.15.4, and wireless point-to-multipoint systems, such as IEEE 801.11ah. Also included are wired device connections, such as IEEE 1901 power line communications. Chapter 4 provides more details on these connectivity technologies.

In many cases, the smart (and sometimes not-so-smart) devices communicate with each other. In other cases, machine-to-machine communication is not necessary, and the devices simply communicate through a field area network (FAN) to use-case-specific apps in the IoT application domain. Therefore, the device domain also includes the gateway device, which provides communications up into the core network and acts as a demarcation point between the device and network domains.

Technical Specifications and Technical Reports published by oneM2M covering IoT functional architecture and other aspects can be found at www.onem2m.org.

The IoT World Forum (IoTWF) Standardized Architecture

In 2014 the IoTWF architectural committee (led by Cisco, IBM, Rockwell Automation, and others) published a seven-layer IoT architectural reference model. While various IoT reference models exist, the one put forth by the IoT World Forum offers a clean, simplified perspective on IoT and includes edge computing, data storage, and access. It provides a succinct way of visualizing IoT from a technical perspective. Each of the seven layers is broken down into specific functions, and security encompasses the entire model. Figure 2-2 details the IoT Reference Model published by the IoTWF.

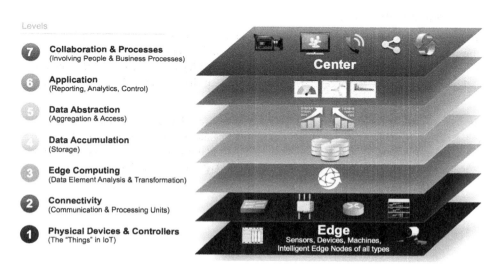

Figure 2-2 *IoT Reference Model Published by the IoT World Forum*

As shown in Figure 2-2, the IoT Reference Model defines a set of levels with control flowing from the center (this could be either a cloud service or a dedicated data center), to the edge, which includes sensors, devices, machines, and other types of intelligent end nodes. In general, data travels up the stack, originating from the edge, and goes northbound to the center. Using this reference model, we are able to achieve the following:

- Decompose the IoT problem into smaller parts

- Identify different technologies at each layer and how they relate to one another

- Define a system in which different parts can be provided by different vendors

- Have a process of defining interfaces that leads to interoperability

- Define a tiered security model that is enforced at the transition points between levels

The following sections look more closely at each of the seven layers of the IoT Reference Model.

Layer 1: Physical Devices and Controllers Layer

The first layer of the IoT Reference Model is the physical devices and controllers layer. This layer is home to the "things" in the Internet of Things, including the various endpoint devices and sensors that send and receive information. The size of these "things" can range from almost microscopic sensors to giant machines in a factory. Their primary function is generating data and being capable of being queried and/or controlled over a network.

Layer 2: Connectivity Layer

In the second layer of the IoT Reference Model, the focus is on connectivity. The most important function of this IoT layer is the reliable and timely transmission of data. More specifically, this includes transmissions between Layer 1 devices and the network and between the network and information processing that occurs at Layer 3 (the edge computing layer).

As you may notice, the connectivity layer encompasses all networking elements of IoT and doesn't really distinguish between the last-mile network (the network between the sensor/endpoint and the IoT gateway, discussed later in this chapter), gateway, and backhaul networks. Functions of the connectivity layer are detailed in Figure 2-3.

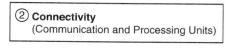

Layer 2 Functions:
- Communications Between Layer 1 Devices
- Reliable Delivery of Information Across the Network
- Switching and Routing
- Translation Between Protocols
- Network Level Security

Figure 2-3 *IoT Reference Model Connectivity Layer Functions*

Layer 3: Edge Computing Layer

Edge computing is the role of Layer 3. Edge computing is often referred to as the "fog" layer and is discussed in the section "Fog Computing," later in this chapter. At this layer, the emphasis is on data reduction and converting network data flows into information that is ready for storage and processing by higher layers. One of the basic principles of this reference model is that information processing is initiated as early and as close to the edge of the network as possible. Figure 2-4 highlights the functions handled by Layer 3 of the IoT Reference Model.

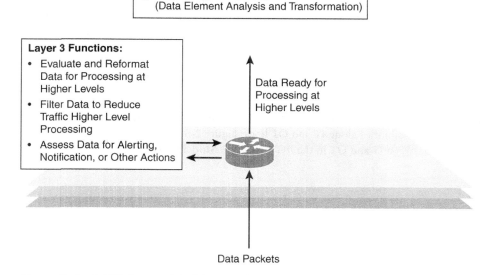

Figure 2-4 *IoT Reference Model Layer 3 Functions*

Another important function that occurs at Layer 3 is the evaluation of data to see if it can be filtered or aggregated before being sent to a higher layer. This also allows for data to be reformatted or decoded, making additional processing by other systems easier. Thus, a critical function is assessing the data to see if predefined thresholds are crossed and any action or alerts need to be sent.

Upper Layers: Layers 4–7

The upper layers deal with handling and processing the IoT data generated by the bottom layer. For the sake of completeness, Layers 4–7 of the IoT Reference Model are summarized in Table 2-2.

Table 2-2   *Summary of Layers 4–7 of the IoTWF Reference Model*

IoT Reference Model Layer	Functions
Layer 4: Data accumulation layer	Captures data and stores it so it is usable by applications when necessary. Converts event-based data to query-based processing.
Layer 5: Data abstraction layer	Reconciles multiple data formats and ensures consistent semantics from various sources. Confirms that the data set is complete and consolidates data into one place or multiple data stores using virtualization.
Layer 6: Applications layer	Interprets data using software applications. Applications may monitor, control, and provide reports based on the analysis of the data.
Layer 7: Collaboration and processes layer	Consumes and shares the application information. Collaborating on and communicating IoT information often requires multiple steps, and it is what makes IoT useful. This layer can change business processes and delivers the benefits of IoT.

IT and OT Responsibilities in the IoT Reference Model

An interesting aspect of visualizing an IoT architecture this way is that you can start to organize responsibilities along IT and OT lines. Figure 2-5 illustrates a natural demarcation point between IT and OT in the IoT Reference Model framework.

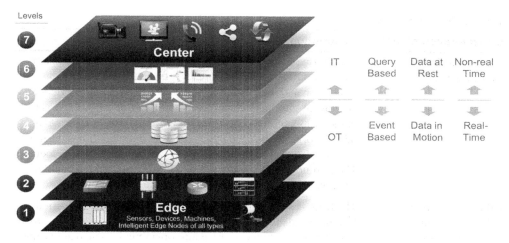

Figure 2-5 *IoT Reference Model Separation of IT and OT*

As demonstrated in Figure 2-5, IoT systems have to cross several boundaries beyond just the functional layers. The bottom of the stack is generally in the domain of OT. For an industry like oil and gas, this includes sensors and devices connected to pipelines, oil rigs, refinery machinery, and so on. The top of the stack is in the IT area and includes things like the servers, databases, and applications, all of which run on a part of the network controlled by IT. In the past, OT and IT have generally been very independent and had little need to even talk to each other. IoT is changing that paradigm.

At the bottom, in the OT layers, the devices generate real-time data at their own rate—sometimes vast amounts on a daily basis. Not only does this result in a huge amount of data transiting the IoT network, but the sheer volume of data suggests that applications at the top layer will be able to ingest that much data at the rate required. To meet this requirement, data has to be buffered or stored at certain points within the IoT stack. Layering data management in this way throughout the stack helps the top four layers handle data at their own speed.

As a result, the real-time "data in motion" close to the edge has to be organized and stored so that it becomes "data at rest" for the applications in the IT tiers. The IT and OT organizations need to work together for overall data management.

Additional IoT Reference Models

In addition to the two IoT reference models already presented in this chapter, several other reference models exist. These models are endorsed by various organizations and standards bodies and are often specific to certain industries or IoT applications. Table 2-3 highlights these additional IoT reference models.

Table 2-3   *Alternative IoT Reference Models*

IoT Reference Model	Description
Purdue Model for Control Hierarchy	The Purdue Model for Control Hierarchy (see www.cisco.com/c/en/us/td/docs/solutions/Verticals/EttF/EttFDIG/ch2_EttF.pdf) is a common and well-understood model that segments devices and equipment into hierarchical levels and functions. It is used as the basis for ISA-95 for control hierarchy, and in turn for the IEC-62443 (formerly ISA-99) cyber security standard. It has been used as a base for many IoT-related models and standards across industry. The Purdue Model's application to IoT is discussed in detail in Chapter 9, "Manufacturing," and in Chapter 10, "Oil & Gas."
Industrial Internet Reference Architecture (IIRA) by Industrial Internet Consortium (IIC)	The IIRA is a standards-based open architecture for Industrial Internet Systems (IISs). To maximize its value, the IIRA has broad industry applicability to drive interoperability, to map applicable technologies, and to guide technology and standard development. The description and representation of the architecture are generic and at a high level of abstraction to support the requisite broad industry applicability. The IIRA distills and abstracts common characteristics, features and patterns from use cases well understood at this time, predominantly those that have been defined in the IIC. For more information, see www.iiconsortium.org/IIRA.htm.
Internet of Things–Architecture (IoT-A)	IoT-A created an IoT architectural reference model and defined an initial set of key building blocks that are foundational in fostering the emerging Internet of Things. Using an experimental paradigm, IoT-A combined top-down reasoning about architectural principles and design guidelines with simulation and prototyping in exploring the technical consequences of architectural design choices. For more information, see https://vdivde-it.de/en.

A Simplified IoT Architecture

Although considerable differences exist between the aforementioned reference models, they each approach IoT from a layered perspective, allowing development of technology and standards somewhat independently at each level or domain. The commonality between these frameworks is that they all recognize the interconnection of the IoT endpoint devices to a network that transports the data where it is ultimately used by applications, whether at the data center, in the cloud, or at various management points throughout the stack.

It is not the intention of this book to promote or endorse any one specific IoT architectural framework. In fact, it can be noted that IoT architectures may differ somewhat depending on the industry use case or technology being deployed, and each has merit in solving the IoT heterogeneity problem discussed earlier. Thus, in this book we present an IoT framework that highlights the fundamental building blocks that are common to most IoT systems and which is intended to help you in designing an IoT network. This framework is presented as two parallel stacks: The IoT Data Management and Compute Stack and the Core IoT Functional Stack. Reducing the framework down to a pair of three-layer stacks in no way suggests that the model lacks the detail necessary to develop a sophisticated IoT strategy. Rather, the intention is to simplify the IoT architecture into its most basic building blocks and then to use it as a foundation to understand key design and deployment principles that are applied to industry-specific use cases. All the layers of more complex models are still covered, but they are grouped here in functional blocks that are easy to understand. Figure 2-6 illustrates the simplified IoT model presented in this book.

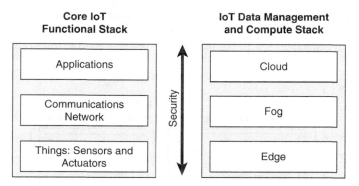

Figure 2-6 *Simplified IoT Architecture*

Nearly every published IoT model includes core layers similar to those shown on the left side of Figure 2-6, including "things," a communications network, and applications. However, unlike other models, the framework presented here separates the core IoT and data management into parallel and aligned stacks, allowing you to carefully examine the functions of both the network and the applications at each stage of a complex IoT system. This separation gives you better visibility into the functions of each layer.

The presentation of the Core IoT Functional Stack in three layers is meant to simplify your understanding of the IoT architecture into its most foundational building blocks. Of course, such a simple architecture needs to be expanded on. The network communications layer of the IoT stack itself involves a significant amount of detail and incorporates a vast array of technologies. Consider for a moment the heterogeneity of IoT sensors and the many different ways that exist to connect them to a network. The network communications layer needs to consolidate these together, offer gateway and backhaul technologies, and ultimately bring the data back to a central location for analysis and processing.

Many of the last-mile technologies used in IoT are chosen to meet the specific requirements of the endpoints and are unlikely to ever be seen in the IT domain. However, the
network between the gateway and the data center is composed mostly of traditional
technologies that experienced IT professionals would quickly recognize. These include
tunneling and VPN technologies, IP-based quality of service (QoS), conventional Layer 3
routing protocols such as BGP and IP-PIM, and security capabilities such as encryption,
access control lists (ACLs), and firewalls.

Unlike with most IT networks, the applications and analytics layer of IoT doesn't
necessarily exist only in the data center or in the cloud. Due to the unique challenges
and requirements of IoT, it is often necessary to deploy applications and data management
throughout the architecture in a tiered approach, allowing data collection, analytics,
and intelligent controls at multiple points in the IoT system. In the model presented in
this book, data management is aligned with each of the three layers of the Core IoT
Functional Stack. The three data management layers are the edge layer (data management
within the sensors themselves), the fog layer (data management in the gateways and transit
network), and the cloud layer (data management in the cloud or central data center). The
IoT Data Management and Compute Stack is examined in greater detail later in this chapter. Figure 2-7 highlights an expanded view of the IoT architecture presented in this book.

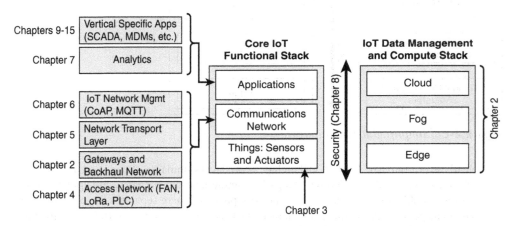

Figure 2-7 *Expanded View of the Simplified IoT Architecture*

As shown in Figure 2-7, the Core IoT Functional Stack can be expanded into sublayers
containing greater detail and specific network functions. For example, the communications layer is broken down into four separate sublayers: the access network, gateways and
backhaul, IP transport, and operations and management sublayers.

The applications layer of IoT networks is quite different from the application layer of
a typical enterprise network. Instead of simply using business applications, IoT often
involves a strong big data analytics component. One message that is stressed throughout

this book is that IoT is not just about the control of IoT devices but, rather, the useful insights gained from the data generated by those devices. Thus, the applications layer typically has both analytics and industry-specific IoT control system components.

You will notice that security is central to the entire architecture, both from network connectivity and data management perspectives. The chapters in Part II, "Engineering IoT Networks," discuss security at each layer. Chapter 8 is dedicated to the subject of securing IoT systems. The industry chapters in Part III, "IoT in Industry," highlight how lessons learned in Parts I, "Introduction to IoT," and II can be applied to specific industries. Each of the Part III chapters examines the issue of IoT security for a particular sector.

The architectural framework presented in Figure 2-7 reflects the flow of the chapters in this book. To help navigate your way through this book, chapter numbers are highlighted next to the various layers of the stack.

The remainder of this chapter provides a high-level examination of each layer of this model and lays the foundation for a detailed examination of the technologies involved at each layer presented in Part II, and it gives you the tools you need to understand how these technologies are applied in key industries in Part III.

The Core IoT Functional Stack

IoT networks are built around the concept of "things," or smart objects performing functions and delivering new connected services. These objects are "smart" because they use a combination of contextual information and configured goals to perform actions. These actions can be self-contained (that is, the smart object does not rely on external systems for its actions); however, in most cases, the "thing" interacts with an external system to report information that the smart object collects, to exchange with other objects, or to interact with a management platform. In this case, the management platform can be used to process data collected from the smart object and also guide the behavior of the smart object. From an architectural standpoint, several components have to work together for an IoT network to be operational:

- **"Things" layer:** At this layer, the physical devices need to fit the constraints of the environment in which they are deployed while still being able to provide the information needed.

- **Communications network layer:** When smart objects are not self-contained, they need to communicate with an external system. In many cases, this communication uses a wireless technology. This layer has four sublayers:

  - **Access network sublayer:** The last mile of the IoT network is the access network. This is typically made up of wireless technologies such as 802.11ah, 802.15.4g, and LoRa. The sensors connected to the access network may also be wired.

■ **Gateways and backhaul network sublayer:** A common communication system organizes multiple smart objects in a given area around a common gateway. The gateway communicates directly with the smart objects. The role of the gateway is to forward the collected information through a longer-range medium (called the backhaul) to a headend central station where the information is processed. This information exchange is a Layer 7 (application) function, which is the reason this object is called a gateway. On IP networks, this gateway also forwards packets from one IP network to another, and it therefore acts as a router.

■ **Network transport sublayer:** For communication to be successful, network and transport layer protocols such as IP and UDP must be implemented to support the variety of devices to connect and media to use.

■ **IoT network management sublayer:** Additional protocols must be in place to allow the headend applications to exchange data with the sensors. Examples include CoAP and MQTT.

■ **Application and analytics layer:** At the upper layer, an application needs to process the collected data, not only to control the smart objects when necessary, but to make intelligent decision based on the information collected and, in turn, instruct the "things" or other systems to adapt to the analyzed conditions and change their behaviors or parameters.

The following sections examine these elements and help you architect your IoT communication network.

Layer 1: Things: Sensors and Actuators Layer

Most IoT networks start from the object, or "thing," that needs to be connected. Chapter 3, "Smart Objects: The 'Things' in IoT," provides more in-depth information about smart objects. From an architectural standpoint, the variety of smart object types, shapes, and needs drive the variety of IoT protocols and architectures. There are myriad ways to classify smart objects. One architectural classification could be:

■ **Battery-powered or power-connected:** This classification is based on whether the object carries its own energy supply or receives continuous power from an external power source. Battery-powered things can be moved more easily than line-powered objects. However, batteries limit the lifetime and amount of energy that the object is allowed to consume, thus driving transmission range and frequency.

■ **Mobile or static:** This classification is based on whether the "thing" should move or always stay at the same location. A sensor may be mobile because it is moved from one object to another (for example, a viscosity sensor moved from batch to batch in a chemical plant) or because it is attached to a moving object (for example, a location sensor on moving goods in a warehouse or factory floor). The frequency of the movement may also vary, from occasional to permanent. The range of mobility (from a few inches to miles away) often drives the possible power source.

- **Low or high reporting frequency:** This classification is based on how often the object should report monitored parameters. A rust sensor may report values once a month. A motion sensor may report acceleration several hundred times per second. Higher frequencies drive higher energy consumption, which may create constraints on the possible power source (and therefore the object mobility) and the transmission range.

- **Simple or rich data:** This classification is based on the quantity of data exchanged at each report cycle. A humidity sensor in a field may report a simple daily index value (on a binary scale from 0 to 255), while an engine sensor may report hundreds of parameters, from temperature to pressure, gas velocity, compression speed, carbon index, and many others. Richer data typically drives higher power consumption. This classification is often combined with the previous to determine the object data throughput (low throughput to high throughput). You may want to keep in mind that throughput is a combined metric. A medium-throughput object may send simple data at rather high frequency (in which case the flow structure looks continuous), or may send rich data at rather low frequency (in which case the flow structure looks bursty).

- **Report range:** This classification is based on the distance at which the gateway is located. For example, for your fitness band to communicate with your phone, it needs to be located a few meters away at most. The assumption is that your phone needs to be at visual distance for you to consult the reported data on the phone screen. If the phone is far away, you typically do not use it, and reporting data from the band to the phone is not necessary. By contrast, a moisture sensor in the asphalt of a road may need to communicate with its reader several hundred meters or even kilometers away.

- **Object density per cell:** This classification is based on the number of smart objects (with a similar need to communicate) over a given area, connected to the same gateway. An oil pipeline may utilize a single sensor at key locations every few miles. By contrast, telescopes like the SETI Colossus telescope at the Whipple Observatory deploy hundreds, and sometimes thousands, of mirrors over a small area, each with multiple gyroscopes, gravity, and vibration sensors.

From a network architectural standpoint, your initial task is to determine which technology should be used to allow smart objects to communicate. This determination depends on the way the "things" are classified. However, some industries (such as manufacturing and utilities) may include objects in various categories, matching different needs. Figure 2-8 provides some examples of applications matching the combination of mobility and throughput requirements.

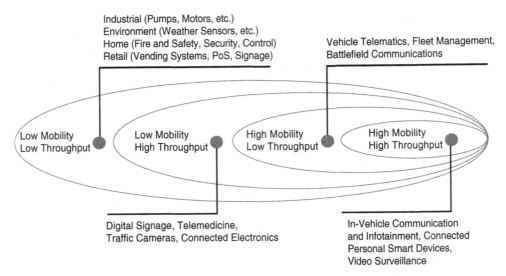

Figure 2-8   *Example of Sensor Applications Based on Mobility and Throughput*

The categories used to classify things can influence other parameters and can also influence one another. For example, a battery-operated highly mobile object (like a heart rate monitor, for example) likely has a small form factor. A small sensor is easier to move or integrate into its environment. At the same time, a small and highly mobile smart object is unlikely to require a large antenna and a powerful power source. This constraint will limit the transmission range and, therefore, the type of network protocol available for its connections. The criticality of data may also influence the form factor and, therefore, the architecture. For example, a missing monthly report from an asphalt moisture sensor may simply flag an indicator for sensor (or battery) replacement. A multi-mirror gyroscope report missing for more than 100 ms may render the entire system unstable or unusable. These sensors either need to have a constant source of power (resulting in limited mobility) or need to be easily accessible for battery replacement (resulting in limited transmission range). A first step in designing an IoT network is to examine the requirements in terms of mobility and data transmission (how much data, how often).

Layer 2: Communications Network Layer

Once you have determined the influence of the smart object form factor over its transmission capabilities (transmission range, data volume and frequency, sensor density and mobility), you are ready to connect the object and communicate.

Compute and network assets used in IoT can be very different from those in IT environments. The difference in the physical form factors between devices used by IT and OT is obvious even to the most casual of observers. What typically drives this is the physical environment in which the devices are deployed. What may not be as inherently obvious, however, is their operational differences. The operational differences must be understood in order to apply the correct handling to secure the target assets.

Temperature variances are an easily understood metric. The cause for the variance is easily attributed to external weather forces and internal operating conditions. Remote external locations, such as those associated with mineral extraction or pipeline equipment can span from the heat of the Arabian Gulf to the cold of the Alaskan North Slope. Controls near the furnaces of a steel mill obviously require heat tolerance, and controls for cold food storage require the opposite. In some cases, these controls must handle extreme fluctuations as well. These extremes can be seen within a single deployment. For example, portions of the Tehachapi, California, wind farms are located in the Mojave Desert, while others are at an altitude of 1800 m in the surrounding mountains. As you can imagine, the wide variance in temperature takes a special piece of hardware that is capable of withstanding such harsh environments.

Humidity fluctuations can impact the long-term success of a system as well. Well heads residing in the delta of the Niger River will see very different conditions from those in the middle of the Arabian Desert. In some conditions, the systems could be exposed to direct liquid contact such as may be found with outdoor wireless devices or marine condition deployments.

Less obvious are the operating extremes related to kinetic forces. Shock and vibration needs vary based on the deployment scenario. In some cases, the focus is on low-amplitude but constant vibrations, as may be expected on a bushing-mounted manufacturing system. In other cases, it could be a sudden acceleration or deceleration, such as may be experienced in peak ground acceleration of an earthquake or an impact on a mobile system such as high-speed rail or heavy-duty earth moving equipment.

Solid particulates can also impact the gear. Most IT environments must contend with dust build-up that can become highly concentrated due to the effect of cooling fans. In less-controlled IT environments, that phenomenon can be accelerated due to higher concentrations of particulates. A deterrent to particulate build-up is to use fanless cooling, which necessitates a higher surface area, as is the case with heat transfer fins.

Hazardous location design may also cause corrosive impact to the equipment. Caustic materials can impact connections over which power or communications travel. Furthermore, they can result in reduced thermal efficiency by potentially coating the heat transfer surfaces.

In some scenarios, the concern is not how the environment can impact the equipment but how the equipment can impact the environment. For example, in a scenario in which volatile gases may be present, spark suppression is a critical design criterion.

There is another class of device differentiators related to the external connectivity of the device for mounting or industrial function. Device mounting is one obvious difference between OT and IT environments. While there are rack mount environments in some industrial spaces, they are more frequently found among IT type assets. Within industrial environments, many compute and communication assets are placed within an enclosed space, such as a control cabinet where they will be vertically mounted on a DIN (Deutsches Institut für Normung) rail inside. In other scenarios, the devices might be mounted horizontally directly on a wall or on a fence.

In contrast to most IT-based systems, industrial compute systems often transmit their state or receive inputs from external devices through an alarm channel. These may drive an indicator light (stack lights) to display the status of a process element from afar. This same element can also receive inputs to initiate actions within the system itself.

Power supplies in OT systems are also frequently different from those commonly seen on standard IT equipment. A wider range of power variations are common attributes of industrial compute components. DC power sources are also common in many environments. Given the criticality of many systems, it is often required that redundant power supplies be built into the device itself. Extraneous power supplies, especially those not inherently mounted, are frowned upon, given the potential for accidental unplugging. In some utility cases, the system must be able to handle brief power outages and still continue to operate.

Access Network Sublayer

There is a direct relationship between the IoT network technology you choose and the type of connectivity topology this technology allows. Each technology was designed with a certain number of use cases in mind (what to connect, where to connect, how much data to transport at what interval and over what distance). These use cases determined the frequency band that was expected to be most suitable, the frame structure matching the expected data pattern (packet size and communication intervals), and the possible topologies that these use cases illustrate.

As IoT continues to grow exponentially, you will encounter a wide variety of applications and special use cases. For each of them, an access technology will be required. IoT sometimes reuses existing access technologies whose characteristics match more or less closely the IoT use case requirements. Whereas some access technologies were developed specifically for IoT use cases, others were not.

One key parameter determining the choice of access technology is the range between the smart object and the information collector. Figure 2-9 lists some access technologies you may encounter in the IoT world and the expected transmission distances.

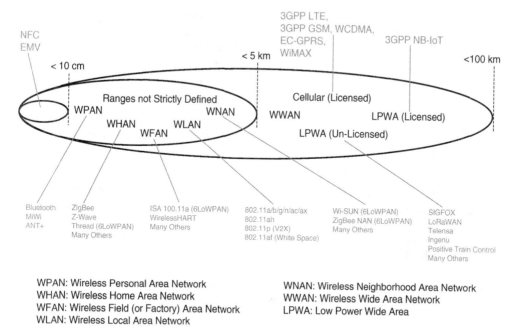

WPAN: Wireless Personal Area Network
WHAN: Wireless Home Area Network
WFAN: Wireless Field (or Factory) Area Network
WLAN: Wireless Local Area Network

WNAN: Wireless Neighborhood Area Network
WWAN: Wireless Wide Area Network
LPWA: Low Power Wide Area

Figure 2-9 *Access Technologies and Distances*

Note that the ranges in Figure 2-9 are inclusive. For example, cellular is indicated for transmissions beyond 5 km, but you could achieve a successful cellular transmission at shorter range (for example, 100 m). By contrast, ZigBee is expected to be efficient over a range of a few tens of meters, but you would not expect a successful ZigBee transmission over a range of 10 km.

Range estimates are grouped by category names that illustrate the environment or the vertical where data collection over that range is expected. Common groups are as follows:

- **PAN (personal area network):** Scale of a few meters. This is the personal space around a person. A common wireless technology for this scale is Bluetooth.

- **HAN (home area network):** Scale of a few tens of meters. At this scale, common wireless technologies for IoT include ZigBee and Bluetooth Low Energy (BLE).

- **NAN (neighborhood area network):** Scale of a few hundreds of meters. The term NAN is often used to refer to a group of house units from which data is collected.

- **FAN (field area network):** Scale of several tens of meters to several hundred meters. FAN typically refers to an outdoor area larger than a single group of house units. The FAN is often seen as "open space" (and therefore not secured and not controlled). A FAN is sometimes viewed as a group of NANs, but some verticals see the FAN as a group of HANs or a group of smaller outdoor cells. As you can see, FAN and NAN may sometimes be used interchangeably. In most cases, the vertical context is clear enough to determine the grouping hierarchy.

■ **LAN (local area network):** Scale of up to 100 m. This term is very common in networking, and it is therefore also commonly used in the IoT space when standard networking technologies (such as Ethernet or IEEE 802.11) are used. Other networking classifications, such as MAN (metropolitan area network, with a range of up to a few kilometers) and WAN (wide area network, with a range of more than a few kilometers), are also commonly used.

Note that for all these places in the IoT network, a "W" can be added to specifically indicate wireless technologies used in that space. For example, HomePlug is a wired technology found in a HAN environment, but a HAN is often referred to as a WHAN (wireless home area network) when a wireless technology, like ZigBee, is used in that space.

Similar achievable distances do not mean similar protocols and similar characteristics. Each protocol uses a specific frame format and transmission technique over a specific frequency (or band). These characteristics introduce additional differences. For example, Figure 2-10 demonstrates four technologies representing WHAN to WLAN ranges and compares the throughput and range that can be achieved in each case. Figure 2-10 supposes that the sensor uses the same frame size, transmit power, and antenna gain. The slope of throughput degradation as distance increases varies vastly from one technology to the other. This difference limits the amount of data throughput that each technology can achieve as the distance from the sensor to the receiver increases.

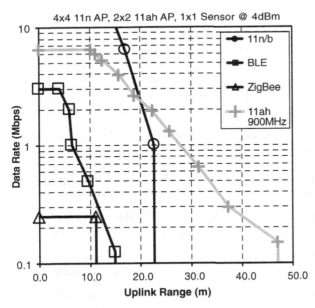

Simulation Assumptions: 1% PER, 4dB NF,
32 Bytes, D-NLOS Fading, Indoor-to-Outdoor
PL Model. 900MHz has12dB propagation gain.

Sensor Antenna Gain: 11ah (-6.5dB)
and 11n (-4dB). AP antenna gain = 2dB.
* BT Long Range Adds 125 kbps and 500 kbps Modes

Figure 2-10   *Range Versus Throughput for Four WHAN to WLAN Technologies*

Increasing the throughput and achievable distance typically comes with an increase in power consumption. Therefore, after determining the smart object requirements (in terms of mobility and data transfer), a second step is to determine the target quantity of objects in a single collection cell, based on the transmission range and throughput required. This parameter in turn determines the size of the cell.

It may be tempting to simply choose the technology with the longest range and highest throughput. However, the cost of the technology is a third determining factor. Figure 2-11 combines cost, range, power consumption, and typical available bandwidth for common IoT access technologies.

The amount of data to carry over a given time period along with correlated power consumption (driving possible limitations in mobility and range) determines the wireless cell size and structure.

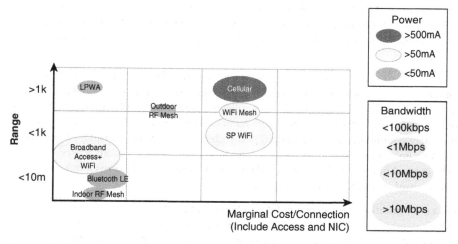

Figure 2-11 *Comparison Between Common Last-Mile Technologies in Terms of Range Versus Cost, Power, and Bandwidth*

Similar ranges also do not mean similar topologies. Some technologies offer flexible connectivity structure to extend communication possibilities:

■ **Point-to-point topologies:** These topologies allow one point to communicate with another point. This topology in its strictest sense is uncommon for IoT access, as it would imply that a single object can communicate only with a single gateway. However, several technologies are referred to as "point-to-point" when each object establishes an individual session with the gateway. The "point-to-point" concept, in that case, often refers to the communication structure more than the physical topology.

■ **Point-to-multipoint topologies:** These topologies allow one point to communicate with more than one other point. Most IoT technologies where one or more than one gateways communicate with multiple smart objects are in this category. However, depending on the features available on each communicating mode, several subtypes need to be considered. A particularity of IoT networks is that some nodes (for example, sensors) support both data collection and forwarding functions, while some other nodes (for example, some gateways) collect the smart object data, sometimes instruct the sensor to perform specific operations, and also interface with other networks or possibly other gateways. For this reason, some technologies categorize the nodes based on the functions (described by a protocol) they implement.

An example of a technology that categorizes nodes based on their function is IEEE 802.15.4, which is covered in depth in Chapter 4. Although 802.15.4 is used as an example in this section, the same principles may apply to many other technologies. Applications leveraging IEEE 802.15.4 commonly rely on the concept of an end device (a sensor) collecting data and transmitting the data to a collector. Sensors need to be small and are often mobile (or movable). When mobile, these sensors are therefore commonly battery operated.

To form a network, a device needs to connect with another device. When both devices fully implement the protocol stack functions, they can form a peer-to-peer network. However, in many cases, one of the devices collects data from the others. For example, in a house, temperature sensors may be deployed in each room or each zone of the house, and they may communicate with a central point where temperature is displayed and controlled. A room sensor does not need to communicate with another room sensor. In that case, the control point is at the center of the network. The network forms a star topology, with the control point at the hub and the sensors at the spokes.

In such a configuration, the central point can be in charge of the overall network coordination, taking care of the beacon transmissions and connection to each sensor. In the IEEE 802.15.4 standard, the central point is called a *coordinator* for the network. With this type of deployment, each sensor is not intended to do anything other than communicate with the coordinator in a master/slave type of relationship. The sensor can implement a subset of protocol functions to perform just a specialized part (communication with the coordinator). Such a device is called a reduced-function device (RFD). An RFD cannot be a coordinator. An RFD also cannot implement direct communications to another RFD.

The coordinator that implements the full network functions is called, by contrast, a fullfunction device (FFD). An FFD can communicate directly with another FFD or with more than one FFD, forming multiple peer-to-peer connections. Topologies where each FFD has a unique path to another FFD are called cluster tree topologies. FFDs in the cluster tree may have RFDs, resulting in a cluster star topology. Figure 2-12 illustrates these topologies.

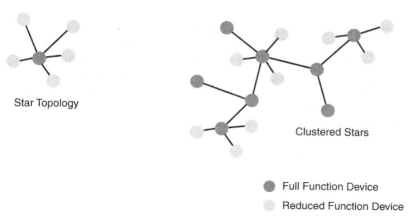

Star Topology

Clustered Stars

● Full Function Device

○ Reduced Function Device

Figure 2-12 *Star and Clustered Star Topologies*

Other point-to-multipoint technologies allow a node to have more than one path to another node, forming a mesh topology. This redundancy means that each node can communicate with more than just one other node. This communication can be used to directly exchange information between nodes (the receiver directly consumes the information received) or to extend the range of the communication link. In this case, an intermediate node acts as a relay between two other nodes. These two other nodes would not be able to communicate successfully directly while respecting the constraints of power and modulation dictated by the PHY layer protocol. Range extension typically comes at the price of slower communications (as intermediate nodes need to spend time relaying other nodes' messages). An example of a technology that implements a mesh topology is Wi-Fi mesh.

Another property of mesh networks is redundancy. The disappearance of one node does not necessarily interrupt network communications. Data may still be relayed through other nodes to reach the intended destination.

Figure 2-13 shows a mesh topology. Nodes A and D are too far apart to communicate directly. In this case, communication can be relayed through nodes B or C. Node B may be used as the primary relay. However, the loss of node B does not prevent the communication between nodes A and D. Here, communication is rerouted through another node, node C.

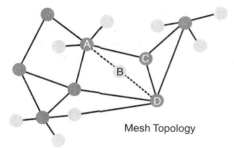

Mesh Topology

Figure 2-13 *Mesh Topology*

Note Figure 2-13 shows a partial mesh topology, where a node can communicate with more than one other node, but not all nodes communicate directly with all other nodes. In a full mesh topology each node communicates with each other node. In the topology shown in Figure 2-13, which has 17 nodes, a full mesh structure would mean that each node would have 16 connections (one to each other node). Full mesh structures are computationally expensive (as each node needs to maintain a connection to each other node). In the IoT space, full mesh deployments are uncommon. In most cases, information has to travel to a target destination rather than being directly distributed to all other nodes. Full mesh topologies also limit the acceptable distance between nodes (as all nodes must be in range of all other nodes).

Note Do not confuse *topology* and *range*. Topology describes the organization of the nodes, while range is dictated by factors such as the frequency or operation, the signal structure, and operational bandwidth. For example, both IEEE 802.15.4 and LoRaWAN implement star topologies, but the range of IEEE 802.15.4 is a few tens of meters, while LoRaWAN can achieve a successful signal over many kilometers. The bandwidth and signal structure (modulation) are very different. Figure 2-11 helps you compare the use cases and implementation considerations (range, cost, available bandwidth) for common IoT access technologies. Chapter 4 describes in detail IEEE 802.15.4, LTE, LoRaWAN, and other competing IoT technologies. However, keep in mind that many technologies that were not initially designed for IoT usage can be leveraged by specific applications. For example, remote sites may need to leverage satellite communications when standard IoT wireless technologies cannot achieve the range required. Also, the adoption of technology can vary widely over time, based on use cases, technology maturity, and other factors. For example, cellular technologies were initially designed for voice communications. The burst of data traffic that accompanied the explosion of mobile devices in the early 2000s brought the development of enhanced standards for cellular communications (with LTE). In turn, this enhancement allowed LTE to grow rapidly as a major connection technology for FANs.

Gateways and Backhaul Sublayer

Data collected from a smart object may need to be forwarded to a central station where data is processed. As this station is often in a different location from the smart object, data directly received from the sensor through an access technology needs to be forwarded to another medium (the backhaul) and transported to the central station. The gateway is in charge of this inter-medium communication.

In most cases, the smart objects are static or mobile within a limited area. The gateway is often static. However, some IoT technologies do not apply this model. For example, dedicated short-range communication (DSRC) allows vehicle-to-vehicle and vehicle-to-infrastructure communication. In this model, the smart object's position relative to the gateway is static. The car includes sensors and one gateway. Communication between the sensors and the gateway may involve wired or wireless technologies. Sensors may also be integrated into the road infrastructure and connect over a wired or wireless technology to a gateway on the side of the road. A wireless technology (DSRC operates in the upper 5 GHz range) is used for backhaul communication, peer-to-peer, or mesh communication between vehicles.

In the DSRC case, the entire "sensor field" is moving along with the gateway, but the general principles of IoT networking remain the same. The range at which DSRC can communicate is limited. Similarly, for all other IoT architectures, the choice of a backhaul technology depends on the communication distance and also on the amount of data that needs to be forwarded. When the smart object's operation is controlled from a local site, and when the environment is stable (for example, factory or oil and gas field), Ethernet can be used as a backhaul. In unstable or changing environments (for example, open mines) where cables cannot safely be run, a wireless technology is used. Wi-Fi is common in this case, often with multiple hops between the sensor field and the operation center. Mesh is a common topology to allow communication flexibility in this type of dynamic environment.

However, throughput decreases as node-to-node distance increases, and it also decreases as the number of hops increases. In a typical Wi-Fi mesh network, throughput halves for each additional hop. Some technologies, like 802.11ah, implement Wi-Fi in a lower band (lower than 1 GHz instead of 2.4 GHz/5 GHz for classical Wi-Fi) with special provisions adapted to IoT, to achieve a longer range (up to about 2 km). Beyond that range, other technologies are needed.

WiMAX (802.16) is an example of a longer-range technology. WiMAX can achieve ranges of up to 50 kilometers with rates of up to 70 Mbps. Obviously, you cannot achieve maximum rate at maximum range; you could expect up to 70 Mbps at short range and 2 to 3 Mbps at maximum range. 802.16d (also called Fixed WiMAX) describes the backhaul implementation of the protocol. Improvements to this aspect have been published (802.16.1), but most WiMAX networks still implement a variation of 802.16d. 802.16 can operate in unlicensed bands, but its backhaul function is often deployed in more-reliable licensed bands, where interferences from other systems are better controlled.

As licensed bands imply the payment of a usability fee, other cellular technologies also grew as competitive solutions for the backhaul part to achieve similar range. The choice of WiMAX or a cellular technology depends on the vertical and the location (local preferences, local costs). Chapter 4 offers an in-depth look at the most commonly deployed protocols for this segment, and Table 2-4 compares the main solutions from an architectural angle.

Table 2-4 *Architectural Considerations for WiMAX and Cellular Technologies*

Technology	Type and Range	Architectural Characteristics
Ethernet	Wired, 100 m max	Requires a cable per sensor/sensor group; adapted to static sensor position in a stable environment; range is limited; link is very reliable
Wi-Fi (2.4 GHz, 5 GHz)	Wireless, 100 m (multipoint) to a few kilometers (P2P)	Can connect multiple clients (typically fewer than 200) to a single AP; range is limited; adapted to cases where client power is not an issue (continuous power or client battery recharged easily); large bandwidth available, but interference from other systems likely; AP needs a cable
802.11ah (HaloW, Wi-Fi in sub-1 GHz)	Wireless, 1.5 km (multipoint), 10 km (P2P)	Can connect a large number of clients (up to 6000 per AP); longer range than traditional Wi-Fi; power efficient; limited bandwidth; low adoption; and cost may be an issue
WiMAX (802.16)	Wireless, several kilometers (last mile), up to 50 km (backhaul)	Can connect a large number of clients; large bandwidth available in licensed spectrum (fee-based); reduced bandwidth in license-free spectrum (interferences from other systems likely); adoption varies on location
Cellular (for example, LTE)	Wireless, several kilometers	Can connect a large number of clients; large bandwidth available; licensed spectrum (interference-free; license-based)

Network Transport Sublayer

The previous section describes a hierarchical communication architecture in which a series of smart objects report to a gateway that conveys the reported data over another medium and up to a central station. However, practical implementations are often flexible, with multiple transversal communication paths. For example, consider the case of IoT for the energy grid. Your house may have a meter that reports the energy consumption to a gateway over a wireless technology. Other houses in your neighborhood (NAN) make the same report, likely to one or several gateways. The data to be transported is small and the interval is large (for example, four times per hour), resulting in a low-mobility, low-throughput type of data structure, with transmission distances up to a mile. Several technologies (such as 802.11ah, 802.15.4, or LPWA) can be used for this collection segment. Other neighborhoods may also connect the same way, thus forming a FAN.

For example, the power utility's headend application server may be regional, and the gateway may relay to a wired or wireless backhaul technology. The structure appears to be hierarchical. Practically, however, this IoT system may achieve more than basic upstream reporting. If your power consumption becomes unusually high, the utility headend application server may need on-demand reporting from your meter at short intervals to follow the consumption trend. From a standard vertical push model, the transport structure changes and becomes bidirectional (downstream pull model instead of upstream push).

Distribution automation (DA) also allows your meter to communicate with neighboring meters or other devices in the electrical distribution grid. With such communication, consumption load balancing may be optimized. For example, your air conditioning pulses fresh air at regular intervals. With DA, your neighbor's AC starts pulsing when your system pauses; in this way, the air in both houses is kept fresh, but the energy consumed from the network is stable instead of spiking up and down with uncoordinated start and stop points. Here again, the transport model changes. From a vertical structure, you are now changing to a possible mesh structure with multiple peer-to-peer exchanges.

Similarly, your smart meter may communicate with your house appliances to evaluate their type and energy demand. With this scheme, your washing machine can be turned on in times of lower consumption from other systems, such as at night, while power to your home theater system will never be deprived, always turning on when you need it. Once the system learns your consumption pattern, charging of your electric car can start and stop at intervals to achieve the same overnight charge without creating spikes in energy demand. When these functions appear, the transport model changes again. A mesh system may appear at the scale of the house. More commonly, a partial mesh appears, with some central nodes connecting to multiple other nodes. Data may flow locally, or it may have to be orchestrated by a central application to coordinate the power budget between houses.

In this smart system, your car's charging system is connected to your energy account. As you plug into a public charging station, your car logs into the system to be identified and uniquely links to your account. At regular intervals, the central system may need to query all the charging stations for status update. The transport structure loses its vertical organization a bit more in this model, as you may be connecting from anywhere. In a managed environment, the headend system needs to upgrade the software on your meter, just as appliance vendors may need to update your oven or washing machine smart energy software. From a bottom-up data transport flow, you now implement top-down data flows.

This communication structure thus may involve peer-to-peer (for example, meter to meter), point-to-point (meter to headend station), point-to-multipoint (gateway or headend to multiple meters), unicast and multicast communications (software update to one or multiple systems). In a multitenant environment (for example, electricity and gas consumption management), different systems may use the same communication pathways. This communication occurs over multiple media (for example, power lines inside your house or a short-range wireless system like indoor Wi-Fi and/or ZigBee), a longer-range wireless system to the gateway, and yet another wireless or wired medium for backhaul transmission.

To allow for such communication structure, a network protocol with specific characteristics needs to be implemented. The protocol needs to be open and standard-based to accommodate multiple industries and multiple media. Scalability (to accommodate thousands or millions of sensors in a single network) and security are also common requirements. IP is a protocol that matches all these requirements. The advantages of IP are covered in depth in Chapter 5.

The flexibility of IP allows this protocol to be embedded in objects of very different natures, exchanging information over very different media, including low-power, lossy, and low-bandwidth networks. For example, RFC 2464 describes how an IPv6 packet gets encapsulated over an Ethernet frame and is also used for IEEE 802.11 Wi-Fi. Similarly, the IETF 6LoWPAN working group specifies how IPv6 packets are carried efficiently over lossy networks, forming an "adaption layer" for IPv6, primarily for IoT networks. Chapter 4 provides more details on 6LoWPAN and its capabilities.

Finally, the transport layer protocols built above IP (UDP and TCP) can easily be leveraged to decide whether the network should control the data packet delivery (with TCP) or whether the control task should be left to the application (UDP). UDP is a much lighter and faster protocol than TCP. However, it does not guarantee packet delivery. Both TCP and UDP can be secured with TLS/SSL (TCP) or DTLS (UDP). Chapter 6 takes a closer look at TCP and UDP for IoT networks.

IoT Network Management Sublayer

IP, TCP, and UDP bring connectivity to IoT networks. Upper-layer protocols need to take care of data transmission between the smart objects and other systems. Multiple protocols have been leveraged or created to solve IoT data communication problems. Some networks rely on a push model (that is, a sensor reports at a regular interval or based on a local trigger), whereas others rely on a pull model (that is, an application queries the sensor over the network), and multiple hybrid approaches are also possible.

Following the IP logic, some IoT implementers have suggested HTTP for the data transfer phase. After all, HTTP has a client and server component. The sensor could use the client part to establish a connection to the IoT central application (the server), and then data can be exchanged. You can find HTTP in some IoT applications, but HTTP is something of a fat protocol and was not designed to operate in constrained environments with low memory, low power, low bandwidth, and a high rate of packet failure. Despite these limitations, other web-derived protocols have been suggested for the IoT space. One example is WebSocket. WebSocket is part of the HTML5 specification, and provides a simple bidirectional connection over a single connection. Some IoT solutions use WebSocket to manage the connection between the smart object and an external application. WebSocket is often combined with other protocols, such as MQTT (described shortly) to handle the IoT-specific part of the communication.

With the same logic of reusing well-known methods, Extensible Messaging and Presence Protocol (XMPP) was created. XMPP is based on instant messaging and presence. It allows the exchange of data between two or more systems and supports presence and contact list maintenance. It can also handle publish/subscribe, making it a good choice for distribution of information to multiple devices. A limitation of XMPP is its reliance on TCP, which may force subscribers to maintain open sessions to other systems and may be a limitation for memory-constrained objects.

To respond to the limits of web-based protocols, another protocol was created by the IETF Constrained Restful Environments (CoRE) working group: Constrained Application

Protocol (CoAP). CoAP uses some methods similar to those of HTTP (such as Get, Post, Put, and Delete) but implements a shorter list, thus limiting the size of the header. CoAP also runs on UDP (whereas HTTP typically uses TCP). CoAP also adds a feature that is lacking in HTTP and very useful for IoT: observation. Observation allows the streaming of state changes as they occur, without requiring the receiver to query for these changes.

Another common IoT protocol utilized in these middle to upper layers is Message Queue Telemetry Transport (MQTT). MQTT uses a broker-based architecture. The sensor can be set to be an MQTT publisher (publishes a piece of information), the application that needs to receive the information can be set as the MQTT subscriber, and any intermediary system can be set as a broker to relay the information between the publisher and the subscriber(s). MQTT runs over TCP. A consequence of the reliance on TCP is that an MQTT client typically holds a connection open to the broker at all times. This may be a limiting factor in environments where loss is high or where computing resources are limited.

Chapter 6 examines in more detail the various IoT application protocols, including CoAP and MQTT. From an architectural standpoint, you need to determine the requirements of your application protocol. Relying on TCP implies maintaining sessions between endpoints. The advantage of reliability comes with the cost of memory and processing resources consumed for session awareness. Relying on UDP delegates the control to the upper layers. You also need to determine the requirements for QoS with different priority levels between the various messages. Finally, you need to evaluate the security of the IoT application protocol to balance the level of security provided against the overhead required. Chapter 8 describes how to evaluate the security aspect of IoT networks.

Layer 3: Applications and Analytics Layer

Once connected to a network, your smart objects exchange information with other systems. As soon as your IoT network spans more than a few sensors, the power of the Internet of Things appears in the applications that make use of the information exchanged with the smart objects.

Analytics Versus Control Applications

Multiple applications can help increase the efficiency of an IoT network. Each application collects data and provides a range of functions based on analyzing the collected data. It can be difficult to compare the features offered. Chapter 7, "Data and Analytics for IoT," provides an in-depth analysis of the various application families. From an architectural standpoint, one basic classification can be as follows:

- **Analytics application:** This type of application collects data from multiple smart objects, processes the collected data, and displays information resulting from the data that was processed. The display can be about any aspect of the IoT network, from historical reports, statistics, or trends to individual system states. The important aspect is that the application processes the data to convey a view of the network that cannot be obtained from solely looking at the information displayed by a single smart object.

■ **Control application:** This type of application controls the behavior of the smart object or the behavior of an object related to the smart object. For example, a pressure sensor may be connected to a pump. A control application increases the pump speed when the connected sensor detects a drop in pressure. Control applications are very useful for controlling complex aspects of an IoT network with a logic that cannot be programmed inside a single IoT object, either because the configured changes are too complex to fit into the local system or because the configured changes rely on parameters that include elements outside the IoT object.

An example of control system architecture is SCADA. SCADA was developed as a universal method to access remote systems and send instructions. One example where SCADA is widely used is in the control and monitoring of remote terminal units (RTUs) on the electrical distribution grid.

Many advanced IoT applications include both analytics and control modules. In most cases, data is collected from the smart objects and processed in the analytics module. The result of this processing may be used to modify the behavior of smart objects or systems related to the smart objects. The control module is used to convey the instructions for behavioral changes. When evaluating an IoT data and analytics application, you need to determine the relative depth of the control part needed for your use case and match it against the type of analytics provided.

Data Versus Network Analytics

Analytics is a general term that describes processing information to make sense of collected data. In the world of IoT, a possible classification of the analytics function is as follows:

■ **Data analytics:** This type of analytics processes the data collected by smart objects and combines it to provide an intelligent view related to the IoT system. At a very basic level, a dashboard can display an alarm when a weight sensor detects that a shelf is empty in a store. In a more complex case, temperature, pressure, wind, humidity, and light levels collected from thousands of sensors may be combined and then processed to determine the likelihood of a storm and its possible path. In this case, data processing can be very complex and may combine multiple changing values over complex algorithms. Data analytics can also monitor the IoT system itself. For example, a machine or robot in a factory can report data about its own movements. This data can be used by an analytics application to report degradation in the movement speeds, which may be indicative of a need to service the robot before a part breaks.

■ **Network analytics:** Most IoT systems are built around smart objects connected to the network. A loss or degradation in connectivity is likely to affect the efficiency of the system. Such a loss can have dramatic effects. For example, open mines use wireless networks to automatically pilot dump trucks. A lasting loss of connectivity may result in an accident or degradation of operations efficiency (automated dump trucks typically stop upon connectivity loss). On a more minor scale, loss of connectivity means that data stops being fed to your data analytics platform, and the system stops making intelligent analyses of the IoT system. A similar consequence is that the control module cannot modify local object behaviors anymore.

Most analytics applications employ both data and network analytics modules. When architecting an IoT system, you need to evaluate the need for each one. Network analytics is necessary for connected systems. However, the depth of analysis depends on your use cases. A basic connectivity view may be enough if the smart objects report occasional status, without expectation for immediate action based on this report. Detailed analysis and trending about network performance are needed if the central application is expected to pilot in near-real-time connected systems.

Data analytics is a wider space with a larger gray area (in terms of needs) than network analytics. Basic systems analytics can provide views of the system state and state trend analysis. More advanced systems can refine the type of data collected and display additional information about the system. The type of collected data and processing varies widely with the use case.

Data Analytics Versus Business Benefits

Data analytics is undoubtedly a field where the value of IoT is booming. Almost any object can be connected, and multiple types of sensors can be installed on a given object. Collecting and interpreting the data generated by these devices is where the value of IoT is realized.

From an architectural standpoint, you can define static IoT networks where a clear list of elements to monitor and analytics to perform are determined. Such static systems are common in industrial environments where the IoT charter is about providing a clear view of the state of the operation. However, a smarter architectural choice may be to allow for an open system where the network is engineered to be flexible enough that other sensors may be added in the future, and where both upstream and downstream operations are allowed. This flexibility allows for additional processing of the existing sensors and also deeper and more efficient interaction with the connected objects. This enhanced data processing can result in new added value for businesses that are not envisioned at the time when the system is initially deployed.

An example of a flexible analytics and control application is Cisco Jasper, which provides a turnkey cloud-based platform for IoT management and monetization. Consider the case of vending machines deployed throughout a city. At a basic level, these machines can be connected, and sensors can be deployed to report when a machine is in an error state. A repair person can be sent to address the issue when such a state is identified. This type of alert is a time saver and avoids the need for the repair team to tour all the machines in turn when only one may be malfunctioning.

This alert system may also avoid delay between the time when a machine goes into the error state and the time when a repair team visits the machine location. With a static platform, this use case is limited to this type of alert. With a flexible platform like Cisco Jasper, new applications may be imagined and developed over time. For example, the machine sensors can be improved to also report when an item is sold. The central application can then be enhanced to process this information and analyze what item is most sold, in what location, at what times. This new view of the machines may allow for an optimization of the items to sell in machines in a given area. Systems may be implemented to adapt the goods to time, season, or location—or many other parameters that may have been analyzed. In short, architecting open systems opens the possibility for new applications.

Smart Services

The ability to use IoT to improve operations is often termed "smart services." This term is generic, and in many cases the term is used but its meaning is often stretched to include one form of service or another where an additional level of intelligence is provided.

Fundamentally, smart services use IoT and aim for efficiency. For example, sensors can be installed on equipment to ensure ongoing conformance with regulations or safety requirements. This angle of efficiency can take multiple forms, from presence sensors in hazardous areas to weight threshold violation detectors on trucks.

Smart services can also be used to measure the efficiency of machines by detecting machine output, speed, or other forms of usage evaluation. Entire operations can be optimized with IoT. In hospitality, for example, presence and motion sensors can evaluate the number of guests in a lobby and redirect personnel accordingly. The same type of action can be taken in a store where a customer is detected as staying longer than the typical amount of time in front of a shelf. Personnel can be deployed to provide assistance. Movement of people and objects on factory floors can be analyzed to optimize the production flow.

Smart services can be integrated into an IoT system. For example, sensors can be integrated in a light bulb. A sensor can turn a light on or off based on the presence of a human in the room. An even smarter system can communicate with other systems in the house, learn the human movement pattern, and anticipate the presence of a human, turning on the light just before the person enters the room. An even smarter system can use smarter sensors that analyze multiple parameters to detect human mood and modify accordingly the light color to adapt to the learned preferences, or to convey either a more relaxing or a more dynamic environment.

Light bulbs are a simple example. By connecting to other systems in the house, efficiencies can be coordinated. For example, the house entry alarm system or the heating system can coordinate with the presence detector in a light bulb to adapt to detected changes. The alarm system can disable volumetric movement alarms in zones where a known person is detected. The heating system can adapt the temperature to human presence or detected personal preferences.

Similar efficiency can be extended to larger systems than a house. For example, smart grid applications can coordinate the energy consumption between houses to regulate the energy demand from the grid. We already mentioned that your washing machine may be turned on at night when the energy demand for heating and cooling is lower. Just as your air conditioning pulses can be coordinated with your neighbor's, your washing machine cycles can be coordinated with the appliances in your house and in the neighborhood to smooth the energy demand spikes on the grid.

Efficiency also applies to M2M communications. In mining environments, vehicles can communicate to regulate the flows between drills, draglines, bulldozers, and dump trucks, for example, making sure that a dump truck is always available when a bulldozer needs it. In smart cities, vehicles communicate. A traffic jam is detected and anticipated automatically by public transportation, and the system can temporarily reroute buses or regulate the number of buses servicing a specific line based on traffic and customer quantity, instantaneous or learned over trending.

Part III of this book provides detailed examples of how IoT is shaping specific industries. The lessons learned are always that architecting open IoT systems allows for increased efficiency over time. New applications and possibilities for an IoT system will appear in the upcoming years. When building an IoT network, you should make sure to keep the system open for the possibility of new smart objects and more traffic on the system.

IoT Data Management and Compute Stack

One of the key messages in the first two chapters of this book is that the massive scale of IoT networks is fundamentally driving new architectures. For instance, Figure 1-2 in Chapter 1 illustrates how the "things" connected to the Internet are continuing to grow exponentially, with a prediction by Cisco that by 2020 there will be more than 50 billion devices connected to some form of an IP network. Clearly, traditional IT networks are not prepared for this magnitude of network devices. However, beyond the network architecture itself, consider the data that is generated by these devices. If the number of devices is beyond conventional numbers, surely the data generated by these devices must also be of serious concern.

In fact, the data generated by IoT sensors is one of the single biggest challenges in building an IoT system. In the case of modern IT networks, the data sourced by a computer or server is typically generated by the client/server communications model, and it serves the needs of the application. In sensor networks, the vast majority of data generated is unstructured and of very little use on its own. For example, the majority of data generated by a smart meter is nothing more than polling data; the communications system simply determines whether a network connection to the meter is still active. This data on its own is of very little value. The real value of a smart meter is the metering data read by the meter management system (MMS). However, if you look at the raw polling data from a different perspective, the information can be very useful. For example, a utility may have millions of meters covering its entire service area. If whole sections of the smart grid start to show an interruption of connectivity to the meters, this data can be analyzed and combined with other sources of data, such as weather reports and electrical demand in the grid, to provide a complete picture of what is happening. This information can help determine whether the loss of connection to the meters is truly a loss of power or whether some other problem has developed in the grid. Moreover, analytics of this data can help the utility quickly determine the extent of the service outage and repair the disruption in a timely fashion.

In most cases, the processing location is outside the smart object. A natural location for this processing activity is the cloud. Smart objects need to connect to the cloud, and data processing is centralized. One advantage of this model is simplicity. Objects just need to connect to a central cloud application. That application has visibility over all the IoT nodes and can process all the analytics needed today and in the future.

However, this model also has limitations. As data volume, the variety of objects connecting to the network, and the need for more efficiency increase, new requirements appear, and those requirements tend to bring the need for data analysis closer to the IoT system. These new requirements include the following:

- **Minimizing latency:** Milliseconds matter for many types of industrial systems, such as when you are trying to prevent manufacturing line shutdowns or restore electrical service. Analyzing data close to the device that collected the data can make a difference between averting disaster and a cascading system failure.

- **Conserving network bandwidth:** Offshore oil rigs generate 500 GB of data weekly. Commercial jets generate 10 TB for every 30 minutes of flight. It is not practical to transport vast amounts of data from thousands or hundreds of thousands of edge devices to the cloud. Nor is it necessary because many critical analyses do not require cloud-scale processing and storage.

- **Increasing local efficiency:** Collecting and securing data across a wide geographic area with different environmental conditions may not be useful. The environmental conditions in one area will trigger a local response independent from the conditions of another site hundreds of miles away. Analyzing both areas in the same cloud system may not be necessary for immediate efficiency.

An important design consideration, therefore, is how to design an IoT network to manage this volume of data in an efficient way such that the data can be quickly analyzed and lead to business benefits. The volume of data generated by IoT devices can be so great that it can easily overrun the capabilities of the headend system in the data center or the cloud. For example, it has been observed that a moderately sized smart meter network of 1 million meters will generate close to 1 billion data points each day (including meter reads and other instrumentation data), resulting in 1 TB of data. For an IT organization that is not prepared to contend with this volume of data storage and real-time analysis, this creates a whole new challenge.

The volume of data also introduces questions about bandwidth management. As the massive amount of IoT data begins to funnel into the data center, does the network have the capacity to sustain this volume of traffic? Does the application server have the ability to ingest, store, and analyze the vast quantity of data that is coming in? This is sometimes referred to as the "impedance mismatch" of the data generated by the IoT system and the management application's ability to deal with that data.

As illustrated in Figure 2-14, data management in traditional IT systems is very simple. The endpoints (laptops, printers, IP phones, and so on) communicate over an IP core network to servers in the data center or cloud. Data is generally stored in the data center, and the physical links from access to core are typically high bandwidth, meaning access to IT data is quick.

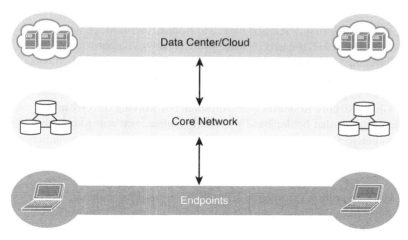

Figure 2-14   *The Traditional IT Cloud Computing Model*

IoT systems function differently. Several data-related problems need to be addressed:

- Bandwidth in last-mile IoT networks is very limited. When dealing with thousands/ millions of devices, available bandwidth may be on order of tens of Kbps per device or even less.

- Latency can be very high. Instead of dealing with latency in the milliseconds range, large IoT networks often introduce latency of hundreds to thousands of milliseconds.

- Network backhaul from the gateway can be unreliable and often depends on 3G/LTE or even satellite links. Backhaul links can also be expensive if a per-byte data usage model is necessary.

- The volume of data transmitted over the backhaul can be high, and much of the data may not really be that interesting (such as simple polling messages).

- Big data is getting bigger. The concept of storing and analyzing all sensor data in the cloud is impractical. The sheer volume of data generated makes real-time analysis and response to the data almost impossible.

Fog Computing

The solution to the challenges mentioned in the previous section is to distribute data management throughout the IoT system, as close to the edge of the IP network as possible. The best-known embodiment of edge services in IoT is fog computing. Any device with computing, storage, and network connectivity can be a fog node. Examples include industrial controllers, switches, routers, embedded servers, and IoT gateways. Analyzing IoT data close to where it is collected minimizes latency, offloads gigabytes of network traffic from the core network, and keeps sensitive data inside the local network.

Note The concept of fog was first developed by Flavio Bonomi and Rodolfo Milito of Cisco Systems. In the world of IoT, fog gets its name from a relative comparison to computing in the cloud layer. Just as clouds exist in the sky, fog rests near the ground. In the same way, the intention of fog computing is to place resources as close to the ground—that is, the IoT devices—as possible. An interesting side note is that the term "fog" was actually coined by Ginny Nichols, Rodolfo's wife. Although not working directly in IoT, she had an excellent grasp of what her husband was developing and was able to quickly draw the comparison between cloud and edge computing. One day she made the suggestion of simply calling it the "fog layer." The name stuck.

An advantage of this structure is that the fog node allows intelligence gathering (such as analytics) and control from the closest possible point, and in doing so, it allows better performance over constrained networks. In one sense, this introduces a new layer to the traditional IT computing model, one that is often referred to as the "fog layer." Figure 2-15 shows the placement of the fog layer in the IoT Data Management and Compute Stack.

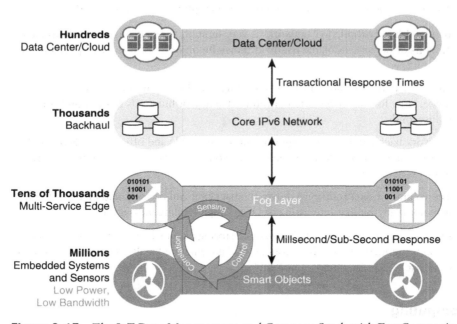

Figure 2-15 *The IoT Data Management and Compute Stack with Fog Computing*

Fog services are typically accomplished very close to the edge device, sitting as close to the IoT endpoints as possible. One significant advantage of this is that the fog node has contextual awareness of the sensors it is managing because of its geographic proximity to those sensors. For example, there might be a fog router on an oil derrick that is monitoring all the sensor activity at that location. Because the fog node is able to analyze information from all the sensors on that derrick, it can provide contextual analysis of the messages it is receiving and may decide to send back only the relevant information over the backhaul network to the cloud. In this way, it is performing distributed analytics such that the volume of data sent upstream is greatly reduced and is much more useful to application and analytics servers residing in the cloud.

In addition, having contextual awareness gives fog nodes the ability to react to events in the IoT network much more quickly than in the traditional IT compute model, which would likely incur greater latency and have slower response times. The fog layer thus provides a distributed edge control loop capability, where devices can be monitored, controlled, and analyzed in real time without the need to wait for communication from the central analytics and application servers in the cloud.

The value of this model is clear. For example, tire pressure sensors on a large truck in an open-pit mine might continually report measurements all day long. There may be only minor pressure changes that are well within tolerance limits, making continual reporting to the cloud unnecessary. Is it really useful to continually send such data back to the cloud over a potentially expensive backhaul connection? With a fog node on the truck, it is possible to not only measure the pressure of all tires at once but also combine this data with information coming from other sensors in the engine, hydraulics, and so on. With this approach, the fog node sends alert data upstream only if an actual problem is beginning to occur on the truck that affects operational efficiency.

IoT fog computing enables data to be preprocessed and correlated with other inputs to produce relevant information. This data can then be used as real-time, actionable knowledge by IoT-enabled applications. Longer term, this data can be used to gain a deeper understanding of network behavior and systems for the purpose of developing proactive policies, processes, and responses.

Fog applications are as diverse as the Internet of Things itself. What they have in common is data reduction—monitoring or analyzing real-time data from network-connected things and then initiating an action, such as locking a door, changing equipment settings, applying the brakes on a train, zooming a video camera, opening a valve in response to a pressure reading, creating a bar chart, or sending an alert to a technician to make a preventive repair.

The defining characteristic of fog computing are as follows:

- **Contextual location awareness and low latency:** The fog node sits as close to the IoT endpoint as possible to deliver distributed computing.

- **Geographic distribution:** In sharp contrast to the more centralized cloud, the services and applications targeted by the fog nodes demand widely distributed deployments.

- **Deployment near IoT endpoints:** Fog nodes are typically deployed in the presence of a large number of IoT endpoints. For example, typical metering deployments often see 3000 to 4000 nodes per gateway router, which also functions as the fog computing node.

- **Wireless communication between the fog and the IoT endpoint:** Although it is possible to connect wired nodes, the advantages of fog are greatest when dealing with a large number of endpoints, and wireless access is the easiest way to achieve such scale.

- **Use for real-time interactions:** Important fog applications involve real-time interactions rather than batch processing. Preprocessing of data in the fog nodes allows upper-layer applications to perform batch processing on a subset of the data.

Edge Computing

Fog computing solutions are being adopted by many industries, and efforts to develop distributed applications and analytics tools are being introduced at an accelerating pace. The natural place for a fog node is in the network device that sits closest to the IoT endpoints, and these nodes are typically spread throughout an IoT network. However, in recent years, the concept of IoT computing has been pushed even further to the edge, and in some cases it now resides directly in the sensors and IoT devices.

Note   Edge computing is also sometimes called "mist" computing. If clouds exist in the sky, and fog sits near the ground, then mist is what actually sits on the ground. Thus, the concept of mist is to extend fog to the furthest point possible, right into the IoT endpoint device itself.

IoT devices and sensors often have constrained resources, however, as compute capabilities increase. Some new classes of IoT endpoints have enough compute capabilities to perform at least low-level analytics and filtering to make basic decisions. For example, consider a water sensor on a fire hydrant. While a fog node sitting on an electrical pole in the distribution network may have an excellent view of all the fire hydrants in a local neighborhood, a node on each hydrant would have clear view of a water pressure drop on its own line and would be able to quickly generate an alert of a localized problem. The fog node, on the other hand, would have a wider view and would be able to ascertain whether the problem was more than just localized but was affecting the entire area. Another example is in the use of smart meters. Edge compute–capable meters are able to communicate with each other to share information on small subsets of the electrical distribution grid to monitor localized power quality and consumption, and they can inform a fog node of events that may pertain to only tiny sections of the grid. Models such as these help ensure the highest quality of power delivery to customers.

The Hierarchy of Edge, Fog, and Cloud

It is important to stress that edge or fog computing in no way replaces the cloud. Rather, they complement each other, and many use cases actually require strong cooperation between layers. In the same way that lower courts do not replace the supreme court of a country, edge and fog computing layers simply act as a first line of defense for filtering, analyzing, and otherwise managing data endpoints. This saves the cloud from being queried by each and every node for each event.

This model suggests a hierarchical organization of network, compute, and data storage resources. At each stage, data is collected, analyzed, and responded to when necessary, according to the capabilities of the resources at each layer. As data needs to be sent to the cloud, the latency becomes higher. The advantage of this hierarchy is that a response to events from resources close to the end device is fast and can result in immediate benefits, while still having deeper compute resources available in the cloud when necessary.

It is important to note that the heterogeneity of IoT devices also means a heterogeneity of edge and fog computing resources. While cloud resources are expected to be homogenous, it is fair to expect that in many cases both edge and fog resources will use different operating systems, have different CPU and data storage capabilities, and have different energy consumption profiles. Edge and fog thus require an abstraction layer that allows applications to communicate with one another. The abstraction layer exposes a common set of APIs for monitoring, provisioning, and controlling the physical resources in a standardized way. The abstraction layer also requires a mechanism to support virtualization, with the ability to run multiple operating systems or service containers on physical devices to support multitenancy and application consistency across the IoT system. Definition of a common communications services framework is being addressed by groups such as oneM2M, discussed earlier. Figure 2-16 illustrates the hierarchical nature of edge, fog, and cloud computing across an IoT system.

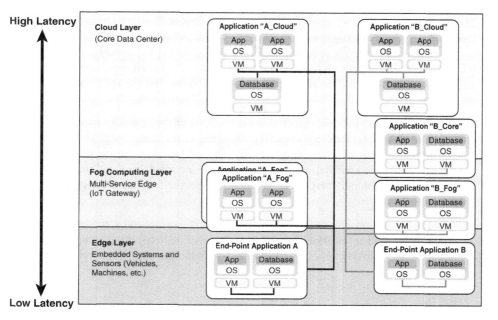

Figure 2-16 *Distributed Compute and Data Management Across an IoT System*

From an architectural standpoint, fog nodes closest to the network edge receive the data from IoT devices. The fog IoT application then directs different types of data to the optimal place for analysis:

- The most time-sensitive data is analyzed on the edge or fog node closest to the things generating the data.

- Data that can wait seconds or minutes for action is passed along to an aggregation node for analysis and action.

- Data that is less time sensitive is sent to the cloud for historical analysis, big data analytics, and long-term storage. For example, each of thousands or hundreds of thousands of fog nodes might send periodic summaries of data to the cloud for historical analysis and storage.

In summary, when architecting an IoT network, you should consider the amount of data to be analyzed and the time sensitivity of this data. Understanding these factors will help you decide whether cloud computing is enough or whether edge or fog computing would improve your system efficiency. Fog computing accelerates awareness and response to events by eliminating a round trip to the cloud for analysis. It avoids the need for costly bandwidth additions by offloading gigabytes of network traffic from the core network. It also protects sensitive IoT data by analyzing it inside company walls.

Summary

The requirements of IoT systems are driving new architectures that address the scale, constraints, and data management aspects of IoT. To address these needs, several IoT-specific reference models have arisen, including the oneM2M IoT model and the IoT World Forum's IoT Reference Model. The commonalities between these models are the interaction of IoT devices, the network that connects them, and the applications that manage the endpoints.

This book presents an IoT framework that uses aspects of these various models and applies them to specific industry use cases. This chapter presents a model based on common concepts in these architectures that breaks the IoT layers into a simplified architecture incorporating two parallel stacks: the Core IoT Functional Stack and the IoT Data Management and Compute Stack. This architecture sets the format for the chapters that follow in this book.

The Core IoT Functional Stack has three layers: the IoT sensors and actuators, networking components, and applications and analytics layers. The networking components and applications layers involve several sublayers corresponding to different parts of the overall IoT system.

The IoT Data Management and Compute Stack deals with how and where data is filtered, aggregated, stored, and analyzed. In traditional IT models, this occurs in the cloud or the data center. However, due to the unique requirements of IoT, data management is distributed as close to the edge as possible, including the edge and fog layers.

References

1. ETSI, *oneM2M*, Accessed December 2016, www.etsi.org/about/what-we-do/global-collaboration/onem2m.

2. oneM2M, *oneM2M Technical Specification*, Accessed December 2016, ftp.onem2m.org/Deliverables/20140801_Candidate%20Release/TS-0002-Requirements-V-2014-08.pdf.

Part II

Engineering IoT Networks

Chapter 3

Smart Objects: The "Things" in IoT

Imagine the IoT-enabled connected vehicle and roadway highlighted in Chapter 1, "What Is IoT?" That car has an impressive ecosystem of sensors that provides an immense amount of data that can be intelligently consumed by a variety of systems and services on the car itself as well as shared externally with other vehicles, the connected roadway infrastructure, or even a whole host of other cloud-based diagnostic and consumer services. From behind the steering wheel, almost everything in the car can be checked (sensed) and controlled. The car is filled with sensors of all types (for example, temperature, location [GPS], pressure, velocity) that are meant to provide a wealth of rich and relevant data to, among many other things, improve safety, simplify vehicle maintenance, and enhance the driver experience.

Such sensors are fundamental building blocks of IoT networks. In fact, they are the foundational elements found in smart objects—the "things" in the Internet of Things. Smart objects are any physical objects that contain embedded technology to sense and/or interact with their environment in a meaningful way by being interconnected and enabling communication among themselves or an external agent.

This chapter provides a detailed analysis of smart objects and their architecture. It also provides an understanding of their design limitations and role within IoT networks. Specifically, the following sections are included:

- **Sensors, Actuators, and Smart Objects:** This section defines sensors, actuators, and smart objects and describes how they are the fundamental building blocks of IoT networks.

- **Sensor Networks:** This section covers the design, drivers for adoption, and deployment challenges of sensor networks.

Sensors, Actuators, and Smart Objects

The following sections describe the capabilities, characteristics, and functionality of sensors and actuators. They also detail how the economic and technical conditions are finally right for IoT to flourish. Finally, you will see how to bring these foundational elements together to form smart objects, which are connected to form the sensor and actuator networks that make most IoT use cases possible.

Sensors

A sensor does exactly as its name indicates: It senses. More specifically, a sensor measures some physical quantity and converts that measurement reading into a digital representation. That digital representation is typically passed to another device for transformation into useful data that can be consumed by intelligent devices or humans.

Naturally, a parallel can be drawn with humans and the use of their five senses to learn about their surroundings. Human senses do not operate independently in silos. Instead, they complement each other and compute together, empowering the human brain to make intelligent decisions. The brain is the ultimate decision maker, and it often uses several sources of sensory input to validate an event and compensate for "incomplete" information.

Sensors are not limited to human-like sensory data. They can measure anything worth measuring. In fact, they are able to provide an extremely wide spectrum of rich and diverse measurement data with far greater precision than human senses; sensors provide superhuman sensory capabilities. This additional dimension of data makes the physical world an incredibly valuable source of information. Sensors can be readily embedded in any physical objects that are easily connected to the Internet by wired or wireless networks. Because these connected host physical objects with multidimensional sensing capabilities communicate with each other and external systems, they can interpret their environment and make intelligent decisions. Connecting sensing devices in this way has ushered in the world of IoT and a whole new paradigm of business intelligence.

There are myriad different sensors available to measure virtually everything in the physical world. There are a number of ways to group and cluster sensors into different categories, including the following:

- **Active or passive:** Sensors can be categorized based on whether they produce an energy output and typically require an external power supply (active) or whether they simply receive energy and typically require no external power supply (passive).

- **Invasive or non-invasive:** Sensors can be categorized based on whether a sensor is part of the environment it is measuring (invasive) or external to it (non-invasive).

- **Contact or no-contact:** Sensors can be categorized based on whether they require physical contact with what they are measuring (contact) or not (no-contact).

- **Absolute or relative:** Sensors can be categorized based on whether they measure on an absolute scale (absolute) or based on a difference with a fixed or variable reference value (relative).

- **Area of application:** Sensors can be categorized based on the specific industry or vertical where they are being used.

- **How sensors measure:** Sensors can be categorized based on the physical mechanism used to measure sensory input (for example, thermoelectric, electrochemical, piezo-resistive, optic, electric, fluid mechanic, photoelastic).

- **What sensors measure:** Sensors can be categorized based on their applications or what physical variables they measure.

Note that this is by no means an exhaustive list, and there are many other classification and taxonomic schemes for sensors, including those based on material, cost, design, and other factors. The most useful classification scheme for the pragmatic application of sensors in an IoT network, as described in this book, is to simply classify based on what physical phenomenon a sensor is measuring. This type of categorization is shown in Table 3-1.

Table 3-1 *Sensor Types*

Sensor Types	Description	Examples
Position	A position sensor measures the position of an object; the position measurement can be either in absolute terms (absolute position sensor) or in relative terms (displacement sensor). Position sensors can be linear, angular, or multi-axis.	Potentiometer, inclinometer, proximity sensor
Occupancy and motion	Occupancy sensors detect the presence of people and animals in a surveillance area, while motion sensors detect movement of people and objects. The difference between the two is that occupancy sensors generate a signal even when a person is stationary, whereas motion sensors do not.	Electric eye, radar
Velocity and acceleration	Velocity (speed of motion) sensors may be linear or angular, indicating how fast an object moves along a straight line or how fast it rotates. Acceleration sensors measure changes in velocity.	Accelerometer, gyroscope
Force	Force sensors detect whether a physical force is applied and whether the magnitude of force is beyond a threshold.	Force gauge, viscometer, tactile sensor (touch sensor)
Pressure	Pressure sensors are related to force sensors, measuring force applied by liquids or gases. Pressure is measured in terms of force per unit area.	Barometer, Bourdon gauge, piezometer
Flow	Flow sensors detect the rate of fluid flow. They measure the volume (mass flow) or rate (flow velocity) of fluid that has passed through a system in a given period of time.	Anemometer, mass flow sensor, water meter

Sensor Types	Description	Examples
Acoustic	Acoustic sensors measure sound levels and convert that information into digital or analog data signals.	Microphone, geophone, hydrophone
Humidity	Humidity sensors detect humidity (amount of water vapor) in the air or a mass. Humidity levels can be measured in various ways: absolute humidity, relative humidity, mass ratio, and so on.	Hygrometer, humistor, soil moisture sensor
Light	Light sensors detect the presence of light (visible or invisible).	Infrared sensor, photodetector, flame detector
Radiation	Radiation sensors detect radiation in the environment. Radiation can be sensed by scintillating or ionization detection.	Geiger-Müller counter, scintillator, neutron detector
Temperature	Temperature sensors measure the amount of heat or cold that is present in a system. They can be broadly of two types: contact and non-contact. Contact temperature sensors need to be in physical contact with the object being sensed. Non-contact sensors do not need physical contact, as they measure temperature through convection and radiation.	Thermometer, calorimeter, temperature gauge
Chemical	Chemical sensors measure the concentration of chemicals in a system. When subjected to a mix of chemicals, chemical sensors are typically selective for a target type of chemical (for example, a CO_2 sensor senses only carbon dioxide).	Breathalyzer, olfactometer, smoke detector
Biosensors	Biosensors detect various biological elements, such as organisms, tissues, cells, enzymes, antibodies, and nucleic acid.	Blood glucose biosensor, pulse oximetry, electrocardiograph

Source: J. Holdowsky et al., *Inside the Internet of Things: A Primer on the Technologies Building the IoT*, August 21, 2015, http://dupress.deloitte.com/dup-us-en/focus/internet-of-things/iot-primer-iot-technologies-applications.html.

Sensors come in all shapes and sizes and, as shown in Table 3-1, can measure all types of physical conditions. A fascinating use case to highlight the power of sensors and IoT is in the area of precision agriculture (sometimes referred to as smart farming), which uses a variety of technical advances to improve the efficiency, sustainability, and profitability of traditional farming practices. This includes the use of GPS and satellite aerial imagery for determining field viability; robots for high-precision planting, harvesting, irrigation, and so on; and real-time analytics and artificial intelligence to predict optimal crop yield, weather impacts, and soil quality.

Among the most significant impacts of precision agriculture are those dealing with sensor measurement of a variety of soil characteristics. These include real-time measurement of soil quality, pH levels, salinity, toxicity levels, moisture levels for irrigation planning, nutrient levels for fertilization planning, and so on. All this detailed sensor data can be analyzed to provide highly valuable and actionable insight to boost productivity and crop yield. Figure 3-1 shows biodegradable, passive microsensors to measure soil and crop and conditions. These sensors, developed at North Dakota State University (NDSU), can be planted directly in the soil and left in the ground to biodegrade without any harm to soil quality.

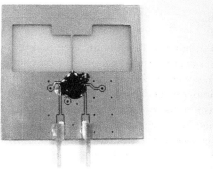 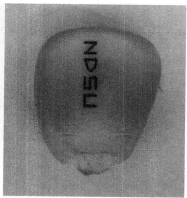

Figure 3-1   *Biodegradable Sensors Developed by NDSU for Smart Farming (Reprinted with permission from NDSU.)*

IoT and, by extension, networked sensors have been repeatedly named among a small number of emerging revolutionary technologies that will change the global economy and shape the future. The staggering proliferation of sensors is the principal driver of this phenomenon. The astounding volume of sensors is in large part due to their smaller size, their form factor, and their decreasing cost. These factors make possible the economic and technical feasibility of having an increased density of sensors in objects of all types. Perhaps the most significant accelerator for sensor deployments is mobile phones. More than a billion smart phones are sold each year, and each one has well over a dozen sensors inside it (see Figure 3-2), and that number continues to grow each year. Imagine the exponential effect of extending sensors to practically every technology, industry, and vertical. For example, there are smart homes with potentially hundreds of sensors, intelligent vehicles with 100+ sensors each, connected cities with thousands upon thousands of connected sensors, and the list goes on and on.

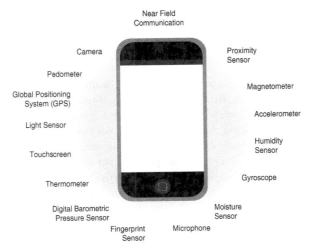

Figure 3-2   *Sensors in a Smart Phone*

It's fascinating to think that that a trillion-sensor economy is around the corner.
Figure 3-3 shows the explosive year-over-year increase over the past several years and
some bold predictions for sensor numbers in the upcoming years. There is a strong belief
in the sensor industry that this number will eclipse a trillion in the next few years. In
fact, many large players in the sensor industry have come together to form industry
consortia, such as the TSensors Summits (www.tsensorssummit.org), to create a strategy
and roadmap for a trillion-sensor economy. The trillion-sensor economy will be of such
an unprecedented and unimaginable scale that it will change the world forever. This is the
power of IoT.

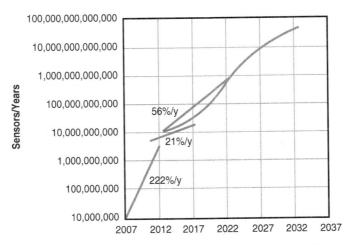

Figure 3-3   *Growth and Predictions in the Number of Sensors*

Actuators

Actuators are natural complements to sensors. Figure 3-4 demonstrates the symmetry and complementary nature of these two types of devices. As discussed in the previous section, sensors are designed to sense and measure practically any measurable variable in the physical world. They convert their measurements (typically analog) into electric signals or digital representations that can be consumed by an intelligent agent (a device or a human). Actuators, on the others hand, receive some type of control signal (commonly an electric signal or digital command) that triggers a physical effect, usually some type of motion, force, and so on.

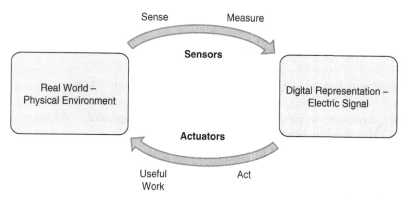

Figure 3-4   *How Sensors and Actuators Interact with the Physical World*

The previous section draws a parallel between sensors and the human senses. This parallel can be extended to include actuators, as shown in Figure 3-5. Humans use their five senses to sense and measure their environment. The sensory organs convert this sensory information into electrical impulses that the nervous system sends to the brain for processing. Likewise, IoT sensors are devices that sense and measure the physical world and (typically) signal their measurements as electric signals sent to some type of microprocessor or microcontroller for additional processing. The human brain signals motor function and movement, and the nervous system carries that information to the appropriate part of the muscular system. Correspondingly, a processor can send an electric signal to an actuator that translates the signal into some type of movement (linear, rotational, and so on) or useful work that changes or has a measurable impact on the physical world. This interaction between sensors, actuators, and processors and the similar functionality in biological systems is the basis for various technical fields, including robotics and biometrics.

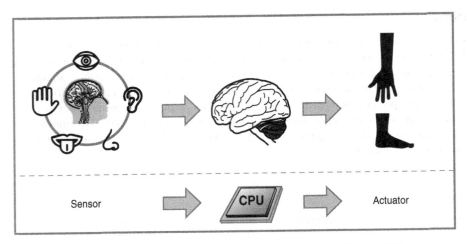

Figure 3-5   *Comparison of Sensor and Actuator Functionality with Humans*

Much like sensors, actuators also vary greatly in function, size, design, and so on. Some common ways that they can be classified include the following:

- **Type of motion:** Actuators can be classified based on the type of motion they produce (for example, linear, rotary, one/two/three-axes).

- **Power:** Actuators can be classified based on their power output (for example, high power, low power, micro power)

- **Binary or continuous:** Actuators can be classified based on the number of stable-state outputs.

- **Area of application:** Actuators can be classified based on the specific industry or vertical where they are used.

- **Type of energy:** Actuators can be classified based on their energy type.

Categorizing actuators is quite complex, given their variety, so this is by no means an exhaustive list of classification schemes. The most commonly used classification is based on energy type. Table 3-2 shows actuators classified by energy type and some examples for each type. Again, this is not a complete list, but it does provide a reasonably comprehensive overview that highlights the diversity of function and design of actuators.

Table 3-2   *Actuator Classification by Energy Type*

Type	Examples
Mechanical actuators	Lever, screw jack, hand crank
Electrical actuators	Thyristor, biopolar transistor, diode
Electromechanical actuators	AC motor, DC motor, step motor

Type	Examples
Electromagnetic actuators	Electromagnet, linear solenoid
Hydraulic and pneumatic actuators	Hydraulic cylinder, pneumatic cylinder, piston, pressure control valves, air motors
Smart material actuators (includes thermal and magnetic actuators)	Shape memory alloy (SMA), ion exchange fluid, magnetorestrictive material, bimetallic strip, piezoelectric bimorph
Micro- and nanoactuators	Electrostatic motor, microvalve, comb drive

Whereas sensors provide the information, actuators provide the action. The most interesting use cases for IoT are those where sensors and actuators work together in an intelligent, strategic, and complementary fashion. This powerful combination can be used to solve everyday problems by simply elevating the data that sensors provide to actionable insight that can be acted on by work-producing actuators.

We can build on the precision agriculture example from the previous section to demonstrate how actuators can complement and enhance a sensor-only solution. For example, the smart sensors used to evaluate soil quality (by measuring a variety of soil, temperature, and plant characteristics) can be connected with electrically or pneumatically controlled valve actuators that control water, pesticides, fertilizers, herbicides, and so on. Intelligently triggering a high-precision actuator based on well-defined sensor readings of temperature, pH, soil/air humidity, nutrient levels, and so on to deliver a highly optimized and custom environment-specific solution is truly smart farming.

Micro-Electro-Mechanical Systems (MEMS)

One of the most interesting advances in sensor and actuator technologies is in how they are packaged and deployed. Micro-electro-mechanical systems (MEMS), sometimes simply referred to as micro-machines, can integrate and combine electric and mechanical elements, such as sensors and actuators, on a very small (millimeter or less) scale. One of the keys to this technology is a microfabrication technique that is similar to what is used for microelectronic integrated circuits. This approach allows mass production at very low costs. The combination of tiny size, low cost, and the ability to mass produce makes MEMS an attractive option for a huge number of IoT applications.

MEMS devices have already been widely used in a variety of different applications and can be found in very familiar everyday devices. For example, inkjet printers use micro-pump MEMS. Smart phones also use MEMS technologies for things like accelerometers and gyroscopes. In fact, automobiles were among the first to commercially introduce MEMS into the mass market, with airbag accelerometers.

Figure 3-6 shows a torsional ratcheting actuator (TRA) that was developed by Sandia National Laboratory as a low-voltage alternative to a micro-engine.

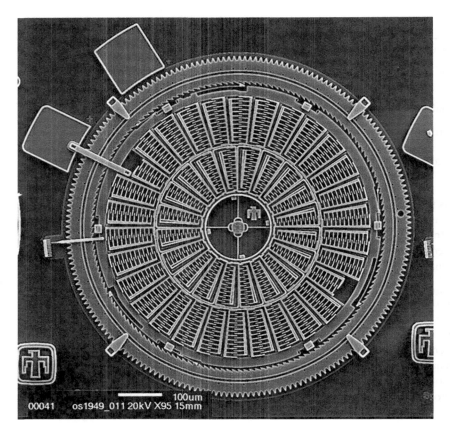

Figure 3-6   *Torsional Ratcheting Actuator (TRA) MEMS (Courtesy Sandia National Laboratories, SUMMiT™ Technologies, www.sandia.gov/mstc.)*

As Figure 3-6 shows, this MEMS is only a few hundred micrometers across; a scanning electron microscope is needed to show the level of detail visible in the figure. Micro-scale sensors and actuators are immensely embeddable in everyday objects, which is a defining characteristic of IoT. For this reason, it is expected that IoT will trigger significant advances in MEMS technology, and manufacturing and will make them pervasive across all industries and verticals as they become broadly commercialized.

Smart Objects

Smart objects are, quite simply, the building blocks of IoT. They are what transform everyday objects into a network of intelligent objects that are able to learn from and interact with their environment in a meaningful way. It can't be stressed enough that the real power of smart objects in IoT comes from being networked together rather than being isolated as standalone objects. This ability to communicate over a network has a multiplicative effect and allows for very sophisticated correlation and interaction between disparate smart objects. For instance, recall the smart farming sensors described previously. If a sensor is a standalone device that simply measures the humidity of the soil, it is interesting and useful, but it isn't revolutionary. If that same sensor is connected as part of an intelligent network that is able to coordinate intelligently with actuators to trigger irrigation systems as needed based on those sensor readings, we have something far more powerful. Extending that even further, imagine that the coordinated sensor/actuator set is intelligently interconnected with other sensor/actuator sets to further coordinate fertilization, pest control, and so on—and even communicate with an intelligent backend to calculate crop yield potential. This now starts to look like a complete system that begins to unlock the power of IoT and provides the intelligent automation we have come to expect from such a revolutionary technology.

Smart Objects: A Definition

Historically, the definition of a smart object has been a bit nebulous because of the different interpretations of the term by varying sources. To add to the overall confusion, the term *smart object*, despite some semantic differences, is often used interchangeably with terms such as *smart sensor*, *smart device*, *IoT device*, *intelligent device*, *thing*, *smart thing*, *intelligent node*, *intelligent thing*, *ubiquitous thing*, and *intelligent product*. In order to clarify some of this confusion, we provide here the definition of *smart object* as we use it in this book. A *smart object*, as described throughout this book, is a device that has, at a minimum, the following four defining characteristics (see Figure 3-7):

- **Processing unit:** A smart object has some type of processing unit for acquiring data, processing and analyzing sensing information received by the sensor(s), coordinating control signals to any actuators, and controlling a variety of functions on the smart object, including the communication and power systems. The specific type of processing unit that is used can vary greatly, depending on the specific processing needs of different applications. The most common is a microcontroller because of its small form factor, flexibility, programming simplicity, ubiquity, low power consumption, and low cost.

- **Sensor(s) and/or actuator(s):** A smart object is capable of interacting with the physical world through sensors and actuators. As described in the previous sections, a sensor learns and measures its environment, whereas an actuator is able to produce some change in the physical world. A smart object does not need to contain both sensors and actuators. In fact, a smart object can contain one or multiple sensors and/or actuators, depending upon the application.

- **Communication device:** The communication unit is responsible for connecting a smart object with other smart objects and the outside world (via the network). Communication devices for smart objects can be either wired or wireless. Overwhelmingly, in IoT networks smart objects are wirelessly interconnected for a number of reasons, including cost, limited infrastructure availability, and ease of deployment. There are myriad different communication protocols for smart objects. In fact, much of this book is dedicated to how smart objects communicate within an IoT network, especially Chapter 4, "Connecting Smart Objects," Chapter 5,

"IP as the IoT Network Layer," and Chapter 6, "Application Protocols for IoT." Thus, this chapter provides only a high-level overview and refers to those other chapters for a more detailed treatment of the subject matter.

■ **Power source:** Smart objects have components that need to be powered. Interestingly, the most significant power consumption usually comes from the communication unit of a smart object. As with the other three smart object building blocks, the power requirements also vary greatly from application to application. Typically, smart objects are limited in power, are deployed for a very long time, and are not easily accessible. This combination, especially when the smart object relies on battery power, implies that power efficiency, judicious power management, sleep modes, ultra-low power consumption hardware, and so on are critical design elements. For long-term deployments where smart objects are, for all practical purposes, inaccessible, power is commonly obtained from scavenger sources (solar, piezoelectric, and so on) or is obtained in a hybridized manner, also tapping into infrastructure power.

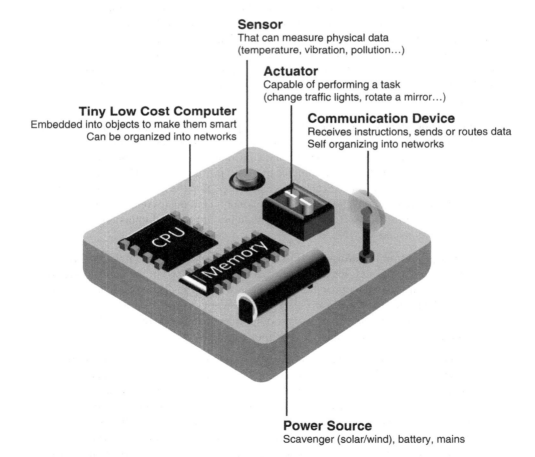

Sensor
That can measure physical data
(temperature, vibration, pollution…)

Actuator
Capable of performing a task
(change traffic lights, rotate a mirror…)

Tiny Low Cost Computer
Embedded into objects to make them smart
Can be organized into networks

Communication Device
Receives instructions, sends or routes data
Self organizing into networks

Power Source
Scavenger (solar/wind), battery, mains

Figure 3-7   *Characteristics of a Smart Object*

Trends in Smart Objects

As this definition reveals, it is perhaps variability that is the key characteristic of smart objects. They vary wildly in function, technical requirements, form factor, deployment conditions, and so on. Nevertheless, there are certain important macro trends that we can infer from recent and planned future smart object deployments. Of course, these do not apply to all smart objects because there will always be application-dependent variability, but these are broad generalizations and trends impacting IoT:

- **Size is decreasing:** As discussed earlier, in reference to MEMS, there is a clear trend of ever-decreasing size. Some smart objects are so small they are not even visible to the naked eye. This reduced size makes smart objects easier to embed in everyday objects.

- **Power consumption is decreasing:** The different hardware components of a smart object continually consume less power. This is especially true for sensors, many of which are completely passive. Some battery-powered sensors last 10 or more years without battery replacement.

- **Processing power is increasing:** Processors are continually getting more powerful and smaller. This is a key advancement for smart objects, as they become increasingly complex and connected.

- **Communication capabilities are improving:** It's no big surprise that wireless speeds are continually increasing, but they are also increasing in range. IoT is driving the development of more and more specialized communication protocols covering a greater diversity of use cases and environments.

- **Communication is being increasingly standardized:** There is a strong push in the industry to develop open standards for IoT communication protocols. In addition, there are more and more open source efforts to advance IoT.

These trends in smart objects begin to paint a picture of increasingly sophisticated devices that are able to perform increasingly complex tasks with greater efficiency. A key enabler of this paradigm is improved communication between interconnected smart objects within a system and between that system and external entities (for example, edge compute, cloud). The power of IoT is truly unlocked when smart objects are networked together in sensor/actuator networks.

Sensor Networks

A sensor/actuator network (SANET), as the name suggests, is a network of sensors that sense and measure their environment and/or actuators that act on their environment. The sensors and/or actuators in a SANET are capable of communicating and cooperating in a productive manner. Effective and well-coordinated communication and cooperation is a prominent challenge, primarily because the sensors and actuators in SANETs are diverse, heterogeneous, and resource-constrained.

SANETs offer highly coordinated sensing and actuation capabilities. Smart homes are a type of SANET that display this coordination between distributed sensors and actuators.

For example, smart homes can have temperature sensors that are strategically networked with heating, ventilation, and air-conditioning (HVAC) actuators. When a sensor detects a specified temperature, this can trigger an actuator to take action and heat or cool the home as needed.

While such networks can theoretically be connected in a wired or wireless fashion, the fact that SANETs are typically found in the "real world" means that they need an extreme level of deployment flexibility. For example, smart home temperature sensors need to be expertly located in strategic locations throughout the home, including at HVAC entry and exit points.

The following are some advantages and disadvantages that a wireless-based solution offers:

- Advantages:
    - Greater deployment flexibility (especially in extreme environments or hard-to-reach places)
    - Simpler scaling to a large number of nodes
    - Lower implementation costs
    - Easier long-term maintenance
    - Effortless introduction of new sensor/actuator nodes
    - Better equipped to handle dynamic/rapid topology changes
- Disadvantages:
    - Potentially less secure (for example, hijacked access points)
    - Typically lower transmission speeds
    - Greater level of impact/influence by environment

Not only does wireless allow much greater flexibility, but it is also an increasingly inexpensive and reliable technology across a very wide spectrum of conditions—even extremely harsh ones. These characteristics are the key reason that wireless SANETs are the ubiquitous networking technology for IoT.

Note   From a terminology perspective, wireless SANETs are typically referred to as wireless sensor and actuator networks (WSANs). Because many IoT deployments are overwhelmingly sensors, WSANs are also often interchangeably referred to as wireless sensor networks (WSNs). In this book, we commonly refer to WSANs as WSNs, with the understanding that actuators are often part of the wireless network.

Wireless Sensor Networks (WSNs)

Wireless sensor networks are made up of wirelessly connected smart objects, which are sometimes referred to as *motes*. The fact that there is no infrastructure to consider with

WSNs is surely a powerful advantage for flexible deployments, but there are a variety of design constraints to consider with these wirelessly connected smart objects. Figure 3-8 illustrates some of these assumptions and constraints usually involved in WSNs.

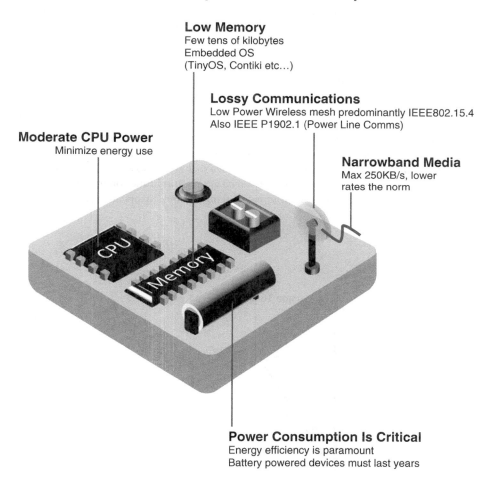

Low Memory
Few tens of kilobytes
Embedded OS
(TinyOS, Contiki etc…)

Lossy Communications
Low Power Wireless mesh predominantly IEEE802.15.4
Also IEEE P1902.1 (Power Line Comms)

Moderate CPU Power
Minimize energy use

Narrowband Media
Max 250KB/s, lower
rates the norm

Power Consumption Is Critical
Energy efficiency is paramount
Battery powered devices must last years

Figure 3-8   *Design Constraints for Wireless Smart Objects*

The following are some of the most significant limitations of the smart objects in WSNs:

- Limited processing power
- Limited memory
- Lossy communication
- Limited transmission speeds
- Limited power

These limitations greatly influence how WSNs are designed, deployed, and utilized. The fact that individual sensor nodes are typically so limited is a reason that they are often deployed in very large numbers. As the cost of sensor nodes continues to decline, the ability to deploy highly redundant sensors becomes increasingly feasible. Because many sensors are very inexpensive and correspondingly inaccurate, the ability to deploy smart objects redundantly allows for increased accuracy.

Note   Smart objects with limited processing, memory, power, and so on are often referred to as *constrained nodes*. Constrained nodes are discussed in more detail in Chapter 5.

Such large numbers of sensors permit the introduction of hierarchies of smart objects. Such a hierarchy provides, among other organizational advantages, the ability to aggregate similar sensor readings from sensor nodes that are in close proximity to each other. Figure 3-9 shows an example of such a data aggregation function in a WSN where temperature readings from a logical grouping of temperature sensors are aggregated as an average temperature reading.

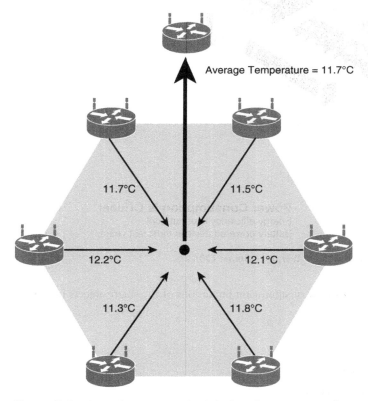

Figure 3-9   *Data Aggregation in Wireless Sensor Networks*

These data aggregation techniques are helpful in reducing the amount of overall traffic (and energy) in WSNs with very large numbers of deployed smart objects. This data aggregation at the network edges is where fog and mist computing, discussed in Chapter 2, "IoT Network Architecture and Design," are critical IoT architectural elements needed to deliver the scale and performance required by so many IoT use cases. While there are certain instances in which sensors continuously stream their measurement data, this is typically not the case. Wirelessly connected smart objects generally have one of the following two communication patterns:

- **Event-driven:** Transmission of sensory information is triggered only when a smart object detects a particular event or predetermined threshold.

- **Periodic:** Transmission of sensory information occurs only at periodic intervals.

The decision of which of these communication schemes is used depends greatly on the specific application. For example, in some medical use cases, sensors periodically send postoperative vitals, such as temperature or blood pressure readings. In other medical use cases, the same blood pressure or temperature readings are triggered to be sent only when certain critically low or high readings are measured.

As WSNs grow to very large numbers of smart objects, there is a trend toward ever-increasing levels of autonomy. For example, manual configuration of potentially thousands of smart objects is impractical and unwieldy, so smart objects in a WSN are typically self-configuring or automated by an IoT management platform in the background. Likewise, additional levels of autonomous functions are required to establish cohesive communication among the multitudinous nodes of large-scale WSNs that are often ad hoc deployments with no regard for uniform node distribution and/or density. For example, there is an increasing trend toward "smart dust" applications, in which very small sensor nodes (that is, MEMS) are scattered over a geographic area to detect vibrations, temperature, humidity, and so on. This technology has practically limitless capabilities, such as military (for example, detecting enemy troop movement), environmental (for example, detecting earthquakes or forest fires), and industrial (for example, detecting manufacturing anomalies, asset tracking). Some level of self-organization is required for networking the scads of wireless smart objects such that these nodes autonomously come together to form a true network with a common purpose. This capability to self-organize is able to adapt and evolve the logical topology of a WSN to optimize communication (among nodes as well as to centralized wireless controllers), simplify the introduction of new smart objects, and improve reliability and access to services.

Additional advantages of being able to deploy large numbers of wireless low-cost smart objects are the inherent ability to provide fault tolerance, reliability, and the capability to extend the life of a WSN, especially in scenarios where the smart objects have limited battery life. Autonomous techniques, such as self-healing, self-protection, and self-optimization, are often employed to perform these functions on behalf of an overall WSN system. IoT applications are often mission critical, and in large-scale WSNs, the overall system can't fail if the environment suddenly changes, wireless communication is temporarily lost, or a limited number of nodes run out of battery power or function improperly.

Communication Protocols for Wireless Sensor Networks

There are literally thousands of different types of sensors and actuators. To further complicate matters, WSNs are becoming increasingly heterogeneous, with more sophisticated interactions. This heterogeneity is manifested in a variety of ways. For instance, WSNs are seeing transitions from homogenous wireless networks made up of mostly a single type of sensor to networks made up of multiple types of sensors that can even be a hybridized mix of many cheap sensors with a few expensive ones used for very specific high-precision functions. WSNs are also evolving from single-purpose networks to more flexible multipurpose networks that can use specific sensor types for multiple different applications at any given time. Imagine a WSN that has multiple types of sensors, and one of those types is a temperature sensor that can be flexibly used concurrently for environmental applications, weather applications, and smart farming applications.

Coordinated communication with sophisticated interactions by constrained devices within such a heterogeneous environment is quite a challenge. The protocols governing the communication for WSNs must deal with the inherent defining characteristics of WSNs and the constrained devices within them. For instance, any communication protocol must be able to scale to a large number of nodes. Likewise, when selecting a communication protocol, you must carefully take into account the requirements of the specific application and consider any trade-offs the communication protocol offers between power consumption, maximum transmission speed, range, tolerance for packet loss, topology optimization, security, and so on. The fact that WSNs are often deployed outdoors in harsh and unpredictable environments adds yet another variable to consider because obviously not all communication protocols are designed to be equally rugged. In addition to the aforementioned technical capabilities, they must also enable, as needed, the overlay of autonomous techniques (for example, self-organization, self-healing, self-configuration) mentioned in the previous section.

Wireless sensor networks interact with their environment. Sensors often produce large amounts of sensing and measurement data that needs to be processed. This data can be processed locally by the nodes of a WSN or across zero or more hierarchical levels in IoT networks. (These hierarchical levels are discussed in detail in Chapter 2.) Communication protocols need to facilitate routing and message handling for this data flow between sensor nodes as well as from sensor nodes to optional gateways, edge compute, or centralized cloud compute. IoT communication protocols for WSNs thus straddle the entire protocol stack. Ultimately, they are used to provide a platform for a variety of IoT smart services.

As with any other networking application, in order to interoperate in multivendor environments, these communication protocols must be standardized. This is a critical dependency for IoT and one of the most significant success factors. IoT is one of those rare technologies that impacts all verticals and industries, which means standardization of communication protocols is a complicated task, requiring protocol definition across multiple layers of the stack, as well as a great deal of coordination across multiple standards development organizations.

Recently there have been focused efforts to standardize communication protocols for IoT, but, as with the adoption of any significant technology movement, there has been some market fragmentation. While there isn't a single protocol solution, there is beginning to be some clear market convergence around several key communication protocols. We do not spend time here discussing these specific protocols and their detailed operation because large chunks of this book are specifically dedicated to such discussion, including Chapters 4, 5, and 6.

Summary

Wireless sensor and actuator networks are a unique computing platform that can be highly distributed and deployed in unique environments where traditional computing platforms are not typically found. This offers unique advantages and opportunities to interact with and influence those environments. This is the basis of IoT, and it opens up a world of possibility, embedding sensors and/or actuators in everyday objects and networking them to enable sophisticated and well-coordinated automations that improves and simplifies our lives.

This chapter introduces the "things" that are the building blocks of IoT. It includes descriptions and practical examples of sensors and how they are able to measure their environment. It provides the same sort of discussion for actuators, which use environmental sensing information in a complementary way to act on their surroundings. This chapter also highlights recent manufacturing trends (such as MEMS) toward making sensors and actuators ever smaller and more embeddable in everyday objects. This chapter also covers smart objects, which are typically highly constrained devices with sensor(s) and/or actuator(s) along with very limited power, transmission, and compute capabilities.

As discussed in this chapter, we unlock the power of IoT by networking smart objects. Sensor and actuator networks (SANETs) are discussed, with particular attention and detail given to the overwhelmingly ubiquitous use case of wireless sensor networks (WSNs). The last topic discussed in this chapter is communication protocols for WSANs, which sets you up for the next chapter, on connecting smart objects.

Chapter 4

Connecting Smart Objects

IoT devices and sensors must be connected to the network for their data to be utilized. In addition to the wide range of sensors, actuators, and smart objects that make up IoT, there are also a number of different protocols used to connect them. This chapter takes a look at the characteristics and communications criteria that are important for the **technologies** that smart objects employ for their connectivity, along with a deeper dive into some of the major technologies being deployed today.

Two main sections divide this chapter. The first main section, "Communications Criteria," describes the characteristics and attributes you should consider when selecting and dealing with connecting smart objects. The various technologies used for connecting sensors can differ greatly depending on the criteria used to analyze them. The following subsections look closely at these criteria:

- **Range:** This section examines the importance of signal propagation and distance.

- **Frequency Bands:** This section describes licensed and unlicensed spectrum, including sub-GHz frequencies.

- **Power Consumption:** This section discusses the considerations required for devices connected to a stable power source compared to those that are battery powered.

- **Topology:** This section highlights the various layouts that may be supported for connecting multiple smart objects.

- **Constrained Devices:** This section details the limitations of certain smart objects from a connectivity perspective.

- **Constrained-Node Networks:** This section highlights the challenges that are often encountered with networks connecting smart objects.

The second main section of this chapter, "IoT Access Technologies," provides an in-depth look at some of the technologies that are considered when connecting smart objects. Currently, the number of technologies connecting smart objects is quite extensive, but you should expect consolidation, with certain protocols eventually winning out over others in the various IoT market segments. This section intentionally limits the discussion of technologies for connecting sensors to the ones that seem to be most promising going forward in the IoT marketplace. Other technologies are mentioned in context when applicable. The following subsections cover technologies for connecting smart objects:

- **IEEE 802.15.4:** This section highlights IEEE 802.15.4, an older but foundational wireless protocol for connecting smart objects.

- **IEEE 802.15.4g and IEEE 802.15.4e:** This section discusses improvements to 802.15.4 that are targeted to utilities and smart cities deployments.

- **IEEE 1901.2a:** This section discusses IEEE 1901.2a, which is a technology for connecting smart objects over power lines.

- **IEEE 802.11ah:** This section discusses IEEE 802.11ah, a technology built on the well-known 802.11 Wi-Fi standards that is specifically for smart objects.

- **LoRaWAN:** This section discusses LoRaWAN, a scalable technology designed for longer distances with low power requirements in the unlicensed spectrum.

- **NB-IoT and Other LTE Variations:** This section discusses NB-IoT and other LTE variations, which are often the choice of mobile service providers looking to connect smart objects over longer distances in the licensed spectrum.

This chapter covers quite a few fundamental IoT technologies and is critical for truly understanding how smart objects handle data transport to and from the network. We encourage you to pay special attention to the protocols and technologies discussed here because they are applied and referenced in many of the other chapters of this book.

Communications Criteria

In the world of connecting "things," a large number of wired and wireless access technologies are available or under development. Before reviewing some of these access technologies, it is important to talk about the criteria to use in evaluating them for various use cases and system solutions.

Wireless communication is prevalent in the world of smart object connectivity, mainly because it eases deployment and allows smart objects to be mobile, changing location without losing connectivity. The following sections take this into account as they discuss various criteria. In addition, wired connectivity considerations are mentioned when applicable.

Range

How far does the signal need to be propagated? That is, what will be the area of coverage for a selected wireless technology? Should indoor versus outdoor deployments be differentiated? Very often, these are the first questions asked when discussing wired and wireless access technologies. The simplest approach to answering these types of questions is to categorize these technologies as shown in Figure 4-1, breaking them down into the following ranges:

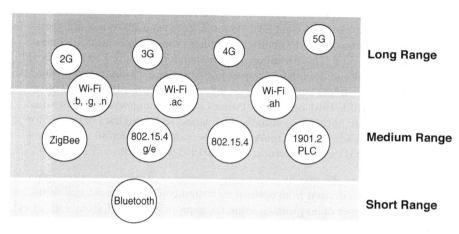

Figure 4-1   *Wireless Access Landscape*

Note   Figure 4-1 focuses on the IoT technologies discussed in this chapter. To avoid adding too much confusion by talking about all of the multitude of IoT technologies in the market today, this chapter discusses only the ones that appear to have the strongest foothold.

- **Short range:** The classical wired example is a serial cable. Wireless short-range technologies are often considered as an alternative to a serial cable, supporting tens of meters of maximum distance between two devices. Examples of short-range wireless technologies are IEEE 802.15.1 Bluetooth and IEEE 802.15.7 Visible Light Communications (VLC). These short-range communication methods are found in only a minority of IoT installations. In some cases, they are not mature enough for production deployment. For more information on these IEEE examples, see http://standards.ieee.org/about/get/802/802.15.html.

- **Medium range:** This range is the main category of IoT access technologies. In the range of tens to hundreds of meters, many specifications and implementations are available. The maximum distance is generally less than 1 mile between two devices, although RF technologies do not have real maximum distances defined, as long as the radio signal is transmitted and received in the scope of the applicable specification. Examples of medium-range wireless technologies include IEEE 802.11 Wi-Fi, IEEE 802.15.4, and 802.15.4g WPAN. Wired technologies such as IEEE 802.3 Ethernet and IEEE 1901.2 Narrowband Power Line Communications (PLC) may also be classified as medium range, depending on their physical media characteristics. (All the medium-range protocols just mentioned are covered in more detail later in this chapter.)

■ **Long range:** Distances greater than 1 mile between two devices require long-range technologies. Wireless examples are cellular (2G, 3G, 4G) and some applications of outdoor IEEE 802.11 Wi-Fi and Low-Power Wide-Area (LPWA) technologies. LPWA communications have the ability to communicate over a large area without consuming much power. These technologies are therefore ideal for battery-powered IoT sensors. (LPWA and the other examples just mentioned are discussed in more detail later in this chapter.) Found mainly in industrial networks, IEEE 802.3 over optical fiber and IEEE 1901 Broadband Power Line Communications are classified as long range but are not really considered IoT access technologies. For more information on these standards, see http://standards.ieee.org/about/get/802/802.3.html and https://standards.ieee.org/findstds/standard/1901-2010.html.

For wireless deployments, the maximum coverage, as expressed in specifications or product descriptions, is often derived from optimal estimated conditions. In the real world, you should perform proper radio planning using the appropriate tools, followed by a field radio survey to better understand the actual conditions over a given area. You also need to consider environmental factors, such as interference and noise, and specific product characteristics such as antenna design and transmit power. Finally, you should be aware of potential landscape and topology changes in the field, such as new buildings, that may interfere with signal transmission.

Frequency Bands

Radio spectrum is regulated by countries and/or organizations, such as the International Telecommunication Union (ITU) and the Federal Communications Commission (FCC). These groups define the regulations and transmission requirements for various frequency bands. For example, portions of the spectrum are allocated to types of telecommunications such as radio, television, military, and so on.

Around the world, the spectrum for various communications uses is often viewed as a critical resource. For example, you can see the value of these frequencies by examining the cost that mobile operators pay for licenses in the cellular spectrum.

Focusing on IoT access technologies, the frequency bands leveraged by wireless communications are split between licensed and unlicensed bands. Licensed spectrum is generally applicable to IoT long-range access technologies and allocated to communications infrastructures deployed by services providers, public services (for example, first responders, military), broadcasters, and utilities.

An important consideration for IoT access infrastructures that wish to utilize licensed spectrum is that users must subscribe to services when connecting their IoT devices. This adds more complexity to a deployment involving large numbers of sensors and other IoT devices, but in exchange for the subscription fee, the network operator can guarantee the exclusivity of the frequency usage over the target area and can therefore sell a better guarantee of service.

Improvements have been made in handling the complexity that is inherent when deploying large numbers of devices in the licensed spectrum. Thanks to the development of IoT platforms, such as the Cisco Jasper Control Center, automating the provisioning, deployment, and management of large numbers of devices has become much easier. Examples of licensed spectrum commonly used for IoT access are cellular, WiMAX, and Narrowband IoT (NB-IoT) technologies.

Note Exceptions exist in the licensed spectrum. For example, the Digital Enhanced Cordless Telecommunications (DECT) wireless technology operates in licensed bands centered on 1.9 GHz, but no royalty fees apply. Therefore, DECT Ultra Low Energy (ULE) is defined as an IoT wireless communication standard in the licensed spectrum, but it does not require a service provider.

The ITU has also defined unlicensed spectrum for the industrial, scientific, and medical (ISM) portions of the radio bands. These frequencies are used in many communications technologies for short-range devices (SRDs). *Unlicensed* means that no guarantees or protections are offered in the ISM bands for device communications. For IoT access, these are the most well-known ISM bands:

- 2.4 GHz band as used by IEEE 802.11b/g/n Wi-Fi

- IEEE 802.15.1 Bluetooth

- IEEE 802.15.4 WPAN

Note The low range of IEEE 802.15.1 Bluetooth limits its usefulness in most IoT deployments.

An unlicensed band, such as those in the ISM range of frequencies, is not *unregulated*. National and regional regulations exist for each of the allocated frequency bands (much as with the licensed bands). These regulations mandate device compliance on parameters such as transmit power, duty cycle and dwell time, channel bandwidth, and channel hopping.

Unlicensed spectrum is usually simpler to deploy than licensed because it does not require a service provider. However, it can suffer from more interference because other devices may be competing for the same frequency in a specific area. This becomes a key element in decisions for IoT deployments. Should an IoT infrastructure utilize unlicensed spectrum available for private networks or licensed frequencies that are dependent on a service provider? Various LPWA technologies are taking on a greater importance when it comes to answering this question. In addition to meeting low power requirements, LPWA communications are able to cover long distances that in the past required the licensed bands offered by service providers for cellular devices.

Some communications within the ISM bands operate in the sub-GHz range. Sub-GHz bands are used by protocols such as IEEE 802.15.4, 802.15.4g, and 802.11ah, and LPWA technologies such as LoRa and Sigfox. (All these technologies are discussed in more detail later in this chapter.)

The frequency of transmission directly impacts how a signal propagates and its practical maximum range. (Range and its importance to IoT access are discussed earlier in this chapter.) Either for indoor or outdoor deployments, the sub-GHz frequency bands allow greater distances between devices. These bands have a better ability than the 2.4 GHz ISM band to penetrate building infrastructures or go around obstacles, while keeping the transmit power within regulation.

The disadvantage of sub-GHz frequency bands is their lower rate of data delivery compared to higher frequencies. However, most IoT sensors do not need to send data at high rates. Therefore, the lower transmission speeds of sub-GHz technologies are usually not a concern for IoT sensor deployments.

For example, in most European countries, the 169 MHz band is often considered best suited for wireless water and gas metering applications. This is due to its good deep building basement signal penetration. In addition, the low data rate of this frequency matches the low volume of data that needs to be transmitted.

Several sub-GHz ranges have been defined in the ISM band. The most well-known ranges are centered on 169 MHz, 433 MHz, 868 MHz, and 915 MHz. However, most IoT access technologies tend to focus on the two sub-GHz frequency regions around 868 MHz and 915 MHz. These main bands are commonly found throughout the world and are applicable to nearly all countries.

Note   Countries may also specify other unlicensed bands. For example, China has provisioned the 779–787 MHz spectrum as documented in the LoRaWAN 1.0 specifications and IEEE 802.15.4g standard.

The European Conference of Postal and Telecommunications Administrations (CEPT), in the European Radiocommunications Committee (ERC) Recommendation 70-03, defines the 868 MHz frequency band. CEPT was established in 1959 as a coordinating body for European state telecommunications and postal organizations. European countries generally apply Recommendation 70-03 to their national telecommunications regulations, but the 868 MHz definition is also applicable to regions and countries outside Europe. For example, India, the Middle East, Africa, and Russia have adopted the CEPT definitions, some of them making minor revisions. Recommendation 70-03 mostly characterizes the use of the 863–870 MHz band, the allowed transmit power, or EIRP (effective isotropic radiated power), and duty cycle (that is, the percentage of time a device can be active in transmission). EIRP is the amount of power that an antenna would emit to produce the peak power density observed in the direction of maximum antenna gain. The 868 MHz band is applicable to IoT access technologies such as IEEE 802.15.4 and 802.15.4g, 802.11ah, and LoRaWAN. (These protocols are covered later in this chapter.)

Note   In the latest version of ERC Recommendation 70-03 (from May 2015), CEPT introduced the new frequency band 870–876 MHz. This band is relevant to IoT wireless access solutions. However, its adoption in local country regulations is still an ongoing process. This new band is referenced in the IEEE 802.15.4v draft and the Wi-SUN 1.0 regional PHY layer parameters. (Wi-SUN 1.0 is discussed later in this chapter.)

Centered on 915 MHz, the 902–928 MHz frequency band is the main unlicensed sub-GHz band available in North America, and it conforms to FCC regulations (FCC-Part-15.247). Countries around the world that do not align on the CEPT ERC 70-03 recommendation generally endorse the use of the 902–928 MHz range or a subset of it in their national regulations. For example, Brazilian regulator ANATEL defines the use of 902–907.5 and 915–928 MHz ranges (ANATEL506), the Japanese regulator ARIB provisions the 920–928 MHz range (ARIB-T108), and in Australia, ACMA provides recommendations for the 915–928 MHz range. As mentioned previously, even though these bands are unlicensed, they are regulated. The regulators document parameters, such as channel bandwidth, channel hopping, transmit power or EIRP, and dwell time.

In summary, you should take into account the frequencies and corresponding regulations of a country when implementing or deploying IoT smart objects. Smart objects running over unlicensed bands can be easily optimized in terms of hardware supporting the two main worldwide sub-GHz frequencies, 868 MHz and 915 MHz. However, parameters such as transmit power, antennas, and EIRP must be properly designed to follow the settings required by each country's regulations.

Power Consumption

While the definition of *IoT device* is very broad, there is a clear delineation between powered nodes and battery-powered nodes. A powered node has a direct connection to a power source, and communications are usually not limited by power consumption criteria. However, ease of deployment of powered nodes is limited by the availability of a power source, which makes mobility more complex.

Battery-powered nodes bring much more flexibility to IoT devices. These nodes are often classified by the required lifetimes of their batteries. Does a node need 10 to 15 years of battery life, such as on water or gas meters? Or is a 5- to 7-year battery life sufficient for devices such as smart parking sensors? Their batteries can be changed or the devices replaced when a street gets resurfaced. For devices under regular maintenance, a battery life of 2 to 3 years is an option.

IoT wireless access technologies must address the needs of low power consumption and connectivity for battery-powered nodes. This has led to the evolution of a new wireless environment known as Low-Power Wide-Area (LPWA). Obviously, it is possible to run just about any wireless technology on batteries. However, in reality, no operational deployment will be acceptable if hundreds of batteries must be changed every month.

Wired IoT access technologies consisting of powered nodes are not exempt from power optimization. In the case of deployment of smart meters over PLC, the radio interface on meters can't consume 5 to 10 watts of power, or this will add up to a 20-million-meter deployment consuming 100 to 200 megawatts of energy for communications.

Topology

Among the access technologies available for connecting IoT devices, three main topology schemes are dominant: star, mesh, and peer-to-peer. For long-range and short-range technologies, a star topology is prevalent, as seen with cellular, LPWA, and Bluetooth networks. Star topologies utilize a single central base station or controller to allow communications with endpoints.

For medium-range technologies, a star, peer-to-peer, or mesh topology is common, as shown in Figure 4-2. Peer-to-peer topologies allow any device to communicate with any other device as long as they are in range of each other. Obviously, peer-to-peer topologies rely on multiple full-function devices. Peer-to-peer topologies enable more complex formations, such as a mesh networking topology.

For example, indoor Wi-Fi deployments are mostly a set of nodes forming a star topology around their access points (APs). Meanwhile, outdoor Wi-Fi may consist of a mesh topology for the backbone of APs, with nodes connecting to the APs in a star topology. Similarly, IEEE 802.15.4 and 802.15.4g and even wired IEEE 1901.2a PLC are generally deployed as a mesh topology. A mesh topology helps cope with low transmit power, searching to reach a greater overall distance, and coverage by having intermediate nodes relaying traffic for other nodes.

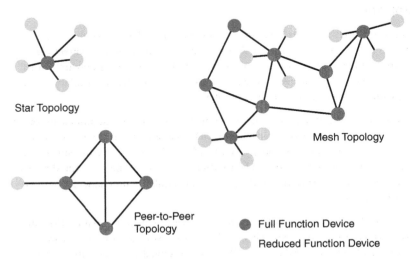

Figure 4-2   *Star, Peer-to-Peer, and Mesh Topologies*

Mesh topology requires the implementation of a Layer 2 forwarding protocol known as *mesh-under* or a Layer 3 forwarding protocol referred to as *mesh-over* on each intermediate node. (See Chapter 5, "IP as the IoT Network Layer," for more information.) As discussed previously in Chapter 2, "IoT Network Architecture and Design," an intermediate node or full-function device (FFD) is simply a node that interconnects other nodes. A node that doesn't interconnect or relay the traffic of other nodes is known as a leaf node, or reduced-function device (RFD). (More information on full-function and reduced-function devices is also presented later in this chapter.)

While well adapted to powered nodes, mesh topology requires a properly optimized implementation for battery-powered nodes. Battery-powered nodes are often placed in a "sleep mode" to preserve battery life when not transmitting. In the case of mesh topology, either the battery-powered nodes act as leaf nodes or as a "last resource path" to relay traffic when used as intermediate nodes. Otherwise, battery lifetime is greatly shortened. For battery-powered nodes, the topology type and the role of the node in the topology (for example, being an intermediate or leaf node) are significant factors for a successful implementation.

Constrained Devices

The Internet Engineering Task Force (IETF) acknowledges in RFC 7228 that different categories of IoT devices are deployed. While categorizing the class of IoT nodes is a perilous exercise, with computing, memory, storage, power, and networking continuously evolving and improving, RFC 7228 gives some definitions of constrained nodes. These definitions help differentiate constrained nodes from unconstrained nodes, such as servers, desktop or laptop computers, and powerful mobile devices such as smart phones.

Constrained nodes have limited resources that impact their networking feature set and capabilities. Therefore, some classes of IoT nodes do not implement an IP stack. According to RFC 7228, constrained nodes can be broken down into the classes defined in Table 4-1.

Table 4-1   *Classes of Constrained Nodes, as Defined by RFC 7228*

Class	Definition
Class 0	This class of nodes is severely constrained, with less than 10 KB of memory and less than 100 KB of Flash processing and storage capability. These nodes are typically battery powered. They do not have the resources required to directly implement an IP stack and associated security mechanisms. An example of a Class 0 node is a push button that sends 1 byte of information when changing its status. This class is particularly well suited to leveraging new unlicensed LPWA wireless technology.

Class	Definition
Class 1	While greater than Class 0, the processing and code space characteristics (approximately 10 KB RAM and approximately 100 KB Flash) of Class 1 are still lower than expected for a complete IP stack implementation. They cannot easily communicate with nodes employing a full IP stack. However, these nodes can implement an optimized stack specifically designed for constrained nodes, such as Constrained Application Protocol (CoAP). This allows Class 1 nodes to engage in meaningful conversations with the network without the help of a gateway, and provides support for the necessary security functions. Environmental sensors are an example of Class 1 nodes.
Class 2	Class 2 nodes are characterized by running full implementations of an IP stack on embedded devices. They contain more than 50 KB of memory and 250 KB of Flash, so they can be fully integrated in IP networks. A smart power meter is an example of a Class 2 node.

Constrained-Node Networks

While several of the IoT access technologies, such as Wi-Fi and cellular, are applicable to laptops, smart phones, and some IoT devices, some IoT access technologies are more suited to specifically connect constrained nodes. Typical examples are IEEE 802.15.4 and 802.15.4g RF, IEEE 1901.2a PLC, LPWA, and IEEE 802.11ah access technologies. (These technologies are discussed in more detail later in this chapter.)

Constrained-node networks are often referred to as low-power and lossy networks (LLNs). (See Chapter 5 for more details on LLNs.) *Low-power* in the context of LLNs refers to the fact that nodes must cope with the requirements from powered and battery-powered constrained nodes. *Lossy networks* indicates that network performance may suffer from interference and variability due to harsh radio environments. Layer 1 and Layer 2 protocols that can be used for constrained-node networks must be evaluated in the context of the following characteristics for use-case applicability: data rate and throughput, latency and determinism, and overhead and payload.

Data Rate and Throughput

The data rates available from IoT access technologies range from 100 bps with protocols such as Sigfox to tens of megabits per second with technologies such as LTE and IEEE 802.11ac. (Sigfox, LTE, and IEEE 802.11ac are discussed later in this chapter.) However, the actual throughput is less—sometimes much less—than the data rate. Therefore, understanding the bandwidth requirements of a particular technology, its applicability to given use cases, the capacity planning rules, and the expected real throughput are important for proper network design and successful production deployment.

Technologies not particularly designed for IoT, such as cellular and Wi-Fi, match up well to IoT applications with high bandwidth requirements. For example, nodes involved with video analytics have a need for high data rates. These nodes are found in retail, airport, and smart cities environments for detecting events and driving actions. Because these types of IoT endpoints are not constrained in terms of computing or network bandwidth, the design guidelines tend to focus on application requirements, such as latency and determinism. (Latency and determinism is discussed in more detail later in this chapter.)

Short-range technologies can also provide medium to high data rates that have enough throughput to connect a few endpoints. For example, Bluetooth sensors that are now appearing on connected wearables fall into this category. In this case, the solutions focus more on footprint and battery lifetime than on data rate.

The IoT access technologies developed for constrained nodes are optimized for low power consumption, but they are also limited in terms of data rate, which depends on the selected frequency band, and throughput.

With the data rate ranging from 100 bps to less than 1 Mbps, you may think back to the years when bandwidth was a scarce resource. You often needed some expertise to understand how to design such networks. Today this sort of expertise is helpful for LPWA networks, which are designed with a certain number of messages per day or per endpoint rather than just having a pure bandwidth usage limit in place. In addition, in an access mesh topology, an application's behavior, such as frequency polling, impacts the design because all devices share the constrained bandwidth capacity.

A discussion of data rate and bandwidth in LLNs must include a look at real throughput, or "goodput," as seen by the application. While it may not be important for constrained nodes that send only one message a day, real throughput is often very important for constrained devices implementing an IP stack. In this case, throughput is a lower percentage of the data rate, even if the node gets the full constrained network at a given time.

For example, let's consider an IEEE 802.15.4g subnetwork implementing 2FSK modulation at 150 kbps for the 915 MHz frequency band. (The IEEE 802.15.4g protocol is covered in more detail later in this chapter.) To cover the border case of distance and radio signal quality, Forward Error Correction (FEC) will be turned on, which lowers the data rate from 150 kbps to 75 kbps. If you now add in the protocol stack overhead, the two-way communication handling, and the variable data payload size, you end up with a maximum throughput of 30 to 40 kbps. This must be considered as the best value because the number of devices simultaneously communicating along with the topology and control plane overhead will also impact the throughput.

Another characteristic of IoT devices is that a majority of them initiate the communication. Upstream traffic toward an application server is usually more common than downstream traffic from the application server. Understanding this behavior also helps when deploying an IoT access technology, such as cellular, that is asymmetrical because the upstream bandwidth must be considered a key parameter for profiling the network capacity.

Latency and Determinism

Much like throughput requirements, latency expectations of IoT applications should be known when selecting an access technology. This is particularly true for wireless networks, where packet loss and retransmissions due to interference, collisions, and noise are normal behaviors.

On constrained networks, latency may range from a few milliseconds to seconds, and applications and protocol stacks must cope with these wide-ranging values. For example, UDP at the transport layer is strongly recommended for IP endpoints communicating over LLNs. In the case of mesh topologies, if communications are needed between two devices inside the mesh, the forwarding path may call for some routing optimization, which is available using the IPv6 RPL protocol. (For more information on RPL, see Chapter 5.)

Note   When latency is a strong concern, emergent access technologies such as Deterministic Ethernet or the Time-Slotted Channel Hopping (TSCH) mode of IEEE 802.15.4e should be considered. However, some of these solutions are not fully mature for production deployment. (For more information on TSCH, see Chapter 5. The 802.15.4e protocol is discussed later in this chapter.)

Overhead and Payload

When considering constrained access network technologies, it is important to review the MAC payload size characteristics required by applications. In addition, you should be aware of any requirements for IP. The minimum IPv6 MTU size is expected to be 1280 bytes. Therefore, the fragmentation of the IPv6 payload has to be taken into account by link layer access protocols with smaller MTUs.

Note   The use of IP on IoT devices is an open topic of discussion. As mentioned earlier in this chapter, the IETF acknowledges the fact that different classes of IoT devices exist. For the more constrained classes of devices, like Class 0 and Class 1 devices, it is usually not possible or optimal to implement a complete IP stack implementation.

For technologies that fall under the LLN definition but are able to transport IP, such as IEEE 802.15.4 and 802.15.4g, IEEE 1901.2, and IEEE 802.11ah, Layer 1 or Layer 2 fragmentation capabilities and/or IP optimization is important. (The protocols IEEE 802.14 and 802.15.4g, IEEE 1901.2, and IEEE 802.11ah are covered later in this chapter.) For example, the payload size for IEEE 802.15.4 is 127 bytes and requires an IPv6 payload with a minimum MTU of 1280 bytes to be fragmented. (For more information on the fragmentation of IPv6, see Chapter 5.) On the other hand, IEEE 802.15.4g enables payloads up to 2048 bytes, easing the support of the IPv6 minimum MTU of 1280 bytes.

Most LPWA technologies offer small payload sizes. These small payload sizes are defined to cope with the low data rate and time over the air or duty cycle requirements of IoT nodes and sensors. For example, payloads may be as little as 19 bytes using LoRaWAN technology or up to 250 bytes, depending on the adaptive data rate (ADR). While this doesn't preclude the use of an IPv6/6LoWPAN payload, as seen on some endpoint implementations, these types of protocols are better suited to Class 0 and 1 nodes, as defined in RFC 7228. (LoRaWAN and ADR are discussed in more detail later in this chapter. RFC 7228 and the node classes it defines are covered earlier in this chapter.)

In conclusion, the communication criteria just covered are fundamental to understanding IoT access technologies, their characteristics, and when they are most applicable. These criteria include range, frequency bands, power consumption, network topology, the presence of constrained devices and/or networks, and data throughput.

From a network engineer perspective, you must make sure an architecture is developed with the proper abstraction for a particular access technology. This is especially true for constrained network nodes, where quite often your choices of protocols and solutions can be limited. The next section reviews the main IoT access technologies dedicated to constrained networks.

IoT Access Technologies

The previous section describes criteria that help you in evaluating IoT constrained network technologies for proper design and operations. This section provides an overview of the main IoT access technologies. The technologies highlighted here are the ones that are seen as having market and/or mind share. Therefore, you should have a basic familiarity with them as they are fundamental to many IoT conversations.

Note Remember that there are many more IoT technologies in the market today than we can discuss here. This chapter focuses on the ones that appear to have the strongest foothold.

For each of the IoT access technologies discussed in this chapter, a common information set is being provided. Particularly, the following topics are addressed for each IoT access technology:

- **Standardization and alliances:** The standards bodies that maintain the protocols for a technology

- **Physical layer:** The wired or wireless methods and relevant frequencies

- **MAC layer:** Considerations at the Media Access Control (MAC) layer, which bridges the physical layer with data link control

- **Topology:** The topologies supported by the technology

- **Security:** Security aspects of the technology

- **Competitive technologies:** Other technologies that are similar and may be suitable alternatives to the given technology

While having a familiarity with these protocols and their capabilities is recommended, you may find that much of the information about these technologies is better used as reference material. When you encounter these protocols, you can use this chapter as a handy overview and quick summary of the important details.

IEEE 802.15.4

IEEE 802.15.4 is a wireless access technology for low-cost and low-data-rate devices that are powered or run on batteries. In addition to being low cost and offering a reasonable battery life, this access technology enables easy installation using a compact protocol stack while remaining both simple and flexible. Several network communication stacks, including deterministic ones, and profiles leverage this technology to address a wide range of IoT use cases in both the consumer and business markets. IEEE 802.15.4 is commonly found in the following types of deployments:

- Home and building automation

- Automotive networks

- Industrial wireless sensor networks

- Interactive toys and remote controls

Criticisms of IEEE 802.15.4 often focus on its MAC reliability, unbounded latency, and susceptibility to interference and multipath fading. The negatives around reliability and latency often have to do with the Collision Sense Multiple Access/Collision Avoidance (CSMA/CA) algorithm. CSMA/CA is an access method in which a device "listens" to make sure no other devices are transmitting before starting its own transmission. If another device is transmitting, a wait time (which is usually random) occurs before "listening" occurs again. Interference and multipath fading occur with IEEE 802.15.4 because it lacks a frequency-hopping technique. Later variants of 802.15.4 from the IEEE start to address these issues. (See the section "IEEE 802.15.4e and 802.15.4g," later in this chapter, for more information.)

Note   Most forms of radio communications are affected by multipath fading to varying degrees. *Multipath fading* refers to multiple copies of the signal hitting the receiver at different points in time because of different signal paths and reflections. The ability to change frequencies can mitigate the effects of multipath fading.

Standardization and Alliances

IEEE 802.15.4 or IEEE 802.15 Task Group 4 defines low-data-rate PHY and MAC layer specifications for wireless personal area networks (WPAN). This standard has evolved over the years and is a well-known solution for low-complexity wireless devices with low data rates that need many months or even years of battery life. For more detailed information on IEEE 802.15.4, visit www.ieee802.org/15/pub/TG4.html.

Since 2003, the IEEE has published several iterations of the IEEE 802.15.4 specification, each labeled with the publication's year. For example, IEEE 802.15.4-2003 was published in 2003, 802.15.4-2006 was released in 2006, and 802.15.4-2011 and 802.15.4-2015 were issued in 2011 and 2015, respectively. Newer releases typically supersede older ones, integrate addendums, and add features or clarifications to previous versions.

While there is no alliance or promotion body for IEEE 802.15.4 per se, the IEEE 802.15.4 PHY and MAC layers are the foundations for several networking protocol stacks. These protocol stacks make use of 802.15.4 at the physical and link layer levels, but the upper layers are different. These protocol stacks are promoted separately through various organizations and often commercialized. Some of the most well-known protocol stacks based on 802.15.4 are highlighted in Table 4-2.

Table 4-2 *Protocol Stacks Utilizing IEEE 802.15.4*

Protocol	Description
ZigBee	Promoted through the ZigBee Alliance, ZigBee defines upper-layer components (network through application) as well as application profiles. Common profiles include building automation, home automation, and healthcare. ZigBee also defines device object functions, such as device role, device discovery, network join, and security. For more information on ZigBee, see the ZigBee Alliance webpage, at www.zigbee.org. ZigBee is also discussed in more detail later in the next Section.
6LoWPAN	6LoWPAN is an IPv6 adaptation layer defined by the IETF 6LoWPAN working group that describes how to transport IPv6 packets over IEEE 802.15.4 layers. RFCs document header compression and IPv6 enhancements to cope with the specific details of IEEE 802.15.4. (For more information on 6LoWPAN, see Chapter 5.)
ZigBee IP	An evolution of the ZigBee protocol stack, ZigBee IP adopts the 6LoWPAN adaptation layer, IPv6 network layer, and RPL routing protocol. In addition, it offers improvements to IP security. ZigBee IP is discussed in more detail later in this chapter.
ISA100.11a	ISA100.11a is developed by the International Society of Automation (ISA) as "Wireless Systems for Industrial Automation: Process Control and Related Applications." It is based on IEEE 802.15.4-2006, and specifications were published in 2010 and then as IEC 62734. The network and transport layers are based on IETF 6LoWPAN, IPv6, and UDP standards.
WirelessHART	WirelessHART, promoted by the HART Communication Foundation, is a protocol stack that offers a time-synchronized, self-organizing, and self-healing mesh architecture, leveraging IEEE 802.15.4-2006 over the 2.4 GHz frequency band. A good white paper on WirelessHART can be found at http://www.emerson.com/resource/blob/system-engineering-guidelines-iec-62591-wirelesshart--data-79900.pdf
Thread	Constructed on top of IETF 6LoWPAN/IPv6, Thread is a protocol stack for a secure and reliable mesh network to connect and control products in the home. Specifications are defined and published by the Thread Group at www.threadgroup.org.

Because of its relatively long history compared to the others, ZigBee is one of the most well-known protocols listed in Table 4-2. In addition, ZigBee has continued to evolve over time as evidenced by the release of Zigbee IP and is representative of how IEEE 802.15.4 can be leveraged at the PHY and MAC layers, independent of the protocol layers above. For these reasons, both Zigbee and Zigbee IP are discussed in more detail in the following sections.

ZigBee

Based on the idea of ZigBee-style networks in the late 1990s, the first ZigBee specification was ratified in 2004, shortly after the release of the IEEE 802.15.4 specification the previous year. While not released as a typical standard, like an RFC, ZigBee still had industry support from more than 100 companies upon its initial publication. This industry support has grown to more than 400 companies that are members of the ZigBee Alliance. Similar to the Wi-Fi Alliance, the Zigbee Alliance is an industry group formed to certify interoperability between vendors and it is committed to driving and evolving ZigBee as an IoT solution for interconnecting smart objects.

ZigBee solutions are aimed at smart objects and sensors that have low bandwidth and low power needs. Furthermore, products that are ZigBee compliant and certified by the ZigBee Alliance should interoperate even though different vendors may manufacture them.

The Zigbee specification has undergone several revisions. In the 2006 revision, sets of commands and message types were introduced, and increased in number in the 2007 (called Zigbee pro) iteration, to achieve different functions for a device, such as metering, temperature, or lighting control. These sets of commands and message types are called clusters. Ultimately, these clusters from different functional domains or libraries form the building blocks of Zigbee application profiles. Vendors implementing pre-defined Zigbee application profiles like Home Automation or Smart Energy can ensure interoperability between their products.

The main areas where ZigBee is the most well-known include automation for commercial, retail, and home applications and smart energy. In the industrial and commercial automation space, ZigBee-based devices can handle various functions, from measuring temperature and humidity to tracking assets. For home automation, ZigBee can control lighting, thermostats, and security functions. ZigBee Smart Energy brings together a variety of interoperable products, such as smart meters, that can monitor and control the use and delivery of utilities, such as electricity and water. These ZigBee products are controlled by the utility provider and can help coordinate usage between homes and businesses and the utility provider itself to provide more efficient operations.

The traditional ZigBee stack is illustrated in Figure 4-3. As mentioned previously, ZigBee utilizes the IEEE 802.15.4 standard at the lower PHY and MAC layers. (The 802.15.4 PHY and MAC layers are covered in detail later in this chapter.) ZigBee specifies the network and security layer and application support layer that sit on top of the lower layers.

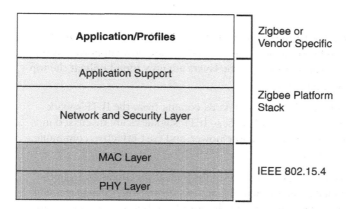

Figure 4-3 *High-Level ZigBee Protocol Stack*

The ZigBee network and security layer provides mechanisms for network startup, configuration, routing, and securing communications. This includes calculating routing paths in what is often a changing topology, discovering neighbors, and managing the routing tables as devices join for the first time. The network layer is also responsible for forming the appropriate topology, which is often a mesh but could be a star or tree as well. From a security perspective, ZigBee utilizes 802.15.4 for security at the MAC layer, using the Advanced Encryption Standard (AES) with a 128-bit key and also provides security at the network and application layers.

Note   ZigBee uses Ad hoc On-Demand Distance Vector (AODV) routing across a mesh network. Interestingly, this routing algorithm does not send a message until a route is needed. Assuming that the next hop for a route is not in its routing table, a network node broadcasts a request for a routing connection. This causes a burst of routing-related traffic, but after a comparison of various responses, the path with the lowest number of hops is determined for the connection. This process is quite different from standard enterprise routing protocols, which usually learn the entire network topology in some manner and then store a consolidated but complete routing table.

The application support layer in Figure 4-3 interfaces the lower portion of the stack dealing with the networking of ZigBee devices with the higher-layer applications. ZigBee predefines many application profiles for certain industries, and vendors can optionally create their own custom ones at this layer. As mentioned previously, Home Automation and Smart Energy are two examples of popular application profiles.

ZigBee is one of the most well-known protocols built on an IEEE 802.15.4 foundation. On top of the 802.15.4 PHY and MAC layers, ZigBee specifies its own network and security layer and application profiles. While this structure has provided a fair degree of interoperability for vendors with membership in the ZigBee Alliance, it has not provided interoperability with other IoT solutions. However, this has started to change with the release of ZigBee IP, which is discussed next.

ZigBee IP

With the introduction of ZigBee IP, the support of IEEE 802.15.4 continues, but the IP and TCP/UDP protocols and various other open standards are now supported at the network and transport layers. The ZigBee-specific layers are now found only at the top of the protocol stack for the applications.

ZigBee IP was created to embrace the open standards coming from the IETF's work on LLNs, such as IPv6, 6LoWPAN, and RPL. (These IETF standards are discussed in Chapter 5.) They provide for low-bandwidth, low-power, and cost-effective communications when connecting smart objects.

ZigBee IP is a critical part of the Smart Energy (SE) Profile 2.0 specification from the ZigBee Alliance. SE 2.0 is aimed at smart metering and residential energy management systems. In fact, ZigBee IP was designed specifically for SE 2.0 but it is not limited to this use case. Any other applications that need a standards-based IoT stack can utilize Zigbee IP. The ZigBee IP stack is shown in Figure 4-4.

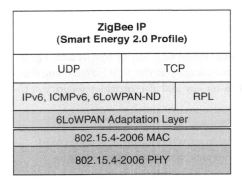

Figure 4-4   *ZigBee IP Protocol Stack*

Unlike traditional ZigBee, discussed in the previous section, ZigBee IP supports 6LoWPAN as an adaptation layer. (The 6LoWPAN protocol is covered in Chapter 5.) The 6LoWPAN mesh addressing header is not required as ZigBee IP utilizes the mesh-over or route-over method for forwarding packets. ZigBee IP requires the support of 6LoWPAN's fragmentation and header compression schemes.

At the network layer, all ZigBee IP nodes support IPv6, ICMPv6, and 6LoWPAN Neighbor Discovery (ND), and utilize RPL for the routing of packets across the mesh network. IPv6 and RPL are discussed in more detail in Chapter 5. Both TCP and UDP are also supported, to provide both connection-oriented and connectionless service.

As you can see, ZigBee IP is a compelling protocol stack offering because it is based on current IoT standards at every layer under the application layer. This opens up opportunities for ZigBee IP to integrate and interoperate on just about any 802.15.4 network with other solutions built on these open IoT standards. The following sections take a deeper dive into 802.15.4 and its PHY and MAC layers.

Physical Layer

The 802.15.4 standard supports an extensive number of PHY options that range from 2.4 GHz to sub-GHz frequencies in ISM bands. (ISM bands are discussed earlier in this chapter.) The original IEEE 802.15.4-2003 standard specified only three PHY options based on direct sequence spread spectrum (DSSS) modulation. DSSS is a modulation technique in which a signal is intentionally spread in the frequency domain, resulting in greater bandwidth. The original physical layer transmission options were as follows:

- 2.4 GHz, 16 channels, with a data rate of 250 kbps

- 915 MHz, 10 channels, with a data rate of 40 kbps

- 868 MHz, 1 channel, with a data rate of 20 kbps

You should note that only the 2.4 GHz band operates worldwide. The 915 MHz band operates mainly in North and South America, and the 868 MHz frequencies are used in Europe, the Middle East, and Africa. IEEE 802.15.4-2006, 802.15.4-2011, and IEEE 802.15.4-2015 introduced additional PHY communication options, including the following:

- **OQPSK PHY:** This is DSSS PHY, employing offset quadrature phase-shift keying (OQPSK) modulation. OQPSK is a modulation technique that uses four unique bit values that are signaled by phase changes. An offset function that is present during phase shifts allows data to be transmitted more reliably.

- **BPSK PHY:** This is DSSS PHY, employing binary phase-shift keying (BPSK) modulation. BPSK specifies two unique phase shifts as its data encoding scheme.

- **ASK PHY:** This is parallel sequence spread spectrum (PSSS) PHY, employing amplitude shift keying (ASK) and BPSK modulation. PSSS is an advanced encoding scheme that offers increased range, throughput, data rates, and signal integrity compared to DSSS. ASK uses amplitude shifts instead of phase shifts to signal different bit values.

These improvements increase the maximum data rate for both 868 MHz and 915 MHz to 100 kbps and 250 kbps, respectively. The 868 MHz support was enhanced to 3 channels, while other IEEE 802.15.4 study groups produced addendums for new frequency bands. For example, the IEEE 802.15.4c study group created the bands 314–316 MHz, 430–434 MHz, and 779–787 MHz for use in China.

Figure 4-5 shows the frame for the 802.15.4 physical layer. The synchronization header for this frame is composed of the Preamble and the Start of Frame Delimiter fields. The Preamble field is a 32-bit 4-byte (for parallel construction) pattern that identifies the start of the frame and is used to synchronize the data transmission. The Start of Frame Delimiter field informs the receiver that frame contents start immediately after this byte.

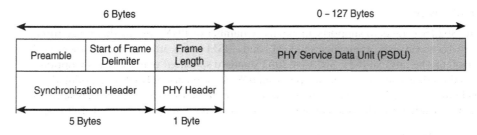

Figure 4-5   *IEEE 802.15.4 PHY Format*

The PHY Header portion of the PHY frame shown in Figure 4-5 is simply a frame length value. It lets the receiver know how much total data to expect in the PHY service data unit (PSDU) portion of the 802.4.15 PHY. The PSDU is the data field or payload.

Note   The maximum size of the IEEE 802.15.4 PSDU is 127 bytes. This size is significantly smaller than the lowest MTU setting of other upper-layer protocols, such as IPv6, which has a minimum MTU setting of 1280 bytes. Therefore, fragmentation of the IPv6 packet must occur at the data link layer for larger IPv6 packets to be carried over IEEE 802.15.4 frames. (See Chapter 5 for more details.)

The various versions and addendums to 802.15.4 over the years through various working groups can make it somewhat difficult to follow. Therefore, you should pay attention to which versions of 802.15.4 particular devices support. Products and solutions must refer to the proper IEEE 802.15.4 specification, frequency band, modulation, and data rate when providing details on their physical layer implementation.

MAC Layer

The IEEE 802.15.4 MAC layer manages access to the PHY channel by defining how devices in the same area will share the frequencies allocated. At this layer, the scheduling and routing of data frames are also coordinated. The 802.15.4 MAC layer performs the following tasks:

- Network beaconing for devices acting as coordinators (New devices use beacons to join an 802.15.4 network)
- PAN association and disassociation by a device
- Device security
- Reliable link communications between two peer MAC entities

The MAC layer achieves these tasks by using various predefined frame types. In fact, four types of MAC frames are specified in 802.15.4:

- **Data frame:** Handles all transfers of data
- **Beacon frame:** Used in the transmission of beacons from a PAN coordinator

- **Acknowledgement frame:** Confirms the successful reception of a frame

- **MAC command frame:** Responsible for control communication between devices

Each of these four 802.15.4 MAC frame types follows the frame format shown in Figure 4-6. In Figure 4-6, notice that the MAC frame is carried as the PHY payload. The 802.15.4 MAC frame can be broken down into the MAC Header, MAC Payload, and MAC Footer fields.

The MAC Header field is composed of the Frame Control, Sequence Number and the Addressing fields. The Frame Control field defines attributes such as frame type, addressing modes, and other control flags. The Sequence Number field indicates the sequence identifier for the frame. The Addressing field specifies the Source and Destination PAN Identifier fields as well as the Source and Destination Address fields.

Note   Within the Frame Control portion of the 802.15.4 header is the Security Enabled field. When this field is set to a value of 0, the frame format matches Figure 4-6. Beginning with the 802.15.4-2006 specification, when this field is set to a value of 1, an Auxiliary Security Header field is added to the 802.15.4 frame, as shown later, in Figure 4-8.

The MAC Payload field varies by individual frame type. For example, beacon frames have specific fields and payloads related to beacons, while MAC command frames have different fields present. The MAC Footer field is nothing more than a frame check sequence (FCS). An FCS is a calculation based on the data in the frame that is used by the receiving side to confirm the integrity of the data in the frame.

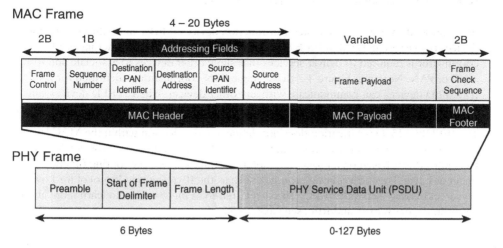

Figure 4-6   *IEEE 802.15.4 MAC Format*

IEEE 802.15.4 requires all devices to support a unique 64-bit extended MAC address, based on EUI-64. However, because the maximum payload is 127 bytes, 802.15.4 also defines how a 16-bit "short address" is assigned to devices. This short address is local to the PAN and substantially reduces the frame overhead compared to a 64-bit extended MAC address. However, you should be aware that the use of this short address might be limited to specific upper-layer protocol stacks.

Topology

IEEE 802.15.4–based networks can be built as star, peer-to-peer, or mesh topologies. Mesh networks tie together many nodes. This allows nodes that would be out of range if trying to communicate directly to leverage intermediary nodes to transfer communications.

Please note that every 802.15.4 PAN should be set up with a unique ID. All the nodes in the same 802.15.4 network should use the same PAN ID. Figure 4-7 shows an example of an 802.15.4 mesh network with a PAN ID of 1.

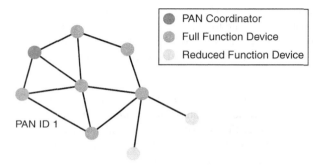

Figure 4-7   *802.15.4 Sample Mesh Network Topology*

As mentioned earlier in this chapter, full-function devices (FFDs) and reduced-function devices (RFDs) are defined in IEEE 802.15.4. A minimum of one FFD acting as a PAN coordinator is required to deliver services that allow other devices to associate and form a cell or PAN. Notice in Figure 4-7 that a single PAN coordinator is identified for PAN ID 1. FFD devices can communicate with any other devices, whereas RFD devices can communicate only with FFD devices.

The IEEE 802.15.4 specification does not define a path selection within the MAC layer for a mesh topology. This function can be done at Layer 2 and is known as *mesh-under*. Generally, this is based on a proprietary solution. Alternatively, the routing function can occur at Layer 3, using a routing protocol, such as the IPv6 Routing Protocol for Low Power and Lossy Networks (RPL). This is referred to as *mesh-over*. (To learn more about mesh-under, mesh-over, and RPL, see Chapter 5.)

Security

The IEEE 802.15.4 specification uses Advanced Encryption Standard (AES) with a 128-bit key length as the base encryption algorithm for securing its data. Established by the US National Institute of Standards and Technology in 2001, AES is a block cipher, which means it operates on fixed-size blocks of data. The use of AES by the US government and its widespread adoption in the private sector has helped it become one of the most popular algorithms used in symmetric key cryptography. (A *symmetric key* means that the same key is used for both the encryption and decryption of the data.)

In addition to encrypting the data, AES in 802.15.4 also validates the data that is sent. This is accomplished by a message integrity code (MIC), which is calculated for the entire frame using the same AES key that is used for encryption.

Enabling these security features for 802.15.4 changes the frame format slightly and consumes some of the payload. Using the Security Enabled field in the Frame Control portion of the 802.15.4 header is the first step to enabling AES encryption. This field is a single bit that is set to 1 for security. Once this bit is set, a field called the Auxiliary Security Header is created after the Source Address field, by stealing some bytes from the Payload field. Figure 4-8 shows the IEEE 802.15.4 frame format at a high level, with the Security Enabled bit set and the Auxiliary Security Header field present.

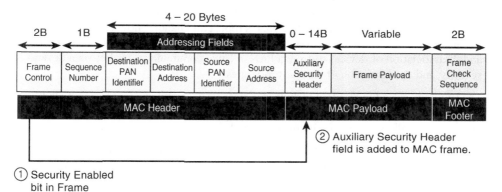

Figure 4-8 *Frame Format with the Auxiliary Security Header Field for 802.15.4-2006 and Later Versions*

Competitive Technologies

As detailed in Table 4-2, the IEEE 802.15.4 PHY and MAC layers are the foundations for several networking profiles that compete against each other in various IoT access environments. These various vendors and organizations build upper-layer protocol stacks on top of an 802.15.4 core. They compete and distinguish themselves based on features and capabilities in these upper layers.

A competitive radio technology that is different in its PHY and MAC layers is DASH7. DASH7 was originally based on the ISO18000-7 standard and positioned for industrial communications, whereas IEEE 802.15.4 is more generic. Commonly employed in active radio frequency identification (RFID) implementations, DASH7 was used by US military forces for many years, mainly for logistics purposes. Active RFID utilizes radio waves generated by a battery-powered tag on an object to enable continuous tracking.

The current DASH7 technology offers low power consumption, a compact protocol stack, range up to 1 mile, and AES encryption. Frequencies of 433 MHz, 868 MHz, and 915 MHz have been defined, enabling data rates up to 166.667 kbps and a maximum payload of 256 bytes.

DASH7 is promoted by the DASH7 Alliance, which has evolved the protocol from its active RFID niche into a wireless sensor network technology that is aimed at the commercial market. For more information on DASH7, see the Dash7 Alliance webpage, at www.dash7-alliance.org.

IEEE 802.15.4 Conclusions

The IEEE 802.15.4 wireless PHY and MAC layers are mature specifications that are the foundation for various industry standards and products (refer to Table 4-2). The PHY layer offers a maximum speed of up to 250 kbps, but this varies based on modulation and frequency. The MAC layer for 802.15.4 is robust and handles how data is transmitted and received over the PHY layer. Specifically, the MAC layer handles the association and disassociation of devices to/from a PAN, reliable communications between devices, security, and the formation of various topologies.

The topologies used in 802.15.4 include star, peer-to-peer, and cluster trees that allow for the formation of mesh networks. From a security perspective, 802.15.4 utilizes AES encryption to allow secure communications and also provide data integrity.

The main competitor to IEEE 802.15.4 is DASH7, another wireless technology that compares favorably. However, IEEE 802.15.4 has an edge in the marketplace through all the different vendors and organizations that utilize its PHY and MAC layers. As 802.15.4 continues to evolve, you will likely see broader adoption of the IPv6 standard at the network layer. For IoT sensor deployments requiring low power, low data rate, and low complexity, the IEEE 802.15.4 standard deserves strong consideration.

IEEE 802.15.4g and 802.15.4e

The IEEE frequently makes amendments to the core 802.15.4 specification, before integrating them into the next revision of the core specification. When these amendments are made, a lowercase letter is appended. Two such examples of this are 802.15.4e-2012 and 802.15.4g-2012, both of which are especially relevant to the subject of IoT. Both of these amendments were integrated in IEEE 802.15.4-2015 but are often still referred to by their amendment names.

The IEEE 802.15.4e amendment of 802.15.4-2011 expands the MAC layer feature set to remedy the disadvantages associated with 802.15.4, including MAC reliability, unbounded latency, and multipath fading. In addition to making general enhancements to the MAC layer, IEEE 802.15.4e also made improvements to better cope with certain application domains, such as factory and process automation and smart grid. Smart grid is associated with the modernization of the power grid and utilities infrastructure by connecting intelligent devices and communications. IEEE 802.15.4e-2012 enhanced the IEEE 802.15.4 MAC layer capabilities in the areas of frame format, security, determinism mechanism, and frequency hopping. (The specific MAC layer enhancements introduced in IEEE 802.15.4e are covered in more detail later in this chapter.)

IEEE 802.15.4g-2012 is also an amendment to the IEEE 802.15.4-2011 standard, and just like 802.15.4e-2012, it has been fully integrated into the core IEEE 802.15.4-2015 specification. The focus of this specification is the smart grid or, more specifically, smart utility network communication. 802.15.4g seeks to optimize large outdoor wireless mesh networks for field area networks (FANs). New PHY definitions are introduced, as well as some MAC modifications needed to support their implementation. This technology applies to IoT use cases such as the following:

- Distribution automation and industrial supervisory control and data acquisition (SCADA) environments for remote monitoring and control (SCADA is covered in more detail in Chapter 6, "Application Protocols for IoT.")

- Public lighting

- Environmental wireless sensors in smart cities

- Electrical vehicle charging stations

- Smart parking meters

- Microgrids

- Renewable energy

Note   The IEEE continues to improve the 802.15.4 specification through amendments. For example, IEEE 802.15.4u defines the PHY layer characteristics for India (865–867 MHz). Meanwhile, IEEE 802.15.4v defines changes to the SUN PHYs, enabling the use of the 870–876 MHz and 915–921 MHz bands in Europe, the 902–928 MHz band in Mexico, the 902–907.5 MHz and 915–928 MHz bands in Brazil, the 915–928 MHz band in Australia/New Zealand, and Asian regional frequency bands that are not in IEEE 802.15.4-2015.

Standardization and Alliances

Because 802.15.4g-2012 and 802.15.4e-2012 are simply amendments to IEEE 802.15.4-2011, the same IEEE 802.15 Task Group 4 standards body authors, maintains, and integrates them into the next release of the core specification. However, the additional capabilities and options provided by 802.15.4g-2012 and 802.15.4e-2012 led to additional difficulty in achieving the interoperability between devices and mixed vendors that users requested.

To guarantee interoperability, the Wi-SUN Alliance was formed. (SUN stands for *smart utility network*.) This organization is not a standards body but is instead an industry alliance that defines communication profiles for smart utility and related networks. These profiles are based on open standards, such as 802.15.4g-2012, 802.15.4e-2012, IPv6, 6LoWPAN, and UDP for the FAN profile. (For more information on 6LoWPAN, see Chapter 5.) In addition, Wi-SUN offers a testing and certification program to further ensure interoperability.

The Wi-SUN Alliance performs the same function as the Wi-Fi Alliance and WiMAX Forum. Each of these organizations has an associated standards body as well as a commercial name, as shown in Table 4-3. For more information on Wi-SUN, visit www.wi-sun.org.

Table 4-3   *Industry Alliances for Some Common IEEE Standards*

Commercial Name/Trademark	Industry Organization	Standards Body
Wi-Fi	Wi-Fi Alliance	IEEE 802.11 Wireless LAN
WiMAX	WiMAX Forum	IEEE 802.16 Wireless MAN
Wi-SUN	Wi-SUN Alliance	IEEE 802.15.4g Wireless SUN

Physical Layer

In IEEE 802.15.4g-2012, the original IEEE 802.15.4 maximum PSDU or payload size of 127 bytes was increased for the SUN PHY to 2047 bytes. This provides a better match for the greater packet sizes found in many upper-layer protocols. For example, the default IPv6 MTU setting is 1280 bytes. Fragmentation is no longer necessary at Layer 2 when IPv6 packets are transmitted over IEEE 802.15.4g MAC frames. Also, the error protection was improved in IEEE 802.15.4g by evolving the CRC from 16 to 32 bits.

The SUN PHY, as described in IEEE 802.15.4g-2012, supports multiple data rates in bands ranging from 169 MHz to 2.4 GHz. These bands are covered in the unlicensed ISM frequency spectrum specified by various countries and regions. Within these bands, data must be modulated onto the frequency using at least one of the following PHY mechanisms to be IEEE 802.15.4g compliant:

- **Multi-Rate and Multi-Regional Frequency Shift Keying (MR-FSK):** Offers good transmit power efficiency due to the constant envelope of the transmit signal

- **Multi-Rate and Multi-Regional Orthogonal Frequency Division Multiplexing (MR-OFDM):** Provides higher data rates but may be too complex for low-cost and low-power devices

- **Multi-Rate and Multi-Regional Offset Quadrature Phase-Shift Keying (MR-O-QPSK):** Shares the same characteristics of the IEEE 802.15.4-2006 O-QPSK PHY, making multi-mode systems more cost-effective and easier to design

Enhanced data rates and a greater number of channels for channel hopping are available, depending on the frequency bands and modulation. For example, for the 902–928 MHz ISM band that is used in the United States, MR-FSK provides 50, 150, or 200 kbps. MR-OFDM at this same frequency allows up to 800 kbps. Other frequencies provide their own settings.

Therefore, products and solutions must refer to the proper IEEE 802.15.4 specification, frequency band, modulation, and data rate when providing details about their PHY implementation. This is important because the availability of chipsets supporting new PHY mechanisms, such as MR-OFDM, may limit the implementation of enhanced data rates. You should look to the Wi-SUN Alliance to mitigate these problems and provide some consistency in terms of implementation, interoperability, and certifications. For example, the Wi-SUN PHY working group publishes a Regional Frequency Bands specification describing the details for various regions and countries.

MAC Layer

While the IEEE 802.15.4e-2012 amendment is not applicable to the PHY layer, it is pertinent to the MAC layer. This amendment enhances the MAC layer through various functions, which may be selectively enabled based on various implementations of the standard. In fact, if interoperability is a "must have," then using profiles defined by organizations such as Wi-SUN is necessary. The following are some of the main enhancements to the MAC layer proposed by IEEE 802.15.4e-2012:

- **Time-Slotted Channel Hopping (TSCH):** TSCH is an IEEE 802.15.4e-2012 MAC operation mode that works to guarantee media access and channel diversity. Channel hopping, also known as frequency hopping, utilizes different channels for transmission at different times. TSCH divides time into fixed time periods, or "time slots," which offer guaranteed bandwidth and predictable latency. In a time slot, one packet and its acknowledgement can be transmitted, increasing network capacity because multiple nodes can communicate in the same time slot, using different channels. A number of time slots are defined as a "slot frame," which is regularly repeated to provide "guaranteed access." The transmitter and receiver agree on the channels and the timing for switching between channels through the combination of a global time slot counter and a global channel hopping sequence list, as computed on each node to determine the channel of each time slot. TSCH adds robustness in noisy environments and smoother coexistence with other wireless technologies, especially for industrial use cases.

Note   Although TSCH is supported in 802.15.4e-2012, implementation of this feature may vary due to industry standardization on how TSCH should be implemented. Implementation of TSCH is tied to the IETF 6TiSCH working group standardization effort, which defines a scheduling algorithm for TSCH. (For more information on 6TiSCH, see Chapter 5.)

- **Information elements:** Information elements (IEs) allow for the exchange of information at the MAC layer in an extensible manner, either as header IEs (standardized) and/or payload IEs (private). Specified in a tag, length, value (TLV) format, the IE field allows frames to carry additional metadata to support MAC layer services. These services may include IEEE 802.15.9 key management, Wi-SUN 1.0 IEs to broadcast and unicast schedule timing information, and frequency hopping synchronization information for the 6TiSCH architecture.

- **Enhanced beacons (EBs):** EBs extend the flexibility of IEEE 802.15.4 beacons to allow the construction of application-specific beacon content. This is accomplished by including relevant IEs in EB frames. Some IEs that may be found in EBs include network metrics, frequency hopping broadcast schedule, and PAN information version.

- **Enhanced beacon requests (EBRs):** Like enhanced beacons, an enhanced beacon request (EBRs) also leverages IEs. The IEs in EBRs allow the sender to selectively specify the request of information. Beacon responses are then limited to what was requested in the EBR. For example, a device can query for a PAN that is allowing new devices to join or a PAN that supports a certain set of MAC/PHY capabilities.

- **Enhanced Acknowledgement:** The Enhanced Acknowledgement frame allows for the integration of a frame counter for the frame being acknowledged. This feature helps protect against certain attacks that occur when Acknowledgement frames are spoofed.

The 802.15.4e-2012 MAC amendment is quite often paired with the 802.15.4g-2012 PHY. Figure 4-9 details this frame format. Notice that the 802.15.4g-2012 PHY is similar to the 802.15.4 PHY in Figure 4-5. The main difference between the two is the payload size, with 802.15.4g supporting up to 2047 bytes and 802.15.4 supporting only 127 bytes.

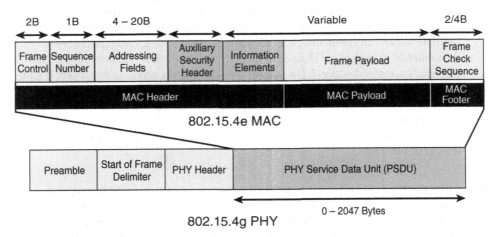

Figure 4-9 *IEEE 802.15.4g/e MAC Frame Format*

The 802.15.4e MAC is similar to the 802.15.4 MAC in Figure 4-6. The main changes shown in the IEEE 802.15.4e header in Figure 4-9 are the presence of the Auxiliary

Security Header and Information Elements field. The Auxiliary Security header provides for the encryption of the data frame. This field is optionally supported in both 802.15.4e-2012 and 802.15.4, starting with the 802.15.4-2006 specification, as shown in Figure 4-8. As discussed earlier in this section, the IE field contains one or more information elements that allow for additional information to be exchanged at the MAC layer.

Topology

Deployments of IEEE 802.15.4g-2012 are mostly based on a mesh topology. This is because a mesh topology is typically the best choice for use cases in the industrial and smart cities areas where 802.15.4g-2012 is applied. A mesh topology allows deployments to be done in urban or rural areas, expanding the distance between nodes that can relay the traffic of other nodes. Considering the use cases addressed by this technology, powered nodes have been the primary targets of implementations. Support for battery-powered nodes with a long lifecycle requires optimized Layer 2 forwarding or Layer 3 routing protocol implementations. This provides an extra level of complexity but is necessary in order to cope with sleeping battery-powered nodes.

Security

Both IEEE 802.15.4g and 802.15.4e inherit their security attributes from the IEEE 802.15.4-2006 specification. Therefore, encryption is provided by AES, with a 128-bit key. In addition to the Auxiliary Security Header field initially defined in 802.15.4-2006, a secure acknowledgement and a secure Enhanced Beacon field complete the MAC layer security. Figure 4-10 shows a high-level overview of the security associated with an IEEE 802.15.4e MAC frame.

The full frame in Figure 4-10 gets authenticated through the MIC at the end of frame. The MIC is a unique value that is calculated based on the frame contents. (The MIC is discussed in more detail earlier in this chapter.) The Security Header field denoted in Figure 4-10 is composed of the Auxiliary Security field and one or more Information Elements fields. Integration of the Information Elements fields allows for the adoption of additional security capabilities, such as the IEEE 802.15.9 Key Management Protocol (KMP) specification. KMP provides a means for establishing keys for robust datagram security. Without key management support, weak keys are often the result, leaving the security system open to attack.

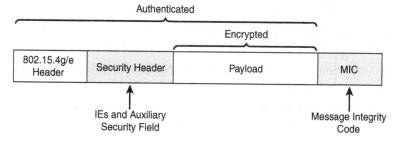

Figure 4-10 *IEEE 802.15.4g/e MAC Layer Security*

Competitive Technologies

Competitive technologies to IEEE 802.15.4g and 802.15.4e parallel the technologies that also compete with IEEE 802.15.4, such as DASH7. (DASH7 is discussed earlier in this chapter.) In many ways, 802.15.4 and its various flavors of upper-layer protocols, as shown in Table 4-2, can be seen as competitors as well. IEEE 802.15.4 is well established and already deployed in many scenarios, mostly indoors.

IEEE 802.15.4g and 802.15.4e Conclusions

It is important to remember that IEEE 802.15.4g and 802.15.4e are simply amendments to the IEEE 802.15.4 standard. They are mature specifications that are integrated into IEEE 802.15.4-2015. They have been successfully deployed in real-world scenarios, and already support millions of endpoints. IEEE 802.15.4g focuses mainly on improvements to the PHY layer, while IEEE 802.15.4e targets the MAC layer. These improvements overcome many of the disadvantages of IEEE 802.15.4, such as latency and vulnerability to multipath fading. In addition, provisions in these amendments make them better suited to handle the unique deployment models in the areas of smart grid/utilities and smart cities.

The Wi-SUN Alliance is an important industry alliance that provides interoperability and certification for industry implementations. Utilizing 802.15.4g as a foundation, the alliance releases profiles, such as the FAN profile, to help promote the adoption of the technology while guaranteeing interoperability between vendors. You should expect to see increasing use of both 802.15.4g and 802.15.4e, especially in the smart grid and smart cities verticals of IoT, where they have already seen strong adoption.

IEEE 1901.2a

While most of the constrained network technologies relate to wireless, IEEE 1901.2a-2013 is a wired technology that is an update to the original IEEE 1901.2 specification. This is a standard for Narrowband Power Line Communication (NB-PLC). NB-PLC leverages a narrowband spectrum for low power, long range, and resistance to interference over the same wires that carry electric power. NB-PLC is often found in use cases such as the following:

- **Smart metering:** NB-PLC can be used to automate the reading of utility meters, such as electric, gas, and water meters. This is true particularly in Europe, where PLC is the preferred technology for utilities deploying smart meter solutions.

- **Distribution automation:** NB-PLC can be used for distribution automation, which involves monitoring and controlling all the devices in the power grid.

- **Public lighting:** A common use for NB-PLC is with public lighting—the lights found in cities and along streets, highways, and public areas such as parks.

- **Electric vehicle charging stations:** NB-PLC can be used for electric vehicle charging stations, where the batteries of electric vehicles can be recharged.

■ **Microgrids:** NB-PLC can be used for microgrids, local energy grids that can disconnect from the traditional grid and operate independently.

■ **Renewable energy:** NB-PLC can be used in renewable energy applications, such as solar, wind power, hydroelectric, and geothermal heat.

All these use cases require a direct connection to the power grid. So it makes sense to transport IoT data across power grid connections that are already in place.

Multiple PLC standards exist, but the formation of IEEE 1901.2a was driven by the absence of a low-frequency PLC solution below 500 kHz. IEEE 1901.2a specifies the use of both alternating and direct current electric power lines. Low- and medium-voltage lines in both indoor and outdoor environments are supported, along with multiple-mile distances. Data rates can scale up to 500 kbps. The IEEE 1901.2a PHY and MAC layers can be mixed with IEEE 802.15.4g/e on endpoints, offering a dual-PHY solution for some use cases.

Standardization and Alliances

The first generations of NB-PLC implementations have generated a lot of interest from utilities in Europe but have often suffered from poor reliability, low throughput (in the range of a few hundred bits per second to a maximum of 2 kbps), lack of manageability, and poor interoperability. This has led several organizations (including standards bodies and alliance consortiums) to develop their own specifications for new generations of NB-PLC technologies. Most recent NB-PLC standards are based on orthogonal frequency-division multiplexing (OFDM). However, different standards from various vendors competing with one another have created a fragmented market. OFDM encodes digital data on multiple carrier frequencies. This provides several parallel streams that suffer less from high frequency attenuation in copper wire and narrowband interference.

The IEEE 1901.2 working group published the IEEE 1901.2a specification in November 2013. Originally leveraging the work done by the G3-PLC (now ITU G.9903) and PRIME (now ITU G.9904) working groups, the IEEE 1901.2 working group only looked at standardizing the NB-PLC PHY and MAC layers (as defined by the IEEE charter and done in other IEEE standards) independently of the upper layers. This differs from G.9903 and G.9904, which were developed for a single use case, smart metering, and focused on running specific application protocols for smart meters.

The IEEE 1901.2a standard does have some alignment with the latest developments done in other IEEE working groups. For example, using the 802.15.4e Information Element fields eases support for IEEE 802.15.9 key management. In addition, a dual-PHY approach is possible when combined with IEEE 802.15.4g/e on endpoints.

The HomePlug Alliance was one of the main industry organizations that drove the promotion and certification of PLC technologies, with IEEE 1901.2a being part of its HomePlug Netricity program. In 2016, the HomePlug Alliance made the decision to offer the alliance's broadband power line networking technology to a broader audience by making its technical specifications publicly available. It has also partnered with other alliances on continuing ongoing work. The HomePlug Alliance has struck a liaison agreement with the Wi-SUN Alliance with the goal of enabling hybrid smart grid networks that support both wireless and power line–wired connectivity. For more information on the HomePlug Alliance and Netricity, see www.homeplug.org.

Physical Layer

NB-PLC is defined for frequency bands from 3 to 500 kHz. Much as with wireless sub-GHz frequency bands, regional regulations and definitions apply to NB-PLC. The IEEE 1901.2 working group has integrated support for all world regions in order to develop a worldwide standard. Specifications include support for CENELEC A and B bands, US FCC-Low and FCC-above-CENELEC, and Japan ARIB bands. CENELEC is the French Comité Européen de Normalisation Électrotechnique, which in English translates to European Committee for Electrotechnical Standardization. This organization is responsible for standardization in the area of electrical engineering for Europe. The CENELEC A and B bands refer to 9–95 kHz and 95–125 kHz, respectively. The FCC is the Federal Communications Commission, a US government organization that regulates interstate and international communications by radio, television, wire, satellite, and cable. The FCC-Low band encompasses 37.5–117.1875 kHz, and the FCC-above-CENELEC band is 154.6875–487.5 kHz. The FCC-above-CENELEC band may become the most useful frequency due to its higher throughput and reduced interference.

Figure 4-11 shows the various frequency bands for NB-PLC. Notice that the most well-known bands are regulated by CENELEC and the FCC, but the Japan Association of Radio Industries and Businesses (ARIB) band is also present. The two ARIB frequency bands are ARIB 1, 37.5–117.1875 kHz, and ARIB 2, 154.6875–403.125 kHz.

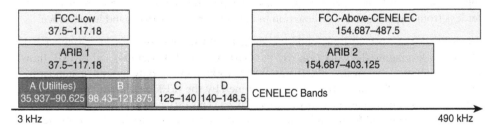

Figure 4-11 *NB-PLC Frequency Bands*

Based on OFDM, the IEEE 1901.2 specification leverages the best from other NB-PLC OFDM technologies that were developed previously. Therefore, IEEE 1901.2a supports the largest set of coding and enables both robustness and throughput. The standard includes tone maps and modulations, such as robust modulation (ROBO), differential binary phase shift keying (DBPSK), differential quadrature phase shift keying (DQPSK), differential 8-point phase shift keying (D8PSK) for all bands, and optionally 16 quadrature amplitude modulation (16QAM) for some bands. ROBO mode transmits redundant information on multiple carriers, and DBPSK, DQPSK, and D8PSK are all variations of phase shift keying, where the phase of a signal is changed to signal a binary data transmission. ROBO utilizes QPSK modulation, and its throughput depends on the degree to which coding is repeated across streams. For example, standard ROBO uses a repetition of 4, and Super-ROBO utilizes a repetition of 6.

With IEEE 1901.2a, the data throughput rate has the ability to dynamically change, depending on the modulation type and tone map. For CENELEC A band, the data rate ranges from 4.5 kbps in ROBO mode to 46 kbps with D8PSK modulation. For the FCC-above-CENELEC frequencies, throughput varies from 21 kbps in ROBO mode to a maximum of 234 kbps using D8PSK.

One major difference between IEEE 802.15.4g/e and IEEE 1901.2a is the full integration of different types of modulation and tone maps by a single PHY layer in the IEEE 1901.2a specification. IEEE 802.15.4g/e doesn't really define a multi-PHY management algorithm. The PHY payload size can change dynamically, based on channel conditions in IEEE 1901.2a. Therefore, MAC sublayer segmentation is implemented. If the size of the MAC payload is too large to fit within one PHY service data unit (PSDU), the MAC payload is partitioned into smaller segments. MAC payload segmentation is done by dividing the MAC payload into multiple smaller amounts of data (segments), based on PSDU size. The segmentation may require the addition of padding bytes to the last payload segment so that the final MPDU fills the PSDU. All forms of addressing (unicast and broadcast) are subject to segmentation.

MAC Layer

The MAC frame format of IEEE 1901.2a is based on the IEEE 802.15.4 MAC frame but integrates the latest IEEE 802.15.4e-2012 amendment, which enables key features to be supported. (For more information on the 802.15.4 MAC frame format, refer to Figure 4-6. For the 802.15.4e MAC frame format, see Figure 4-9.) One of the key components brought from 802.15.4e to IEEE 1901.2a is information elements. With IE support, additional capabilities, such as IEEE 802.15.9 Key Management Protocol and SSID, are supported. Figure 4-12 provides an overview of the general MAC frame format for IEEE 1901.2. Note that the numeric value above each field in the frame shows the size of the field, in bytes.

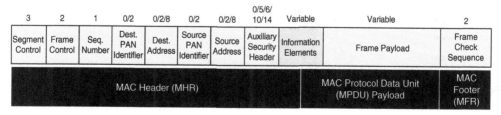

Figure 4-12   *General MAC Frame Format for IEEE 1901.2*

As shown in Figure 4-12, IEEE 1901.2 has a Segment Control field. This is a new field that was not present in our previous discussions of the MAC frame for 802.15.4 and 802.15.4e. This field handles the segmentation or fragmentation of upper-layer packets with sizes larger than what can be carried in the MAC protocol data unit (MPDU). The rest of the fields are discussed earlier in this chapter and shown in Figures 4-6, 4-8, and 4-9. Refer to these figures if you need further information on these fields.

Topology

Use cases and deployment topologies for IEEE 1901.2a are tied to the physical power lines. As with wireless technologies, signal propagation is limited by factors such as noise, interference, distortion, and attenuation. These factors become more prevalent with distance, so most NB-PLC deployments use some sort of mesh topology. Mesh networks offer the advantage of devices relaying the traffic of other devices so longer distances can be segmented. Figure 4-13 highlights a network scenario in which a PLC mesh network is applied to a neighborhood.

The IEEE 1901.2a standard offers the flexibility to run any upper-layer protocol. So, implementations of IPv6 6LoWPAN and RPL IPv6 protocols are supported. These protocols enable the use of network layer routing to create mesh networks over PLC. (For more information on 6LoWPAN and RPL, see Chapter 5.)

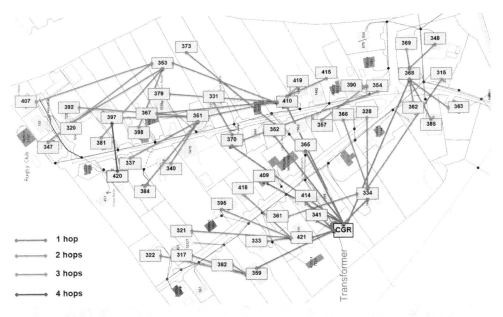

Figure 4-13 *IPv6 Mesh in NB-PLC*

Security

IEEE 1901.2a security offers similar features to IEEE 802.15.4g. Encryption and authentication are performed using AES. In addition, IEEE 1901.2a aligns with 802.15.4g in its ability to support the IEEE 802.15.9 Key Management Protocol. However, some differences exist. These differences are mostly tied to the PHY layer fragmentation capabilities of IEEE 1901.2a and include the following:

- The Security Enabled bit in the Frame Control field should be set in all MAC frames carrying segments of an encrypted frame. (The Security Enabled bit is shown in Figure 4-8.)

- If data encryption is required, it should be done before packet segmentation. During packet encryption, the Segment Control field should not be included in the input to the encryption algorithm.

- On the receiver side, the data decryption is done after packet reassembly.

- When security is enabled, the MAC payload is composed of the ciphered payload and the message integrity code (MIC) authentication tag for non-segmented payloads. If the payload is segmented, the MIC is part of the last packet (segment) only. The MIC authentication is computed using only information from the MHR of the frame carrying the first segment.

Competitive Technologies

In the domain of NB-PLC, two technologies compete against IEEE 1901.2a: G3-PLC (now ITU G.9903) and PRIME (now ITU G.9904). Both of these technologies were initially developed to address a single use case: smart metering deployment in Europe over the CENELEC A band.

As mentioned previously, IEEE 1901.2a leverages portions of G3-PLC and PRIME, and it also competes with them. More specifically, G3-PLC is really close to IEEE 1901.2. The main differences include the fact that G3-PLC mandates data link layer protocol options for bootstrapping and allocating device addresses, and it is incompatible with IEEE 802.15.4g/e and an end-to-end IPv6 model. This means there is no information element support and no global IPv6 address support. PRIME is more like an ATM approach, with a Layer 7 protocol (that is, DLMS/COSEM) that runs directly on top of Layer 2. Adding IP support requires that Layer 3 protocols be added.

Following the IEEE 1901.2 working group efforts, new versions of G3-PLC and PRIME were published. These newer versions add a similar feature set, such as FCC and ARIB band support, ROBO for PRIME, and Super-ROBO and 16QAM for G3-PLC. As these competitive technologies continue to evolve and borrow from one another, it seems there might be a convergence toward compatibility at some point in the future.

IEEE 1901.2a Conclusions

IEEE 1901.2a is an open PHY and MAC standard approach to enable the use of Narrowband Power Line Communication. The set of use cases for this standard depends on and also benefits from the physical power lines that interconnect the devices.

The IEEE 1901.2a standard leverages the earlier standards G3-PLC (now ITU G.9903) and PRIME (now ITU G.9904). Supporting a wide range of frequencies at the PHY layer,

IEEE 1901.2a also has a feature-rich MAC layer, based on 802.15.4. This flexibility in the MAC layer lends readily to the support of mesh topologies.

The HomePlug Alliance's Netricity program and the liaison agreement with the Wi-SUN Alliance provide industry support for IEEE 1901.2a by means of a profile definition and a certification program. However, IEEE 1901.2a faces competition from G3-PLC and PRIME as they are more established standards that continue to evolve.

Widespread adoption of IEEE 1901.2a depends on implementation from vendors. Most chipsets offer support for IEEE 1901.2a, G3-PLC, and PRIME because they are the three competitive OFDM-based PLC technologies. If end-to-end IP communication or dual-PHY integration with IEEE 802.15.4g/e is expected, IEEE 1901.2a becomes the protocol of choice.

IEEE 802.11ah

In unconstrained networks, IEEE 802.11 Wi-Fi is certainly the most successfully deployed wireless technology. This standard is a key IoT wireless access technology, either for connecting endpoints such as fog computing nodes, high-data-rate sensors, and audio or video analytics devices or for deploying Wi-Fi backhaul infrastructures, such as outdoor Wi-Fi mesh in smart cities, oil and mining, or other environments. However, Wi-Fi lacks sub-GHz support for better signal penetration, low power for battery-powered nodes, and the ability to support a large number of devices. For these reasons, the IEEE 802.11 working group launched a task group named IEEE 802.11ah to specify a sub-GHz version of Wi-Fi. Three main use cases are identified for IEEE 802.11ah:

- **Sensors and meters covering a smart grid:** Meter to pole, environmental/agricultural monitoring, industrial process sensors, indoor healthcare system and fitness sensors, home and building automation sensors

- **Backhaul aggregation of industrial sensors and meter data:** Potentially connecting IEEE 802.15.4g subnetworks

- **Extended range Wi-Fi:** For outdoor extended-range hotspot or cellular traffic offloading when distances already covered by IEEE 802.11a/b/g/n/ac are not good enough

Standardization and Alliances

In July 2010, the IEEE 802.11 working group decided to work on an "industrial Wi-Fi" and created the IEEE 802.11ah group. The 802.11ah specification would operate in unlicensed sub-GHz frequency bands, similar to IEEE 802.15.4 and other LPWA technologies.

The industry organization that promotes Wi-Fi certifications and interoperability for 2.4 GHz and 5 GHz products is the Wi-Fi Alliance. The Wi-Fi Alliance is a similar body to the Wi-SUN Alliance. For more information on the Wi-Fi Alliance, see its webpage, at www.wi-fi.org

For the 802.11ah standard, the Wi-Fi Alliance defined a new brand called Wi-Fi HaLow. This marketing name is based on a play on words between "11ah" in reverse and "low power." It is similar to the word "hello" but it is pronounced "hay-low." The HaLow brand exclusively covers IEEE 802.11ah for sub-GHz device certification. You can think of Wi-Fi HaLow as a commercial designation for products incorporating IEEE 802.11ah technology. For more information on W-Fi HaLow, visit www.wi-fi.org/discover-wi-fi/wi-fi-halow.

Physical Layer

IEEE 802.11ah essentially provides an additional 802.11 physical layer operating in unlicensed sub-GHz bands. For example, various countries and regions use the following bands for IEEE 802.11ah: 868–868.6 MHz for EMEAR, 902–928 MHz and associated subsets for North America and Asia-Pacific regions, and 314–316 MHz, 430–434 MHz, 470–510 MHz, and 779–787 MHz for China.

Based on OFDM modulation, IEEE 802.11ah uses channels of 2, 4, 8, or 16 MHz (and also 1 MHz for low-bandwidth transmission). This is one-tenth of the IEEE 802.11ac channels, resulting in one-tenth of the corresponding data rates of IEEE 802.11ac. The IEEE 802.11ac standard is a high-speed wireless LAN protocol at the 5 GHz band that is capable of speeds up to 1 Gbps. While 802.11ah does not approach this transmission speed (as it uses one-tenth of 802.11ac channel width, it reaches one-tenth of 802.11ac speed), it does provide an extended range for its lower speed data. For example, at a data rate of 100 kbps, the outdoor transmission range for IEEE 802.11ah is expected to be 0.62 mile.

MAC Layer

The IEEE 802.11ah MAC layer is optimized to support the new sub-GHz Wi-Fi PHY while providing low power consumption and the ability to support a larger number of endpoints. Enhancements and features specified by IEEE 802.11ah for the MAC layer include the following:

- **Number of devices:** Has been scaled up to 8192 per access point.

- **MAC header:** Has been shortened to allow more efficient communication.

- **Null data packet (NDP) support:** Is extended to cover several control and management frames. Relevant information is concentrated in the PHY header and the additional overhead associated with decoding the MAC header and data payload is avoided. This change makes the control frame exchanges efficient and less power-consuming for the receiving stations.

- **Grouping and sectorization:** Enables an AP to use sector antennas and also group stations (distributing a group ID). In combination with RAW and TWT, this mechanism reduces contention in large cells with many clients by restricting which group, in which sector, can contend during which time window. (Sectors are described in more detail in the following section.)

■ **Restricted access window (RAW):** Is a control algorithm that avoids simultaneous transmissions when many devices are present and provides fair access to the wireless network. By providing more efficient access to the medium, additional power savings for battery-powered devices can be achieved, and collisions are reduced.

■ **Target wake time (TWT):** Reduces energy consumption by permitting an access point to define times when a device can access the network. This allows devices to enter a low-power state until their TWT time arrives. It also reduces the probability of collisions in large cells with many clients.

■ **Speed frame exchange:** Enables an AP and endpoint to exchange frames during a reserved transmit opportunity (TXOP). This reduces contention on the medium, minimizes the number of frame exchanges to improve channel efficiency, and extends battery life by keeping awake times short.

You can see from this feature list that the 802.11ah MAC layer is focused on power consumption and mechanisms to allow low-power Wi-Fi stations to wake up less often and operate more efficiently. This sort of MAC layer is ideal for IoT devices that often produce short, low-bit-rate transmissions.

Topology

While IEEE 802.11ah is deployed as a star topology, it includes a simple hops relay operation to extend its range. This relay option is not capped, but the IEEE 802.11ah task group worked on the assumption of two hops. It allows one 802.11ah device to act as an intermediary and relay data to another. In some ways, this is similar to a mesh, and it is important to note that the clients and not the access point handle the relay function.

This relay operation can be combined with a higher transmission rate or modulation and coding scheme (MCS). This means that a higher transmit rate is used by relay devices talking directly to the access point. The transmit rate reduces as you move further from the access point via relay clients. This ensures an efficient system that limits transmission speeds at the edge of the relays so that communications close to the AP are not negatively affected.

Sectorization is a technique that involves partitioning the coverage area into several sectors to get reduced contention within a certain sector. This technique is useful for limiting collisions in cells that have many clients. This technique is also often necessary when the coverage area of 802.11ah access points is large, and interference from neighboring access points is problematic. Sectorization uses an antenna array and beam-forming techniques to partition the cell-coverage area. Figure 4-14 shows an example of 802.11ah sectorization.

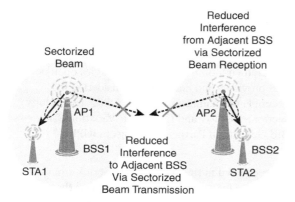

Figure 4-14   *IEEE 802.11ah Sectorization*

Security

No additional security has been identified for IEEE 802.11ah compared to other IEEE 802.11 specifications. (The other IEEE protocols are discussed earlier in this chapter.) These protocols include IEEE 802.15.4, IEEE 802.15.4e, and IEEE 1901.2a, and the security information for them is also applicable to IEEE 802.11ah.

Competitive Technologies

Competitive technologies to IEEE 802.11ah are IEEE 802.15.4 and IEEE 802.15.4e, along with the competitive technologies highlighted in each of their sections. (For more information on these competing technologies, see the sections "IEEE 802.15.4" and "IEEE 802.15.4g and IEEE 802.15.4e," earlier in this chapter.)

IEEE 802.11ah Conclusions

The IEEE 802.11ah access technology is an ongoing effort of the IEEE 802.11 working group to define an "industrial Wi-Fi." Currently, this standard is just at the beginning of its evolution, and it is not clear how the market will react to this new Wi-Fi standard.

This specification offers a longer range than traditional Wi-Fi technologies and provides good support for low-power devices that need to send smaller bursts of data at lower speeds. At the same time, it has the ability to scale to higher speeds as well.

IEEE 802.11ah is quite different in terms of current products and the existing Wi-Fi technologies in the 2.4 GHz and 5 GHz frequency bands. To gain broad adoption and compete against similar technologies in this space, it will need an ecosystem of products and solutions that can be configured and deployed at a low cost.

LoRaWAN

In recent years, a new set of wireless technologies known as Low-Power Wide-Area (LPWA) has received a lot of attention from the industry and press. Particularly well adapted for long-range and battery-powered endpoints, LPWA technologies open new business opportunities to both services providers and enterprises considering IoT solutions. This section discusses an example of an unlicensed-band LPWA technology, known as LoRaWAN, and the next section, "NB-IoT and Other LTE Variations," reviews licensed-band alternatives from the 3rd Generation Partnership Project (3GPP).

Note   Other technologies could have been covered in this section of the book from an LPWA perspective, but currently this part of the IoT world is still evolving, and there are a lot of available options. We chose to cover LoRaWAN because it is one of the few options that is established, and it is backed by an industry alliance supported by a substantial number of companies.

Standardization and Alliances

Initially, LoRa was a physical layer, or Layer 1, modulation that was developed by a French company named Cycleo. Later, Cycleo was acquired by Semtech. Optimized for long-range, two-way communications and low power consumption, the technology evolved from Layer 1 to a broader scope through the creation of the LoRa Alliance. For more information on the LoRa Alliance, visit www.lora-alliance.org.

The LoRa Alliance quickly achieved industry support and currently has hundreds of members. Published LoRaWAN specifications are open and can be accessed from the LoRa Alliance website.

Semtech LoRa as a Layer 1 PHY modulation technology is available through multiple chipset vendors. To differentiate from the physical layer modulation known as LoRa, the LoRa Alliance uses the term LoRaWAN to refer to its architecture and its specifications that describe end-to-end LoRaWAN communications and protocols.

Figure 4-15 provides a high-level overview of the LoRaWAN layers. In this figure, notice that Semtech is responsible for the PHY layer, while the LoRa Alliance handles the MAC layer and regional frequency bands.

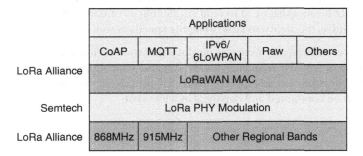

Figure 4-15   *LoRaWAN Layers*

Overall, the LoRa Alliance owns and manages the roadmap and technical development of the LoRaWAN architecture and protocol. This alliance also handles the LoRaWAN endpoint certification program and technology promotion through its certification and marketing committees.

Physical Layer

Semtech LoRa modulation is based on chirp spread spectrum modulation, which trades a lower data rate for receiver sensitivity to significantly increase the communication distance. In addition, it allows demodulation below the noise floor, offers robustness to noise and interference, and manages a single channel occupation by different spreading factors. This enables LoRa devices to receive on multiple channels in parallel.

LoRaWAN 1.0.2 regional specifications describe the use of the main unlicensed sub-GHz frequency bands of 433 MHz, 779–787 MHz, 863–870 MHz, and 902–928 MHz, as well as regional profiles for a subset of the 902–928 MHz bandwidth. For example, Australia utilizes 915–928 MHz frequency bands, while South Korea uses 920–923 MHz and Japan uses 920–928 MHz.

Note Semtech LoRa chipsets support additional frequency bands, such as 169 MHz, that are not supported by LoRaWAN specifications. Additional regional profiles and bands are under development and are being considered by the LoRa Alliance.

Understanding LoRa gateways is critical to understanding a LoRaWAN system. A LoRa gateway is deployed as the center hub of a star network architecture. It uses multiple transceivers and channels and can demodulate multiple channels at once or even demodulate multiple signals on the same channel simultaneously. LoRa gateways serve as a transparent bridge relaying data between endpoints, and the endpoints use a single-hop wireless connection to communicate with one or many gateways.

The data rate in LoRaWAN varies depending on the frequency bands and adaptive data rate (ADR). ADR is an algorithm that manages the data rate and radio signal for each endpoint. The ADR algorithm ensures that packets are delivered at the best data rate possible and that network performance is both optimal and scalable. Endpoints close to the gateways with good signal values transmit with the highest data rate, which enables a shorter transmission time over the wireless network, and the lowest transmit power. Meanwhile, endpoints at the edge of the link budget communicate at the lowest data rate and highest transmit power.

Note LoRaWAN best practices recommend the use of ADR for fixed endpoints, and a fixed data rate or spreading factor for mobile endpoints. Data rate management is not practical when mobile endpoints cause quick changes in their radio environment.

An important feature of LoRa is its ability to handle various data rates via the spreading factor. Devices with a low spreading factor (SF) achieve less distance in their communications but transmit at faster speeds, resulting in less airtime. A higher SF provides slower transmission rates but achieves a higher reliability at longer distances. Table 4-4 illustrates how LoRaWAN data rates can vary depending on the associated spreading factor for the two main frequency bands, 863–870 MHz and 902–928 MHz.

Table 4-4   *LoRaWAN Data Rate Example*

Configuration	863–870 MHz bps	902–928 MHz bps
LoRa: SF12/125 kHz	250	N/A
LoRa: SF11/125 kHz	440	N/A
LoRa: SF10/125 kHz	980	980
LoRa: SF9/125 kHz	1760	1760
LoRa: SF8/125 kHz	3125	3125
LoRa: SF7/125 kHz	5470	5470
LoRa: SF7/250 kHz	11,000	N/A
FSK: 50 kbps	50,000	N/A
LoRa: SF12/500 kHz	N/A	980
LoRa: SF11/500 kHz	N/A	1760
LoRa: SF10/500 kHz	N/A	3900
LoRa: SF9/500 kHz	N/A	7000
LoRa: SF8/500 kHz	N/A	12,500
LoRa: SF7/500 kHz	N/A	21,900

In Table 4-4, notice the relationship between SF and data rate. For example, at an SF value of 12 for 125 kHz of channel bandwidth, the data rate is 250 bps. However, when the SF is decreased to a value of 7, the data rate increases to 5470 bps.

Channel bandwidth values of 125 kHz, 250 kHz, and 500 kHz are also evident in Table 4-4. The effect of increasing the bandwidth is that faster data rates can be achieved for the same spreading factor.

MAC Layer

As mentioned previously, the MAC layer is defined in the LoRaWAN specification. This layer takes advantage of the LoRa physical layer and classifies LoRaWAN endpoints to optimize their battery life and ensure downstream communications to the LoRaWAN endpoints. The LoRaWAN specification documents three classes of LoRaWAN devices:

- **Class A:** This class is the default implementation. Optimized for battery-powered nodes, it allows bidirectional communications, where a given node is able to receive downstream traffic after transmitting. Two receive windows are available after each transmission.

■ **Class B:** This class was designated "experimental" in LoRaWAN 1.0.1 until it can be better defined. A Class B node or endpoint should get additional receive windows compared to Class A, but gateways must be synchronized through a beaconing process.

■ **Class C:** This class is particularly adapted for powered nodes. This classification enables a node to be continuously listening by keeping its receive window open when not transmitting.

LoRaWAN messages, either uplink or downlink, have a PHY payload composed of a 1-byte MAC header, a variable-byte MAC payload, and a MIC that is 4 bytes in length. The MAC payload size depends on the frequency band and the data rate, ranging from 59 to 230 bytes for the 863–870 MHz band and 19 to 250 bytes for the 902–928 MHz band. Figure 4-16 shows a high-level LoRaWAN MAC frame format.

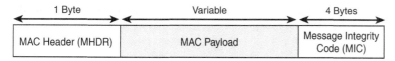

Figure 4-16 *High-Level LoRaWAN MAC Frame Format*

In version 1.0.x, LoRaWAN utilizes six MAC message types. LoRaWAN devices use join request and join accept messages for over-the-air (OTA) activation and joining the network. The other message types are unconfirmed data up/down and confirmed data up/down. A "confirmed" message is one that must be acknowledged, and "unconfirmed" signifies that the end device does not need to acknowledge. "up/down" is simply a directional notation identifying whether the message flows in the uplink or downlink path. Uplink messages are sent from endpoints to the network server and are relayed by one or more LoRaWAN gateways. Downlink messages flow from the network server to a single endpoint and are relayed by only a single gateway. Multicast over LoRaWAN is being considered for future versions.

LoRaWAN endpoints are uniquely addressable through a variety of methods, including the following:

■ An endpoint can have a global end device ID or DevEUI represented as an IEEE EUI-64 address.

■ An endpoint can have a global application ID or AppEUI represented as an IEEE EUI-64 address that uniquely identifies the application provider, such as the owner, of the end device.

■ In a LoRaWAN network, endpoints are also known by their end device address, known as a DevAddr, a 32-bit address. The 7 most significant bits are the network identifier (NwkID), which identifies the LoRaWAN network. The 25 least significant bits are used as the network address (NwkAddr) to identify the endpoint in the network.

Note   The LoRa Alliance maintains a list of companies that have registered for network identifiers (NwkIDs). The LoRa Alliance also allocates new NwkIDs. When the LoRaWAN 1.1 specification is released, a NetID field will uniquely identify a network operator. This code is also managed by the LoRa Alliance. The seven least significant bits of the NetID contain the NwkID. The NwkIDs in the DevAddr field and the NetID field are the same so the 7 most significant bits found in the DevAddr field must match the 7 least significant bits of the NetID.

Topology

LoRaWAN topology is often described as a "star of stars" topology. As shown in Figure 4-17, the infrastructure consists of endpoints exchanging packets through gateways acting as bridges, with a central LoRaWAN network server. Gateways connect to the backend network using standard IP connections, and endpoints communicate directly with one or more gateways.

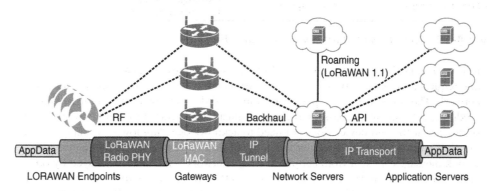

Figure 4-17   *LoRaWAN Architecture*

In Figure 4-17, LoRaWAN endpoints transport their selected application data over the LoRaWAN MAC layer on top of one of the supported PHY layer frequency bands. The application data is contained in upper protocol layers. These upper layers are not the responsibility of the LoRa Alliance, but best practices may be developed and recommended. These upper layers could just be raw data on top of the LoRaWAN MAC layer, or the data could be stacked in multiple protocols. For example, you could have upper-layer protocols, such as ZigBee Control Layer (ZCL), Constrained Application Protocol (CoAP), or Message Queuing Telemetry Transport (MQTT), with or without an IPv6/6LoWPAN layer. (The CoAP and MQTT protocols are covered in Chapter 6.)

Figure 4-17 also shows how LoRaWAN gateways act as bridges that relay between endpoints and the network servers. Multiple gateways can receive and transport the same packets. When duplicate packets are received, de-duplication is a function of the network server.

Note Semtech, developer of the LoRa PHY, has specified two generations of LoRaWAN gateways. The first generation was simple, and the next generation, known as version 2, adds new features, such as geolocation. Geolocation works by having version 2 LoRaWAN gateways share an accurate time source and then adding a high-resolution timestamp to each received LoRa packet. The endpoint's geolocation can be determined by using time differential of arrival (TDoA) algorithms.

The LoRaWAN network server manages the data rate and radio frequency (RF) of each endpoint through the adaptive data rate (ADR) algorithm. ADR is a key component of the network scalability, performance, and battery life of the endpoints. The LoRaWAN network server forwards application data to the application servers, as depicted in Figure 4-17.

In future versions of the LoRaWAN specification, roaming capabilities between LoRaWAN network servers will be added. These capabilities will enable mobile endpoints to connect and roam between different LoRaWAN network infrastructures.

Security

Security in a LoRaWAN deployment applies to different components of the architecture, as detailed in Figure 4-18. LoRaWAN endpoints must implement two layers of security, protecting communications and data privacy across the network.

The first layer, called "network security" but applied at the MAC layer, guarantees the authentication of the endpoints by the LoRaWAN network server. Also, it protects LoRaWAN packets by performing encryption based on AES.

Each endpoint implements a network session key (NwkSKey), used by both itself and the LoRaWAN network server. The NwkSKey ensures data integrity through computing and checking the MIC of every data message as well as encrypting and decrypting MAC-only data message payloads.

The second layer is an application session key (AppSKey), which performs encryption and decryption functions between the endpoint and its application server. Furthermore, it computes and checks the application-level MIC, if included. This ensures that the LoRaWAN service provider does not have access to the application payload if it is not allowed that access.

Endpoints receive their AES-128 application key (AppKey) from the application owner. This key is most likely derived from an application-specific root key exclusively known to and under the control of the application provider.

For production deployments, it is expected that the LoRaWAN gateways are protected as well, for both the LoRaWAN traffic and the network management and operations over their backhaul link(s). This can be done using traditional VPN and IPsec technologies that demonstrate scaling in traditional IT deployments. Additional security add-ons are under evaluation by the LoRaWAN Alliance for future revisions of the specification.

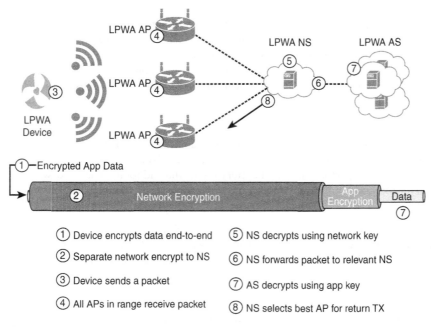

Figure 4-18 *LoRaWAN Security*

LoRaWAN endpoints attached to a LoRaWAN network must get registered and authenticated. This can be achieved through one of the two join mechanisms:

- **Activation by personalization (ABP):** Endpoints don't need to run a join procedure as their individual details, including DevAddr and the NwkSKey and AppSKey session keys, are preconfigured and stored in the end device. This same information is registered in the LoRaWAN network server.

- **Over-the-air activation (OTAA):** Endpoints are allowed to dynamically join a particular LoRaWAN network after successfully going through a join procedure. The join procedure must be done every time a session context is renewed. During the join process, which involves the sending and receiving of MAC layer join request and join accept messages, the node establishes its credentials with a LoRaWAN network server, exchanging its globally unique DevEUI, AppEUI, and AppKey. The AppKey is then used to derive the session NwkSKey and AppSKey keys.

Competitive Technologies

LPWA solutions and technologies are split between unlicensed and licensed bands. The licensed-band technologies are dedicated to mobile service providers that have acquired spectrum licenses; they are discussed in the next section. In addition, several technologies are targeting the unlicensed-band LPWA market to compete against LoRaWAN. The LPWA market is quickly evolving. Table 4-5 evaluates two of the best-established vendors known to provide LPWA options.

Table 4-5 *Unlicensed LPWA Technology Comparison*

Characteristic	LoRaWAN	Sigfox	Ingenu Onramp
Frequency bands	433 MHz, 868 MHz, 902–928 MHz	433 MHz, 868 MHz, 902–928 MHz	2.4 GHz
Modulation	Chirp spread spectrum	Ultra-narrowband	DSSS
Topology	Star of stars	Star	Star; tree supported with an RPMA extender
Data rate	250 bps–50 kbps (868 MHz) 980 bps–21.9 kbps (915 MHz)	100 bps (868 MHz) 600 bps (915 MHz)	6 kbps
Adaptive data rate	Yes	No	No
Payload	59–230 bytes (868 MHz) 19–250 bytes (915 MHz)	12 bytes	6 bytes–10 KB
Two-way communications	Yes	Partial	Yes
Geolocation	Yes (LoRa GW version 2 reference design)	No	No
Roaming	Yes (LoRaWAN 1.1)	No	Yes
Specifications	LoRA Alliance	Proprietary	Proprietary

Table 4-5 gives you a good overview of two of the most established LoRaWAN competitors. This is a good starting point, but you should perform additional research to further differentiate these technologies if you are interested in deploying an LPWAN.

LoRaWAN Conclusions

The LoRaWAN wireless technology was developed for LPWANs that are critical for implementing many new devices on IoT networks. The term LoRa refers to the PHY layer, and LoRaWAN focuses on the architecture, the MAC layer, and a unified, single standard for seamless interoperability. LoRaWAN is managed by the LoRa Alliance, an industry organization.

The PHY and MAC layers allow LoRaWAN to cover longer distances with a data rate that can change depending on various factors. The LoRaWAN architecture depends on gateways to bridge endpoints to network servers. From a security perspective, LoRaWAN offers AES authentication and encryption at two separate layers.

Unlicensed LPWA technologies represent new opportunities for implementing IoT infrastructures, solutions, and use cases for private enterprise networks, broadcasters, and mobile and non-mobile service providers. The ecosystem of endpoints is rapidly growing and will certainly be the tie-breaker between the various LPWA technologies and solutions, including LoRaWAN. Smart cities operators, broadcasters, and mobile and non-mobile services providers, which are particularly crucial to enabling use cases for the consumers' markets, are addressing the need for regional or national IoT infrastructures.

As private enterprises look at developing LPWA networks, they will benefit from roaming capabilities between private and public infrastructures. These can be deployed similarly to Wi-Fi infrastructures and can coexist with licensed-band LPWA options. Overall, LoRaWAN and other LPWA technologies answer a definite need in the IoT space and are expected to continue to grow as more and more "things" need to be interconnected.

NB-IoT and Other LTE Variations

Existing cellular technologies, such as GPRS, Edge, 3G, and 4G/LTE, are not particularly well adapted to battery-powered devices and small objects specifically developed for the Internet of Things. While industry players have been developing unlicensed-band LPWA technologies, 3GPP and associated vendors have been working on evolving cellular technologies to better address IoT requirements. The effort started with the definition of new LTE device categories. The aim was to both align with specific IoT requirements, such as low throughput and low power consumption, and decrease the complexity and cost of the LTE devices. This resulted in the definition of the LTE-M work item.

Note   3rd Generation Partnership Project (3GPP) is a standards organization that unites multiple telecommunications standards development organizations to provide a stable environment to produce the reports and specifications that define 3GPP technologies. For more information on 3GPP, visit www.3gpp.org.

Because the new LTE-M device category was not sufficiently close to LPWA capabilities, in 2015 3GPP approved a proposal to standardize a new narrowband radio access technology called Narrowband IoT (NB-IoT). NB-IoT specifically addresses the requirements of a massive number of low-throughput devices, low device power consumption, improved indoor coverage, and optimized network architecture. The following sections review the proposed evolution of cellular technologies to better support the IoT opportunities by mobile service providers.

Standardization and Alliances

The 3GPP organization includes multiple working groups focused on many different aspects of telecommunications (for example, radio, core, terminal, and so on). Many service providers and vendors make up 3GPP, and the results of their collaborative work in these areas are the 3GPP specifications and studies. The workflow within 3GPP involves receiving contributions related to licensed LPWA work from the involved vendors. Then, depending on the access technology that is most closely aligned, such as 3G, LTE, or

GSM, the IoT-related contribution is handled by either 3GPP or the GSM EDGE Radio Access Networks (GERAN) group.

Mobile vendors and service providers are not willing to lose leadership in this market of connecting IoT devices. Therefore, a couple intermediate steps have been pushed forward, leading to the final objectives set for NB-IoT and documented by 3GPP. At the same time, another industry group, the GSM Association (GSMA), has proposed the Mobile IoT Initiative, which "is designed to accelerate the commercial availability of LPWA solutions in licensed spectrum." For more information on the Mobile IoT Initiative, go to www.gsma.com/connectedliving/mobile-iot-initiative/.

LTE Cat 0

The first enhancements to better support IoT devices in 3GPP occurred in LTE Release 12. A new user equipment (UE) category, Category 0, was added, with devices running at a maximum data rate of 1 Mbps. Generally, LTE enhancements target higher bandwidth improvements. Category 0 includes important characteristics to be supported by both the network and end devices. Meanwhile, the UE still can operate in existing LTE systems with bandwidths up to 20 MHz. These Cat 0 characteristics include the following:

- **Power saving mode (PSM):** This new device status minimizes energy consumption. Energy consumption is expected to be lower with PSM than with existing idle mode. PSM is defined as being similar to "powered off" mode, but the device stays registered with the network. By staying registered, the device avoids having to reattach or reestablish its network connection. The device negotiates with the network the idle time after which it will wake up. When it wakes up, it initiates a tracking area update (TAU), after which it stays available for a configured time and then switches back to sleep mode or PSM. A TAU is a procedure that an LTE device uses to let the network know its current tracking area, or the group of towers in the network from which it can be reached. Basically, with PSM, a device can be practically powered off but not lose its place in the network.

- **Half-duplex mode:** This mode reduces the cost and complexity of a device's implementation because a duplex filter is not needed. Most IoT endpoints are sensors that send low amounts of data that do not have a full-duplex communication requirement.

Note   Recent LTE chipsets should have support for LTE Cat 0 because vendors began advertising LTE Cat 0 support on their chipsets starting in 2015. However, ecosystem and market acceptance still have to be demonstrated.

LTE-M

Following LTE Cat 0, the next step in making the licensed spectrum more supportive of IoT devices was the introduction of the LTE-M category for 3GPP LTE Release 13. These are the main characteristics of the LTE-M category in Release 13:

- **Lower receiver bandwidth:** Bandwidth has been lowered to 1.4 MHz versus the usual 20 MHz. This further simplifies the LTE endpoint.

- **Lower data rate:** Data is around 200 kbps for LTE-M, compared to 1 Mbps for Cat 0.

- **Half-duplex mode:** Just as with Cat 0, LTE-M offers a half-duplex mode that decreases node complexity and cost.

- **Enhanced discontinuous reception (eDRX):** This capability increases from seconds to minutes the amount of time an endpoint can "sleep" between paging cycles. A paging cycle is a periodic check-in with the network. This extended "sleep" time between paging cycles extends the battery lifetime for an endpoint significantly.

LTE-M requires new chipsets and additional software development. Commercial deployment is expected in 2017. Mobile carriers expect that only new LTE-M software will be required on the base stations, which will prevent re-investment in hardware.

NB-IoT

Recognizing that the definition of new LTE device categories was not sufficient to support LPWA IoT requirement, 3GPP specified Narrowband IoT (NB-IoT). The work on NB-IoT started with multiple proposals pushed by the involved vendors, including the following:

- Extended Coverage GSM (EC-GSM), Ericsson proposal

- Narrowband GSM (N-GSM), Nokia proposal

- Narrowband M2M (NB-M2M), Huawei/Neul proposal

- Narrowband OFDMA (orthogonal frequency-division multiple access), Qualcomm proposal

- Narrowband Cellular IoT (NB-CIoT), combined proposal of NB-M2M and NB-OFDMA

- Narrowband LTE (NB-LTE), Alcatel-Lucent, Ericsson, and Nokia proposal

- Cooperative Ultra Narrowband (C-UNB), Sigfox proposal

Consolidation occurred with the agreement to specify a single NB-IoT version based on orthogonal frequency-division multiple access (OFDMA) in the downlink and a couple options for the uplink. OFDMA is a modulation scheme in which individual users are assigned subsets of subcarrier frequencies. This enables multiple users to transmit low-speed data simultaneously. For more information on the uplink options, refer to the 3GPP specification TR 36.802.

Three modes of operation are applicable to NB-IoT:

- **Standalone:** A GSM carrier is used as an NB-IoT carrier, enabling reuse of 900 MHz or 1800 MHz.

■ **In-band:** Part of an LTE carrier frequency band is allocated for use as an NB-IoT frequency. The service provider typically makes this allocation, and IoT devices are configured accordingly. You should be aware that if these devices must be deployed across different countries or regions using a different service provider, problems may occur unless there is some coordination between the service providers, and the NB-IoT frequency band allocations are the same.

■ **Guard band:** An NB-IoT carrier is between the LTE or WCDMA bands. This requires coexistence between LTE and NB-IoT bands.

In its Release 13, 3GPP completed the standardization of NB-IoT. Beyond the radio-specific aspects, this work specifies the adaptation of the IoT core to support specific IoT capabilities, including simplifying the LTE attach procedure so that a dedicated bearer channel is not required and transporting non-IP data. Subsequent releases of 3GPP NB-IoT will introduce additional features and functionality, such as multicasting, and will be backward compatible with Release 13.

Mobile service providers consider NB-IoT the target technology as it allows them to leverage their licensed spectrum to support LPWA use cases. For instance, NB-IoT is defined for a 200-kHz-wide channel in both uplink and downlink, allowing mobile service providers to optimize their spectrum, with a number of deployment options for GSM, WCDMA, and LTE spectrum, as shown in Figure 4-19.

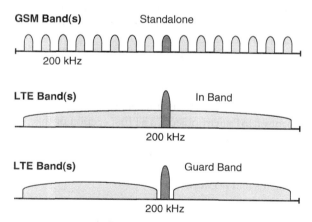

Figure 4-19 *NB-IoT Deployment Options*

In an LTE network, resource blocks are defined with an effective bandwidth of 180 kHz, while on NB-IoT, tone or subcarriers replace the LTE resource blocks. The uplink channel can be 15 kHz or 3.75 kHz or multi-tone (n*15 kHz, n up to 12). At Layer 1, the maximum transport block size (TBS) for downlink is 680 bits, while uplink is 1000 bits. At Layer 2, the maximum Packet Data Convergence Protocol (PDCP) service data unit (SDU) size is 1600 bytes.

NB-IoT operates in half-duplex frequency-division duplexing (FDD) mode with a maximum data rate uplink of 60 kbps and downlink of 30 kbps.

Topology

NB-IoT is defined with a link budget of 164 dB; compare this with the GPRS link budget of 144 dB, used by many machine-to-machine services. The additional 20 dB link budget increase should guarantee better signal penetration in buildings and basements while achieving battery life requirements.

Competitive Technologies

In licensed bands, it is expected that 3GPP NB-IoT will be the adopted LPWA technology when it is fully available. Competitive technologies are mostly the unlicensed-band LPWA technologies such as LoRaWAN. The main challenge faced by providers of the licensed bands is the opportunity for non-mobile service providers to grab market share by offering IoT infrastructure without buying expensive spectrum.

NB-IoT and Other LTE Variations Conclusions

NB-IoT represents the future of LPWA technology for the mobile service providers who own licensed-band spectrum. IoT-related specifications must be completed and published by 3GPP to enable vendors, mobile service providers, and applications to successfully and widely endorse the technology. Evolution to eSIMs, which are still not widely supported, should be tied to NB-IoT as managing millions of SIM cards may not be an acceptable path for the market. An eSIM card is compliant across multiple operators and also reconfigurable. This means that it is a permanent part of the device and is easily rewritten if the device is switched to a different provider.

Summary

This chapter reviews the communications criteria and the significant and most recent technologies supporting the deployment of IoT smart objects. The first section of this chapter provides criteria for evaluating smart objects and what is needed for their connectivity. These criteria included the transmission range, frequency bands, power consumption, topology, and constrained devices and networks. It is critical to evaluate these criteria when dealing with IoT deployments and networks.

The second section of this chapter provides a detailed discussion of the main technologies for connecting sensors. While various technologies are available for this purpose, many of them are in their infancy and will evolve over the years. This chapter provides a comprehensive look at the technologies that are the most promising going forward, based on current market trends, industry support, and market share. The technologies covered in the second part of this chapter included IEEE 802.15.4, IEEE 802.15.4g and IEEE 802.15.4e, IEEE 1901.2a, IEEE 802.11ah, LoRaWAN, and NB-IoT. You should have an awareness and base knowledge of these technologies, as they are fundamental to connecting IoT smart objects; in addition, understanding these technologies will provide a foundation for you to understand new technologies. Table 4-6 summarizes and compares some of the main characteristics of the access technologies discussed in this chapter.

Table 4-6 *Main Characteristics of Access Technologies Discussed in This Chapter*

Characteristic	IEEE 802.15.4	IEEE 802.15.4g and IEEE 802.15.4e	IEEE 1901.2a	IEEE 802.11ah	LoRaWAN	NB-IoT
Wired or wireless	Wireless	Wireless	Wired	Wireless	Wireless	Wireless
Frequency bands	Unlicensed 2.4 GHz and sub-GHz	Unlicensed 2.4 GHz and sub-GHz	Unlicensed CENELEC A and B, FCC, ARIB	Unlicensed sub-GHz	Unlicensed sub-GHz	Licensed
Topology	Star, mesh	Star, mesh	Mesh	Star	Star	Star
Range	Medium	Medium	Medium	Medium	Long	Long
Data rate	Low	Low	Low	Low–high	Low	Low

Chapter 5

IP as the IoT Network Layer

In Chapter 4, "Connecting Smart Objects," you learned about the important consider-ations in creating an IoT network and common protocols employed by smart objects to access and communicate with a network. Chapter 4 focuses on connectivity at Layer 1 (PHY) and Layer 2 (MAC). In this chapter, we move up the protocol stack and extend the conversation to network layer connectivity, which is commonly referred to as Layer 3. Referring back to the Core IoT Functional Stack introduced in Figure 2-7, this chapter covers the network transport layer sublayer that is part of the communications net-work layer. Alternatively, you can also align this chapter with the network layer of the oneM2M architecture shown in Figure 2-1 or the connectivity layer of the IoT World Forum architecture detailed in Figure 2-3 if these models are preferable.

This chapter is composed of the following sections:

- **The Business Case for IP:** This section discusses the advantages of IP from an IoT perspective and introduces the concepts of adoption and adaptation.

- **The Need for Optimization:** This section dives into the challenges of constrained nodes and devices when deploying IP. This section also looks at the migration from IPv4 to IPv6 and how it affects IoT networks.

- **Optimizing IP for IoT:** This section explores the common protocols and technolo-gies in IoT networks utilizing IP, including 6LoWPAN, 6TiSCH, and RPL.

- **Profiles and Compliances:** This section provides a summary of some of the most significant organizations and standards bodies involved with IP connectivity and IoT.

This chapter builds on many of the technologies introduced in previous ones. In fact, protocols and technologies from these chapters are often paired together and developed with this pairing in mind. For example, 802.15.4 and 6LoWPAN are a combination that is paired together frequently for many applications.

This chapter has a deliberate focus on IP, which has become the de facto standard in many areas of IoT. With support from numerous standards and industry organizations, IP and its role as the network layer transport for IoT is a foundational element that you should be familiar with.

The Business Case for IP

Data flowing from or to "things" is consumed, controlled, or monitored by data center servers either in the cloud or in locations that may be distributed or centralized. Dedicated applications are then run over virtualized or traditional operating systems or on network edge platforms (for example, fog computing). These lightweight applications communicate with the data center servers. Therefore, the system solutions combining various physical and data link layers call for an architectural approach with a common layer(s) independent from the lower (connectivity) and/or upper (application) layers. This is how and why the Internet Protocol (IP) suite started playing a key architectural role in the early 1990s. IP was not only preferred in the IT markets but also for the OT environment.

The Key Advantages of Internet Protocol

One of the main differences between traditional information technology (IT) and operational technology (OT) is the lifetime of the underlying technologies and products. (For more information on IT and OT, refer to Chapter 1, "What Is IoT?") An entire industrial workflow generally mandates smooth, incremental steps that evolve, with operations itself being the most time- and mission-critical factor for an organization.

One way to guarantee multi-year lifetimes is to define a layered architecture such as the 30-year-old IP architecture. IP has largely demonstrated its ability to integrate small and large evolutions. At the same time, it is able to maintain its operations for large numbers of devices and users, such as the 3 billion Internet users.

Note   Using the Internet Protocol suite does not mean that an IoT infrastructure running IP has to be an open or publicly accessible network. Indeed, many existing mission-critical but private and highly secure networks, such as inter-banking networks, military and defense networks, and public-safety and emergency-response networks, use the IP architecture.

Before evaluating the pros and cons of IP adoption versus adaptation, this section provides a quick review of the key advantages of the IP suite for the Internet of Things:

- **Open and standards-based:** Operational technologies have often been delivered as turnkey features by vendors who may have optimized the communications through closed and proprietary networking solutions. The Internet of Things creates a new paradigm in which devices, applications, and users can leverage a large set of devices and functionalities while guaranteeing interchangeability and interoperability, security, and management. This calls for implementation, validation, and deployment of open, standards-based solutions. While many standards development organizations (SDOs) are working on Internet of Things definitions, frameworks, applications, and technologies, none are questioning the role of the Internet Engineering Task Force (IETF) as the foundation for specifying and optimizing the network and transport layers. The IETF is an open standards body that focuses on the development of the Internet Protocol suite and related Internet technologies and protocols.

■ **Versatile:** A large spectrum of access technologies is available to offer connectivity of "things" in the last mile. Additional protocols and technologies are also used to transport IoT data through backhaul links and in the data center. Even if physical and data link layers such as Ethernet, Wi-Fi, and cellular are widely adopted, the history of data communications demonstrates that no given wired or wireless technology fits all deployment criteria. Furthermore, communication technologies evolve at a pace faster than the expected 10- to 20-year lifetime of OT solutions. So, the layered IP architecture is well equipped to cope with any type of physical and data link layers. This makes IP ideal as a long-term investment because various protocols at these layers can be used in a deployment now and over time, without requiring changes to the whole solution architecture and data flow.

■ **Ubiquitous:** All recent operating system releases, from general-purpose computers and servers to lightweight embedded systems (TinyOS, Contiki, and so on), have an integrated dual (IPv4 and IPv6) IP stack that gets enhanced over time. In addition, IoT application protocols in many industrial OT solutions have been updated in recent years to run over IP. While these updates have mostly consisted of IPv4 to this point, recent standardization efforts in several areas are adding IPv6. In fact, IP is the most pervasive protocol when you look at what is supported across the various IoT solutions and industry verticals.

■ **Scalable:** As the common protocol of the Internet, IP has been massively deployed and tested for robust scalability. Millions of private and public IP infrastructure nodes have been operational for years, offering strong foundations for those not familiar with IP network management. Of course, adding huge numbers of "things" to private and public infrastructures may require optimizations and design rules specific to the new devices. However, you should realize that this is not very different from the recent evolution of voice and video endpoints integrated over IP. IP has proven before that scalability is one of its strengths.

■ **Manageable and highly secure:** Communications infrastructure requires appropriate management and security capabilities for proper operations. One of the benefits that comes from 30 years of operational IP networks is the well-understood network management and security protocols, mechanisms, and toolsets that are widely available. Adopting IP network management also brings an operational business application to OT. Well-known network and security management tools are easily leveraged with an IP network layer. However, you should be aware that despite the secure nature of IP, real challenges exist in this area. Specifically, the industry is challenged in securing constrained nodes, handling legacy OT protocols, and scaling operations.

■ **Stable and resilient:** IP has been around for 30 years, and it is clear that IP is a workable solution. IP has a large and well-established knowledge base and, more importantly, it has been used for years in critical infrastructures, such as financial and defense networks. In addition, IP has been deployed for critical services, such as voice and video, which have already transitioned from closed environments to open IP standards. Finally, its stability and resiliency benefit from the large ecosystem of IT professionals who can help design, deploy, and operate IP-based solutions.

■ **Consumers' market adoption:** When developing IoT solutions and products targeting the consumer market, vendors know that consumers' access to applications and devices will occur predominantly over broadband and mobile wireless infrastructure. The main consumer devices range from smart phones to tablets and PCs. The common protocol that links IoT in the consumer space to these devices is IP.

■ **The innovation factor:** The past two decades have largely established the adoption of IP as a factor for increased innovation. IP is the underlying protocol for applications ranging from file transfer and e-mail to the World Wide Web, e-commerce, social networking, mobility, and more. Even the recent computing evolution from PC to mobile and mainframes to cloud services are perfect demonstrations of the innovative ground enabled by IP. Innovations in IoT can also leverage an IP underpinning.

In summary, the adoption of IP provides a solid foundation for the Internet of Things by allowing secured and manageable bidirectional data communication capabilities between all devices in a network. IP is a standards-based protocol that is ubiquitous, scalable, versatile, and stable. Network services such as naming, time distribution, traffic prioritization, isolation, and so on are well-known and developed techniques that can be leveraged with IP. From cloud, centralized, or distributed architectures, IP data flow can be developed and implemented according to business requirements. However, you may wonder if IP is an end-to-end requirement; this is covered in the next section.

Adoption or Adaptation of the Internet Protocol

How to implement IP in data center, cloud services, and operation centers hosting IoT applications may seem obvious, but the adoption of IP in the last mile is more complicated and often makes running IP end-to-end more difficult.

If we look at the historical trend of IP adoption by IT in general, we can glean some insight into how IP adoption in the last mile should unfold. Before IPv4 was widely accepted and deployed in IT networks, many different protocol stacks overlapped with IP. For example, X.25/X.75 was standardized and promoted by service providers, while computer manufacturers implemented their own proprietary protocols, such as SNA, DECnet, IPX, and AppleTalk. Multiprotocol routers were needed to handle this proliferation of network layer protocols.

The use of numerous network layer protocols in addition to IP is often a point of contention between computer networking experts. Typically, one of two models, adaptation or adoption, is proposed:

■ *Adaptation* means application layered gateways (ALGs) must be implemented to ensure the translation between non-IP and IP layers.

■ *Adoption* involves replacing all non-IP layers with their IP layer counterparts, simplifying the deployment model and operations.

A similar transition is now occurring with IoT and its use of IP connectivity in the last mile. While IP is slowly becoming more prevalent, alternative protocol stacks are still often used. Let's look at a few examples in various industries to see how IP adaptation and adoption are currently applied to IoT last-mile connectivity.

In the industrial and manufacturing sector, there has been a move toward IP adoption. Solutions and product lifecycles in this space are spread over 10+ years, and many protocols have been developed for serial communications. While IP and Ethernet support were not specified in the initial versions, more recent specifications for these serial communications protocols integrate Ethernet and IPv4.

Supervisory control and data acquisition (SCADA) applications are typical examples of vertical market deployments that operate both the IP adaptation model and the adoption model. Found at the core of many modern industries, SCADA is an automation control system for remote monitoring and control of equipment. Implementations that make use of IP adaptation have SCADA devices attached through serial interfaces to a gateway tunneling or translating the traffic. With the IP adoption model, SCADA devices are attached via Ethernet to switches and routers forwarding their IPv4 traffic. (For more information on SCADA, see Chapter 6, "Application Protocols for IoT.")

Another example is a ZigBee solution that runs a non-IP stack between devices and a ZigBee gateway that forwards traffic to an application server. (For more information on ZigBee, see Chapter 4.) A ZigBee gateway often acts as a translator between the ZigBee and IP protocol stacks.

As highlighted by these examples, the IP adaptation versus adoption model still requires investigation for particular last-mile technologies used by IoT. You should consider the following factors when trying to determine which model is best suited for last-mile connectivity:

■ **Bidirectional versus unidirectional data flow:** While bidirectional communications are generally expected, some last-mile technologies offer optimization for unidirectional communication. For example, as introduced in Chapter 4, different classes of IoT devices, as defined in RFC 7228, may only infrequently need to report a few bytes of data to an application. These sorts of devices, particularly ones that communicate through LPWA technologies, include fire alarms sending alerts or daily test reports, electrical switches being pushed on or off, and water or gas meters sending weekly indexes. LPWA is further discussed in Chapter 4. For these cases, it is not necessarily worth implementing a full IP stack. However, it requires the overall end-to-end architecture to solve potential drawbacks; for example, if there is only one-way communication to upload data to an application, then it is not possible to download new software or firmware to the devices. This makes integrating new features and bug and security fixes more difficult.

■ **Overhead for last-mile communications paths:** IP adoption implies a layered architecture with a per-packet overhead that varies depending on the IP version. IPv4 has 20 bytes of header at a minimum, and IPv6 has 40 bytes at the IP network layer. For the IP transport layer, UDP has 8 bytes of header overhead, while TCP has a minimum of 20 bytes. If the data to be forwarded by a device is infrequent and only a few bytes, you can potentially have more header overhead than device data—again, particularly in the case of LPWA technologies. Consequently, you need to decide whether the IP adoption model is necessary and, if it is, how it can be optimized. This same consideration applies to control plane traffic that is run over IP for low-bandwidth, last-mile links. Routing protocol and other verbose network services may either not be required or call for optimization.

■ **Data flow model:** One benefit of the IP adoption model is the end-to-end nature of communications. Any node can easily exchange data with any other node in a network, although security, privacy, and other factors may put controls and limits on the "end-to-end" concept. However, in many IoT solutions, a device's data flow is limited to one or two applications. In this case, the adaptation model can work because translation of traffic needs to occur only between the end device and one or two application servers. Depending on the network topology and the data flow needed, both IP adaptation and adoption models have roles to play in last-mile connectivity.

■ **Network diversity:** One of the drawbacks of the adaptation model is a general dependency on single PHY and MAC layers. For example, ZigBee devices must only be deployed in ZigBee network islands. This same restriction holds for ITU G.9903 G3-PLC nodes. Therefore, a deployment must consider which applications have to run on the gateway connecting these islands and the rest of the world. Integration and coexistence of new physical and MAC layers or new applications impact how deployment and operations have to be planned. This is not a relevant consideration for the adoption model.

The Need for Optimization

As discussed in the previous section, the Internet of Things will largely be built on the Internet Protocol suite. However, challenges still exist for IP in IoT solutions. In addition to coping with the integration of non-IP devices, you may need to deal with the limits at the device and network levels that IoT often imposes. Therefore, optimizations are needed at various layers of the IP stack to handle the restrictions that are present in IoT networks.

The following sections take a detailed look at why optimization is necessary for IP. Both the nodes and the network itself can often be constrained in IoT solutions. Also, IP is transitioning from version 4 to version 6, which can add further confinements in the IoT space.

Constrained Nodes

As documented in Table 4-1 in Chapter 4, in IoT solutions, different classes of devices coexist. Depending on its functions in a network, a "thing" architecture may or may not offer similar characteristics compared to a generic PC or server in an IT environment.

Another limit is that this network protocol stack on an IoT node may be required to communicate through an unreliable path. Even if a full IP stack is available on the node, this causes problems such as limited or unpredictable throughput and low convergence when a topology change occurs.

Finally, power consumption is a key characteristic of constrained nodes. Many IoT devices are battery powered, with lifetime battery requirements varying from a few months to 10+ years. This drives the selection of networking technologies since high-speed ones, such as Ethernet, Wi-Fi, and cellular, are not (yet) capable of multi-year battery life. Current capabilities practically allow less than a year for these technologies on battery-powered nodes. Of course, power consumption is much less of a concern on nodes that do not require batteries as an energy source.

You should also be aware that power consumption requirements on battery-powered nodes impact communication intervals. To help extend battery life, you could enable a "low-power" mode instead of one that is "always on." Another option is "always off," which means communications are enabled only when needed to send data.

While it has been largely demonstrated that production IP stacks perform well in constrained nodes, classification of these nodes helps when evaluating the IP adoption versus adaptation model selection. IoT constrained nodes can be classified as follows:

- **Devices that are very constrained in resources, may communicate infrequently to transmit a few bytes, and may have limited security and management capabilities:** This drives the need for the IP adaptation model, where nodes communicate through gateways and proxies.

- **Devices with enough power and capacities to implement a stripped-down IP stack or non-IP stack:** In this case, you may implement either an optimized IP stack and directly communicate with application servers (adoption model) or go for an IP or non-IP stack and communicate through gateways and proxies (adaptation model).

- **Devices that are similar to generic PCs in terms of computing and power resources but have constrained networking capacities, such as bandwidth:** These nodes usually implement a full IP stack (adoption model), but network design and application behaviors must cope with the bandwidth constraints.

You probably already realize that the definition of constrained nodes is evolving. The costs of computing power, memory, storage resources, and power consumption are generally decreasing. At the same time, networking technologies continue to improve and offer more bandwidth and reliability. In the future, the push to optimize IP for constrained nodes will lessen as technology improvements and cost decreases address many of these challenges.

Constrained Networks

In the early years of the Internet, network bandwidth capacity was restrained due to technical limitations. Connections often depended on low-speed modems for transferring data. However, these low-speed connections demonstrated that IP could run over low-bandwidth networks.

Fast forward to today, and the evolution of networking has seen the emergence of high-speed infrastructures. However, high-speed connections are not usable by some IoT devices in the last mile. The reasons include the implementation of technologies with low bandwidth, limited distance and bandwidth due to regulated transmit power, and lack of or limited network services. When link layer characteristics that we take for granted are not present, the network is constrained. A constrained network can have high latency and a high potential for packet loss.

> **Note**   Constrained networks are often referred to as low-power and lossy networks (LLNs). *Lossy* in this context refers to network unreliability that is caused by disruptions in the data flow or packet loss. LLNs were defined by the IETF's Routing over Low-Power and Lossy Networks (RoLL) working group when developing the IPv6 RPL protocol. An IETF working group is an open discussion group of individuals in a particular technology area. They have a charter that defines their focus and what they are expected to produce. If you are interested in the work of the RoLL working group, see https://datatracker.ietf.org/wg/roll/documents/. (RPL is discussed in more detail later in this chapter.)

Constrained networks have unique characteristics and requirements. In contrast with typical IP networks, where highly stable and fast links are available, constrained networks are limited by low-power, low-bandwidth links (wireless and wired). They operate between a few kbps and a few hundred kbps and may utilize a star, mesh, or combined network topologies, ensuring proper operations.

With a constrained network, in addition to limited bandwidth, it is not unusual for the packet delivery rate (PDR) to oscillate between low and high percentages. Large bursts of unpredictable errors and even loss of connectivity at times may occur. These behaviors can be observed on both wireless and narrowband power-line communication links, where packet delivery variation may fluctuate greatly during the course of a day.

Unstable link layer environments create other challenges in terms of latency and control plane reactivity. One of the golden rules in a constrained network is to "underreact to failure." Due to the low bandwidth, a constrained network that overreacts can lead to a network collapse—which makes the existing problem worse.

Control plane traffic must also be kept at a minimum; otherwise, it consumes the bandwidth that is needed by the data traffic. Finally, you have to consider the power consumption in battery-powered nodes. Any failure or verbose control plane protocol may reduce the lifetime of the batteries.

In summary, constrained nodes and networks pose major challenges for IoT connectivity in the last mile. This in turn has led various standards organizations to work on optimizing protocols for IoT. This optimization for IP is discussed in more detail later in this chapter.

Note   In addition to optimizing protocols for IoT, the IETF is publishing guidelines for IoT implementation. Much of this work is occurring in the IETF Light-Weight Implementation Guidance (LWIG) working group. For more information on the work of this working group, see https://datatracker.ietf.org/wg/lwig/documents/.

IP Versions

For 20+ years, the IETF has been working on transitioning the Internet from IP version 4 to IP version 6. The main driving force has been the lack of address space in IPv4 as the Internet has grown. IPv6 has a much larger range of addresses that should not be exhausted for the foreseeable future. Today, both versions of IP run over the Internet, but most traffic is still IPv4 based.

Note   A full discussion of the benefits and characteristics of IPv6 is beyond the scope of this book. For a more detailed look at IPv6, please refer to the Cisco Press book *IPv6 Fundamentals: A Straightforward Approach to Understanding IPv6.*

While it may seem natural to base all IoT deployments on IPv6, you must take into account current infrastructures and their associated lifecycle of solutions, protocols, and products. IPv4 is entrenched in these current infrastructures, and so support for it is required in most cases. Therefore, the Internet of Things has to follow a similar path as the Internet itself and support both IPv4 and IPv6 versions concurrently. Techniques such as tunneling and translation need to be employed in IoT solutions to ensure interoperability between IPv4 and IPv6.

A variety of factors dictate whether IPv4, IPv6, or both can be used in an IoT solution. Most often these factors include a legacy protocol or technology that supports only IPv4. Newer technologies and protocols almost always support both IP versions. The following are some of the main factors applicable to IPv4 and IPv6 support in an IoT solution:

- **Application Protocol:** IoT devices implementing Ethernet or Wi-Fi interfaces can communicate over both IPv4 and IPv6, but the application protocol may dictate the choice of the IP version. For example, SCADA protocols such as DNP3/IP (IEEE 1815), Modbus TCP, or the IEC 60870-5-104 standards are specified only for IPv4, as discussed in Chapter 6. So, there are no known production implementations by vendors of these protocols over IPv6 today. For IoT devices with application protocols defined by the IETF, such as HTTP/HTTPS, CoAP, MQTT, and XMPP, both IP versions are supported. (For more information on these IoT application layer protocols, see Chapter 6.) The selection of the IP version is only dependent on the implementation.

■ **Cellular Provider and Technology:** IoT devices with cellular modems are dependent on the generation of the cellular technology as well as the data services offered by the provider. For the first three generations of data services—GPRS, Edge, and 3G—IPv4 is the base protocol version. Consequently, if IPv6 is used with these generations, it must be tunneled over IPv4. On 4G/LTE networks, data services can use IPv4 or IPv6 as a base protocol, depending on the provider.

■ **Serial Communications:** Many legacy devices in certain industries, such as manufacturing and utilities, communicate through serial lines. Data is transferred using either proprietary or standards-based protocols, such as DNP3, Modbus, or IEC 60870-5-101. In the past, communicating this serial data over any sort of distance could be handled by an analog modem connection. However, as service provider support for analog line services has declined, the solution for communicating with these legacy devices has been to use local connections. To make this work, you connect the serial port of the legacy device to a nearby serial port on a piece of communications equipment, typically a router. This local router then forwards the serial traffic over IP to the central server for processing. Encapsulation of serial protocols over IP leverages mechanisms such as raw socket TCP or UDP. While raw socket sessions can run over both IPv4 and IPv6, current implementations are mostly available for IPv4 only.

■ **IPv6 Adaptation Layer:** IPv6-only adaptation layers for some physical and data link layers for recently standardized IoT protocols support only IPv6. While the most common physical and data link layers (Ethernet, Wi-Fi, and so on) stipulate adaptation layers for both versions, newer technologies, such as IEEE 802.15.4 (Wireless Personal Area Network), IEEE 1901.2, and ITU G.9903 (Narrowband Power Line Communications) only have an IPv6 adaptation layer specified. (For more information on these physical and data link layers, see Chapter 4.) This means that any device implementing a technology that requires an IPv6 adaptation layer must communicate over an IPv6-only subnetwork. This is reinforced by the IETF routing protocol for LLNs, RPL, which is IPv6 only. The RPL routing protocol is discussed in more detail later in this chapter.

Note Transition mechanisms such as Mapping of Address and Port using Translation (MAP-T) allow IPv4 traffic to be forwarded over an IPv6 network. Such techniques enable older, industrial end devices and applications to continue running IPv4 even though the network providing connectivity is IPv6. Often these legacy devices and applications do not even have the ability to be upgraded to support IPv6. Please see Chapter 6 to learn more about MAP-T. For even more detailed information on MAP-T, see IETF RFC 7599, at https://tools.ietf.org/html/rfc7599.

Optimizing IP for IoT

While the Internet Protocol is key for a successful Internet of Things, constrained nodes and constrained networks mandate optimization at various layers and on multiple protocols of the IP architecture. The following sections introduce some of these optimizations already available from the market or under development by the IETF. Figure 5-1 highlights the TCP/IP layers where optimization is applied.

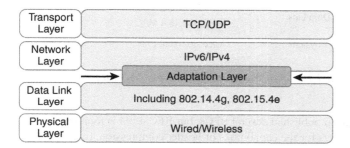

Figure 5-1 *Optimizing IP for IoT Using an Adaptation Layer*

From 6LoWPAN to 6Lo

In the IP architecture, the transport of IP packets over any given Layer 1 (PHY) and Layer 2 (MAC) protocol must be defined and documented. The model for packaging IP into lower-layer protocols is often referred to as an *adaptation layer*.

Unless the technology is proprietary, IP adaptation layers are typically defined by an IETF working group and released as a Request for Comments (RFC). An RFC is a publication from the IETF that officially documents Internet standards, specifications, protocols, procedures, and events. For example, RFC 864 describes how an IPv4 packet gets encapsulated over an Ethernet frame, and RFC 2464 describes how the same function is performed for an IPv6 packet.

IoT-related protocols follow a similar process. The main difference is that an adaptation layer designed for IoT may include some optimizations to deal with constrained nodes and networks. (See the sections "Constrained Nodes" and "Constrained Networks," earlier in this chapter.)

The main examples of adaptation layers optimized for constrained nodes or "things" are the ones under the 6LoWPAN working group and its successor, the 6Lo working group. The initial focus of the 6LoWPAN working group was to optimize the transmission of IPv6 packets over constrained networks such as IEEE 802.15.4. (For more information on IEEE 802.15.4, see Chapter 4.) Figure 5-2 shows an example of an IoT protocol stack using the 6LoWPAN adaptation layer beside the well-known IP protocol stack for reference.

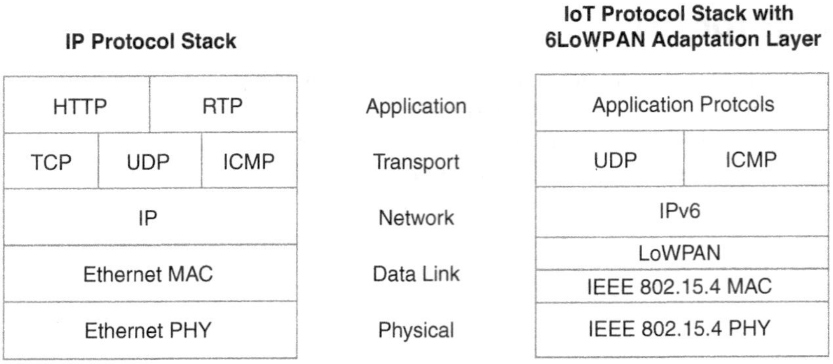

IP Protocol Stack

IoT Protocol Stack with 6LoWPAN Adaptation Layer

HTTP		RTP		Application		Application Protcols	
TCP	UDP	ICMP		Transport		UDP	ICMP
IP				Network		IPv6	
Ethernet MAC				Data Link		LoWPAN	
						IEEE 802.15.4 MAC	
Ethernet PHY				Physical		IEEE 802.15.4 PHY	

Figure 5-2   *Comparison of an IoT Protocol Stack Utilizing 6LoWPAN and an IP Protocol Stack*

The 6LoWPAN working group published several RFCs, but RFC 4994 is foundational because it defines frame headers for the capabilities of header compression, fragmentation, and mesh addressing. These headers can be stacked in the adaptation layer to keep these concepts separate while enforcing a structured method for expressing each capability. Depending on the implementation, all, none, or any combination of these capabilities and their corresponding headers can be enabled. Figure 5-3 shows some examples of typical 6LoWPAN header stacks.

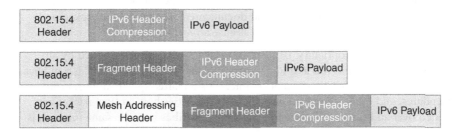

Figure 5-3   *6LoWPAN Header Stacks*

Figure 5-3 shows the subheaders related to compression, fragmentation, and mesh addressing. You'll learn more about these capabilities in the following subsections.

Note   The 6LoWPAN working group also published RFC 6775. This document defines neighbor discovery and autoconfiguration, and you are encouraged to refer directly to RFC 6775 for more information on this part of 6LoWPAN. For a full listing of all the documents produced by the 6LoWPAN working group, see https://datatracker.ietf.org/wg/6lowpan/documents/.

Header Compression

IPv6 header compression for 6LoWPAN was defined initially in RFC 4944 and subsequently updated by RFC 6282. This capability shrinks the size of IPv6's 40-byte headers and User Datagram Protocol's (UDP's) 8-byte headers down as low as 6 bytes combined in some cases.

Note that header compression for 6LoWPAN is only defined for an IPv6 header and not IPv4. The 6LoWPAN protocol does not support IPv4, and, in fact, there is no standardized IPv4 adaptation layer for IEEE 802.15.4.

6LoWPAN header compression is stateless, and conceptually it is not too complicated. However, a number of factors affect the amount of compression, such as implementation of RFC 4944 versus RFC 6922, whether UDP is included, and various IPv6 addressing scenarios. It is beyond the scope of this book to cover every use case and how the header fields change for each. However, this chapter provides an example that shows the impact of 6LoWPAN header compression.

At a high level, 6LoWPAN works by taking advantage of shared information known by all nodes from their participation in the local network. In addition, it omits some standard header fields by assuming commonly used values. Figure 5-4 highlights an example that shows the amount of reduction that is possible with 6LoWPAN header compression.

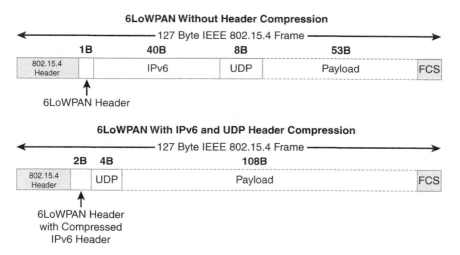

Figure 5-4   *6LoWPAN Header Compression*

At the top of Figure 5-4, you see a 6LoWPAN frame without any header compression enabled: The full 40-byte IPv6 header and 8-byte UDP header are visible. The 6LoWPAN header is only a single byte in this case. Notice that uncompressed IPv6 and UDP headers leave only 53 bytes of data payload out of the 127-byte maximum frame size in the case of IEEE 802.15.4.

The bottom half of Figure 5-4 shows a frame where header compression has been enabled for a best-case scenario. The 6LoWPAN header increases to 2 bytes to accommodate the compressed IPv6 header, and UDP has been reduced in half, to 4 bytes from 8. Most importantly, the header compression has allowed the payload to more than double, from 53 bytes to 108 bytes, which is obviously much more efficient. Note that the 2-byte header compression applies to intra-cell communications, while communications external to the cell may require some field of the header to not be compressed.

Note   While nothing precludes running TCP over IPv6/6LoWPAN, no TCP header compression is defined. The main reason is because TCP's congestion-avoidance algorithms could overreact to LLN's packet drops and/or round-trip delay variance.

Fragmentation

The maximum transmission unit (MTU) for an IPv6 network must be at least 1280 bytes. The term *MTU* defines the size of the largest protocol data unit that can be passed. For IEEE 802.15.4, 127 bytes is the MTU. You can see that this is a problem because IPv6, with a much larger MTU, is carried inside the 802.15.4 frame with a much smaller one. To remedy this situation, large IPv6 packets must be fragmented across multiple 802.15.4 frames at Layer 2.

Note   You may recall from Chapter 4 that the IEEE 802.15.4g standard specifically is not bounded by the short 127-byte MTU limitation while using the 6LoWPAN adaptation layer. Our discussion on fragmentation and its necessity in this section obviously excludes this variant of 802.15.4.

The fragment header utilized by 6LoWPAN is composed of three primary fields: Datagram Size, Datagram Tag, and Datagram Offset. The 1-byte Datagram Size field specifies the total size of the unfragmented payload. Datagram Tag identifies the set of fragments for a payload. Finally, the Datagram Offset field delineates how far into a payload a particular fragment occurs. Figure 5-5 provides an overview of a 6LoWPAN fragmentation header.

6LoWPAN Fragmentation Header

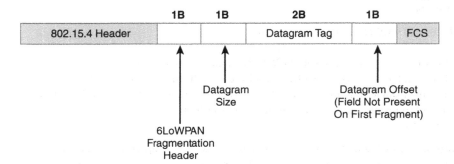

Figure 5-5   *6LoWPAN Fragmentation Header*

In Figure 5-5, the 6LoWPAN fragmentation header field itself uses a unique bit value to identify that the subsequent fields behind it are fragment fields as opposed to another capability, such as header compression. Also, in the first fragment, the Datagram Offset field is not present because it would simply be set to 0. This results in the first fragmentation header for an IPv6 payload being only 4 bytes long. The remainder of the fragments have a 5-byte header field so that the appropriate offset can be specified.

Mesh Addressing

The purpose of the 6LoWPAN mesh addressing function is to forward packets over multiple hops. Three fields are defined for this header: Hop Limit, Source Address, and Destination Address. Analogous to the IPv6 hop limit field, the hop limit for mesh addressing also provides an upper limit on how many times the frame can be forwarded. Each hop decrements this value by 1 as it is forwarded. Once the value hits 0, it is dropped and no longer forwarded.

The Source Address and Destination Address fields for mesh addressing are IEEE 802.15.4 addresses indicating the endpoints of an IP hop. Figure 5-6 details the 6LoWPAN mesh addressing header fields.

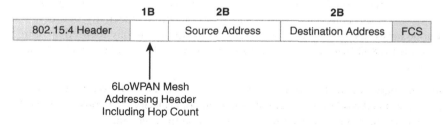

Figure 5-6   *6LoWPAN Mesh Addressing Header*

Note that the mesh addressing header is used in a single IP subnet and is a Layer 2 type of routing known as mesh-under. The concept of mesh-under is discussed in the next section. Keep in mind that RFC 4944 only provisions the function in this case as the definition of Layer 2 mesh routing specifications was outside the scope of the 6LoWPAN working group, and the IETF doesn't define "Layer 2 routing." An implementation performing Layer 3 IP routing does not need to implement a mesh addressing header unless required by a given technology profile.

Mesh-Under Versus Mesh-Over Routing

For network technologies such as IEEE 802.15.4, IEEE 802.15.4g, and IEEE 1901.2a that support mesh topologies and operate at the physical and data link layers, two main options exist for establishing reachability and forwarding packets. With the first option, mesh-under, the routing of packets is handled at the 6LoWPAN adaptation layer.

The other option, known as "mesh-over" or "route-over," utilizes IP routing for getting packets to their destination.

With mesh-under routing, the routing of IP packets leverages the 6LoWPAN mesh addressing header discussed in the previous section to route and forward packets at the link layer. The term *mesh-under* is used because multiple link layer hops can be used to complete a single IP hop. Nodes have a Layer 2 forwarding table that they consult to route the packets to their final destination within the mesh. An edge gateway terminates the mesh-under domain. The edge gateway must also implement a mechanism to translate between the configured Layer 2 protocol and any IP routing mechanism implemented on other Layer 3 IP interfaces.

In mesh-over or route-over scenarios, IP Layer 33 routing is utilized for computing reachability and then getting packets forwarded to their destination, either inside or outside the mesh domain. Each full-functioning node acts as an IP router, so each link layer hop is an IP hop. When a LoWPAN has been implemented using different link layer technologies, a mesh-over routing setup is useful. While traditional IP routing protocols can be used, a specialized routing protocol for smart objects, such as RPL, is recommended. RPL is discussed in more detail later in this chapter.

6Lo Working Group

With the work of the 6LoWPAN working group completed, the 6Lo working group seeks to expand on this completed work with a focus on IPv6 connectivity over constrained-node networks. While the 6LoWPAN working group initially focused its optimizations on IEEE 802.15.4 LLNs, standardizing IPv6 over other link layer technologies is still needed.

Therefore, the charter of the 6Lo working group, now called the IPv6 over Networks of Resource-Constrained Nodes, is to facilitate the IPv6 connectivity over constrained-node networks. In particular, this working group is focused on the following:

- **IPv6-over-foo adaptation layer specifications using 6LoWPAN technologies (RFC4944, RFC6282, RFC6775) for link layer technologies:** For example, this includes:

  - IPv6 over Bluetooth Low Energy

  - Transmission of IPv6 packets over near-field communication

  - IPv6 over 802.11ah

  - Transmission of IPv6 packets over DECT Ultra Low Energy

  - Transmission of IPv6 packets on WIA-PA (Wireless Networks for Industrial Automation–Process Automation)

  - Transmission of IPv6 over Master Slave/Token Passing (MS/TP)

■ **Information and data models such as MIB modules:** One example is RFC 7388, "Definition of Managed Objects for IPv6 over Low-Power Wireless Personal Area Networks (6LoWPANs)."

■ **Optimizations that are applicable to more than one adaptation layer specification:** For example, this includes RFC 7400, "6LoWPAN-GHC: Generic Header Compression for IPv6 over Low-Power Wireless Personal Area Networks (6LoWPANs)."

■ **Informational and maintenance publications needed for the IETF specifications in this area**

In summary, the 6Lo working group is standardizing the 6LoWPAN adaptation layer that initially focused on the IEEE 802.15.4 Layer 2 protocol to others that are commonly found with constrained nodes. In fact, based on the work of the 6LoWPAN working group and now the 6Lo working group, the 6LoWPAN adaptation layer is becoming the de factor standard for connecting constrained nodes in IoT networks.

6TiSCH

Many proprietary wireless technologies have been developed and deployed in various industry verticals over the years. However, the publication of the IEEE 802.15.4 physical and data link layer specifications, followed by IEEE 802.15.4e amendments, has opened the path to standardized, deterministic communications over wireless networks.

IEEE 802.15.4e, Time-Slotted Channel Hopping (TSCH), is an add-on to the Media Access Control (MAC) portion of the IEEE 802.15.4 standard, with direct inheritance from other standards, such as WirelessHART and ISA100.11a.

Devices implementing IEEE 802.15.4e TSCH communicate by following a Time Division Multiple Access (TDMA) schedule. An allocation of a unit of bandwidth or time slot is scheduled between neighbor nodes. This allows the programming of predictable transmissions and enables deterministic, industrial-type applications. In comparison, other 802.15.4 implementations do not allocate slices of bandwidth, so communication, especially during times of contention, may be delayed or lost because it is always best effort.

To standardize IPv6 over the TSCH mode of IEEE 802.15.4e (known as 6TiSCH), the IETF formed the 6TiSCH working group. This working group works on the architecture, information model, and minimal 6TiSCH configuration, leveraging and enhancing work done by the 6LoWPAN working group, RoLL working group, and CoRE working group. The RoLL working group focuses on Layer 3 routing for constrained networks. The work of the RoLL working group is discussed in more detail in the upcoming section "RPL." The CoRE working group is covered in Chapter 6.

An important element specified by the 6TiSCH working group is 6top, a sublayer that glues together the MAC layer and 6LoWPAN adaptation layer. This sublayer provides commands to the upper network layers, such as RPL. In return, these commands enable functionalities including network layer routing decisions, configuration, and control procedures for 6TiSCH schedule management.

The IEEE 802.15.4e standard defines a time slot structure, but it does not mandate a scheduling algorithm for how the time slots are utilized. This is left to higher-level protocols like 6TiSCH. Scheduling is critical because it can affect throughput, latency, and power consumption. Figure 5-7 shows where 6top resides in relation to IEEE 802.15.4e, 6LoWPAN HC, and IPv6. 6LoWPAN HC is covered earlier in this chapter, in the section "Header Compression."

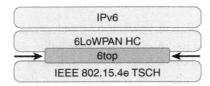

Figure 5-7 *Location of 6TiSCH's 6top Sublayer*

Schedules in 6TiSCH are broken down into cells. A cell is simply a single element in the TSCH schedule that can be allocated for unidirectional or bidirectional communications between specific nodes. Nodes only transmit when the schedule dictates that their cell is open for communication. The 6TiSCH architecture defines four schedule management mechanisms:

- **Static scheduling:** All nodes in the constrained network share a fixed schedule. Cells are shared, and nodes contend for slot access in a slotted aloha manner. Slotted aloha is a basic protocol for sending data using time slot boundaries when communicating over a shared medium. Static scheduling is a simple scheduling mechanism that can be used upon initial implementation or as a fallback in the case of network malfunction. The drawback with static scheduling is that nodes may expect a packet at any cell in the schedule. Therefore, energy is wasted idly listening across all cells.

- **Neighbor-to-neighbor scheduling:** A schedule is established that correlates with the observed number of transmissions between nodes. Cells in this schedule can be added or deleted as traffic requirements and bandwidth needs change.

- **Remote monitoring and scheduling management:** Time slots and other resource allocation are handled by a management entity that can be multiple hops away. The scheduling mechanism leverages 6top and even CoAP in some scenarios. For more information on the application layer protocol CoAP, see Chapter 6. This scheduling mechanism provides quite a bit of flexibility and control in allocating cells for communication between nodes.

- **Hop-by-hop scheduling:** A node reserves a path to a destination node multiple hops away by requesting the allocation of cells in a schedule at each intermediate node hop in the path. The protocol that is used by a node to trigger this scheduling mechanism is not defined at this point.

In addition to schedule management functions, the 6TiSCH architecture also defines three different forwarding models. Forwarding is the operation performed on each packet by a node that allows it to be delivered to a next hop or an upper-layer protocol. The forwarding decision is based on a preexisting state that was learned from a routing computation. There are three 6TiSCH forwarding models:

- **Track Forwarding (TF):** This is the simplest and fastest forwarding model. A "track" in this model is a unidirectional path between a source and a destination. This track is constructed by pairing bundles of receive cells in a schedule with a bundle of receive cells set to transmit. So, a frame received within a particular cell or cell bundle is switched to another cell or cell bundle. This forwarding occurs regardless of the network layer protocol.

- **Fragment forwarding (FF):** This model takes advantage of 6LoWPAN fragmentation to build a Layer 2 forwarding table. Fragmentation within the 6LoWPAN protocol is covered earlier in this chapter, in the section "Fragmentation." As you may recall, IPv6 packets can get fragmented at the 6LoWPAN sublayer to handle the differences between IEEE 802.15.4 payload size and IPv6 MTU. Additional headers for RPL source route information can further contribute to the need for fragmentation. However, with FF, a mechanism is defined where the first fragment is routed based on the IPv6 header present. The 6LoWPAN sublayer learns the next-hop selection of this first fragment, which is then applied to all subsequent fragments of that packet. Otherwise, IPv6 packets undergo hop-by-hop reassembly. This increases latency and can be power- and CPU-intensive for a constrained node.

- **IPv6 Forwarding (6F):** This model forwards traffic based on its IPv6 routing table. Flows of packets should be prioritized by traditional QoS (quality of service) and RED (random early detection) operations. QoS is a classification scheme for flows based on their priority, and RED is a common congestion avoidance mechanism.

For many IoT wireless networks, it is not necessary to be able to control the latency and throughput for sensor data. However, when some sort of determinism is needed, 6TiSCH provides an open, IPv6-based standard solution for ensuring predictable communications over wireless sensor networks. However, its adoption by the industry is still an ongoing effort.

RPL

The IETF chartered the RoLL (Routing over Low-Power and Lossy Networks) working group to evaluate all Layer 3 IP routing protocols and determine the needs and requirements for developing a routing solution for IP smart objects. After study of various use cases and a survey of existing protocols, the consensus was that a new routing protocol should be developed for use by IP smart objects, given the characteristics and requirements of constrained networks. This new distance-vector routing protocol was named the IPv6 Routing Protocol for Low Power and Lossy Networks (RPL). The RPL specification was published as RFC 6550 by the RoLL working group.

Note   In addition to the main RPL standard (RFC 6550), RPL is also addressed across a number of other RFCs published by the RoLL working group. These RFCs include RPL use cases, RPL-specific terms with definitions, and other enhancements or clarifications to the protocol. This section provides a high-level overview of RPL and how it works, but you should refer to the RFCs listed here for a more in-depth study of RPL: https://datatracker. ietf.org/wg/roll/documents/.

In an RPL network, each node acts as a router and becomes part of a mesh network. Routing is performed at the IP layer. Each node examines every received IPv6 packet and determines the next-hop destination based on the information contained in the IPv6 header. No information from the MAC-layer header is needed to perform next-hop determination. Remember from earlier in this chapter that this is referred to as mesh-over routing.

To cope with the constraints of computing and memory that are common characteristics of constrained nodes, the protocol defines two modes:

■ **Storing mode:** All nodes contain the full routing table of the RPL domain. Every node knows how to directly reach every other node.

■ **Non-storing mode:** Only the border router(s) of the RPL domain contain(s) the full routing table. All other nodes in the domain only maintain their list of parents and use this as a list of default routes toward the border router. This abbreviated routing table saves memory space and CPU. When communicating in non-storing mode, a node always forwards its packets to the border router, which knows how to ultimately reach the final destination.

RPL is based on the concept of a directed acyclic graph (DAG). A DAG is a directed graph where no cycles exist. This means that from any vertex or point in the graph, you cannot follow an edge or a line back to this same point. All of the edges are arranged in paths oriented toward and terminating at one or more root nodes. Figure 5-8 shows a basic DAG.

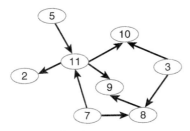

Figure 5-8   *Example of a Directed Acyclic Graph (DAG)*

A basic RPL process involves building a destination-oriented directed acyclic graph (DODAG). A DODAG is a DAG rooted to one destination. In RPL, this destination occurs at a border router known as the DODAG root. Figure 5-9 compares a DAG and a DODAG. You can see that that a DAG has multiple roots, whereas the DODAG has just one.

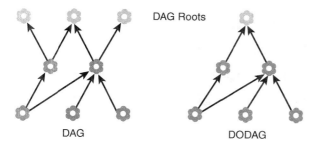

Figure 5-9 *DAG and DODAG Comparison*

In a DODAG, each node maintains up to three parents that provide a path to the root. Typically, one of these parents is the preferred parent, which means it is the preferred next hop for upward routes toward the root.

The routing graph created by the set of DODAG parents across all nodes defines the full set of upward routes. RPL protocol implementation should ensure that routes are loop free by disallowing nodes from selected DODAG parents that are positioned further away from the border router.

Upward routes in RPL are discovered and configured using DAG Information Object (DIO) messages. Nodes listen to DIOs to handle changes in the topology that can affect routing. The information in DIO messages determines parents and the best path to the DODAG root.

Nodes establish downward routes by advertising their parent set toward the DODAG root using a Destination Advertisement Object (DAO) message. DAO messages allow nodes to inform their parents of their presence and reachability to descendants.

In the case of the non-storing mode of RPL, nodes sending DAO messages report their parent sets directly to the DODAG root (border router), and only the root stores the routing information. The root uses the information to then determine source routes needed for delivering IPv6 datagrams to individual nodes downstream in the mesh.

For storing mode, each node keeps track of the routing information that is advertised in the DAO messages. While this is more power- and CPU-intensive for each node, the benefit is that packets can take shorter paths between destinations in the mesh. The nodes can make their own routing decisions; in non-storing mode, on the other hand, all packets must go up to the root to get a route for moving downstream.

RPL messages, such as DIO and DAO, run on top of IPv6. These messages exchange and advertise downstream and upstream routing information between a border router and the nodes under it. As illustrated in Figure 5-10, DAO and DIO messages move both up and down the DODAG, depending on the exact message type.

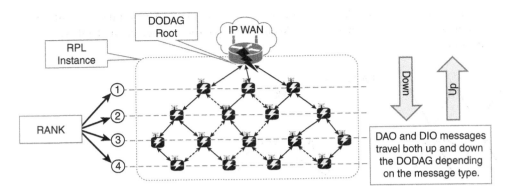

Figure 5-10   *RPL Overview*

Objective Function (OF)

An objective function (OF) defines how metrics are used to select routes and establish a node's rank. Standards such as RFC 6552 and 6719 have been published to document OFs specific to certain use cases and node types.

For example, nodes implementing an OF based on RFC 6719's Minimum Expected Number of Transmissions (METX) advertise the METX among their parents in DIO messages. Whenever a node establishes its rank, it simply sets the rank to the current minimum METX among its parents.

Rank

The rank is a rough approximation of how "close" a node is to the root and helps avoid routing loops and the count-to-infinity problem. Nodes can only increase their rank when receiving a DIO message with a larger version number. However, nodes may decrease their rank whenever they have established lower-cost routes. While the rank and routing metrics are closely related, the rank differs from routing metrics in that it is used as a constraint to prevent routing loops.

RPL Headers

Specific network layer headers are defined for datagrams being forwarded within an RPL domain. One of the headers is standardized in RFC 6553, "The Routing Protocol for Low-Power and Lossy Networks (RPL) Option for Carrying RPL Information in Data-Plane Datagrams," and the other is discussed in RFC 6554, "An IPv6 Routing Header for Source Routes with the Routing Protocol for Low-Power and Lossy Networks (RPL)."

RFC 6553 defines a new IPv6 option, known as the RPL option. The RPL option is carried in the IPv6 Hop-by-Hop header. The purpose of this header is to leverage data-plane packets for loop detection in a RPL instance. As discussed earlier, DODAGs only have single paths and should be loop free.

RFC 6554 specifies the Source Routing Header (SRH) for use between RPL routers. A border router or DODAG root inserts the SRH when specifying a source route to deliver datagrams to nodes downstream in the mesh network.

Metrics

RPL defines a large and flexible set of new metrics and constraints for routing in RFC 6551. Developed to support powered and battery-powered nodes, RPL offers a far more complete set than any other routing protocol. Some of the RPL routing metrics and constraints defined in RFC 6551 include the following:

- **Expected Transmission Count (ETX):** Assigns a discrete value to the number of transmissions a node expects to make to deliver a packet.

- **Hop Count:** Tracks the number of nodes traversed in a path. Typically, a path with a lower hop count is chosen over a path with a higher hop count.

- **Latency:** Varies depending on power conservation. Paths with a lower latency are preferred.

- **Link Quality Level:** Measures the reliability of a link by taking into account packet error rates caused by factors such as signal attenuation and interference.

- **Link Color:** Allows manual influence of routing by administratively setting values to make a link more or less desirable. These values can be either statically or dynamically adjusted for specific traffic types.

- **Node State and Attribute:** Identifies nodes that function as traffic aggregators and nodes that are being impacted by high workloads. High workloads could be indicative of nodes that have incurred high CPU or low memory states. Naturally, nodes that are aggregators are preferred over nodes experiencing high workloads.

- **Node Energy:** Avoids nodes with low power, so a battery-powered node that is running out of energy can be avoided and the life of that node and the network can be prolonged.

- **Throughput:** Provides the amount of throughput for a node link. Often, nodes conserving power use lower throughput. This metric allows the prioritization of paths with higher throughput.

In addition to the metrics and constraints listed in RFC 6551, others can also be implemented. For example, let's look at a scenario in which two constraints are used as a filter for pruning links that do not satisfy the specified conditions.

One of the constraints is ETX. ETX, which is described in RFC 6551, is defined earlier in this chapter. The other constraint, Relative Signal Strength Indicator (RSSI), specifies the power present in a received radio signal. Signals with low strength are generally less reliable and more susceptible to interference, resulting in packet loss.

In this scenario, a DODAG root and nodes form an IEEE 802.15.4 mesh. When a node finds a potential parent, it enters the neighbor into its routing table. However, it does not yet use the new neighbor for routing. Instead, the node must first establish that the link quality to its neighbor is sufficient for forwarding datagrams.

The node determines whether the link quality to a potential parent is sufficient by looking at its programmed constraints. In this example, the configured constraints are ETX and RSSI. If the RSSI in both directions exceeds a threshold and the ETX falls below a threshold, then the node confirms that the link quality to the potential parent is sufficient.

Once a node has determined that the link quality to a potential parent is sufficient, it adds the appropriate default route entry to its forwarding table. Maintaining RSSI and ETX for neighboring nodes is done at the link layer and stored in the link layer neighbor table.

The results from all link layer unicast traffic are fed into the RSSI and ETX computation for neighboring devices. If the link quality is not sufficient, then the link is not added to the forwarding table and is therefore not used for routing packets.

To illustrate, Example 5-1 displays a simple RPL routing tree on a Cisco CGR-1000 router connecting an IEEE 802.15.4g mesh 6LoWPAN-based subnetwork. The first IPv6 address in this example, which ends in **1CC5**, identifies the DODAG root for the RPL tree. This DODAG root has branches to two nodes, indicated by the two IPv6 addresses ending in **924D** and **6C35**.

Example 5-1   show wpan <interface> rpl tree *Command from a Cisco CGR-1000*

```
pat1# show wpan 3/1 rpl tree

--------------------------- WPAN RPL TREE FIGURE [3] ---------------------------
[2013:DB8:9999:8888:207:8108:B8:1CC5] (2)
\--- 2013:DB8:9999:8888:89C6:F7C9:D551:924D
\--- 2013:DB8:9999:8888:95DF:2AD4:C1B1:6C35
RPL TREE: Num.DataEntries 2, Num.GraphNodes 3
```

RPL integration in a routing domain follows the same rules as more traditional IP routing protocols. Route redistribution, filtering, load balancing, and dynamic rerouting can be implemented the same way as other well-known protocols. For example, in IoT routers, you could see routes learned via RPL being redistributed into more well-known routing protocols, such as BGP and EIGRP.

In summary, RPL is a new routing protocol that enables an IPv6 standards-based solution to be deployed on a large scale while being operated in a similar way to today's IP infrastructures. RPL was designed to meet the requirements of constrained nodes and networks, and this has led to it becoming one of the main network layer IPv6-based routing protocols in IoT sensor networks.

Authentication and Encryption on Constrained Nodes

IoT security is a complex topic that often spawns discussions and debates across the industry. While IoT security is the focus of Chapter 8, "Securing IoT," we have discussed constrained nodes and networks extensively in this chapter. So it is worth mentioning here the IETF working groups that are focused on their security: ACE and DICE.

ACE

Much like the RoLL working group, the Authentication and Authorization for Constrained Environments (ACE) working group is tasked with evaluating the applicability of existing authentication and authorization protocols and documenting their suitability for certain constrained-environment use cases. Once the candidate solutions are validated, the ACE working group will focus its work on CoAP with the Datagram Transport Layer Security (DTLS) protocol. (The CoAP protocol is covered in Chapter 6, and RFC 6437 defines the DTLS security protocol.) The ACE working group may investigate other security protocols later, with a particular focus on adapting whatever solution is chosen to HTTP and TLS.

The ACE working group expects to produce a standardized solution for authentication and authorization that enables authorized access (Get, Put, Post, Delete) to resources identified by a URI and hosted on a resource server in constrained environments. An unconstrained authorization server performs mediation of the access. Aligned with the initial focus, access to resources at a resource server by a client device occurs using CoAP and is protected by DTLS.

DICE

New generations of constrained nodes implementing an IP stack over constrained access networks are expected to run an optimized IP protocol stack. For example, when implementing UDP at the transport layer, the IETF Constrained Application Protocol (CoAP) should be used at the application layer. (See Chapter 6 for more details on CoAP.)

In constrained environments secured by DTLS, CoAP can be used to control resources on a device. (Constrained environments are network situations where constrained nodes and/or constrained networks are present. Constrained networks and constrained nodes are discussed earlier in this chapter, in the sections "Constrained Nodes" and "Constrained Networks.")

The DTLS in Constrained Environments (DICE) working group focuses on implementing the DTLS transport layer security protocol in these environments. The first task of the DICE working group is to define an optimized DTLS profile for constrained nodes. In addition, the DICE working group is considering the applicability of the DTLS record layer to secure multicast messages and investigating how the DTLS handshake in constrained environments can get optimized.

Profiles and Compliances

As discussed throughout this chapter, leveraging the Internet Protocol suite for smart objects involves a collection of protocols and options that must work in coordination with lower and upper layers. Therefore, profile definitions, certifications, and promotion by alliances can help implementers develop solutions that guarantee interoperability and/ or interchangeability of devices.

This section introduces some of the main industry organizations working on profile definitions and certifications for IoT constrained nodes and networks. You can find various documents and promotions from these organizations in the IoT space, so it is worth being familiar with them and their goals.

Internet Protocol for Smart Objects (IPSO) Alliance

Established in 2008, the Internet Protocol for Smart Objects (IPSO) Alliance has had its objective evolve over years. The alliance initially focused on promoting IP as the premier solution for smart objects communications. Today, it is more focused on how to use IP, with the IPSO Alliance organizing interoperability tests between alliance members to validate that IP for smart objects can work together and properly implement industry standards. The IPSO Alliance does not define technologies, as that is the role of the IETF and other standard organizations, but it documents the use of IP-based technologies for various IoT use cases and participates in educating the industry. As the IPSO Alliance declares in its value and mission statement, it wants to ensure that "engineers and product builders will have access to the necessary tools for 'how to build the IoT RIGHT.'" For more information on the IPSO Alliance, visit www.ipso-alliance.org.

Wi-SUN Alliance

The Wi-SUN Alliance is an example of efforts from the industry to define a communication profile that applies to specific physical and data link layer protocols. Currently, Wi-SUN's main focus is on the IEEE 802.15.4g protocol and its support for multiservice and secure IPv6 communications with applications running over the UDP transport layer.

The utilities industry is the main area of focus for the Wi-SUN Alliance. The Wi-SUN field area network (FAN) profile enables smart utility networks to provide resilient, secure, and cost-effective connectivity with extremely good coverage in a range of topographic environments, from dense urban neighborhoods to rural areas. (FANs are described in more detail in Chapter 11, "Utilities."). You can read more about the Wi-SUN Alliance and its certification programs at the Wi-SUN Alliance website, www.wi-sun.org.

Thread

A group of companies involved with smart object solutions for consumers created the Thread Group. This group has defined an IPv6-based wireless profile that provides the best way to connect more than 250 devices into a low-power, wireless mesh network.

The wireless technology used by Thread is IEEE 802.15.4, which is different from Wi-SUN's IEEE 802.15.4g. Please see Chapter 4 for more information on 802.15.4 and 802.15.4g and their differences. For additional information on Thread and its specifications, visit http://threadgroup.org.

IPv6 Ready Logo

Initially, the IPv6 Forum ensured the promotion of IPv6 around the world. Once IPv6 implementations became widely available, the need for interoperability and certification led to the creation of the IPv6 Ready Logo program.

The IPv6 Ready Logo program has established conformance and interoperability testing programs with the intent of increasing user confidence when implementing IPv6. The IPv6 Core and specific IPv6 components, such as DHCP, IPsec, and customer edge router certifications, are in place. These certifications have industry-wide recognition, and many products are already certified. An IPv6 certification effort specific to IoT is currently under definition for the program.

Summary

The IP protocol suite has been deployed in private and public networks over the past three decades, interconnecting billions of IP devices and users. The architecture has proven to be highly flexible, and it has protected investments in many ways. For example, new link types have been adapted, new routing and transport protocols have been specified and deployed, and the number of supported applications has exceeded all expectations by an order of magnitude.

The vast majority of the IP protocols and technologies, including addressing, address provisioning, QoS, transport, reliability, and so on, can be reused as is by IoT solutions. Where IP may fall short is in scenarios where IoT devices are constrained nodes and/or connect to constrained networks. This is especially the case for some highly constrained devices that use LPWA technologies for last-mile communications.

To remedy these scenarios, the IETF, the main standards organization in charge of the TCP/IP architecture, is now engaged through several working groups to optimize IP for IoT and smart objects communications. These working groups have often had to develop new protocols, such as RPL, or adaptation layers, such as 6LoWPAN, to handle the constrained environments where IoT sensor networks are often deployed.

As highlighted in this chapter, the foundation for the network layer in IoT implementations is firmly in place. The IETF and other standards bodies continue to work on defining the networks, protocols, and use cases that are necessary for advancing the Internet of Things.

Chapter 6

Application Protocols for IoT

As with the wired and wireless access technologies discussed in Chapter 5, "IP as the IoT Network Layer," the IoT application protocols you select should be contingent on the use cases and vertical industries they apply to. In addition, IoT application protocols are dependent on the characteristics of the lower layers themselves. For example, application protocols that are sufficient for generic nodes and traditional networks often are not well suited for constrained nodes and networks.

This chapter focuses on how higher-layer IoT protocols are transported. Specifically, this chapter includes the following sections:

- **The Transport Layer:** IP-based networks use either TCP or UDP. However, the constrained nature of IoT networks requires a closer look at the use of these traditional transport mechanisms.

- **IoT Application Transport Methods:** This section explores the various types of IoT application data and the ways this data can be carried across a network.

As in traditional networks, TCP or UDP are utilized in most cases when transporting IoT application data. The transport methods are covered in depth and form the bulk of the material in this chapter. You will notice that, as with the lower-layer IoT protocols, there are typically multiple options and solutions presented for transporting IoT application data. This is because IoT is still developing and maturing and has to account for the transport of not only new application protocols and technologies but legacy ones as well.

The Transport Layer

This section reviews the selection of a protocol for the transport layer as supported by the TCP/IP architecture in the context of IoT networks. With the TCP/IP protocol, two main protocols are specified for the transport layer:

- **Transmission Control Protocol (TCP):** This connection-oriented protocol requires a session to get established between the source and destination before exchanging data. You can view it as an equivalent to a traditional telephone conversation, in which two phones must be connected and the communication link established before the parties can talk.

- **User Datagram Protocol (UDP):** With this connectionless protocol, data can be quickly sent between source and destination—but with no guarantee of delivery. This is analogous to the traditional mail delivery system, in which a letter is mailed to a destination. Confirmation of the reception of this letter does not happen until another letter is sent in response.

With the predominance of human interactions over the Internet, TCP is the main protocol used at the transport layer. This is largely due to its inherent characteristics, such as its ability to transport large volumes of data into smaller sets of packets. In addition, it ensures reassembly in a correct sequence, flow control and window adjustment, and retransmission of lost packets. These benefits occur with the cost of overhead per packet and per session, potentially impacting overall packet per second performances and latency.

In contrast, UDP is most often used in the context of network services, such as Domain Name System (DNS), Network Time Protocol (NTP), Simple Network Management Protocol (SNMP), and Dynamic Host Control Protocol (DHCP), or for real-time data traffic, including voice and video over IP. In these cases, performance and latency are more important than packet retransmissions because re-sending a lost voice or video packet does not add value. When the reception of packets must be guaranteed error free, the application layer protocol takes care of that function.

When considering the choice of a transport layer by a given IoT application layer protocol, it is recommended to evaluate the impact of this choice on both the lower and upper layers of the stack. For example, most of the industrial application layer protocols, as discussed later in this chapter, are implemented over TCP, while their specifications may offer support for both transport models. The reason for this is that often these industrial application layer protocols are older and were deployed when data link layers were often unreliable and called for error protection.

While the use of TCP may not strain generic compute platforms and high-data-rate networks, it can be challenging and is often overkill on constrained IoT devices and networks. This is particularly true when an IoT device needs to send only a few bytes of data per transaction. When using TCP, each packet needs to add a minimum of 20 bytes of TCP overhead, while UDP adds only 8 bytes. TCP also requires the establishment and potential maintenance of an open logical channel.

IoT nodes may also be limited by the intrinsic characteristics of the data link layers. For example, low-power and lossy networks (LLNs), as discussed in Chapter 5, may not cope well with supporting large numbers of TCP sessions.

This may explain why a new IoT application protocol, such as Constrained Application Protocol (CoAP), almost always uses UDP and why implementations of industrial application layer protocols may call for the optimization and adoption of the UDP transport layer if run over LLNs. For example, the Device Language Message Specification/Companion Specification for Energy Metering (DLMS/COSEM) application layer protocol, a popular protocol for reading smart meters in the utilities space, is the de facto standard in Europe. Adjustments or optimizations to this protocol should be made depending on the IoT transport protocols that are present in the lower layers. For example, if you compare the transport of DLMS/COSEM over a cellular network versus an LLN deployment, you should consider the following:

- Select TCP for cellular networks because these networks are typically more robust and can handle the overhead. For LLNs, where both the devices and network itself are usually constrained, UDP is a better choice and often mandatory.

- DLMS/COSEM can reduce the overhead associated with session establishment by offering a "long association" over LLNs. *Long association* means that sessions stay up once in place because the communications overhead necessary to keep a session established is much less than is involved in opening and closing many separate sessions over the same time period. Conversely, for cellular networks, a short association better controls the costs by tearing down the open associations after transmitting.

- When transferring large amounts of DLMS/COSEM data, cellular links are preferred to optimize each open association. Smaller amounts of data can be handled efficiently over LLNs. Because packet loss ratios are generally higher on LLNs than on cellular networks, keeping the data transmission amounts small over LLNs limits the retransmission of large numbers of bytes.

Multicast requirements are also impacted by the protocol selected for the transport layer. With multicast, a single message can be sent to multiple IoT devices. This is useful in the IoT context for upgrading the firmware of many IoT devices at once. Also, keep in mind that multicast utilizes UDP exclusively.

To guarantee interoperability, certification and compliance profiles, such as Wi-SUN, need to specify the stack from Layer 1 to Layer 4. This enables the chosen technology to be compatible with the different options of the stack while also being compatible with IP. (Chapter 4, "Connecting Smart Objects," provides more information on Wi-SUN.)

In summary, TCP and UDP are the two main choices at the transport layer for the TCP/IP protocol. The performance and scalability of IoT constrained devices and networks is impacted by which one of these is selected.

IoT Application Transport Methods

Because of the diverse types of IoT application protocols, there are various means for transporting these protocols across a network. Sometimes you may be dealing with legacy utility and industrial IoT protocols that have certain requirements, while other times you might need to consider the transport requirements of more modern application layer protocols. To make these decisions easier, it makes sense to categorize the common IoT application protocols and then focus on the transport methods available for each category. The following categories of IoT application protocols and their transport methods are explored in the following sections:

- **Application layer protocol not present:** In this case, the data payload is directly transported on top of the lower layers. No application layer protocol is used.

- **Supervisory control and data acquisition (SCADA):** SCADA is one of the most common industrial protocols in the world, but it was developed long before the days of IP, and it has been adapted for IP networks.

- **Generic web-based protocols:** Generic protocols, such as Ethernet, Wi-Fi, and 4G/ LTE, are found on many consumer- and enterprise-class IoT devices that communicate over non-constrained networks.

- **IoT application layer protocols:** IoT application layer protocols are devised to run on constrained nodes with a small compute footprint and are well adapted to the network bandwidth constraints on cellular or satellite links or constrained 6LoWPAN networks. Message Queuing Telemetry Transport (MQTT) and Constrained Application Protocol (CoAP), covered later in this chapter, are two well-known examples of IoT application layer protocols.

Application Layer Protocol Not Present

As introduced in Chapter 4, IETF RFC 7228 devices defined as class 0 send or receive only a few bytes of data. For myriad reasons, such as processing capability, power constraints, and cost, these devices do not implement a fully structured network protocol stack, such as IP, TCP, or UDP, or even an application layer protocol. Class 0 devices are usually simple smart objects that are severely constrained. Implementing a robust protocol stack is usually not useful and sometimes not even possible with the limited available resources.

For example, consider low-cost temperature and relative humidity (RH) sensors sending data over an LPWA LoRaWAN infrastructure. (LPWA and LoRaWAN are discussed in Chapter 4.) Temperature is represented as 2 bytes and RH as another 2 bytes of data. Therefore, this small data payload is directly transported on top of the LoRaWAN MAC layer, without the use of TCP/IP. Example 6-1 shows the raw data for temperature and relative humidity and how it can be decoded by the application.

Example 6-1 *Decoding Temperature and Relative Humidity Sensor Data*

```
Temperature data payload over the network: Tx = 0x090c
Temperature conversion required by the application
T = Tx/32 - 50  to  T = 0x090c/32 - 50  to  T = 2316/32 - 50 = 22.4°
RH data payload over the network: RHx = 0x062e
RH conversion required by the application:
100RH = RHx/16-24  to 100RH = 0x062e/16-24 = 74.9  to RH = 74.9%
```

While many constrained devices, such as sensors and actuators, have adopted deployments that have no application layer, this transportation method has not been standardized. This lack of standardization makes it difficult for generic implementations of this transport method to be successful from an interoperability perspective.

Imagine expanding Example 6-1 to different kinds of temperature sensors from different manufacturers. These sensors will report temperature data in varying formats. A temperature value will always be present in the data transmitted by each sensor, but decoding this data will be vendor specific. If you scale this scenario out across hundreds or thousands of sensors, the problem of allowing various applications to receive and interpret temperature values delivered in different formats becomes increasingly complex. The solution to this problem is to use an IoT data broker, as detailed in Figure 6-1. An IoT data broker is a piece of middleware that standardizes sensor output into a common format that can then be retrieved by authorized applications. (The concept of the IoT data broker is introduced in Chapter 1, "What Is IoT?")

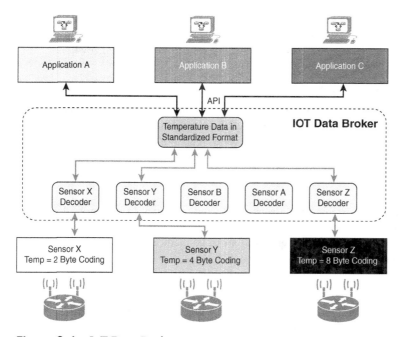

Figure 6-1 *IoT Data Broker*

In Figure 6-1, Sensors X, Y, and Z are all temperature sensors, but their output is encoded differently. The IoT data broker understands the different formats in which the temperature is encoded and is therefore able to decode this data into a common, standardized format. Applications A, B, and C in Figure 6-1 can access this temperature data without having to deal with decoding multiple temperature data formats.

You should note that IoT data brokers are also utilized from a commercial perspective to distribute and sell IoT data to third parties. Companies can provide access to their data broker from another company's application for a fee. This makes an IoT data broker a possible revenue stream, depending on the value of the data it contains.

In summary, while directly transporting data payload without a structured network stack clearly optimizes data transmission over low-data-rate networks, the lack of a data model implies that each application needs to know how to interpret the data-specific format. This becomes increasingly complex for larger networks of devices with different data payload formats. Furthermore, it makes the IoT application environment challenging in terms of evolution, development, interoperability, and so on, and often calls for structured data models and data broker applications.

SCADA

In the world of networking technologies and protocols, IoT is relatively new. Combined with the fact that IP is the de facto standard for computer networking in general, older protocols that connected sensors and actuators have evolved and adapted themselves to utilize IP.

A prime example of this evolution is supervisory control and data acquisition (SCADA). Designed decades ago, SCADA is an automation control system that was initially implemented without IP over serial links, before being adapted to Ethernet and IPv4.

A Little Background on SCADA

For many years, vertical industries have developed communication protocols that fit their specific requirements. Many of them were defined and implemented when the most common networking technologies were serial link-based, such as RS-232 and RS-485. This led to SCADA networking protocols, which were well structured compared to the protocols described in the previous section, running directly over serial physical and data link layers.

At a high level, SCADA systems collect sensor data and telemetry from remote devices, while also providing the ability to control them. Used in today's networks, SCADA systems allow global, real-time, data-driven decisions to be made about how to improve business processes.

SCADA networks can be found across various industries, but you find SCADA mainly concentrated in the utilities and manufacturing/industrial verticals. Within these specific industries, SCADA commonly uses certain protocols for communications between devices and applications. For example, Modbus and its variants are industrial protocols used to monitor and program remote devices via a master/slave relationship. Modbus is also found in building management, transportation, and energy applications. The DNP3 and International Electrotechnical Commission (IEC) 60870-5-101 protocols are found mainly in the utilities industry, along with DLMS/COSEM and ANSI C12 for advanced meter reading (AMR). Both DNP3 and IEC 60870-5-101 are discussed in more detail later in this chapter.

As mentioned previously, these protocols go back decades and are serial based. So, transporting them over current IoT and traditional networks requires that certain accommodations be made from both protocol and implementation perspectives. These accommodations and other adjustments form various SCADA transport methods that are the focus of upcoming sections.

Adapting SCADA for IP

In the 1990s, the rapid adoption of Ethernet networks in the industrial world drove the evolution of SCADA application layer protocols. For example, the IEC adopted the Open System Interconnection (OSI) layer model to define its protocol framework. Other protocol user groups also slightly modified their protocols to run over an IP infrastructure. Benefits of this move to Ethernet and IP include the ability to leverage existing equipment and standards while integrating seamlessly the SCADA subnetworks to the corporate WAN infrastructures.

To further facilitate the support of legacy industrial protocols over IP networks, protocol specifications were updated and published, documenting the use of IP for each protocol. This included assigning TCP/UDP port numbers to the protocols, such as the following:

- DNP3 (adopted by IEEE 1815-2012) specifies the use of TCP or UDP on port 20000 for transporting DNP3 messages over IP.

- The Modbus messaging service utilizes TCP port 502.

- IEC 60870-5-104 is the evolution of IEC 60870-5-101 serial for running over Ethernet and IPv4 using port 2404.

- DLMS User Association specified a communication profile based on TCP/IP in the DLMS/COSEM Green Book (Edition 5 or higher), or in the IEC 62056-53 and IEC 62056-47 standards, allowing data exchange via IP and port 4059.

Note The DNP3 protocol is based on the IEC 60870-5 standard. So, while DNP3 is not interoperable with IEC 60870-5, it is very similar in its operation and functionality. Both are associated with SCADA networks, with DNP3 found predominantly in the United States and Canada and IEC 60870-5 in Europe. See Chapter 11, "Utilities," for a discussion of how these SCADA protocols are used in utilities networks.

These legacy serial protocols have adapted and evolved to utilize IP and TCP/UDP as both networking and transport mechanisms. This has allowed utilities and other companies to continue leveraging their investment in equipment and infrastructure, supporting these legacy protocols with modern IP networks. Let's dig deeper into how these legacy serial protocols have evolved to use IP by looking specifically at DNP3 as a representative use case.

Like many of the other SCADA protocols, DNP3 is based on a master/slave relationship. The term *master* in this case refers to what is typically a powerful computer located in the control center of a utility, and a *slave* is a remote device with computing resources found in a location such as a substation. DNP3 refers to slaves specifically as *outstations*.

Outstations monitor and collect data from devices that indicate their state, such as whether a circuit breaker is on or off, and take measurements, including voltage, current, temperature, and so on. This data is then transmitted to the master when it is requested, or events and alarms can be sent in an asynchronous manner. The master also issues control commands, such as to start a motor or reset a circuit breaker, and logs the incoming data.

The IEEE 1815-2012 specification describes how the DNP3 protocol implementation must be adapted to run either over TCP (recommended) or UDP. This specification defines connection management between the DNP3 protocol and the IP layers, as shown in Figure 6-2. Connection management links the DNP3 layers with the IP layers in addition to the configuration parameters and methods necessary for implementing the network connection. The IP layers appear transparent to the DNP3 layers as each piece of the protocol stack in one station logically communicates with the respective part in the other. This means that the DNP3 endpoints or devices are not aware of the underlying IP transport that is occurring.

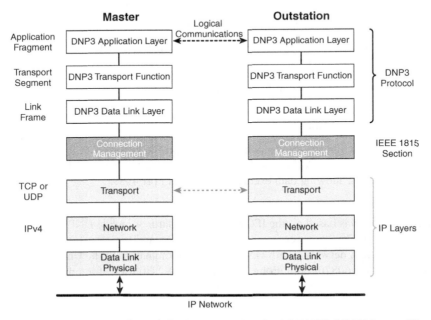

Figure 6-2 *Protocol Stack for Transporting Serial DNP3 SCADA over IP*

In Figure 6-2, the master side initiates connections by performing a TCP active open. The outstation listens for a connection request by performing a TCP passive open. *Dual endpoint* is defined as a process that can both listen for connection requests and perform an active open on the channel if required.

Master stations may parse multiple DNP3 data link layer frames from a single UDP datagram, while DNP3 data link layer frames cannot span multiple UDP datagrams. Single or multiple connections to the master may get established while a TCP keepalive timer monitors the status of the connection. Keepalive messages are implemented as DNP3 data link layer status requests. If a response is not received to a keepalive message, the connection is deemed broken, and the appropriate action is taken.

Tunneling Legacy SCADA over IP Networks

Deployments of legacy industrial protocols, such as DNP3 and other SCADA protocols, in modern IP networks call for flexibility when integrating several generations of devices or operations that are tied to various releases and versions of application servers. Native support for IP can vary and may require different solutions. Ideally, end-to-end native IP support is preferred, using a solution like IEEE 1815-2012 in the case of DNP3. Otherwise, transport of the original serial protocol over IP can be achieved either by tunneling using raw sockets over TCP or UDP or by installing an intermediate device that performs protocol translation between the serial protocol version and its IP implementation.

A raw socket connection simply denotes that the serial data is being packaged directly into a TCP or UDP transport. A socket in this instance is a standard application programming interface (API) composed of an IP address and a TCP or UDP port that is used to access network devices over an IP network. More modern industrial application servers may support this capability, while older versions typically require another device or piece of software to handle the transition from pure serial data to serial over IP using a raw socket. Figure 6-3 details raw socket scenarios for a legacy SCADA server trying to communicate with remote serial devices.

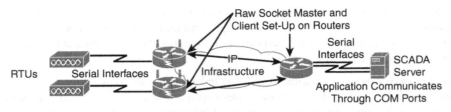

Scenario A: Raw Socket between Routers – no change on SCADA server

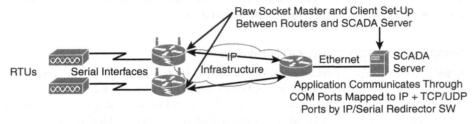

Scenario B: Raw Socket between Router and SCADA Server – no SCADA application change on server but IP/Serial Redirector software and Ethernet interface to be added

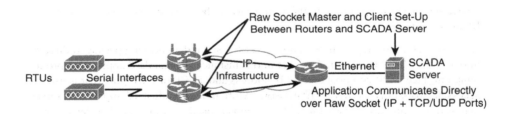

Scenario C: Raw Socket between Router and SCADA Server – SCADA application knows how to directly communicate over a Raw Socket and Ethernet interface

Figure 6-3 *Raw Socket TCP or UDP Scenarios for Legacy Industrial Serial Protocols*

In all the scenarios in Figure 6-3, notice that routers connect via serial interfaces to the remote terminal units (RTUs), which are often associated with SCADA networks. An RTU is a multipurpose device used to monitor and control various systems, applications, and devices managing automation. From the master/slave perspective, the RTUs are the slaves. Opposite the RTUs in each Figure 6-3 scenario is a SCADA server, or master, that varies its connection type. In reality, other legacy industrial application servers could be shown here as well.

In Scenario A in Figure 6-3, both the SCADA server and the RTUs have a direct serial connection to their respective routers. The routers terminate the serial connections at both ends of the link and use raw socket encapsulation to transport the serial payload over the IP network.

Scenario B has a small change on the SCADA server side. A piece of software is installed on the SCADA server that maps the serial COM ports to IP ports. This software is commonly referred to as an IP/serial redirector. The IP/serial redirector in essence terminates the serial connection of the SCADA server and converts it to a TCP/IP port using a raw socket connection.

In Scenario C in Figure 6-3, the SCADA server supports native raw socket capability. Unlike in Scenarios A and B, where a router or IP/serial redirector software has to map the SCADA server's serial ports to IP ports, in Scenario C the SCADA server has full IP support for raw socket connections.

Note   While the examples shown here highlight tunneling of older serial-based SCADA protocols over IP using raw sockets, this mechanism can also be used to tunnel other legacy serial communication protocols that are not part of SCADA.

SCADA Protocol Translation

As mentioned earlier, an alternative to a raw socket connection for transporting legacy serial data across an IP network is protocol translation. With protocol translation, the legacy serial protocol is translated to a corresponding IP version. For example, Figure 6-4 shows two serially connected DNP3 RTUs and two master applications supporting DNP3 over IP that control and pull data from the RTUs. The IoT gateway in this figure performs a protocol translation function that enables communication between the RTUs and servers, despite the fact that a serial connection is present on one side and an IP connection is used on the other.

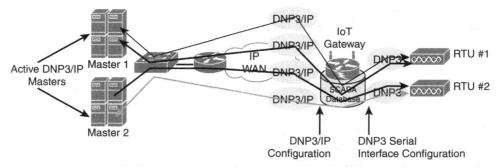

Figure 6-4   *DNP3 Protocol Translation*

By running protocol translation, the IoT gateway connected to the RTUs in Figure 6-4 is implementing a computing function close to the edge of the network. Adding computing functions close to the edge helps scale distributed intelligence in IoT networks. This can be accomplished by offering computing resources on IoT gateways or routers, as shown in this protocol translation example. Alternatively, this can also be performed directly on a node connecting multiple sensors. In either case, this is referred to as fog computing. (For more information on fog computing, see Chapter 2, "IoT Network Architecture and Design.")

Note   In Figure 6-4, DNP3 is shown as the protocol being translated. However, the scenario in this figure is just as applicable to IEC 60870-5. For example, instead of the RTU using DNP3 to connect to the IoT gateway, IEC 60870-5-101 or T101 could be used. On the opposite side, IEC 60870-5-104 or T104 would replace DNP3/IP.

SCADA Transport over LLNs with MAP-T

Due to the constrained nature of LLNs, the implementation of industrial protocols should at a minimum be done over UDP. This in turn requires that both the application servers and devices support and implement UDP. While the long-term evolution of SCADA and other legacy industrial protocols is to natively support IPv6, it must be highlighted that most, if not all, of the industrial devices supporting IP today support IPv4 only. When deployed over LLN subnetworks that are IPv6 only, a transition mechanism, such as MAP-T (Mapping of Address and Port using Translation, RFC 7599), needs to be implemented. This allows the deployment to take advantage of native IPv6 transport transparently to the application and devices.

Figure 6-5 depicts a scenario in which a legacy endpoint is connected across an LLN running 6LoWPAN to an IP-capable SCADA server. The legacy endpoint could be running various industrial and SCADA protocols, including DNP3/IP, Modbus/TCP, or IEC 60870-5-104. In this scenario, the legacy devices and the SCADA server support only IPv4 (typical in the industry today). However, IPv6 (with 6LoWPAN and RPL) is being used for connectivity to the endpoint. As discussed in Chapter 5, 6LoWPAN is a standardized protocol designed for constrained networks, but it only supports IPv6. In this situation, the end devices, the endpoints, and the SCADA server support only IPv4, but the network in the middle supports only IPv6.

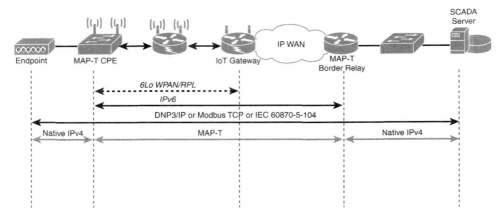

Figure 6-5   *DNP3 Protocol over 6LoWPAN Networks with MAP-T*

The solution to this problem is to use the protocol known as MAP-T, introduced in Chapter 5. MAP-T makes the appropriate mappings between IPv4 and the IPv6 protocols. This allows legacy IPv4 traffic to be forwarded across IPv6 networks. In other words, older devices and protocols can continue running IPv4 even though the network is requiring IPv6.

In Figure 6-5 the IPv4 endpoint on the left side is connected to a Customer Premise Equipment (CPE) device. The MAP-T CPE device has an IPv6 connection to the RPL mesh. On the right side, a SCADA server with native IPv4 support connects to a MAP-T border gateway. The MAP-T CPE device and MAP-T border gateway are thus responsible for the MAP-T conversion from IPv4 to IPv6.

Legacy implementations of SCADA and other industrial protocols are still widely deployed across many industries. While legacy SCADA has evolved from older serial connections to support IP, we can still expect to see mixed deployments for many years. To address this challenge, OT networks require mechanisms such as raw sockets and protocol translation to transport legacy versions over modern IP networks. Even when the legacy devices have IPv4 capability, the constrained portions of the network often require IPv6, not IPv4. In these cases, a MAP-T solution can be put in place to enable IPv4 data to be carried across an IPv6 network.

Generic Web-Based Protocols

Over the years, web-based protocols have become common in consumer and enterprise applications and services. Therefore, it makes sense to try to leverage these protocols when developing IoT applications, services, and devices in order to ease the integration of data and devices from prototyping to production.

The level of familiarity with generic web-based protocols is high. Therefore, programmers with basic web programming skills can work on IoT applications, and this may lead to innovative ways to deliver and handle real-time IoT data. For example, an IoT device generating an event can have the result of launching a video capture, while at the same time a notification is sent to a collaboration tool, such as a Cisco Spark room. This notification allows technicians and engineers to immediately start working on this alert. In addition to a generally high level of familiarity with web-based protocols, scaling methods for web environments are also well understood—and this is crucial when developing consumer applications for potentially large numbers of IoT devices.

Once again, the definition of constrained nodes and networks must be analyzed to select the most appropriate protocol. (Constrained nodes and networks are discussed in Chapter 5.) On non-constrained networks, such as Ethernet, Wi-Fi, or 3G/4G cellular, where bandwidth is not perceived as a potential issue, data payloads based on a verbose data model representation, including XML or JavaScript Object Notation (JSON), can be transported over HTTP/HTTPS or WebSocket. This allows implementers to develop their IoT applications in contexts similar to web applications.

The HTTP/HTTPS client/server model serves as the foundation for the World Wide Web. Recent evolutions of embedded web server software with advanced features are now implemented with very little memory (in the range of tens of kilobytes in some cases). This enables the use of embedded web services software on some constrained devices.

When considering web services implementation on an IoT device, the choice between supporting the client or server side of the connection must be carefully weighed. IoT devices that only push data to an application (for example, an Ethernet- or Wi-Fi-based weather station reporting data to a weather map application or a Wi-Fi–enabled body weight scale that sends data to a health application) may need to implement web services on the client side. The HTTP client side only initiates connections and does not accept incoming ones.

On the other hand, some IoT devices, such as a video surveillance camera, may have web services implemented on the server side. However, because these devices often have limited resources, the number of incoming connections must be kept low. In addition, advanced development in data modeling should be considered as a way to shift the work-load from devices to clients, including web browsers on PCs, mobile phones, tablets, and cloud applications.

Interactions between real-time communication tools powering collaborative applications, such as voice and video, instant messaging, chat rooms, and IoT devices, are also emerging. This is driving the need for simpler communication systems between people and IoT devices. One protocol that addresses this need is Extensible Messaging and Presence Protocol (XMPP). (For more information on XMPP-IoT, see www.xmpp-iot.org.)

Note   In IoT networks, it is common to see both Simple Object Access Protocol (SOAP) and representational state transfer (REST) utilized as web services access protocols. Based on Extensible Markup Language (XML), SOAP is verbose and complex from a coding perspective, with a slow parsing speed, but it is versatile and has built-in error handling that can make resolving issues easier. XML is a specification that details a set of rules for encoding documents and other data structures in a way that is readable by both humans and computers.

As a simple, lightweight alternative to SOAP, REST often implements a simple URI or JSON instead of XML for requests. JSON is easier to read and understand than XML. Also, REST itself is not a standard-based protocol like SOAP but an architectural style.

A detailed discussion of the intricacies of SOAP and REST is beyond the scope of this book, but each of them has a place in performing web services in IoT networks. From a high-level perspective, the simplicity of REST makes it suited more for applications on lightweight clients, such as mobile and embedded devices. SOAP, on the other hand, has better adherence to enterprise and business applications and has stronger security requirements. Many coders have the opinion that REST is the future, but at the same time you will find that SOAP is still quite prevalent in certain applications.

In summary, the Internet of Things greatly benefits from the existing web-based protocols. These protocols, including HTTP/HTTPS and XMPP, ease the integration of IoT devices in the Internet world through well-known and scalable programming techniques.

However, to fully address constrained devices and networks, optimized IoT protocols are required. These protocols are discussed in the next sections.

IoT Application Layer Protocols

When considering constrained networks and/or a large-scale deployment of constrained nodes, verbose web-based and data model protocols, as discussed in the previous section, may be too heavy for IoT applications. To address this problem, the IoT industry is working on new lightweight protocols that are better suited to large numbers of constrained nodes and networks. Two of the most popular protocols are CoAP and MQTT. Figure 6-6 highlights their position in a common IoT protocol stack.

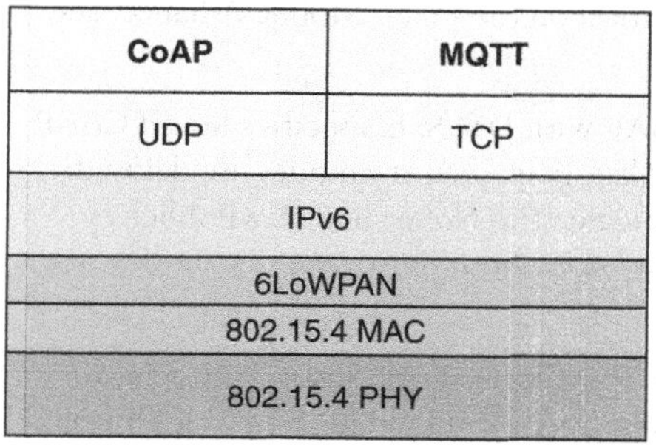

CoAP	MQTT
UDP	TCP
IPv6	
6LoWPAN	
802.15.4 MAC	
802.15.4 PHY	

Figure 6-6   *Example of a High-Level IoT Protocol Stack for CoAP and MQTT*

In Figure 6-6, CoAP and MQTT are naturally at the top of this sample IoT stack, based on an IEEE 802.15.4 mesh network. While there are a few exceptions, you will almost always find CoAP deployed over UDP and MQTT running over TCP. The following sections take a deeper look at CoAP and MQTT.

CoAP

Constrained Application Protocol (CoAP) resulted from the IETF Constrained RESTful Environments (CoRE) working group's efforts to develop a generic framework for resource-oriented applications targeting constrained nodes and networks. (For more information on the IETF CoRE working group, see https://datatracker.ietf.org/wg/core/charter/.) Constrained nodes and networks are discussed in Chapter 5.

The CoAP framework defines simple and flexible ways to manipulate sensors and actuators for data or device management. The IETF CoRE working group has published multiple standards-track specifications for CoAP, including the following:

- **RFC 6690:** Constrained RESTful Environments (CoRE) Link Format
- **RFC 7252:** The Constrained Application Protocol (CoAP)

- **RFC 7641:** Observing Resources in the Constrained Application Protocol (CoAP)

- **RFC 7959:** Block-Wise Transfers in the Constrained Application Protocol (CoAP)

- **RFC 8075:** Guidelines for Mapping Implementations: HTTP to the Constrained Application Protocol (CoAP)

The CoAP messaging model is primarily designed to facilitate the exchange of messages over UDP between endpoints, including the secure transport protocol Datagram Transport Layer Security (DTLS). (UDP is discussed earlier in this chapter.) The IETF CoRE working group is studying alternate transport mechanisms, including TCP, secure TLS, and WebSocket. CoAP over Short Message Service (SMS) as defined in Open Mobile Alliance for Lightweight Machine-to-Machine (LWM2M) for IoT device management is also being considered. (For more information on the Open Mobile Alliance, see http://openmobilealliance.org.)

RFC 7252 provides more details on securing CoAP with DTLS. It specifies how a CoAP endpoint is provisioned with keys and a filtering list. Four security modes are defined: NoSec, PreSharedKey, RawPublicKey, and Certificate. The NoSec and RawPublicKey implementations are mandatory. (For more information about these security modes, see https://tools.ietf.org/html/rfc7252.)

From a formatting perspective, a CoAP message is composed of a short fixed-length Header field (4 bytes), a variable-length but mandatory Token field (0–8 bytes), Options fields if necessary, and the Payload field. Figure 6-7 details the CoAP message format, which delivers low overhead while decreasing parsing complexity.

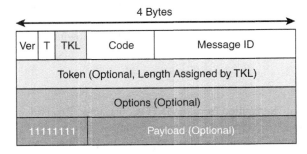

Figure 6-7   *CoAP Message Format*

As you can see in Figure 6-7, the CoAP message format is relatively simple and flexible. It allows CoAP to deliver low overhead, which is critical for constrained networks, while also being easy to parse and process for constrained devices. Table 6-1 provides an overview of the various fields of a CoAP message. (For more details on these fields, see https://tools.ietf.org/html/rfc7252.)

Table 6-1 *CoAP Message Fields*

CoAP Message Field	Description
Ver (Version)	Identifies the CoAP version.
T (Type)	Defines one of the following four message types: Confirmable (CON), Non-confirmable (NON), Acknowledgement (ACK), or Reset (RST). CON and ACK are highlighted in more detail in Figure 6-9.
TKL (Token Length)	Specifies the size (0–8 Bytes) of the Token field.
Code	Indicates the request method for a request message and a response code for a response message. For example, in Figure 6-9, GET is the request method, and 2.05 is the response code. For a complete list of values for this field, refer to RFC 7252.
Message ID	Detects message duplication and used to match ACK and RST message types to Con and NON message types.
Token	With a length specified by TKL, correlates requests and responses.
Options	Specifies option number, length, and option value. Capabilities provided by the Options field include specifying the target resource of a request and proxy functions.
Payload	Carries the CoAP application data. This field is optional, but when it is present, a single byte of all 1s (0xFF) precedes the payload. The purpose of this byte is to delineate the end of the Options field and the beginning of Payload.

CoAP can run over IPv4 or IPv6. However, it is recommended that the message fit within a single IP packet and UDP payload to avoid fragmentation. For IPv6, with the default MTU size being 1280 bytes and allowing for no fragmentation across nodes, the maximum CoAP message size could be up to 1152 bytes, including 1024 bytes for the payload. In the case of IPv4, as IP fragmentation may exist across the network, implementations should limit themselves to more conservative values and set the IPv4 Don't Fragment (DF) bit.

While most sensor and actuator traffic utilizes small-packet payloads, some use cases, such as firmware upgrades, require the capability to send larger payloads. CoAP doesn't rely on IP fragmentation but defines (in RFC 7959) a pair of Block options for transferring multiple blocks of information from a resource representation in multiple request/response pairs.

As illustrated in Figure 6-8, CoAP communications across an IoT infrastructure can take various paths. Connections can be between devices located on the same or different constrained networks or between devices and generic Internet or cloud servers, all operating over IP. Proxy mechanisms are also defined, and RFC 7252 details a basic HTTP mapping for CoAP. As both HTTP and CoAP are IP-based protocols, the proxy function can be located practically anywhere in the network, not necessarily at the border between constrained and non-constrained networks.

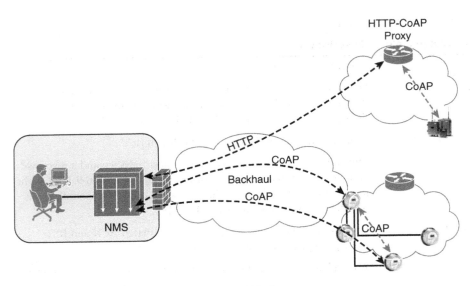

Figure 6-8   *CoAP Communications in IoT Infrastructures*

Just like HTTP, CoAP is based on the REST architecture, but with a "thing" acting as both the client and the server. Through the exchange of asynchronous messages, a client requests an action via a method code on a server resource. A uniform resource identifier (URI) localized on the server identifies this resource. The server responds with a response code that may include a resource representation. The CoAP request/response semantics include the methods GET, POST, PUT, and DELETE.

Example 6-2 shows the CoAP URI format. You may notice that the CoAP URI format is similar to HTTP/HTTPS. The **coap/coaps** URI scheme identifies a resource, including host information and optional UDP port, as indicated by the **host** and **port** parameters in the URI.

Example 6-2   *CoAP URI format*

```
coap-URI = "coap:" "//" host [":" port] path-abempty ["?" query]
coaps-URI = "coaps:" "//" host [":" port] path-abempty ["?" query]
```

CoAP defines four types of messages: confirmable, non-confirmable, acknowledgement, and reset. Method codes and response codes included in some of these messages make them carry requests or responses. CoAP code, method and response codes, option numbers, and content format have been assigned by IANA as Constrained RESTful Environments (CoRE) parameters. (For more information on these parameters, see www.iana.org/assignments/core-parameters/core-parameters.xhtml.)

While running over UDP, CoAP offers a reliable transmission of messages when a CoAP header is marked as "confirmable." In addition, CoAP supports basic congestion control with a default time-out, simple stop and wait retransmission with exponential back-off mechanism, and detection of duplicate messages through a message ID. If a request or response is tagged as confirmable, the recipient must explicitly either acknowledge or reject the message, using the same message ID, as shown in Figure 6-9. If a recipient can't process a non-confirmable message, a reset message is sent.

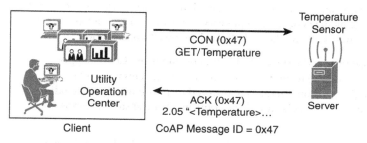

Figure 6-9   *CoAP Reliable Transmission Example*

Figure 6-9 shows a utility operations center on the left, acting as the CoAP client, with the CoAP server being a temperature sensor on the right of the figure. The communication between the client and server uses a CoAP message ID of 0x47. The CoAP Message ID ensures reliability and is used to detect duplicate messages.

The client in Figure 6-9 sends a GET message to get the temperature from the sensor. Notice that the 0x47 message ID is present for this GET message and that the message is also marked with CON. A CON, or confirmable, marking in a CoAP message means the message will be retransmitted until the recipient sends an acknowledgement (or ACK) with the same message ID.

In Figure 6-9, the temperature sensor does reply with an ACK message referencing the correct message ID of 0x47. In addition, this ACK message piggybacks a successful response to the GET request itself. This is indicated by the 2.05 response code followed by the requested data.

CoAP supports data requests sent to a group of devices by leveraging the use of IP Multicast. Implementing IP Multicast with CoAP requires the use of all-CoAP-node multicast addresses. For IPv4 this address is 224.0.1.187, and for IPv6 it is FF0X::FD. These multicast addresses are joined by CoAP nodes offering services to other endpoints while listening on the default CoAP port, 5683. Therefore, endpoints can find available CoAP services through multicast service discovery. A typical use case for multicasting is deploying a firmware upgrade for a group of IoT devices, such as smart meters.

With often no affordable manual configuration on the IoT endpoints, a CoAP server offering services and resources needs to be discovered by the CoAP clients. Services from a CoAP server can either be discovered by learning a URI in a namespace or through the "All CoAP nodes" multicast address. When utilizing the URI scheme for discovering services, the default port 5683 is used for non-secured CoAP, or **coap**, while port 5684 is utilized for DTLS-secured CoAP, or **coaps**. The CoAP server must be in listening state on these ports, unless a different port number is associated with the URI in a namespace.

Much as with accessing web server resources, CoAP specifications provide a description of the relationships between resources in RFC 6690, "Constrained RESTful Environments (CoRE) Link Format." This standard defines the CoRE Link format carried as a payload with an assigned Internet media type. A default entry point for listing to a CoAP server's resource links is to set a well-known relative URI, such as **/.well-known/core**.

To improve the response time and reduce bandwidth consumption, CoAP supports caching capabilities based on the response code. To use a cache entry, a CoAP endpoint must validate the presented request and stored response matches, including all options (unless marked as NoCacheKey). This confirms that the stored response is fresh or valid.

A wide range of CoAP implementations are available. Some are published with open source licenses, and others are part of vendor solutions. A good resource for CoAP implementations is http://coap.technology/impls.html.

In summary, CoAP is a key application protocol adapted to the IoT framework. Because its standardization is led by the IETF CoRE working group, it closely coordinates with other IETF working groups, in particular those looking at constrained nodes and networks, such as 6Lo, 6TiSCH, LWIG, RoLL, ACE, and COSE. Therefore, CoAP is fully optimized for IoT constrained nodes and networks, while leveraging traditional web programming techniques to make it easily understandable by the development community. (For more information on CoAP resources, see http://coap.technology/.)

Message Queuing Telemetry Transport (MQTT)

At the end of the 1990s, engineers from IBM and Arcom (acquired in 2006 by Eurotech) were looking for a reliable, lightweight, and cost-effective protocol to monitor and control a large number of sensors and their data from a central server location, as typically used by the oil and gas industries. Their research resulted in the development and implementation of the Message Queuing Telemetry Transport (MQTT) protocol that is now standardized by the Organization for the Advancement of Structured Information Standards (OASIS). (For more information on OASIS, see www.oasis-open.org.)

Considering the harsh environments in the oil and gas industries, an extremely simple protocol with only a few options was designed, with considerations for constrained nodes, unreliable WAN backhaul communications, and bandwidth constraints with variable latencies. These were some of the rationales for the selection of a client/server and publish/subscribe framework based on the TCP/IP architecture, as shown in Figure 6-10.

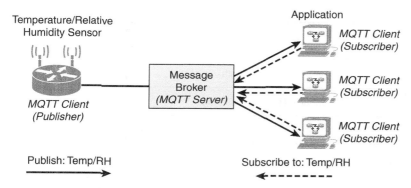

Figure 6-10 *MQTT Publish/Subscribe Framework*

An MQTT client can act as a publisher to send data (or resource information) to an MQTT server acting as an MQTT message broker. In the example illustrated in Figure 6-10, the MQTT client on the left side is a temperature (Temp) and relative humidity (RH) sensor that publishes its Temp/RH data. The MQTT server (or message broker) accepts the network connection along with application messages, such as Temp/RH data, from the publishers. It also handles the subscription and unsubscription process and pushes the application data to MQTT clients acting as subscribers.

The application on the right side of Figure 6-10 is an MQTT client that is a subscriber to the Temp/RH data being generated by the publisher or sensor on the left. This model, where subscribers express a desire to receive information from publishers, is well known. A great example is the collaboration and social networking application Twitter.

With MQTT, clients can subscribe to all data (using a wildcard character) or specific data from the information tree of a publisher. In addition, the presence of a message broker in MQTT decouples the data transmission between clients acting as publishers and subscribers. In fact, publishers and subscribers do not even know (or need to know) about each other. A benefit of having this decoupling is that the MQTT message broker ensures that information can be buffered and cached in case of network failures. This also means that publishers and subscribers do not have to be online at the same time.

MQTT control packets run over a TCP transport using port 1883. TCP ensures an ordered, lossless stream of bytes between the MQTT client and the MQTT server. Optionally, MQTT can be secured using TLS on port 8883, and WebSocket (defined in RFC 6455) can also be used.

MQTT is a lightweight protocol because each control packet consists of a 2-byte fixed header with optional variable header fields and optional payload. You should note that a control packet can contain a payload up to 256 MB. Figure 6-11 provides an overview of the MQTT message format.

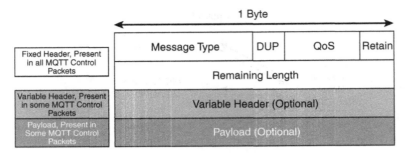

Figure 6-11   *MQTT Message Format*

Compared to the CoAP message format in Figure 6-7, you can see that MQTT contains a smaller header of 2 bytes compared to 4 bytes for CoAP. The first MQTT field in the header is Message Type, which identifies the kind of MQTT packet within a message. Fourteen different types of control packets are specified in MQTT version 3.1.1. Each of them has a unique value that is coded into the Message Type field. Note that values 0 and 15 are reserved. MQTT message types are summarized in Table 6-2.

Table 6-2   *MQTT Message Types*

Message Type	Value	Flow	Description
CONNECT	1	Client to server	Request to connect
CONNACK	2	Server to client	Connect acknowledgement
PUBLISH	3	Client to server Server to client	Publish message
PUBACK	4	Client to server Server to client	Publish acknowledgement
PUBREC	5	Client to server Server to client	Publish received
PUBREL	6	Client to server Server to client	Publish release
PUBCOMP	7	Client to server Server to client	Publish complete
SUBSCRIBE	8	Client to server	Subscribe request
SUBACK	9	Server to client	Subscribe acknowledgement
UNSUBSCRIBE	10	Client to server	Unsubscribe request

Message Type	Value	Flow	Description
UNSUBACK	11	Server to client	Unsubscribe acknowledgement
PINGREQ	12	Client to server	Ping request
PINGRESP	13	Server to client	Ping response
DISCONNECT	14	Client to server	Client disconnecting

The next field in the MQTT header is DUP (Duplication Flag). This flag, when set, allows the client to notate that the packet has been sent previously, but an acknowledgement was not received.

The QoS header field allows for the selection of three different QoS levels. These are discussed in more detail later in this chapter.

The next field is the Retain flag. Only found in a PUBLISH message (refer to Table 6-2), the Retain flag notifies the server to hold onto the message data. This allows new subscribers to instantly receive the last known value without having to wait for the next update from the publisher.

The last mandatory field in the MQTT message header is Remaining Length. This field specifies the number of bytes in the MQTT packet following this field.

MQTT sessions between each client and server consist of four phases: session establishment, authentication, data exchange, and session termination. Each client connecting to a server has a unique client ID, which allows the identification of the MQTT session between both parties. When the server is delivering an application message to more than one client, each client is treated independently.

Subscriptions to resources generate SUBSCRIBE/SUBACK control packets, while unsubscription is performed through the exchange of UNSUBSCRIBE/UNSUBACK control packets. Graceful termination of a connection is done through a DISCONNECT control packet, which also offers the capability for a client to reconnect by re-sending its client ID to resume the operations.

A message broker uses a topic string or topic name to filter messages for its subscribers. When subscribing to a resource, the subscriber indicates the one or more topic levels that are used to structure the topic name. The forward slash (/) in an MQTT topic name is used to separate each level within the topic tree and provide a hierarchical structure to the topic names. Figure 6-12 illustrates these concepts with **adt/lora.adeunis** being a topic level and **adt/lora/adeunis/0018B2000000023A** being an example of a topic name.

Figure 6-12 *MQTT Subscription Example*

Wide flexibility is available to clients subscribing to a topic name. An exact topic can be subscribed to, or multiple topics can be subscribed to at once, through the use of wildcard characters. A subscription can contain one of the wildcard characters to allow subscription to multiple topics at once.

The pound sign (#) is a wildcard character that matches any number of levels within a topic. The multilevel wildcard represents the parent and any number of child levels. For example, subscribing to **adt/lora/adeunis/#** enables the reception of the whole subtree, which could include topic names such as the following:

- adt/lora/adeunis/0018B20000000E9E

- adt/lora/adeunis/0018B20000000E8E

- adt/lora/adeunis/0018B20000000E9A

The plus sign (+) is a wildcard character that matches only one topic level. For example, **adt/lora/+** allows access to **adt/lora/adeunis/** and **adt/lora/abeeway** but not to **adt/lora/adeunis/0018B20000000E9E**.

Topic names beginning with the dollar sign ($) must be excluded by the server when subscriptions start with wildcard characters (# or +). Often, these types of topic names are utilized for message broker internal statistics. So messages cannot be published to these topics by clients. For example, a subscription to **+/monitor/Temp** does not receive any messages published to **$SYS/monitor/Temp**. This topic could be the control channel for this temperature sensor.

PINGREQ/PINGRESP control packets are used to validate the connections between the client and server. Similar to ICMP pings that are part of IP, they are a sort of keepalive that helps to maintain and check the TCP session.

Securing MQTT connections through TLS is considered optional because it calls for more resources on constrained nodes. When TLS is not used, the client sends a clear-text username and password during the connection initiation. MQTT server implementations may also accept anonymous client connections (with the username/password being "blank"). When TLS is implemented, a client must validate the server certificate for proper authentication. Client authentication can also be performed through certificate exchanges with the server, depending on the server configuration.

The MQTT protocol offers three levels of quality of service (QoS). QoS for MQTT is implemented when exchanging application messages with publishers or subscribers, and it is different from the IP QoS that most people are familiar with. The delivery protocol is symmetric. This means the client and server can each take the role of either sender or receiver. The delivery protocol is concerned solely with the delivery of an application message from a single sender to a single receiver. These are the three levels of MQTT QoS:

- **QoS 0:** This is a best-effort and unacknowledged data service referred to as "at most once" delivery. The publisher sends its message one time to a server, which transmits it once to the subscribers. No response is sent by the receiver, and no retry is performed by the sender. The message arrives at the receiver either once or not at all.

- **QoS 1:** This QoS level ensures that the message delivery between the publisher and server and then between the server and subscribers occurs at least once. In PUBLISH and PUBACK packets, a packet identifier is included in the variable header. If the message is not acknowledged by a PUBACK packet, it is sent again. This level guarantees "at least once" delivery.

- **QoS 2:** This is the highest QoS level, used when neither loss nor duplication of messages is acceptable. There is an increased overhead associated with this QoS level because each packet contains an optional variable header with a packet identifier. Confirming the receipt of a PUBLISH message requires a two-step acknowledgement process. The first step is done through the PUBLISH/PUBREC packet pair, and the second is achieved with the PUBREL/PUBCOMP packet pair. This level provides a "guaranteed service" known as "exactly once" delivery, with no consideration for the number of retries as long as the message is delivered once.

As mentioned earlier, the QoS process is symmetric in regard to the roles of sender and receiver, but two separate transactions exist. One transaction occurs between the publishing client and the MQTT server, and the other transaction happens between the MQTT server and the subscribing client. Figure 6-13 provides an overview of the MQTT QoS flows for the three different levels.

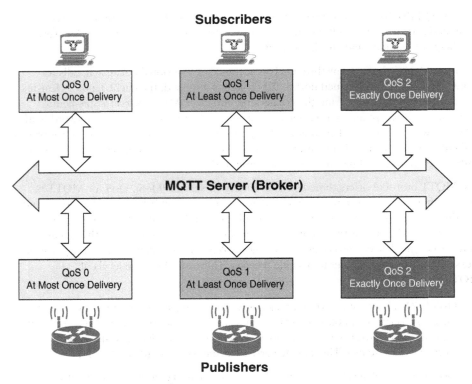

Figure 6-13   *MQTT QoS Flows*

Note   The client on each side of the MQTT flow sets the QoS level. The publishing client side sets the QoS level for communications to the MQTT server. On the other side, the client subscriber sets the QoS level through the subscription with the MQTT server. As illustrated in Figure 6-13, in most cases, QoS remains the same between clients and broker end to end. However, you should be aware that in some scenarios, QoS levels change and are not the same end to end.

As with CoAP, a wide range of MQTT implementations are now available. They are either published as open source licenses or integrated into vendors' solutions, such as Facebook Messenger. For more information on MQTT implementations, see either the older MQTT.org site, at http://mqtt.org, or check out the MQTT community wiki, at https://github.com/mqtt/mqtt.github.io/wiki.

Note   A free tool for working and experimenting with MQTT is MQTT.fx (shown in Figure 6-12). For more information on MQTT.fx, see www.mqttfx.org.

Now that both CoAP and MQTT have been discussed in detail, you can face questions like "Which protocol is better for a given use case?" and "Which one should I used in my IoT network?" Unfortunately, the answer is not always clear, and both MQTT and CoAP have their place. Table 6-3 provides an overview of the differences between MQTT and CoAP, along with their strengths and weaknesses from an IoT perspective.

Table 6-3 *Comparison Between CoAP and MQTT*

Factor	CoAP	MQTT
Main transport protocol	UDP	TCP
Typical messaging	Request/response	Publish/subscribe
Effectiveness in LLNs	Excellent	Low/fair (Implementations pairing UDP with MQTT are better for LLNs.)
Security	DTLS	SSL/TLS
Communication model	One-to-one	many-to-many
Strengths	Lightweight and fast, with low overhead, and suitable for constrained networks; uses a RESTful model that is easy to code to; easy to parse and process for constrained devices; support for multicasting; asynchronous and synchronous messages	TCP and multiple QoS options provide robust communications; simple management and scalability using a broker architecture
Weaknesses	Not as reliable as TCP-based MQTT, so the application must ensure reliability.	Higher overhead for constrained devices and networks; TCP connections can drain low-power devices; no multicasting support

In summary, MQTT is different from the "one-to-one" CoAP model in its "many-to-many" subscription framework, which can make it a better option for some deployments. MQTT is TCP-based, and it ensures an ordered and lossless connection. It has a low overhead when optionally paired with UDP and flexible message format, supports TLS for security, and provides for three levels of QoS. This makes MQTT a key application layer protocol for the successful adoption and growth of the Internet of Things.

Summary

This chapter completes the discussion of the IoT protocol stack. Chapter 4 covers the IoT options for the PHY and MAC layers, and Chapter 5 details the options at the network layer. This chapter focuses on the transport of application protocols in IoT networks.

This chapter begins with a discussion of TCP and UDP. Both of these protocols have their place in IoT networks, depending on the application.

The rest of this chapter focuses on the various methods for transporting IoT application data. The first method discussed is application layer protocol not present, in which the data payload is directly transported on top of the lower layers. An IoT data broker is needed to scale this method of transporting application data.

The second method discussed is IP-adapted application layer. This technique utilizes an IP adaptation layer to transport application data that comes from a non-IP stack. Legacy industrial protocols, such as DNP3, fall in this category and require capabilities like raw sockets and protocol translation to successfully communicate across an IP network.

The next method discussed is generic web-based protocols (such as HTTP), which can be used with non-constrained networks, such as Ethernet and Wi-Fi.

The last approach discussed for handling IoT application data at the upper layers is IoT application layer protocols. This method handles constrained nodes and networks and is recommended for most IoT networks. Special protocols, like CoAP and MQTT, handle the IoT application data requirements and are quite efficient for smart objects with a small compute footprint that need to communicate over a low-bandwidth network.

Chapter 7

Data and Analytics for IoT

In one of the famous episodes of the classic American science fiction TV series *Star Trek*, a harmless furry alien creature known as a "tribble" is brought aboard the starship *Enterprise*. At first, the cute little tribble is treated like a pet, but then its unusual property shows up: It is able to multiply itself at an alarming rate, to the point that the ship soon becomes so filled with tribbles that they consume all supplies on board and begin interfering with the ship's systems.

The problems of data generated by IoT networks might well resemble "The Trouble with Tribbles." At first, IoT data is just a curiosity, and it's even useful if handled correctly. However, given time, as more and more devices are added to IoT networks, the data generated by these systems becomes overwhelming. Not only does this data begin to consume precious network bandwidth but server resources are increasingly taxed in their attempt to process, sort, and analyze the data.

Traditional data management systems are simply unprepared for the demands of what has come to be known as "big data." As discussed throughout this book, the real value of IoT is not just in connecting things but rather in the data produced by those things, the new services you can enable via those connected things, and the business insights that the data can reveal. However, to be useful, the data needs to be handled in a way that is organized and controlled. Thus, a new approach to data analytics is needed for the Internet of Things.

This chapter provides an overview of the field of data analytics from an IoT perspective, including the following sections:

- **An Introduction to Data Analytics for IoT:** This section introduces the subject of analytics for IoT and discusses the differences between structured and unstructured data. It also discusses how analytics relates to IoT data.

- **Machine Learning:** Once you have the data, what do you do with it, and how can you gain business insights from it? This section delves into the major types of machine learning that are used to gain business insights from IoT data.

- **Big Data Analytics Tools and Technology:** *Big data* is one of the most commonly used terms in the world of IoT. This section examines some of the most common technologies used in big data today, including Hadoop, NoSQL, MapReduce, and MPP.

- **Edge Streaming Analytics:** IoT requires that data be processed and analyzed as close to the endpoint as possible, in real-time. This section explores how streaming analytics can be used for such processing and analysis.

- **Network Analytics:** The final section of this chapter investigates the concept of network flow analytics using Flexible NetFlow in IoT systems. NetFlow can help you better understand the function of the overall system and heighten security in an IoT network.

An Introduction to Data Analytics for IoT

In the world of IoT, the creation of massive amounts of data from sensors is common and one of the biggest challenges—not only from a transport perspective but also from a data management standpoint. A great example of the deluge of data that can be generated by IoT is found in the commercial aviation industry and the sensors that are deployed throughout an aircraft.

Modern jet engines are fitted with thousands of sensors that generate a whopping 10GB of data per second.[1] For example, modern jet engines, similar to the one shown in Figure 7-1, may be equipped with around 5000 sensors. Therefore, a twin engine commercial aircraft with these engines operating on average 8 hours a day will generate over 500 TB of data daily, and this is just the data from the engines! Aircraft today have thousands of other sensors connected to the airframe and other systems. In fact, a single wing of a modern jumbo jet is equipped with 10,000 sensors.

Figure 7-1   *Commercial Jet Engine*

The potential for a petabyte (PB) of data per day per commercial airplane is not far-fetched—and this is just for *one* airplane. Across the world, there are approximately 100,000 commercial flights per day. The amount of IoT data coming just from the commercial airline business is overwhelming.

This example is but one of many that highlight the big data problem that is being exacerbated by IoT. Analyzing this amount of data in the most efficient manner possible falls under the umbrella of data analytics. Data analytics must be able to offer actionable insights and knowledge from data, no matter the amount or style, in a timely manner, or the full benefits of IoT cannot be realized.

Note Another example regarding the amount of data being generated by IoT, and thus the need for data analytics, is the utility industry. Even moderately sized smart meter networks can provide over 1 billion data points each day. For more details about this data challenge, refer to Chapter 2, "IoT Network Architecture and Design."

Before diving deeper into data analytics, it is important to define a few key concepts related to data. For one thing, not all data is the same; it can be categorized and thus analyzed in different ways. Depending on how data is categorized, various data analytics tools and processing methods can be applied. Two important categorizations from an IoT perspective are whether the data is structured or unstructured and whether it is in motion or at rest.

Structured Versus Unstructured Data

Structured data and unstructured data are important classifications as they typically require different toolsets from a data analytics perspective. Figure 7-2 provides a high-level comparison of structured data and unstructured data.

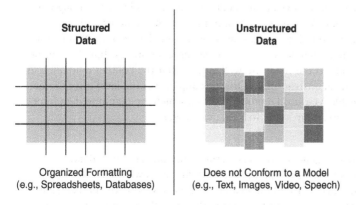

Structured Data

Unstructured Data

Organized Formatting
(e.g., Spreadsheets, Databases)

Does not Conform to a Model
(e.g., Text, Images, Video, Speech)

Figure 7-2 *Comparison Between Structured and Unstructured Data*

Structured data means that the data follows a model or schema that defines how the data is represented or organized, meaning it fits well with a traditional relational database management system (RDBMS). In many cases you will find structured data in a simple tabular form—for example, a spreadsheet where data occupies a specific cell and can be explicitly defined and referenced.

Structured data can be found in most computing systems and includes everything from banking transaction and invoices to computer log files and router configurations. IoT sensor data often uses structured values, such as temperature, pressure, humidity, and so on, which are all sent in a known format. Structured data is easily formatted, stored, queried, and processed; for these reasons, it has been the core type of data used for making business decisions.

Because of the highly organizational format of structured data, a wide array of data analytics tools are readily available for processing this type of data. From custom scripts to commercial software like Microsoft Excel and Tableau, most people are familiar and comfortable with working with structured data.

Unstructured data lacks a logical schema for understanding and decoding the data through traditional programming means. Examples of this data type include text, speech, images, and video. As a general rule, any data that does not fit neatly into a predefined data model is classified as unstructured data.

According to some estimates, around 80% of a business's data is unstructured.[2] Because of this fact, data analytics methods that can be applied to unstructured data, such as cognitive computing and machine learning, are deservedly garnering a lot of attention. With machine learning applications, such as natural language processing (NLP), you can decode speech. With image/facial recognition applications, you can extract critical information from still images and video. The handling of unstructured IoT data employing machine learning techniques is covered in more depth later in this chapter.

Note   A third data classification, semi-structured data, is sometimes included along with structured and unstructured data. As you can probably guess, semi-structured data is a hybrid of structured and unstructured data and shares characteristics of both. While not relational, semi-structured data contains a certain schema and consistency. Email is a good example of semi-structured data as the fields are well defined but the content contained in the body field and attachments is unstructured. Other examples include JavaScript Object Notation (JSON) and Extensible Markup Language (XML), which are common data interchange formats used on the web and in some IoT data exchanges.

Smart objects in IoT networks generate both structured and unstructured data. Structured data is more easily managed and processed due to its well-defined organization. On the other hand, unstructured data can be harder to deal with and typically requires very different analytics tools for processing the data. Being familiar with both of these data classifications is important because knowing which data classification you are working with makes integrating with the appropriate data analytics solution much easier.

Data in Motion Versus Data at Rest

As in most networks, data in IoT networks is either in transit ("data in motion") or being held or stored ("data at rest"). Examples of data in motion include traditional client/server exchanges, such as web browsing and file transfers, and email. Data saved to a hard drive, storage array, or USB drive is data at rest.

From an IoT perspective, the data from smart objects is considered data in motion as it passes through the network en route to its final destination. This is often processed at the edge, using fog computing. When data is processed at the edge, it may be filtered and deleted or forwarded on for further processing and possible storage at a fog node or in the data center. Data does not come to rest at the edge. (For more information on edge and fog computing, refer to Chapter 2.)

When data arrives at the data center, it is possible to process it in real-time, just like at the edge, while it is still in motion. Tools with this sort of capability, such as Spark, Storm, and Flink, are relatively nascent compared to the tools for analyzing stored data. Later sections of this chapter provide more information on these real-time streaming analysis tools that are part of the Hadoop ecosystem.

Data at rest in IoT networks can be typically found in IoT brokers or in some sort of storage array at the data center. Myriad tools, especially tools for structured data in relational databases, are available from a data analytics perspective. The best known of these tools is Hadoop. Hadoop not only helps with data processing but also data storage. It is discussed in more detail later in this chapter.

IoT Data Analytics Overview

The true importance of IoT data from smart objects is realized only when the analysis of the data leads to actionable business intelligence and insights. Data analysis is typically broken down by the types of results that are produced. As shown in Figure 7-3, there are four types of data analysis results:

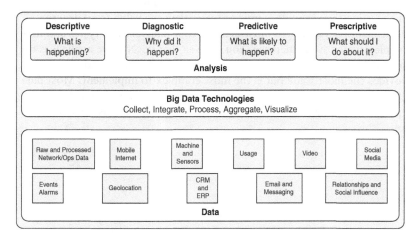

Figure 7-3   *Types of Data Analysis Results*

- **Descriptive:** Descriptive data analysis tells you what is happening, either now or in the past. For example, a thermometer in a truck engine reports temperature values every second. From a descriptive analysis perspective, you can pull this data at any moment to gain insight into the current operating condition of the truck engine. If the temperature value is too high, then there may be a cooling problem or the engine may be experiencing too much load.

- **Diagnostic:** When you are interested in the "why," diagnostic data analysis can provide the answer. Continuing with the example of the temperature sensor in the truck engine, you might wonder why the truck engine failed. Diagnostic analysis might show that the temperature of the engine was too high, and the engine overheated. Applying diagnostic analysis across the data generated by a wide range of smart objects can provide a clear picture of why a problem or an event occurred.

- **Predictive:** Predictive analysis aims to foretell problems or issues before they occur. For example, with historical values of temperatures for the truck engine, predictive analysis could provide an estimate on the remaining life of certain components in the engine. These components could then be proactively replaced before failure occurs. Or perhaps if temperature values of the truck engine start to rise slowly over time, this could indicate the need for an oil change or some other sort of engine cooling maintenance.

- **Prescriptive:** Prescriptive analysis goes a step beyond predictive and recommends solutions for upcoming problems. A prescriptive analysis of the temperature data from a truck engine might calculate various alternatives to cost-effectively maintain our truck. These calculations could range from the cost necessary for more frequent oil changes and cooling maintenance to installing new cooling equipment on the engine or upgrading to a lease on a model with a more powerful engine. Prescriptive analysis looks at a variety of factors and makes the appropriate recommendation.

Both predictive and prescriptive analyses are more resource intensive and increase complexity, but the value they provide is much greater than the value from descriptive and diagnostic analysis. Figure 7-4 illustrates the four data analysis types and how they rank as complexity and value increase. You can see that descriptive analysis is the least complex and at the same time offers the least value. On the other end, prescriptive analysis provides the most value but is the most complex to implement. Most data analysis in the IoT space relies on descriptive and diagnostic analysis, but a shift toward predictive and prescriptive analysis is understandably occurring for most businesses and organizations.

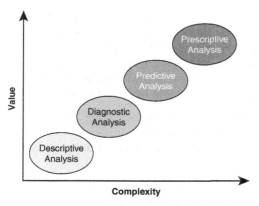

Figure 7-4 *Application of Value and Complexity Factors to the Types of Data Analysis*

IoT Data Analytics Challenges

As IoT has grown and evolved, it has become clear that traditional data analytics solutions were not always adequate. For example, traditional data analytics typically employs a standard RDBMS and corresponding tools, but the world of IoT is much more demanding. While relational databases are still used for certain data types and applications, they often struggle with the nature of IoT data. IoT data places two specific challenges on a relational database:

■ **Scaling problems:** Due to the large number of smart objects in most IoT networks that continually send data, relational databases can grow incredibly large very quickly. This can result in performance issues that can be costly to resolve, often requiring more hardware and architecture changes.

■ **Volatility of data:** With relational databases, it is critical that the schema be designed correctly from the beginning. Changing it later can slow or stop the database from operating. Due to the lack of flexibility, revisions to the schema must be kept at a minimum. IoT data, however, is volatile in the sense that the data model is likely to change and evolve over time. A dynamic schema is often required so that data model changes can be made daily or even hourly.

To deal with challenges like scaling and data volatility, a different type of database, known as NoSQL, is being used. Structured Query Language (SQL) is the computer language used to communicate with an RDBMS. As the name implies, a NoSQL database is a database that does not use SQL. It is not set up in the traditional tabular form of a relational database. NoSQL databases do not enforce a strict schema, and they support a complex, evolving data model. These databases are also inherently much more scalable. (For more information on NoSQL, see the section "NoSQL Databases" later in the chapter.)

In addition to the relational database challenges that IoT imposes, with its high volume of smart object data that frequently changes, IoT also brings challenges with the live streaming nature of its data and with managing data at the network level. Streaming data, which is generated as smart objects transmit data, is challenging because it is usually of a very high volume, and it is valuable only if it is possible to analyze and respond to it in real-time. Real-time analysis of streaming data allows you to detect patterns or anomalies that could indicate a problem or a situation that needs some kind of immediate response. To have a chance of affecting the outcome of this problem, you naturally must be able to filter and analyze the data while it is occurring, as close to the edge as possible.

The market for analyzing streaming data in real-time is growing fast. Major cloud analytics providers, such as Google, Microsoft, and IBM, have streaming analytics offerings, and various other applications can be used in house. (Edge streaming analytics is discussed in depth later in this chapter.)

Another challenge that IoT brings to analytics is in the area of network data, which is referred to as *network analytics*. With the large numbers of smart objects in IoT networks that are communicating and streaming data, it can be challenging to ensure that these data flows are effectively managed, monitored, and secure. Network analytics tools such as Flexible NetFlow and IPFIX provide the capability to detect irregular patterns or other problems in the flow of IoT data through a network. Network analytics, including both Flexible NetFlow and IPFIX, is covered in more detail later in this chapter.

Machine Learning

One of the core subjects in IoT is how to makes sense of the data that is generated. Because much of this data can appear incomprehensible to the naked eye, specialized tools and algorithms are needed to find the data relationships that will lead to new business insights. This brings us to the subject of machine learning (ML).

Machine learning, *deep learning*, *neural networks*, and *convolutional networks* are words you have probably heard in relation to big data and IoT. ML is indeed central to IoT. Data collected by smart objects needs to be analyzed, and intelligent actions need to be taken based on these analyses. Performing this kind of operation manually is almost impossible (or very, very slow and inefficient). Machines are needed to process information fast and react instantly when thresholds are met. For example, every time a new advance is made in the field of self-driving vehicles, abnormal pattern recognition in a crowd, or any other automated intelligent and machine-assisted decision system, ML is named as the tool that made the advance possible. But ML is not new. It was invented in the middle of the twentieth century and actually fell out of fashion in the 1980s. So what has happened in ML that makes it the new tool of choice for IoT and data analytics?

Machine Learning Overview

Machine learning is, in fact, part of a larger set of technologies commonly grouped under the term *artificial intelligence* (*AI*). This term used to make science fiction amateurs dream of biped robots and conscious machines, or of a *Matrix*-like world where machines would enslave humankind. In fact, AI includes any technology that allows a computing system to mimic human intelligence using any technique, from very advanced logic to basic "if-then-else" decision loops. Any computer that uses rules to make decisions belongs to this realm. A simple example is an app that can help you find your parked car. A GPS reading of your position at regular intervals calculates your speed. A basic threshold system determines whether you are driving (for example, "if speed > 20 mph or 30 kmh, then start calculating speed"). When you park and disconnect from the car Bluetooth system, the app simply records the location when the disconnection happens. This is where your car is parked. Beyond the appearance of artificial intelligence (the computer knows that you are parked and where this happened), the ruleset is very simple.

In more complex cases, static rules cannot be simply inserted into the program because they require parameters that can change or that are imperfectly understood. A typical example is a dictation program that runs on a computer. The program is configured to recognize the audio pattern of each word in a dictionary, but it does not know your voice's specifics—your accent, tone, speed, and so on. You need to record a set of predetermined sentences to help the tool match well-known words to the sounds you make when you say the words. This process is called machine learning. ML is concerned with any process where the computer needs to receive a set of data that is processed to help perform a task with more efficiency. ML is a vast field but can be simply divided in two main categories: supervised and unsupervised learning.

Supervised Learning

In supervised learning, the machine is trained with input for which there is a known correct answer. For example, suppose that you are training a system to recognize when there is a human in a mine tunnel. A sensor equipped with a basic camera can capture shapes and return them to a computing system that is responsible for determining whether the shape is a human or something else (such as a vehicle, a pile of ore, a rock, a piece of wood, and so on.). With supervised learning techniques, hundreds or thousands of images are fed into the machine, and each image is labeled (human or nonhuman in this case). This is called the *training set*. An algorithm is used to determine common parameters and common differences between the images. The comparison is usually done at the scale of the entire image, or pixel by pixel. Images are resized to have the same characteristics (resolution, color depth, position of the central figure, and so on), and each point is analyzed. Human images have certain types of shapes and pixels in certain locations (which correspond to the position of the face, legs, mouth, and so on). Each new image is compared to the set of known "good images," and a deviation is calculated to determine how different the new image is from the average human image and, therefore, the probability that what is shown is a human figure. This process is called *classification*.

After training, the machine should be able to recognize human shapes. Before real field deployments, the machine is usually tested with unlabeled pictures—this is called the validation or the test set, depending on the ML system used—to verify that the recognition level is at acceptable thresholds. If the machine does not reach the level of success expected, more training is needed.

In other cases, the learning process is not about classifying in two or more categories but about finding a correct value. For example, the speed of the flow of oil in a pipe is a function of the size of the pipe, the viscosity of the oil, pressure, and a few other factors. When you train the machine with measured values, the machine can predict the speed of the flow for a new, and unmeasured, viscosity. This process is called *regression*; regression predicts numeric values, whereas classification predicts categories.

Unsupervised Learning

In some cases, supervised learning is not the best method for a machine to help with a human decision. Suppose that you are processing IoT data from a factory manufacturing small engines. You know that about 0.1% of the produced engines on average need adjustments to prevent later defects, and your task is to identify them before they get mounted into machines and shipped away from the factory. With hundreds of parts, it may be very difficult to detect the potential defects, and it is almost impossible to train a machine to recognize issues that may not be visible. However, you can test each engine and record multiple parameters, such as sound, pressure, temperature of key parts, and so on. Once data is recorded, you can graph these elements in relation to one another (for example, temperature as a function of pressure, sound versus rotating speed over time). You can then input this data into a computer and use mathematical functions to find groups. For example, you may decide to group the engines by the sound they make at a given temperature. A standard function to operate this grouping, *K-means clustering*, finds the mean values for a group of engines (for example, mean value for temperature, mean frequency for sound). Grouping the engines this way can quickly reveal several types of engines that all belong to the same category (for example, small engine of chainsaw type, medium engine of lawnmower type). All engines of the same type produce sounds and temperatures in the same range as the other members of the same group.

There will occasionally be an engine in the group that displays unusual characteristics (slightly out of expected temperature or sound range). This is the engine that you send for manual evaluation. The computing process associated with this determination is called *unsupervised learning*. This type of learning is unsupervised because there is not a "good" or "bad" answer known in advance. It is the variation from a group behavior that allows the computer to learn that something is different. The example of engines is, of course, very simple. In most cases, parameters are multidimensional. In other words, hundreds or thousands of parameters are computed, and small cumulated deviations in multiple dimensions are used to identify the exception. Figure 7-5 shows an example of such grouping and deviation identification logic. Three parameters are graphed (components 1, 2, and 3), and four distinct groups (clusters) are found. You can see some points that are far from the respective groups. Individual devices that display such "out of cluster" characteristics should be examined more closely individually.

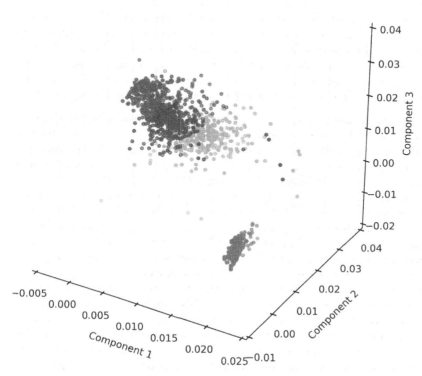

Figure 7-5   *Clustering and Deviation Detection Example*

Neural Networks

Processing multiple dimensions requires a lot of computing power. It is also difficult to determine what parameters to input and what combined variations should raise red flags. Similarly, supervised learning is efficient only with a large training set; larger training sets usually lead to higher accuracy in the prediction. This requirement is partly what made ML fade away somewhat in the 1980s and 1990s. Training the machines was often deemed too expensive and complicated.

Since the 2000s, cheaper computing power along with access to very large data sets (shared over the Internet) rejuvenated the possibilities of ML. At the same time, immense progress has been made in the efficiency of the algorithms used. Take the case of the human shape recognition for mining operations. Distinguishing between a human and a car is easy. The computer can recognize that humans have distinct shapes (such as legs or arms) and that vehicles do not. Distinguishing a human from another mammal is much more difficult (although nonhuman mammals are not common occurrences in mines). The same goes for telling the difference between a pickup truck and a van. You can tell when you see one, but training a machine to differentiate them requires more than basic shape recognition.

This is where neural networks come into the picture. Neural networks are ML methods that mimic the way the human brain works. When you look at a human figure, multiple zones of your brain are activated to recognize colors, movements, facial expressions, and so on. Your brain combines these elements to conclude that the shape you are seeing is human. Neural networks mimic the same logic. The information goes through different algorithms (called *units*), each of which is in charge of processing an aspect of the information. The resulting value of one unit computation can be used directly or fed into another unit for further processing to occur. In this case, the neural network is said to have several layers. For example, a neural network processing human image recognition may have two units in a first layer that determines whether the image has straight lines and sharp angles—because vehicles commonly have straight lines and sharp angles, and human figures do not. If the image passes the first layer successfully (because there are no or only a small percentage of sharp angles and straight lines), a second layer may look for different features (presence of face, arms, and so on), and then a third layer might compare the image to images of various animals and conclude that the shape is a human (or not). The great efficiency of neural networks is that each unit processes a simple test, and therefore computation is quite fast. This model is demonstrated in Figure 7-6.

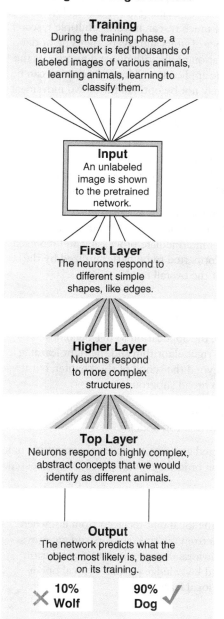

How Neural Networks Recognize a Dog in a Photo

Training
During the training phase, a neural network is fed thousands of labeled images of various animals, learning animals, learning to classify them.

Input
An unlabeled image is shown to the pretrained network.

First Layer
The neurons respond to different simple shapes, like edges.

Higher Layer
Neurons respond to more complex structures.

Top Layer
Neurons respond to highly complex, abstract concepts that we would identify as different animals.

Output
The network predicts what the object most likely is, based on its training.

10% Wolf

90% Dog

Figure 7-6   *Neural Network Example*

By contrast, old supervised ML techniques would compare the human figure to potentially hundreds of thousands of images during the training phase, pixel by pixel, making them difficult and expensive to implement (with a lot of training needed) and slow to operate. Neural networks have been the subject of much research work. Multiple research and optimization efforts have examined the number of units and layers, the type of data processed at each layer, and the type and combination of algorithms used to process the data to make processing more efficient for specific applications. Image processing can be optimized with certain types of algorithms that may not be optimal for crowd movement classification. Another algorithm may be found in this case that would revolutionize the way these movements are processed and analyzed. Possibilities are as numerous as the applications where they can be used.

In a sense, neural networks rely on the idea that information is divided into key components, and each component is assigned a weight. The weights compared together decide the classification of this information (no straight lines + face + smile = human).

When the result of a layer is fed into another layer, the process is called deep learning ("deep" because the learning process has more than a single layer). One advantage of deep learning is that having more layers allows for richer intermediate processing and representation of the data. At each layer, the data can be formatted to be better utilized by the next layer. This process increases the efficiency of the overall result.

Machine Learning and Getting Intelligence from Big Data

When the principles of machine learning are clear, the application to IoT becomes obvious. The difficulty resides in determining the right algorithm and the right learning model for each use case. Such an analysis goes beyond the scope of this chapter, but it can be useful to organize ML operations into two broad subgroups:

- **Local learning:** In this group, data is collected and processed locally, either in the sensor itself (the edge node) or in the gateway (the fog node).

- **Remote learning:** In this group, data is collected and sent to a central computing unit (typically the data center in a specific location or in the cloud), where it is processed.

Note   Associated with these two subgroups, you will encounter the term *inherited learning*. This term refers to results of learning that the local unit received from elsewhere. For example, a processing computer may collect data from multiple sensors and gateways, perform ML on this data, and send the resulting behavioral change request or conclusion back to the gateway and the sensor. This new received knowledge optimizes local operations and is inherited learning (as opposed to simple local learning).

Regardless of the location where (and, therefore, the scale at which) data is processed, common applications of ML for IoT revolve around four major domains:

- **Monitoring:** Smart objects monitor the environment where they operate. Data is processed to better understand the conditions of operations. These conditions can refer to external factors, such as air temperature, humidity, or presence of carbon dioxide in a mine, or to operational internal factors, such as the pressure of a pump, the viscosity of oil flowing in a pipe, and so on. ML can be used with monitoring to detect early failure conditions (for example, K-means deviations showing out-of-range behavior) or to better evaluate the environment (such as shape recognition for a robot automatically sorting material or picking goods in a warehouse or a supply chain).

- **Behavior control:** Monitoring commonly works in conjunction with behavior control. When a given set of parameters reach a target threshold—defined in advance (that is, supervised) or learned dynamically through deviation from mean values (that is, unsupervised)—monitoring functions generate an alarm. This alarm can be relayed to a human, but a more efficient and more advanced system would trigger a corrective action, such as increasing the flow of fresh air in the mine tunnel, turning the robot arm, or reducing the oil pressure in the pipe.

- **Operations optimization:** Behavior control typically aims at taking corrective actions based on thresholds. However, analyzing data can also lead to changes that improve the overall process. For example, a water purification plant in a smart city can implement a system to monitor the efficiency of the purification process based on which chemical (from company A or company B) is used, at what temperature, and associated to what stirring mechanism (stirring speed and depth). Neural networks can combine multiples of such units, in one or several layers, to estimate the best chemical and stirring mix for a target air temperature. This intelligence can help the plant reduce its consumption of chemicals while still operating at the same purification efficiency level. As a result of the learning, behavior control results in different machine actions. The objective is not merely to pilot the operations but to improve the efficiency and the result of these operations.

- **Self-healing, self-optimizing:** A fast-developing aspect of deep learning is the closed loop. ML-based monitoring triggers changes in machine behavior (the change is monitored by humans), and operations optimizations. In turn, the ML engine can be programmed to dynamically monitor and combine new parameters (randomly or semi-randomly) and automatically deduce and implement new optimizations when the results demonstrate a possible gain. The system becomes self-learning and self-optimizing. It also detects new K-means deviations that result in predetection of new potential defects, allowing the system to self-heal. The healing is not literal, as external factors (typically human operators) have to intervene, but the diagnosis is automated. In many cases, the system can also automatically order a piece of equipment that is detected as being close to failure or automatically take corrective actions to avoid the failure (for example, slow down operations, modify a machine's movement to avoid fatigue on a weak link).

For all these operations, a specific aspect of ML for IoT is the scale. A weather sensor mounted on a light pole in a street can provide information about the local pollution level. At the scale of the entire city, the authorities can monitor moving pollution clouds, and the global and local effects of mist or humidity, pressure, and terrain. All this information can be combined with traffic data to globally regulate traffic light patterns, reduce emissions from industrial pollution sources, or increase the density of mass transit vehicles along the more affected axes. Meanwhile, at the local level, the LED on the light pole can increase or reduce its luminosity and change its color to adapt to local conditions. This change can be driven by either local condition processing (local learning) or inherited learning.

The ability to combine fog computing on specific and specialized systems with cloud computing on data coming from multiple sources and derive global or local corrective actions is what makes ML so powerful for IoT. With open systems and the explosion of smart objects, the possibilities of correlations and cross-optimizations are very wide.

Predictive Analytics

Machine learning and big data processing for IoT fit very well into the digitization described in Chapter 1, "What Is IoT?" The advanced stages of this model see the network self-diagnose and self-optimize. In the IoT world, this behavior is what the previous section describes. When data from multiple systems is combined and analyzed together, predictions can be made about the state of the system. For example, Chapter 13, "Transportation," examines the case of sensors deployed on locomotives. Multiple smart objects measure the pull between carriages, the weight on each wheel, and multiple other parameters to offer a form of cruise control optimization for the driver. At the same time, cameras observe the state of the tracks ahead, audio sensors analyze the sound of each wheel on the tracks, and multiple engine parameters are measured and analyzed. All this data can be returned to a data processing center in the cloud that can re-create a virtual twin of each locomotive. Modeling the state of each locomotive and combining this knowledge with anticipated travel and with the states (and detected failures) of all other locomotives of the same type circulating on the tracks of the entire city, province, state, or country allows the analytics platform to make very accurate predictions on what issue is likely to affect each train and each locomotive. Such predictive analysis allows preemptive maintenance and increases the safety and efficiency of operations.

Similarly, sensors combined with big data can anticipate defects or issues in vehicles operating in mines, in manufacturing machines, or any system that can be monitored, along with other similar systems.

Big Data Analytics Tools and Technology

It is a common mistake for individuals new to the world of data management to use the terms *big data* and *Hadoop* interchangeably. Though it's true that Hadoop is at the core of many of today's big data implementations, it's not the only piece of the puzzle. Big data analytics can consist of many different software pieces that together collect, store, manipulate, and analyze all different data types. It helps to better understand the land-scape by defining what big data is and what it is not. Generally, the industry looks to the "three Vs" to categorize big data:

- **Velocity:** *Velocity* refers to how quickly data is being collected and analyzed. Hadoop Distributed File System is designed to ingest and process data very quickly. Smart objects can generate machine and sensor data at a very fast rate and require database or file systems capable of equally fast ingest functions.

- **Variety:** *Variety* refers to different types of data. Often you see data categorized as structured, semi-structured, or unstructured. Different database technologies may only be capable of accepting one of these types. Hadoop is able to collect and store all three types. This can be beneficial when combining machine data from IoT devices that is very structured in nature with data from other sources, such as social media or multimedia, that is unstructured.

- **Volume:** *Volume* refers to the scale of the data. Typically, this is measured from gigabytes on the very low end to petabytes or even exabytes of data on the other extreme. Generally, big data implementations scale beyond what is available on locally attached storage disks on a single node. It is common to see clusters of serv-ers that consist of dozens, hundreds, or even thousands of nodes for some large deployments.

The characteristics of big data can be defined by the sources and types of data. First is machine data, which is generated by IoT devices and is typically unstructured data. Second is transactional data, which is from sources that produce data from transactions on these systems, and, have high volume and structured. Third is social data sources, which are typically high volume and structured. Fourth is enterprise data, which is data that is lower in volume and very structured. Hence big data consists of data from all these separate sources.

An additional point to consider while reviewing data sources is the amount of data ingested from each source, which determines the data storage layer design. You should also consider the mechanism to get the data from the ingest systems—namely push or pull. The type of data source—database, file, web service, stream—also needs to be considered as it also determines the structure of data.

Data ingest is the layer that connects data sources to storage. It's the layer that prepro-cesses, validates, extracts, and stores data temporarily for further processing. There are several patterns to consider for data ingest. First is multisource ingestion, which connects multiple data sources to ingest systems. In this pattern, ingest nodes receive streams of data from multiple sources and do processing before passing the data to intermediate nodes and to final store nodes. This pattern is typically implemented in batch systems and (less often, due to the delay of data availability) in real-time systems.

Data collection and analysis are not new concepts in the industries that helped define IoT. Industrial verticals have long depended on the ability to get, collect, and record data from various processes in order to record trends and track performance and quality.

For example, many industrial automation and control systems feed data into two distinct database types, relational databases and historians. Relational databases, such as Oracle and Microsoft SQL, are good for transactional, or process, data. Their benefit is being able to analyze complex data relationships on data that arrives over a period of time. On the other hand, historians are optimized for time-series data from systems and processes. They are built with speed of storage and retrieval of data at their core, recording each data point in a series with the pertinent information about the system being logged. This data may consist of a sensor reading, the quantity of a material, a temperature reading, or flow data.

Relational databases and historians are mature technologies that have been with us for many years, but new technologies and techniques in the data management market have opened up new possibilities for sensor and machine data. These database technologies broadly fit into a few categories that each have strengths and potential drawbacks when used in an IoT context. The three most popular of these categories are massively parallel processing systems, NoSQL, and Hadoop.

Massively Parallel Processing Databases

Enterprises have used relational databases for storing structured, row and column style data types for decades. Relational databases are often grouped into a broad data storage category called data warehouses. Though they are the centerpiece of most data architectures, they are often used for longer-term archiving and data queries that can often take minutes or hours. An example of this would be asking for all the items produced in the past year that had a particular specification. Depending on the number of items in the database and the complexity of the question being asked, the response could be slow to return.

Massively parallel processing (MPP) databases were built on the concept of the relational data warehouses but are designed to be much faster, to be efficient, and to support reduced query times. To accomplish this, MPP databases take advantage of multiple nodes (computers) designed in a scale-out architecture such that both data and processing are distributed across multiple systems.

MPPs are sometimes referred to as *analytic databases* because they are designed to allow for fast query processing and often have built-in analytic functions. As the name implies, these database types process massive data sets in parallel across many processors and nodes. An MPP architecture (see Figure 7-7) typically contains a single master node that is responsible for the coordination of all the data storage and processing across the cluster. It operates in a "shared-nothing" fashion, with each node containing local processing, memory, and storage and operating independently. Data storage is optimized across the nodes in a structured SQL-like format that allows data analysts to work with the data using common SQL tools and applications. The earlier example of a complex SQL query could be distributed and optimized, resulting in a significantly faster response. Because data stored on MPPs must still conform to this relational structure, it may not be the only database type used in an IoT implementation. The sources and types of data may vary, requiring a database that is more flexible than relational databases allow.

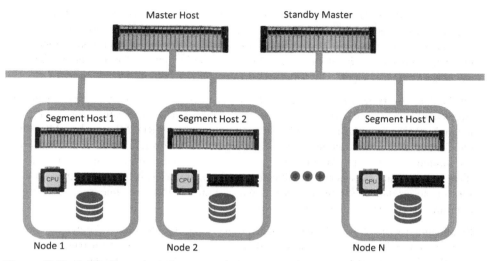

Figure 7-7 *MPP Shared-Nothing Architecture*

NoSQL Databases

NoSQL ("not only SQL") is a class of databases that support semi-structured and unstructured data, in addition to the structured data handled by data warehouses and MPPs. NoSQL is not a specific database technology; rather, it is an umbrella term that encompasses several different types of databases, including the following:

- **Document stores:** This type of database stores semi-structured data, such as XML or JSON. Document stores generally have query engines and indexing features that allow for many optimized queries.

- **Key-value stores:** This type of database stores associative arrays where a key is paired with an associated value. These databases are easy to build and easy to scale.

- **Wide-column stores:** This type of database stores similar to a key-value store, but the formatting of the values can vary from row to row, even in the same table.

- **Graph stores:** This type of database is organized based on the relationships between elements. Graph stores are commonly used for social media or natural language processing, where the connections between data are very relevant.

NoSQL was developed to support the high-velocity, urgent data requirements of modern web applications that typically do not require much repeated use. The original intent was to quickly ingest rapidly changing server logs and clickstream data generated by web-scale applications that did not neatly fit into the rows and columns required by relational databases. Similar to other data stores, like MPPs and Hadoop (discussed later), NoSQL is built to scale horizontally, allowing the database to span multiple hosts, and can even be distributed geographically.

Expanding NoSQL databases to other nodes is similar to expansion in other distributed data systems, where additional hosts are managed by a master node or process. This expansion can be automated by some NoSQL implementations or can be provisioned manually. This level of flexibility makes NoSQL a good candidate for holding machine and sensor data associated with smart objects.

Of the database types that fit under the NoSQL category, key-value stores and document stores tend to be the best fit for what is considered "IoT data." Key-value store is the technology that provides the foundation for many of today's RDBMSs, such as MS SQL, Oracle, and DB2.[3] However, unlike traditional RDBMSs, key-value stores on NoSQL are not limited to a single monolithic system. NoSQL key-value stores are capable of handling indexing and persistence simultaneously at a high rate. This makes it a great choice for time-series data sets, which record a value at a given interval of time, such as a temperature or pressure reading from a sensor.

By allowing the database schema to change quickly, NoSQL document databases tend to be more flexible than key-value store databases. Semi-structured or unstructured data that does not neatly fit into rows and columns can share the same database with organized time-series data. Unstructured data can take many forms; two examples are a photograph of a finished good on a manufacturing line used for QA and a maintenance report from a piece of equipment.

Many NoSQL databases provide additional capabilities, such as being able to query and analyze data within the database itself, eliminating the need to move and process it elsewhere. They also provide a variety of ways to query the database through an API, making it easy to integrate them with other data management applications.

Hadoop

Hadoop is the most recent entrant into the data management market, but it is arguably the most popular choice as a data repository and processing engine. Hadoop was originally developed as a result of projects at Google and Yahoo!, and the original intent for Hadoop was to index millions of websites and quickly return search results for open source search engines. Initially, the project had two key elements:

- **Hadoop Distributed File System (HDFS):** A system for storing data across multiple nodes

- **MapReduce:** A distributed processing engine that splits a large task into smaller ones that can be run in parallel

Both of these elements are still present in current Hadoop distributions and provide the foundation for other projects that are discussed later in this chapter.

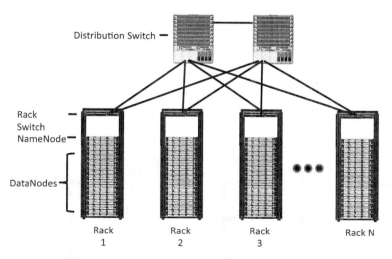

Figure 7-8 *Distributed Hadoop Cluster*

Much like the MPP and NoSQL systems discussed earlier, Hadoop relies on a scale-out architecture that leverages local processing, memory, and storage to distribute tasks and provide a scalable storage system for data. Both MapReduce and HDFS take advantage of this distributed architecture to store and process massive amounts of data and are thus able to leverage resources from all nodes in the cluster. For HDFS, this capability is handled by specialized nodes in the cluster, including NameNodes and DataNodes (see Figure 7-8):

■ **NameNodes:** These are a critical piece in data adds, moves, deletes, and reads on HDFS. They coordinate where the data is stored, and maintain a map of where each block of data is stored and where it is replicated. All interaction with HDFS is coordinated through the primary (active) NameNode, with a secondary (standby) NameNode notified of the changes in the event of a failure of the primary. The NameNode takes write requests from clients and distributes those files across the available nodes in configurable block sizes, usually 64 MB or 128 MB blocks. The NameNode is also responsible for instructing the DataNodes where replication should occur.

■ **DataNodes:** These are the servers where the data is stored at the direction of the NameNode. It is common to have many DataNodes in a Hadoop cluster to store the data. Data blocks are distributed across several nodes and often are replicated three, four, or more times across nodes for redundancy. Once data is written to one of the DataNodes, the DataNode selects two (or more) additional nodes, based on replication policies, to ensure data redundancy across the cluster. Disk redundancy techniques such as Redundant Array of Independent Disks (RAID) are generally not used for HDFS because the NameNodes and DataNodes coordinate block-level redundancy with this replication technique.

Figure 7-9 shows the relationship between NameNodes and DataNodes and how data blocks are distributed across the cluster.

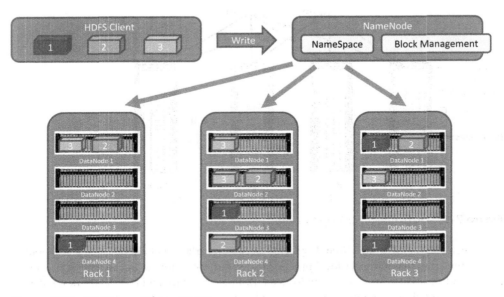

Figure 7-9   *Writing a File to HDFS*

MapReduce leverages a similar model to batch process the data stored on the cluster nodes. Batch processing is the process of running a scheduled or ad hoc query across historical data stored in the HDFS. A query is broken down into smaller tasks and distributed across all the nodes running MapReduce in a cluster. While this is useful for understanding patterns and trending in historical sensor or machine data, it has one significant drawback: time. Depending on how much data is being queried and the complexity of the query, the result could take seconds or minutes to return. If you have a real-time process running where you need a result at a moment's notice, MapReduce is not the right data processing engine for that. (Real-time streaming analytics is discussed later in this chapter.)

YARN

Introduced with version 2.0 of Hadoop, YARN (Yet Another Resource Negotiator) was designed to enhance the functionality of MapReduce. With the initial release, MapReduce was responsible for batch data processing and job tracking and resource management across the cluster. YARN was developed to take over the resource negotiation and job/task tracking, allowing MapReduce to be responsible only for data processing.

With the development of a dedicated cluster resource scheduler, Hadoop was able to add additional data processing modules to its core feature set, including interactive SQL and real-time processing, in addition to batch processing using MapReduce.

The Hadoop Ecosystem

As mentioned earlier, Hadoop plays an increasingly big role in the collection, storage, and processing of IoT data due to its highly scalable nature and its ability to work with large volumes of data. Many organizations have adopted Hadoop clusters for storage and processing of data and have looked for complimentary software packages to add additional functionality to their distributed Hadoop clusters. Since the initial release of Hadoop in 2011, many projects have been developed to add incremental functionality to Hadoop and have collectively become known as the *Hadoop ecosystem*.

Hadoop may have had meager beginnings as a system for distributed storage and processing, but it has since grown into a robust collection of projects that, combined, create a very complete data management and analytics framework. Hadoop now comprises more than 100 software projects under the Hadoop umbrella, capable of nearly every element in the data lifecycle, from collection, to storage, to processing, to analysis and visualization. Each of these individual projects is a unique piece of the overall data management solution. The following sections describe several of these packages and discuss how they are used to collect or process data.

Apache Kafka

Part of processing real-time events, such as those commonly generated by smart objects, is having them ingested into a processing engine. The process of collecting data from a sensor or log file and preparing it to be processed and analyzed is typically handled by messaging systems. Messaging systems are designed to accept data, or messages, from where the data is generated and deliver the data to stream-processing engines such as Spark Streaming or Storm. Apache Kafka is a distributed publisher-subscriber messaging system that is built to be scalable and fast. It is composed of topics, or message brokers, where producers write data and consumers read data from these topics. Figure 7-10 shows the data flow from the smart objects (producers), through a topic in Kafka, to the real-time processing engine. Due to the distributed nature of Kafka, it can run in a clustered configuration that can handle many producers and consumers simultaneously and exchanges information between nodes, allowing topics to be distributed over multiple nodes. The goal of Kafka is to provide a simple way to connect to data sources and allow consumers to connect to that data in the way they would like. The following sections describe several of these packages and discusses how they are used to collect or process data.

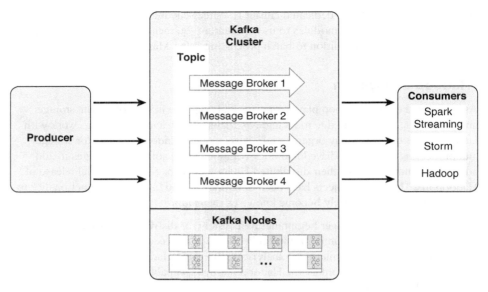

Figure 7-10   *Apache Kafka Data Flow*

Apache Spark

Apache Spark is an in-memory distributed data analytics platform designed to accelerate processes in the Hadoop ecosystem. The "in-memory" characteristic of Spark is what enables it to run jobs very quickly. At each stage of a MapReduce operation, the data is read and written back to the disk, which means latency is introduced through each disk operation. However, with Spark, the processing of this data is moved into high-speed memory, which has significantly lower latency. This speeds the batch processing jobs and also allows for near-real-time processing of events.

Real-time processing is done by a component of the Apache Spark project called Spark Streaming. Spark Streaming is an extension of Spark Core that is responsible for taking live streamed data from a messaging system, like Kafka, and dividing it into smaller microbatches. These microbatches are called discretized streams, or DStreams. The Spark processing engine is able to operate on these smaller pieces of data, allowing rapid insights into the data and subsequent actions. Due to this "instant feedback" capability, Spark is becoming an important component in many IoT deployments. Systems that control safety and security of personnel, time-sensitive processes in the manufacturing space, and infrastructure control in traffic management all benefit from these real-time streaming capabilities.

Apache Storm and Apache Flink

As you work with the Hadoop ecosystem, you will inevitably notice that different projects are very similar and often have significant overlap with other projects. This is the case with data streaming capabilities. For example, Apache Spark is often used for both distributed streaming analytics and batch processing. Apache Storm and Apache Flink are other Hadoop ecosystem projects designed for distributed stream processing and are commonly deployed for IoT use cases. Storm can pull data from Kafka and process it in a near-real-time fashion, and so can Apache Flink. This space is rapidly evolving, and projects will continue to gain and lose popularity as they evolve.

Lambda Architecture

Ultimately the key elements of a data infrastructure to support many IoT use cases involves the collection, processing, and storage of data using multiple technologies. Querying both data in motion (streaming) and data at rest (batch processing) requires a combination of the Hadoop ecosystem projects discussed. One architecture that is currently being leveraged for this functionality is the Lambda Architecture. Lambda is a data management system that consists of two layers for ingesting data (Batch and Stream) and one layer for providing the combined data (Serving). These layers allow for the packages discussed previously, like Spark and MapReduce, to operate on the data independently, focusing on the key attributes for which they are designed and optimized. Data is taken from a message broker, commonly Kafka, and processed by each layer in parallel, and the resulting data is delivered to a data store where additional processing or queries can be run. Figure 7-11 shows this parallel data flow through the Lambda Architecture.

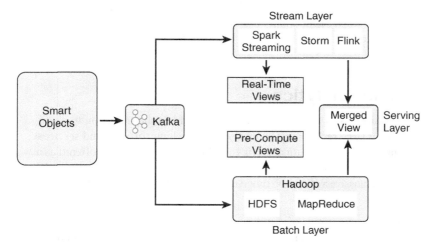

Figure 7-11 *Lambda Architecture*

The Lambda Architecture is not limited to the packages in the Hadoop ecosystem, but due to its breadth and flexibility, many of the packages in the ecosystem fill the requirements of each layer nicely:

- **Stream layer:** This layer is responsible for near-real-time processing of events. Technologies such as Spark Streaming, Storm, or Flink are used to quickly ingest, process, and analyze data on this layer. Alerting and automated actions can be triggered on events that require rapid response or could result in catastrophic outcomes if not handled immediately.

- **Batch layer:** The Batch layer consists of a batch-processing engine and data store. If an organization is using other parts of the Hadoop ecosystem for the other layers, MapReduce and HDFS can easily fit the bill. Other database technologies, such as MPPs, NoSQL, or data warehouses, can also provide what is needed by this layer.

- **Serving layer:** The Serving layer is a data store and mediator that decides which of the ingest layers to query based on the expected result or view into the data. If an aggregate or historical view is requested, it may invoke the Batch layer. If real-time analytics is needed, it may invoke the Stream layer. The Serving layer is often used by the data consumers to access both layers simultaneously.

The Lambda Architecture can provide a robust system for collecting and processing massive amounts of data and the flexibility of being able to analyze that data at different rates. One limitation of this type of architecture is its place in the network. Due to the processing and storage requirements of many of these pieces, the vast majority of these deployments are either in data centers or in the cloud. This could limit the effectiveness of the analytics to respond rapidly enough if the processing systems are milliseconds or seconds away from the device generating the data. When this is the case, a distributed edge-processing architecture may be needed to augment the central data center infrastructure.

Edge Streaming Analytics

A major area of evolution for IT in the past few years has been the transition to cloud services. Nearly every large technology company is now selling software and services from the cloud, and this includes data analytics systems, whether they are offered as a service from a public cloud operator or are built in massive private data center clouds. However, analyzing a massive volume of time-sensitive IoT data in a centralized cloud is often not ideal.

In the world of IoT, vast quantities of data are generated on the fly and often need to be analyzed and responded to immediately. Not only is the volume of data generated at the edge immense—meaning the bandwidth requirements to the cloud or data center need to be engineered to match—but the data may be so time sensitive that it needs immediate attention, and waiting for deep analysis in the cloud simply isn't possible.

One industry where data analytics is used extensively is the world of automobile racing. For example, in Formula One racing, each car has between 150 to 200 sensors that, combined, generate more than 1000 data points per second, resulting in hundreds of gigabytes of raw data per race. The sensor data is transmitted from the car and picked up by track-side wireless sensors. During a race, weather conditions may vary, tire conditions change, and accidents or other racing incidents almost always require an adaptable and flexible racing strategy. As the race develops, decisions such as when to pit, what tires to use, when to pass, and when to slow down all need to be made in seconds. Teams have found that enormous insights leading to better race results can be gained by analyzing data on the fly—and the data may come from many different sources, including trackside sensors, car telemetry, and weather reports.

Most teams use sophisticated data analytics systems to enhance racing strategy, but in many cases, this equipment resides back in the team's data center, far away from the track. For a team that has its analytics software in a data center in the UK, the latency to Australia (the most remote race) is several hundred milliseconds away. The time it takes to collect and analyze this data as a batch process in a distant part of the world is not only inefficient but can mean the difference between a successful race strategy that adapts to changing conditions and one that lacks the flexibility and agility to send meaningful instructions to the drivers. In short, it can mean the difference between winning and losing a race.

Comparing Big Data and Edge Analytics

When you hear the term *big data*, it is usually in reference to unstructured data that has been collected and stored in the cloud. The data is collected over time so that it can be analyzed through batch-processing tools, such as an RDBMS, Hadoop, or some other tool, at which point business insights are gained, and value is drawn from the data. Tools like Hadoop and MapReduce are great at tackling problems that require deep analytics on a large and complex quantity of unstructured data; however, due to their distance from the IoT endpoints and the bandwidth required to bring all the data back to the cloud, they are generally not well suited to real-time analysis of data as it is generated.

In applying data analytics to the car racing example discussed earlier, big data analytics is used to examine all the statistics of the racing team and players based on their performance in the data center or cloud. While big data can apply analytics in real-time (as discussed earlier), it is mainly focused on batch-job analytics on large volumes of data. Streaming analytics involves analyzing a race while it is happening and trying to figure out who is going to win based on the actual performance in real-time—and this analysis is typically performed as close to the edge as possible. Streaming analytics allows you to continually monitor and assess data in real-time so that you can adjust or fine-tune your predictions as the race progresses.

In the context of IoT, with streaming analytics performed at the edge (either at the sensors themselves or very close to them, in a fog node that is, for example, integrated into the gateway), it is possible to process and act on the data in real-time without waiting for the results from a future batch-processing job in the cloud. Does this mean that streaming analytics replaces big data analytics in the cloud? Not at all. They both have roles to play and both contribute to improved business insights and processes.

In one sense, if raw data is generated in the data center, it makes sense to analyze it there. But what if the majority of data is being generated in remote locations by sensors that are spread all over a wide area? To be truly effective at the moment it is created, the data needs to be analyzed and responded to as close to the edge as possible. Once it has been analyzed and reduced at the edge, the resultant data can be sent to the cloud and used to gain deeper insights over time. It is also important to remember that the edge isn't in just one place. The edge is highly distributed, which means analytics at the edge needs to be highly coordinated and structured. This also implies a communications system where edge/fog nodes are able to communicate with each other when necessary and report results to a big data system in the cloud.

From a business perspective, streaming analytics involves acting on data that is generated while it is still valuable, before it becomes stale. For example, roadway sensors combined with GPS wayfinding apps may tell a driver to avoid a certain highway due to traffic. This data is valuable for only a small window of time. Historically, it may be interesting to see how many traffic accidents or blockages have occurred on a certain segment of highway or to predict congestion based on past traffic data. However, for the driver in traffic receiving this information, if the data is not acted upon immediately, the data has little value.

From a security perspective, having instantaneous access to analyzed and preprocessed data at the edge also allows an organization to realize anomalies in its network so those anomalies can be quickly contained before spreading to the rest of the network.

To summarize, the key values of edge streaming analytics include the following:

- **Reducing data at the edge:** The aggregate data generated by IoT devices is generally in proportion to the number of devices. The scale of these devices is likely to be huge, and so is the quantity of data they generate. Passing all this data to the cloud is inefficient and is unnecessarily expensive in terms of bandwidth and network infrastructure.

- **Analysis and response at the edge:** Some data is useful only at the edge (such as a factory control feedback system). In cases such as this, the data is best analyzed and acted upon where it is generated.

- **Time sensitivity:** When timely response to data is required, passing data to the cloud for future processing results in unacceptable latency. Edge analytics allows immediate responses to changing conditions.

Edge Analytics Core Functions

To perform analytics at the edge, data needs to be viewed as real-time flows. Whereas big data analytics is focused on large quantities of data at rest, edge analytics continually processes streaming flows of data in motion. Streaming analytics at the edge can be broken down into three simple stages:

- **Raw input data:** This is the raw data coming from the sensors into the analytics processing unit.

- **Analytics processing unit (APU):** The APU filters and combines data streams (or separates the streams, as necessary), organizes them by time windows, and performs various analytical functions. It is at this point that the results may be acted on by micro services running in the APU.

- **Output streams:** The data that is output is organized into insightful streams and is used to influence the behavior of smart objects, and passed on for storage and further processing in the cloud. Communication with the cloud often happens through a standard publisher/subscriber messaging protocol, such as MQTT.

Figure 7-12 illustrates the stages of data processing in an edge APU.

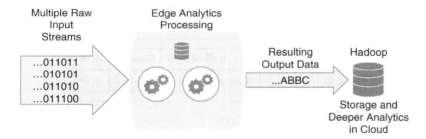

Figure 7-12   *Edge Analytics Processing Unit*

In order to perform analysis in real-time, the APU needs to perform the following functions:

- **Filter:** The streaming data generated by IoT endpoints is likely to be very large, and most of it is irrelevant. For example, a sensor may simply poll on a regular basis to confirm that it is still reachable. This information is not really relevant and can be mostly ignored. The filtering function identifies the information that is considered important.

- **Transform:** In the data warehousing world, Extract, Transform, and Load (ETL) operations are used to manipulate the data structure into a form that can be used for other purposes. Analogous to data warehouse ETL operations, in streaming analytics, once the data is filtered, it needs to be formatted for processing.

- **Time:** As the real-time streaming data flows, a timing context needs to be established. This could be to correlated average temperature readings from sensors on a minute-by-minute basis. For example, Figure 7-13 shows an APU that takes input data from multiple sensors reporting temperature fluctuations. In this case, the APU is programmed to report the average temperature every minute from the sensors, based on an average of the past two minutes. (An example where this may be used is in real-time monitoring of food in a grocery store, where rolling averages of the temperature in open-air refrigeration units needs to be monitored to ensure the safety of the food.) Note that on the left side is the cleaned stream data. This data is presented as streams to the analytics engine (note the syntax at the bottom right of the figure) that establishes the time window and calculates the average temperature over the past two minutes. The results are reported on a per-minute basis (on the right side of the figure).

Defining Streams and Windows

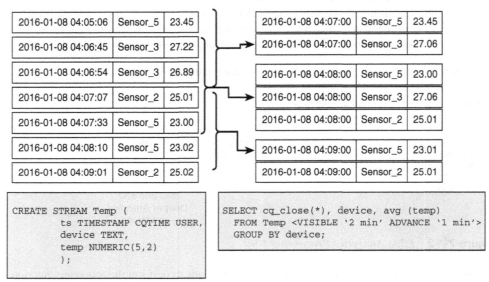

Figure 7-13 *Example: Establishing a Time Window for Analytics of Average Temperature from Sensors*

- **Correlate:** Streaming data analytics becomes most useful when multiple data streams are combined from different types of sensors. For example, in a hospital, several vital signs are measured for patients, including body temperature, blood pressure, heart rate, and respiratory rate. These different types of data come from different instruments, but when this data is combined and analyzed, it provides an invaluable picture of the health of the patient at any given time.[4] However, correlation goes beyond just combining real-time data streams. Another key aspect is combining and correlating real-time measurements with preexisting, or historical, data. For example, historical data may include the patient's past medical history, such as blood test results. Combining historical data gives the live streaming data a powerful context and promotes more insights into the current condition of the patient (see Figure 7-14).

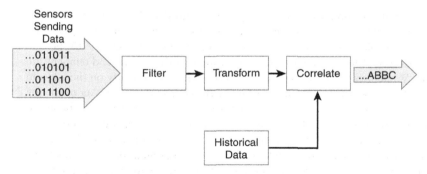

Figure 7-14 *Correlating Data Streams with Historical Data*

■ **Match patterns:** Once the data streams are properly cleaned, transformed, and cor-related with other live streams as well as historical data sets, pattern matching opera-tions are used to gain deeper insights to the data. For example, say that the APU has been collecting the patient's vitals for some time and has gained an understanding of the expected patterns for each variable being monitored. If an unexpected event arises, such as a sudden change in heart rate or respiration, the pattern matching operator recognizes this as out of the ordinary and can take certain actions, such as generating an alarm to the nursing staff. The patterns can be simple relationships, or they may be complex, based on the criteria defined by the application. Machine learning may be leveraged to identify these patterns.

■ **Improve business intelligence:** Ultimately, the value of edge analytics is in the improvements to business intelligence that were not previously available. For example, conducting edge analytics on patients in a hospital allows staff to respond more quickly to the patient's changing needs and also reduces the volume of unstruc-tured (and not always useful) data sent to the cloud. Over time, the resulting changes in business logic can produce improvements in basic operations, bringing in higher levels of care as well as better efficiencies for the hospital.

Distributed Analytics Systems

Depending on the application and network architecture, analytics can happen at any point throughout the IoT system. Streaming analytics may be performed directly at the edge, in the fog, or in the cloud data center. There are no hard-and-fast rules dictating where analytics should be done, but there are a few guiding principles. We have already discussed the value of reducing the data at the edge, as well as the value of analyzing information so it can be responded to before it gets stale. There is also value in stepping back from the edge to gain a wider view with more data. It's hard to see the forest when you are standing in the middle of it staring at a tree. In other words, sometimes better insights can be gained and data responded to more intelligently when we step back from the edge and look at a wider data set.

This is the value of fog computing. (Fog computing is introduced in Chapter 2.) Fog analytics allows you to see beyond one device, giving you visibility into an aggregation of edge nodes and allowing you to correlate data from a wider set. Figure 7-15 shows an example of an oil drilling company that is measuring both pressure and temperature on an oil rig. While there may be some value in doing analytics directly on the edge, in this example, the sensors communicate via MQTT through a message broker to the fog analytics node, allowing a broader data set. (MQTT is discussed in depth in Chapter 6, "Application Protocols for IoT.") The fog node is located on the same oil rig and performs streaming analytics from several edge devices, giving it better insights due to the expanded data set. It may not be able to respond to an event as quickly as analytics performed directly on the edge device, but it is still close to responding in real-time as events occur. Once the fog node is finished with the data, it communicates the results to the cloud (again through a message broker via MQTT) for deeper historical analysis through big data analytics tools.

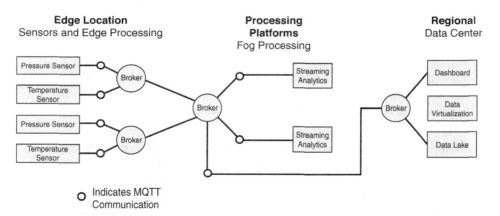

Figure 7-15   *Distributed Analytics Throughout the IoT System*

Network Analytics

Another form of analytics that is extremely important in managing IoT systems is network-based analytics. Unlike the data analytics systems previously discussed that are concerned with finding patterns in the data generated by endpoints, network analytics is concerned with discovering patterns in the communication flows from a network traffic perspective. Network analytics has the power to analyze details of communications patterns made by protocols and correlate this across the network. It allows you to understand what should be considered normal behavior in a network and to quickly identify anomalies that suggest network problems due to suboptimal paths, intrusive malware, or excessive congestion. Analysis of traffic patterns is one of the most powerful tools in an IoT network engineer's troubleshooting arsenal.

As discussed in Chapter 6, IoT endpoints, contrary to generic computing platforms, are designed to directly communicate with a very small number of specific application servers, such as an IoT message or data broker, or specific application servers and network management systems. Therefore, it could be said that IoT solutions and use cases tightly couple devices and applications. Figure 7-16 shows field area network (FAN) traffic analytics performed on the aggregation router in a smart grid.

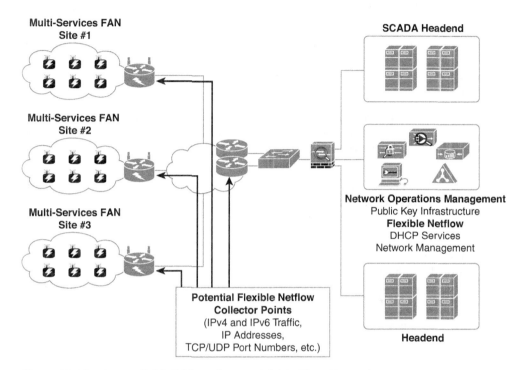

Figure 7-16   *Smart Grid FAN Analytics with NetFlow Example*

This behavior represents a key aspect that can be leveraged when performing network analytics: Network analytics offer capabilities to cope with capacity planning for scalable IoT deployment as well as security monitoring in order to detect abnormal traffic volume and patterns (such as an unusual traffic spike for a normally quiet protocol) for both centralized or distributed architectures, such as fog computing.

Consider that an IoT device sends its traffic to specific servers, either directly to an application or an IoT broker with the data payload encapsulated in a given protocol. This represents a pair of source and destination addresses, as well as application layer–dependent TCP or UDP port numbers, which can be used for network analytics.

One of the drivers of the adoption of an IP architectural framework for IoT is to leverage tools and processes largely known and deployed by Internet service providers (ISPs) as well as private corporate enterprise networks. To monitor network infrastructure, de facto industry standards and protocols allow pervasive characterization of IP traffic flows, including identification of source and/or destination addresses, data timing and volume, and application types within a network infrastructure. Flow statistics can be collected at different locations in the network. For example, centralized routers or switches that aggregate subnetworks as well as nodes that are highly distributed and connect the last mile of the infrastructure can be used to collect flow information. After data is collected in a known format, it can be sent to an external network analytics tools that delivers unique services to network managers, like security and performance monitoring and capacity planning.

In the context of IoT infrastructure deployments, for technologies discussed in Chapter 4, "Connecting Smart Objects," Chapter 5, "IP as the IoT Network Layer," and Chapter 6, the benefits of flow analytics, in addition to other network management services, are as follows:

- **Network traffic monitoring and profiling:** Flow collection from the network layer provides global and distributed near-real-time monitoring capabilities. IPv4 and IPv6 networkwide traffic volume and pattern analysis helps administrators proactively detect problems and quickly troubleshoot and resolve problems when they occur.

- **Application traffic monitoring and profiling:** Monitoring and profiling can be used to gain a detailed time-based view of IoT access services, such as the application-layer protocols, including MQTT, CoAP, and DNP3, as well as the associated applications that are being used over the network.

- **Capacity planning:** Flow analytics can be used to track and anticipate IoT traffic growth and help in the planning of upgrades when deploying new locations or services by analyzing captured data over a long period of time. This analysis affords the opportunity to track and anticipate IoT network growth on a continual basis.

- **Security analysis:** Because most IoT devices typically generate a low volume of traffic and always send their data to the same server(s), any change in network traffic behavior may indicate a cyber security event, such as a denial of service (DoS) attack. Security can be enforced by ensuring that no traffic is sent outside the scope of the IoT domain. For example, with a LoRaWAN gateway, there should be no reason to see traffic sent or received outside the LoRaWAN network server and network management system. Such traffic could indicate an attack of some sort.

- **Accounting:** In field area networks, routers or gateways are often physically isolated and leverage public cellular services and VPNs for backhaul. Deployments may have thousands of gateways connecting the last-mile IoT infrastructure over a cellular network. Flow monitoring can thus be leveraged to analyze and optimize the billing, in complement with other dedicated applications, such as Cisco Jasper, with a broader scope than just monitoring data flow.

- **Data warehousing and data mining:** Flow data (or derived information) can be warehoused for later retrieval and analysis in support of proactive analysis of multiservice IoT infrastructures and applications.

Flexible NetFlow Architecture

Flexible NetFlow (FNF) and IETF IPFIX (RFC 5101, RFC 5102) are examples of protocols that are widely used for networks. This section examines the fundamentals of FNF and how it may be used in an IoT deployment.

FNF is a flow technology developed by Cisco Systems that is widely deployed all over the world. Key advantages of FNF are as follows:

- Flexibility, scalability, and aggregation of flow data

- Ability to monitor a wide range of packet information and produce new information about network behavior

- Enhanced network anomaly and security detection

- User-configurable flow information for performing customized traffic identification and ability to focus and monitor specific network behavior

- Convergence of multiple accounting technologies into one accounting mechanism

FNF Components

FNF has the following main components, as shown in Figure 7-17:

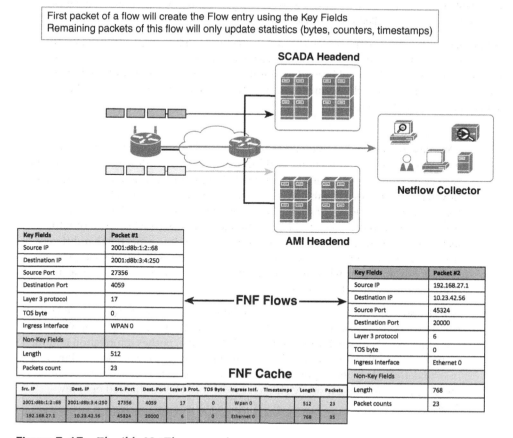

Figure 7-17   *Flexible NetFlow overview*

- **FNF Flow Monitor (NetFlow cache):** The FNF Flow Monitor describes the NetFlow cache or information stored in the cache. The Flow Monitor contains the flow record definitions with key fields (used to create a flow, unique per flow record: match statement) and non-key fields (collected with the flow as attributes or characteristics of a flow) within the cache. Also, part of the Flow Monitor is the Flow Exporter, which contains information about the export of NetFlow information, including the destination address of the NetFlow collector. The Flow Monitor includes various cache characteristics, including timers for exporting, the size of the cache, and, if required, the packet sampling rate.

Note   Each packet that is forwarded within a router or switch is examined for a set of IP packet attributes. These attributes are the IP packet identity, or *key fields*, for the flow and determine whether the packet information is unique or similar to other packets. If packet key fields are unique, a new entry in the flow record is created. The first packet of a flow creates the flow entry, using the key fields. Remaining packets of this flow only update statistics (bytes, counters, timestamps). This methodology of flow characterization is scalable because a large amount of network information is condensed into a database of NetFlow information called the *NetFlow cache*.

Additional information (non-key fields) can be added to the Flow Record and exported. The non-key fields are not used to create or characterize the flows but are exported and just added to the flow. If a field is non-key, normally only the first packet of the flow is used for the value in this field. Examples include flow timestamps, next-hop IP addresses, subnet masks, and TCP flags.

- **FNF flow record:** A flow record is a set of key and non-key NetFlow field values used to characterize flows in the NetFlow cache. Flow records may be predefined for ease of use or customized and user defined. A typical predefined record aggregates flow data and allows users to target common applications for NetFlow. User-defined records allow selections of specific key or non-key fields in the flow record. The user-defined field is the key to Flexible NetFlow, allowing a wide range of information to be characterized and exported by NetFlow. It is expected that different network management applications will support specific user-defined and predefined flow records based on what they are monitoring (for example, security detection, traffic analysis, capacity planning).

- **FNF Exporter:** There are two primary methods for accessing NetFlow data: Using the **show** commands at the command-line interface (CLI), and using an application reporting tool. NetFlow Export, unlike SNMP polling, pushes information periodically to the NetFlow reporting collector. The Flexible NetFlow Exporter allows the user to define where the export can be sent, the type of transport for the export, and properties for the export. Multiple exporters can be configured per Flow Monitor.

■ **Flow export timers:** Timers indicate how often flows should be exported to the collection and reporting server.

■ **NetFlow export format:** This simply indicates the type of flow reporting format.

■ **NetFlow server for collection and reporting:** This is the destination of the flow export. It is often done with an analytics tool that looks for anomalies in the traffic patterns.

Figure 7-18 illustrates the analysis reported from the FNF records on a smart grid FAN. In this example, the FNF collector is able to see the patterns of traffic for various applications as well as management traffic on the FAN.

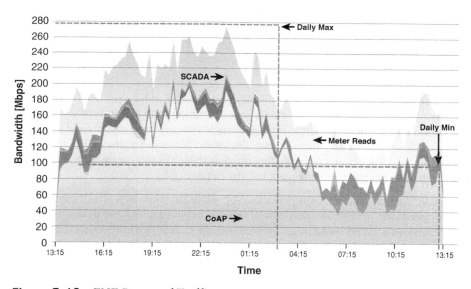

Figure 7-18   *FNF Report of Traffic on a Smart Grid FAN*

Flexible NetFlow in Multiservice IoT Networks

In the context of multiservice IoT networks, it is recommended that FNF be configured on the routers that aggregate connections from the last mile's routers. This gives a global view of all services flowing between the core network in the cloud and the IoT last-mile network (although not between IoT devices). FNF can also be configured on the last-mile gateway or fog nodes to provide more granular visibility. However, care must be taken in terms of how much northbound data is consumed through reporting.

However, flow analysis at the gateway is not possible with all IoT systems. For example, LoRaWAN gateways simply forward MAC-layer sensor traffic to the centralized LoRaWAN network server, which means flow analysis (based on Layer 3) is not possible at this point. A similar problem is encountered when using an MQTT server that sends data through an IoT broker. Some other challenges with deploying flow analytics tools in an IoT network include the following:

- The distributed nature of fog and edge computing may mean that traffic flows are processed in places that might not support flow analytics, and visibility is thus lost.

- IPv4 and IPv6 native interfaces sometimes need to inspect inside VPN tunnels, which may impact the router's performance.

- Additional network management traffic is generated by FNF reporting devices. The added cost of increasing bandwidth thus needs to be reviewed, especially if the backhaul network uses cellular or satellite communications.

In summary, existing network analytics protocols and tools may be leveraged to provide great value for IoT environments, helping to both automate and secure them.

Summary

IoT systems are producing vast volumes of data—far more than has ever been available in the past. This new paradigm of continual data generation from all forms of connected and networked instruments has created an opportunity to gain new insights and improve efficiencies like never before. The business value of IoT is not just in the ability to connect devices but comes from understanding the data these devices create. A new form of data management has therefore emerged: IoT data analytics.

Traditionally data management was performed by relational databases, which cared for well-structured data in tables where the relationships between tables and data structures were well understood and could be easily accessed through SQL. However, the majority of data generated by IoT devices is unstructured. As the IoT data is collected over time, it becomes big data and requires special handling in order to reveal the patterns within the lake of data.

To unlock the value of the data, special algorithms that perform machine learning are required to process the data and find patterns. Different types of machine learning can be used for specific purposes, including supervised, unsupervised, and neural networks.

Processing of aggregate IoT data happens in the cloud or data center and is performed by big data analytics systems, such as NoSQL, Hadoop, and MPP. These systems are specifically designed to deal with the vast volume, velocity, and variety of data generated by IoT systems.

Over time, streaming edge analytics systems have been developed to not only filter and reduce the data generated by IoT devices but also to allow near-real-time response to the IoT deices as close to the edge of the network as possible.

Finally, a different form of analytics, network analytics, is discussed in this chapter. Network analytics doesn't look at the content of the data but rather is used to discover patterns in the communications behavior of the network, helping identify and prevent security vulnerabilities, plan network evolution, and better understand the behavior of the various network elements.

In summary, network analytics comes in many shapes and forms. Each of them plays a key role in the world of IoT and helps define the true value that comes from connecting things.

References

1. Bhoopathi Rapolu, *Internet of Aircraft Things: An Industry Set to Be Transformed*, January 18, 2016, http://aviationweek.com/connected-aerospace/internet-aircraft-things-industry-set-be-transformed.

2. Goutam Chakraborty and Murali Krishna Pagolu, *Analysis of Unstructured Data: Applications of Text Analytics and Sentiment Mining*, https://support.sas.com/resources/papers/proceedings14/1288-2014.pdf

3. Bernard Marr, *That's Data Science: Airbus Puts 10,000 Sensors in Every Single Wing!* April 9, 2015, www.datasciencecentral.com/profiles/blogs/that-s-data-science-airbus-puts-10-000-sensors-in-every-single.

4. William Vorhies, *Stream Processing and Streaming Analytics—How It Works*, October 29, 2015, www.datasciencecentral.com/profiles/blogs/stream-processing-and-streaming-analytics-how-it-works.

Chapter 8

Securing IoT

It is often said that if World War III breaks out, it will be fought in cyberspace. As IoT brings more and more systems together under the umbrella of network connectivity, security has never been more important. From the electrical grid system that powers our world, to the lights that control the flow of traffic in a city, to the systems that keep airplanes flying in an organized and efficient way, security of the networks, devices, and the applications that use them is foundational and essential for all modern communications systems. Providing security in such a world is not easy. Security is among the very few, if not the only, technology disciplines that must operate with external forces continually working against desired outcomes. To further complicate matters, these external forces are able to leverage traditional technology as well as nontechnical methods (for example, physical security, operational processes, and so on) to meet their goals. With so many potential attack vectors, information and cybersecurity is a challenging, but engaging, topic that is of critical importance to technology vendors, enterprises, and service providers alike.

Information technology (IT) environments have faced active attacks and information security threats for many decades, and the incidents and lessons learned are well-known and documented. By contrast, operational technology (OT) environments were traditionally kept in silos and had only limited connection to other networks. Thus, the history of cyber attacks on OT systems is much shorter and has far fewer incidents documented. Therefore, the learning opportunities and the body of cataloged incidents with their corresponding mitigations are not as rich as in the IT world. Security in the OT world also addresses a wider scope than in the IT world. For example, in OT, the word *security* is almost synonymous with *safety*. In fact, many of the industrial security standards that form the foundation for industrial IoT security also incorporate equipment and personnel safety recommendations.

It is for these reasons that this chapter focuses on the core principles of securing OT environments. IT security is a vast domain with many books dedicated to its various aspects. An exhaustive treatment of the subject is simply not possible in one chapter, so we instead focus on OT security and the elements of IT security that are fundamental to OT security. In addition, the industry-specific chapters in Part III, "IoT in Industry," discuss the application of security to specific industry verticals.

This chapter provides a historical perspective of OT security, how it has evolved, and some of the common challenges it faces. It also details some of the key differences between securing IT and OT environments. Finally, this chapter explores a number of practical steps for creating a more secure industrial environment, including best practices in introducing modern IT network security into legacy industrial environments. It includes the following sections:

■ **A Brief History of OT Security:** This section provides an overview of how OT environments have evolved and the impact that the evolution has had on securing operational networks.

■ **Common Challenges in OT Security:** This section provides a synopsis of different security challenges in operational environments, including legacy systems and insecure protocols and assets.

■ **How IT and OT Security Practices and Systems Vary:** This section provides a comparison between the security practices in enterprise IT environments and operational industrial environments.

■ **Formal Risk Analysis Structures: OCTAVE and FAIR:** This section provides a holistic view of securing an operational environment and a risk assessment framework that includes the people, processes, and vendor ecosystem components that make up a control system.

■ **The Phased Application of Security in an Operational Environment:** This section provides a description of a phased approach to introducing modern network security into largely preexisting legacy industrial networks.

A Brief History of OT Security

To better understand the current situation in industrial environments, it is important to differentiate between assumptions and realities. Few topics in information technology inspire more fear, uncertainty, or doubt than cybersecurity. This chapter is therefore limited to incidents and data sources from official sources rather than public media reports or uncorroborated third-party accounts.

More than in most other sectors, cybersecurity incidents in industrial environments can result in physical consequences that can cause threats to human lives as well as damage to equipment, infrastructure, and the environment. While there are certainly traditional IT-related security threats in industrial environments, it is the physical manifestations and impacts of the OT security incidents that capture media attention and elicit broad-based public concern.

One example of a reported incident where physical damage was caused by a cybersecurity attack is the Stuxnet malware that damaged uranium enrichment systems in Iran. Another example is an event that damaged a furnace in a German smelter. In both incidents, multiple steps led to the undesirable outcomes. Many of the security policies and mitigation procedures that were in place went unheeded; however, if properly implemented, they could have impeded or possibly stopped the attacks entirely. For example, Stuxnet is thought to have been deployed on USB memory sticks up to two years before it was finally identified and discovered.

In addition to physical damage, operational interruptions have occurred in OT environments due to cybersecurity incidents. For example, in 2000, the sewage control system of Maroochy Shire in Queensland, Australia, was accessed remotely, and it released 800,000 liters of sewage into the surrounding waterways. In 2015, the control systems of the Ukrainian power distribution operator Kyiv Oblenergo were remotely accessed by attackers, causing an outage that lasted several hours and resulted in days of degraded service for thousands of customers. In both cases, known mitigation techniques could have been applied to detect the attacks earlier or block the ability to hijack production systems and affect service.

Historically, attackers were skilled individuals with deep knowledge of technology and the systems they were attacking. However, as technology has advanced, tools have been created to make attacks much easier to carry out. To further complicate matters, these tools have become more broadly available and more easily obtainable. Compounding this problem, many of the legacy protocols used in IoT environments are many decades old, and there was no thought of security when they were first developed. This means that attackers with limited or no technical capabilities now have the potential to launch cyber attacks, greatly increasing the frequency of attacks and the overall threat to end operators. It is, however, a common misconception that attackers always have the advantage and that end operators lack effective defensive capabilities. An important advantage for operators is the fact that they are far more familiar with their environment and have a better understanding of their processes, and can thus leverage multiple technologies and capabilities to defend their networks against attack. This is critical as networks will continue to face ever-evolving and changing methods of attack that will be increasingly difficult to defend against and respond to.

Communication networks, both local and geographically dispersed, have been used in industrial environments for decades. For example, remote monitoring of substations in utilities and communications between semi-autonomous systems in manufacturing are long-standing examples of such OT networks. These OT-specific communication systems have typically been standalone and physically isolated from the traditional IT enterprise networks in the same companies. While it follows the traditional logic of "security through obscurity," this form of network compartmentalization has led to the independent evolution of IT and OT networks, with interconnections between the environments strictly segregated and monitored.

The isolation between industrial networks and the traditional IT business networks has been referred to as an "air gap," suggesting that there are no links between the two. While there are clearly examples of such extreme isolation in some industries, it is actually not an accurate description of most IoT networks today. Broadly speaking, there is a varying amount of interconnection between OT and IT network environments, and many interdependencies between the two influence the level of interconnection.

In addition to the policies, regulations, and governance imposed by the different industrial environments, there is also a certain amount of end-user preference and deployment-specific design that determines the degree of isolation between IT and OT environments. While some organizations continue to maintain strict separation, others are starting to allow certain elements of interconnection. One common example of this is the use of Ethernet and IP to transport control systems in industrial environments. As much as IT and OT networks are still operated and managed separately in a good portion of the world, the prevailing trend is to consolidate networks based on IT-centric technologies such as TCP/IP, Ethernet, and common APIs.

This evolution of ever-increasing IT technologies in the OT space comes with the benefits of increased accessibility and a larger base of skilled operators than with the nonstandard and proprietary communication methods in traditional industrial environments. The challenges associated with these well-known IT standards is that security vulnerabilities are more widely known, and abuse of those systems is often easier and occurs on a much larger scale. This accessibility and scale makes security a major concern, particularly because many systems and devices in the operational domain were never envisioned to run on a shared, open standards–based infrastructure, and they were not designed and developed with high levels of built-in security capabilities.

Projects in industrial environments are often capital intensive, with an expected life span that can be measured in decades. Unlike in IT-based enterprises, OT-deployed solutions commonly have no reason to change as they are designed to meet specific (and often single-use) functions, and have no requirements or incentives to be upgraded. A huge focus and priority in OT is system uptime and high availability, so changes are typically only made to fix faults or introduce new system capabilities in support of that goal. As a result, deployed OT systems often have slower development and upgrade cycles and can quickly become out of sync with traditional IT network environments. The outcome is that both OT technologies and the knowledge of those looking after those operational systems have progressed at a slower pace than their IT counterparts.

Most of the industrial control systems deployed today, their components, and the limited associated security elements were designed when adherence to published and open standards were rare. The proprietary nature of these systems meant that threats from the outside world were unlikely to occur and were rarely addressed. There has, however, been a growing trend whereby OT system vulnerabilities have been exposed and reported. This increase is depicted in Figure 8-1, which shows the history of vulnerability disclosures in industrial control systems (ICSs) since 2010. While the number of reports has been increasing over the past years, it is likely that there are still many others that are not reported or discovered.

ICS Reported Vulnerabilities

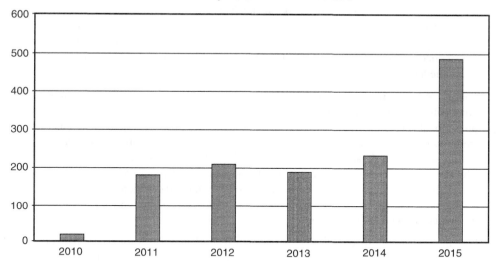

Figure 8-1 *History of Vulnerability Disclosures in Industrial Control Systems Since 2010 (US Industrial Control Systems Cyber Emergency Response Team (ICS-CERT) https://ics-cert.us-cert.gov).*

Given the slow rate of change and extended upgrade cycles of most OT environments, the investment in security for industrial communication and compute technologies has historically lagged behind the investment in securing traditional IT enterprise environments.

Common Challenges in OT Security

The security challenges faced in IoT are by no means new and are not limited to specific industrial environments. The following sections discuss some of the common challenges faced in IoT.

Erosion of Network Architecture

Two of the major challenges in securing industrial environments have been initial design and ongoing maintenance. The initial design challenges arose from the concept that networks were safe due to physical separation from the enterprise with minimal or no connectivity to the outside world, and the assumption that attackers lacked sufficient knowledge to carry out security attacks. In many cases, the initial network design is sound and even follows well-defined industrial best practices and standards, such as the Purdue Model for Control Hierarchy that was introduced in Chapter 2, "IoT Network Architecture and Design." The challenge, and the biggest threat to network security, is standards and best practices either being misunderstood or the network being poorly maintained. In fact, from a security design perspective, it is better to know that communication paths are insecure than to not know the actual communication paths. It is more common that, over time, what may have been a solid design to begin with is eroded through ad hoc updates and individual changes to hardware and machinery without consideration for the broader network impact. This kind of organic growth has led to miscalculations of expanding networks and the introduction of wireless communication in a standalone fashion, without consideration of the impact to the original security design. These uncontrolled or poorly controlled OT network evolutions have, in many cases, over time led to weak or inadequate network and systems security.

There is a wide variety in secured network designs within and across different industries. For example, power utilities have a strong history of leveraging modern technologies for operational activities, and in North America there are regulatory requirements in place from regulatory authorities, such as North American Electric Reliability Corporation's (NERC's) Critical Infrastructure Protection (CIP), discussed in greater detail in Chapter 11, "Utilities"), to implement secure network connectivity and control with reasonably prescriptive actions. By contrast, in other industries, there are often no legislative requirements or compliance policies, which has resulted in widespread differences in security capabilities.

In many industries, the control systems consist of packages, skids, or components that are self-contained and may be integrated as semi-autonomous portions of the network. These packages may not be as fully or tightly integrated into the overall control system, network management tools, or security applications, resulting in potential risk.

Pervasive Legacy Systems

Due to the static nature and long lifecycles of equipment in industrial environments, many operational systems may be deemed legacy systems. For example, in a power utility environment, it is not uncommon to have racks of old mechanical equipment still operating alongside modern intelligent electronic devices (IEDs). In many cases, legacy components are not restricted to isolated network segments but have now been consolidated into the IT operational environment. From a security perspective, this is potentially dangerous as many devices may have historical vulnerabilities or weaknesses that have not been patched and updated, or it may be that patches are not even available due to the age of the equipment.

Beyond the endpoints, the communication infrastructure and shared centralized compute resources are often not built to comply with modern standards. In fact, their communication methods and protocols may be generations old and must be interoperable with the oldest operating entity in the communications path. This includes switches, routers, firewalls, wireless access points, servers, remote access systems, patch management, and network management tools. All of these may have exploitable vulnerabilities and must be protected.

Insecure Operational Protocols

Many industrial control protocols, particularly those that are serial based, were designed without inherent strong security requirements. Furthermore, their operation was often within an assumed secure network. In addition to any inherent weaknesses or vulnerabilities, their operational environment may not have been designed with secured access control in mind.

Industrial protocols, such as supervisory control and data acquisition (SCADA) (refer to Chapter 6, "Application Protocols for IoT"), particularly the older variants, suffer from common security issues. Three examples of this are a frequent lack of authentication between communication endpoints, no means of securing and protecting data at rest or in motion, and insufficient granularity of control to properly specify recipients or avoid default broadcast approaches. These may not be as critical in self-contained systems, but between zones or on longer network segments, such as a WAN (particularly a public WAN), they may be significant considerations.

The structure and operation of most of these protocols is often publicly available. While they may have been originated by a private firm, for the sake of interoperability, they are typically published for others to implement. Thus, it becomes a relatively simple matter to compromise the protocols themselves and introduce malicious actors that may use them to compromise control systems for either reconnaissance or attack purposes that could lead to undesirable impacts in normal system operation.

The following sections discuss some common industrial protocols and their respective security concerns. Note that many have serial, IP, or Ethernet-based versions, and the security challenges and vulnerabilities are different for the different variants.

Modbus

Modbus is commonly found in many industries, such as utilities and manufacturing environments, and has multiple variants (for example, serial, TCP/IP). It was created by the first programmable logic controller (PLC) vendor, Modicon, and has been in use since the 1970s. It is one of the most widely used protocols in industrial deployments, and its development is governed by the Modbus Organization. For more details on Modbus, refer to Chapter 6.

The security challenges that have existed with Modbus are not unusual. Authentication of communicating endpoints was not a default operation because it would allow an inappropriate source to send improper commands to the recipient. For example, for a message to reach its destination, nothing more than the proper Modbus address and function call (code) is necessary.

Some older and serial-based versions of Modbus communicate via broadcast. The ability to curb the broadcast function does not exist in some versions. There is potential for a recipient to act on a command that was not specifically targeting it. Furthermore, an attack could potentially impact unintended recipient devices, thus reducing the need to understand the details of the network topology.

Validation of the Modbus message content is also not performed by the initiating application. Instead, Modbus depends on the network stack to perform this function. This could open up the potential for protocol abuse in the system.

DNP3 (Distributed Network Protocol)

DNP3 is found in multiple deployment scenarios and industries. It is common in utilities and is also found in discrete and continuous process systems. Like many other ICS/SCADA protocols, it was intended for serial communication between controllers and simple IEDs. (For more detailed information on DNP3, refer to Chapter 6.)

There is an explicit "secure" version of DNP3, but there also remain many insecure implementations of DNP3 as well. DNP3 has placed great emphasis on the reliable delivery of messages. That emphasis, while normally highly desirable, has a specific weakness from a security perspective. In the case of DNP3, participants allow for unsolicited responses, which could trigger an undesired response. The missing security element here is the ability to establish trust in the system's state and thus the ability to trust the veracity of the information being presented. This is akin to the security flaws presented by Gratuitous ARP messages in Ethernet networks, which has been addressed by Dynamic ARP Inspection (DAI) in modern Ethernet switches.

ICCP (Inter-Control Center Communications Protocol)

ICCP is a common control protocol in utilities across North America that is frequently used to communicate between utilities. Given that it must traverse the boundaries between different networks, it holds an extra level of exposure and risk that could expose a utility to cyber attack.

Unlike other control protocols, ICCP was designed from inception to work across a WAN. Despite this role, initial versions of ICCP had several significant gaps in the area of security. One key vulnerability is that the system did not require authentication for communication. Second, encryption across the protocol was not enabled as a default condition, thus exposing connections to man-in-the-middle (MITM) and replay attacks.

OPC (OLE for Process Control)

OPC is based on the Microsoft interoperability methodology Object Linking and Embedding (OLE). This is an example where an IT standard used within the IT domain and personal computers has been leveraged for use as a control protocol across an industrial network.

In industrial control networks, OPC is limited to operation at the higher levels of the control space, with a dependence on Windows-based platforms. Concerns around OPC begin with the operating system on which it operates. Many of the Windows devices in the operational space are old, not fully patched, and at risk due to a plethora of well-known vulnerabilities. The dependence on OPC may reinforce that dependence. While newer versions of OPC have enhanced security capabilities, they have also opened up new communications modes, which have both positive and negative security potential.

Of particular concern with OPC is the dependence on the Remote Procedure Call (RPC) protocol, which creates two classes of exposure. The first requires you to clearly understand the many vulnerabilities associated with RPC, and the second requires you to identify the level of risk these vulnerabilities bring to a specific network.

International Electrotechnical Commission (IEC) Protocols

The IEC 61850 standard was created to allow vendor-agnostic engineering of power utility systems, which would, in turn, allow interoperability between vendors and standardized communication protocols. Three message types were initially defined: MMS (Manufacturing Message Specification), GOOSE (Generic Object Oriented Substation Event), and SV (Sampled Values). Web services was a fourth protocol that was added later. Here we provide a short summary of each, but for more information on IEC protocols, see Chapter 11:

- **MMS (61850-8.1):** MMS is a client/server protocol that leverages TCP/IP and operates at Layer 3. It provides the same functionality as other SCADA protocols, such as IEC 60870 and Modbus.

- GOOSE (61850-8.1): GOOSE is a Layer 2 protocol that operates via multicast over Ethernet. It allows IEDs to exchange data "horizontally," between bays and between substations, especially for interlocking, measurement, and tripping signals.

- SV (61850-9-2): SV is a Layer 2 protocol that operates via multicast over Ethernet. It carries voltage and current samples, typically on the process bus, but it can also flow over the station bus.

Both GOOSE and SV operate via a publisher/subscriber model, with no reliability mechanism to ensure that data has been received.

IEC 61850 has several known security deficiencies that could be leveraged by skilled attackers to compromise a control system. Authentication is embedded in MMS, but it is based on clear-text passwords, and authentication is not available in GOOSE or SV. Firmware is typically not signed, which means there is no way to verify its authenticity or integrity. GOOSE and SV have limited message integrity, which makes it relatively easy to impersonate a publisher.

When the standard was first released, there was minimal security capability in these protocols, but this is being addressed by IEC 62351 with the introduction of well-known IT-based security measures, such as certificate exchange.

IEC 60870 is widely used for SCADA telecontrol in Europe, particularly in the power utility industry, and for widely geographically dispersed control systems. Part 5 of the standard outlines the communication profiles used between endpoints to exchange telecontrol messages. 60870-5-101 is the serial implementation profile, 60870-5-104 is the IP implementation profile, and 60870-5-103 is used for protection equipment. Again, in the early iterations of IEC 60870-5, security was lacking. This is now being addressed by IEC 62351, with the 60870-5-7 security extensions work, applicable to 60870-101 and 60870-104.

Other Protocols

At times, discussions about the security of industrial systems are decidedly focused on industrial control protocols as if they were the sum total of what would be observed or considered. This assumption is narrow-minded and problematic on many levels. In fact, it is highly recommended that a security practitioner passively identify all aspects of the traffic traversing the network prior to implementing any kind of controls or security measures therein. Of particular importance are proper accounting, handling, and understanding of the most basic protocols, transport mechanisms, and foundational elements of any network, including ARP, UDP, TCP, IP, and SNMP.

Some specialized environments may also have other background control protocols. For example, many IoT networks reach all the way to the individual sensors, so protocols such as Constrained Application Protocol (CoAP) (see Chapter 6) and Datagram Transport Layer Security (DTLS) are used, and have to be considered separately from a security perspective.

Device Insecurity

Beyond the communications protocols that are used and the installation base of legacy systems, control and communication elements themselves have a history of vulnerabilities. As mentioned earlier in this chapter (see Figure 8-1), prior to 2010, the security community paid little attention to industrial compute, and as a result, OT systems have not gone through the same "trial by fire" as IT systems. Figure 8-2 shows this graphically by simply overlaying the count of industrial security topics presented at the Black Hat security conference with the number of vulnerabilities reported for industrial control systems. The correlation between presentations on the subject of OT security at Black Hat and the number of vulnerabilities discovered is obvious, including the associated slowing of discoveries.

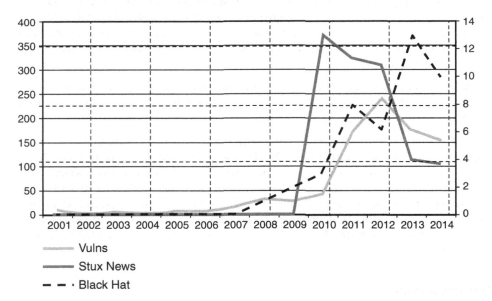

Figure 8-2 *Correlation of Industrial Black Hat Presentations with Discovered Industrial Vulnerabilities (US Industrial Control Systems Cyber Emergency Response Team (ICS-CERT) https://ics-cert.us-cert.gov).*

To understand the nature of the device insecurity, it is important to review the history of what vulnerabilities were discovered and what types of devices were affected. A review of the time period 2000 to 2010 reveals that the bulk of discoveries were at the higher levels of the operational network, including control systems trusted to operate plants, transmission systems, oil pipelines, or whatever critical function is in use.

It is not difficult to understand why such systems are frequently found vulnerable. First, many of the systems utilize software packages that can be easily downloaded and worked against. Second, they operate on common hardware and standard operating systems, such as Microsoft Windows. Third, Windows and the components used within those applications are well known to traditionally IT-focused security researchers. There is little need to develop new tools or techniques when those that have long been in place are sufficiently adequate to breach the target's defenses. For example, Stuxnet, the most famous of the industrial compute-based attacks, was initially successful because it was able to exploit a previously unknown vulnerability in Windows.

The ICS vendor community is also lagging behind IT counterparts with regard to security capabilities and practices, as well as cooperation with third-party security researchers. That said, this situation is beginning to get significant industry focus and is improving through a number of recent initiatives designed to formally address security vulnerability and system testing in the industrial environment. While there are some formal standards, such as ISO/IEC 15408 (Common Criteria), ISO/IEC 19790, and a few others, there remain few formal security testing entities. Beyond formal testing, there is little regulatory enforcement of common criteria that address device security testing.

It was not too long ago that the security research community was viewed as a threat, rather than as a valued and often free service to expose potential dangers. While the situation has improved, operational efforts still significantly lag behind IT-based initiatives, such as bug bounty reward programs and advanced vulnerability preparation programs, along the lines of something like the Microsoft Active Protections Program (MAPP). To go a step further, in the industrial realm, there aren't even parallels to the laws that protect individuals' private data. While many states and countries require notification if an individual's personal and financial data is possibly exposed, outside the electrical utility industry, very few laws require the reporting of incidents that may have put lives at risk.

Dependence on External Vendors

While modern IT environments may be outsourcing business operations or relegating certain processing or storage functions to the cloud, it is less common for the original equipment manufacturers of the IT hardware assets to be required to operate the equipment. However, that level of vendor dependence is not uncommon in some industrial spaces.

Direct and on-demand access to critical systems on the plant floor or in the field are sometimes written directly into contracts or are required for valid product warranties. This has clear benefits in many industries as it allows vendors to remotely manage and monitor equipment and to proactively alert the customer if problems are beginning to creep in. While contracts may be written to describe equipment monitoring and management requirements with explicit statements of what type of access is required and under what conditions, they generally fail to address questions of shared liability for security breaches or processes to ensure communication security.

Such vendor dependence and control are not limited to remote access. Onsite management of non-employees that are to be granted compute and network access are also required, but again, control conditions and shared responsibility statements are yet to be observed.

Security Knowledge

In the industrial operations space, the technical investment is primarily in connectivity and compute. It has seen far less investment in security relative to its IT counterpart. According to the research firm Infonetics, the industrial firewall market in 2015 was only approximately 4% the size of the overall firewall market.

Another relevant challenge in terms of OT security expertise is the comparatively higher age of the industrial workforce. According to a study by the US Bureau of Labor, in North America the average age gap between manufacturing workers and other non-farm workers doubled between 2000 and 2012, and the trend shows no sign of reversing. Simultaneously, new connectivity technologies are being introduced in OT industrial environments that require up-to-date skills, such as TCP/IP, Ethernet, and wireless that are quickly replacing serial-based legacy technologies. The rapid expansion of extended communications networks and the need for an industrial controls-aware workforce creates an equally serious gap in security awareness.

This gap in OT security knowledge is actively being addressed. Education for industrial security environments has grown steadily, particularly in the electrical utility space, where regulations such as NERC CIP (CIP 004) and IEC 62351 (01) require ongoing training.

Due to the importance of security in the industrial space, all likely attack surfaces are treated as unsafe. Unfortunately, considering the potential massive public impact of breaching these systems, there remains a healthy paranoia concerning the connection of IT-centric technologies and external connections, despite the massive amount of investment in security in these areas. Bringing industrial networks up to the latest and most secure levels is a slow process due to deep historical cultural and philosophical differences between OT and IT environments.

How IT and OT Security Practices and Systems Vary

The differences between an enterprise IT environment and an industrial-focused OT deployment are important to understand because they have a direct impact on the security practice applied to them. Some of these areas are touched on briefly earlier in this chapter, and they are more explicitly discussed in the following sections.

The Purdue Model for Control Hierarchy

Regardless of where a security threat arises, it must be consistently and unequivocally treated. IT information is typically used to make business decisions, such as those in process optimization, whereas OT information is instead characteristically leveraged to make physical decisions, such as closing a valve, increasing pressure, and so on. Thus, the operational domain must also address physical safety and environmental factors as part of its security strategy—and this is not normally associated with the IT domain. Organizationally, IT and OT teams and tools have been historically separate, but this has begun to change, and they have started to converge, leading to more traditionally IT-centric solutions being introduced to support operational activities. For example, systems such as firewalls and intrusion prevention systems (IPS) are being used in IoT networks.

As the borders between traditionally separate OT and IT domains blur, they must align strategies and work more closely together to ensure end-to-end security. The types of devices that are found in industrial OT environments are typically much more highly optimized for tasks and industrial protocol-specific operation than their IT counterparts. Furthermore, their operational profile differs as well.

Industrial environments consist of both operational and enterprise domains. To understand the security and networking requirements for a control system, the use of a logical framework to describe the basic composition and function is needed. The Purdue Model for Control Hierarchy, introduced in Chapter 2, is the most widely used framework across industrial environments globally and is used in manufacturing, oil and gas, and many other industries. It segments devices and equipment by hierarchical function levels and areas and has been incorporated into the ISA99/IEC 62443 security standard, as shown in Figure 8-3. For additional detail on how the Purdue Model for Control Hierarchy is applied to the manufacturing and oil and gas industries, see Chapter 9, "Manufacturing," and Chapter 10, "Oil and Gas."

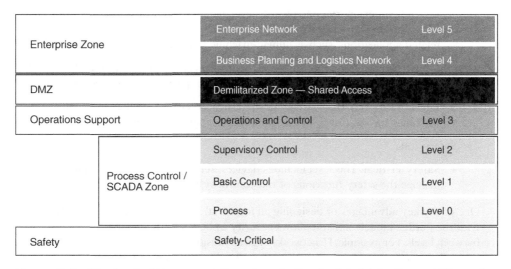

Figure 8-3 *The Logical Framework Based on the Purdue Model for Control Hierarchy*

This model identifies levels of operations and defines each level. The enterprise and operational domains are separated into different zones and kept in strict isolation via an industrial demilitarized zone (DMZ):

- Enterprise zone

  - **Level 5: Enterprise network:** Corporate-level applications such as Enterprise Resource Planning (ERP), Customer Relationship Management (CRM), document management, and services such as Internet access and VPN entry from the outside world exist at this level.

  - **Level 4: Business planning and logistics network:** The IT services exist at this level and may include scheduling systems, material flow applications, optimization and planning systems, and local IT services such as phone, email, printing, and security monitoring.

- Industrial demilitarized zone

  - **DMZ:** The DMZ provides a buffer zone where services and data can be shared between the operational and enterprise zones. It also allows for easy segmentation of organizational control. By default, no traffic should traverse the DMZ; everything should originate from or terminate on this area.

- Operational zone

  - **Level 3: Operations and control:** This level includes the functions involved in managing the workflows to produce the desired end products and for monitoring and controlling the entire operational system. This could include production scheduling, reliability assurance, systemwide control optimization, security management, network management, and potentially other required IT services, such as DHCP, DNS, and timing.

  - **Level 2: Supervisory control:** This level includes zone control rooms, controller status, control system network/application administration, and other control-related applications, such as human-machine interface (HMI) and historian.

  - **Level 1: Basic control:** At this level, controllers and IEDs, dedicated HMIs, and other applications may talk to each other to run part or all of the control function.

  - **Level 0: Process:** This is where devices such as sensors and actuators and machines such as drives, motors, and robots communicate with controllers or IEDs.

- Safety zone

  - **Safety-critical:** This level includes devices, sensors, and other equipment used to manage the safety functions of the control system.

One of the key advantages of designing an industrial network in structured levels, as with the Purdue model, is that it allows security to be correctly applied at each level and between levels. For example, IT networks typically reside at Levels 4 and 5 and use security principles common to IT networks. The lower levels are where the industrial systems and

IoT networks reside. As shown in Figure 8-3, a DMZ resides between the IT and OT levels. Clearly, to protect the lower industrial layers, security technologies such as firewalls, proxy servers, and IPSs should be used to ensure that only authorized connections from trusted sources on expected ports are being used. At the DMZ, and, in fact, even between the lower levels, industrial firewalls that are capable of understanding the control protocols should be used to ensure the continuous operation of the OT network.

Although security vulnerabilities may potentially exist at each level of the model, it is clear that due to the amount of connectivity and sophistication of devices and systems, the higher levels have a greater chance of incursion due to the wider attack surface. This does not mean that lower levels are not as important from a security perspective; rather, it means that their attack surface is smaller, and if mitigation techniques are implemented properly, there is potentially less impact to the overall system. As shown in Figure 8-4, a review of published vulnerabilities associated with industrial security in 2011 shows that the assets at the higher levels of the framework had more detected vulnerabilities.

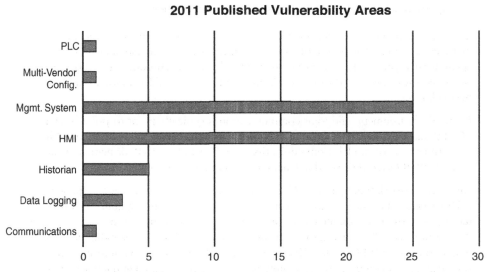

Figure 8-4 *2011 Industrial Security Report of Published Vulnerability Areas (US Industrial Control Systems Cyber Emergency Response Team (ICS-CERT) https://ics-cert.us-cert.gov).*

OT Network Characteristics Impacting Security

While IT and OT networks are beginning to converge, they still maintain many divergent characteristics in terms of how they operate and the traffic they handle. These differences influence how they are treated in the context of a security strategy. For example, compare the nature of how traffic flows across IT and OT networks:

- **IT networks:** In an IT environment, there are many diverse data flows. The communication data flows that emanate from a typical IT endpoint travel relatively far. They frequently traverse the network through layers of switches and eventually make their way to a set of local or remote servers, which they may connect to directly. Data in the form of email, file transfers, or print services will likely all make its way to the central data center, where it is responded to, or triggers actions in more local services, such as a printer. In the case of email or web browsing, the endpoint initiates actions that leave the confines of the enterprise network and potentially travel around the earth.

- **OT networks:** By comparison, in an OT environment (Levels 0–3), there are typically two types of operational traffic. The first is local traffic that may be contained within a specific package or area to provide local monitoring and closed-loop control. This is the traffic that is used for real-time (or near-real-time) processes and does not need to leave the process control levels. The second type of traffic is used for monitoring and control of areas or zones or the overall system. SCADA traffic is a good example of this, where information about remote devices or summary information from a function is shared at a system level so that operators can understand how the overall system, or parts of it, are operating. They can then implement appropriate control commands based on this information.

When IT endpoints communicate, it is typically short and frequent conversations with many connections. The nature of the communications is open, and almost anybody can speak with anybody else, such as with email or browsing. Although there are clearly access controls, most of those controls are at the application level rather than the network level.

In an OT environment, endpoint communication is typically point-to-point, such as a SCADA master to SCADA slave, or uses multicast or broadcast, leveraging a publisher/subscriber type of model. Communication could be TCP or UDP or neither (as in the case of PROFINET, discussed in Chapter 9, "Manufacturing").

Although network timing in the OT space typically mirrors that of the enterprise with NTP/SNTP used for device clocking against a master time source, a number of use cases require an extremely accurate clock source and extremely accurate time/synchronization distribution, as well as measurable and consistent latency/jitter. Some industrial applications require timing via IEEE 1588, PTP (Precision Time Protocol), so that information from source and destination can be accurately measured and compared at microsecond intervals with communication equipment introducing delays of no more than 50 nanoseconds. Jitter for the sending and receiving of information must also be minimized to ensure correct operation. By way of comparison, in the enterprise space, voice is often considered the highest-priority application, with a typical one-way delay of 150 milliseconds or more. In a number of operational environments for oil and gas, manufacturing, and power utilities, delay must be under 10 microseconds. Security attacks that cause delay, such as denial of service (DoS) attacks, can cause systems to malfunction purely by disrupting the timing mechanism.

IT networks are typically more mature and use up-to-date technologies. These mature modern networking practices are critical to meet the high degree of flexibility required in the IT environment. Virtual networking, virtual workspaces, and virtual servers are commonplace. It is likely that there are a wide variety of device types actively participating in any given network at any one time. Flexible interoperability is thus critical. To achieve interoperability, there is usually minimal proprietary communication activity, and the emphasis is typically on open standards. The movement to IPv6 continues to progress, and higher-order network services, such as quality of service (QoS), are normal as well. Endpoints are not just promiscuous in their communications, but they operate a wide number of applications from a large number of diverse vendors. The open nature of these compute systems means a wide range of protocols are traversing the OT network.

Industrial networks often still rely on serial communication technologies or have mixed serial and Ethernet. This means that not only do many devices lack IP capabilities, but it is not even possible to monitor and secure the serial traffic in the same way you do for IP or Ethernet. In some environments, the network remains very static, meaning a baseline of traffic patterns can be built up and monitored for changes. In static environments, the visibility of devices, protocols, and traffic flows can be managed and secured more easily. However, there is a continued growth of mobile devices and ad hoc connectivity, especially in industries such as transportation and smart cities, as well as a rise in mobile fleet assets across a plethora of other industries. These dynamic and variable networks are much more difficult to baseline, monitor, and secure.

Security Priorities: Integrity, Availability, and Confidentiality

Security priorities are driven by the nature of the assets in each environment. In an IT realm, the most critical element and the target of attacks has been information. In an OT realm, the critical assets are the process participants: workers and equipment. Security priorities diverge based on those differences.

In the IT business world, there are legal, regulatory, and commercial obligations to protect data, especially data of individuals who may or may not be employed by the organization. This emphasis on privacy focuses on the confidentiality, integrity, and availability of the data—not necessarily on a system or a physical asset. The impact of losing a compute device is considered minimal compared to the information that it could hold or provide access to. By way of comparison, in the OT world, losing a device due to a security vulnerability means production stops, and the company cannot perform its basic operation. Loss of information stored on these devices is a lower concern, but there are certainly confidential data sets in the operating environment that may have economic impacts, such as formulations and processes.

In an operational space, the safety and continuity of the process participants is considered the most critical concern. Thus, the goal is the continued uptime of devices and the safety of the people who operate them. The result is to emphasize availability, integrity, and confidentiality. The impact of loss here extends even to loss of life.

Security Focus

Security focus is frequently driven by the history of security impacts that an organization has experienced. In an IT environment, the most painful experiences have typically been intrusion campaigns in which critical data is extracted or corrupted. The result has been a significant investment in capital goods and humanpower to reduce these external threats and minimize potential internal malevolent actors.

In the OT space, the history of loss due to external actors has not been as long, even though the potential for harm on a human scale is clearly significantly higher. The result is that the security events that have been experienced have come more from human error than external attacks. Interest and investment in industrial security have primarily been in the standard access control layers. Where OT has diverged, to some degree, is to emphasize the application layer control between the higher-level controller layer and the receiving operating layer. Later in this chapter you will learn more about the value and risks associated with this approach.

Formal Risk Analysis Structures: OCTAVE and FAIR

Within the industrial environment, there are a number of standards, guidelines, and best practices available to help understand risk and how to mitigate it. IEC 62443 is the most commonly used standard globally across industrial verticals. It consists of a number of parts, including 62443-3-2 for risk assessments, and 62443-3-3 for foundational requirements used to secure the industrial environment from a networking and communications perspective. Also, ISO 27001 is widely used for organizational people, process, and information security management. In addition, the National Institute of Standards and Technology (NIST) provides a series of documents for critical infrastructure, such as the NIST Cybersecurity Framework (CSF). In the utilities domain, the North American Electric Reliability Corporation's (NERC's) Critical Infrastructure Protection (CIP) has legally binding guidelines for North American utilities, and IEC 62351 is the cybersecurity standard for power utilities.

The key for any industrial environment is that it needs to address security holistically and not just focus on technology. It must include people and processes, and it should include all the vendor ecosystem components that make up a control system.

In this section, we present a brief review of two such risk assessment frameworks:

- OCTAVE (Operationally Critical Threat, Asset and Vulnerability Evaluation) from the Software Engineering Institute at Carnegie Mellon University

- FAIR (Factor Analysis of Information Risk) from The Open Group

These two systems work toward establishing a more secure environment but with two different approaches and sets of priorities. Knowledge of the environment is key to determining security risks and plays a key role in driving priorities.

OCTAVE

OCTAVE has undergone multiple iterations. The version this section focuses on is OCTAVE Allegro, which is intended to be a lightweight and less burdensome process to implement. Allegro assumes that a robust security team is not on standby or immediately at the ready to initiate a comprehensive security review. This approach and the assumptions it makes are quite appropriate, given that many operational technology areas are similarly lacking in security-focused human assets. Figure 8-5 illustrates the OCTAVE Allegro steps and phases.

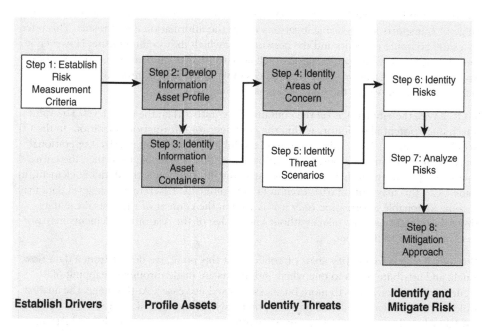

Figure 8-5   *OCTAVE Allegro Steps and Phases (see https://blog.compass-security.com/ 2013/04/lean-risk-assessment-based-on-octave-allegro/).*

The first step of the OCTAVE Allegro methodology is to establish a risk measurement criterion. OCTAVE provides a fairly simple means of doing this with an emphasis on impact, value, and measurement. The point of having a risk measurement criterion is that at any point in the later stages, prioritization can take place against the reference model. (While OCTAVE has more details to contribute, we suggest using the FAIR model, described next, for risk assessment.)

The second step is to develop an information asset profile. This profile is populated with assets, a prioritization of assets, attributes associated with each asset, including owners, custodians, people, explicit security requirements, and technology assets. It is important to stress the importance of process. Certainly, the need to protect information does not disappear, but operational safety and continuity are more critical.

Within this asset profile, process are multiple substages that complete the definition of the assets. Some of these are simply survey and reporting activities, such as identifying the asset and attributes associated with it, such as its owners, custodians, human actors with which it interacts, and the composition of its technology assets. There are, however, judgment-based attributes such as prioritization. Rather than simply assigning an arbitrary ranking, the system calls for a justification of the prioritization. With an under-standing of the asset attributes, particularly the technical components, appropriate threat mitigation methods can be applied. With the application of risk assessment, the level of security investment can be aligned with that individual asset.

The third step is to identify information asset containers. Roughly speaking, this is the range of transports and possible locations where the information might reside. This refer-ences the compute elements and the networks by which they communicate. However, it can also mean physical manifestations such as hard copy documents or even the people who know the information. Note that the operable target here is information, which includes data from which the information is derived.

In OCTAVE, the emphasis is on the container level rather than the asset level. The value is to reduce potential inhibitors within the container for information operation. In the OT world, the emphasis is on reducing potential inhibitors in the containerized operational space. If there is some attribute of the information that is endemic to it, then the entire container operates with that attribute because the information is the defining element. In some cases this may not be true, even in IT environments. Discrete atomic-level data may become actionable information only if it is seen in the context of the rest of the data. Similarly, operational data taken without knowledge of the rest of the elements may not be of particular value either.

The fourth step is to identify areas of concern. At this point, we depart from a data flow, touch, and attribute focus to one where judgments are made through a mapping of security-related attributes to more business-focused use cases. At this stage, the analyst looks to risk profiles and delves into the previously mentioned risk analysis. It is no longer just facts, but there is also an element of creativity that can factor into the evaluation. History both within and outside the organization can contribute. References to similar operational use cases and incidents of security failures are reasonable associations.

Closely related is the fifth step, where threat scenarios are identified. Threats are broadly (and properly) identified as potential undesirable events. This definition means that results from both malevolent and accidental causes are viable threats. In the context of operational focus, this is a valuable consideration. It is at this point that an explicit identification of actors, motives, and outcomes occurs. These scenarios are described in threat trees to trace the path to undesired outcomes, which, in turn, can be associated with risk metrics.

At the sixth step risks are identified. Within OCTAVE, risk is the possibility of an unde-sired outcome. This is extended to focus on how the organization is impacted. For more focused analysis, this can be localized, but the potential impact to the organization could extend outside the boundaries of the operation.

The seventh step is risk analysis, with the effort placed on qualitative evaluation of the impacts of the risk. Here the risk measurement criteria defined in the first step are explic-itly brought into the process.

Finally, mitigation is applied at the eighth step. There are three outputs or decisions to be taken at this stage. One may be to accept a risk and do nothing, other than document the situation, potential outcomes, and reasons for accepting the risk. The second is to mitigate the risk with whatever control effort is required. By walking back through the threat scenarios to asset profiles, a pairing of compensating controls to mitigate those threat/risk pairings should be discoverable and then implemented. The final possible action is to defer a decision, meaning risk is neither accepted nor mitigated. This may imply further research or activity, but it is not required by the process.

OCTAVE is a balanced information-focused process. What it offers in terms of discipline and largely unconstrained breadth, however, is offset by its lack of security specificity. There is an assumption that beyond these steps are seemingly means of identifying specific mitigations that can be mapped to the threats and risks exposed during the analysis process.

FAIR

FAIR (Factor Analysis of Information Risk) is a technical standard for risk definition from The Open Group. While information security is the focus, much as it is for OCTAVE, FAIR has clear applications within operational technology. Like OCTAVE, it also allows for non-malicious actors as a potential cause for harm, but it goes to greater lengths to emphasize the point. For many operational groups, it is a welcome acknowledgement of existing contingency planning. Unlike with OCTAVE, there is a significant emphasis on naming, with risk taxonomy definition as a very specific target.

FAIR places emphasis on both unambiguous definitions and the idea that risk and associated attributes are measurable. Measurable, quantifiable metrics are a key area of emphasis, which should lend itself well to an operational world with a richness of operational data.

At its base, FAIR has a definition of risk as the probable frequency and probable magnitude of loss. With this definition, a clear hierarchy of sub-elements emerges, with one side of the taxonomy focused on frequency and the other on magnitude.

Loss even frequency is the result of a threat agent acting on an asset with a resulting loss to the organization. This happens with a given frequency called the threat event frequency (TEF), in which a specified time window becomes a probability. There are multiple sub-attributes that define frequency of events, all of which can be understood with some form of measurable metric. Threat event frequencies are applied to a vulnerability. *Vulnerability* here is not necessarily some compute asset weakness, but is more broadly defined as the probability that the targeted asset will fail as a result of the actions applied. There are further sub-attributes here as well.

The other side of the risk taxonomy is the probable loss magnitude (PLM), which begins to quantify the impacts, with the emphasis again being on measurable metrics. The FAIR specification makes it a point to emphasize how ephemeral some of these cost estimates can be, and this may indeed be the case when information security is the target of the discussion. Fortunately for the OT operator, a significant emphasis on operational efficiency and analysis makes understanding and quantifying costs much easier.

FAIR defines six forms of loss, four of them externally focused and two internally focused. Of particular value for operational teams are productivity and replacement loss. Response loss is also reasonably measured, with fines and judgments easy to measure but difficult to predict. Finally, competitive advantage and reputation are the least measurable.

Note   The discussion of OCTAVE Allegro and FAIR is meant to give you a grounding in formal risk analysis processes. While there are others, both represent mechanics that can be applied in an OT environment.

The Phased Application of Security in an Operational Environment

It is a security practitioner's goal to safely secure the environment for which he or she is responsible. For an operational technologist, this process is different because the priorities and assets to be protected are highly differentiated from the better-known IT environment. The differences have been discussed at length in this chapter, but many of the processes used by IT security practitioners still have validity and can be used in an OT environment. If there is one key concept to grasp, it is that security for an IoT environment is an ongoing process in which steps forward can be taken, but there is no true finish line.

The following sections present a phased approach to introduce modern network security into largely preexisting legacy industrial networks.

Secured Network Infrastructure and Assets

Given that networks, compute, or operational elements in a typical IoT or industrial system have likely been in place for many years and given that the physical layout largely defines the operational process, this phased approach to introducing modern network security begins with very modest, non-intrusive steps.

As a first step, you need to analyze and secure the basic network design. Most automated process systems or even hierarchical energy distribution systems have a high degree of correlation between the network design and the operational design. It is a basic tenet of ISA99 and IEC 62443 that functions should be segmented into zones (cells) and that communication crossing the boundaries of those zones should be secured and controlled through the concept of conduits. In response to this, it is suggested that a security professional discover the state of his or her network and all communication channels.

Figure 8-6 illustrates inter-level security models and inter-zone conduits in the process control hierarchy.

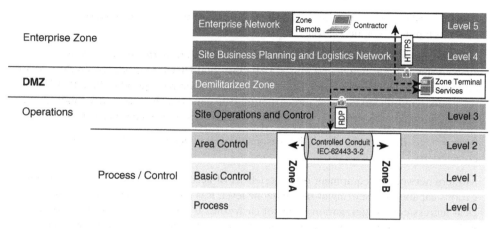

Figure 8-6   *Security Between Levels and Zones in the Process Control Hierarchy Model*

Normal network discovery processes can be highly problematic for older networking equipment. In fact, the discovery process in pursuit of improved safety, security, and operational state can result in degradation of all three. Given that condition, the network discovery process may require manual inspection of physical connections, starting from the highest accessible aggregation point and working all the way down to the last access layer. This discovery activity must include a search for wireless access points. For the sake of risk reduction, any on-wire network mapping should be done passively as much as possible.

It is fair to note that this prescribed process is much more likely to succeed in a smaller confined environment such as a plant floor. In geographically distributed environments, it may not be possible to trace the network, and in such cases, the long-haul connections may not be physical or may be carried by an outside communication provider. For those sections of the operational network, explicit partnering with other entities is required.

A side activity of this network tracing process is to note the connectivity state of the physical connections. This is not just an exercise to see what fiber or cables are in what ports but to observe the use or operational state of other physical connections, such as USB, SD card, alarm channel, serial, or other connections, at each network appliance. For more modern environments where updated networking devices and protocols are used, tools like NetFlow and IPFIX can also be used to discover the network communication paths.

As the network mapping reaches the aggregation point, it is worthwhile to continue to the connected asset level.

Normally, in an IT environment, the very first stage of discovery is focused on assets connected to the network. Assets remain critical, but from an efficiency and criticality perspective, it is generally recommended to find data paths into and between zones (cells) rather than the serial links between devices within a zone. One thing to continually be on the lookout for is the ever-dangerous, unsecured, and often undocumented convenience port.

Any physical port that is not physically locked down or doesn't have an enforceable protection policy is an uncontrolled threat vector.

Once the network is physically mapped, the next step is to perform a connectivity analysis through the switch and router ARP tables and DHCP requests within the network infrastructure. This should help further illuminate connectivity, good or bad, that has occurred. Firewall and network infrastructure data can contribute to understanding what devices are talking to other devices and the traffic paths over which this is done.

At this stage, the network should be reasonably well understood and prepared for secure connectivity.

Modern networking equipment offers a rich set of access control and secured communications capabilities. Starting at the cell/zone level, it is important to ensure that there is a clear ingress/egress aggregation point for each zone. If your communications patterns are well identified, you can apply access control policies to manage who and what can enter those physical portions of the process. If you are not comfortable explicitly controlling the traffic, then begin with alert-only actions. With time, you should be confident enough in your knowledge to apply controls.

At upstream levels, consider traffic controls such as denial of service (DoS) protection, traffic normalization activities, and quality of service (QoS) controls (such as marking and black-holing or rate-limiting scavenger-class traffic). The goal here is to ensure that these aggregated traffic segments are carrying high-priority traffic without impediment.

Network infrastructure should also provide the ability to secure communications between zones via secured conduits (see Figure 8-6). The primary method is encrypted communications in the form of virtual private networks (VPNs). VPNs can come in multiple forms, such as site-to-site, which would be appropriate between a utility substation and a control center, or perhaps in cell-to-cell communications. Remote access controls can be established in more ad hoc situations and utilize the convenience of browser-based VPNs with Secure Sockets Layer (SSL)–based VPNs. If latency concerns are not particularly high, you can use Media Access Control Security (MACSec) hop-by-hop encryption to allow for potential controls and visibility at key junctions.

The next discovery phase should align with the software and configurations of the assets on the network. At this point, the rights and roles of the network administrator may be insufficient to access the required information. Certainly, the network infrastructure and its status are within the network admin's view, but the individual assets likely are not. At this point, organizational cooperation is required for success. For an experienced IT-based network practitioner, this is not an unusual situation. It is very common, especially in larger enterprises, to see a separation of responsibilities and controls between the communications transport and the assets to which they are connected. At the operations level, similar cooperation is required with those responsible for the maintenance of the OT assets.

There are reasonable sources of information describing the configuration state of OT assets. The control systems associated with the processes hold historical data describing what is connected and what those assets are doing. A review of historical data should provide an idea of what assets are present and what operations are being performed on them, and it should identify such things as firmware updates and health status. The volume of data to analyze may be challenging, but if it is organized correctly, it would be valuable for understanding asset operation.

With an initial asset inventory completed, you can initiate a risk analysis based on the network and assets, and determine an initial scope of security needs.

Deploying Dedicated Security Appliances

The next stage is to expand the security footprint with focused security functionality. The goal is to provide visibility, safety, and security for traffic within the network. Visibility provides an understanding of application and communication behavior. With visibility, you can set policy actions that reflect the desired behaviors for inter-zone and conduit security.

While network elements can provide simplified views with connection histories or some kind of flow data, you get a true understanding when you look within the packets on the network. This level of visibility is typically achieved with deep packet inspection (DPI) technologies such as intrusion detection/prevention systems (IDS/IPS). These technologies can be used to detect many kinds of traffic of interest, from simply identifying what applications are speaking, to whether communications are being obfuscated, to whether exploits are targeting vulnerabilities, to passively identifying assets on the network.

With the goal of identifying assets, an IDS/IPS can detect what kind of assets are present on the network. Passive OS identification programs can capture patterns that expose the base operating systems and other applications communicating on the network. The organizationally unique identifier (OUI) in a captured MAC address, which could have come from ARP table exploration, is yet another means of exposure. Coupled with the physical and historical data mentioned before, this is a valuable tool to expand on the asset inventory without having to dangerously or intrusively prod critical systems.

Application-specific protocols are also detectable by IDS/IPS systems. For more IT-like applications, user agents are of value, but traditionally, combinations of port numbers and other protocol differentiators can contribute to identification. Some applications have behaviors that are found only in certain software releases. Knowledge of those differences can help to determine the software version being run on a particular asset.

Within applications and industrial protocols are well-defined commands and, often, associated parameter values. Again, an IDS/IPS can be configured to identify those commands and values to learn what actions are being taken and what associated settings are being changed.

All these actions can be done from a non-intrusive deployment scenario. Modern DPI implementations can work out-of-band from a span or tap. Viewing copies of packets has no impact on traffic performance or latency. It is easily the safest means of getting deep insight into the activities happening on a network.

Visibility and an understanding of network connectivity uncover the information necessary to initiate access control activity. Access control is typically achieved with access control lists (ACLs), which are available on practically all modern network equipment. For improved scalability, however, a dedicated firewall would be preferred. Providing strong segmentation and zone access control is the first step. Access control, however, is not just limited to the typical address and protocol identifiers. Modern firewalls have the ability to discern attributes associated with the user accessing the network, allowing controls to be placed on the "who" element also. In addition, access control can be aligned with applications and application behaviors. Equipped with the right toolset, a modern OT practitioner can ensure that only those operators in a certain user class can initiate any external commands to that particular asset.

Safety is a particular benefit as application controls can be managed at the cell/zone edge through an IDS/IPS. The same technologies that observe the who and what can also manage the values being passed to the target asset. For example, in a manufacturing scenario where a robot operates, there may be an area frequented by workers who are within the potential range of the robot's operation. The range is unique to the physical layout of the cell, and parameter changes could cause physical harm to a plant worker. With an IDS/IPS, the system can detect that a parameter value exceeds the safety range and act accordingly to ensure worker safety.

Safety and security are closely related linguistically (for example, in German, the same word, Sicherheit, can be used for both), but for a security practitioner, security is more commonly associated with threats. Threat identification and protection is a key attribute of IPSs using DPI.

Mature IPSs have thousands of threat identifiers, which address the complete range of asset types where remotely exploitable vulnerabilities are known. In some cases, the nature of the threat identifier is generic enough that it addresses a common technique without having to be associated with a particular application instance of the vulnerability type.

Placement priorities for dedicated security devices vary according to the security practitioner's perception of risk. If visibility is incomplete and concern dictates that further knowledge is necessary prior to creating a proactive defense, the security device should be placed where that gap is perceived. It is important to note that the process of gaining visibility or addressing risk is dynamic. Networks change, and as knowledge is gained, new priorities (either in the form of visible threats or a reduction of gaps) creates new points of emphasis. Given this dynamism, consider the idea that placement of a dedicated security device can change as well. In other words, just because you start with a device in one location does not mean you can't move it later to address security gaps.

Inevitably a decision must be made. Here we discuss some of the relative merits of different placement locations. Placement at the operational cell is likely the most fine-grained deployment scenario. By *fine-grained* we mean that it is the lowest portion of a network that gives network-based access to the lowest level of operational assets. As discussed earlier, the nature of the deployment—out-of-band or in-line—depends on the organization's comfort level for in-line operation and desire to actually exert control. In either case, the industrial security appliance should be attached directly to the switch, which denotes the access point into the cell. This location gives the greatest level of control for safety controls, visibility, and threats. If network design has properly segmented to a single zone entry point, then this is an optimal deployment location. For safety considerations, application control can be exerted to ensure that application changes will not allow for dangerous settings. Threats can be mitigated as they traverse the device, and traffic entering and exiting the cell can be made visible.

A particularly valuable function is enabled if a security device can terminate VPNs in addition to performing deep packet inspection. Secured communication, potentially from a vendor representative outside the organization, can be terminated at the ingress to the device and then inspected. The time cost of the termination would be similar to what would be done on the switch, and then inspection of what that remote user accessing the network is doing is viable. Naturally, any potential threat traffic can be halted as well.

If the zone/cell houses critical infrastructure and remote operation is requisite, a redundant high-availability configuration for both the network and security infrastructure is advised.

For the purposes of pure visibility, hanging off a mirror or span port from the switch would be optimal. For control capabilities, one must be in-line to truly act on undesired traffic. In most cases, the preferred location is upstream of the zone/cell access switch between the aggregation layer and the zone switch. It may be viable to have the security device between the zone assets and the zone access switch as well.

For broader, less detailed levels of control, placement of dedicated security devices upstream of the aggregation switches is the preferred approach. If the network has multiple zones going through the aggregation switch with mostly redundant functionality but with no communication between them, this may be a more efficient point of deployment.

At some point, a functional layer above the lowest zone layer becomes connected to the network, and there should be a device located between those functions and their OT charges in the zones/cells. At that next layer up, there may be HMIs or other lower-level operational tools. For safety considerations, a control point between that layer and the cell is valuable.

At the higher level of the network are a good number of higher-function assets, such as standard network elements (for example, directory servers, network monitoring tools, remote access plus proxy servers, print servers, security control elements). More operationally focused functionality involves elements such as engineering workstations and operations control applications. Depending on the diversity and network topologies at play, these operational structures could be replicated within their own subzones (subnets) at the same level. There may be justification for using a dedicated security device between the subzones, depending on the need to control access, but for the most part, this is a zone that needs controls placed above and below.

Below is where industrial awareness and, potentially, hardware ruggedization is more likely to be needed. With some amount of industrial traffic traversing this layer, a dedicated and security-aware tool would be advisable.

Above this highest level, a dedicated security device with IT-centric threat controls is recommended. If the applications hosted here are similar in nature to those found in IT environments (for example, Windows- or Linux-based applications), this requires common networking infrastructure, web-based access, and so on for proper visibility, control, and protection. Applying such controls to all ingress points (above and below) is important. There should be no assumptions made that an IT-centric threat can only emanate from the IT/enterprise layer above the DMZ. Attackers would not limit themselves to such thinking.

There is evidence that end-of-life OS and software components exist in operational environments. An all-too-common and unfortunate attribute of such systems is that further patching for security vulnerabilities is likely unavailable. To protect those systems after their official end-of-support date, the concept of a "virtual patch" layer may be possible. The idea is that protections for vulnerabilities can be applied through the network path by which these systems communicate. While this is not a substitute for keeping abreast of patching, it may be a mitigation approach that fits your organization's risk acceptance policy.

At the logical edge of the operational space is the DMZ (demilitarized zone)—a security boundary between two diverged compute realms. Assets in this area are meant to bridge communications in a secure fashion between the enterprise's IT realm and the industrial OT realm. Security should be applied both above and below this layer.

Before we leave the second phase of operational security, it is important to reemphasize that security, in whatever location, is an ongoing process. The policies applied and the knowledge gained should never stagnate. Conditions will inevitably change, so security deployments and sometimes networks themselves must change to adapt. Where you place your security enforcement products and the policies they employ must be ready to change with them.

Higher-Order Policy Convergence and Network Monitoring

So far we have focused on very basic concepts that are common and easily implemented by network engineering groups. Finding network professionals with experience performing such functions or even training those without prior experience is not difficult.

Another security practice that adds value to a networked industrial space is convergence, which is the adoption and integration of security across operational boundaries. This means coordinating security on both the IT and OT sides of the organization. Convergence of the IT and OT spaces is merging, or at least there is active coordination across formerly distinct IT and OT boundaries. From a security perspective, the value follows the argument that most new networking and compute technologies coming to the operations space were previously found and established in the IT space. It is expected to also be true that the practices and tools associated with those new technologies are likely to be more mature in the IT space.

There are advanced enterprise-wide practices related to access control, threat detection, and many other security mechanisms that could benefit OT security. As stated earlier, the key is to adjust the approach to fit the target environment.

Several areas are more likely to require some kind of coordination across IT and OT environments. Two such areas are remote access and threat detection. For remote access, most large industrial organizations backhaul communication through the IT network. Some communications, such as email and web browsing, are obvious communication types that are likely to touch shared IT infrastructure. Often vendors or consultants who require some kind of remote access to OT assets also traverse the IT side of the network. Given this, it would be of significant value for an OT security practitioner to coordinate access control policies from the remote initiator across the Internet-facing security layers, through the core network, and to a handoff point at the industrial demarcation and deeper, toward the IoT assets. The use of common access controls and operational conditions eases and protects network assets to a greater degree than having divergent groups creating ad hoc methods. Using location information, participant device security stance, user identity, and access target attributes are all standard functions that modern access policy tools can make use of. Such sophistication is a relatively new practice in industrial environments, and so, if these functions are available, an OT security practitioner would benefit from coordination with his or her IT equivalents.

Network security monitoring (NSM) is a process of finding intruders in a network. It is achieved by collecting and analyzing indicators and warnings to prioritize and investigate incidents with the assumption that there is, in fact, an undesired presence.

The practice of NSM is not new, yet it is not implemented often or thoroughly enough even within reasonably mature and large organizations. There are many reasons for this underutilization, but lack of education and organizational patience are common reasons. To simplify the approach, there is a large amount of readily available data that, if reviewed, would expose the activities of an intruder.

It is important to note that NSM is inherently a process in which discovery occurs through the review of evidence and actions that have already happened. This is not meant to imply that it is a purely postmortem type of activity. If you recognize that intrusion activities are, much like security, an ongoing process, then you see that there is a similar set of stages that an attacker must go through. The tools deployed will slow that process and introduce opportunities to detect and thwart the attacker, but there is rarely a single event that represents an attack in its entirety. NSM is the discipline that will most likely discover the extent of the attack process and, in turn, define the scope for its remediation.

Summary

As industries modernize in pursuit of operational efficiencies, improved safety, and competitive agilities, they must do so securely. Modernization processes frequently initiate greater connectivity in the context of older and highly vulnerable OT assets and processes. Security is a process that must be applied throughout the lifecycle of that change and operation. To achieve security, an organization must be able to define risks and make informed choices about how best to address them.

Fortunately, much of what is available to minimize risks from threats is readily available. Network connectivity can be made secure with the right equipment and policies. Threats from unsafe practices, attacks, and remote access needs can be identified and controlled with dedicated industrial security appliances and practices. With time, there are opportunities to expand risk reduction through convergence and cooperation. Learning from the more extensive and mature security practices and tools in IT environments as well as coordinating layers of defense to protect critical industrial assets are key security enablers for operational environments.

Part III

IoT in Industry

Chapter 9

Manufacturing

Business imperatives are changing for every industry, and manufacturing is no exception. Controlling costs and improving efficiency have always been important to manufacturers, but as industry models change and competition heats up, the primary focus is now shifting toward innovation and improved business models. After decades of squeezing costs out of production systems and the supply chain, manufacturers are recognizing that further cost containment may only impede customer service and open the door to competition.

These economic changes are igniting a massive disruption in the manufacturing industry, led by advances in digitization and IoT. This chapter explores these disruptive forces and looks at innovative architectures that are being used to digitize factories and connect machines. This chapter includes the following sections:

- **An Introduction to Connected Manufacturing:** The chapter opens by examining the technologies that are creating digital disruption in manufacturing. This section also discusses a strategy for the connected factory and the business benefits to manufacturers.

- **An Architecture for the Converged Factory:** Industrial automation and control systems (IACS) networking technologies are converging, with the aid of Ethernet and IP. This section explores a connected factory framework, with a focus on the Converged Plantwide Ethernet (CPwE) architecture that was jointly developed by Cisco and Rockwell Automation.

- **Industrial Automation Control Protocols:** This section discusses the wide variety of networking and control protocols used in manufacturing, including EtherNet/IP, PROFINET, and Modbus/TCP.

- **Connected Factory Security:** This section examines key security considerations in the connected factory and how they can be addressed with the correct design methodology.

- **Edge Computing in the Connected Factory:** The data generated by connected machines is massive. This section examines ways to implement edge computing in the connected factory to improve data management and visibility.

An Introduction to Connected Manufacturing

In a recent SCM World survey of more than 400 manufacturing business leaders, approximately 80% of participants stated that their top challenges were to meet customer delivery dates and respond to unforeseen events.[1] Figure 9-1 shows the results of this survey.

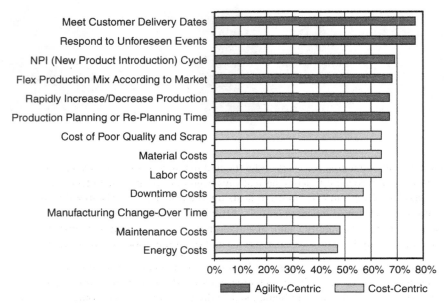

Figure 9-1   *Shifting Focus from Cost to Agility*

Source: SCM World /Cisco, *Smart Manufacturing and the Internet of Things 2015 Survey of 418 Manufacturing Business Line and Executives and Plant Managers Across 17 Vertical Industries.*

In a dynamic economy, manufacturers recognize the need to quickly turn around projects. They require the ability to scale, align, and adjust production capacities quickly in response to market demands. All too often, however, between economic fluctuations and long cycles of asset investment, manufacturers are saddled with aging production facilities that encumber and reduce their flexibility. For example, it is estimated that the average age of automation infrastructure in the United States is the highest it has been since 1938. Nearly 75% of US plants are more than 20 years old. Factories around the world are facing a similar challenge: Their aging assets not only slow innovation but also cost billions in unplanned downtime.

Connecting previously unconnected machines to intelligent data systems and, in turn, using the data generated by machines to better utilize existing investments in a more productive way is seen as the "low-hanging fruit" of factory modernization. The opportunity in front of manufacturers is massive. By some estimates, there are 60 million machines in factories throughout the world. Of them, 90% are not connected, and the vast majority of the machines are more than 15 years old.[2-4] There is an increasing urgency to connect these machines and better utilize the data they generate.

At the heart of the manufacturing digital disruption are several IoT-related technologies:

- **Data-driven manufacturing:** Big data is changing the face of manufacturing. Manufacturers want access to all data generated from machines to monitor real-time quality control, improve overall equipment effectiveness (OEE), and reduce unplanned downtime. OEE is a well-known metric that indicates manufacturing productivity. Manufacturers are also exploring ways to use this data to support rapid retooling when market fluctuations or other needs occur.

- **OT and IT convergence:** In the context of IoT in a factory setting, operational technology is made up of programmable logic controllers (PLCs), computers, and other technology that is often like the technology used in IT but is operated and owned by business operations outside IT. IP networking is enabling closer integration between machines and factories, and the line between factory and enterprise networks is becoming less distinct. Manufacturers are moving beyond traditional silos and looking for ways to bring their operations together under a single networking infrastructure. (For more information on OT and IT convergence, see Chapter 1, "What Is IoT?")

- **Improved technology with lower costs:** New technologies are creating conditions for scaled, automated, and platform-based machine connectivity, monitoring, and optimization. In this evolved technology state, machine operations can be viewed as part of a fully connected network system instead of an air-gapped point system. The convergence of compute, switching, routing, and security has the potential to drive down the cost of connecting machines.

- **Machine builder OEMs focused on new priorities:** Original equipment manufacturers (OEMs) are facing disruption by new cloud-based providers that intend to provide Machines as a Service (MaaS), where machines can be deployed quickly on the plant floor through zero-touch deployment from the cloud, which offers remote connectivity and monitoring of those machines. This is driving a new focus on providing better customer experience and emphasizing after-sales products and services. Manufacturers are looking toward near 100% uptime and zero-touch deployments. They are also exploring ways to control support costs through remote connectivity and monitoring.

An IoT Strategy for Connected Manufacturing

How do manufacturers respond to the challenges of connecting their factories? The drive toward agility and mass customization requires drastic improvements in technology to factories that are aging due to decades of cost containment. Digital transformation requires embracing key information technology advances, many of which have already been proven and widely adopted in other industries.

Perhaps the most important trend in manufacturing is the ubiquity of software. The lines between software and hardware are increasingly being dissolved. Many things that previously required hardware in our daily lives can now be achieved with software. Remember answering machines? The little recording boxes with miniature cassette tapes used by answering machines now reside as software in your smart phone or cloud-based servers hosted by your service provider. The same is happening in industrial settings, and an increasing number of physical controls are now residing as software available through the human–machine interface (HMI). In some factories, the only remaining physical control is the emergency stop button. The advantage of software over hardware is that new features and software patches are more simply and cost-effectively managed.

We are now entering a world where machine builders remotely troubleshoot and repair a machine that is causing unplanned downtime by simply sending a software update to the machine. Moreover, through artificial intelligence (AI), machines are now able to self-diagnose problems. Issues are revealed several days before an interruption occurs, and the machine repairs itself through a software update during a planned maintenance window. According to Jeff Immelt, CEO of General Electric, "If you went to bed last night as an industrial company, you're going to wake up today as a software and analytics company."

Software analytics are also playing an essential role in enabling manufacturing improvements in agility and efficiency. Manufacturers need to have full visibility to key performance indicators (KPIs) that unify activities on the plant floor, in the enterprise, and across the supply chain. This real-time data collection and analysis is a major focus of IoT initiatives for leading manufacturers.

One recent study of manufacturing executives asked them to rank the barriers to achieving their IoT and digital manufacturing objectives.[1] The top three barriers related to a lack of visibility to data and data access to the machine, plant floor, and supply chain. Figure 9-2 displays the full results from this survey.

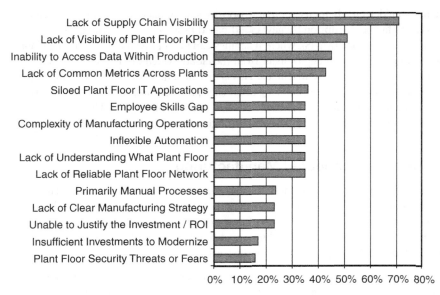

Figure 9-2   *Primary barriers related to information visibility*

Source: SCM World /Cisco, *Smart Manufacturing and the Internet of Things 2015 Survey of 418 Manufacturing Business Line and Executives and Plant Managers Across 17 Vertical Industries.*

Some have described a future state of manufacturing where factories won't require any humans and will run "lights out." In these factories, robotics and AI systems will fully automate production functions. All machines will be able to self-diagnose and self-repair. Pervasive analytics will be able to provide real-time visibility into all aspects of the production process and across the supply chain. All this will be enabled by software and an Ethernet-based connected factory infrastructure. We may be some years away from achieving this vision, but the technology foundations do exist today, and are now starting to be deployed in discrete manufacturing environments.

Note   In the world of manufacturing, there are generally two classes: discrete and process manufacturing. *Discrete manufacturing* refers to the production of distinct items, such as computers, fishing rods, and hand tools. *Process manufacturing* refers to the production of goods that are produced in bulk, such as foods, cement, and chemicals.

Business Improvements Driven Through IoT

The encouraging news for manufacturers is that, while technology and business models are changing dramatically, and the convergence of IT and OT production networks is inevitable, the same metrics that were the focus of business process improvements and quality efforts in the past are still in force with IoT and digital manufacturing initiatives today.

Note   An example of the manufacturing industry's drive for quality is illustrated by the Six Sigma methodology. Six Sigma is a set of data-driven manufacturing techniques used to reduce defects. The name is taken from the goal of limiting any process to less than six standard deviations between the mean and nearest specification limit, aiming for a defect-free product 99.99966% of the time. The approach was first introduced by Bill Smith, an engineer working at Motorola, and was later a key focus of GE CEO Jack Welch. Six Sigma today is a set of tools and methods used for constant quality improvement.

Manufacturers are expecting profound improvements in key manufacturing metrics as visibility increases through improved connectivity to assets in the factory and across the enterprise. Improvements include reduced unplanned downtime, improved quality, and improved OEE.

In one case where a leading robot manufacturer implemented a real-time data analysis and predictive maintenance application for a leading auto manufacturer, unplanned downtime on several thousand robots was completely eliminated. This saved the manufacturer approximately $40 million in downtime in just a few weeks. Examples like this are leading to raised expectations of what is possible through the digital transformation of manufacturing.

An Architecture for the Connected Factory

In the past, traditional factory networks were deployed ad hoc. They were isolated and air-gapped from the enterprise IT network. In addition, network security in the factory was typically limited to an industrial DMZ, leaving the machines mostly unprotected. Factories rarely deployed network-level security systems that included identity policies and secure remote access tools that allowed plant-level data to be securely extended to the cloud. This is starting to change. Companies are beginning to tie together their industrial automation and control systems (IACS) with IT applications and analytics tools to provide control and analytics capabilities that are driving operational and business benefits.

CPwE is an architectural framework that provides network services to IACS devices and equipment and promotes secure integration into the enterprise network. Before the CPwE framework can be discussed in detail, it is important to define several key terms and review the IACS reference model, which CPwE heavily leverages.

Industrial Automation and Control Systems Reference Model

For several decades, manufacturing environments have relied on many different types of technologies to enable communication in the plant. These often have depended on vendor-specific proprietary communications protocols, which have, in turn, required purpose-built and vendor-specific networks.

Today, Ethernet and IP have become the standard for IACS communication systems. The IACS reference model uses a logical framework to describe the network and security functions of the manufacturing system. Following the Purdue Model for Control Hierarchy developed in the 1990s by the Purdue University Consortium for Computer Integrated Manufacturing, the manufacturing industry segments devices and equipment into hierarchical functions. The Purdue Model for Control Hierarchy is discussed in Chapter 8, "Securing IoT." The International Society of Automation (ISA99) Committee for Manufacturing and Control Systems Security (now IEC-26443) has identified a logical framework for manufacturing based on this hierarchy, shown in Figure 9-3.

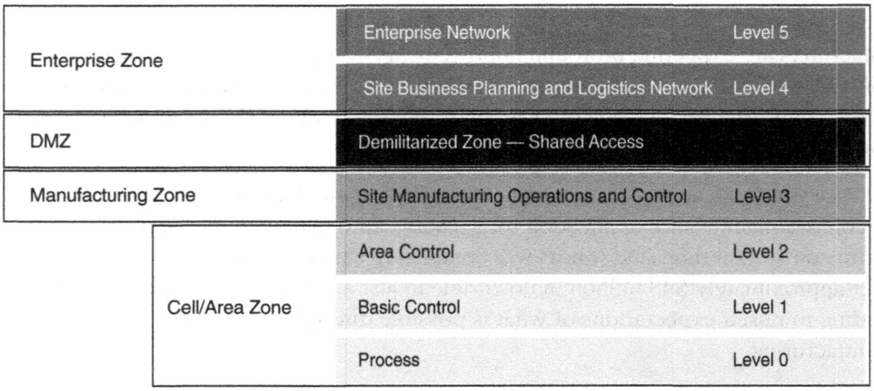

Enterprise Zone	Enterprise Network	Level 5
	Site Business Planning and Logistics Network	Level 4
DMZ	Demilitarized Zone — Shared Access	
Manufacturing Zone	Site Manufacturing Operations and Control	Level 3
Cell/Area Zone	Area Control	Level 2
	Basic Control	Level 1
	Process	Level 0

Figure 9-3   *The ISA99 / IEC-62443 IACS Logical Framework, Based on the Purdue Model for Control Hierarchy*

The IACS logical framework identifies functional zones and levels of the manufacturing plant and defines operations at each level. (Note that the naming convention used here is "levels," not "layers," to avoid confusion with protocol stack models, such as the OSI model.) These zones are defined as follows:

- **Safety zone:** Systems in the safety zone are typically hard-wired and air-gapped from the IACS network. The safety system's function in this zone is to provide an IACS shutdown (a "stop" button) in case of an emergency. You can think of this as a hardwired fail-safe used to protect personnel and equipment if a dangerous event occurs.

- **Manufacturing zone:** The manufacturing zone is composed of the cell/area zones (Levels 0–2) and site-level manufacturing (Level 3) activities. The manufacturing zone is important because all IACS applications, devices, and controllers critical to monitoring and controlling plant IACS operations are here. To support secure plant operations and functioning of the IACS applications, there is a secure separation of the manufacturing zone and the enterprise zone (Levels 4 and 5).

- **Cell/area zone:** The cell/area zone is the machine area within a plant. There are typically multiple cell/area zones within a single plant. For example, in an electronics plant, a cell/area may be the assembly process area. The cell/area zone might consist of just a single controller and associated devices, or it could be many controllers on a large assembly line.

  A single factory may in fact have many cell/areas. For the purposes of the CPwE architecture, a cell/area zone is a set of IACS devices and controllers that are involved in the real-time control of a functional aspect of the manufacturing process. To control the functional process, IACS devices need to be in real-time communication with other IACS devices, meaning the network connecting them needs to be fast and reliable. This zone has essentially three levels of activity:

  - **Level 0: Process:** Level 0 is the "things" level in manufacturing IoT and consists of sensors and actuators involved in the manufacturing process. These IoT devices perform IACS functions, such as moving a manufacturing robot, spraying, driving a motor, and welding. These devices are in communication with the basic control devices in Level 1.

  - **Level 1: Basic control:** Level 1 is where the controllers that direct the manufacturing process live. These controllers interact with Level 0 IoT devices. In discrete manufacturing, a controller is usually a PLC, and in process manufacturing, it is known as a distributed control system (DCS).

  - **Level 2: Area supervisory control:** Level 2 includes functions within the cell/area zone that require runtime supervision and operation. Some examples include HMIs, alarms, and control workstations.

Figure 9-4 illustrates the types of device and corresponding interfaces in Levels 0–2.

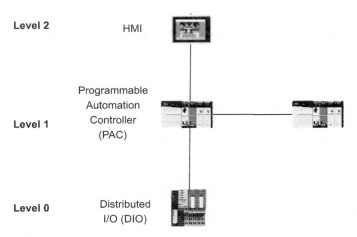

Figure 9-4 *IACS Controller Traffic Flow*

- **Level 3: Site level:** The applications and functions at Level 3 include SCADA systems, file servers, control room workstations, scheduling systems, and reporting systems. Note that this level is not a subset of the cell/area zone but is part of the larger manufacturing zone.

- **Demilitarized zone (DMZ):** The DMZ is the CPwE demarcation between the plant operational network and the traditional network. DMZ security is critical to plant operations as it protects the machines at the lower level from malicious activity that may occur in the traditional enterprise network.

- **Enterprise zone:** Levels 4 and 5 in the enterprise zone relate to traditional IT/enterprise networking functions, including file services, Internet connectivity, and email systems.

The CPwE Reference Model

With the manufacturing industry's acceptance of Ethernet for industrial applications, several new communications protocols have emerged that take advantage of both Ethernet and TCP/IP. In response to this trend, Cisco and Rockwell Automation began co-development of the Converged Plantwide Ethernet (CPwE) reference model, which is primarily focused on the transport of EtherNet/IP (discussed later in this chapter).

The CPwE solution is designed to enable the convergence of IACS applications with enterprise IT systems. Figure 9-5 illustrates the overall CPwE network architecture. In this framework, the cell/area zone contains the IACS devices from Levels 0 to 2. Devices that reside here, such as HMIs and controllers, belong to a single cell/area network. An HMI is simply the interface between the machine and the human operator. In the CPwE architecture, IACS devices communicate with EtherNet/IP and real-time control traffic throughout the cell/area using Ethernet. CPwE Ethernet networks come in various topologies, including redundant star, bus/star, and ring. A more detailed discussion of CPwE topologies and the redundancy technologies they utilize is provided later in this chapter.

Ethernet infrastructure devices in the cell/area zone are predominantly industrial-grade access switches that are ruggedized and hardened against electrostatic discharge, are fanless, and support an extended temperature range. As shown in Figure 9-5, the distribution switches between the cell/area and industrial zones form a demarcation point. Because these distribution switches touch the same Ethernet segment as the access switches in the cell/area, they are also considered cell/area infrastructure devices and are typically required to be ruggedized devices. The distribution switch is also the demarcation point between Layer 2 and Layer 3.

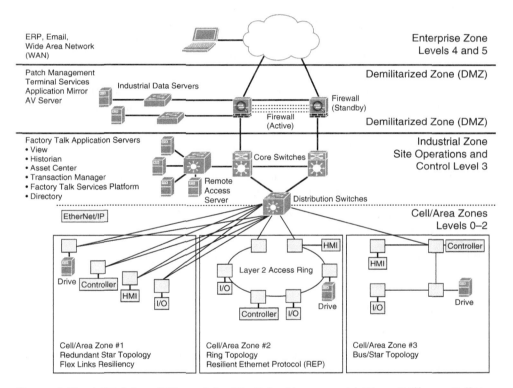

Figure 9-5   *A High-Level View of the CPwE Architecture with Three Different Cell/Area Zone Ethernet Topologies*

The industrial zone is analogous to Level 3 of the IACS reference model and is also very similar to a traditional campus network. Most plants have only a single industrial zone. As with most campus networks, the industrial zone incorporates access switches for plant IT operations and employee services, and it includes core network functions. The industrial zone provides network connectivity through routed distribution switches to multiple cell/area zones as required. The industrial zone also supports IP routing capabilities for IACS devices that require Level 3 application support.

The demilitarized zone (DMZ) is the zone that sits between the industrial and enterprise zones and is used to securely manage traffic flows between networks in the adjacent zones. This is also the point where a plant firewall is typically implemented to control traffic flow into and out of the plant network.

CPwE Resilient Network Design

Due to sensitive controller and application requirements in IACS networks, network resiliency between IACS devices is a mandatory requirement within cell/area zones. Resilient IACS networks need to support the following capabilities:

- **Availability:** LAN topology design is critical in supporting IACS application uptime and business continuity. IACS applications have stringent requirements that must be considered for the LAN design, including network availability, performance, and distance between equipment. For critical operations where uptime is crucial, a fully redundant physical path in the IACS Ethernet network topology should be chosen.

- **Predictable performance:** Meeting the predictable, reliable, and real-time traffic requirements of IACS applications is a requirement for successful CPwE deployments.

- **Fast network reconvergence:** In the event of equipment or link failure, network restoration times need to be minimized so that other IACS devices are not impacted by the failure. Typical IACS application interruption tolerance limits are on the order of less than 100 ms, with minimal jitter.

- **Industrial protocol support:** CPwE IACS devices and networking equipment need to support industrial application protocol requirements.

The following are examples of communication patterns that require network resiliency:

- Controller to HMI

- Controller to controller

- Controller to input/output (I/O; the sensor and controller modules for machines)

- Controller to variable frequent drives (VFDs; adjustable electromechanical drives to control a motor)

- Controller to motor control centers (MCCs; used in factories to control a large number of motors from one central controller)

As illustrated in Figure 9-5, several different Ethernet topologies may be used in the cell/area zone, but in all cases, high availability of the Ethernet segment within the zone is a requirement. Depending on the Ethernet topology that is implemented, different high-availability technologies may be used to achieve application continuity. For example, in a simple redundant-star topology, network resiliency technologies such as Flex Links or cross-stack EtherChannel are popular. Flex Links have dual uplinks where one is active and one is standby. If the active link fails for some reason, the backup link takes over.

With EtherChannel, both the uplinks are used simultaneously, and traffic is load balanced across the two links. If either of them fails, the other is still active, but with half the available uplink bandwidth.

Consider the example of how the CPwE model was used to improve the manufacturing system of one of the largest motorcycle manufacturers in the world. The company was building hundreds of motorcycles each shift, but it was dealing with significant manufacturing challenges due to the complexity of supporting different vehicle configurations. The company's key objective was to improve agility in the manufacturing process. It was able to address this by bringing machine data into a central dashboard over the Ethernet network. This approach allowed the company to collate data from across the factory, allowing better response situations on the plant floor and, ultimately, a substantial reduction in machine downtime.

Having the ability to quickly bring new machines online and connect them to the Ethernet network has yielded much greater flexibility and has significantly reduced new model and new product introduction, thus improving the overall time to market.

Resilient Ethernet Protocol (REP)

In the CPwE reference architecture, Resilient Ethernet Protocol (REP) is used in the cell/area zone to achieve high-speed protection of ring topologies.

Similar to Spanning Tree Protocol (STP), standardized in IEEE 802.1D and its successors that support higher-speed convergence, REP controls a group of ports connected to an Ethernet segment to ensure that no bridging loops exist and that the Ethernet segment is able to respond to topology changes. When used on a fiber infrastructure, REP is able to achieve sub-50 ms convergence times when a link in a segment is broken or some other topology change occurs (such as a switch failure). Another key advantage of REP is that it is not limited to a small number of devices on a single Ethernet segment. Traditional STP is limited to only seven devices per segment, a number that can quickly become the limiting factor on the plant floor. Conversely, REP has no fixed upper limit on the number of nodes per segment, thus supporting large ring topologies.

For each REP segment, one switch is designated as a master node that controls the overall ring. The master node requires three critical pieces of information:

- Identification of the REP control VLAN, which allows the REP control messages to be communicated throughout the segment

- The location of the edges of the REP segment

- The preferred place to break the ring under normal conditions, which is called the "alternate port" (If none is configured, REP automatically selects the alternate port, making the decision nondeterministic.)

A REP segment is a chain of ports on an Ethernet segment configured with a segment ID. When all ports in the ring segment are active, one port is identified as the alternate port, meaning it is in the blocking state, thus preventing the ring from becoming a Layer 2 bridging loop. If any other port in the REP segment fails, the alternate port is signaled to change state into the forwarding state, repairing the broken Ethernet ring segment and allowing communications to continue.

REP uses a loss of signal (LOS) detection mechanism to learn of adjacent neighbor failures on the segment. When a switch port detects a REP segment failure (such as a fiber break or a physical switch failure), notification messages indicating a link failure are sent to all the other REP switches. In addition to notifying the alternate port to change to a forwarding state, these notification messages signal that the MAC addresses in content addressable memory (CAM) of all switches must be flushed. In this manner, a new bridging path is formed. Figures 9-6 and 9-7 illustrate the REP failure notification and repair mechanism.

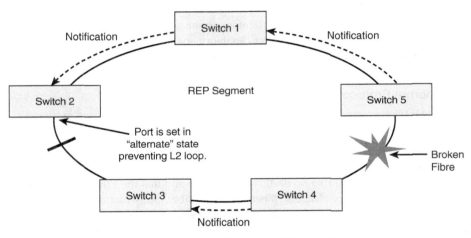

Figure 9-6 *REP Notification When a Topology Change Occurs*

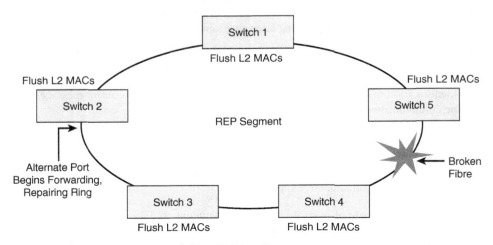

Figure 9-7 *Reconvergence of the REP Ring Segment*

Note   Although there are many proprietary Ethernet Ring Protection Switching (ERPS) technologies available on the market today (including REP), there has also been an effort to standardize high-speed ERPS. This effort has been led by the ITU-T under G.8032. G.8032 has many similarities to REP, including sub-50 ms ring protection times and the support for a multitiered ladder topology. While the industry is now beginning to move toward G.8032 as the standard for high-speed ERPS, G.8032 still struggles with limited commercial availability.

As plant network convergence drives significant change in manufacturing organizations, systems, and networks, REP plays an important role in improving application availability. In the event of a network disruption, REP networks support continued IACS functionality and reduced downtime costs while preserving throughput productivity and sustained operations. Applications deployed in a REP environment support a wide variety of manufacturing disciplines, including batch, discrete, process, and hybrid manufacturing.

Business Value of Resiliency in Converged Networks

Designing a factory with network resiliency has a significantly positive business impact for a manufacturer. Increasing numbers of devices are being connected on the plant floor. These devices are being connected using the same network technology as the Internet. Devices, such as sensors, embedded into manufacturing devices that collect data are now used as tools to better understand complex processes. Today, when work on cell/area zone network devices requires significant planning and outage, a resilient network design allows a single device to be taken out of service without impacting the rest of the cell/area network. The network is thus more forgiving of single-point outages, allowing flexibility in network upgrades and maintenance.

REP-based architectures enhance the production network's resilience and ability to support systems that connect people, processes, and data to real-time applications, even during a network disruption. In manufacturing, Ethernet networks are driving a new generation of connected, intelligent machines with improved network visibility into the plant.

CPwE Wireless

While CPwE is often deployed with wired Ethernet access switches, plantwide architectures are increasingly using Wi-Fi (IEEE 802.11) for critical IACS applications. These applications have similar network requirements to their wired Ethernet brethren in that they demand reliable data transfer and quality of service (QoS) handling with minimal latency and jitter for critical applications.

CPwE wireless networks can be used to manage machines, handheld devices, and automated guided vehicles (AGVs). Wireless brings the flexibility to quickly change a manufacturing line or move assets as needs arise, without worrying about the physical wiring. In addition, location-based tags and sensors are now being used to provide visibility to assets and goods moving around the plant floor.

CPwE Wireless Network Architecture

Wi-Fi networks differ significantly from traditional wired LANs in their use of shared radio frequencies, susceptibility to interference, and coverage impairments. Deploying a Wi-Fi network requires thoughtful planning and design, as well as periodic monitoring to meet expectations for bandwidth, QoS handling, throughput, reliability, and security. Most importantly, an industrial wireless local area network (WLAN) design and implementation must meet the performance requirements of IACS applications.

Wi-Fi is a wireless technology where stations need to "contend," or compete, for their chance to send a frame over the air. This means that latency varies, depending on several factors, including how many stations are associated to the AP, how much traffic they are sending (including how busy the AP is), and interference. This could pose a serious problem for certain IACS applications that are latency sensitive. In cases where a control system needs predictable latency, alternate wireless technologies that use Time-Sensitive Networking (TSN), such as WirelessHART or ISA100.11a, are preferable over Wi-Fi. (These technologies are discussed in Chapter 4, "Connecting Smart Objects.") The downside of these technologies is that they support much smaller bandwidth than Wi-Fi.

If Wi-Fi is chosen for the plant floor, the WLAN systems needs to be tailored to IACS use cases for Wi-Fi networking within the plant. The WLAN should integrate the IACS into the broader manufacturing environment, and a wide range of client device types and applications should be taken into consideration, along with the strictness of the latency required by the IACS application.

One such architecture that uses a centralized wireless LAN controller (WLC) to manage the APs distributed throughout the plant is illustrated in Figure 9-8. By using a WLC, a centralized management model is created, thus introducing security and self-healing mechanisms to the wireless network.

Note   While the focus in this chapter is on centralized controller-based WLANs, the CPwE design and implementation guides provide details of autonomous AP deployment models in the connected factory. While controller-based Wi-Fi deployments are becoming very popular, you are likely to see many factories still using autonomous APs that do not use a controller.

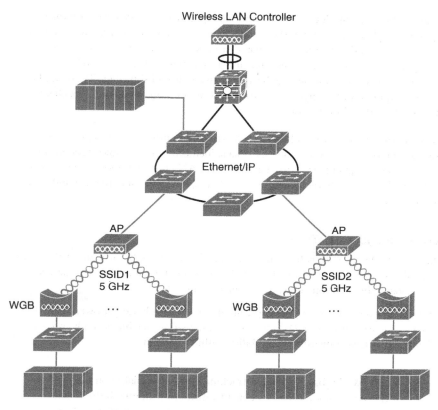

Figure 9-8   *A Factory Wireless LAN Architecture*

The following are several use-case examples where Wi-Fi is used in manufacturing environments:

■ **Fixed-position devices:** Fixed-position devices in the WLAN have a permanent operational location and are also known as "static." Fixed-position wireless is an alternative to a wired connection for hard-to-reach and remote locations where cabling is too expensive or impossible to install. Usage areas include process control, machine condition monitoring, fixed environmental monitoring, and energy industries. In the manufacturing environment, a common use case is a standalone original equipment manufacturer (OEM) machine or skid that needs to be integrated into a production line over a wireless link.

■ **Nomadic devices:** Nomadic equipment stays in place while operating and then moves to a new location in the shutdown state. After relocation, a new wireless connection commonly needs to be established. Examples are process skids, storage tanks, reactors, and portable manufacturing equipment.

■ **Operational relocation devices:** Some mobile equipment changes position during an operation, while remaining in the same wireless coverage zone. Examples include rotary platforms and turntables, automated storage and retrieval systems (ASRS), assembly systems, overhead cranes, and similar machinery that uses wireless as a replacement for wired solutions, such as inductive rails and slip rings. These applications may require rapid changes in position and orientation of the wireless client relative to the AP within the coverage area.

Deploying a factory Wi-Fi network based on centralized controller design principles allows you to overcome many common challenges, including shared radio frequencies, interference, and coverage impairments. The wireless LAN controller model also allows you to easily deploy key technology features, such as QoS, Wi-Fi security capabilities, and location services.

Real-Time Location System (RTLS)

When a factory Wi-Fi network is fully in place and offers thorough coverage of the plant floor, it may also be leveraged as an RTLS. RTLS solves a common problem in factories: the need to manage the location and status of plant materials.

Wi-Fi–based location tracking systems typically include active battery-powered Wi-Fi radio frequency identification (RFID) tags that are attached to machines, skids, vehicles, or other devices that have a measure of mobility within the plant.

Note There are various Wi-Fi–based location tracking systems available on the market, and the accuracy of these technologies varies considerably. For example, RSSI/distance-based location techniques require data from several access points to calculate a device's location. RSSI stands for received signal strength indicator and is simply a measurement of the power in an incoming radio wave. In contrast, Wi-Fi–based angulation (also known as angle of arrival) techniques use an array of antennas on a single AP to measure the angle of arrival, and can typically produce much more accurate location estimates than the RSSI/distance measurement approach. Many RFID tags use a small battery and send a message at a configurable interval (which can range from a few seconds to every hour), thus changing the accuracy in the time dimension. Larger devices may include a bigger battery, allowing for a signal to be sent each second or more often. For this reason, RTLS is often referred to as nRTLS, or Near Real-Time Location System.

By using RTLS and a graphical location visualization tool, it is possible for assembly workers, shift supervisors, and plant managers to view the location of plant materials and assets through tablets and smart phones. With real-time visibility into track production, floor managers are also able to track each line's output and determine whether production is meeting daily targets.

A good example of RTLS in practice comes from one of the world's leading airplane manufacturers. This manufacturer decided to equip all the safety equipment on its planes with RFID tags. When an aircraft goes through maintenance, one job is to inspect each piece of equipment and verify that it is accounted for. Without RFID tags, this job took on average 6.5 hours per plane. With RFID tags in place, the time dropped to 20 minutes per plane. On the factory floor, using RFID tags to locate airplane parts has allowed the company to assemble planes faster by using movement optimization software that moves parts where they are needed and removes objects that may reduce access to other parts. The company estimate its gain per year per factory at $100 million.

Using RTLS also allows plant managers to monitor how quickly employees are completing their respective stages in the production process. The business value of RTLS in manufacturing is that it helps factory managers better understand how to increase efficiency and lower costs associated with inventory. By tracking inventory and the location of materials, RTLS is also able to help improve customer service by providing accurate delivery schedules.

Industrial Automation Control Protocols

Industrial automation application systems use a unique set of protocols for control, motion, synchronization, and safety. The development of these industrial protocols began long before the days of Ethernet and IP, but in recent years, efforts have been made to adapt these automation protocols to take advantage of the benefits of modern transport mechanisms.

The list of available automation control protocols is very long, but the three with the largest market adoption are discussed in the following sections: EtherNet/IP, PROFINET, and Modbus/TCP.

EtherNet/IP and CIP

EtherNet/IP is an open standard for industrial automation systems that was developed by Rockwell Automation and is now managed by the Open DeviceNet Vendors Association (ODVA). Note that in the case of EtherNet/IP, "IP" stands for "Industrial Protocol," not "Internet Protocol." Industrial Protocols are specifically used to handle industrial automation applications, such as those for control, safety, motion, and configuration.

EtherNet/IP adapts the Common Industrial Protocol (CIP) to standard Ethernet and TCP/IP technology. CIP is a communications protocol used for I/O control, device configuration, and data collection in automation and control systems. CIP includes capabilities for the following types of communications:

- **Implicit messaging:** This type of messaging involves real-time I/O data, functional safety data, motion control data, and often UDP multicast.
- **Explicit messaging:** This type of messaging involves configuration, diagnostics, and data collection, and it is based on TCP unicast messaging.

Figure 9-9 illustrates a manufacturing network based on EtherNet/IP. As discussed in the previous section, REP is used as a resiliency mechanism between the industrial Ethernet switches (IESs) to pass CIP Class 1 (real-time Ethernet) and Class 3 (TCP) messages.

EtherNet/IP also specifies a redundancy protocol known as Device Level Ring (DLR), which is used when the system requires continuous operation and is able to achieve high-speed reconvergence in the case of a ring break. DLR is optimally deployed where devices have an integrated two-port switch and do not require separate industrial Ethernet switches.

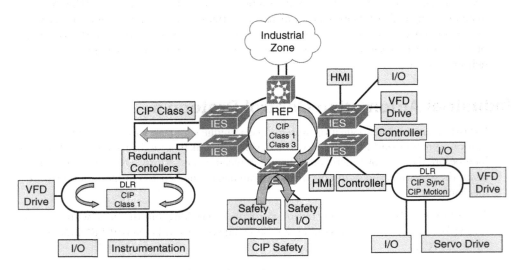

Figure 9-9   *A Factory Network Based on EtherNet/IP*

Note   The CPwE reference architecture for industrial applications discussed earlier is largely based on EtherNet/IP and CIP.

PROFINET

PROFINET (Process Field Net) is a widely used industrial technology for the exchange of data between controllers and devices. One of the key advantages of PROFINET is that it exchanges messages in a deterministic manner over high-speed Ethernet links. Unlike Modbus TCP, which uses TCP to communicate between devices (thus requiring devices to establish and maintain a TCP socket connection), or EtherNet/IP, which uses UDP, PROFINET is able to send and receive data directly to the application layer, without having to wait for processing in the TCP/IP stack, which has the potential of introducing variable delay.

Note   How does PROFINET compare with EtherNet/IP? EtherNet/IP and PROFINET are different standards for industrial automation and are the two leaders in the industrial Ethernet fieldbus market. In a nutshell, EtherNet/IP is supported by ODVA and was developed by Rockwell Automation, which is a leader in the manufacturing industry, especially in North America. PROFINET is supported by PROFINET International (PI) and is the market leader in Europe and the Middle East; it is supported by Siemens and other vendors.

From a networking perspective, a key difference is in how the two standards approach deterministic networking and real-time communications. EtherNet/IP leverages UDP/IP for real-time communications (similar to Voice over IP applications), whereas PROFINET uses a unique EtherType to bypass the UDP/IP layers of the stack to allow direct application communication.

PROFINET is fully compatible with standard IEEE 802.3 Ethernet, which means regular Ethernet devices can coexist with PROFINET I/O devices and controllers on the same segment. However, PROFINET also has some significant differences from standard Ethernet. For example, PROFINET is a deterministic protocol, which means frames are sent and received at specific times. This is especially important in discrete manufacturing, when a controller needs to send a message to a device to stop or change operation.

PROFINET applications are time sensitive. Network services, applications, and devices are all dependent on command and control traffic being delivered within strict delay tolerances, which means any network-induced delay is a critical design consideration. To address this, PROFINET networks are designed to support real-time PROFINET communications with minimal latency, while supporting network resiliency at the manufacturing plant floor. PROFINET architectures consist of the following:

- **Industrial automation devices:** These include robots, sensors, actuators, and drives.

- **HMIs:** HMIs provide visual status reports and control of the industrial automation devices.

- **Controllers:** Examples include PLCs and distributed I/O devices.

A well-designed PROFINET architecture provides the following operational benefits:

- It reduces the risk of production downtime through the use of a resilient network architecture capable of network convergence based on the IEC 62439-2 standard. IEC 62439-2 is covered in more detail later in this chapter, in the section "Media Redundancy Protocol (MRP)."

- It improves plant uptime through validated reference architectures, with a focus on application availability.

- It enriches critical information access from machines and applications through better managed network resources.

■ It enhances single-pane management compliance, using industry standard general system description (GSD) files and supervisor applications of PROFINET-compliant devices. GSD files contain a device's capabilities and characteristics, and they enable efficient integration, configuration, and management of that device in a PROFINET network.

The PROFINET Architecture

The PROFINET architecture for the connected factory is similar in many ways to the CPwE architecture discussed previously, including support for network resiliency services provided to devices, equipment, and applications in an industrial automation environment.

Similar to CPwE, PROFINET leverages the Purdue Model for Control Hierarchy. The cell/area zone (Levels 0–2) is where most of the real-time PROFINET traffic moves between industrial automation system devices. The upper manufacturing zone acts as an aggregation point for one or more cell/area zones.

The PROFINET architecture utilizes strict traffic segregation methods to protect industrial automation applications from external and internal interruptions. Disruptions in the control network—even short ones lasting just milliseconds—can create significant impacts on the functioning of a production facility.

Network resiliency is the primary consideration in the PROFINET architecture shown in Figure 9-10.

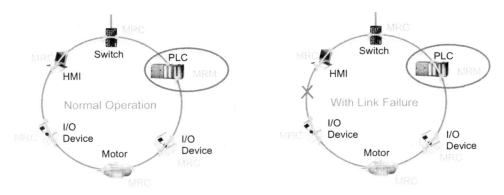

Figure 9-10   *PROFINET MRP Operation*

Much as with CPwE, the cell/area zone is the primary zone where most of the industrial automation activities are performed. It is important to consider this zone as an isolated entity of the manufacturing environment where availability and performance are the most important considerations.

Media Redundancy Protocol (MRP)

Determinism and network performance are key requirements for PROFINET stability in the cell/area zone. Determinism in industrial automation ensures that Ethernet frames are sent and arrive when required. While the PROFINET device is responsible for scheduling and transmitting the Ethernet frame, the network's main impact on a system's determinism is based on the following performance characteristics:

- **Latency:** The average amount of time a message takes to be transmitted and processed from originating node to destination node

- **Jitter:** The amount of variance in the latency

- **Packet Loss:** The number of packets, usually expressed as a percentage, lost in a transmission from one device to another

Industrial automation networks need to have low levels of latency and jitter, and they need to support reliable data transmission for real-time applications. In industrial automation implementations, an application's timing requirements often vary, depending on the underlying process, system, or devices.

Industrial automation networks must adhere to the following requirements for real-time applications:

- **Machine and process cycle times:** This includes the frequency with which the industrial automation application moves from one operation to the next.

- **Request packet interval (RPI) or I/O update time:** This is the frequency at which input and outputs are sent and received.

- **Packet-loss tolerance:** This is the number of consecutive packet intervals lost before an application generates errors or fails into a safe state.

To meet these strict requirements and protect against application layer issues of link or switch failure, PROFINET supports a ring resiliency protocol known as Media Redundancy Protocol (MRP). MRP is an industry protocol defined in the IEC 62439-2 standard. MRP allows rings of industrial Ethernet switches to overcome a single segment failure with recovery times similar to those of REP. MRP is suitable for industrial Ethernet applications and is natively supported in PROFINET.

PROFINET-compliant industrial Ethernet switches support two roles in an MRP ring. In a ring topology, only one switch or industrial automation device can act as a media redundancy manager (MRM), and all other devices act as media redundancy clients (MRCs). The purpose of the MRM is to keep the ring loop free and provide redundancy when failure happens. The MRM does this by sending control packets or test frames from one ring port and receiving them on its other ring port. During normal operation, the control packets are received, and the MRM keeps a port blocked to prevent a loop. If the MRM does not receive its own control packet, this means the loop is not intact, and a network failure has occurred. The MRM informs the MRCs about the network failure.

It unblocks its port and starts forwarding to provide connectivity until the network failure is resolved (refer to Figure 9-10).

Table 9-1 provides a list of resiliency protocols and their interoperability with types of topology and convergence requirements.

Table 9-1   *A Comparison of Ethernet Ring Resiliency Protocols*

Protocol	Topology	Number of Nodes	Typical Convergence	Comments
802.1D STP	Any	Max 7 hops	50 s	Not suited for industrial automation due to slow convergence time, which affects real-time applications
Rapid Spanning Tree (802.1w)	Any	Max 20 hops	~2-3 seconds −6 s	Not well suited for ring topologies
MRP	Ring	50	30–500 ms	Part of PROFINET
ITU G.8032	Ring	16 recommended (250 max)	50 ms	ITU standard, similar to REP
DLR (Device Level Ring)	Ring	50	3 ms	Predictable convergence
REP	Ring	Unlimited	50–250 ms	Cisco proprietary but widely deployed in manufacturing, utilities, and other industrial use cases

Modbus/TCP

Modbus was originally introduced in the 1970s by Modicon (now Schneider). It is a serial communications protocol that is widely used in manufacturing, utilities, and many other industries. In the manufacturing world, Modbus is most commonly used for management of PLCs in a master/slave configuration. Much like other automation control standards, Modbus has been adapted to modern communications standards, including Ethernet and TCP/IP.

Modbus is popular due to the fact that the protocol is an open published standard and is well established throughout the world. The Modbus master/slave configuration is well suited to the connection-oriented nature of TCP, but this mode of communication tends to introduce extra latency and is generally not as flexible as either EtherNet/IP or PROFINET.

Modbus/TCP is discussed in greater detail in Chapter 6, "Application Protocols for IoT."

Connected Factory Security

Manufacturing has become one of the top industries targeted by cyber criminals. Often, the solution has been simply to air-gap the factory floor network by disconnecting it from the IT enterprise network. However, a network disconnected from higher-layer functions is limited in its capabilities and business improvements that may be achieved through IoT. In addition, many threats arise from the plant floor computers and workstations that are physically accessible by contractors or employees with unfettered access. For example, consider the Stuxnet worm, mentioned in Chapter 2, "IoT Network Architecture and Design," and Chapter 8, which is thought to have been introduced through a physical USB device on the internal network.

A Holistic Approach to Industrial Security

No single product, technology, or methodology can fully secure industrial applications from cyber attack. Protecting IACS assets requires a "defense-in-depth" security approach that addresses internal and external threats. This approach implements multiple layers of defense (physical, procedural, and electronic) at each IACS level.

A comprehensive IACS security framework should serve as a natural extension to the industrial control system network. However, for existing IACS deployments that have little in the way of security, the same defense-in-depth model can be applied incrementally to help improve the security posture of the IACS.

In most cases, holistic factory security requires that different stakeholders work together, including control system engineers, IT network engineers, and the IT security architects. Responsibilities for these different stakeholders include the following:

- Control system engineers:
  - IACS device hardening (that is, physical and electronic)
  - Infrastructure device hardening (for example, port security)
  - Network segmentation
  - IACS application authentication, authorization, and accounting (for example, AAA)
- Control system engineers in collaboration with IT network engineers:
  - Zone-based policy firewalls at the IACS application
  - Operating system hardening
  - Network device hardening (for example, access control, resiliency)
  - Wireless LAN access control policies
- IT security architects in collaboration with control systems engineers:
  - Identity services (wired and wireless)

- Directory services

- Remote access servers

- Plant firewalls

- Industrial demilitarized zone (IDMZ) design best practices

Figure 9-11 illustrates an overall holistic security architecture for the connected factory and highlights places where each of these security considerations need to be implemented.

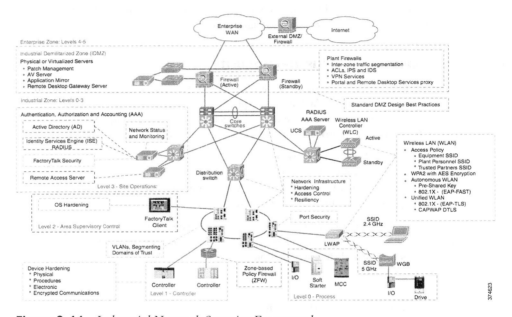

Figure 9-11   *Industrial Network Security Framework*

While industrial network security is a vast subject, it can be treated only briefly in this book. The following sections address three aspects of factory security:

- Network Address Translation in the factory

- The industrial DMZ

- Factory security identity services

Network Address Translation in the Factory

Whether you are an end user, an OEM, or a system integrator, IP addresses in your IACS application may need to be reused. Network Address Translation (NAT) enables the reuse of IP addressing without introducing duplicate IP address errors into your IACS application architecture.

Technology and business aspects drive the decision to use NAT:

- **Business drivers:** Machine builder OEMs often produce similar machines that all have the same IP address and rely on NAT to enable the rapid deployment and replication of skids and machines, including IP addressing. This helps reduce development and commissioning costs.

- **Technology drivers:** NAT is used when the IP address space in the plantwide network infrastructure is limited and not every device needs to communicate outside the skid or machine-level network.

Plantwide architectures require unique IP addressing for each device. NAT is a networking technology that enables control system engineers to build IACS applications that reuse IP addresses, while allowing those IACS applications to integrate into the larger plantwide architecture.

NAT can be configured to translate specific IP addresses from inside the IACS application to the outside plant network. Doing so provides the added benefit of effectively hiding the inside IP addressing scheme of the IACS application. NAT translations have two forms: one-to-one (1:1) and one-to-many (1:n).

It is important to note that the NAT design needs to be scalable because multiple cells/areas may be present in a factory network.

A common use case, as depicted in Figure 9-12, is the coordination of control functions of an OEM machine by a line controller. In this case, there are multiple machines, each with its own machine controller. Note, however, that there is one line controller on the outside, used for both machines. Both IACS devices have been deployed with the same IP address and require NAT to communicate with the line controller.

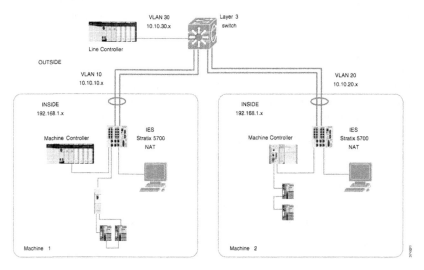

Figure 9-12 *Multiple Machines Deployed with the Same IP Addresses Requiring NAT*

VLAN 10 is deployed for Machine 1, VLAN 20 for Machine 2, and VLAN 30 for the line controller. Machine 1's NAT switch translates the inside IP address (192.168.1.x) of the machine controller to an outside IP address (10.10.10.x) on VLAN 10. The NAT switch also translates the outside IP address of the default gateway (the Layer 3 switch) to an inside IP address. Correspondingly, Machine 2's NAT switch translates the inside IP address (192.168.1.x) of the machine controller to an outside IP address (10.10.20.x) on VLAN 20. Likewise, Machine 2's NAT switch also translates the outside IP address of the default gateway to an inside IP address.

Between the Layer 3 switch and the NAT switches is a unique VLAN for each machine, and each controller has a unique outside IP address. The Layer 3 switch on the outside routes the outside IP address of each machine controller either to the line controller (vertical interlocking) on VLAN 30 or to the other machine VLAN (horizontal interlocking).

This scalable use case enables the integration of multiple skids or machines with a duplicated IP addressing scheme into the same line controller VLAN. For this use case, a NAT-capable industrial Ethernet switch is required for each skid or machine. A Layer 3 distribution-layer switch is also required to enable routing between the VLANs.

The Industrial DMZ

IACS networks run a manufacturing business. Although several attack vectors into IACS systems exist, penetration from the enterprise zone continues to be a key focus of the security architecture. To deal with this threat, many organizations and standards bodies recommend segmenting the business system networks from the plant networks by deploying an industrial demilitarized zone (IDMZ).

The IDMZ is a buffer that enforces data security policies between a trusted network (industrial zone) and an untrusted network (enterprise zone). The demilitarized zone concept is commonplace in traditional IT networks but is still in early adoption for IACS applications.

The IDMZ exists as a separate network located at a level between the industrial (identified as the manufacturing zone in the Purdue model in Figure 9-3) and enterprise zones, commonly referred to as Level 3.5. An IDMZ environment consists of numerous infrastructure devices, including firewalls, VPN servers, IACS application mirrors, and reverse proxy servers, in addition to network switches, routers, and virtualized services.

For secure IACS data sharing, the IDMZ contains assets that act as brokers between zones. Multiple methods to broker IACS data across the IDMZ exist:

- A reverse proxy server

- An application mirror, which is similar to a proxy server—essentially a facsimile of the actual application running outside the protected data center

- Remote desktop services (such as Microsoft RDP)

Key IDMZ design principles include the following:

- All IACS network traffic from either side of the IDMZ terminates in the IDMZ; no IACS traffic directly traverses the IDMZ, leaving no direct path between the industrial and enterprise zones.

- Industrial control traffic does not enter the IDMZ; it remains within the industrial zone.

- Primary services are not permanently stored in the IDMZ.

- All data is transient, meaning the IDMZ does not permanently store data.

- Functional subzones are used within the IDMZ to segment access to IACS data and network services (for example, partner access to resources).

- A properly designed IDMZ also supports the capability of being unplugged if compromised, while still allowing the industrial zone to operate without disruption.

Factory Security Identity Services

As access methods to the industrial network expand, the complexity of managing network access security and controlling unknown risks continues to increase. With a growing demand for in-plant access by contractors (such as OEMs and system integrators), plantwide networks face continued security threats.

In addition, IACS networks need to be secured against untrusted (and potentially compromised) computers, such as those used by contractors or partner vendors. With the proliferation of contractor devices in manufacturing plants and constrained plantwide operational resources, the potential impact of failing to identify and remediate security threats introduces a significant risk to plantwide operations.

Network identity services provide an additional layer of network access and control by identifying the type of computer, operating system, and user that is accessing the network. Based on the identity and applying a corresponding policy, identity services are able to push security policies to the network infrastructure that the computer is accessing. Since identity services are typically tied to directory services (such as LDAP or Microsoft Active Directory), the common practice is to use a centrally managed identity services model, with the IT department maintaining management of the identity system that operates from the industrial zone.

It is important to note that the security architecture likely needs to support both wired and wireless access methods by plant personnel and contractors. This is achieved by deploying a centralized identity services system that is capable of establishing a trust boundary on all network access points.

This approach provides the following benefits:

- A comprehensive centralized policy for network access in both the manufacturing and enterprise zones

- Streamlined device onboarding

- Policy-driven rules and access control policies

- Guest portal services for contractors and guests

Through the incorporation of a centralized identity system, policies can be applied across the network in real time so users experience consistent access to their services from both wired and wireless connections. In addition, unknown devices are directed to an administratively defined safe destination with no access to local resources in the plantwide operations, whereas trusted devices are granted access to essential platforms in the industrial zone.

Identity service tools also enable centralized guest portal services as well as policies for self-service registration of plant personnel, vendors, partners, and guests.

Edge Computing in the Connected Factory

Machines on the plant floor are capable of producing a massive amount of data. One way many factories have dealt with this challenge is to deploy PCs to collect this data. Collecting data from PCs on the plant floor has led to maintenance and security challenges, since each PC requires patching and operating system upgrades. Hardware failures are also common because the devices are often not ruggedized for factory conditions. Clearly, this approach makes it very difficult for factory operations to aggregate, digest, and respond to the data effectively. Such an approach is a major impediment to the visibility and the latent business benefits that could result from factory data analytics.

New trends in compute capacity at the network edge are helping resolve these dilemmas. With machine-embedded and near-machine edge compute devices that include switching, routing, and security features in a single ruggedized form factor, manufacturers are beginning to realize the value of connecting machines and edge compute services.

Connected Machines and Edge Computing

Connecting machines to plant-level applications requires a communications model and data scheme that is extensible, secure, and easy to implement. Several open manufacturing communications protocols have been developed that provide interoperability between devices and software, allowing you to monitor and then harvest data from the production floor. These protocols are generally based on XML or HTTP.

Different data standards exist for different machine types, so you should expect some heterogeneity in data protocols on the plant floor. For example, MTConnect is common for computer numerical control (CNC) machines, OPC UA is widely used in industrial automation, and PackML is used in packaging machines.

New developments in edge computing platforms combine switching, NAT, routing, and security features into a single ruggedized edge appliance. This edge services approach reduces costs for secure machine data collection and optimizes available network resources and bandwidth by analyzing data on the plant floor prior to transmitting it to the data center or cloud for further analysis.

The edge appliance typically includes a basic open source and efficient operating system like Linux, which runs a streaming analytics application and the required standard data agents needed for the respective machine types.

Hardware adapters for standard protocols are installed on the machine that define I/O tags for each machine and broadcast change of state for each tag to the agent on the edge appliance. The agent that resides on the edge appliance is configured to listen to specific adapters and buffer the predefined tags. Edge streaming analytics can be configured to parse the data and determine what is useful for further consideration and analysis. The refined data is then sent over HTTP or XML to an on-premises or cloud-based data center running a big data consumption and processing engine, such as Hadoop.

OEE analytics tools can be used for data visualization. (OEE is defined earlier in this chapter, in the section "An Introduction to Connected Manufacturing.") In some cases, OEM machine builders produce custom analytics software that can be delivered on-premises or through the cloud. Figure 9-13 illustrates the machine hardware adapter being used to pass data to an agent on the edge node/edge appliance for analysis and then only refined data being sent to the cloud for further analysis.

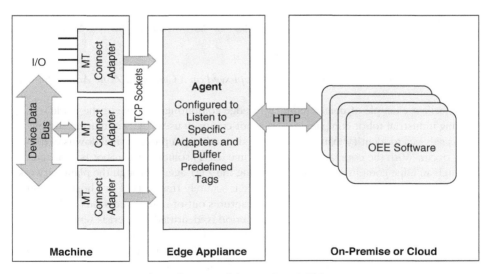

Figure 9-13   *Connected Machine Model Based on MTConnect*

Because the data can be sourced from disparate resources, it may be preferable to manage the applications in an enterprise portal environment with identity management capabilities. As machine builders mature in their delivery of OEE analytics for preventive maintenance, it is anticipated that they will increasingly deliver web services using

RESTful APIs that can be consumed in a connected machine's web portal for end-user manufacturers. Modern portal applications allow these services to be consumed from disparate sources with secure identity and Single Sign-On (SSO) capabilities.

For large manufacturers with heterogeneous plant floors, the task of identifying data standards for each machine type and working with machine builders to architect a solution can be daunting. Meanwhile, when enabled by a resilient, secure, and converged connected factory infrastructure with industrial Ethernet edge switches, the benefits of edge computing and storage can be realized in a reasonable timeframe. Figure 9-14 shows an example of how edge computing can be deployed on a ruggedized industrial switch directly attached to machines in the manufacturing zone.

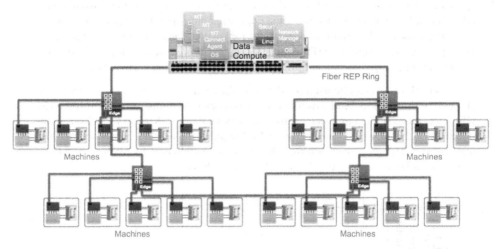

Figure 9-14 *Example of Edge Computing Deployed on a Cell/Area Zone Access Switch*

An excellent example of connected factory edge computing is in one of the world's leading industrial robot companies. This robot company uses edge computing and big data analytics to identify maintenance procedures that can prevent breakdowns before they occur. With the company's zero downtime (ZDT) solution, the robot is connected through an edge computing appliance running the ZDT agent through the plant network. The data relevant for optimizing maintenance is securely transmitted to a hosted cloud environment, where the analytics software captures out-of-range exceptions and predicts needed maintenance. When a maintenance period is identified, an alert is sent from the cloud application to service personnel, alerting them to the need for service. The required parts are then shipped to the factory in time for the next scheduled maintenance window. With thousands of robots connected through the ZDT application for one major auto manufacturer, this has helped save millions of dollars in unplanned downtime.

Summary

The world of manufacturing is rapidly moving toward digital transformation. Manufacturers are migrating disparate independent systems toward converged networks and control protocols. The ISA99 Committee for Manufacturing and Control has outlined an architectural model known as IACS model that is built on the Purdue Model for Control Hierarchy (ISA99/IEC-62443), in which a series of zones and levels identify protocol sets, security boundaries, and operational models for the manufacturing plant. Converged Plantwide Ethernet (CPwE), championed by Cisco and Rockwell, builds on this model and defines a set of guidelines for IACS wired and wireless network design.

Fundamental to converged factory architectures are cell/area zone Ethernet resiliency protocols, such as REP, DLR, and MRP, which allow rapid Ethernet ring convergence. To support automation control requirements, specific control protocols have been developed for manufacturing that utilize standard communications protocols. Three of the most popular control protocols are EtherNet/IP, PROFINET, and Modbus/TCP.

When machines and other devices are connected to the cell/area zone within a factory, their security is paramount. To address this, private addresses are often used, thus requiring NAT services within the cell/area zone. In addition, centralized access control and device/user profiling through an identity service tool is highly recommended to ensure that untrusted computers and devices are not used within the industrial zone on networks.

Finally, manufacturers are beginning to benefit from edge computing within the cell/area zone. Manufacturing-specific edge applications are now being deployed that process machine data at the machine and send only relevant data to the cloud or data center.

References

1. SCM World/Cisco, *Smart Manufacturing and the Internet of Things 2015 Survey of 418 Manufacturing Business Line and Executives and Plant Managers Across 17 Vertical Industries.*

2. IHS 2014 Machines Report for Cisco.

3. PWC Internet of Things in Manufacturing 2015.

4. McKinsey Disruptive Technologies 2013 Report.

Chapter 10

Oil and Gas

Oil and gas are among the most critical resources used in modern society. Almost every aspect of modern life, from transportation systems to the supply of plastics, relies on the availability of these commodities. Today, the major focus of oil and gas companies is on ways to reduce cost, improve efficiency and speed, and get more from existing investments. Among the most important key performance indicators (KPIs) of the industry include controlling production costs and improving the overall health and safety of hazardous environments.

This is an industry where an increasing number of cyber attacks is compromising security and generating losses. This is occurring in a context where profound technological evolutions are disrupting traditional ways of working and driving rapid changes in productivity. The unprecedented growth of data, advance analytics, increased automation, and connectivity are fundamentally bringing a paradigm shift in how and where work is achieved.

As with other industries, oil and gas companies are using IoT for a wide variety of applications, including the following:

- Monitoring the status or behavior of industrial devices in order to provide visibility and control

- Optimizing processes and resource use

- Improving business decision making

This chapter explores IoT in oil and gas and how digitization is a disruptive force in this industry. It looks at use cases and innovative architectures that are being used to digitize this industry. This chapter includes the following sections:

- **An Introduction to the Oil and Gas Industry:** The section opens by defining oil and gas and then describes the value chain as well as key market players in this industry.

This chapter looks at the oil and gas industry's well-understood vulnerability to price fluctuations as well as the most important industry trends and associated impacts and the opportunities they represent for IoT.

■ **Industry Key Challenges as Digitization Drivers:** This section illustrates the challenges the oil and gas industry is facing, some of them influenced by global economic conditions, as well as how new technologies are disrupting older ways of doing things.

■ **Improving Operational Efficiency:** This section examines key operational efficiency considerations, use cases, and technologies used in oil and gas IoT systems.

■ **IoT Architectures for Oil and Gas:** This section examines key security considerations, use cases, and technologies in the oil and gas industry, as well as how they can be addressed with the correct design methodology.

An Introduction to the Oil and Gas Industry

In order to understand any industry and become a relevant player in its business transformation, it is important to have some background understanding of the industry, including its products, processes, key stakeholders, and current trends. The following sections introduce these fundamental prerequisites for the oil and gas industry.

Defining Oil and Gas

Oil and gas are hydrocarbon materials that originate from organic matter, principally small plankton and algae. In the energy value chain, oil and gas are primary energies. The first level of classification used in the industry is related to the notions of *conventional* and *unconventional*, which refer to the methods that are used for extraction and also refer to the types of rock from which the oil and natural gas are produced.

Conventional oil and natural gas are found in pools in which wells can be drilled so that oil and natural gas flow naturally or can be pumped to the surface. Conventional oil and gas are found in sandstone that can be extracted using traditional methods. The oil and gas resources are usually from another formation but move into the sandstone and are trapped by an impermeable cap rock. Conventional petroleum resources are extracted using traditional methods of drilling through the cap rock and allowing the petroleum to flow up the well, as illustrated in the Figure 10-1.

Unconventional oil and natural gas do not flow naturally through the rock, and they are therefore much more difficult to extract. They usually require extensive well fields and surface infrastructure due to low permeability and porosity. They are produced or extracted using special techniques such as fracking, which is the process of injecting liquid at very high pressure into subterranean rocks in order to force open existing fissures and extract oil or gas.

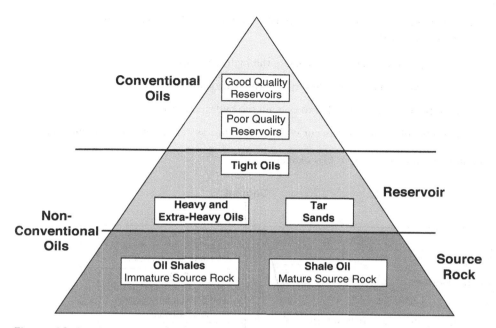

Figure 10-1   *Conventional Versus Unconventional Oil and Gas*

Source: Oil and Gas IoT Service Vertical, based on IFP Energies Nouvelles [IFPEN].

Oil has various compositions and types, such as rock oil, mineral oil, and crude oil, and is usually classified based on its density, viscosity, and sulfur content. Some examples of oil classification include the following (refer to Figure 10-1):

- **Tight oils:** Tight oils are liquid hydrocarbons contained in reservoirs with very low porosity and equally low permeability.

- **Heavy and extra-heavy oils:** These resources are referred to as heavy because of their high density and viscosity, which make it impossible for them to be extracted in the traditional way.

- **Oil sands:** These deposits are made up of sand and tar mixed together.

- **Oil shales:** Shales are a source rock that has not yet been transformed into hydrocarbon and needs to be heated to be recovered.

- **Shale oil:** With shale oil, the source rock is sufficiently far below the surface that the organic material it contains has been transformed into liquid hydrocarbons. However, as a result of its very low porosity and impermeability, these liquid hydrocarbons remain trapped in the source rock. The extraction of these trapped liquid hydrocarbons requires the use of horizontal drilling and hydraulic fracturing techniques to artificially increase the permeability of the rock.

The following are four elements that must exist for oil and gas to accumulate in "economic" quantities:

- A source rock is needed to generate the hydrocarbons.

- A suitable reservoir is needed to bear the hydrocarbons.

- A trap with a seal is needed to contain the hydrocarbons.

- All three elements must occur within a dynamic system where they can interact.

Figure 10-2 illustrates these four elements.

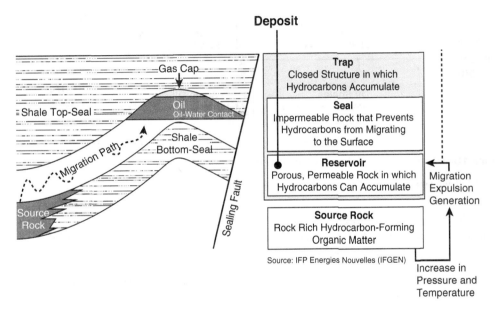

Figure 10-2 *From Organic Matter to Oil and Gas*

Source: IFP Energies Nouvelles [IFPEN].

Unlike oil, gas has very low density and viscosity, and it cannot be transported at normal temperature and pressure conditions. Raw natural gas from a well consists of methane as well as many other smaller fractions of heavier hydrocarbons and various other components, such as the following:

- Ethane

- Propane

- Butane

- Alkenes

- Acid gases

- Nitrogen

- Helium

- Water

- Trace pollutants

Natural gas is characterized in several ways, depending on the composition of these components, into the following basic categories:

- **Wet gas:** Raw gas with a methane content less than 85%

- **Dry gas:** Raw or treated natural gas that contains less than 15 liters of condensate per 1000 standard cubic meter

- **Sour gas:** Raw gas with a content of more than 5.7 mg hydrogen sulfide (H_2S) per standard cubic meter

- **Acid gas:** Gas with a high content of acidic gases, such as hydrogen sulfide

- **Condensate:** A mixture of hydrocarbons and other chemical components

Raw gas is processed into various products, including the following:

- **Natural gas:** Typically 90% methane, with 10% other light alkenes

- **Natural gas liquids (NGL):** Processed purified product that serves as a raw material for the petrochemical industry

- **Liquefied petroleum gas (LPG):** Propane or butane or a mixture of these gases that has been compressed to liquid at normal temperature

- **Liquefied natural gas (LNG):** Natural gas that is refrigerated and liquefied at below −162°C for storage and transport

- **Compressed natural gas (CNG):** Natural gas that is compressed to less than 1% of volume at atmospheric pressure

The Oil and Gas Value Chain

Now that you know what raw materials are at stake, this section examines the value chain through which oil and gas are transformed, from primary energy sources to final products. The oil and gas value chain is divided into three main segments, as shown in Figure 10-3.

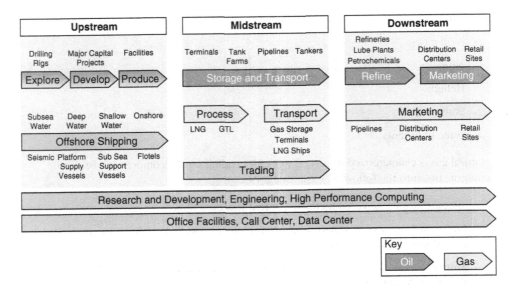

Figure 10-3   *The Oil and Gas Value Chain*

■ **Upstream segment:** This segment is focused on operations related to exploration, capital project development, and production of crude oil and natural gas. In the case of offshore rigs, shipping is also considered. Exploration includes prospecting, seismic, and drilling activities that take place before the development of a field.

■ **Midstream segment:** This segment is focused on operations related to process (gas), transport (pipeline, tanker/barge, truck, and rail), and storage of oil and gas. It is where oil and condensates are processed into products with defined specifications such as gasoline or diesel. This segment is where the fundamental differences between oil and gas impact the cost of transport and storage. Pipeline installations consist of driving compressors and pumps, valve stations, and pig receive and launch facilities. In order to control and operate the pipeline, a SCADA system and pipeline management system are also required. (SCADA is introduced in Chapter 6, "Application Protocols for IoT.") Transporting gas and oil is thus a complex and expensive process.

■ **Downstream segment:** This segment is focused on operations related to refining, marketing, distribution, and commercialization. It is important to note that in this segment, the success of a modern refinery depends on economies of scale and the ability to process a wide range of crudes into the maximum quantity of high-value fuels and feedstock.

Current Trends in the Oil and Gas Industry

One of the most important factors influencing the oil and gas industry is price volatility. At the heart of this volatility is the supply and demand imbalance. This section examines the main trends that have led to this imbalance, as well as the consequences on the industry.

Low-carbon climate policies are creating a resource-abundant world. Renewable energy technologies, a critical element of the low-carbon pillar of global energy supply, are rapidly gaining ground, aided by global subsidies and climate policies. In many parts of the world, this trend has had the effect of reducing demand for conventional primary energy sources, including oil, gas, and coal.

In January 2014, the European Commission proposed a climate and energy policy framework goal for the European Union for 2030. Its centerpiece is the goal to reduce greenhouse gas emissions by 40% below 1990 levels and to reduce emissions by at least 80% by 2050. If these targets are to be met, renewable energy resources need to play a major role.

Figure 10-4 shows the EU's projected demand in million tons of oil equivalent (Mtoe) for primary energies from 1990 to 2040 (the ton of oil equivalent is a unit of energy defined as the amount of energy released by burning 1 ton of crude oil). Notice that the demand for cleaner primary energies is expected to grow, whereas the demand for more polluting ones (coal, oil, and so on) is projected to decrease.

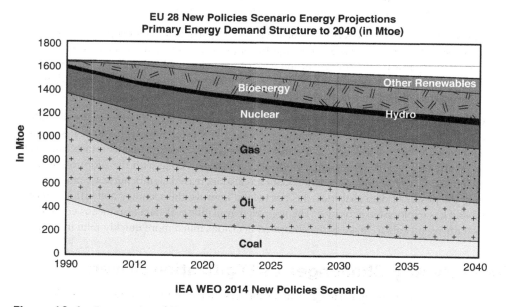

Figure 10-4   *International Energy Agency World Energy Outlook (IEA WEO) 2014 New Policies Scenario*

Source: IEA, WEO 2014, Deloitte.

Figure 10-5 shows the percentage of primary energy lost (coal source in this case) from production to final consumption. In this example, the energy required to power a light bulb results in almost 98% loss of energy through the cost of production and transmission. This model is clearly inefficient and ripe for improvements through technology.

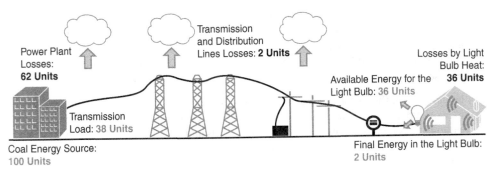

Figure 10-5   *Energy Inefficiency from Generation to Consumption*

Energy markets are notoriously volatile, often because of the imbalance between energy supply and demand. Many of the oil-producing countries have been pumping out oil at record levels, leading to low global energy prices. This situation has resulted in a significant focus on cost, efficiency, and speed, with oil and gas firms striving to get more from their existing investments and resisting new ones.

Another trend is the production of shale gas and, in particular, technological break-throughs in fracking that have led to significant production increases in recent years. The relatively low production costs and ease of entry for smaller producers has meant an easy path to production ramp-up or decrease in response to the slightest market dynamic changes, thus causing further instability.

Other trends related to the use of technology have emerged and are influencing the indus-try as a whole. For example, the enhanced connectivity offered by technology has meant an increase in the number of cyber attacks in this sector. A serious cyber attack can result in significant financial losses and can impact operations. Along with the adoption of IoT technologies, the amount of available data has also increased significantly. Combined with the power of data analytics, this has helped improve the accuracy and efficiency of oil and gas exploration activities. The improved availability of data also means company executives are able to make better-informed decisions much more quickly than in the past.

Industry Key Challenges as Digitization Drivers

The oil and gas industry is facing many challenges, many of them influenced by global economic conditions. In addition, new technologies are disrupting older ways of doing things, bringing new efficiencies and new expectations. Challenges can bring opportunity. IoT and digitization—the process of leveraging innovations in information technology to build new solutions and technologies for operations, work processes, and methods—are opening the way to new (and previously unheard of) improvements in efficiency and new business models.

This section addresses a series of challenges by category and establishes a mapping with the underlying digitization requirement. In its 2014 report *Top 10 Technology Trends*

Impacting the Oil and Gas Industry in 2014,[1] Gartner identified the following key digitization trends:

- Advanced analytics and modeling (business asset planning and optimization)

- Big data (business asset planning and optimization)

- IT/OT convergence (digital oil fields)

- Smart machines (digital oil fields)

- Extended infrastructure (digital oil fields)

- Mobility (intuitive workflow)

- Upstream modeling suites (intuitive workflow)

- Collaboration (intuitive workflow)

- Cloud (oil and gas business systems)

- Asset performance management (oil and gas business systems)

In Table 10-1, notice how these digitization trends are mapped to specific IoT capabilities. The oil and gas industry's main challenges can be organized into three main categories:

- Operational efficiency and cost reductions

- Security

- Faster and better decision making

These categories can be split into subcategories and mapped to corresponding digitization requirements, as shown in Table 10-1.

Table 10-1   *Challenges and Requirements of the Oil and Gas Industry*

Challenge	Digitization Requirements
Operational efficiency in a context of low investment	
■ People effective collaboration	■ Available and reliable real-time communications
	■ Device-agnostic and integrated collaboration
	■ Real-time access to relevant information
	■ Cost-effective access to experts
	■ Increased productivity through digital labor
■ Process optimization	■ Process automation
	■ Reduced downtime and increased process integrity
■ Asset management and maintenance	■ Increased real-time monitoring and control of assets
	■ Predictive maintenance

Challenge	Digitization Requirements
Security in a context of sophisticated attacks	
■ Secure operations	■ Patch management
	■ Compliance monitoring
	■ Secure remote access
■ Network reliability	■ Availability
	■ Scalability
	■ Data management
	■ Bandwidth
	■ QoS
	■ Cybersecurity
■ Asset safety and security	■ Physical safety and security
	■ Protection against overpressures
	■ Shutdown management
■ People safety and security	■ People monitoring and worker down tracking
	■ Physical safety and security
■ Business continuity	■ Operations dashboard and remediation
	■ Process automation
■ Cybersecurity risk and vulnerabilities	■ Intrusion prevention and detection
	■ Proactive incident monitoring
Improved decision making in a context of data storm	
■ Faster and better decision making	■ Data analytics
	■ Decentralized computing and data storage
■ Knowledge management and skills shortage	■ People training
	■ Knowledge management

The challenges listed in Table 10-1 have forced the industry to adopt new technologies that have brought improvements in the areas of safety, downtime, efficiency, environmental protection, and asset integrity. Figure 10-6 illustrates these value propositions in the oil and gas industry.

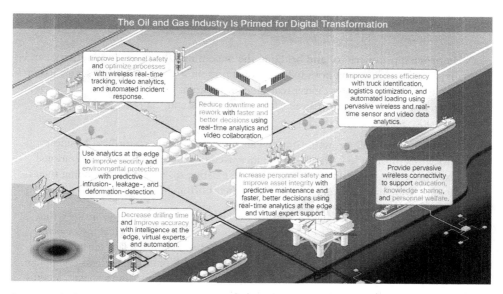

Figure 10-6 *Use Cases and Digitization Capabilities*

IoT and the Oil and Gas Industry

The oil and gas industry was one of the first industrial sectors to start leveraging the power of technology. The nature of its activities, processes, and dependence on data has forced widespread use of data analytics, from exploration techniques to industrial preventive maintenance and beyond. In general, oil and gas fields are risky zones for human beings, hence the paramount importance given to health, safety, and the environment. In this context, having digital intelligence capabilities with machine-to-machine communications can help achieve operations without the need for physical human presence, thus making the environment safer and more secure. IoT is therefore a must for this industry.

IoT and digitization are bringing about significant improvements in the oil and gas industry, including the following:

■ **Enabling feasible data acquisition:** Cost-effective and pervasive communication technologies such as industrial Wi-Fi, LTE, and LoRa are enabling the industry to acquire data from certain assets either for the first time or in real time. This, in turn, enables entirely new decision-making capability.

■ **Driving cost savings throughout the value chain—upstream, midstream, and downstream:** Cost savings can be achieved by utilizing digital convergence of IT and OT to eliminate silos in the business and reengineering operations to deliver reduced costs, increased production efficiencies, and improved utilization of existing assets.

■ **Increasing agility and risk mitigation:** Analytics can be used to convert real-time data created by the IoT infrastructure into predictive and actionable insights that facilitate faster and better decisions, increased worker safety, and improved cybersecurity.

- **Improving productivity and bridging the oncoming talent gap:** Productivity can be improved by leveraging both IoT and collaboration systems to extend scarce expertise to remote locations, deliver real-time information to the right teams at the right time, and provide an effective mechanism to attract and train the next generation of workers.

- **Enabling profitable growth:** Growth can be achieved by transforming business processes through IoT. Thanks to the increased productivity through operational excellence and the ability to better leverage existing assets (hence extending their lives), oil and gas companies can improve their bottom line.

Well-defined business outcomes are critical because oil and gas margins are very thin. Therefore, operators require a compelling business case for technological investments. Technologies that help extend the life of current assets or improve their uptime and efficiency are getting the greatest prioritization. Forward-looking oil and gas companies believe that today's turbulent market landscape provides an opportunity to gain a competitive advantage by harnessing new technologies.

The largest driver of IoT value for an oil and gas firm relies heavily on asset monitoring and data management capabilities to gather accurate and timely information from the field of operations. Value also comes from the ability to perform automatic analyses, diagnostics, and optimization in real time. This implies the need to integrate data from multiple sources, automate the collection of data, and analyze data quickly so that actionable insights can be identified.

The second area of IoT value generation comes from advanced sensors, machine-to-machine connections, and big data analytics that help the company anticipate equipment failures and maintenance requirements, thus minimizing downtime.

Digital transformation is not an easy journey for any oil or gas company, and some obstacles should be foreseen, such as the complexity of integrating old and new technologies. For example, most new technologies take advantage of IP, but many legacy technologies are not capable of this. Other challenges include the following:

- The need to automate the extraction of insights and quickly determine—and execute—resulting actions

- The increasing volume of data produced by devices on pipelines, refineries, oil wells, and so on

- Expanded security vulnerabilities

- Siloed networks and departments

Figure 10-7 provides a view of some capabilities that can help mitigate these obstacles and demonstrates the increased business value of each as time goes by. IoT is at the core of each of them.

Solution Framework for the Digital Journey

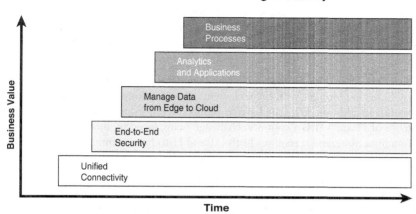

Figure 10-7 *IoT and Value Drivers*

Improving Operational Efficiency

IoT is helping solve some of the main challenges of the oil and gas industry, including the following:

- Operational efficiency in the context of cost reduction
- Security of operations in the context of increased industrial cyber attacks
- Faster and better decision making

As discussed earlier, the value chain of the oil and gas industry has the three main sectors: upstream, midstream, and downstream. These three sectors share similar challenges in their operational flow. IoT can help address them in a variety of different use cases.

The Purdue Model for Control Hierarchy in Oil and Gas Networks

Before delving into specific IoT use cases for the oil and gas industry, it is important to revisit the Purdue Model for Control Hierarchy that is discussed in Chapter 2, "IoT Network Architecture and Design," and Chapter 8, "Securing IoT," and applied to the manufacturing industry in Chapter 9, "Manufacturing."

In a process control network (PCN), automation equipment is attached to a network (typically a combination of hardware and software) that has command and control responsibility for critical infrastructure, such as refineries, oil and gas pipelines, nuclear plants, and many others.

The PCN automation equipment (and its associated components) form a control system known as an industrial control network (ICN). ICNs monitor physical processes that perform a variety of functions in a production environment, including control, protection, safety, and situational awareness.

Examples of control systems are supervisory control and data acquisition (SCADA) and distributed control systems (DCSs). Some of the functions they perform include pipeline operations such as remotely controlling valves along a pipeline (closing or opening them as required) and monitoring the operations of pumps that are used to move the product along a pipeline.

As ICNs have evolved over time, from standalone isolated entities into more connected networks, they have also brought with them elements of technology that have been adopted by IT networks. In addition, OT staff have recognized the need to access IT systems. This convergence of IT and OT is a common challenge being faced by most industries adopting IoT architectures, and it requires both OT and IT to have communication interfaces that allow mutual access and the exchange of information between systems.

The interaction of these components in such a complex system requires a framework to define the flow of communication between components, which are dependent on the functions they perform in the process. A well-known framework used by many industries today is the Purdue Model for Control Hierarchy. This model is briefly introduced in Chapter 2 and applied specifically to the manufacturing industry in Chapter 9. In this chapter we look at how the Purdue Model for Control Hierarchy can be adapted to IoT for the oil and gas industry.

The Purdue Model for Control Hierarchy has three main components: facilities, people, and control and information systems. Within the control and information systems component are levels that define and further separate the various areas in the OT (control systems) and IT (information systems) of an enterprise or organization (see Figure 10-8). These levels are specifically referenced throughout this chapter in relation to oil and gas use cases.

Levels 0–2 represent batch, continuous, and discrete control; Level 3 is where we find the manufacturing operations and control; and Levels 4 and above are where business planning and logistics reside.

The Purdue Model for Control Hierarchy is also used to define the hierarchy and the objects in the ISA99/IEC-62443 standards that define cybersecurity.

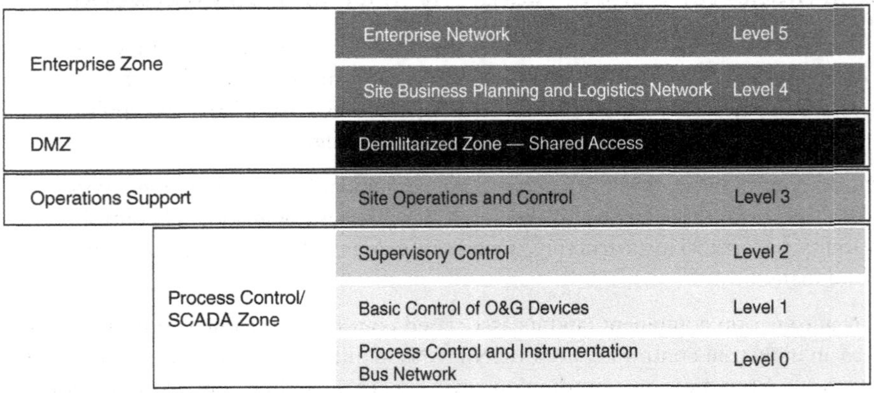

Enterprise Zone	Enterprise Network	Level 5
	Site Business Planning and Logistics Network	Level 4
DMZ	Demilitarized Zone — Shared Access	
Operations Support	Site Operations and Control	Level 3
Process Control/ SCADA Zone	Supervisory Control	Level 2
	Basic Control of O&G Devices	Level 1
	Process Control and Instrumentation Bus Network	Level 0

Figure 10-8 *Purdue Model for Control Hierarchy Applied to Oil and Gas Processing*

Looking at the levels in more detail, you can see that the functionality they provide to devices has been layered in a way that describes the information flow from bottom to top as far as process control is concerned. The levels of the model can be divided into three separate groups:

- **Operational levels (Levels 0–3):** Level 0 is where you can find the "things" of IoT, such as sensors, motors, actuators, and instrumentation. Level 1 is where the programmable logic controllers (PLCs) in a refinery can be found, as well as remote terminal units (RTUs) used for SCADA management on a pipeline, and control processors. These devices are responsible for programming or extracting readings from the Level 0 devices, which are at the production/process level. Level 2 is where engineering workstations or data historians reside; they are responsible for logging, collecting, and populating the databases that keep a history of process data. Level 3 is where the human-machine interface (HMI) devices operate; servers run software that provides a graphical user interface to represent processes and their operations, readings of sensors, and specified thresholds that help monitor a process, display alerts, and so on.

- **Business levels (Levels 4 and 5):** These are the levels where the traditional IT systems are located, including file and print servers, corporate email applications, HR systems, and so on, as well as the corporate Internet connection or VPN access to the enterprise network.

- **Demilitarized zone (DMZ):** The DMZ, also referred to as Level 3.5, is the zone that separates the OT and IT domains. The systems and applications that typically reside in the DMZ are remote access solutions, antivirus and patch management servers, reporting dashboard applications, and so on.

Oil and Gas Use Cases for IoT

Improving operational efficiency is a top-of-mind item for many industry executives, especially considering the costs involved in exploration and extraction of hydrocarbons, from processing to the final product distribution to the end consumer.

In an effort to drive down costs and increase efficiency, IoT architectures need to be tailored to different use cases in key oil and gas sectors, including the connected refinery, the connected oil field, and the connected pipeline. These use cases illustrate how technology can be adopted within the operational workflow of the oil and gas industry in order to optimize productivity, reduce cost, and help make the operational decision process swifter and better informed.

The Connected Oil Field

A typical example of an IoT architecture built to support the oil and gas industry for upstream operations is the connected oil field, as shown in Figure 10-9.

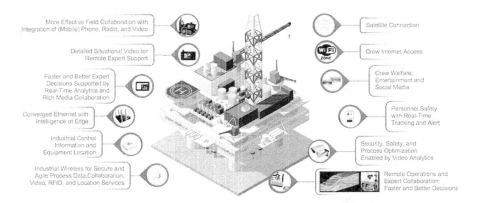

Figure 10-9   *Connected Oil Field IoT Use Cases*

An oil field is an area, either onshore or offshore, where a number of wells extract crude oil below ground or from the seabed. Typically, offshore oil fields are located in remote areas or in the middle of the sea, making them difficult to access and communicate with. As a result, the need for a robust but self-contained communications infrastructure is critical. The offshore oil rig's infrastructure needs to support situational awareness for the operation of the drilling system, communications with head office locations, and health, safety, and environmental monitoring systems, just to name a few. Also, because the personnel working at the oil field are living on the premises for extended periods of time, communications for entertainment and social media purposes are also required.

Due to the remote and isolated nature of oil fields, much of their communications infrastructure is based on wireless technology.

The Connected Pipeline

One of the key assets in the midstream portion of the oil and gas value chain is the pipeline. Pipelines are important because they are links between the exploration, extraction, and refining operations. Pipelines ensure that product is continually supplied and refined on a 24x7 basis. The operational challenges are many, and they vary in nature. The following are some examples of the challenges:

- **Long distances and large geographic area of coverage:** Pipelines can be very long. For example, the current world record holder for longest gas pipeline spans China east–west, and its longest segment is 9100 km.

- **Harsh environments:** Pipelines can span great distances underwater, through deserts, over mountains, and in other inhospitable environments.

- **Isolation from general infrastructure:** Pipelines are often far away from major roads or highways, which makes communicating with sensors and instrumentation on the pipeline a challenge.

- **Leaks:** Oil and gas pipelines carry highly flammable content. It is important to have the ability to detect leaks along the pipeline length so that fires, explosions, and contamination of the surrounding area can be avoided.

- **Earthquakes and landslides:** Landslides and earthquakes can affect the integrity of a pipeline, so a pipeline must be monitored for seismic activity.

- **Theft and vandalism:** Theft and vandalism are becoming commonplace along pipelines, with thieves tapping into pipelines and extracting product. Other than the obvious financial implications, there are also risks associated with theft and vandalism that can cause significant damage to the environment and infrastructure.

Figure 10-10 illustrates some common IoT use cases for the connected pipeline.

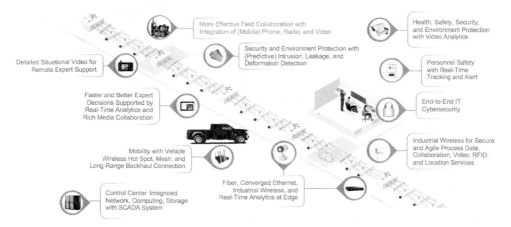

Figure 10-10 *Connected Pipeline IoT Use Cases*

The guiding principle in implementing any of these use cases is to ensure that a connected pipeline communication network supports the following characteristics:

- High availability and redundancy

- Multilevel security (both cyber and physical)

- Adherence to open standards

- Multiservice support (for both the control room and the operational network using the connected pipeline communications network)

The Connected Refinery

Refineries and processing plants are typically large complexes with multiple buildings, storage tanks, and interconnected underground and aboveground piping systems. Like oil fields, refineries are operational on a 24x7 basis, with complex systems constantly monitoring operational parameters such as flow, tank level, temperature, vibration, pressure, and even the presence of dangerous or explosive gases that are produced during the process of refining crude oil.

Figure 10-11 highlights some of the common IoT use cases in a modern oil or gas refinery.

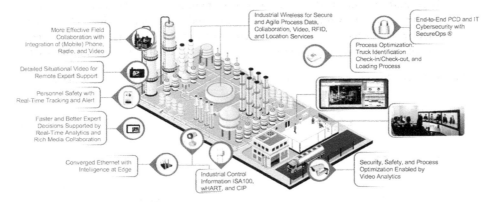

Figure 10-11   *Connected Refinery IoT Use Cases*

Refineries are workplaces for permanent staff as well as external companies and contractors that work on a variety of tasks around a plant. Process control operators ensure that refinery processes are working as expected; they monitor and optimize the processes where appropriate. Refineries also include maintenance staff who keep the refinery equipment in good working order and perform repairs when needed. All these systems and people are kept working in an effective, efficient, and safe manner through the implementation of control, safety, and management systems. These systems require communications systems that are fast and reliable.

IoT Architectures for Oil and Gas

To address the various IoT use cases in the oil and gas sector, this section maps various network and security functions to the Purdue Model discussed earlier. For example, the connected refinery reference architecture shown in Figure 10-12 illustrates how wired and wireless communication systems are interconnected in order to provide fast and reliable operations.

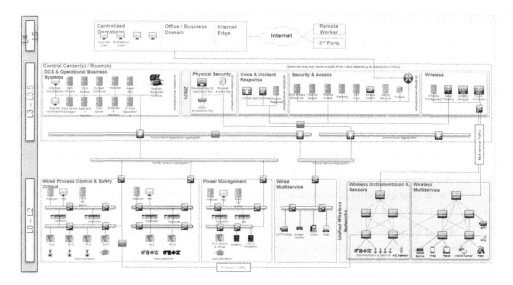

Figure 10-12   *An Oil and Gas Reference Architecture*

The architecture is built using the different systems of the refinery infrastructure, following the ISA99/IEC-62443 standard, which is based on the Purdue Model for Control Hierarchy. These systems could be divided into three main categories: control room networks, wired networks, and wireless networks.

Control Room Networks for Oil and Gas

Control room networks operate out of the control room(s) of the refinery. The control room is designed to offer centralized visibility and control for site operations. Some examples of control room networks include the following:

- **Distributed control systems:** Distributed control systems are deployed throughout a plant using autonomous controllers, and their operational control is performed centrally.

- **Physical security:** This includes video surveillance/CCTV systems, access control systems, and so on.

- **Centralized wireless management:** This category describes software applications used for managing wireless networks deployed in the plant, such as network management applications, asset and people location-based services, and so on.

- **Security and access services:** Because the control room is the point of connection between the refinery and the outside world, networks and services here typically require intrusion detection and prevention systems and firewalls.

Wired Networks for Oil and Gas

The wired network infrastructure at a refinery or processing plant can be categorized as follows:

- **Wired process control:** Wired process control networks support the process control equipment, including the sensors, controllers, and instrumentation used to monitor and optimize production processes.

- **Wired safety critical:** Safety-critical systems, as the name implies, are systems that are responsible for normal or emergency shutdown or are operating specific critical functions of the production process.

- **Wired energy management:** These systems are responsible for energy integration at the production facility.

- **Wired multiservice:** This category includes systems that are providing collaboration or physical security, and the technologies that are typically used are voice and video.

Wireless Networks for Oil and Gas

While the wired infrastructure (both LAN and WAN) is key in implementing the architecture, wireless is often one of the most common network elements used in refineries. Two main types of industrial wireless networks are typically found in oil and gas environments:

- **Wireless multiservice:** These networks, including IEEE 802.11/Wi-Fi, LTE, and so on, provide the platform for wireless connectivity to a number of multiprotocol devices.

- **Wireless process control:** These networks typically feature deterministic IEEE 802.15.4 devices (such as ISA100.11a or WirelessHART).

These two types of industrial wireless networks can be combined into a unified architecture, as discussed later in this chapter.

Wireless Multiservice: IEEE 802.11 Mesh Networks

IEEE 802.11 wireless mesh networks are very popular in oil and gas environments. One of the key advantages of 802.11 mesh is that it doesn't require each access point (AP) to be physically wired to the Ethernet network. As you can imagine, cable installation in a petrochemical refinery or an oil rig can be very costly. Installation activities are very time-consuming and sometimes extremely complicated. For example, installation of fiber or copper cables on an oil rig often requires drilling through metal walls or bulkhead on the structure of the vessel, which is often not allowed. Digging around production plants that have explosive gas or powder requires production to stop while the installation activities occur. Very often, the cost of installing data cables exceeds the cost of the equipment itself by several orders of magnitude.

However, with mesh networks, an AP only needs to be powered, and it forms a wireless backhaul connection with other APs. With 802.11 mesh, once the initial infrastructure has been deployed, it is relatively simple to extend its coverage by adding extra access points. For further details on 802.11 wireless mesh, see Chapter 14, "Mining."

Wireless Process Control

A wireless field network (WFN) consists of a self-organizing mesh of wireless devices (of various types—sensors and actuators, field mobile devices, and field endpoints) and gateways, serving a small contiguous area (typically 50–100 m radius from the WFN gateways), that are connected to LANs to provide monitoring and control of process systems over radio channels.

Figure 10-13 shows an example of a WFN mesh architecture. At the field level, a mesh of sensors have been deployed to measure and provide readings to the PCN applications at the control network. The sensors are communicating with the sensor gateways, which are responsible for performing protocol translation from 802.15.4 (WirelessHART, ISA100.11, and so on) to IP.

The sensor gateway then communicates with the wireless network infrastructure, which is responsible for forwarding traffic upstream, where the applications that are consuming and reporting on the sensor data reside. The same wireless LAN infrastructure can be used in parallel to provide a variety of other use cases, such as voice and location services.

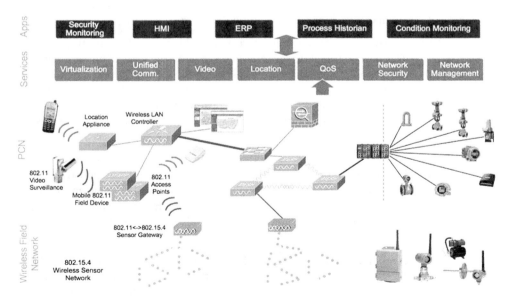

Figure 10-13   *WFN Mesh Architecture in an 802.11 Wireless Mesh*

WFN mesh networks are often based on (but can vary from) industry-standard IEEE 802.15.4 wireless network technology, which in turn forms the foundation for several other wireless standards, including WirelessHART (IEC-62591) and ISA100.11a.

IEEE 802.15.4–based sensors can supply important process control information, such as gas flow through a pipeline, temperature of a flare in a refinery, level of a kerosene tank, or vibration of a compressor. These types of deterministic networks are also used to control pumps and motors in a very predictable way—something that contention-based Wi-Fi is not able to accomplish.

To deploy a deterministic wireless network built on 802.15.4, several components are required, including the following:

- A wireless sensor gateway, which provides the interconnection between the wireless field network and control systems

- Network controllers to provide orchestration of the wireless field network(s)

- Protocol gateways to translate between protocol stacks implemented within the wireless field network and PLCs

WirelessHART and ISA100.11a wireless field instruments operate at ISA95 Level 0 in an industrial network. Both WirelessHART and ISA100.11a implement the IEEE 802.15.4 radio protocols, operating at 2.4 gigahertz (GHz). The radios employ direct sequence spread spectrum (DSSS) technology and channel hopping for communication security and reliability, as well as time division multiple access (TDMA) to ensure latency-controlled communications between devices on the network.

802.15.4-based networks are favorable in process control networks because they are deterministic. This means that all devices are time-synchronized and communicate in predefined, prescheduled, fixed time slots. These time slots are grouped together in superframes, which are repeated according to a specified rate. The advantage is that a latency-sensitive control system does not have to deal with congestion on the air and wait to transmit its frame. When the controller says it's time to transmit, the system does so without any delay.

Deterministic control of wireless access has a major impact on reliability. For example, WirelessHART is capable of providing end-to-end reliability of 99.9% in industrial process environments.[2] This is achieved through the use of channel hopping and self-healing capabilities of the mesh network. When paths deteriorate or become obstructed, the network takes action to conduct auto-repair and finds alternative paths around the obstacle(s) blocking the path.

WFN technologies operate in the 2.4 GHz ISM "unlicensed" public-use spectrum. These systems must share the same RF spectrum with other wireless systems, such as Wi-Fi, DECT, Bluetooth, and Ultra Wideband (UWB), and they are subject to interference from other devices that emit in the 2.4 GHz spectrum (for example, microwave ovens, USB 3.0 devices and cables, car alarms). However, the deterministic mechanisms used by WirelessHART and ISA100.11 greatly help in minimizing the impact of interference, frequency hopping, multipath mesh routing, channel whitelisting/blacklisting, and other factors that can impact wireless field network performance and reliability.

Because the applications that use these types of networks require only minimal bandwidth but at the same time demand predictable low-latency communications, WirelessHART- and ISA100.11-based systems are more appropriate for control systems than Wi-Fi or equivalent systems. The typical maximum bandwidth that 802.15.4 networks deliver is about 250 Kbps, which is very slow compared to the newest Wi-Fi standards. However, the trade-off with lower bandwidth is greater range, which is one of the benefits of these types of systems.

WirelessHART and ISA100.11a gateways operate at Level 1 in an industrial network (refer to Figure 10-8). Wireless field networks must be connected to the LAN to provide communications between wireless sensor/control devices, ISA95 control systems (such as PLCs), and wireless sensor network control systems.

WFN-to-wired infrastructure communications occur via wireless field network gateways. Wireless field network gateways translate wireless sensor protocols (such as ISA100.11 and WirelessHART) into LAN-routable protocol suites that are suitable for communicating with PLCs.

Wireless field networks can also be dual-homed (that is, two wireless sensor gateways for each wireless field network) to LAN access switches via Ethernet, providing alternate-path homing for all wireless field network devices. When dual-homing wireless field networks, each wireless sensor gateway must connect to separate LAN access switches that are in turn connected to separate LAN distribution switches, ensuring dual network paths for wireless field network devices.

Depending on the vendor product implementation, WFN device-to-PLC communications may occur in one of three ways:

- Wireless field network gateways may connect directly with PLC Ethernet ports for control traffic. In this deployment mode, wireless field network gateways are connected directly to PLC Ethernet ports.

- Wireless field network gateways may be integrated with dual wireless radio access systems (for example, WirelessHART and IEEE 802.11) combined in a single wireless access point. In this deployment configuration, the dual-technology wireless access point must present an IEEE 802.1Q VLAN tagged Ethernet port to a LAN access switch. Traffic destined for IEEE 802.11 wireless LAN controllers (CAPWAP tunnels; see RFC 5415) flows over one VLAN to the central wireless LAN controller, and wireless sensor communications flow over a separate VLAN in the terminating port LAN access switch to a directly connected PLC control Ethernet port. An alternative variation would be for the dual-technology wireless access point to present two physical Ethernet ports—one for connection to a port LAN access switch for traffic destined for IEEE 802.11 wireless LAN controllers and a separate Ethernet port for connection to a controlling PLC. Figure 10-14 illustrates a combined Wi-Fi with ISA100.11 network in a refinery. In this example, ISA100.11 is used to establish a control loop between sensors and actuators, and the same APs also offer Wi-Fi mesh services at the facility.

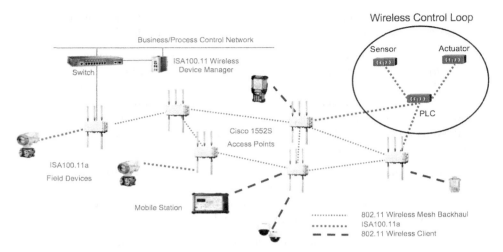

Figure 10-14   *An Example of a Combined Wi-Fi with ISA100.11 Network*

- Some wireless field network vendors require wireless field network devices control-ling PLC traffic to pass through protocol converters (such as an ISA100.11a IPv6-to-IPv4 protocol conversion). The resulting protocol-converted communications flows are then forwarded through intrusion detection and firewall functions before being forwarded across IEEE 802.1Q trunks to a VLAN on access switches and then finally to the controlling PLC via a PLC control Ethernet port.

Wireless Use Cases in the Oil and Gas Industry

The following sections look at some of the most popular applications of industrial wire-less networks in the oil and gas industry, which are based on 802.11 WLAN technology.

Mobile Process Control Network Operator

In a mobile process control network operator scenario, the facility (for example, a plant, a pipeline, an oil rig) has either ubiquitous or partial wireless coverage at strategic areas in a given location. One area of responsibility for the PCN operator is to ensure that the processes at the plant are adequately optimized and operating reliably. Fulfilling this task requires tools and applications for the monitoring and management of the informa-tion systems used at that site. While the HMIs where these applications are running are located in the control room of the plant, the PCN operator is sometimes required to be physically outdoors in different areas of the plant so he or she can troubleshoot or main-tain different systems.

The combination of portable operator technology (such as tablets, laptops, smart phones, or wearables) that can be used in hazardous areas together with ubiquitous Wi-Fi cover-age significantly helps optimize the productivity of the PCN operator. For example, with seamless Wi-Fi coverage, the PCN operator has access to work orders, schematics, and operational manuals from anywhere in the facility.

Plant Turnaround

Turnarounds are scheduled periods during which a plant stops production for inspections and maintenance, which require normal operation shutdown. During this period, the facilities are not refining product, which has an obvious negative (and significant) financial impact because time to return to operation is extremely critical.

During the turnaround, plant employees, equipment vendors, and external contractors work on high-risk and complex activities around the clock to try to get the plant in operation as quickly as possible and without any HSE (health, safety, and environment) incidents. Depending on the size of the turnaround, there could be thousands of workers present at the height of activities.

Traditionally, turnarounds have been a two-way a process, with engineers working on tasks around the plant communicating back to a central engineer via radio, and the engineer providing support and signoff for tasks. Deploying a wireless infrastructure and providing workers with tools and processes for independent and remote work saves time and money. Wireless mobility technologies allow engineering tools and applications for job tasks to be linked directly to central workflow and completion tools.

In addition, the majority of workers who are brought in for a turnaround are often unfamiliar with the site, permitting processes, and so on; as a result, productivity suffers, and HSE risk factors increase dramatically. Using industrial pervasive wireless, combined with enterprise data sources such as project work scopes, HR data, gate access control data, and worker information, productivity can be tracked and optimized in real time rather than after project completion. Location tracking of people and equipment can be monitored, managed, and adjusted in real time. Electronic permitting and equipment tracking can also be enabled, and human performance factors such as fatigue monitoring can be analyzed and acted upon.

Plant turnaround use cases help to greatly speed up completion, workflow, activity records, safety, and compliance.

Remote Expert

One of the biggest challenges with a refinery, a pipeline, or an oil rig is loss of productivity and profitability due to unforeseen outages and downtime. With a younger workforce and fewer experienced workers available, particularly for older systems and infrastructure, ensuring that the right resources are available in the right place and at the right time is challenging and often not possible. Companies may need a number of subject matter experts from different disciplines to collaborate on situations in real time—and they may want to avoid the expense and having to wait for them all to travel to the same location.

Leveraging video, voice, and collaboration technologies to connect onsite plant workers with remote experts across an optimized communications infrastructure makes expertise available on demand. Experienced operators and staff members with specific skills are able to instantly help with support tasks, training, and emergencies, regardless of their location, and they can be instantly connected to control room or onsite workers.

This creates a centralized pool of specialists available when they are needed to consult, guide, and advise. To comply with risk management and regulations, all aspects of the interaction can be captured on a timeline via digital voice, video, and messaging recordings. These recordings can then also be used as training tools.

Personnel Safety

The many chemicals used in the refining and processing process, in addition to those used for plant maintenance, wastewater treatment, and product treatments, mean potential safety risks caused by accidental leaks in the plant that may affect employees, contractors, and first responders, as well as local communities around the facility.

Hydrogen sulfide (H_2S), sulfur dioxide (SO_2), and volatile organic compound (VOC) leaks may happen due to pipe failures, tank leaks, faulty equipment, and spills during transportation. Such events can have catastrophic effects, both in terms of the environment and loss of life. For example, during the *Deepwater Horizon* oil spill in May 2010, 11 people lost their lives, and 4.9 million barrels of crude oil were spilled into the Gulf of Mexico. As another example, in the Bhophal disaster at the UCIL plant in India in December 1984, an accident that caused a gas leak at the plant led to more than half a million people being exposed to toxic gas; the death toll exceeded 2000 people, and many thousands more suffered severe injuries.

In addition, trips, falls, and injuries due to falling or moving objects are common risks to employee safety. Being able to monitor fixed locations for gas leaks and liquid spills and also monitor mobile workers for potential exposure to leaks is an essential safety function. Being able to quickly detect and isolate hazardous areas saves lives and helps meet regulatory compliance. In addition, having a precise understanding of the physical locations of employees around the plant helps ensure that those impacted in the leak zone are identified and evacuated and others outside the zone are prevented from entering.

Fixed wireless gas sensors can be installed in key locations where leaks are potential hazards, and workers can be provided with portable gas detectors that communicate across the wireless infrastructure. Location tracking of employees can be achieved via RFID tags either integrated into a device like the gas detector or a mobile handset or via a separate locator tag. Both fixed and wireless sensors can be overlaid on a map of the plant for real-time visibility, and information can be backhauled across the wireless infrastructure to a centralized control room.

For worker-down scenarios, it is possible to leverage an accelerometer in a mobile device or tag to quickly detect personnel who are downed due to trips or falls. Information can be sent back to a central monitoring location and can even be tied into live video feeds from the mobile device to show whether it is a real incident or perhaps just a dropped device. Again, information is sent across the wireless infrastructure.

Asset Location Tracking

Asset location tracking through RFID tags on a Wi-Fi network is a key enabler of many industrial applications. With integrated location tracking, plant administrators, security personnel, users, asset owners, and health and safety staff have realized great benefits in location-based services that allow them to better address a number of key issues in the plant, including the following:

- Quickly and efficiently locating valuable assets and key personnel

- Improving productivity via effective asset and personnel allocation

- Increasing personnel safety via portable gas detectors and sensors, as well as worker-down indicators

- Reducing theft loss due to unauthorized removal of assets from company premises

- Coordinating Wi-Fi device location with security policy enforcement and determining the locations of rogue devices

- Monitoring the health and status of key assets in their environment and receiving prompt notification of changes

Managing the locations of key assets and personnel throughout a plant is key to improving operational efficiency. By tagging equipment, vehicles, and containers with active RFID tags and deploying portable gas detectors and sensors across the infrastructure, a plant can greatly enhance its operational efficiency, employee safety, and regulatory compliance.

The Risk Control Framework for Cybersecurity in IoT

The number-one need of process automation teams is uptime and process integrity. In this light, cybersecurity is ultimately a means of protecting uptime and integrity; in fact, process automation teams are often willing to endure a compromised state of cybersecurity in favor of process uptime and integrity. Oil and gas and almost all other automated industries have historically relied on physical separation for protection of their OT production networks. Historically, SCADA networks and the distributed control systems (DCSs) required to control and monitor manufacturing, utility, power generation, and other systems were designed to be physically separate from all other networks.

It was believed that this air-gap separation protected against cyber attacks, which presumably originated outside the network. (This was obviously not applicable to legacy serial SCADA systems which are totally isolated.) In addition, little was done to defeat cyber attacks that may have already breached the separation, as the deployed systems were not systematically updated with the latest antivirus signatures and did not have their operating systems patched against known vulnerabilities.

Thanks to the rapid growth of Ethernet and IP technologies in recent years, this air-gap model is clearly no longer viable. As oil and gas companies continue to adopt new technologies and new use cases, new and diverse devices are being connected to converged networks. This brings with it the potential challenge of a wider set of security attack challenges (intentional, unintentional, external, and internal), and companies need to broaden their response beyond mere physical segmentation, often called "security by obscurity."

Physical separation did not help prevent Stuxnet, and similar attacks have proven that even the most segregated networks can be vulnerable through local access by malware introduced on USB flash drives. Furthermore, the need for better information flow and decision making requires the interconnection of industrial networks with systems and data applications. Reporting, compliance monitoring, and controlling the status of the systems deployed in the PCN environment can provide necessary insights into the level of risk and exposure of the OT environment at any given time.

Cost savings are an equally important driver, along with improved monitoring and the ability to facilitate business agility via secure, flexible, and standardized platforms. The ability to safely update operating systems and AV signatures instead of employing an army of field technicians moving between locations and using fixed media can significantly lower operational expenses. All these developments have raised the importance of cybersecurity, making it one of the top priorities for many CIOs in the oil and gas industry.

A risk control framework is used for PCNs to better secure critical OT systems. This framework maps a set of practices and controls to combat the most significant attack vectors in the PCN. These controls and practices are illustrated in Figure 10-15.

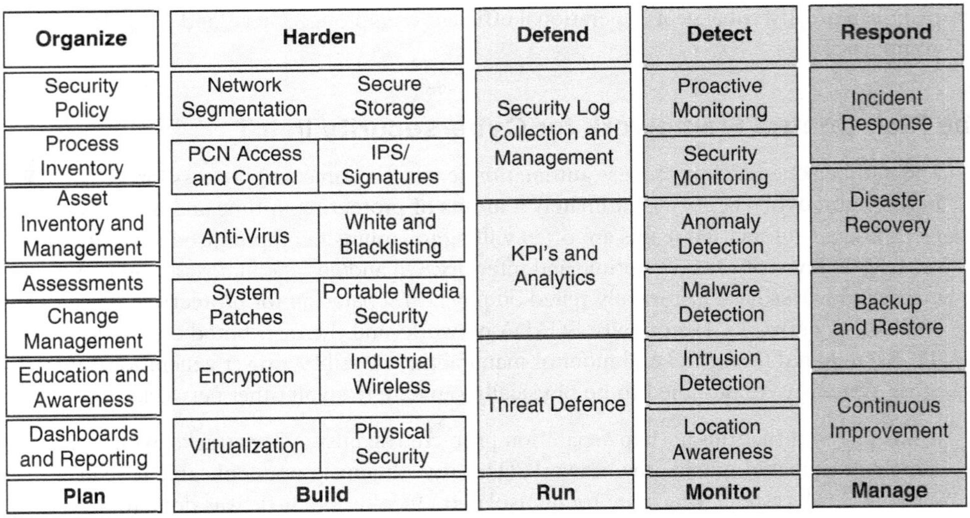

Organize	Harden		Defend	Detect	Respond
Security Policy	Network Segmentation	Secure Storage	Security Log Collection and Management	Proactive Monitoring	Incident Response
Process Inventory	PCN Access and Control	IPS/ Signatures		Security Monitoring	
Asset Inventory and Management	Anti-Virus	White and Blacklisting	KPI's and Analytics	Anomaly Detection	Disaster Recovery
Assessments	System Patches	Portable Media Security		Malware Detection	Backup and Restore
Change Management				Intrusion Detection	
Education and Awareness	Encryption	Industrial Wireless	Threat Defence		Continuous Improvement
Dashboards and Reporting	Virtualization	Physical Security		Location Awareness	
Plan	Build		Run	Monitor	Manage

Figure 10-15 *PCN Risk Control Framework*

Using the risk control framework, a more robust layered security paradigm is possible. This paradigm seeks to enable systems connectivity while also ensuring that connectivity is handled securely and limits an attacker's ability to exploit systems.

The main areas that the risk control framework addresses are categorized as five main pillars:

■ **Organize:** As part of the planning phase, policies and processes need to be established and followed throughout the lifecycle of a network or system, with necessary levels of dashboards and reports complementing them. The inventory of components comprising various systems needs to be accurate and detailed.

- **Harden:** This pillar involves the implementation of network segmentation, which separates IT and OT environments and controls the communication flow between them. System patching, AV protection, and portable media security ensure protection against known threats, while physical security prevents access to equipment from unauthorized individuals.

- **Detect:** This is part of the monitor phase, during which you look for any anomalous behavior within the PCN and identify controls for the detection of malware or other security threats.

- **Defend:** The areas included in this pillar ensure that there is sufficient collection of forensic data, which can be analyzed to determine threats and the responses to them.

- **Respond:** The last pillar is responsible for ensuring that the necessary hygiene is in place, with the right backup and restore policies and disaster recovery implemented.

The risk control framework for PCNs is a new paradigm that provides defense-in-depth measures to organize, block, collect, defend, detect, and respond to cybersecurity threats. Because process control network equipment stays in the field for years, this paradigm must address existing equipment as well as new systems.

Securing the Oil and Gas PCN: Background

One of the most important goals of the risk control framework for PCNs is to support the industry's need for maintaining a "clean slate" in terms of HSE (health, safety, and environment) incidents as well as in terms of unplanned disruptions to projects and/or product losses that result from cyber incidents.

In order to support this objective, a number of detailed requirements needs to be met. These specific requirements are designed to do the following:

- Maintain a centralized solution for the monitoring, management, and reporting of the compliance status of equipment in the field

- Provide a simplified, standardized solution across businesses

- Introduce a superior level of flexibility and agility into the environment

- Maintain a level of operational security deemed acceptable by the businesses

By meeting these requirements, a number of stakeholders in the business can reap the benefits of the security architecture. The emphasis given to confidentiality, integrity, and high availability highlight the fact that these stakeholders operate critical infrastructure that should not be compromised under any circumstance. Major accidents and disasters that can cause loss of life or severe environmental damage need to be avoided at all costs. Therefore, even though these control systems (even those deployed years ago that have limited security capabilities) now need to be connected, at the same time the interfaces need to be kept to a minimum and remain carefully controlled at all times. Figure 10-16 shows an example of a PCN security reference architecture for the oil and gas industry.

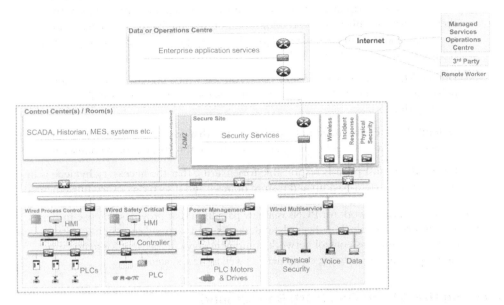

Figure 10-16   *Security Operations Reference Architecture*

This reference architecture includes two main components: the secure center and the secure site (which are hosting the main uses cases that help secure the oil and gas PCN). The guiding principle here is to use the secure center not only as the central point for visibility into the security posture of the PCN environment but also as the single entry point into the environment. A centralized point for compliance and reporting can give visibility to the entire site estate—sometimes across the globe—enabling a view of oil rigs, pipelines, and refineries from a single location. The key advantage of this approach is that it greatly reduces the risk involved in controlling multiple entry points.

Securing the Oil and Gas PCN: Use Cases and Requirements

A risk control framework needs to be flexible as well as capable of enforcing controls and collecting information and reports on those controls. The main use cases, as discussed in the following sections, are asset inventory, remote access control, patch management, antivirus control, and security intelligence.

Real-Time Asset Inventory

Asset inventory provides visibility into deployed OT assets throughout the different PCN systems across the oil and gas facility. The ability to identify OT assets and their attributes provides the foundation for the implementation of other security management, such as patch management. Asset inventory capabilities also need to support accurate maintenance records.

Asset information should be consolidated at the central OT asset database and should enable visibility of the software installed at each component, and support proactive and corrective management of incidents and/or problems. Additional information may be collected in order to support other business practices or requirements. The asset inventory is typically stored in a relational database that allows querying and integration with external reporting tools.

Remote Access Control

External remote access to a PCN should support connections from within an organization's intranet and from external vendors, and access should align with the requirements defined in the risk control framework. Enabling secure PCN access (including remote access) relies on a combination of encryption technologies and strong authentication methods to ensure that the identity of the user or system is restricted to the appropriate PCN components.

By enforcing a central entry point into the PCN environment, and by ensuring that connectivity between the operations center and the sites is established by using virtual private networking (using layered technologies such as IPSec, RDP, VNC, or SSH), access can be carefully controlled and is easier to manage. Figure 10-17 shows an example of a flow between a third party or a remote worker to a PCN asset at a secure site.

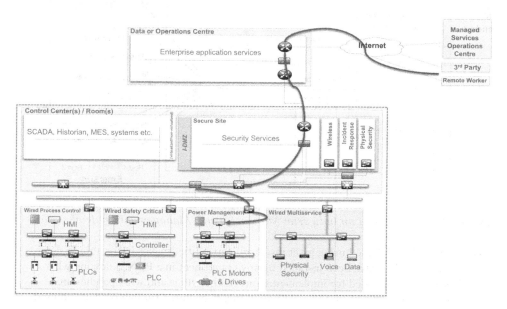

Figure 10-17 *Remote Access Session Flow into the PCN*

Patch Management

Operating system patches are crucial to the overall security of the OT environment, and they are closely associated with IT components deployed in the PCN. Patch management ensures that known vulnerabilities have been addressed and are not potential backdoors for unauthorized access or used to conduct malicious activities.

In order to most effectively interface with Microsoft Windows–based components (which are predominately used in the PCN), Windows Server Update Services (WSUS) should be implemented with additional logic to ensure simplified management and the ability to produce meaningful reports. These reports can aid in the identification of potential weaknesses in the PCN.

Such a solution can assist in the delivery of accurate qualified PCN vendor patches, which tend to come out on a regular basis. The solution can link qualified patch lists (QPLs) to groups within the patching solution, assuring improved patching process response times as well as reducing the possibility of error by removing manual QPL creation. Figure 10-18 illustrates a Microsoft WSUS patch management solution deployed in a refinery and supporting a variety of third-party industrial systems.

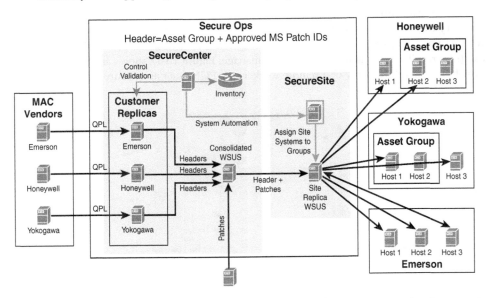

Figure 10-18 *Example of an Industrial Microsoft Patch Management Implementation*

The information collected using asset inventory capabilities makes it possible to determine which patches have been installed on any component in a PCN. Knowing what patches are recommended for implementation (via the QPLs) and what patches are currently installed on a given OT asset within the PCN allows for mapping of required and missing patches to individual assets.

Antivirus (AV) Management

Much as with the solution just offered for OS security patching, there needs to be a process for AV signature updates. Management solutions offered by standard AV providers could be leveraged to deploy approved AV signature file updates in combination with the asset inventory capabilities. After matching specific equipment to signature update requirements, AV signatures can be pushed out by the AV management solution.

A robust AV patch management system is extremely important in ensuring that the OT assets in a PCN are protected against known threats and vulnerabilities, especially since many of these systems run on well-known OSs, such as Microsoft Windows. In many cases breaches have been achieved through known vulnerabilities where the asset was not correctly patched.

Security Intelligence and Anomaly Detection

Accurate asset inventory is critical because, as it is said, "you can't secure what you don't know." Asset inventory allows you to monitor the delta between all the assets deployed in the PCN estate and your desired baseline in terms of OS patches and AV signatures, as well as what needs to be done in order to remediate any inconsistencies. It is not, however, the entire story. Monitoring the activity of these assets on the network and the ability to report anomalies or unexpected changes in network or device behavior allows for meaningful management of the passive defense mechanism and the processes and procedures required to defend against cyber threats.

Note   *Passive defense* refers to systems or components that can provide a defense mechanism without requiring human intervention.

Important challenges need to be addressed because of the nature of PCN environments. For example, a large variety of different PCN solutions and systems are used in most oil and gas facilities, and a variety of industrial protocols and access methods have been implemented on different networking technologies. An effective system needs to be able to move around this variability and present all the information in a clear and concise manner so it can be managed and actioned in a timely fashion. If a centralized security operations center (SOC) is also monitoring the devices, OS and network logs also have to be collected and uploaded to a SIEM (security information and event management) system for further analysis.

Data Analytics for Predictive Asset Monitoring

Performing real-time data analysis on plant machinery and assets (such as motors, valves, and pumps) is an invaluable way to optimize performance and proactively detect issues before they occur.

Traditionally, equipment is assessed on a preventive time-based schedule, or, in the worst-case scenario, equipment is fixed or replaced after issues occur. In many cases, equipment or parts may be replaced even if they do not need to be based on an estimated lifetime use. For example, a pressure sensor might be in perfect working order and could potentially last another 10 years, but due to a rigid replacement schedule, it gets replaced years before it needs to be, introducing unnecessary costs and lost efficiency. In addition, physical inspection can be expensive—especially inside pipelines and other hard-to-reach areas. The lack of real-time information about the status of equipment can easily lead to equipment failure, costly unplanned maintenance, and lost processing time, not to mention the danger of accidents or emergencies resulting from failed equipment.

Analytics can be leveraged to make equipment monitoring, management, and maintenance more effective. Models can be created for each equipment type to help predict component failures and also to optimize performance characteristics. Wireless sensors and plant monitoring equipment can be used to measure characteristics such as temperature, vibration, alignment, pressure, viscosity, and lubricant condition in real time and compare these measurements with historical models to assess how equipment is performing and the likelihood of failure.

From a predictive maintenance perspective, equipment can be fixed or replaced based on its actual condition rather than a preset timeline or agenda. This can potentially provide savings on replacement costs and also allows for equipment that may fail before the scheduled maintenance window to be fixed, and prevent accidents or downtime. In addition, optimized equipment performance based on real-time feedback of equipment parameters may be realized, with even small efficiency improvements returning savings. (For more details on analytics in IoT, refer to Chapter 7, "Data and Analytics for IoT.")

Summary

As technology has advanced, the oil and gas industry has begun innovating through connectivity to assets and insights gained through the data produced. IoT solutions are helping drive better access to existing data sources, as well as meeting compliance requirements and increasing the safety of employees. Many view IoT technologies as a key enabler, particularly with the adoption of wireless technology.

It is essential to understand that a single technology cannot enable the oil and gas industry to meet these requirements. Only a properly architected, secure integration of technologies and applications will help reduce costs, improve efficiencies, keep workers safe, and continue to drive innovation.

The oil and gas industry is building new IoT solutions for the connected refinery, control center, pipeline, and oil rig. These solutions follow the Purdue Model for Control Hierarchy, which helps identify the architectural levels and security zones.

Because of the nature of oil and gas facilities and work environments, wireless technology is widely used to connect sensors, workers, and industrial control systems. Wi-Fi and deterministic wireless systems such as ISA100.11 and WirelessHART are popular in this industry, and they solve very specific challenges.

Security is also paramount in the oil and gas industry, and adhering to a risk management framework enhances security. Security should be managed through a comprehensive defense-in-depth strategy that incorporates authentication, encryption, remote access controls, AV, and OS patch management.

References

1. Gartner, *Top 10 Technology Trends Impacting the Oil and Gas Industry in 2014*, 2014.

2. http://robotics.eecs.berkeley.edu/~pister/publications/dissertations/ZatsSamuel_MSReport2010.pdf.

Chapter 11

Utilities

Utilities are a mainstay of the modern world. Be it electric power, gas, or water, utility companies provide the services that run our cities, businesses, and, indeed, entire economy. One power company executive was recently asked to explain his company's core business function in one sentence. He replied: "We supply electric power for the enjoyment of our customers." It may seem strange to think of "enjoying" electric power; it's one of those things we tend to take for granted—but there is truth in the comment: Reliable electrical power allows us to enjoy many things in life. When the power goes off, we are suddenly without access to our treasured electronic devices and find ourselves desperately looking for candles and matches. It feels like we have been abruptly thrown back into the Dark Ages, trying to figure out how people used to entertain themselves before electric power. Some people joke that the function of the power company is simply to "keep the lights on." For most of us, that is exactly what we expect because when the lights go out, our normal life screeches to an abrupt halt. We experience similar challenges when our gas and water services stop.

The importance of utilities to the basic function of society is evident as many governments categorize them as "critical infrastructure," and most countries have strict laws to ensure their safety, protection, continued operation, and quality.

The size and scale of utility networks can be truly massive. Consider that each home connected to a utility company's services requires a meter for each service. As each meter in the utility network becomes automated through IP and IoT, the scale of that network becomes huge. Imagine a midsized city with half a million homes and businesses that receive electric, water, and gas service from different utilities. If you assume one IP address for each type of meter, the network has already scaled to 1.5 million endpoints, not to mention the network infrastructure supporting these nodes. However, this example is actually very small compared to the size of some modern smart meter networks, which now scale into the tens of millions. From a pure IP perspective, very few organizations have dealt with the challenges involved in designing, deploying, and managing a network of this size.

The main focus of this chapter is on the digitization journey of electric power companies and, in particular, how IoT is being used to build smart grid networks. This is not to imply that gas or water utilities are less important, but rather reflects the fact that electric utilities have been the first to embrace the potential of grid automation and analytics through IoT. In addition, many of the technologies commonly found in electric power grids lend themselves very well to the automation benefits of IoT. That being said, many of the principles discussed in this chapter are also applicable to other types of utilities.

This chapter introduces the concept of the smart grid and explores some of the underlying IoT technologies that are transforming the way power is generated, transmitted, and delivered. It includes the following sections:

- **An Introduction to the Power Utility Industry:** This section describes the power utility industry and provides a better understanding of its business models and technical challenges.

- **The GridBlocks Reference Model:** GridBlocks is a foundational architecture for the smart grid. This section discusses this reference model and how it can be used to build a coherent smart grid strategy.

- **The Primary Substation GridBlock and Substation Automation:** The substation is the place where power is transmitted and distributed. Assets in the substation are becoming highly connected and automated. This section explores automation solutions and the IoT building blocks that are now being deployed in substations.

- **System Control GridBlock: The Substation WAN:** The utility WAN allows interconnection between substations and to the control center. The utility WAN is now transitioning from tradition TDM transport to IP packet-based networks. This section examines design considerations that allow the utility WAN to carry some of the most sensitive applications of any industry.

- **The Field Area Network (FAN) GridBlock:** This section explores the FAN as a foundational element to connect intelligent devices, including smart meters and devices on the distribution grid, allowing utilities to harness the power of automation and data analytics.

- **Securing the Smart Grid:** The electric grid is considered "critical infrastructure." This section explores concepts such as SCADA security, NERC CIP, and security best practices for the distribution grid.

- **The Future of the Smart Grid:** IoT has already had a profound impact on power utilities worldwide, resulting in new processes and business models. In the future, distributed energy generation, clean energy, and electric vehicles will further disrupt grid technology.

An Introduction to the Power Utility Industry

If someone were to ask you the name of the electric company that serves your home or business, you would probably answer with the name of the power company that sends bills to you. However, this is only part of the answer, and in many cases, the billing company is only part of the last mile of the power supply chain. Power delivery to your home typically comes in three stages, and in many parts of the world these stages are supported by entirely different companies, or at least separate divisions of one large power company. The three stages of the power supply–chain are generation, transmission, and distribution:

- **Generation:** Power generation is where the electricity gets produced. Power production typically includes nuclear, hydroelectric, gas, and coal pants. Once generated, high-voltage (HV) electrical power is sent through high-voltage transmission lines into the transmission system. The generation company is also responsible for responding to the fluctuating power demands of the end customers.

- **Transmission:** Power transmission takes the HV power over long distances— typically 115 kV and above over distances of 50 km and greater. Transmission lines include aerial lines and also submarine cables that transmit HV electrical power over long distances underwater. The transmission system is responsible for connecting HV lines from generation stations to substations throughout the service area. When you see large metal towers along the highway supporting long power cables, these are the transmission lines bringing power from the generation plant to the substations.

- **Distribution:** Power distribution includes the part of the utility network from the substation to your home or business. This includes the medium-voltage (12.5 kV, for example) powerlines you see on poles around your neighborhood, including pad mount transformers. Note that power is stepped down to low-voltage at the transformers near your home and typically runs at a couple hundred volts toward the end customer. It is important to note that there are some differences between the North American and European distribution grid models. For example, in Europe, it is common to see secondary substations. Also, low-voltage is 240 V in Europe and 110 V in North America.

Figure 11-1 illustrates how generation, transmission, and distribution work together to bring power to end customers.

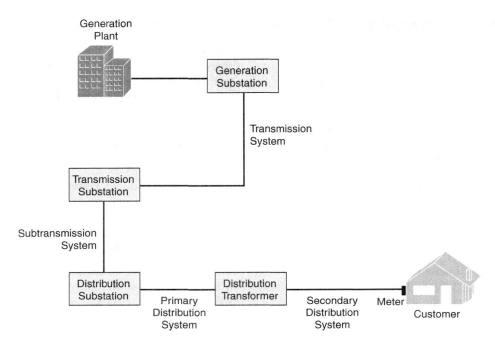

Figure 11-1 *Traditional Generation, Transmission, and Distribution Stages in a Power Utility Network*

Note   Vertically integrated utilities own and operate the entire electric power supply chain—generation, transmission, and distribution (as well as retail or direct sales) to all classes of customers. Depending on the country, governments and utility regulators have split the major utility operations into separate companies, although the specific separation and operations strategy depends on the region or country. Depending on government regulations, a utility holding company can have ownership of multiple operations even though they've been separated into different legal entities. Thus, a utility may be either vertically integrated or separated, depending on the area.

The IT/OT Divide in Utilities

The power engineering side of the utility had its beginnings long before there were inexpensive microprocessors, industry communications standards, and IP networks. What was an engineer to do if he or she needed to gather data from a sensor and take some type of action? The very early days of utility OT networks connected remote dials and indicators so that operators and engineers could make readings without having to travel to remote locations. This allowed them to make readings of many sensors from one conveniently located control room. Power grid control rooms today echo those beginnings, with graphical displays that tile entire walls.

As inexpensive and reliable serial communications became widely available, more capabilities came, at lower prices, allowing for wide deployment. When Ethernet first became available, no one dreamed that it would become cheaper than serial or that comput-ing would become so inexpensive and powerful that it could be used almost anywhere throughout the grid instead of being a centrally located behemoth-sized mainframe in a glass-walled control room.

Given the longevity of electrical control and monitoring systems, as well as the vast scale of utility networks, it is simply not economical to replace all legacy utility systems when new technologies become available. However, as new systems with new capabilities are installed, and as equipment and system prices decline, they are bringing greater reliability and cost benefits to utilities.

While OT networks are not as flexible as their IT counterparts, OT engineering depart-ments have continually adapted to take advantage of newer technologies supporting the power grid. This has included developing ways to support many generations of legacy systems on new networks. OT engineers are always looking for better, more cost-effective ways to do things, and this often includes utilizing IT technology whenever possible. IT technology has the benefit of wide adoption in the industry, which means it is easy to find qualified people to design and support networks and application servers. The chal-lenge was, and continues to be, understanding the OT physical systems and making sure that general-purpose IT, which is primarily based on IP networking technology, is up to the job. (IT and OT are introduced and defined in Chapter 1, "What Is IoT?")

Note   The term *OT* is not universally used by utilities. In many parts of the world, the operational telecommunications engineering role is done by protection and control engineers, but for simplicity, the term *OT* is used in this book.

As the utility OT networks begin to migrate to IP communications and use IoT architectures, the sizes of the OT networks become orders of magnitude larger than those of IT counterparts. Take, for example, advanced metering infrastructure (AMI), where the electric meters become "smart" IP-enabled devices that are connected to a single network. The AMI network alone may have millions of nodes, all of which may become IPv6 routable endpoints. A question arises: Who designs, operates, and manages the AMI network, along with other IP-based OT networks? Is it the OT team, which has the skills to understand utility applications, or is it the IT team, which has experience in IP networking?

These challenges become even more evident as the IT and OT networks become interconnected. Concerns that need to be addressed include the following:

- How can network resiliency and redundancy be supported for mission-critical OT applications that keep the lights on?

- Who will support remote access to distributed systems on the grid that must transit both the IT and OT networks?

- How will security be governed in both the OT networks and the interconnection points between the IT and OT networks? Is this the responsibility of the traditional IT security department, or is a new paradigm required?

- Will change management be governed in the same way as it is for IT systems, or does the criticality of the OT applications require a new set of rules to ensure the continuity of business?

Different organizations respond in different ways to these challenges. In the past, IT and OT were completely separate groups—ships in the night that rarely needed to interface with each other. Today, as networks converge, OT and IT need to work closely together. Some OT engineers are learning the IP skills needed to build and support complex OT systems, and IT engineers are learning important aspects of the utility's core OT system. However, the expertise and knowledge that each party has acquired over many years has been hard won; this knowledge is not easy to transfer between departments in a short period of time. How long would it take an IT engineer to learn the intricacies of electrical protection and control systems? Likewise, how long would it take for protection and control engineers to lean the intricacies of Ethernet resiliency and IP routing, which are today forming the network transport of the applications they are responsible for? These skills take many years to develop and mature.

These challenges have ushered in the age of the smart grid—the combination of the electric power grid and the information and communications technology (ICT) that operates the grid, with objectives of efficiently delivering sustainable, economic, and secure electricity supplies.

Utility companies are now grappling with the IT/OT convergence challenge, and this is perhaps the first major industry to be confronted with the rigors of integrating IT and OT at such a large scale into a converged network with cohesive governance. In addition, the utility industry is now faced with the challenge of developing new industry standards that allow the secure interconnection of millions of substation and distribution OT devices into the enterprise IT network. To accomplish this successfully, an architectural approach must be followed. The GridBlocks reference model provides such an architecture for utilities and is discussed next.

The GridBlocks Reference Model

Cisco was one of the first companies to recognize that a systematic architecture was needed to integrate systems at all stages of the electrical supply chain into modern communications systems. The architecture must take into account the rapid modernization of smart grid technologies while at the same time supporting a host of legacy technologies that are likely to be in place for many years to come.

In response to this need, Cisco developed the GridBlocks reference model. While other reference models exist, GridBlocks offers an easy-to-understand model for both novice and advanced users working in the utility space. The GridBlocks reference model, shown in Figure 11-2, depicts the entire bulk electricity supply chain, from wide area bulk power entities through generation, control centers, transmission grids, substations, distribution grids, and integration of distributed energy resources at the edge of the grid. The model is forward-looking and is intended to be a generalized end-state reference framework that can help assist in deploying and designing end-to-end secure energy communications solutions for all aspects of the grid, thus facilitating a new and powerful foundation for utilities—the *smart grid*.

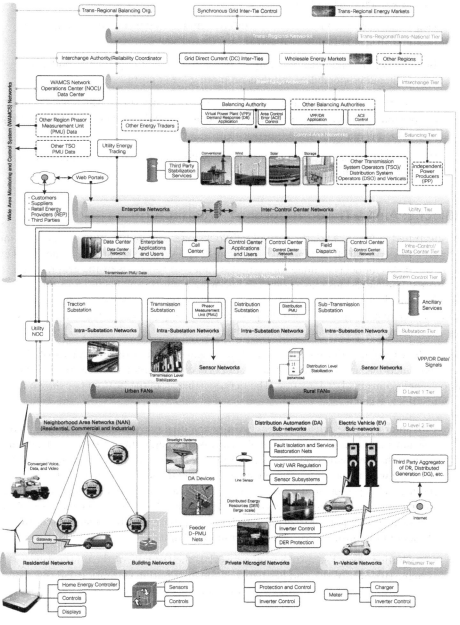

Figure 11-2   *The GridBlocks Reference Architecture*

The GridBlocks reference architecture provides the following benefits to utility operators:

- Details a flexible, tier-based model that supports incremental improvements to logical sections (tiers) of the grid

- Helps enable secure integration of both new and legacy technologies, improving overall manageability and visibility of network elements

- Builds on open standards, primarily IP, preventing vendor dependency and also supporting interoperability and thus promoting lower costs

- Enables the consolidation and convergence of utility networks, which has the effect of streamlining operations and reducing operational and capital costs while creating new value through increased functionality

- Provides a digitization roadmap for utilities, allowing them to modernize different parts of the grid in stages

GridBlocks: An 11-Tiered Reference Architecture

As illustrated in Figure 11-2, the Cisco GridBlocks reference architecture is organized into 11 parts (or tiers), which network all aspects of the power delivery supply chain. The key strategy of this model is to unite formerly disconnected functions of the grid through network communications into a converged network architecture. Each tier of the grid may be owned and operated by different divisions of the same power company, or even entirely different companies along the power deliver supply chain, while at the same time supporting secure interconnections between each tier.

While the GridBlocks tier-based model allows segmentation of the utility's capabilities and functional areas into tiers, it also supports consolidation of network elements into a single converged architecture. The tiers, starting from the bottom tier shown in Figure 11-2, are as follows:

- **Prosumer tier:** The prosumer tier combines the dual roles of energy producer and consumer and encompasses external elements that might impact the grid. These are devices that are neither owned by the utility nor part of its infrastructure, but that interface with it somehow. This includes distributed energy resources (DERs) that produce local power from solar or some other means. This could also include energy storage systems and responsive loads in electric vehicles or industrial facilities. This rapidly maturing part of smart grid technology promises to be a major disruptive element in the future, as discussed later in this chapter.

- **Distribution tiers:** The distribution network is the last mile of the power delivery system. This part of the grid lies between the distribution substation and the end user. For simplicity, it is broken into two subtiers, as follows:

■ **Distribution Level 2 tier:** This lower-level distribution tier is the last mile, or neighborhood area network (NAN), of the power delivery system. This part of the smart grid network supports metering systems, demand response systems, electric vehicle (EV) recharging stations, remote terminal units that are part of the distribution automation system, and many other types of devices.

■ **Distribution Level 1 tier:** Level 1 of the distribution tier connects the Level 2 tier networks to the distribution substation and provides backhaul services to the utility control center via the system control tier.

■ **Substation tier:** This tier includes all substation networks, including those in both the transmission and distribution substations. Transmission substations connect multiple transmission lines and typically involve higher voltages (115 kV and above), and feed power toward distribution stations. Distribution substations receive an input of typically 115 kV and above (or whatever is common in the service area) and feed power at 25 kV or less toward the end customer. Networks at this tier have a wide variety of requirements, from basic secondary substations to complex primary substations that provide critical power delivery functions, such as teleprotection (discussed in detail later in this chapter). Inside the substation, there are often strict network requirements, including resiliency, performance, time synchronization, and security. These substation requirements have resulted in the separation of functions, with independent buses for each (for example, the station and process bus functions). Primary distribution substations may also include distribution aggregation.

■ **System control tier:** This tier includes the wide area networks (WANs) that connect substations with each other and with control centers. The WAN connections in this tier require some of the most stringent latency and resiliency performance metrics of any industry. The substation WANs require flexibility and scalability and may involve different media types, including fiber or microwave. The system control tier supports connectivity for remote SCADA (supervisory control and data acquisition, covered later in this chapter) devices to the control center, event messaging, and teleprotection services between the relays within the substations.

■ **Intra-control center/intra-data center tier:** This is the tier inside the utility data centers and control centers. Both data centers and control centers are at the same logical level, but they have very different requirements. A data center is very familiar to the IT engineers, as it contains enterprise-level applications and services. A control center contains real-time systems that operate and control the grid itself, including power distribution and transmission systems, monitoring, and demand response. This tier needs to be connected to the substation through the system control tier so that important data can be collected and run by both IT and OT systems in the substations.

- **Utility tier:** This tier is home to the enterprise campus networks. (Although the name implies that there is some grid-related function here, this is an IT-focused tier.) The utility tier is the connection point between the control center and the enterprise network, and it utilizes firewalls with the appropriate security policies to ensure that only trusted traffic from the enterprise network enters into the control center. (Note that firewalls are used throughout this architecture and between tiers, and this is but one example.) It is also important to note that most utilities operate multiple control centers and have highly dispersed enterprise networks, meaning that these networks must be securely connected through either metro networks or WANs (possibly reusing a WAN network as the system control tier).

- **Balancing tier:** This tier supports connections between third-party power-generation operators and balancing authorities (as well as connections to independent power producers [IPPs]). In an electric utility, demand from customers may not always meet the generation supply. To manage load and demand, most utilities are interconnected with other utilities and can buy and sell electrical energy from each other when necessary. At times, there may be an excess of power in one utility and a shortage of electricity in another. The balancing authority has the delicate responsibility of managing electrical demand versus supply on the grid. If electrical demand and supply fall out of balance, blackouts can occur. The sensitive nature of the balancing tier highlights the need for a communications network that enables different parties to collaborate effectively and securely.

- **Interchange tier:** The network at this tier allows electricity to be bought and sold between utility operators. In the utility world, electricity is transacted in much the same way as other commodities, such as oil and gas. The sale or purchase of electricity needs to happen in real time. Networks at this tier allow the utility to not only buy electrical energy when needed but also make a profit by selling excess power to other utilities when there is an opportunity to do so.

- **Trans-regional/trans-national tier:** Most utility grids are interconnected with much larger supergrids. For example, Figure 11-3 shows how the utilities in different countries and regions are interconnected with one another to form what is known as the Synchronous Grid of Continental Europe. In North America, this is known as the North American Interconnection, and it is composed of interconnection points between the Texas Grid, Western Interconnection, Eastern Interconnection, and Quebec Interconnection, as shown in Figure 11-4. At this tier are the network connections between synchronous grids for power interchange as well grid monitoring and power flow management.

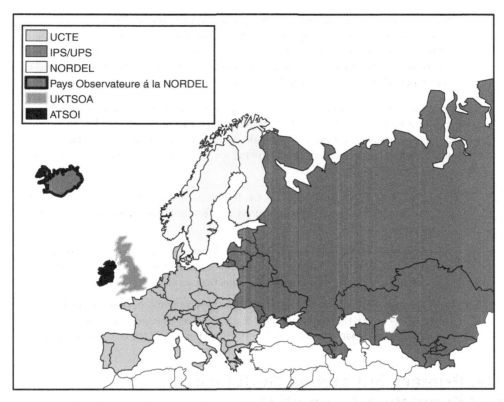

Figure 11-3 *The Synchronous Electrical Grid of Continental Europe*

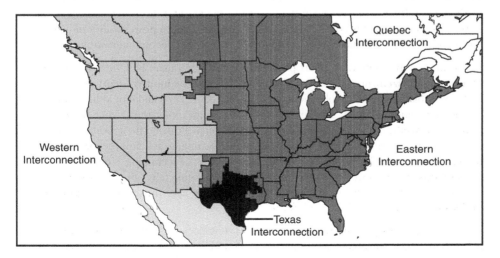

Figure 11-4 *Interconnections of the North American Electric Power Grid*

■ **Wide area measurement and control system (WAMCS) tier:** This tier includes connections to a critical component of the power grid, power management units (PMUs), which are responsible for wide area power measurements across the grid. Due to the scope of this tier, it needs to connect to several of the other tiers and is thus depicted as a vertical tier in Figure 11-2.

The GridBlocks reference model is a useful tool and blueprint that can be used as a foundation to build network elements within the tiers and link them to other tiers. It also provides a fundamental grouping of network capabilities into "grid blocks" that can be expanded in much greater detail. The following are some examples that are discussed in subsequent sections of this chapter:

■ **Primary substation GridBlock:** This GridBlock delves into the subject of substation automation and the interconnection of process bus and station bus devices within the substation.

■ **System control GridBlock:** This GridBlock connects substations to one another and with the control center. One of the key focus areas of this GridBlock is supporting WAN architectures that can deliver teleprotection services.

■ **Field area network (FAN) GridBlock:** The FAN is a rapidly developing area of the utility IoT network that supports the connection and management of distant distribution elements, smart meters, distribution automation, demand response, and more.

The Primary Substation GridBlock and Substation Automation

Thomas Edison and Alexander Graham Bell were contemporaries and are considered two of the most influential inventors in the history of the world. Edison invented electrical power distribution and is considered the father of the modern power utility industry. Bell invented the telephone and is considered the father of the telecommunications industry.

If you were to give a modern smart phone to Alexander Graham Bell, he would likely look at it in amazement and wonder. The capabilities of the modern smart phone bear little resemblance to the simple telephone he invented in 1876 and would likely be considered something from another one of his contemporaries, the science fiction writer H.G. Wells. However, if you were to take Thomas Edison into a modern power generation or electrical substation, he would likely be able to tell you the exact function of nearly everything he could see. Indeed, the progress of technology in the electrical power industry has moved at a much slower rate than in the telecommunications industry. However, this is beginning to change—and we have the technical beginnings of Alexander Graham Bell to thank for it.

One of the greatest progressive leaps in the past few decades in the electrical power industry has been the ability to connect devices and control them through telecommunications networks, and IoT is now taking this leap to a whole new level.

SCADA

SCADA is a system by which remote devices can be monitored and controlled by a central server. SCADA plays a critical role in the substation, allowing (as the name suggests) controls and data acquisition from remote devices, known as remote terminal units (RTUs) and intelligent electronic devices (IEDs). RTUs and IEDs are microprocessor-controlled devices attached to power grid hardware, such as electric relays, load controllers, circuit breaker controllers, capacitor bank controllers, and so on. In the world of SCADA, the remote device is called a *SCADA slave*, and the server is called a *SCADA master*.

SCADA had its beginnings back in the 1950s, long before computer networks existed. It was intended to be a system in which an operator could manage remote industrial devices from a central point (often a mainframe computer system). In these early days, SCADA systems were independent, with no connectivity to other systems, and they relied almost entirely on proprietary protocols. Over time, remote WAN networks allowed SCADA connectivity to extend to RTUs, but these connections were typically point-to-point serial links that utilized RS-232 or RS-485 interfaces and were transported over TDM circuits.

Over time, SCADA transport began to adopt standards-based protocols and an open network architecture. Instead of relying on dedicated serial links connecting every SCADA slave, the substation LAN began to be leveraged for transport, with a local SCADA master residing at each substation. As high-speed, resilient, and flexible IP WAN networks became available, SCADA services began to be dispersed throughout the network and could use a centralized SCADA master in the control center.

The most widely deployed legacy SCADA communication protocols are Modbus, IEC 60870-5, and Distributed Network Protocol (DNP3).

Note   Modbus, the oldest of these protocols, was developed in 1979 for programmable logic controller (PLC) devices but eventually found its way into SCADA for power systems. IEC 60870-5-101, completed in 1995, was designed for distributed SCADA systems over serial links. DNP3 was originally developed by GE Harris in Canada in 1990 and is now managed by the DNP Users Group. DNP3 has been adopted by the IEEE as a standard for SCADA communications. Historically, DNP3 has been the dominant SCADA protocol in North America, while IEC 60870 has been the leading protocol in Europe. Today, these protocols have TCP/IP variants, allowing them to be natively transported over IP networks.

Figure 11-5 illustrates a legacy substation where the electrical relays are attached via serial (RS-232 or RS-485) connections to RTUs, which are in turn connected to a SCADA gateway device that is connected to the substation Ethernet network. A SCADA gateway device typically functions in one of two ways. The first way is protocol translation, such as translation of native serial to IP encapsulation. Examples of this include DNP3 to DNP3/IP or IEC 60870-5-101 (serial) to 60870-5-104 (TCP/IP). The second way a gateway device may work is to tunnel the serial traffic through the IP network (for example, with raw sockets). For a more in-depth discussion of Modbus, IEC 60870-5, and DNP3, along with the transport concepts of protocol translation and raw sockets, refer to Chapter 6, "Application Protocols for IoT."

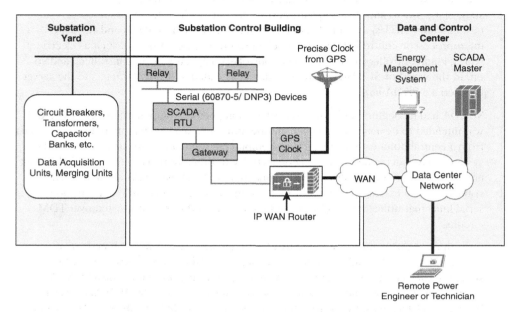

Figure 11-5 *A Traditional Substation SCADA Network with Serial Attached RTUs*

While we expect these legacy SCADA transport mechanisms to exist for many years to come, long term, traditional SCADA systems are being replaced by a new technology standard that natively takes advantage of Ethernet and TCP/IP: IEC 61850.

IEC 61850: The Modernization of Substation Communication Standards

Existing serial-based SCADA systems running on Modbus, IEC 60870-5-101, or DNP3 are ill-equipped to support next-generation capabilities of modern IEDs. Even with IP-based protocol translation services, they still lack deployment flexibility and ultimately rely on aging serial communications at the RTU. In an effort to modernize substation communication and leverage protocols that can take advantage of Ethernet and IP, the IEC Technical Committee 57 (TC57) developed the IEC 61850 standard. IEC 61850 is not simply a redevelopment of former serial-based protocols utilizing Ethernet and IP for transport. Instead, IEC 61850 was built from the ground up on modern standards and technologies and offers a host of new capabilities to IEDs in the substation.

IEC 61850 overcomes some of the most challenging vendor and network interoperability challenges in the substation and beyond. With 61850, dedicated serial links are replaced with Ethernet and IP, which means the copper wiring plant in the substation can be greatly reduced. The inherent flexibility of Ethernet means that IEDs can easily communicate directly with one another and with other elements of the communications infrastructure. Another key advantage offered by the flexibility of Ethernet is that interfaces are cheap and are being added by equipment vendors to all modern assets, which means unsupervised gear in the substation is now becoming a thing of the past.

IEC 61850 Station Bus

IEC 61850 defines substation communications in two key areas of the substation—the station level and the process level—as illustrated in Figure 11-6. At the station level is equipment that needs to communicate with the IEDs (typically SCADA communications). The station bus is the network interconnection between the devices in the station level and IEDs in the bay level, where you find protection and electrical control assets, metering gear, and other key systems.

The bay level, shown in Figure 11-6, relates to high-voltage devices that make connections to power and current transformers, switching gear, and so on. These devices make connections into the measurement system for protection and control. Devices in the bay level typically have two different types of network interfaces: one for SCADA management connected to the station bus and another connected to the process bus.

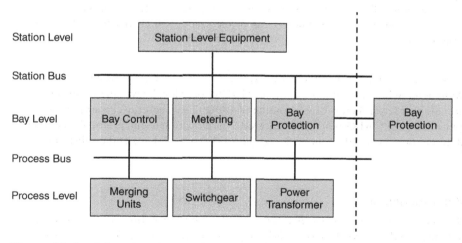

Figure 11-6 *Substation Automation Hierarchy*

While a primary focus of the station bus is on SCADA transport over Ethernet and IP, IEC 61850 goes far beyond. The IEC 61850 communications structure defines three main traffic classes:

- **Manufacturing Message Specification (MMS; IEC 61850-8-1):** MMS supports client/server communications over IP and is used for SCADA. MMS traffic is typically found on the station bus.

- **Generic Object Oriented Substation Event (GOOSE; IEC 61850-8-1):** GOOSE uses Ethernet-based multicast (one-to-many) communications in which IEDs can communicate with each other and between bays. GOOSE is often used for passing power measurements and between protection relays, as well as for tripping and interlocking circuits. GOOSE is typically used over the station bus.

■ **Sampled Values (SVs; IEC 61850-9-2):** SVs are typically used on the process bus to carry voltage and current samples. A common use for SVs is for bus-bar protection and synchrophasors.

Note *Synchrophasors* are time-synchronized electrical numbers that monitor phase and power. They are measured by devices called *phase measurement units* (*PMUs*) in the substation.

In the world of substation automation, GOOSE is an extremely important tool, as it is the primary 61850 message type used between electrical protection and control systems. Protection and control systems are among the most important gear found in a substation, as they are used to continually monitor power being delivered by transmission lines and feeders. If power is disrupted for some reason, the measurement system detects it within a few milliseconds and passes GOOSE messages through the Ethernet network to a peer relay that switches power delivery to an alternate line or feeder. If the GOOSE messages are not delivered correctly or within the required timeframe, the electrical relays can become confused, and power can be incorrectly switched, causing blackouts or even worse.

Note Substation GOOSE uses Ethernet multicast messages that are transmitted between IEDs. Although the initial intention was to use GOOSE only locally within the substation (meaning that Layer 3 inter-VLAN routing of GOOSE was never necessary), recent developments with IEC 61850-90-5 have allowed a modification to the protocol that allows GOOSE to be routed over IP on the wide area network. GOOSE has left the substation!

IEC 61850 Process Bus

At the time of this writing (early 2017), most 61850 implementations worldwide have been limited to the station bus, but this is only part of what IEC 61850 delivers. The other focus area of IEC 61850 is the process bus. In the past, devices such as current transformers (CTs), potential transformers (PTs), and data acquisition units (DAUs) passed a continual stream of data to measurement systems. These devices are critical to the function of a substation as they not only measure the balance and quality of electrical power but effectively keep an eye on the overall function of their part of the grid. This part of the substation is considered so sensitive that the network connections have historically been hard-wired and kept entirely isolated from any other network.

IEC 61850-9 defines process bus communications in which critical process-level equipment may communicate messages over Ethernet. Any upstream metering, protection, or measurement devices may then use this data as necessary.

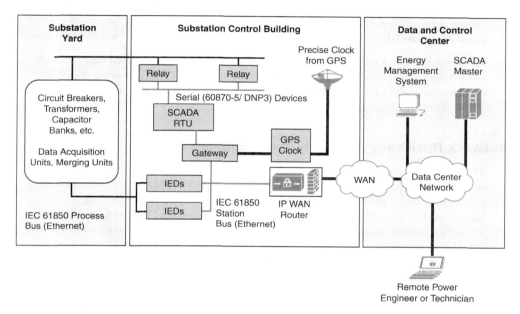

Figure 11-7 *The IEC 61850-Based Substation Architecture*

Figure 11-7 illustrates a possible IEC 61850 substation automation design. As shown in this illustration, two separate Ethernet segments are used: the station bus and process bus. The station bus allows inter-IED communication for things like GOOSE messages for protection and control as well as SCADA communications. According to 61850, the process bus uses an entirely different set of Ethernet switches for the critical substation automation functions. This area of the substation cannot simply use a separate VLAN from the same switches on the station bus; it must use distinct physical switches for each bus. One reason is that the network resiliency requirements of the process bus go far beyond what standard Ethernet is capable of and require a new generation of resiliency protocols, described later in this chapter.

Migration to IEC 61850

DNP3, Modbus, and IEC 60870-5-101 are legacy protocols that rely on point-to-point serial communications and seem incompatible with modern networking technologies. However, they are still very widely deployed and must be supported, even in modern substations.

IEC 61850 is still a relatively new standard for communications within the substation and beyond. Thus, an immediate migration from legacy systems and protocols is not likely.

Utility assets often have 20- to 30-year replacement or upgrade cycles, and migration to newer equipment takes time. In many cases, you can expect a substation to have a mixture of legacy serial-connected RTUs alongside modern IEDs that can take advantage of the Ethernet framework offered by IEC 61850. In time, it is expected that the substation process bus will also begin to adopt the 61850 capabilities. Recent developments in standards also allow 61850 to be routed outside the substation, as defined in the 61850-90-5.

Figure 11-7 shows a hybrid substation where both legacy RTUs are used together with more modern 61850-capable devices. Over time, as the availability of serial and TDM parts becomes difficult, it is expected that IEC 61850 solutions will dominate substation OT networks in all parts of the substation.

Network Resiliency Protocols in the Substation

The IEC 61850 process bus has some of the most stringent resiliency requirements of any application in any industry. Even the loss of one packet or Ethernet frame cannot be tolerated. Modern Ethernet redundancy protocols that feature fast reconvergence capabilities, such as Rapid Spanning Tree, ITU G.8032, and Resilient Ethernet Protocol (REP), are not capable of handling the job. (REP is covered in Chapter 9, "Manufacturing.") The solution to this challenge is a new breed of network resiliency protocols developed by the IEC, including Parallel Redundancy Protocol (PRP) and High-Availability Seamless Redundancy (HSR), which are primarily designed for use in substations.

Parallel Redundancy Protocol

PRP is an IEC standard for implementing highly available automation networks which ensures that the network never loses even a single Ethernet frame, even in the event of a network outage. The protocol, standardized in IEC 62439-3 Clause 4, leverages the principle of parallel redundancy. Instead of just sending one frame onto an Ethernet segment and letting the network quickly converge in the event of a failure (as in the case of REP or G.8032), a PRP-enabled dual-attached IED is capable of sending redundant copies of the same frame on different but parallel Ethernet VLAN segments.

The Ethernet frames originating from the IED are bridged to both network interfaces and are given a sequence number. The two frames then traverse the two parallel network paths until they arrive at the receiving IED, again on two separate NICs. The receiving IED selects a preferred (active) interface and discards the frame received on the nonpreferred (backup) interface. In the event of a failure in one of the parallel networks, this approach guarantees that at least one of the packets will always arrive at the destination IED.

Note   In the case of the 61850 GOOSE protocol, an additional layer of resiliency is added for electrical protection systems where the sending IED transmits each frame multiple times. This ensures that at least one frame arrives correctly at the destination.

The scenario just presented assumes that the IEDs themselves are PRP capable and are thus able to make and remove multiple copies of each frame. This may not always be feasible because it would require not only an upgrade of the IEDs themselves to support PRP but also the deployment of dual redundant Ethernet networks.

A similar but slightly different approach is to single-attach an existing IED to a PRP-capable access switch. In this case, the PRP access switch acts as the redundancy box (or RedBox), making dual copies of the Ethernet frame and sending the copies over different VLANs on opposing sides of the network. The receiving PRP switch then forwards a single copy of the Ethernet frame to the relay and removes the duplicate copy. Note that one of the key advantages of PRP is that the intermediary switches do not need to be PRP capable. In this scenario, only the sending and receiving RedBoxes actually participate in the PRP redundancy, as detailed in Figure 11-8.

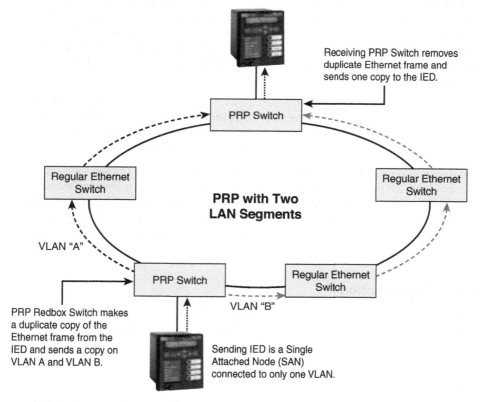

Figure 11-8 *PRP Deployment Example*

High-Availability Seamless Redundancy

Another resiliency protocol that has been developed for utilities is HSR. Unlike PRP, which relies on parallel network segments, HSR was designed for Ethernet ring topologies. HSR shares many similarities with PRP and was standardized in IEC 62439-3

Clause 5. While PRP is very flexible and can be deployed in a variety of topologies, HSR was specifically designed for ring topologies.

Much as in the preceding PRP RedBox example, with HSR, the IED has only a single attachment to the HSR RedBox Ethernet switch. With HSR, instead of making duplicate copies of the Ethernet frame and sending them over different VLANs, the HSR RedBox sends out duplicate copies on the same VLAN but on opposing sides of the ring. One key constraint of HSR is that all intermediary switches in the ring must be capable of understanding HSR to remove the duplicate copy after the primary frame is switched on toward its destination.

System Control GridBlock: The Substation WAN

With the rise of substation automation, the WAN interconnecting the substations and the control center has become responsible for carrying applications that are intrinsic to the operation of the utility. These traffic types include not only traditional IT systems traffic but also physical security system traffic, SCADA, and teleprotection communications. Among all of these, the teleprotection application is the most sensitive to latency, jitter, and packet loss, and it requires careful WAN design.

Protection, according to IEC 60384, is defined as "the provision for detecting faults or other abnormal conditions in a power system, for enabling fault clearance, for terminating abnormal conditions, and for initiating signals or indications." Teleprotection is the mechanism by which this information is transported over a network.

Teleprotection is used by almost every utility in the world between transmission substations and between primary distribution substations. Teleprotection is used by utilities to signal between protection relays and ensure that power is continually delivered, even when part of the electrical grid is out. In the context of IoT, the protection relays are the endpoints that digitize important data which is then transported by the IP transport network.

Defining Teleprotection

In practice, there are two common types of protection: distance protection and current differential line protection. Whatever the protection scheme, a communication system is always required between the relays.

Distance Protection

Distance protection monitors unacceptable variations in circuit impedance over a predetermined distance. If a relay sees a change in the impedance beyond acceptable thresholds, the relay determines that there is a fault on the line. The communications network between the relays transmits the status of the measurements, and is used to determine not only whether a fault occurred but where. In most cases, this information is also used to clear the fault and restore power.

Distance protection uses the concept that the impedance of an electric circuit is proportional to its length (the distance of the line). Thus, for a known line distance, the relay simply needs to measure the impedance of the line at key points, and then a calculation can show where the break is. If the measured impedance is different from what is expected, the relay can signal to the switch to either enable or disable a feeder line. Because line protection uses simple impedance measurements, latency or jitter between the communication relays is not a major concern.

Figure 11-9 illustrates a simple distance protection scheme with multiple zones. The relays measure impedance in the different zones and use this to isolate the location of the fault. Zones may overlap and extend beyond the zone line length to provide 100% primary trip protection and also to provide backup trip protection for adjacent lines. For example, in Figure 11-9, Zones B1 and B2 overlap to provide redundant protection.

Distance Protection

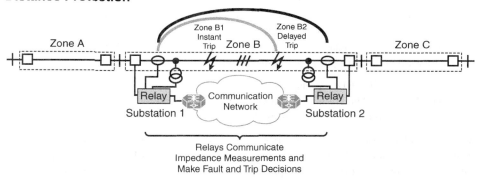

Figure 11-9   *A Sample Distance Protection Scheme*

Current Differential (87L) Protection

Unlike distance protection, current differential protection compares current samples between two distant relays in different substations. For example, a nonzero differential in the current implies that there is a fault somewhere on the line that will cause the relays to trip.

Of course, with alternating current systems, current measurements vary over time, so current differential protection requires that timing be synchronized between substations. If the timing is not synchronized, current measurements between relays may be different at a given point in time, falsely indicating either a loss of current or overcurrent, thus causing the relay to signal a change to the switch that results in a power outage.

Two mechanisms are commonly used to synchronize relays to ensure that current samples are aligned. The first option is to use GPS-based synchronization. The second option, called channel-based synchronization, is based on two-way time transfer and utilizes the communication channel to exchange timestamped messages between relays. The channel-based synchronization technique is typically proprietary to the relay manufacturer.

Common methods of timing synchronization include SyncE and IEEE 1588 Precision Timing Protocol (PTP). Figure 11-10 illustrates a current differential protection scheme that measures current vectors.

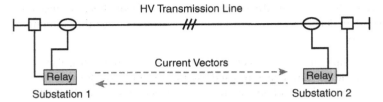

Figure 11-10   *Current Differential Protection Scheme for High-Voltage Transmission Lines*

The need for synchronization between relays also implies that the communications path between the relays has to be deterministic and predictable. Due to the timing sync requirement, current differential protection has very strict telecommunications requirements related to packet delay and jitter, which means that all such schemes require symmetric forward and return path communication between the relays.

In the days before IEC 61850, relays were connected back-to-back between substations using TDM circuits. The amount of data communicated between the relays is actually very small, and typically a DS0 (or 56/64 kbps link) was all that was needed.

Various standards for interfaces have been developed for teleprotection relays over the years. These include ITU-T G.703 for copper connections and IEEE C37.94 for optical. These legacy interface types are unique and customized to the teleprotection application. In addition, ITU-T X.21 and E&M interfaces are also used for some legacy teleprotection relays. Often referred to as "ear and mouth," E&M is a supervisory line signaling method that you may be familiar with from its use with analog voice trunks. In recent years, companies have started to deploy modern IEC 61850-90-12-based protection systems that take advantage of Ethernet interfaces.

The time synchronization requirement of current differential protection imposes an enormous requirement on the network. IEC 61850-90-12 states that end-to-end latency between relays should be no more than 10 ms. This includes the interface processing latency within the relay, the processing at the router, and the speed of light time across the link. This form of teleprotection includes another challenge: managing path symmetry. Just as it is important to manage one-way latency, the difference in bidirectional latency is even more sensitive. Typical relays can tolerate forward and reverse differential communications latency of no more than 500 µs–1 ms. If a protection circuit were to have different forward and reverse paths due to optimal IP routing issues, the relays could misinterpret the communications sync issue and trip the breakers, thus causing a loss of power. Truly, managing the end-to-end teleprotection latency budget is one of the most challenging aspects of a protection and control engineer's job.

Designing a WAN for Teleprotection

In years past, when protection and control engineers used TDM circuits to communicate between pairs of relays in different substations, the latency could be measured and was predictably the same at all times in both directions. These were simple, point-to-point circuits. However, most modern utilities are now migrating to multipurpose packet networks such as MPLS to transport nearly all their applications, including teleprotection. MPLS packet-based networks have huge benefits: They are flexible, easy to scale, multi-tenant, and multiservice; they are able to carry a host of different applications; and they can even transport legacy protocols through channel emulation and tunneling services.

While IP-based WANs are a mostly positive development in the utility world, they do have one downside when it comes to teleprotection: While they use IP routing mechanisms to inherently find the shortest path to a destination, they by default do not use a predictable path with a known latency. If an MPLS network is able to find a better path to a destination, it will take it, without regard for the latency sensitivities of the underlying application it is carrying. There is a delicate balance here: While end-to-end latency must be minimized, it must also be bidirectionally consistent.

In response to this need, in 2008 the IETF and ITU jointly began working on a variation of MPLS that would be able to take advantage of all the benefits of traditional label switching but at the same time incorporate key elements of carrier switching and operations, administration, and management (OAM) that would allow applications such as teleprotection to be transported over MPLS. The result was MPLS–Transport Profile (MPLS-TP), which brings capabilities for traffic engineering, automatic protection switching (APS), and OAM.

MPLS-TP transports a point-to-point pseudo-wire (a virtual circuit transported over MPLS) over a prescriptive label switch path (LSP). The hop-by-hop LSP is programmed by a protection and control engineer such that the exact forward and reverse LSPs are the same (see Figure 11-11). This has the benefit of making latency predictable and symmetrical, and it also keeps jitter to a minimum. The pseudo-wire endpoints terminate at the teleprotection relays.

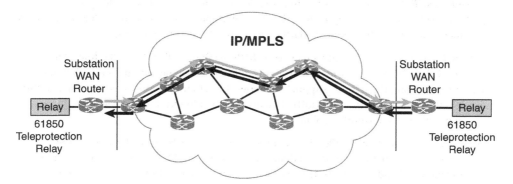

Figure 11-11 *Symmetrical Forward and Reverse MPLS-TP LSPs for Teleprotection Relays, Providing Predictable Latency and Jitter*

MPLS-TP also supports APS by identifying a known backup LPS path in case of a prima-ry LSP failure. In this case, the backup LSP is deployed such that it also has predictable latency and path symmetry in case of failure.

One of the key benefits of MPLS-TP is that it supports end-to-end OAM. OAM allows for fault detection of the pseudo-wire at any point and is used as the trigger mechanism to fail over to a backup LSP. MPLS-TP implements in-band OAM capabilities using a generic associated channel (G-ACh) based on RFC 5085 (Virtual Circuit Connectivity Verification [VCCV]). The in-band OAM channel is like a point-to-point management/control circuit that can detect link or node failures and can signal backup LSP failover on the order of 50 ms or less. Figure 11-12 illustrates the G-ACh within the MPLS-TP pseudo-wire.

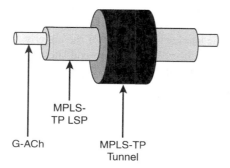

MPLS-TP LSP

G-ACh

MPLS-TP Tunnel

Figure 11-12   *OAM Generic Associated Channel (G-ACh) Within an MPLS-TP Pseudo-wire*

MPLS-TP is able to meet the requirements of teleprotection, but what about other simi-lar MPLS modalities, such as MPLS–Traffic Engineering (MPLS-TE)? MPLS-TE was developed many years ago to explicitly and dynamically define a label switch path (LSP) through an MPLS network. As such, it has many similarities with MPLS-TP. However, although MPLS-TE can be used to meet the predictable latency and path engineering requirements of teleprotection, there is one downside: MPLS-TE does not have OAM capabilities. With MPLS-TE, it is still possible to create deterministic and symmetrical paths, as well as provide support for APS, but the implementation with MPLS-TP tends to be much simpler and has more similarities to carrier Ethernet switching.

MPLS-TE does has one key advantage over MPLS-TP: Its ability for call admission control (CAC). With CAC, the edge router is able to determine whether enough band-width exists along the path to support the requested circuit. In most cases, this capability is not critical for teleprotection traffic because the bandwidth requirements are minimal, but in practice it is a useful capability.

A new MPLS variant called Flex-LSP combines the best of both of these. Flex-LSP supports all the benefits of MPLS-TP, such as APS and OAM for pseudo-wires, while also supporting CAC and Layer 3 traffic engineering, much like MPLS-TE. As technology continues to improve, other MPLS modalities, such as segment routing, may also be appropriate for teleprotection in the future.

The Field Area Network (FAN) GridBlock

The electrical utility industry is at the leading edge of IoT. Nowhere else has this been demonstrated more than in the last-mile distribution grid, referred to as the field area network (FAN).

Note There is some overlap between the terms *neighborhood area network* (*NAN*) and *field area network* (*FAN*). Although these terms are used almost interchangeably, there are some subtle differences. NAN refers strictly to the last-mile network itself, whereas the FAN includes the NAN plus devices connected to the field area router. Figure 11-13 shows a graphical depiction of where the FAN area resides.

The FAN is designed to enable pervasive monitoring and control of all utility elements between the distribution substation and the end customer. This section of the grid includes metering applications for both customers and the distribution network system itself, and it also includes management of the electrical distribution network devices that help enhance energy delivery and build a low-carbon society.

The FAN GridBlock is built to be multiservice, meaning that it is not based on any vendor-specific, proprietary technologies that would limit its use to a single purpose, like so many legacy OT systems. In the past, Internet standards simply did not exist to build metering or distribution automation (DA) networks based on open standards. It was necessary to build a dedicated and independent network for each application. However, modern open standards and network compliance alliances (such as the Wi-UN and HomePlug Alliances) have helped establish interoperability standards that allow a single multiservice network to be deployed, supporting a wide array of applications and vendors. In the same way that the Wi-Fi Alliance has helped establish interoperability among Wi-Fi access points and end clients, these alliances are also establishing interoperability standards. It will soon be possible to have a fully functioning FAN network with various components supplied by different vendors, all using the same standards.

Note Both the Wi-SUN and HomePlug Alliances are discussed earlier in this book. For more information on Wi-UN Alliance, refer to Chapter 4, "Connecting Smart Objects," and Chapter 5, "IP as the IoT Network Layer." The HomePlug Alliance is introduced in Chapter 4.

The FAN GridBlock leverages many of the standards discussed in Chapters 4, 5, and 6, including IPv6, IEEE 802.15.4 mesh, CoAP, and LTE. This flexible and open standards approach promotes multivendor plug-and-play capabilities with a well-understood framework for security, quality of service, resilience, and network management services. The result is a wide array of capabilities that go far beyond trivial metering use cases.

Figure 11-13 demonstrates a multiservice grid FAN supporting applications such as EV recharging stations, connected street lights, demand response endpoints, smart meters, and connections to remote SCADA RTUs in the distribution network.

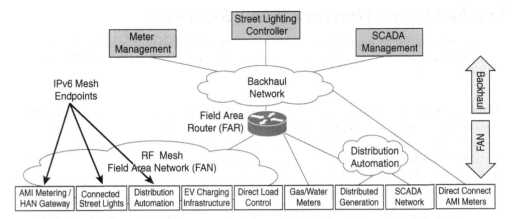

Figure 11-13 *The FAN Multiservice Grid Network*

To summarize, the key advantages of the modern FAN that make it attractive for utilities include the following:

- **Open and standards based:** Core components of the network, transport, and application layers have been standardized by organizations such as the IETF and the IEEE and are interoperable with other compliant devices.

- **Versatile endpoint support:** IPv6-based IoT endpoints are flexible and can be used in a wide variety of locations, including AMI (meters), street lighting modules, demand response devices, and distribution automation endpoints, such as SCADA RTUs.

- **Flexible headend deployment options:** Because the FAN uses IPv6 transport, the headend aggregation points and security system can either be deployed on-premises or hosted in the cloud.

- **Flexible backhaul options:** The FAN typically requires a field area router (FAR) that is mounted on the utility pole or in some other convenient location. The FAR is the termination point of the mesh network. A wide variety of backhaul options are typically available, including LTE, 3G, WiMAX, fiber optics, and even satellite backhaul in very remote communities.

- **Support for legacy applications:** Through the use of a gateway, legacy devices (such as serial RTUs) can be connected to the IPv6 FAN at scale.

- **Scalable:** IPv6 is capable of scaling to tens of millions of endpoints, easily managing the meters and street lights in a large utility network.

- **Highly secure:** The FAN GridBlock incorporates multiple layers of security, including application and network layer encryption as well as endpoint authentication.

- **Stable and resilient:** Thanks to the flexibility of IPv6, a well-designed FAN is able to offer strong network availability and resiliency. For example, if a FAR has its primary backhaul through Wi-Fi, LTE can be used as secondary backup, and IP routing protocols can be used to figure out the optimal path. In addition, using IP routing, the FAR can form redundant connections to both primary and secondary headend sites.

The following sections examine the application of the FAN in two key areas: advanced metering infrastructure (AMI) and distribution automation (DA).

Advanced Metering Infrastructure

By the end of 2016, approximately 700 million smart meters had been installed globally.[1] Smart meters are microprocessor-based sensors and controllers that exchange information such as device authentication, security, and management, using two-way communication processes. In the past, power companies had to dispatch teams of technicians to read their customers' meters in order to send them usage-based bills. In many cases the utility would be doing very well if the meter were read three or four times per year. In addition, many meters were in hard-to-reach areas and were sometimes even dangerous for technicians to access.

With the advent of smart meters, it is now possible to read meters several times per day. In the case of commercial and industrial (C&I) meters, readings can be done every few minutes to provide up-to-the-minute visibility into power consumption. This has been extremely valuable for customers as they are now able to get highly accurate, per-month billing reports. Customers can also view their power consumption on an hourly basis through a web portal. Some utilities have implemented time-of-day billing, in which the cost of power is higher during peak periods. Having near-instantaneous feedback helps families understand their consumption patterns and save money on their electric bill. This demonstrates the power of IoT.

Figure 11-14 illustrates a smart meter web portal launched by a Canadian utility that has fully deployed IPv6 smart meters in its FAN.

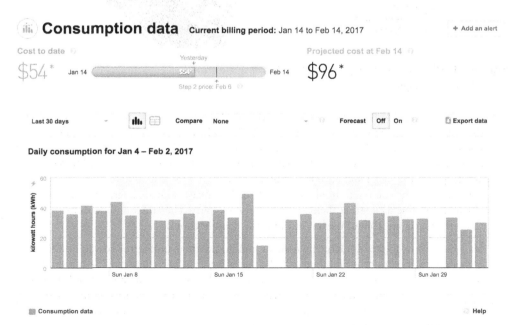

Figure 11-14 *A Smart Meter Web Portal Daily Report*

Smart meters have several other unique benefits. For example, it's now possible to remotely shut off a meter at will through a remote disconnect switch. While this could be viewed as a security concern, the benefit to the utility is that customers who haven't paid their bills or who are stealing power can be shut off or restored without even dispatching a crew. This reduction in truck rolls saves an incredible amount of money and many labor hours.

In addition, most smart meters also come with an internal home area network (HAN) radio that is able to communicate with electrical devices inside the home, often through ZigBee. (For more information on ZigBee, refer to Chapter 4.) This allows the home or business owner to track power consumption on a per-appliance or per-device basis.

Figure 11-15 illustrates the anatomy of a modern smart meter.

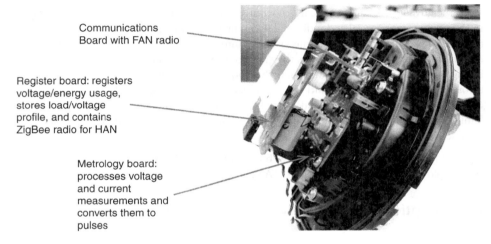

Communications
Board with FAN radio

Register board: registers
voltage/energy usage,
stores load/voltage
profile, and contains
ZigBee radio for HAN

Metrology board:
processes voltage
and current
measurements and
converts them to
pulses

Figure 11-15 *The Anatomy of a Smart Meter*
(Photo by Dave Deyagher)

In an IEEE 802.15.4 network utilizing an RPL mesh, the meters are mesh nodes and are thus repeaters. For more information on 802.15.4 and RPL, refer to Chapters 4 and 5. Each meter runs the IPv6 protocol stack and endeavors to find its place in the mesh through RPL. In a large mesh, only a handful of meters link directly to the FAR. Most are deeper in the mesh and have links between them. In this case, unlike most Layer 2 networks, where you try to limit the size of the broadcast domain, a large mesh is actually a good thing as it strengthens the mesh connectivity. The larger and denser the mesh, the further you are able to push it out into the neighborhood.

Consider the example of a large apartment building with an underground vault containing all the meters for that building (called a meter farm). While there may be hundreds of meters in the farm, representing each apartment or unit, only one meter needs to have an upstream RPL link to a parent node leading to the FAR. The rest are children of that meter. Figure 11-16 illustrates such an underground meter farm in a concrete vault. These underground meters simply form a branch off the main mesh.

Figure 11-16   *A Subterranean Meter Farm in an Apartment Building*
(Photo by Robert Barton)

Other Use Cases

A FAN is designed to be multiservice, supporting a wide array of applications on a single converged network. However, FANs have some key limitations, including limited bandwidth and high latency between nodes (on the order of hundreds of milliseconds per hop), meaning they are not well suited for media-rich applications such as video surveillance, and certainly are not good candidates for teleprotection. However, there are many lower-bandwidth applications that make FANs ideal for utilities and other industries, including smart connected cities.

Note   The Wi-SUN (Wireless Smart Utility Network) Alliance is the most prominent vendor capability alliance for 802.15.4 FANs. The Wi-SUN 1.0 compatibility specification supports up to 150 Kbps link speeds, based on a traditional modulation scheme for encoding data. However, you should be aware that work is underway to significantly improve this to several hundred Kbps, using higher-performance modulation schemes.

Beyond smart metering, there are countless further use cases for FANs, as indicated in Figure 11-13. Two interesting use cases are discussed in more detail in the following sections: demand response and distribution automation.

Demand Response

Balancing availability with demand for electrical power is one of the main challenges of a utility. Electricity needs to flow. It is not typically stored in giant battery units throughout the distribution network, to be dispersed when there is a sudden increase in demand. If demand exceeds availability, something must give. For example, a large number of air-conditioning units during a hot summer can tax a utility to the limit and may cause rolling blackouts.

Over time, utility engineers have addressed this problem by controlling electrical usage on less critical systems during peak periods so that electricity can still be available to customers throughout the grid. This has been accomplished through a mechanism called *demand response* (DR), which involves deploying remotely controlled devices that turn off the flow of electricity to certain devices on the grid during peak power use periods. For example, during peak usage periods, the utility can send out a broadcast message to customers using certain types of electric devices (such as electric water heaters) to automatically reduce the power consumption on those devices, thus making more power available for the rest of the grid.

In the past, DR controllers were nothing more than simple wireless pagers that would receive signals from the DR management system and then automatically shut off devices when instructed. They would then receive other signals when power became available and turn the devices back on (using a binary on/off type of operation).

Although there are many ways to reach a DR controller that is attached to an electric appliance (including cellular and 1901.2 PLC), a FAN can also be used for this application. In this case, the utility uses the FAN's IPv6 network to communicate to DR controllers in specific parts of the grid where demand is reaching peak usage, and can centrally control their power consumption as necessary. Figure 11-17 shows an electric water heater fitted with a FAN mesh DR controller.

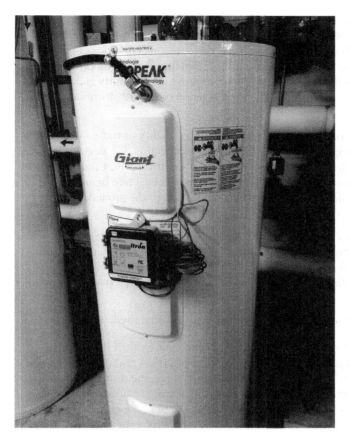

Figure 11-17 *An Electric Water Heater Connected to a FAN Demand Response Controller*
(Photo by Robert Barton)

Distribution Automation

Much as the substation is being automated through network connectivity, the distribution network from the substation to the end customer is also undergoing a connectivity revolution. The distribution network tends to be geographically very large, making network connectivity a significant challenge. If you look up at a utility pole and notice the variety and quantity of electrical devices, you will probably notice that the number is quite significant. Multiplied by the total number of poles in a utility's serving area, this is a very large number of devices. Electrical distribution devices include reclosers, load switches, and capacitor bank controllers. These devices all play key roles in electrical distribution grid services.

Due to the challenge of connecting distribution control and automation devices to a central network, they have, by and large, been designed to work as autonomous devices, in many cases with enough intelligence to operate without any supervisory control. However, as wireless network technology and availability have improved, it has become possible to connect distribution devices that sense the operating conditions of the grid to a communication network, thus greatly improving visibility into conditions of the distribution grid. This has also helped significantly improve the reliability and quality of electrical power in the distribution grid and has ushered in the age of distribution automation (DA).

DA seeks to improve the conditions, reliability, and power quality of the grid and is thus able to reduce costs and improve customer uptime and satisfaction. DA devices perform many different functions, from measuring the quality of electrical power to clearing temporary faults in lines. An example of a temporary fault would be a tree branch falling on a line, causing a temporary short before the branch finally falls to the ground. Clearing this kind of fault is the function of a recloser.

Layering these devices on a communications network causes the level of automation to increase dramatically. Not only does the utility gain the ability to determine the conditions of distribution grid devices through SCADA, but it can begin to collate and analyze the data generated by the thousands of DA devices to gain a better picture of the conditions of the overall grid.

The following are some examples of how FAN-based DA is being used:

■ **Distribution SCADA systems:** Earlier in this chapter, you learned that SCADA within the substation is enabling automation of the electrical grid. Through the use of FANs, the same level of management is now possible on the distribution grid for devices outside the substation. While several technologies are suitable for connecting to these IoT devices (including LTE and Wi-Fi), the scale capabilities of the FAN, along with the low bandwidth requirements of SCADA, make the FAN an ideal network platform. When the SCADA endpoints are remote, the communications can be either aggregated at the substation and then sent back to the control center or sent directly to the control center, bypassing the substation altogether.

Note Beyond FAN solutions for DA, several other wireless technologies can be considered, including 4G and NB-IoT cellular options.

■ **Fault location, isolation, and service restoration (FLISR):** In the past, power outages were discovered when someone called the power company to say that his or her power was out. Not only did this waste valuable restoration time, it didn't help much in finding out where the system fault actually occurred. FLISR systems are designed to identify, locate, and diagnose problems so the utility knows instantly when an outage has occurred, and in some cases they even allow the circuits to self-heal. Circuit breakers, smart meters, and switches for fault clearing are all part of a FLISR system. Since many of these "things" are remote and require only minimal bandwidth, FANs make an ideal choice for transporting FLISR communications.

■ **Integrated volt/VAR control (IVVC):** Volt/VAR systems are used in the distribution grid to monitor and control voltage levels during peak periods and help conserve electrical usage. In the past, due to communications challenges outside the substation as well as availability of voltage sensors in the grid, volt/VAR optimization (VVO) deployments were limited. In recent years, communication systems such as cellular and FAN mesh networks have made it possible to collect information from voltage sensors and use that information to adjust voltage-regulating equipment such as capacitor banks in real time.

Figure 11-18 illustrates these various use cases, connected to a single multiservice field area network. In this illustration, many different applications are using a single FAN. However, the application servers that control functions for SCADA, FLISR, and IVVC all reside in the distribution management system located in the data center or in the control center.

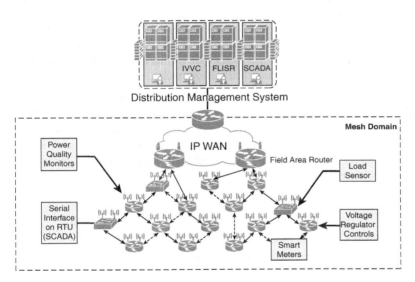

Figure 11-18   *Various DA Devices, Including SCADA, FLISR, and Integrated Volt/VAR Control Systems Connected Using a Single Multiservice FAN Grid Network*

Securing the Smart Grid

When SCADA protocols were first developed, little thought was given to security; it simply wasn't needed because SCADA connections to remote devices used dedicated serial links that were physically isolated and had no connection to any other type of network. In this bygone era, the concept of cyber hacking was not something that utility engineers had even started thinking about. However, as SCADA matured and began using Ethernet and IP as transport technologies, the nature of SCADA protocols led to significant security concerns and, eventually, opportunities for clever new attack vectors.

The 2015 Ukrainian power attack discussed in Chapter 2, "IoT Network Architecture and Design," that cut power to 103 cities and towns (and affected 186 more) involved a sophisticated simultaneous attack on six power companies. This attack, which affected the power grid's SCADA network, began as malware on company computers and spread to the OT system. Today, utility companies are left with this decades-old management protocol that was not designed with security in mind.

To say that the Ukrainian attack left a deep impression on security teams in utility companies around the world would not be an overstatement. Due to this attack, and other less-well-known ones, utility companies are rushing to secure their newly converged and legacy systems as fast as possible.

According to a Cisco Security Capabilities benchmark study, 73% of utility IT security professionals say they've suffered a security breach, compared with an average of 55% in other industries. Certainly, utilities are a high-value target for cybercriminals. In 2015 Lloyds of London modeled the economic impact of a large-scale coordinated cyberattack on northeastern US utilities. The impact was predicted to be $243 million to $1 trillion. While such a widespread attack may seem unlikely, recent cyber attacks, such as the one on the Ukrainian power grid, show that such attacks are technically feasible and should be of concern to both utility operators and their customers.[2]

Different utility-based security architectures have been proposed. One such effort is IEC 62351, which was developed by IEC TC57 to support the security needs of IEC 60870 and 61850, and which encompasses a fairly wide scope. The North American Electric Reliability Corporation's (NERC's) Critical Infrastructure Protection (CIP) is a security model that was developed to protect bulk systems, and it continues to be one of the most important security subjects for North American utilities.

NERC CIP

IoT is a driving force for a new generation of security in utilities. In response to the threat of cyber crimes against power utilities, the US government's Federal Energy Regulatory Commission (FERC) mandated that all power companies comply with NERC's CIP v6 standard by July 1, 2016. Although NERC CIP is a security standard that focuses on American utilities (and power companies that sell power to the United States, such as those in Canada), the principles laid down by this compliance regime provide a useful reference model for utilities around the world.

NERC CIP uses a risk-assessment security approach. Instead of using an exhaustive list of prescriptive recommendations and enforcing them through audits, NERC provides a clear vision of the security end state. This is a powerful methodology as it removes attention from just passing the audit by checking all the right boxes without truly trying to actually protect the networks. Rather, NERC CIP v6 helps utilities focus on what is actually important: securing their networks against attack, from both the inside and the outside. For example, instead of mandating a certain type and level of antivirus, NERC CIP v6 is more principle driven, requiring "malware protection."

NERC CIP is primarily focused on establishing security policies, programs, and procedures. A key concept in this model is the assessment of the impact level that a security breach may have on assets in the utility. Utilities need to properly identify what impact level each asset fits into, with levels defined as high, medium, low, or no impact at all. Assets in scope are defined as ones that "If rendered unavailable, degraded, or misused, would adversely impact the reliable operation of the Bulk Electric System (BES) within 15 minutes of the activation or exercise of the compromise."

NERC CIP v6 also requires intrusion detection/prevention systems (IDS/IPS) or some form of deep packet inspection (DPI). The standard also mandates that an electronic security perimeter (ESP) be defined where assets within the EPS are protected by two distinct security measures, such as a firewall *and* an IPS. In addition, a physical security perimeter (PSP) is defined, which includes other aspects, such as video surveillance and building access systems, and aims to protect the station against physical attack.

Note   On April 16, 2013, the Pacific Gas and Electric (PG&E) Metcalf substation near San Jose, California, was attacked by snipers. In this attack, gunmen fired shots at 17 transformers, resulting in $15 million in damages. This was a highly organized, well-planned attack, but to date the culprits are still at large. Incidents such as this have helped shape the PSP aspects of NERC CIP v6.

A key aspect of NERC CIP is that an ESP must be established for all high- and medium-impact BES cyber systems connected to a routable network, regardless of whether the segment containing the BES cyber system has external connectivity to any other network. Figure 11-19 illustrates a primary substation network, highlighting the ESP and PSP components.

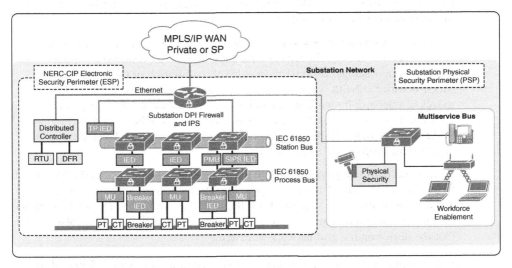

Figure 11-19   *A Primary Substation Network with NERC CIP v6 Electronic and Physical Security Perimeters*

Compliance with a standard is no guarantee of security, but it certainly goes a long way in raising awareness and enforcing accountability for a utility's security posture. NERC CIP v6 is a large and complex subject, and its details are beyond the scope of this book. NERC CIP touches on areas of malicious code prevention, configuration and change management, vulnerability assessments, and security event monitoring. For further details on the current state of NERC CIP, see www.nerc.com.

Smart Grid Security Considerations

The distribution grid is considered beyond the scope of NERC CIP, and thus FANs are not covered by this compliance standard. However, the distribution network is still a critical area that needs security protection, especially because the assets on this part of the grid are so widely dispersed and are in generally unprotected areas.

FAN security is aligned to the following principles:

- **Access control:** FAN devices reside in generally insecure locations, so the devices themselves need to have highly secure access control. If a grid IoT endpoint were maliciously added to a FAN, it could be a backdoor to the network. To this end, FAN endpoints and routers are recommended to support X.509 certificates, with both a factory-level certificate and a utility-specific certificate once the device is enrolled in the network. The ITU-T X.509 standard defines a structure for handling secure certificates and keys, and you may recognize it because it is commonly used to secure web and email communications.

- **Data integrity and confidentiality:** FAN devices need encryption. Last-mile FANs often use unlicensed wireless technologies that could be easily sniffed. Encryption at each layer of the stack is strongly recommended. In addition, configuration files in FAN devices, such as the FAR, should be encrypted to prevent a hacker from accessing information from a stolen device.

- **Threat detection and mitigation:** One way threat detection and mitigation are accomplished is through the logical separation of the FAN headend components and systems from other critical systems in either the substation or the control center. Much as with the NERC CIP v6 requirements mentioned earlier, it is a good idea to follow a defense-in-depth model and use more than one layer of deep packet inspection, such as a firewall and an IPS that understand industrial protocols, like SCADA. (Note that if FAN endpoints encrypt at the application layer, this limits visibility for deep packet inspection.)

- **Device and platform physical integrity:** The field area assets, such as the FAR, need to be physically secured as much as possible. The routers should be tamper proof and have door alarms. In addition, IEEE 802.1AR (Secure Unique Device Identifier) is becoming standard on remote routers to not only speed deployment but also ensure that the device on the grid network is trusted.

Securing the smart grid is a complex and ever-evolving task, especially in highly distributed and public environments such as electrical distribution networks. While NERC CIP is primarily focused on securing generation and substation assets, security for the utility ultimately needs a wider lens. This must be addressed at each tier of the GridBlocks architecture, with a special focus on utility-specific protocols, such as SCADA, that were not designed with security in mind but today are transported over highly interconnected networks.

The Future of the Smart Grid

Since the beginning of the electric power industry, the model involving large-scale generation, transmission, and distribution has been the most cost-effective way to deliver reliable power to customers. However, there have been challenges along the way, including concerns about pollution emitted by generation plants, consumers' insatiable appetite for more power, and the associated costs of constantly expanding the electric grid infrastructure, not to mention the apparent fragility of an increasingly complex grid.

Now, more than ever before, the industry is being challenged on multiple fronts. Some of these challenges are disruptive and threaten the future of the industry. These challenges include requirements to incorporate electric power generated by inherently variable renewable resources, such as wind and solar, as well as integrated distributed energy resources (DERs), such as solar photovoltaic (PV) cells that are installed and owned by the customer rather than the utility but sell power back to the utility grid.

An interesting example of this is in Hawaii, where the average electric bill is more than three times greater than anywhere else in North America. The high cost of electricity has driven many Hawaiians to deploy solar PV panels to take advantage of the abundant sunshine. In fact, by 2016, more than 12% of Hawaiians had solar panels on their homes. While solar is a great way to generate clean energy, the challenge of integrating power produced by these homes into an island power grid that is isolated from any other power grid is extremely difficult. In addition, as more people add solar power to their homes, the power company has fewer paying customers; solar-powered homes connected to the grid become distributed generation nodes, and the power company has to pay customers for the use of their electricity.[3] With fewer paying customers, there is less revenue to maintain the system. In 2016 these economic realities resulted in Hawaii putting a halt to further solar DER deployments on the island.

Some analysts project that over time, the growth of customer-owned generation could undermine the economic basis of utilities to a degree that they would be disrupted—much as we have seen happen with the Internet and music, retailing, and other industries. Some regard the potential for disruption by DERs not owned by the utility as threatening. Others see it as the transformation the grid needs to herald in the age of higher reliability, lower costs, and lower carbon emissions.

The age of distributed generation and renewable energy builds a very strong case for the smart grid. You can't introduce renewable energies, particularly at the medium-/low-voltage layers, if you don't control and monitor them. For example, an interesting challenge that utilities are facing with the rise of DERs is how power will be balanced and controlled on a grid where power generation is highly dispersed. For example, DERs such as PV cells generate DC power. However, the electrical grid runs on AC, where both current frequency and voltage/current phase are key elements in the delivery of high-quality power. For a DER to provide energy back to the grid, DC power needs to be converted to AC through a power inverter. While this seems simple enough, there are challenges to consider, such as how power will be balanced throughout the grid with so much distributed power generation by third parties. This underscores the need to have a reliable network system that is able to communicate between elements in the utility's grid and IoT devices at the DER, such as the inverter or the smart meter.

Another disruptive change we are seeing is the rise of EVs. As more and more electric cars are introduced, they will require more power from the grid, and there is also the potential to use these fully-charged car batteries as remote power storage units. Engineers are looking for ways to use these EV batteries as a DR solution that could support the grid during peak power periods. This completely changes the concept of demand response and how power can be selectively used. Again, car batteries are DC powered, so the power needs to be converted to AC, and such a system would require both inverters and system metering to track the flow of power, both in and out of the utility's grid. All this highlights the criticality of a reliable IoT communications network in the smart grid.

Regardless of how disruption and transformation play out around the world, the electric power industry will undergo more change in the next 10 to 20 years than it has seen in the past century.

Summary

Reliable electric power is essential to modern civilization. While utilities around the world rely heavily on legacy technology and protocols, disruptive technologies and new demands on the electrical grid are making power utilities some of the earliest adopters of IoT.

IoT technologies are driving digital transformation in all aspects of the electrical grid, from generation to transmission to distribution, and are bringing in the era of the smart grid. A vendor-neutral holistic reference model for networking OT elements of the electrical grid into a single architecture is GridBlocks. GridBlocks divides various functions of the electrical grid into 11 tiers, allowing utilities to digitize in a systematic and methodical way.

This chapter discusses several elements of the GridBlocks architecture, including the primary substation GridBlock, and includes a discussion of substation automation techniques. This discussion focuses on the use of SCADA and the drive toward standardization through the IEC 61850 standard. This standardization focuses on supporting the station and process buses within the substation and various Ethernet switching designs that can be used to meet the rigorous requirements of IEC 61850.

This chapter also examines the system control GridBlock, with a particular focus on teleprotection systems over an MPLS WAN. Teleprotection relays have some of the most sensitive application-layer latency and jitter requirements in the world. This chapter discusses different design recommendations to meet these requirements.

This chapter also covers the field area network GridBlock, including how multipurpose FANs are driving a multiservice distribution grid network. Use cases such as AMI, DA, and DR are examined.

Smart grid security is a top-of-mind subject for many in the utility industry, especially as grid devices are being connected through IP. This chapter introduces key concepts of NERC CIP v6, as well as strategies for securing elements outside NERC's scope, such as the distribution FAN network.

This chapter provides a glimpse into the future of the utility industry. Disruptive technologies such as distributed energy generation, microgrids, and electrically powered cars are not only challenging existing power grids in new ways but are major forces for digital disruption that will create new opportunities for innovation in the twenty-first-century smart grid.

References

1. "Global trends in smart metering," *Metering & Smart Energy International*, November 30, 2016, www.metering.com/magazine_articles/global-trends-in-smart-metering/.

2. Intel and Cisco, *Utility Security: Exceeding Mandates to Mitigate Risk*, 2016, www.cisco.com/c/dam/en_us/solutions/industries/energy/docs/greentech-white-paper.pdf.

3. Robert Fares, "3 reasons Hawaii put the brakes on solar—And why the same won't happen in your state," *Scientific American*, December 15, 2015, https://blogs.scientificamerican.com/plugged-in/3-reasons-hawaii-put-the-brakes-on-solar-and-why-the-same-won-t-happen-in-your-state/.

Chapter 12

Smart and Connected Cities

The world is rapidly urbanizing, and this trend is slated to continue. Less than one-third of the world's population lived in cities in 1950; by 2050, two-thirds of our planet's population will be city dwellers. Africa and Asia, which today account for 90% of the world's rural population, are projected to have 56% and 64%, respectively, of their populations urbanize. Today, the percentage of people in North America, Europe, Latin America, and the Caribbean who live in cities already exceeds 70%. In terms of raw numbers, the urban population of the world has grown to nearly 4 billion, from just 746 million in 1950. By 2050, this figure will grow by another 2.5 billion.

Most cities started as small urban centers and grew organically. Very few of them were initially designed to immediately accommodate a very large population. Rapid growth typically strains city infrastructure. Roads, bridges, and sewer systems often reach their maximum capacity, making access to urban services challenging. The question of how to provide basic necessities such as water and housing while reducing the carbon footprint has begun to dominate the agendas of city planners and civic leaders everywhere.

As the world population grows, emissions and consumption also increase. When the population concentrates in limited geographic areas, the environment's ability to absorb emissions and wastes becomes challenged. The triggers for climate change are exacerbated by increased emissions and waste. Today, cities are responsible for 60% to 80% of the world's energy and greenhouse emissions and consume 60% of all potable water, losing as much as 20% in leakage.[1] One key concern of city leaders around the world is to optimize resources (water, power, communication infrastructure efficiency, and so on), waste, and emissions processing.

However, city leaders also know that the increasing population in a city provides an opportunity to capitalize on the city's potential. Within the new population pouring into cities every hour of every day, there are people with skills, talents, and dedicated mentalities that will be assets to whatever city they end up living in. The sheer population density will generate more commerce for all residents. Research from Massachusetts Institute of Technology (MIT) predicts that cities in the future will account for nearly

90% of global population growth, 80% of wealth creation, and 60% of total energy consumption. The goal is not to limit the growth but to manage population increase more effectively. Improved management efficiency means providing better and more efficient urban services and ensuring better life experiences to city inhabitants—in short, capitalizing on the economic benefits of large urban populations while mitigating the social and environmental difficulties that come with them. http://web.mit.edu/professional/international-programs/courses/beyond_smart_cities/index.html.

Where will the cities of tomorrow find the resources they need to sustain themselves? There are no easy answers—but there are smart solutions. This chapter covers some of these solutions, in the following sections:

■ **An IoT Strategy for Smarter Cities:** This section defines how IoT technologies can be leveraged to improve the lives of citizens and the efficient management of urban centers.

■ **Smart City IoT Architecture:** This section describes the four main layers for integration of IoT for smart cities.

■ **Smart City Security Architecture:** This section examines the primary constraints and considerations to secure IoT for smart cities, both in terms of communication and in terms of acceptable use of the collected data.

■ **Smart City Use-Case Examples:** This section details four use cases of IoT for smart cities: street lighting, smart parking, traffic, and smart environment. Chapter 13, "Transportation," and Chapter 15, "Public Safety," provide two other use cases that apply to smart cities that are big enough to require dedicated chapters.

An IoT Strategy for Smarter Cities

Managing a city bears some resemblance to managing a corporate enterprise. As the need for efficiency increases, new tools help increase operational efficiency. For cities, just as for businesses, digitization transforms the perspective on operations. New ideas emerge, bringing different approaches to solving management issues. Scalable solutions utilizing information and communications technology (ICT) can alleviate many issues urban centers face today by increasing efficiency, which reduces costs and enhances quality of life. Cities that take this approach are commonly referred to as *smart cities*, a concept often discussed in urban planning and city policy circles worldwide.

Vertical IoT Needs for Smarter Cities

There are many differing approaches and solutions for city management. All these solutions typically start at the street level, with sensors that capture data on everything from parking space availability to water purity. Data analytics is also used extensively— for example, to reduce crime or improve traffic flows. Citizens can use tools to leverage their smart mobile devices, such as to report problems and make recommendations for improving urban life or locate available parking spaces. When enabled through connectivity, these smart solutions can have a transformative impact on quality of life. Information and communications technology connects people, data, things, and processes together in networks of billions or even trillions of connections. These connections create vast amounts of data, some of which has never been accessible before. When this data is analyzed and used intelligently, the possibilities to correlate, analyze, and optimize services and processes that deliver a better quality of life for people are practically endless. However, the growth of IoT applications for urban centers not only delivers unique benefits for each issue it solves but also enhances a city's ability to develop efficient services.

Cities are expected to generate almost two-thirds (63%) of IoT's overall civilian benefits worldwide over the next decade.[2] To maximize value, smart cities can combine use cases through a shared-revenue business model together with special partners to monetize city location services for retail and tourism, as well as city planning, parking, and water management.

A recent Cisco study, as illustrated in Figure 12-1, expects IoT to have the following economic impact over a 10-year period:[3]

- **Smart buildings:** Smart buildings have the potential to save $100 billion by lowering operating costs by reducing energy consumption through the efficient integration of heating, ventilation, and air-conditioning (HVAC) and other building infrastructure systems. Note that the financial gain applies to city budgets only when a building is city owned. However, the reduced emissions benefit the city regardless of who owns the buildings.

- **Gas monitoring:** Monitoring gas could save $69 billion by reducing meter-reading costs and increasing the accuracy of readings for citizens and municipal utility agencies. The financial benefit is obvious for users and utility companies when the utility is managed by the city. There are also very important advantages in terms of safety, regardless of who operates the utility. In cases of sudden consumption increase, a timely alert could lead to emergency response teams being dispatched sooner, thus increasing the safety of the urban environment.

- **Smart parking:** Smart parking could create $41 billion by providing real-time visibility into parking space availability across a city. Residents can identify and reserve the closest available space, traffic wardens can identify noncompliant usage, and municipalities can introduce demand-based pricing.

- **Water management:** Smart water management could save $39 billion by connecting household water meters over an IP network to provide remote usage and status information. The benefit is obvious, with features such as real-time consumption visibility and leak detection. In addition, smart meters can be used to coordinate and automate private and public lawn watering, initiating the watering programs at times when water consumption is lower or in accordance with water restrictions imposed by civic authorities. At a city scale, IoT can be used to manage water supply equipment and report status (for example, open or closed, on or off, reservoir level, output speed vs. input). A gate or a pump can be opened and closed remotely and automatically in real time, based on a variety of flow input and output analytics data. Vibrations can be measured to detect and predict potential equipment failures. Repair teams can be dispatched proactively before equipment failure occurs. These efficiency gains directly translate into operational gains.

- **Road pricing:** Cities could create $18 billion in new revenues by implementing automatic payments as vehicles enter busy city zones while improving overall traffic conditions. Real-time traffic condition data is very valuable and actionable information that can also be used to proactively reroute public transportation services or private users.

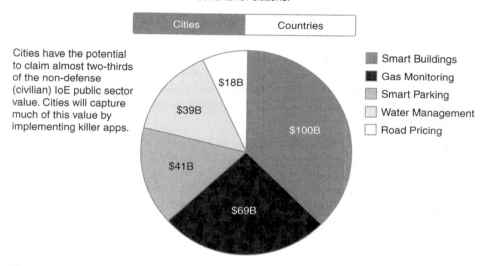

Who Benefits?

By enabling new and more meaningful connections, governments and other public-sector agencies worldwide can benefit and ultimately create quantifiable benefits for citizens.

| Cities | Countries |

Cities have the potential to claim almost two-thirds of the non-defense (civilian) IoE public sector value. Cities will capture much of this value by implementing killer apps.

$18B
$39B
$41B
$100B
$69B

- Smart Buildings
- Gas Monitoring
- Smart Parking
- Water Management
- Road Pricing

Figure 12-1 *Key Use Cases for Smart Cities*

Source: Cisco, Smart+Connected Cities Playbook, 2013

To maximize the return on investment (ROI) on their energy and environmental investments, smart cities can employ strategies that combine water management, smart grid, waste management, particulate monitoring, and gas monitoring.

A smart city can use these technological advances to improve its livability index, which can help attract and retain talent amid increasingly competitive labor markets. The growth in jobs and talent influences the amount of foreign investment and how many top companies come to settle in a city, which in turn leads to higher economic impact and improves the potential for future investments.

Global vs. Siloed Strategies

The main obstacle in implementing smart solutions in today's traditional infrastructure is the complexity of how cities are operated, financed, regulated, and planned. Cities attempting to upgrade their infrastructure to match the growing needs of the citizen population often invest in one problem at a time, and they do it independently. Even cities using IoT technology break up city assets and service management into silos that are typically unable to communicate or rely on each other.

The independent investment model results in the following problems:

- Isolation of infrastructure and IT resources
- No sharing of intelligence and information, such as video feeds and data from sensors.
- Waste and duplication in investment and effort
- Difficulty scaling infrastructure management

This fragmented approach is not scalable, efficient, or economically viable, and it does not benefit from cross-functional sharing of data and services. For example, in traditional city infrastructure, parking, lighting, and traffic departments are all administratively independent and run separately, with their own budgets used to invest in upgrading their respective infrastructures. This introduces duplication of investments made on the same infrastructure, with only minor details tailored to specific department oversights. This is highly inefficient money management and wastes public resources that could instead go toward benefitting the community. However, integrating and expanding disparate IoT systems with different vendors and data protocols creates challenges.

Cities need to begin with a solution that can extend systems across vendors, technologies, and data types, and they should approach their infrastructure investment with a horizontal solution that addresses their issues cohesively. A comparison can be made to a highway system: Cities do not have different road systems for cars, trucks, and emergency vehicles because it is much more efficient to use a unified road network. This idea can be applied to data flowing over the network: Multiple networks are less efficient than a single unified network. A city needs an open IoT solution that allows all public services (garbage, parking, pollution, and so on) to use a common network and, possibly, exchange data for cross-optimization.

City issues are typically large-scale. They require collection of large amounts of diverse data sets in real time. For instance, managing traffic flows and congestion in a city involves understanding patterns of traffic in real time. This means that data from traffic sensors, traffic cameras, parking sensors, and more has to be collected and analyzed in real time so that decision making can be optimized around signal timing, rerouting, and so on.

All these requirements pose technological challenges, including the following:

- How do you collect the data? What are the various sources of data, including hardware endpoints and software?

- How do you make sure that any data collection devices, such as sensors, can be maintained without high costs?

- Where do you analyze the data? What data do you carry back to the cloud, and what data do you analyze locally?

- What kind of network connectivity is best suited for each type of data to collect?

- What kind of power availability and other infrastructure, such as storage, is required?

- How do you aggregate data from different sources to create a unified view?

- How do you publish the data and make it available for applications to consume?

- How do you make the end analysis available to specialized smart city personnel, such as traffic operators, parking enforcement officers, street lighting operators, and so on at their logical decision points?

- How do you present the long-term analysis to city planners?

Each smart city needs a tailored and structured computing model that allows distributed processing of data with the level of resiliency, scale, speed, and mobility required to efficiently and effectively deliver the value that the data being generated can create when properly processed across the network.

In this context, a combination of cloud and fog computing makes sense. (Chapter 2, "IoT Network Architecture and Design," provides more architectural details on cloud vs. fog computing.) Data that needs to be processed locally stays at the edge of the network. For example, local and real-time information about available parking spaces is only locally available. Metrics about traffic can also be processed locally to regulate and synchronize traffic lights or redirect public mass transit vehicles around congestion. In contrast, global statistics and analytics about peak times and structure can be sent to the cloud to be processed at the scale of the entire city. This allows city planners to better organize the growth of various activity centers in the city and also plan for increases in public transportation availability, waste collection shift times, and so on.

Smart City IoT Architecture

A smart city IoT infrastructure is a four-layered architecture, as shown in Figure 12-2. Data flows from devices at the street layer to the city network layer and connect to the data center layer, where the data is aggregated, normalized, and virtualized. The data center layer provides information to the services layer, which consists of the applications that provide services to the city.

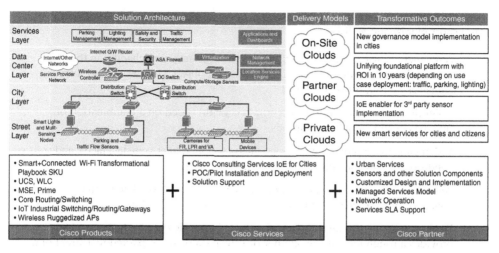

Figure 12-2   *Smart Cities Layered Architecture*

In smart cities, multiple services may use IoT solutions for many different purposes. These services may use different IoT solutions, with different protocols and different application languages. Therefore, data flow from sensor to application involves a translation process into a normalized language that can be exposed through APIs for other service application consumption. This translation ensures a single language for all devices in the cloud. This common language simplifies communication and data management and allows solutions to inform each other. Leveraging this exchange allows smart cities to develop new solutions that span services, without requiring further infrastructure, and future-proofs the system. With a normalized language and open APIs, cities can invest in new solutions, knowing that the new solutions will easily interact with existing solutions. In contrast, a closed format would limit the exchanges and the ability to leverage part of a solution to improve another one.

The following sections discuss various high-level considerations for choosing sensors for specific applications and provide examples of technological networking requirements to support sensors and drive real-time solutions through information and communication technology (ICT) connectivity.

Street Layer

The street layer is composed of devices and sensors that collect data and take action based on instructions from the overall solution, as well as the networking components needed to aggregate and collect data.

A sensor is a data source that generates data required to understand the physical world. Sensor devices are able to detect and measure events in the physical world. ICT connectivity solutions rely on sensors to collect the data from the world around them so that it can be analyzed and used to operationalize use cases for cities. (See Chapter 3, "Smart Objects: The 'Things' in IoT," for an in-depth discussion of smart objects.)

A variety of sensors are used at the street layer for a variety of smart city use cases. Here is a short representative list:

- A magnetic sensor can detect a parking event by analyzing changes in the surrounding magnetic field when a heavy metal object, such as a car or a truck, comes close to it (or on top of it).

- A lighting controller can dim and brighten a light based on a combination of time-based and ambient conditions.

- Video cameras combined with video analytics can detect vehicles, faces, and traffic conditions for various traffic and security use cases.

- An air quality sensor can detect and measure gas and particulate matter concentrations to give a hyper-localized perspective on pollution in a given area.

- Device counters give an estimate of the number of devices in the area, which provides a rough idea of the number of vehicles moving or parked in a street or a public parking area, of pedestrians on a sidewalk, or even of birds in public parks or on public monuments—for cities where bird control has become an issue.

For each type of data to collect, there are a variety of solutions and possible approaches. The choice of sensor technology depends on the exact nature of the problem, the accuracy and cost trade-offs appropriate for it, and any installation limitations posed by the physical environment. Another consideration is the requirement to interact with other IoT systems in the same physical space. For example, parking space availability sensors may be part of a closed system available to users through an app, or they may have to interact through open APIs with other systems, such as towing companies, public law enforcement agencies, parking meters, and so on. A holistic solution would make the data open and integrated, bringing together disparate systems through a single and open platform.

One of the key aspects to consider when choosing a sensing device is its lifetime maintenance costs. Some sensors are mounted on city infrastructure, such as light poles. These sensors can benefit from the power, and possibly the network connectivity, of their mounting location. However, other sensors may be installed in the ground or in other inaccessible locations. Once they are installed, the cost of pulling them out to deal with an issue is very high. At installation time, drawing a power line to the sensor location is typically also extremely costly. Thus, such sensors are normally battery operated and energy efficient so they have long life expectancy, and they are ruggedized to avoid maintenance costs.

Another key aspect to consider when choosing the right technology for a smart city is edge analytics. The many sensors and their data must be managed through the network in a way that securely processes data with minimal delay—and often in real time. Distinguishing between events in order to send only relevant pieces of data is a key component with the large data intakes inherent in a smart city's design. For example, a car-counting sensor does not need to send an update for each car detected; it may send only a cumulative count every minute. Similarly, a pollution sensor may process chemical sensing all the time but send status reports only at intervals. To maximize processing speed and minimize server requirements, the amount of data that goes through cloud servers must be event based. (Refer to Chapter 2 for an in-depth look at cloud vs. fog data processing.)

Event-driven systems allow the city infrastructure to be contextually intelligent so that only targeted events trigger data transfer to the cloud. This flexibility allows the infrastructure to monitor a large number of systems without the risk of overloading the network with uneventful status update messages. Analytics processed on the edge distributes the computing and storage requirements for the cloud, maximizing data transfer speeds and minimizing server requirement and cost.

Finally, for sensor characteristics, storage is a key consideration that depends on the method, location, and length of time the data has to be archived. This varies based on legal requirements on a per-country basis as well as use case; the difference is significant between storing video for weeks and using a set of event-based triggers, and it has a big impact on the analytics that can be included in the limited physical capacity of the device. In addition, given the scale of city deployments and the needs related to long-term planning, the storage requirements might be higher than in traditional deployments, and event-driven approaches help avoid putting pressure on the supporting network. Cities must figure out the best approach to address their storage requirements as well as determine how long they need to keep their data, and choose devices appropriately based on those criteria.

Data collection and storage also have an important impact on privacy. A video sensor used to count entities may be able to read car registration numbers or record the faces of pedestrians. Legal and privacy considerations play a major role in choosing a system. There may be a mandate to record this type of data for public safety reasons. On the other side of the spectrum, there may be a conditional mandate that devices can be counted only if they cannot be individually identified (with privacy as a requirement). In this last case, a sensor may be specifically chosen for its limited image resolution or inability to identify objects beyond their general shape or silhouette. The communication system may also be designed to forbid more than device count transport (low bandwidth, for example). The scope of the privacy requirements must be clearly understood and scoped at the time of design.

Regardless of the type of system chosen, sensor data is transported and processed by the IoT system. Although IoT systems use common APIs and normalized language in the cloud, they may use different network protocols. To physically connect the data streams from so many devices, it is critical to have a network infrastructure that can communicate with devices using the variety of communication protocols operating at the street level. Cellular technologies are core to ICT, as cities typically allow for easy and dense cellular connectivity. However, other technologies are present.

Note Chapter 2 examines in more detail the general architectural considerations of IoT. Chapter 4, "Connecting Smart Objects," provides a deeper **examination** of the various protocols that may be used for the different type of ranges and applications encountered in smart cities. The last part of this chapter also provides targeted examples and specific smart city use cases.

In all cases, the network for a smart city has to be ruggedized for outdoor conditions and must be able to withstand harsh weather conditions. In order to support the ICT solutions a smart city deploys, the network must meet standards for outdoor electronic devices and provide maintenance faults for simplified issue isolation.

Another issue that network planning must take into account is the required level of agnosticism of smart city networks. LoRaWAN is growing as a major protocol for smart city sensors, across multiple verticals. LoRaWAN is well adapted to the type of ranges required in an urban environment and the types of data exchanges that most smart city sensors need. (Chapter 4 provides detailed information about LoRaWAN.) However, multiple use cases mean that multiple protocols may be deployed. A heterogeneous array of sensors for different domains and from different technology vendors utilizes different communication protocols to drive certain benefits and features. Many sensors come with their own gateways that are compatible with their specific hardware. However, the network needs to be broad and vendor-agnostic enough to enable these gateways to communicate with a larger network and with end nodes that can bridge low-power consumption protocols, such as ZigBee to IP, and meet a host of other communication requirements. All these protocols and systems have to work together and be transported over the same network infrastructure.

Smart city networks also have to make possible local analysis and closed-loop decision making, which also means that computing capacity at end nodes needs to be higher than for typical deployments. The size and complexity of the network grows with the size of the smart city deployment, as well as with the number and types of sensors utilized by the city. The IoT network infrastructure is the backbone of any cohesive smart solution for a city; device connectivity is the key to the utility of digitized public services.

City Layer

At the city layer, which is above the street layer, network routers and switches must be deployed to match the size of city data that needs to be transported. This layer aggregates all data collected by sensors and the end-node network into a single transport network.

The city layer may appear to be a simple transport layer between the edge devices and the data center or the Internet. However, one key consideration of the city layer is that it needs to transport multiple types of protocols, for multiple types of IoT applications. Some applications are delay- and jitter-sensitive, and some other applications require a deterministic approach to frame delivery. A missed packet may generate an alarm or result in an invalid status report. As a result, the city layer must be built around resiliency, to ensure that a packet coming from a sensor or a gateway will always be forwarded successfully to the headend station. Figure 12-3 shows a common way of achieving this goal.

City Layer

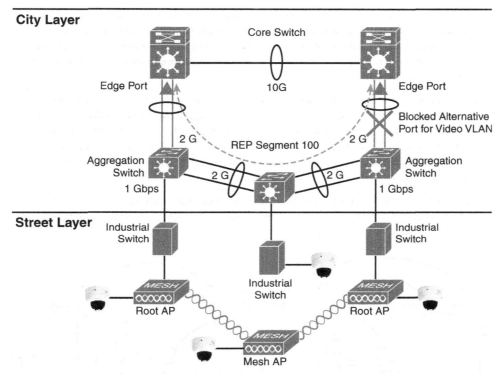

Figure 12-3 *Street Layer Resiliency*

In this model, at least two paths exist from any aggregation switch to the data center layer. A common protocol used to ensure this resiliency is Resilient Ethernet Protocol (REP). (REP is examined in detail in Chapter 9, "Manufacturing.")

Data Center Layer

Ultimately, data collected from the sensors is sent to a data center, where it can be processed and correlated. Based on this processing of data, meaningful information and trends can be derived, and information can be provided back. For example, an application in a data center can provide a global view of the city traffic and help authorities decide on the need for more or less common transport vehicles. At the same time, an automated response can be generated. For example, the same traffic information can be processed to automatically regulate and coordinate the street light durations at the scale of the entire city to limit traffic congestion.

The key technology in creating any comprehensive smart solution with services is the cloud. With a cloud infrastructure, data is not stored in a data center owned directly or indirectly by city authorities. Instead, data is stored in rented logical containers accessed through the Internet. Because the containers can be extended or reduced based on needs, the storage size and computing power are flexible and can adapt to changing requirements or budget conditions. In addition, multiple contractors can store and process data at the same time, without the complexity of exclusively owned space. This proximity and flexibility also facilitate the exchange of information between smart systems and allow for the deployment of new applications that can leverage information from several IoT systems.

The cloud model is the chief means of delivering storage, virtualization, adaptability, and the analytics know-how that city governments require for the technological mashup and synergy of information embodied in a smart city. Traditional city networks simply cannot keep up with the real-time data needs of smart cities; they are encumbered by their physical limitations. The cloud enables data analytics to be taken to server farms with large and extensible processing capabilities.

Figure 12-4 shows the vision of utilizing the cloud in smart solutions for cities. The cloud provides a scalable, secure, and reliable data processing engine that can handle the immense amount of data passing through it.

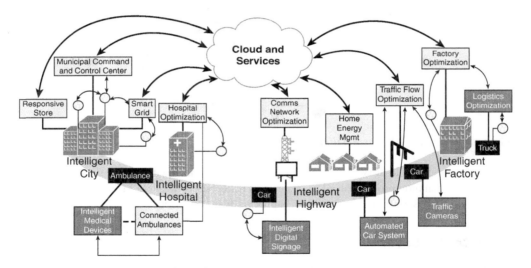

Figure 12-4   *The Role of the Cloud for Smart City Applications*

Smart city issues require not just efficient use of infrastructure, which the cloud helps enable, they also require new data processing and management models. For example, cloud services allow for Software as a Service (SaaS) models that create cyclical returns on investment. With the cloud approach shown in Figure 12-4, smart cities can also take advantage of operating expense–based consumption models to overcome any financial hurdles in adopting solutions to their most critical issues. Critical data, such as air condition (humidity, temperature, pollution) levels monitoring, can be processed initially. Then, as the efficiency of IoT is scaled up, richer data processing can be enabled in the cloud applications. For example, the humidity level can be used to regulate the color and luminosity of street lights. In times when city budgets are strained, data processing can be scaled down to essential services.

In the layered architecture just discussed, a platform can be enabled by the cloud service; this platform would aggregate, normalize, and expose city data through APIs consumable by applications that drive services.

However, not all data is processed in the central cloud-based data center. Most of the real-time and locally significant data can be directly processed at the edge of the network, leveraging a fog architecture. In this model, processing and analytics capabilities are made available at the top of the street layer, where gateways operate. In this way, data coming from multiple sensors (of the same type or of multiple different types) can be processed locally at the edge. Decisions are locally significant and can be made without unnecessary interactions with the cloud. The results from the locally processed data are then sent to the cloud to provide a more global perspective.

Services Layer

Ultimately, the true value of ICT connectivity comes from the services that the measured data can provide to different users operating within a city. Smart city applications can provide value to and visibility for a variety of user types, including city operators, citizens, and law enforcement. The collected data should be visualized according to the specific needs of each consumer of that data and the particular user experience requirements and individual use cases. For example, parking data indicating which spots are and aren't currently occupied can drive a citizen parking app with a map of available spots, as well as an enforcement officer's understanding of the state (utilization and payment) of the public parking space, while at the same time helping the city operator's perspective on parking problem areas in the city at any given time. With different levels of granularity and scale, the same data performs three different functions for three different users. Along the same lines, traffic information can be used by individual car drivers to find the least congested route. A variation of the same information can be made available to public transportation users to estimate travel times. Public transportation systems, such as buses, can be rerouted around known congestion points. The number of subway trains can be increased dynamically to respond to an increase in traffic congestion, anticipating the decisions of thousands or even millions of commuters to take public transportation instead of cars on days when roads are very congested. Here again, the same type of data is utilized by different types of users in different ways based on their specific use cases. (Chapter 13 provides more examples and details on this type of traffic information processing.)

With the architecture described in this section, a smart city can incorporate any number of applications that can consume normalized data from a cloud-hosted platform or from fog applications. Because the entire architecture operates with compatible APIs, these applications can even enable cross-domain benefits. As an example of such cross-domain benefits, at known traffic congestion points, parking spots could be removed from availability maps, waste management routes could be properly rerouted, and street lighting could be increased. These types of cross-domain data correlations can be developed and improved by the system, inside the layered architecture, since there is a horizontal level of aggregation and normalization.

The architecture provides application developers and sensor vendors with the tools necessary to innovate and invent new community experiences via open APIs, software development kits (SDKs), city information models, and more to develop city-qualified applications that drive high-value smart city services. This enables tailored, customized smart city solutions that can also be developed by citizens themselves, for their cities.

On-Premises vs. Cloud

Different cities and regions have different data hosting requirements based on security or legal policies. A key consideration in developing ICT connectivity solutions is whether a city has requirements about where data should be hosted. Data can be hosted on-premises or in the cloud. Fog architectures provide an intermediate layer. The data resulting from fog processing can be sent to the cloud or to a data center operated locally (on-premises). On-premises encompasses traditional networks, and all their limitations, whereas cloud hosting encompasses a whole host of security risks if the proper measures are not taken to secure citizen data. When data is sent to the cloud, data sovereignty laws may restrict the physical location where this data is actually stored.

Ideally, a smart city utilizing ICT connectivity would use the cloud in its architecture, but if this is impossible, the city would need to invest far more in the city layer's networking components (for example, switches, routers) and still may not be able to drive the same cross-domain value propositions and scalability in its design.

A city could begin with traditional networking designs and on-premises hosting, with the intent to protect the data, but then it might quickly conclude that the capabilities of on-premises data centers lag behind what cloud-hosting data management can enable for the city. In that case, a hybrid hosting approach could be implemented, whereby some data may be migrated to the cloud while other data stays on-premises. For example, images from individual street cameras may be stored locally, while the analytics about pedestrian or car flows and the associated metadata may be hosted in the cloud.

Smart City Security Architecture

A serious concern of most smart cities and their citizens is data security. Vast quantities of sensitive information are being shared at all times in a layered, real-time architecture, and cities have a duty to protect their citizens' data from unauthorized access, collection, and tampering.

In general, citizens feel better about data security when the city itself, and not a private entity, owns public or city-relevant data. It is up to the city and the officials who run it to determine how to utilize this data. When a private entity owns city-relevant data, the scope of the ownership may initially be very clear. However, later considerations or changes in the private entity strategy may shift the way the data is used. It may then be more difficult for city authorities or the citizens to oppose this new direction, simply because they do not have any stake in the decision-making process of the private entity. In addition, private entities may have financial interests and political motivations, and they may not have the security standards or the accountability matrix city governments commonly possess or acquire through public vetting and votes. For example, suppose that a private contractor is in charge of collecting and managing parking sensor data. One possible way to increase the profitability of such data is to sell it to insurance companies looking to charge an additional premium to car owners parking in the street (vs. in a covered and secured garage). Such deviations from the original mandate are less likely to happen when cities own the data and when citizens have a way to vote against such usages.

Traditionally, network deployments use a siloed approach and do not always follow open security standards. Agencies may run applications and servers on the public cloud, have limited security safeguards implemented, and use cloud-based collaboration tools without proper security. Hence there is a need for a centralized, cloud-based, compliance-based security mechanism to address the needs of service providers and end users. Security is obviously an end-to-end problem, starting with where and how data is collected, and spanning pervasively throughout the entire data processing lifecycle.

A security architecture for smart cities must utilize security protocols to fortify each layer of the architecture and protect city data. Figure 12-5 shows a reference architecture, with specific security elements highlighted. Security protocols should authenticate the various components and protect data transport throughout. For example, hijacking traffic sensors to send false traffic data to the system regulating the street lights may result in dramatic congestion issues. The benefit for the offender may be the ability to get "all greens" while traveling, but the overall result would typically be dangerous and detrimental to the city. The security architecture should be able to evolve with the latest technology and incorporate regional guidelines (for example, city by-laws, county or regional security regulations). Network partners may also have their own compliance standards, security policies, and governance requirements that need to be added to the local city requirements.

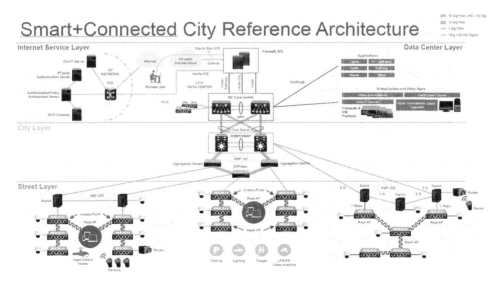

Figure 12-5 *Key Smart and Connected Cities Reference Architecture*

Starting from the street level, sensors should have their own security protocols. Some industry-standard security features include device/sensor identification and authorization; device/sensor data encryption; Trusted Platform Module, which enables self-destruction when the sensor is physically handled; and user ID authentication and authorization. Sensor identification and authorization typically requires a pre-installed factory X.509 certificate and public key infrastructure (PKI) at the organization level, where a new certificate is installed through a zero-touch deployment process. This additional processing may slow the deployment but ensures the security of the exchanges.

Another consideration may be the type of data that the sensor is able to collect and process. For example, a roadside car counter may include a Bluetooth sensor that uniquely identifies each driver or pedestrian. Security considerations should determine whether this information should even be collected. If it is collected, a decision should be made on whether this data is processed using an "online process" (in which information is used for analytics, but individual identifying data is not stored and is therefore forgotten immediately) or a more classical analytical process (in which data is stored temporarily, either because the algorithm needs to avoid duplicates or because trajectory determination is part of data processing). Data should be secured both at rest and in motion, but when data is stored, additional security needs to be put in place to ensure that information will not be tampered with, abused, or stolen. This is true regardless of the location where data is stored—at the gateway (fog) or in the cloud.

The city layer transports data between the street layer and the data center layer. It acts as the network layer. The following are common industry elements for security on the network layer:

- **Firewall:** A firewall is located at the edge, and it should be IPsec- and VPN-ready, and include user- and role-based access control. It should also be integrated with the architecture to give city operators remote access to the city data center.

- **VLAN:** A VLAN provides end-to-end segmentation of data transmission, further protecting data from rogue intervention. Each service/domain has a dedicated VLAN for data transmission.

- **Encryption:** Protecting the traffic from the sensor to the application is a common requirement to avoid data tampering and eavesdropping. In most cases, encryption starts at the sensor level. In some cases, the sensor-to-gateway link uses one type of encryption, and the gateway-to-application connection uses another encryption (for example, a VPN).

Multiple specific elements (such as switch-to-switch encryption) may be required by each deployed IoT solution to increase the reliability of the system. At the data center layer, having secure virtual private clouds is a common requirement. Creating dynamic perimeters around applications, clients, hosts, and shared resources can further obfuscate data from prying eyes. Integrating the latest technology frameworks, such as mutual Transport Layer Security (mTLS) or OAuth 2.0 for device attestation and identity-based access, is key to ensuring the integrity of a city solution.

Note   mTLS is bidirectional, which means that both the client and the server identities are ascertained during the authentication phase. This bidirectionality presents the advantage of preventing unauthorized clients from accessing the network, and also increases system flexibility by allowing each side to act as a client or a server. For example, a sensor may be a client in a connection to the cloud application but may also be a server for the gateway or other sensors. (See the IETF mTLS draft at https://tools.ietf.org/html/draft-badra-hajjeh-mtls-06.)

OAuth is an authorization framework that enables applications to obtain a limited and controlled access to target services, using HTTP. (See the OAuth definition at https://tools.ietf.org/html/rfc6749.)

Following and prioritizing the security logic in the layered architecture will reduce the chances of a serious network security breach or privacy violation of city data.

Smart City Use-Case Examples

There are multiple ways a smart city can improve its efficiency and the lives of its citizens. The following sections examine some of the applications commonly used as starting points to implement IoT in smart cities: connected street lighting, smart parking, smart traffic control, and connected environment. While each of these solutions could fill an entire chapter, for the sake of brevity, we keep these discussions high-level and tied to the conceptual architecture discussed in this chapter. Additional chapters cover public safety (Chapter 15) and transportation (Chapter 13), topics that also apply to smart cities. In addition, we encourage you to refer to the rest of Part 2, "Engineering IoT Networks," to get more in-depth information about smart objects at the various layers, and also about the general architectures and protocols required to support these use cases. Other vertical-specific chapters in Part 3, "IoT in Industry," also provide valuable information about applications that are implemented at city levels, such as utilities (Chapter 11), "Utilities."

Connected Street Lighting

Of all urban utilities, street lighting comprises one of the largest expenses in a municipality's utility bill, accounting for up to 40% of the total, according to the New York State Department of Environmental Conservation.[4] Maintenance of street lights is an operational challenge, given the large number of lights and their vast geographic distribution.

Connected Street Lighting Solution

Cities commonly look for solutions to help reduce lighting expenses and at the same time improve operating efficiencies while minimizing upfront investment. The installation of a smart street lighting solution can provide significant energy savings and can also be leveraged to provide additional services. In this regard, light-emitting diode (LED) technology leads the transition from traditional street lighting to smart street lighting:

- LEDs require less energy to produce more light than legacy lights, and they have a much longer life span and a longer maintenance cycle.

- A leading lighting company estimates that a complete switch to LED technology can reduce individual light bills by up to 70%.[5]

- LEDs are well suited to smart solution use cases. For example, LED color or light intensity can be adapted to site requirements (for example, warmer color and lower intensity in city centers, sun-like clarity on highways, time- and weather-adaptive intensity and color).

Figure 12-6 shows how electricity prices rise, while LED prices decrease and their unit sales rise.

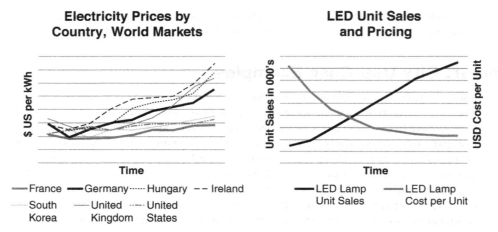

Figure 12-6 *Electricity Cost vs. LED Cost and Sales*

Source: Energy Information Agency, International Energy Agency

The global transition to LED is a key enabler for smart cities to begin the moving toward ICT connectivity solutions. As electricity bills rise and prices for LEDs drop, this hardware transition can open the door to a complete smart lighting solution.

A comprehensive smart lighting solution enables a converged and networked system that incorporates LED-based fixtures and dynamic lighting control, supported by the layered smart city architecture discussed earlier in this chapter that is easily extensible to support other use cases and solutions to benefit the city.

Street Lighting Architecture

Connected lighting uses a light management application to manage street lights remotely by connecting to the smart city's infrastructure. This application attaches to LED lights, monitors their management and maintenance, and allows you to view the operational status of each light. In most cases, a sensor gateway acts as an intermediate system between the application and the lights (light control nodes). The gateway relays instructions from the application to the lights and stores the local lights' events for the application's consumption. The controller and LED lights use the cloud to connect to the smart city's infrastructure, as shown in Figure 12-7.

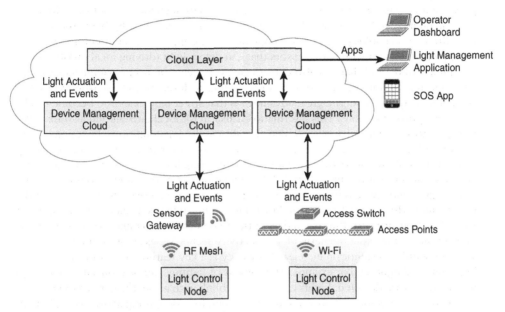

Figure 12-7   *Connected Lighting Architecture*

Source: Cisco, Smart+Connected Lighting

A human or automated operator can use a cloud application to perform automated scheduling for lights and even get light sensors to perform automated dimming or brightening, as needed. The schedule can also impact the light intensity level and possibly the color, depending on environmental conditions, weather, time of year, time of day, location within the city, and so on.

Lighting nodes vary widely in the industry, especially with respect to elements such as what communication protocol they use (for example, Wi-Fi, cellular, ZigBee, 802.15.4g [Wi-SUN], LoRaWAN), level of ruggedization, and on-board sensor capabilities. These features are optimized for different circumstances and conditions; no single lighting node can support all environments ideally. For example, city centers may be locations where Wi-Fi is easy to deploy (due to proximity to Ethernet or Internet backbones, ranges on the order of 100 meters, and high urban furniture density offering a large choice of relays and gateway points), whereas highways may mandate longer-range solutions such as cellular or LoRaWAN. Many solutions leverage wired connectivity, either by using the existing city cable infrastructure or by adding a cable adjacent to the power cable. In cases where cabling is not practical, wireless technologies may bring interesting capabilities. For example, 802.15.4g controllers can be used to form a mesh and extend the network. This extension is used not only to connect other light poles but also to connect smart meters from neighboring houses. In all cases, the built-in versatility offered by the four-layer architecture shown in Figure 12-2 ensures that all the different types of technologies optimized to fit any city topology can be flexibly incorporated into the solution.

Lighting, as an ICT connectivity solution, utilizes an existing city asset with an existing power source. Enabling that asset with ICT connectivity technologies not only drives revenue on its own but can also drive an ICT connectivity solution by being the asset that different technology pieces use to operate. For example, LED light bulbs are commonly equipped with basic sensors that can detect light (driving local on/off and dimming actions) and that can also detect many other environmental parameters, such as temperature, motion, pressure, or humidity. Adding such functions to sensors typically adds only marginal cost. The great advantage is that street lights can also become local weather reporting stations. This information is useful for local citizens and also for city transportation systems that need to detect real-time driving conditions. Functions such as monitoring power, measuring the oxygen and carbon dioxide levels, measuring the amount of pollution or particulate matter, and detecting levels of long-wave ultraviolet A (UVA) and short-wave ultraviolet B (UVB) radiation can also be added to provide additional values and services (for example, pollution monitoring, pollen alerts, energy grid monitoring). More specialized capabilities can also be embedded, such as basic audio or video functionality with filtering and analytics to detect traffic congestion or car crashes in real time. In this case, the network connectivity technologies are important as usage and bandwidth consumption increase. Efficiency is a key feature of smart cities, including connected lighting. For example, the amount of lighting can be reduced on highways where no cars are detected. Lights can be set to blink with a specific pattern to help police locate a specific GPS location quickly. Using IoT for lighting allows for a plethora of useful applications, and for this reason, lighting is often used as an introductory IoT function for smart city deployments. Municipalities often start with the energy cost savings as a primary priority and soon realize that sensors added to the already deployed IoT lighting infrastructure can add major benefits and advantages to city management.

Smart Parking

Parking is a universal challenge for cities around the globe. According to urban planning researchers, up to 30% of cars driving in congested downtown traffic are searching for parking spaces. Ineffective parking access and administration make parking in urban areas a constant struggle and affect cities in many ways. http://shoup.bol.ucla.edu/CruisingForParkingAccess.pdf

Smart Parking Use Cases

Added traffic congestion is one consequence of drivers looking for parking space, and it has several consequences:

- **Contributes to pollution:** Tons of extra carbon emissions are released into the city's environment due to cars driving around searching for parking spots when they could be parked.

- **Causes motorist frustration:** In most cities, parking spot scarcity causes drivers to lose patience and waste time, leading to road rage, inattention, and other stress factors.

- **Increases traffic incidents:** Drivers searching for parking spots cause increased congestion in the streets and that, in turn, causes increased accidents and other traffic incidents.

Revenue loss is another consequence of drivers looking unsuccessfully for parking space, and it also has various negative side effects:

- **Cities often lose revenue:** As a result of inadequate parking meter enforcement and no-parking, no-standing, and loading-zone violations, cities lose revenue.

- **Parking administration employee productivity suffers:** Employees waste time roaming the streets, attempting to detect parking rules offenders.

- **Parking availability affects income:** Local shops and businesses lose customers because of the decreased accessibility caused by parking space shortages.

As we look at ways to apply technology to tackle some of the most pressing issues facing cities today, parking is an area where improvement is clearly needed and can be easily quantified. As cities continue to grow in number, size, and complexity, urban infrastructure and the services that rely on it are increasingly stressed. The issues described above become more pressing as urban population and density increase. The difficulties of parking in urban areas impact citizens' quality of life and make living in the city less desirable due to increased travel times, stress, noise, pollution, and so on.

One option for solving urban center traffic issues is to repurpose dense urban space to create additional parking infrastructure. However, such an option is often challenging, primarily because of the costs, financial and otherwise. Instead of resorting to utilizing valuable city real estate to create more parking spaces, cities often have the option of optimizing the usage efficiency of existing parking assets to better manage citizen needs. This option often provides the quickest relief to the parking issue, while minimizing the need for new investment and limiting the impact on urban architecture.

Smart Parking Architecture

A variety of parking sensors are available on the market, and they take different approaches to sensing occupancy for parking spots. Examples include in-ground magnetic sensors, which use embedded sensors to create a magnetic detection field in a parking spot; video-based sensors, which detect events based on video computing (vehicle movements or presence); and radar sensors that sense the presence of vehicles (volumetric detection). Most sensors installed in the ground must rely on battery power, since running a power line is typically too expensive. These sensors commonly react to changes, such as a change in the magnetic field, triggering a sensor to awaken and send an event report. Because these events are not too frequent, the battery can last a very long time. Based on the energy consumed by each report, a life span of 600,000 reports is not uncommon for a typical parking sensor. A very busy parking spot, where a car enters or leaves every 10 minutes, would allow a 10-year battery span—and it is unusual to see parking spots with usage that heavy. In high-density environments (for example, indoor parking, parking decks), one or several gateways per floor may connect to the parking sensors, using shorter-range protocols such as ZigBee or Wi-Fi. The gateway may then use another protocol (wired or wireless) to connect to the control station. In larger (for example, outdoor) environments, a longer-range Low Power Wide Area (LPWA) protocol is common, as shown in Figure 12-8.

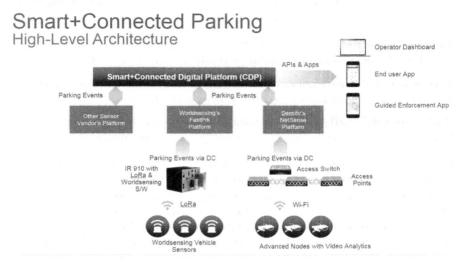

Figure 12-8   *Connected Parking Architecture*

Technology innovations are happening all the time, making the holistic ICT connectivity architecture even more important. For example, new detection technologies rely on sensing the radio emissions (Bluetooth and others) coming from a vehicle. The adoption of such new technologies implies that the communication architecture is open enough to accommodate the needs of these new systems. (Refer to Chapter 2 for more details on such an open architecture.) Combining these technologies in innovative ways also expands the possibilities of the services IoT systems can deliver; this certainly holds true for smart parking. For example, sensors can be installed in disabled parking spots. An application can be used for drivers to register their disability and then locate these spots more easily. When a user parks, the sensor can communicate with the application on the driver's smart phone to validate the disability status and limit fraudulent use of these parking spaces.

Regardless of the technology used, parking sensors are typically event-driven objects. A sensor detects an event and identifies it based on time or analysis. The event is transmitted through the device's communication protocol to an access point or gateway, which forwards the event data through the city layer. The gateway sends it to the cloud or a fog application, where it is normalized. An application shows the parking event on operator dashboards, or personal smart phones, where an action can be taken. For example, a driver can book a nearby parking spot, or a parking operator can remove it from the list of available parking spaces in target locations. This action triggers data to be sent back to the parking sensor to modify its availability status based on the received instructions. In turn, the sensor may interact with nearby systems. For example, in response to these instructions, lights above parking spaces can be turned red, orange, or green to display a free, booked, or occupied spot, thus facilitating a driver's search for an available parking spot. Similarly, a parking sensor can send a status to a general parking spot counter at the entrance of the parking deck to display how many spots are available in a given area, such as on a particular floor of a parking deck. This communication may be direct but often goes through a gateway, the network, and the application that communicates with the other systems through APIs. The user may also access the data from the cloud or fog-based applications to see the list of spots available in a particular city district or neighborhood. Smart data can also be embedded—for example, to increase the discount on more distant parking spots or increase the cost of parking spots closer to venues at particular times (such as sporting events or concerts).

As discussed earlier in this chapter, smart parking has three users that applications must support through aggregated data: city operators, parking enforcement personnel, and citizens. The true value of data normalization is that all parking data, regardless of technology or vendor, would be visible in these applications for the different users to support their particular experiences. The following are some potential user experiences for these three user types:

- **City operators:** These users might want a high-level map of parking in the city to maintain perspective on the city's ongoing parking situation. They would also need information on historical parking data patterns to understand congestion and pain points in order to be able to effectively influence urban planning.

- **Parking enforcement officers:** These users might require real-time updates on parking changes in a certain area to be able to take immediate action on enforcement activities, such as issuing tickets or sending warnings to citizens whose time is nearing expiration. Their focus is driving revenue creation for the city and minimizing wasted time by performing parking monitoring and enforcement at scale (that is, not needing to look at each individual vehicle situation since only a small percentage of the inspected vehicles actually require an action).

- **Citizens:** These users might want an application with a map (such as a built-in parking app in their car) showing available parking spots, reservation capabilities, and online payment. Their focus would be on minimizing the time to get a parking spot and avoiding parking tickets. The application could warn when parking duration limits approach, allowing the driver to move the vehicle before the timer expires or pay a parking timer extension fee without having to go back to the vehicle.

Smart Traffic Control

Traffic is one the most well-understood pain points for any city. It is the leading cause of accidental death globally, causes immense frustration, and heavily contributes to pollution around the globe. A smart city traffic solution would combine crowd counts, transit information, vehicle counts, and so on and send events regarding incidents on the road so that other controllers on the street could take action.

Smart Traffic Control Architecture

In the architecture shown in Figure 12-9, a video analytics sensor computes traffic events based on a video feed and only pushes events (the car count, or metadata, not the individual images) through the network. These events go through the architectural layers and reach the applications that can drive traffic services. These services include traffic light coordination and also license plate identification for toll roads. Some sensors can also recognize abnormal patterns, such as vehicles moving in the wrong direction or a reserved lane. In that case, the video feed itself may be uploaded to traffic enforcement agencies.

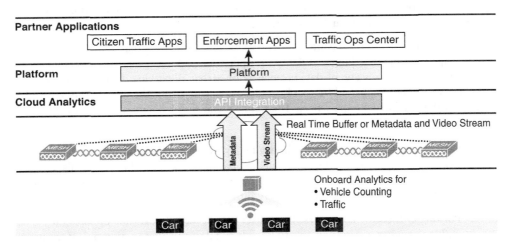

Figure 12-9   *Smart City Traffic Architecture*

Other types of sensors that are part of traffic control solutions include Bluetooth vehicle counters, real-time speed and vehicle counters, and lighting control systems. These sensors provide a real-time perspective while also offering data collection services for historical data trending and correlation purposes. Communication techniques are as varied as sensor form factors. For example, counters installed in light fixtures or traffic lights may use a wired or wireless technology and any number of communication protocols. When a sensor is not coupled with another IoT urban application, wireless technologies are typically used.

Smart Traffic Applications

Traffic applications can be enabled to take immediate action with other sensors to manage traffic and to reduce pain points. Historical data can be used to develop more efficient urban planning to reduce the amount of traffic a city experiences. A common traffic pain point is stop-and-go, where traffic flow suddenly comes to a halt and then flows again. This wavelike traffic pattern is a natural result of the unpredictability of the traffic speed ahead and has long been studied by public and private organizations. (For more information, see http://trafficwaves.org.) A consequence of such traffic waves is a large increase in local accidents, usually benign, but with the effect of worsening the overall congestion.

A well-known remedy for stop-and-go traffic is to regulate the standard flow speed based on car density. As density increases, car speed is forced down to avoid the wave effect. An application that measures traffic density in real time can take action by regulating the street light cycle duration to control the number of cars added to the flow of the main routes, thus limiting or suppressing the wave effect. From the driver's standpoint, there is a wait time before being able to get on the highway or main street, and traffic on the main route is slow but steady. The impression is that traffic is slow but moving, and the overall result is a better commute experience, with lowered and less stressful commute time, as well as a reduced number of accidents.

Information can also be shared with drivers. Countless applications leverage crowd sourcing or sensor-sourced information to provide real-time travel time estimates, suggest rerouting options to avoid congestion spots, or simply find the best way between two points, while taking into account traffic, road work, and so on.

Understanding a city's real-time traffic patterns and being able to effectively mitigate traffic issues can drive tremendous value for a city. Many IoT systems deployed in the street, even for other purposes, can do something with traffic information; specifically, waste, parking, lighting, and environment can all drive traffic outcomes. Sensors counting devices or cars, sensors detecting movements, and sensors measuring gas concentration in the air can all be leveraged to provide an estimate of traffic conditions. The resulting estimate can be leveraged in many ways, such as at a city level to regulate traffic flows and at a citizen level to have a better driving experience.

Connected Environment

As of 2017, 50% of the world's population has settled on less than 2% of the earth's surface area. Such densely populated closed spaces can see spikes in dangerous gas molecules at any given moment. More than 90% of the world's urban population breathes in air with pollutant levels that are much higher than the recommended thresholds, and one out of every eight deaths worldwide is a result of polluted air.[6]

The Need for a Connected Environment

Most large cities monitor their air quality. Data is often derived from enormous air quality monitoring stations that are expensive and have been around for decades. These stations are highly accurate in their measurements but also highly limited in their range, and a city is likely to have many blind spots in coverage. Given the price and size of air quality monitoring stations, cities cannot afford to purchase the number of stations required to give accurate reports on a localized level and follow the pollution flows as they move through the city over time.

To fully address the air quality issues in the short term and the long term, a smart city would need to understand air quality on a hyper-localized, real-time, distributed basis at any given moment. To get those measurements, smart cities need to invest in the following:

- Open-data platforms that provide current air quality measurements from existing air quality monitoring stations

- Sensors that provide similar accuracy to the air quality stations but are available at much lower prices

- Actionable insights and triggers to improve air quality through cross-domain actions

- Visualization of environmental data for consumers and maintenance of historical air quality data records to track emissions over time

Connected Environment Architecture

Figure 12-10 shows an architecture in which all connected environment elements overlay on the generalized four-layer smart city IoT architecture presented earlier in this chapter.

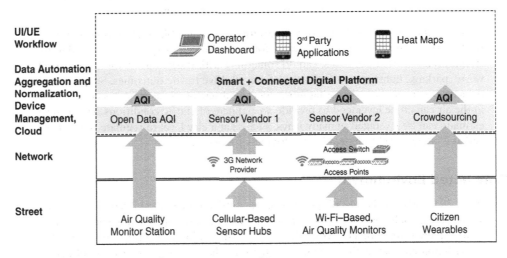

Figure 12-10   *Connected Environment Architecture*

As shown in Figure 12-10, at the street layer there are a variety of multivendor sensor offerings, using a variety of communication protocols. Connected environment sensors might measure different gases, depending on a city's particular air quality issues, and may include weather and noise sensors. These sensors may be located in a variety of urban fixtures, such as in street lights, as explained earlier. They may also be embedded in the ground or in other structures or smart city infrastructure. Even mobile sources of information can be included through connected wearables that citizens might choose to purchase and carry with them to understand the air quality around them at any given moment. Crowdsourcing may make this information available to the global system.

Communication technologies depend on the location of the sensors. Wearables typically communicate via a short-range technology (such as Bluetooth) with a nearby collecting device (such as a phone). That device, in turn, forwards the collected data to the infrastructure (for example, through cellular data). Sensors that are installed in urban fixtures also use a variety of communication technologies. Sensors included in street lighting systems may utilize the same communication infrastructure as the street light control application.

Independent and standalone sensors typically use wireless technologies. In dense urban environments, ZigBee and Wi-Fi are common. However, Wi-Fi is not very well adapted for networks where reports are sporadic because Wi-Fi requires an 802.11 connection to be maintained, which consumes battery resources. (However, new implementations of Wi-Fi, such as Wi-Fi Alliance IoT Low Power and 802.11ah can alleviate this issue.) In larger environments, LPWA technologies, such as NB-IoT and LoRaWAN, are used, unless the sensor is able to use a wired technology (for example, when connecting to the wired lighting infrastructure), but this is much rarer because of the cost.

In addition to all the air quality sensor and wearable data, the data center layer or application layer represented on the left side of Figure 12-10 also receives the open data from existing weather stations as an additional data input. All these data inputs come together to provide a highly accurate sense of the air quality in the city at any given moment. This information can be visualized in applications that include heat maps of particulates, concentrates, and specific information on the dangers of such gaseous anomalies. Different pollution levels can be communicated, and gases can be tracked as they move throughout the city, either because of the wind or because of the movement of gas sources (for example, the systematic pendulum swing of commuter movements in the morning vs. the evening creates pollution patterns along the denser traffic routes).

From this pollution and environmental data and the analytics applied to it, the city can track problem areas and take action in long-term urban planning to reduce the effects of air quality disturbances. This action can take many forms, from increasing public transit availability along the more polluted routes to encouraging the displacement of businesses toward living areas to limit the need to commute daily. With this pollution information, citizens can also take short-term actions, such as turning on their air purifiers at a given moment or simply stepping inside if pollutant concentrations are becoming serious. Strategic coordinated joint actions are also possible, such as restricting traffic along certain routes or on certain days, and encouraging citizens to share vehicles or use the public transportation system.

Summary

This chapter reviews the main components of IoT for smart cities. Urban centers are labeled "smart" when they leverage technologies to improve the management of common resources, such as street space or waste collection, and improve the quality of urban life for citizens. With the increase of urban density, new and more efficient solutions have to be found to maintain or increase the livability of fast-growing urban centers.

IoT technologies deploy sensors at the street layer to collect local data. A city layer conveys the collected information to data centers, where the information is processed. Action can then be taken, automatically or based on machine learning. Signals are sent back to the street layer to modify the sensors' state, modify street light patterns, and so on. In addition, citizens may be able to access the process information and take action (for example, find a parking spot or take an alternate route to avoid traffic).

A key concern for such smart city solutions is security. One requirement for smart cities is to isolate and protect data exchanges with the street level devices and also secure the exchanges with databases and processed data. Another requirement is to use a common transport architecture for multiple services and a common cloud infrastructure to facilitate the exchanges between applications. A great advantage of this exchange is that the same information can be leveraged by multiple users, each with different concerns or perspectives, such as individual citizens, emergency responders, and city planners. Balancing the need for security with the need for exchanges is an ongoing challenge.

A typical example of smart city IoT applications is connected lighting; IoT can reduce city energy costs dramatically while using existing lighting infrastructure and coupling with other smart city applications (pollution or traffic detection, for example) for a very small premium. Smart parking is another case where IoT provides great benefit, reducing city congestion and increasing the quality of life for driving citizens. Correlated with parking, smart traffic control is another smart city solution that can be used to regulate car flows and offer optimal route options in real time. Controlling traffic and improving parking also benefit the environment. Connected environment smart city solutions can measure, manage, and monitor air quality and pollution directly through distributed sensors or crowd sourcing.

References

1. World Business Council on Sustainable Development, *Water: Facts and Trends*, 2006, http://www.unwater.org/downloads/Water_facts_and_trends.pdf.

2. J. Bradley, et al., *Internet of Everything: A $4.6 Trillion Public-Sector Opportunity* (white paper), Cisco, 2013, http://internetofeverything.cisco.com/sites/default/files/docs/en/ioe_public_sector_vas_white paper_121913final.pdf.

3. Cisco, *Private Sector Value at Stake*, http://ioeassessment.cisco.com/learn/value-stake-analysis. Accessed November 23, 2016.

4. New York State Department of Environmental Conservation, *Reduce Utility Bills for Municipal Facilities and Operations*, www.dec.ny.gov/energy/64089.html. Accessed November 23, 2016.

5. R20, *The LED Future: Outdoor Lighting for Sustainable, Living Cities* (white paper), http://regions20.org/wp-content/uploads/2016/08/TheLEDFuture.pdf. Accessed November 23, 2016.

6. World Health Organization, *Ambient Air Pollution: A Global Assessment of Exposure and Burden of Disease*, 2016, www.who.int/phe/publications/air-pollution-global-assessment/en/.

Chapter 13

Transportation

Efficient transportation has revolutionized the way people communicate and interact. With more powerful and cheaper engines, the number of commercial vehicles, passenger cars, buses, trains (including underground, above-ground, trackways, and tramways), and planes of various sizes all grew exponentially during the twentieth century. This explosion brought increased congestion, accidents, and pollution. Today, the main issue affecting the transportation industry is no longer development and growth but rather managing overgrowth and journey experience. IoT and automation can assist individual drivers by providing real-time information on vehicle performance and anticipated journey conditions. IoT can also help entire cities and countries optimize traffic and transportation exchanges.

This chapter includes the following sections:

- **Transportation and Transports:** This section provides a view of the transportation industry and its subsectors.

- **Transportation Challenges:** This section describes challenges that affect road and train travel, for both individuals and mass transit vehicles.

- **IoT Use Cases for Transportation:** This section provides multiple examples of how IoT can dramatically change the transportation industry and the travel experience.

- **An IoT Architecture for Transportation:** This section details the IoT architecture for the transportation industries covered in this chapter: individual vehicles on roads and mass transit buses and trains.

Transportation and Transports

The transportation industry includes multiple subsectors: mass transit (which can include subways, light rails, tramways, trolleys, ferries, and buses), rail, roadways, aviation, maritime, freight and logistics, and passenger vehicles. Each subsector or mode of transport can also include multiple specialized domains. For example, air transport includes airports, regional or national air traffic control authorities, airlines, maintenance companies of multiple sorts. and, of course, plane manufacturers. Figure 13-1 illustrates the common transportation subsectors.

Connected Transportation Sectors

Figure 13-1   *Transportation Subsectors*

Some of the considerations covered in other chapters also apply to these sectors. For example, most IoT solutions for manufacturing can apply to vehicle manufacturers. (Refer to Chapter 9, "Manufacturing," for an in-depth discussion on IoT for manufacturing industries.) Similarly, smart and connected cities leverage many IoT solutions for their transportation infrastructure and emergency vehicles. (Refer to Chapter 12, "Smart and Connected Cities," for a detailed discussion on IoT for public infrastructure, and to Chapter 15, "Public Safety," for a detailed discussion on IoT for emergency services.) The entire transportation industry is too large to be covered in this book. This book focuses on specific verticals and specific aspects of transportation. Three subsectors of transportation are used as illustrations of how IoT is transforming this industry:

- **Roadways:** Roadways involve individual vehicles, managed fleets, and the entire roadways infrastructure: traffic lights, roadside cameras, roadway sensors, toll plazas, digital signage, etc. Because of the powerful and direct effect on individuals' lives, IoT improvements for roadways are massive and very visible.

- **Mass transit:** Mass transit extends individual vehicles to collective transportation. This subsector acts as a catalyst for changes in the other subsectors.

- **Rail:** Although mass transit includes subways and light rails, inter-city train traffic also includes freight, which can be a large part of rail activity.

The transformations described for these three examples can be successfully applied to other transportation subsectors (such as aviation, maritime for passengers, and freight/logistics).

However, keep in mind that each subsector has specific characteristics that may or may not apply to other sectors.

Similarly, this chapter focuses on aspects of IoT for transportation that have an impact on passenger experience, workforce optimization and operational efficiency, safety, and security. Many other aspects of transportation are seeing massive changes as well, due to optimizations made possible by IoT. For example, smart sensors can adapt a car steering wheel's stiffness to detected road conditions, which directly increases the lifetime of the car's tires. Tire lifetime optimization through IoT is a fascinating field, and covering all relationships between IoT and vehicles would take an entire book. In the context of roadways, this chapter focuses on how the interaction between vehicles and the roadways infrastructure can improve the travel experience and also the operational efficiency for the teams in charge of managing fleets.

Transportation Challenges

As means of transportation multiplied, challenges related to scale appeared. With more vehicles, managing and maintaining roads and railways becomes more difficult. Maintaining high safety levels while traffic density increases requires optimized management efficiency. At a scale of a single user, maintaining a vehicle is rather easy. At a scale of a large enterprise or a public transport agency, maintaining an entire fleet is much more challenging. Tracking each vehicle's location and maintenance state requires proactive ways of monitoring each vehicle. These challenges are common to all vehicles and transport media (air, sea, rail, or road). However, each transportation subsector has unique challenges, detailed in the following sections.

Roadways

Challenges on roadways are probably the most commonly known because most adults are potential drivers and because road issues are often reported in the news. Some of the biggest challenges facing roadway operators today are in the areas of safety, mobility, and the environment:

- **Safety:** According to the US Department of Transportation, 6.3 million crashes were reported in the United States in 2015, resulting in more than 33,000 fatalities and 2.4 million people injured.[1,2]

- **Mobility:** With over 1 billion cars on the roads worldwide, congestion has become a major issue. The World Health Organization (WHO, the public health arm of the United Nations) has estimated that 5.5 billion hours of travel delays are caused worldwide by congestion. These delays represent a cost of $101 billion in the US alone.[3] The consequences can be extreme. A 60-mile traffic jam in China in 2012 was so severe that it took three days to untangle.

- **Environment:** According to the American Public Transportation Association, each year congestion generates more than 3 billion gallons of wasted fuel in the United States. In addition, transportation creates nearly one-third of greenhouse gas emissions.[4]

The challenges are obvious at a large scale, but they are also present at the scale of an individual driver. Driving at night or in difficult weather conditions is dangerous. Lack of visibility, slow vehicles, unexpected obstacles, and other drivers add to the challenges. These issues are not new. However, automobiles have become an obvious mode of transportation for the twenty-first century. Individuals expect cars and motorcycles to have the same level of intelligence that they see in a smart phone or in navigation systems. Cars are expected to be clever tools, not just basic sets of tires moved by an engine. In this field, IoT can help improve the journey experience by providing detailed information about the vehicle state and anticipating the fatigue or failure of any element. Smart objects can also help a vehicle and its driver communicate with the larger roadways infrastructure, to anticipate obstacles or have better visibility into the journey conditions. This enhanced visibility facilitates mobility and reduces pollution by rerouting around congestion, and also increases safety with collision avoidance and failure warning mechanisms.

This expectation for vehicle cleverness is also present for any organization managing fleets. With hundreds or thousands of deployed vehicles and crews, organizations need to be able to know where each vehicle is, be warned of mechanical issues, and, in short, be able to view and manage the fleet as a whole without having to rely on occasional verbal input from each vehicle driver. Here again, IoT provides powerful tools to combine individual vehicle monitoring (for the benefit of the vehicle crew) with central reporting to help the fleet management team automate maintenance requirement warnings, locate each vehicle and optimize team rotations, and use big data to manage the fleet operations efficiently.

Mass Transit

Mass transit is typically intra-urban—that is, within a city. It is a collective transport system that connects different locations of a given urban area. The term *urban* can refer to a single city or to a group of neighboring cities that are close enough to share a common collective transport infrastructure. Mass transit can refer to buses, tramways, trolleys, subways, and above-ground trains and light rails. As such, mass transit includes trains. However, the rail subsector is treated in a distinct section of this chapter because inter-city trains include both cargo and passenger trains (while intra-city trains typically primarily carry passengers), and also because urban mass transit in general includes challenges that are not always visible for rail transport alone.

- **Trains always run on tracks.** Mass transit (buses, tramways) may share the street with other vehicles and are therefore often subject to the same challenges relative to congestion. Leaving your car at home to take the bus offers limited incentive if the bus is stuck in the same congested traffic that you would experience in your car.

- **Trains cover multiple realities.** Some of them travel between cities. Mass transit systems (including light rails, metros, buses, and so on) travel over shorter distances but with a much higher frequency. An incident on one mass transit line can be disruptive to passengers in multiple other lines, thus affecting the travel of potentially millions of people. By contrast, an incident on an inter-city track is likely to affect only traffic on that path.

- **Mass transit passengers may use more than one transit system or one transit line when they travel.** For example, traveling on a suburban train and then on a bus (or vice versa) can be a normal part of a daily commute. Basically, the traveler's concern is to find the fastest route between two points. When events affect the efficiency of one system, the traveler must be able to evaluate alternate solutions and adapt in real time. In contrast, inter-city lines typically offer fewer alternative options between two given points.

- **Sizing is an issue.** A train that travels daily between two cities is likely to have the same approximate quantity of cargo and/or number of passengers each day, with predictable peaks and valleys (such as for weekdays vs. weekends and holidays). By contrast, an intra-urban mass transit system will also have well-known peaks (business peak hours), but external events can suddenly change the load on the system. A concert in a particular location may bring thousands of new passengers. A disruption on another mass transit system may re-route thousands of travelers to a parallel system. In this context, planning for load and frequency is much more difficult than for inter-city trains. The transport administration must react in real time to maintain the efficiency of the system.

Rail

Seen from the outside, the rail industry seems to be quite simple in principle. You lay track to connect places. Once the tracks are laid, you position trains at regular intervals in specific directions. Proper timing is all it takes to ensure customer satisfaction and safety.

Reality is a bit more complex, however. For example, the United States tends to prefer air travel to trains. Yet, the United States includes 140,000 miles of track across the country.[5] These are inter-city tracks (and don't include city transportation) that are used by thousands of trains every day, belonging to multiple companies, carrying passengers or freight or both. Even with the best timing tables, things become complex as soon as an unexpected event occurs (for example, an animal or tree on the tracks, a broken piece of equipment forcing a train to stop). Even without accounting for the unexpected, coordinating times and positions is complex. Complexity increases even more where tracks intersect.

Looking at an individual train also shows this complexity. Suppose you are in charge of operating a train daily between two cities that are not too far apart. Passengers or cargo are expected to leave on time and arrive on time. Freight customers or passengers should not worry about weather conditions. The train should achieve the same performance when heavy rain falls, when the track gets covered by blocks of ice, or when twisters or hurricanes blow objects on the path. They also should not worry about mischievous individuals positioning objects on the tracks or stealing signals or cables.

Signals have been used along the track as long as trains have been running. These signals can let the engineer know if the train is approaching a junction or crossing, and different signal colors indicate whether the junction barriers are up or down. With magnetometers, these signals can also detect a passing train and remain on "other train close by" warning for a specific duration.

Making sure a train gets to its destination safely and on time involves the coordination of multiple signals and systems. A major challenge is to ensure the efficiency of all these systems and to make sure that the information is available in a coordinated manner. If a signal is missing or defective, how will the maintenance team know? What should the locomotive engineer do? If a train has to stop because of an issue on the track, should the train behind get this information in order to stop? If the track issue requires heavy repairs, can the trains be routed to a possible alternate path around the affected segment? For such purposes, IoT can dramatically improve the safety and efficiency of operations, tracking the positions of trains and their speed, and collecting data on the state of the tracks, signals, power lines, and other infrastructure elements along the tracks. Having a real-time view into the state of the rail infrastructure considerably reduces the risks of delays or accidents.

If these concerns appear at the scale of a single train, imagine how complex they get when brought to the level of the entire journey. Rail is usually only one part of the journey of goods. Cargo needs to be delivered on time, or the entire supply chain may be affected.

Similarly, a passenger getting to a train station expects an up-to-date and accurate train timetable (which takes into account the "unexpected events of the day" that could not have been compensated for) and a planner option to choose the best alternative, if needed. Once onboard, the passenger also expects a variety of services that go beyond simple transportation (for example, working and clean toilets, food, comfortable temperature, Internet connectivity). As a result, the train industry faces multiple challenges: Ensure passenger safety, run trains on schedule despite any unexpected events, and offer an onboard passenger experience of high enough quality and comfort that travelers will want to take the train again. IoT can be used to track goods, offer a real-time view into the journey (delays, expected arrival, and so on), and also help optimize the travel experience by tracking and reporting the onboard equipment conditions (from defective toilet alarms to number of sandwiches sold) to allow efficient and targeted maintenance at the next stop.

Challenges for Transportation Operators and Users

When you think about the challenges of public and private transportation, you can see that there are different actors, operating at different scales, with different needs.

The users are the first field-level actors. When you get in your car, you want to have a comfortable, predictable, and efficient journey. Your car has to function correctly. (Despite what romantic movies may try to tell you, a car breakdown is usually not a pleasant experience.) When elements of your car are wearing out or on the verge of failure, you want to be informed before the failure occurs. Sensors can provide a clear view of your car's condition. Intelligent algorithms can anticipate wear and warn you long before breakdown. As you start a journey, you also want to have an idea of the travel duration and conditions, including traffic, road status, and weather. Your car has to be able to operate in comfortable conditions in (almost) any weather. If traffic slows your journey, your car's system should be able to inform you (before traffic gets heavy) and offer alternate options. In short, you need your car to provide information about its own operational state, anticipate its degradation, and compensate for changing external conditions. You also need information about the journey and the environment where the journey takes place. With IoT, your car can communicate with the roadways infrastructure, be warned about any approaching issue (accident, road blocks, and so on), and also provide you with a view of the expected journey (travel time, weather conditions, and so on).

What is true at the scale of a single driver is also true at the scale of an entire fleet. Imagine that you are running a cable TV company, a power utility, or any other company with a fleet of vehicles. You also need to be able to tell your customers how long it is going to take for the truck to reach them and incorporate traffic density into each crew's daily workload, based on time and location of travel. The concerns of an individual driver get multiplied by the number of vehicles you have to manage. Being able to track each vehicle in real time or near real time solves this challenge. With smart objects, a vehicle can also report tools and equipment levels to ensure that the crew is always optimally equipped to perform the next mission. If a required tool is missing, the vehicle can be routed to a collection point, or a nearby crew can be sent instead while the other team is routed to another mission for which the vehicle has the appropriate equipment.

The same type of needs appears when you, as an individual traveler, embark on a mass transit journey. In this case, you are free from the need to care about the vehicle. The transit operators are in charge of the journey. Although the state of the transit vehicle does affect your journey, you do not need to care directly about the vehicle; you can just complain if the operators did not take care of it, and the vehicle breaks down. But you still want to have information about the journey (such as transit time and conditions).

Mass transit operators inherit the same worries regarding vehicle state and general traffic conditions. They also operate a fleet and have the same fleet management concerns as private organizations. However, they also operate at a higher level than private drivers. Degradations of driving conditions not only affect many of the vehicles they operate, they also potentially generate more pollution and reduce customer satisfaction. As mass transit is more effective than individual vehicles (in terms of quantity of passengers transported over units of road or track space), these operators have to balance the quantity of vehicles on the road to the cost of operating the vehicles. They also have to balance the travel lines and collect as many passengers as possible, thus maintaining an economically sound solution (if that is their mandate) while being useful to the city population.

At an even higher level, cities either operate the mass transit system directly or have a stake in the mass transit organizations. As such, city authorities (and often citizens who vote on new funding for public transit) have a say in which new tracks need to be built, which street will be made available, and over which travel path, to complement other transportation systems. At this scale, transportation management is not about individual vehicles. It is about congestion and coexistence. More mass transit lines reduce congestion, but only if they fulfill the needs of the citizens. (A transit line between locations that no citizens care about is just a waste of resources.) Incentives to use transit systems can be developed using toll systems and revenue from public transport fares. When congestion occurs, emergency vehicles must have a way to circulate through traffic. Just behind them, mass transit vehicles should have better access to the infrastructure to favor mass transit over individual vehicles.

The same preoccupations are visible for trains. The main differences lie in the distance traveled and alternate transportation options. If a bus breaks down, you may be able to get on another bus or take the subway. If a train breaks down between two cities, passengers and cargo are stuck, sometimes for hours. The effect of issues on the passenger experience is worse. Customer satisfaction is a higher concern with trains than with urban mass transit because there are no immediate alternatives when things go wrong. However, it is much easier for a traveler to decide to use another option for travel (drive or fly) the next time. Cargo customers are not as flexible as passengers, but they may also study alternate transport options if freight is notoriously delayed on a given route. In urban mass transit, travelers may decide to drive instead of use public transit, but immediate alternative options (another bus or the subway) are usually more readily available to limit the extent of the poor traveler experience. As a result, train operators are usually very sensitive about customer experience and travel reliability. This does not mean, of course, that mass transit operators are not sensitive to the traveler experience. They compete every day against alternative transport options and also focus heavily on the passenger experience to maintain and improve their revenue stream.

IoT Use Cases for Transportation

For all the needs just described, IoT brings formidable advantages: collecting local data, sharing this data over any distance, and providing tools to process the collected data in order to better optimize vehicles and the entire transportation infrastructure.

People can optimize resources available to them, but localized information in possession of individual drivers is not always sufficient. Sharing this information over radios and other communication means still provides a limited view of the overall conditions.

The story is well known (in the somewhat self-contained circles of mass transit optimization specialists) of a large city in South America whose authorities thought of delegating the task of optimizing public bus travel efficiency to individual drivers. They thought that because the drivers are in the street, they have a better view on local conditions than any higher authority. The mass transit administration therefore enacted a rule that would tie the driver's pay to his or her performance. Performance would be measured in the time taken to travel each bus from the start to the end of the line and in the number of passengers transported along the way. The reasoning was that this system would encourage drivers to help expedite boarding and alighting of passengers and to find ways around local congestions.

However, stating the objectives that way had a different effect than what was desired. After just a few weeks, buses stopped following the intended bus routes. Drivers would simply take shortcuts, bypassing congested streets—and also bypassing the stops they knew had small numbers of passengers (and not caring about the passengers' expectation to stop at smaller stops), and would engage in road wars and races to be the first to get to large bus stops, where they knew they would collect the largest numbers of passengers. The drivers did fulfill the mandate as specified, but the overall gain on mass transit efficiency was not achieved.

IoT provides a better solution because information can be local and global at the same time, and it can be made available to multiple stakeholders, who can all benefit from the knowledge gained from the system.

Connected Cars

One location where IoT can alleviate transportation challenges is obviously the vehicle itself. Modern cars are highly computerized, with hundreds of sensors to assess everything from tire pressure to a loose gas cap. This information is displayed on the dashboard to help the driver have a better travel experience. This is an example of smart objects but not IoT. One limitation of this implementation is that the information is available only locally. Therefore, it cannot be correlated with information coming from other vehicles to draw a better and larger picture. If you get a flat tire, it is an unfortunate local event. But if 20 cars over the past hour got a flat tire in the same area, then there is a major issue on this portion of the road. If you are traveling toward that zone, you would want to be warned in advance and probably have an onboard system suggest an alternate route. The same logic applies when your car slips over black ice, when your onboard radar detects a pocket of mist, or when knowledge of any other local condition would benefit other drivers.

IoT allows smart objects to communicate and to deliver valuable services based on that communication. Any information discovered by your car's sensors can be shared with systems outside your car. When the information is valid locally, it should be made available locally. When other cars approach a given area, they are warned about congestion due to a local accident, slippery conditions because of oil spilled on the pavement, or difficult traffic due to a broken street light or faulty railroad junction system. This communication implies that there must be a car-to-car, or vehicle-to-vehicle (V2V), information exchange system (one that protects your privacy while providing useful information) and also a vehicle-to-infrastructure (V2I) information exchange system so that local information can be made available where it is relevant.

When the information is relevant solely to your car, it can be made locally available but may be shared with third-party systems. For example, getting a warning that your car is due for an oil change is great, but wouldn't it be better if your dashboard also popped up possible appointment slots available at your local car care provider? Similarly, if your car maker launches a recall for a defective piece of equipment, wouldn't it be useful to get an indication on your dashboard if your car is affected? Such communication requires an always-on connection between the vehicle and the Internet.

The reason apps on your phone are able to provide optimal navigation is because your phone is connected to the Internet, and traffic data is updated in real time. However, your phone has no connection to the car's onboard systems. Connecting the car directly to the

Internet or to your phone brings all the advantages of connectivity to your travel experience. Applications are endless. For example, your car manufacturer can map weather forecasts to a very granular level and dynamically adjust car engine settings to adapt to local conditions and save fuel. In a more palpable manner, startups have begun making smart windshields and smart headlights. The lights blink very fast (50 times per second), faster than the eye can detect. For the driver, there is continuous light on the road. At the same time, the windshield is covered by a transparent screen that can turn black. When two equipped cars face each other, they synchronize their lights and screens. When the lights of the car coming in your direction are on, your screen is darkened, and it becomes transparent when the lights blink off. Because the blinking rate is faster than persistence of vision, the result is that both drivers see the road lightened by the beams, but neither of them get blinded by the oncoming lights. This technology optimizes the driving experience for your eyes and greatly improves safety. Inventions of a similar nature are too many to list, but all of them share the same concept: Your car can communicate with the infrastructure and other cars to exchange information that makes your travel experience easier.

Note   For more applications of connected cars, visit http://local.iteris.com/cvria/html/applications/applications.html.

Connected Fleets

Connected vehicles improve more than individual drivers' journeys. Imagine a storm leaving thousands of households without power. As explained in Chapter 11, "Utilities," the electricity company knows in real time all the points where power lines are ruptured. Hundreds of repair trucks are deployed. With IoT solutions, the dispatch center also knows in real time where each truck is. It knows if a truck is moving toward a rupture point or if the bucket is deployed and the crew is working on a repair. The state of each truck is closely monitored. Armed with this information, the utility company knows exactly the progress of the emergency repair operation. Video cameras can also monitor a truck's surroundings to help assess the need for additional dispatch (to clear the road, add a pole, and so on) and ensure the safety of operations. The dispatch center can redirect trucks where they are most needed, manage maintenance and crew breaks, supply or replace power cables or other equipment, and so on. The efficiency difference is massive. The same benefits apply to any other fleet. A taxi company can optimize the cab density at the scale of an entire city, based on measured customer density, weather, and travel patterns. A car rental company can track cars to optimize yard operations or even recover a lost vehicle. The same benefits apply to bus operators or any other company managing a fleet of vehicles.

Infrastructure and Mass Transit

At a larger level, an information exchange system means the infrastructure can communicate with vehicles, collect information from them (for example, location, speed, vehicle operational state) based on hundreds of sensors, and relay it to the Internet—and it can also send the vehicles information about local conditions. When the infrastructure itself includes sensors, the information can be richer (including weather, detected upcoming traffic density, accidents, and so on). This information is already available in multiple way-finding apps. These apps collect information from multiple users. This information is sent to the cloud, where useful patterns can be derived. Congestion zones and times can be measured and returned to the app to display the expected travel time. However, these apps are limited in terms of the benefits to local users. They can tell you the current state of the traffic, and they can incorporate predictive traffic condition changes and modify their predictions accordingly, but they cannot modify the states of the roads or coordinate the responses sent to multiple users. With IoT, information about each car, as well as programmed travel from each navigation system in each car, can be analyzed in a coordinated fashion in the cloud. The result is better traffic anticipation that can also return different information to different users. If 1000 users are navigating toward the same congested segment, IoT can dynamically suggest different routes to different users to avoid congestion in the first place (instead of simply telling you that congestion is already there and suggesting rerouting at that time). Such a dynamic system can be coupled with dynamic adaptive toll and high-occupancy-vehicle (HOV) rules. (In many cities, HOV lanes are reserved for vehicles carrying two or more occupants.) For an individual driver driving to work every day, the result may be a slightly different route suggested from the navigation system each day but a smoother commute involving overall less congestion.

This IoT intelligence also has a direct effect on a mass transit user. When walking toward a bus station, a text message to a special number (mentioning the bus ID) or a phone app can display the closest bus stop location and estimated wait time. When waiting at the bus stop, a smart panel can display the expected wait time until the next bus and an estimation of the travel time to any destination. This estimation is real time and smart (based on current traffic conditions and also factoring in the anticipated changes in traffic density in the upcoming hours). At the scale of a city, a journey planner informs you about the travel conditions across the city and across all transit systems and can suggest the best route to your destination. Many other IoT use cases allow for better management of city congestion. (Refer to Chapter 12 for more examples.)

Another effect of IoT on vehicle-to-infrastructure communication is increased safety. For example, a major contributor to car accidents in congested traffic is stop-and-go conditions (when traffic runs at moderate or high speed and then suddenly comes to a stop and becomes fast again a bit farther down the road). The causes of stop-and-go are well known: traffic density (merging lanes), roadside distractions (car accidents, unusual phenomena on the side of the road), inclement weather (patches of rain or mist), poorly coordinated street lights, and reduced lane sizes. Some elements are structural to sections of a road (merging lanes, reduced lane width), and others are occasional. The combined effect of these elements can create stop-and-go effects for many kilometers.

A common way to reduce stop-and-go traffic is to carefully regulate the flow of cars entering the various sections of the road. An optimal injection rate speeds up the overall road traffic, resulting in a more fluid flow (and more cars injected to and traveled on the road per unit of distance and time). IoT coupled with machine learning is a formidable combination for achieving this goal. Traffic density information collected from sensors in the vehicles and on the infrastructure—for example, vehicle-counting cameras, pressure cables recording vehicles and speed, or optic cables in the asphalt that can measure traffic density by estimating the deviation of the light beam due to local vehicle pressure on the asphalt—can dynamically adapt to local conditions and coordinate lights to solve stop-and-go issues and increase overall car flow. At the same time, a sudden drop in traffic fluidity (which may indicate an accident) can trigger an alarm in traffic authority control centers. This alarm can be relayed to emergency organizations, allowing emergency vehicles to be dispatched faster. At the same time, a circle of awareness can be drawn around the accident area, with multiple benefits:

- Approaching drivers are warned about the accident zone (infrastructure feedback into the vehicle smart system).

- Road entrance ramp traffic lights are adjusted to let fewer cars per minute access the affected section.

- Drivers who are near but outside the zone can dynamically receive alternate route suggestions. This has to be done in a centralized, and therefore intelligent, manner. Today, your navigation app can alert you if the road ahead has a slowdown. However, thousands of drivers around you receive exactly the same information and choose exactly the same suggested alternate route, resulting in no overall benefit. Centralizing the system allows for live monitoring and smart distribution of alternate routes; several alternate routes can be distributed for re-routing load balancing.

- Emergency service vehicles can ignore the redundant calls they receive reporting the accident. When an accident occurs on a busy road, hundreds and sometimes thousands of drivers call emergency services to report the accident, and emergency services must determine if each call is about a new accident or about an event for which teams have already been dispatched. The circle of awareness can be used to associate similar and overlapping calls from within the circle to the same event. At the same time, smart sensors can detect if another accident happens nearby, thus simplifying event de-duplication.

Roadside sensors can do much more than just count cars. Air quality can be measured, and so can weather conditions. This information can be relayed to central systems for monitoring and alerting. Other sensors can be implemented into the road infrastructure and objects to improve maintenance and safety. For example, sensors in the road can measure the amount of water penetrating the asphalt and evaluate the wear of the surface. On bridges, structural sensors can evaluate the strain and stresses on structural steel members, and tiltmeters can measure the settlement and relative displacement of a bridge and the tilt of piers and abutments. Accelerometers can measure the vibrations and dynamic responses to traffic, wind, or even seismic activity. Figure 13-2 shows an example of these sensors applied to a bridge.

Figure 13-2 *Smart Objects Monitoring a Bridge*

All this information can be reported to roadway maintenance centers, where proactive maintenance can be planned before disruptive events result in accidents or blocked roads. The same types of sensors can be installed on the sides of mountain roads. In short, IoT allows transit authorities to not only monitor and optimize traffic conditions but also proactively monitor the infrastructure.

This information also implies fog and cloud computing. A bridge may incorporate multiple sensors. Not all of them need to report detailed information. A simple "green" status may be a sufficient summary most of the time. Similarly, a standard modern car has multiple sensors generating data. Part of this data is significant only for the driver and should stay in the car. Part of this data is only locally significant and should be processed by roadside fog computing systems. Only the part of the information that is relevant to larger systems (car data for your manufacturer, for example) should be relayed to the cloud (with or without preprocessing in the fog).

With IoT, individual drivers can benefit from a safer and more predictable journey. Traffic authorities can better regulate the flow of vehicles and better manage the roadways infrastructure. These IoT solutions also benefit bus intra-city travelers by providing accurate transit information, smart maps, and journey planners.

IoT applied to mass transportation vehicles can also massively improve travel experience. Monitoring a bus's performance is an obvious use case, similar to car preventive maintenance. The same logic also applies to railways. For example, many types of trains are powered by electric cables hanging over the track (or, for subways, positioned near the track). Any damage to a cable or any object on the power line can eventually result in trains stopping. Fast passing trains can increase the damage (or break the object, which then becomes a hazard on the track). In the past, traditional rail maintenance was all about visual inspection, which takes time and may render portions of the railway unusable (while inspectors slowly and carefully examine each meter of power line). With IoT, smart sensors are installed on the power bar on top of the train (called a pantograph). As soon as the contact to the power line varies from acceptable limits (based on multiple trips used as a baseline), the sensor automatically sends an alert with the exact GPS coordinate, allowing a maintenance crew to be dispatched before damage becomes severe.

With the same logic, smart sensors can be installed on the wheels of locomotives and cars to process the sound of the wheels on the track and identify any abnormality that may indicate wheel or track wear. Locomotive performance is measured in real time and compared from one trip to the next for track maintenance needs. Inter-car connection systems measure the next-car pull force to track abnormalities (an engaged break, an abnormal cargo load, and so on). On the side of the track, detectors can read information sent by tags installed on cars. As the train passes, each car is identified, along with its order in the train (train cars have a tendency to be swapped from one train to the other, making individual car tracking a very challenging task), and also useful data such as the level of water available in the car toilet reservoir, the details of food sold, or identifiers for the carried cargo. This information is communicated in real time to the control center, where proactive action can be ordered (for example, car inspected, toilet reservoir refilled at the next stop, food supply replenished, cargo location tracked).

Other sensors on the trackside can observe the environment and compare it to known parameters. Such systems can measure water table levels (which affect rail embankments if the ground becomes waterlogged) and landslides, and they can also compare the picture of the passing train to averages and thus detect unusual side bending or other abnormalities. Junctions are also a key location for IoT, and sensors can be used at junctions to detect an approaching train (along with its speed), a failing signal or barrier, or a vehicle on the track, and generate proactive alarms or emergency stops.

IoT can also be extended to the carriage itself, and these applications span across all mass transit systems. Cameras linked to big data processing engines can detect crowd density and can anticipate peak hours, and they are also able to detect abnormal movements that are categorized automatically (unstable cargo load, aggression, accident, fall, and so on) and can trigger the right alarm for the right team. Intersection with social media is used often to predict traffic on particular lines and sections. At a simpler level, this data can be used to provide optimal journey planners. These planners help predict more than the duration of the journey; they can also predict the conditions of the journey that affect the customer's satisfaction and can impact business. Not having a seat in a train or having to be pressed into a crowd in the subway or a bus is likely to yield negative feedback on mass transit. Being able to use big data and analytics to plan for the right density of trains or buses is key to improving travel conditions. But just being able to proactively inform the traveler is already a giant step. In general, travelers are less likely to feel negatively about conditions of their journey if they are warned in advance about those conditions.

For all these use cases, and many more invented each day, IoT helps improve safety and improve comfort on the journey.

An IoT Architecture for Transportation

It is clear that IoT for transportation covers different needs and therefore requires different architectures, depending on factors such as the mode of transport. These architectures intersect and overlap in several places, including the following:

- **Individual vehicles** need an architecture to exchange information with the rest of the world. Range can be short or long, with information being local or destined for the cloud. In most cases, both short- and long-range communications are used, depending on the purpose. Similarly, some information is processed locally (fog computing), while some information is sent to and processed in the cloud. Communication also needs to happen between vehicles and between the vehicles and the infrastructure.

- **Mass transit** systems using roadways (buses, tramways, and so on) benefit from an individual vehicle architecture. This architecture can be globally labeled IoT for roadways. Road mass transit organizations also need a more global architecture to manage fleets (for example, a maintenance yard) and to manage or react at a larger scale to changing road conditions.

- **Railways** need their own architecture to allow for traffic, safety, and fleet management. Inter-city railways display a particular sensitivity to the onboard passenger experience as travel durations are longer than intra-city travels.

IoT Technologies for Roadways

An IoT architecture for roadways starts at the vehicle level and allows communication with roadside systems and other vehicles. In the IoT world, this communication is called V2V (vehicle-to-vehicle) and V2I (vehicle-to-infrastructure), or sometimes V2X (vehicle-to-everything) to also include V2P (vehicle-to-pedestrian), V2N (vehicle-to-network), and other variants. Because the vehicle movement is not constrained (in tracks, for example), this communication necessarily relies on wireless technologies. Several technologies are possible, which cover different use cases.

Bluetooth

For short-range communications (for example, vehicle to passenger smart phone), Bluetooth is the technology of choice. Most of the time, class 2 radios are used.

Note   Class 1 radios achieve a range of up to 1 m, class 2 radios 10 meters, and class 3 radios 100 meters.

In some rare cases, class 3 radios are installed to allow V2I communication. In this case, a common application is for traffic lights to interact with public transport systems (emergency vehicles or mass transit) and privilege those vehicles over the rest of the traffic. This application is known as traffic signal prioritization (TSP). Although it can use Bluetooth, a more common technology for TSP is DSRC, detailed later in this chapter. Another application is class 3 Bluetooth radios installed on the side of the road that detect and read the unique MAC addresses of Bluetooth systems in passing cars. This allows for vehicle counting and speed estimation on the equipped section of the road. Although Bluetooth class 3 allows this type of exchange, Bluetooth is a minor player outside the vehicle (initially because of range limitations).

Cellular/LTE

Cellular technologies are used for some V2X applications, but they are more common for roadside-to-infrastructure communications (sensors and objects installed in the road or on roadside objects communicating their status with the network). (Refer to Chapter 4, "Connecting Smart Objects," for detailed discussion and examples of cellular technologies applicable to this space.) Notice that cellular technologies applied to IoT typically use low bandwidth to achieve a longer range.

Another technology worth mentioning is WiMAX (802.16e). Although WiMAX does have its place in some last-mile or backhaul applications for IoT, and although it could fit well in the IoT for roadways space (as the specifications in Figure 13-3 show), it failed to get initial wide adoption in this space. With the competition of other technologies, the future of WiMAX for V2X is unclear.

An Introduction to DSRC and WAVE

V2X aims at facilitating vehicle-to-infrastructure communications and leverages several elements and protocols, such as DSRC, IEEE P1609, and WAVE. These protocols are explained later in this chapter. They distinguish three elements working together:

- **OBU (onboard unit):** The system onboard the vehicle

- **RSU (roadside unit):** The system on the side of the road that communicates with the passing OBU

- **WAVE interface:** The radio and communication system

Both OBU and RSU include a WAVE interface, allowing them to communicate.

V2V and V2I communications are possible, as shown in Figure 13-3. DSRC also allows a vehicle to relay information from another vehicle to a nearby RSU.

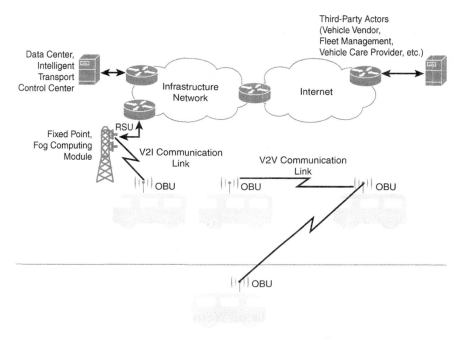

Figure 13-3 *DSRC General Communication Architecture*

Communication can occur through several possible channels. At 90 km/h, establishing communications between a vehicle and a roadside system may be challenging. In most cases, the vehicle first needs to be aware of the presence of the roadside RSU. To simplify operations, the RSU uses a predefined static channel (channel 178 for DSRC in the United States) to announce to passing OBUs at 100 ms intervals what applications it supports on which channel. There are two types of applications: safety and non-safety (detailed later in the chapter). The OBU listens on the static channel (178), authenticates the RSU digital signature, executes safety applications first (if any), and then switches channels and executes non-safety applications. The OBU then returns to channel 178 to listen for the next RSU announcements.

The OBU matches the messages it receives from the RSU and other vehicles OBUs with its own GPS location and trajectory to calculate the position of the RSU or of other emitting OBUs. The RSU can also send specialized messages. Typical and common messages are as follows:

- **Traveler information:** Curve speed, height restriction, icy road conditions, collision ahead, red light on, rail crossing, work zone warning, road hazard warning, and so on

- **Non-DSRC vehicle approaching:** A vehicle that is not smart and will not warn or be warned about other vehicles' positions and trajectories, which means an extra margin needs to be taken

- **Pedestrian alert:** Pedestrian with a DSRC-enabled smart phone detected

Each channel is designated for specific use cases. For example, channel 184 is used exclusively for high-power, long-distance communications for public safety applications.

Emergency services typically use channel 184 to warn other vehicles of their approach. Public safety vehicles also use this channel to get green lights for street lights up to half a kilometer away. Such cases mandate that the vehicle be equipped with DSRC equipment and that the communication occur within less than half a kilometer. With DSRC, channel 172 is used exclusively for V2V safety communications (accident avoidance and mitigation). On channel 172, each vehicle broadcasts its core state information in a basic safety message (BSM) 10 times per second. Upon reception of the BSM, each other vehicle in range builds a model of each neighbor's trajectory, assesses potential collision risks, and warns the driver (or takes control) in case of emergency. Typical applications are as follows:

■ A vehicle ahead of you (directly in front of you or a few vehicles ahead) stops or brakes. That car's OBU broadcasts the stopped or brake status, allowing following vehicles to evaluate the proximity and risk of collision and automatically apply brakes, even if the driver does not see the stopped vehicle yet. This situation is illustrated in Figure 13-4.

Forward Collision Warning (FCW)

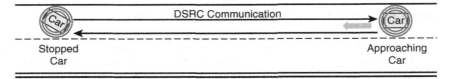

Emergency Electronic Brake Lights (EEBL)

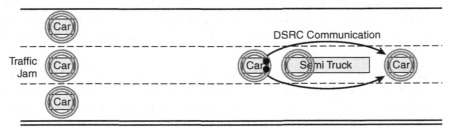

Figure 13-4   *DSRC Emergency Brake Warnings*

■ You want to change lanes. From the neighboring car's OBU messages, your car knows that there is a vehicle in your blind spot and displays an alarm when you turn the steering wheel.

Similarly, you want to pass a slower vehicle, and turn the wheel to change lanes. Your OBU detects approaching cars' signals in the other travel direction and displays an alarm (or takes control for collision avoidance). These cases are illustrated in Figure 13-5.

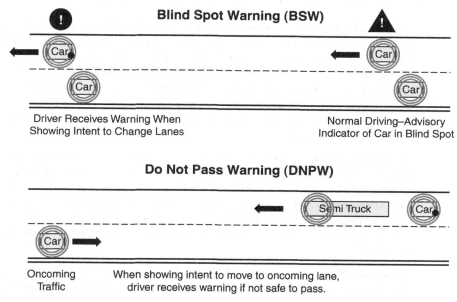

Figure 13-5 *DSRC Blind Spot and Do-Not-Pass Warning System*

■ You approach a road intersection with low visibility because of buildings. Your OBU already has a map of positions and trajectories of other vehicles and can help avoid collisions.

These applications are obvious for the safety of vehicles on the road. However, IoT for connected roadways is about more than just safety. Private apps can be implemented to ask the RSU to relay data to the Internet. The RSU is in this case is just an IP forwarder (it does not necessarily process the data). The example of vehicle diagnostics forwarded to the car maker is provided in the previous section, but many other applications are possible. V2I applications fulfill many requirements of fleet management. In the example provided above of the utility company deploying a fleet after a storm, V2I allows the trucks to communicate through RSUs on the side of the road with the utility company control center to complement direct cellular connections. When a vehicle is sent for maintenance, it automatically uploads its status and log data (service record, recalls, past maintenance, and so on) to better target the maintenance tasks at hand. When coming back to base, trucks can upload their records (speeds, load details, travel duration, and so on). Identifying approaching vehicles may also be very useful for restricted parking access control or even automatic toll collections. Similarly, a rental car company can track each vehicle on the parking lot, along with mileage, fuel level, and many other relevant information, expediting the rental operations.

DSRC/WAVE Protocol and Architecture

The previous section focuses on DSRC. However, mainstream solutions for V2X also use 802.11. You will also read different terms, such as Wi-Fi, 802.11p, WAVE, DSRC, and ASTM Standard E2213-03. Clarifying their relationship might be useful:

- **Dedicated Short Range Communication (DSRC):** This is the name of a band allocated in the 5.9 GHz region of the spectrum by regulatory bodies around the world for the needs of the vehicle industry, to be used by intelligent transportation systems (ITSs). The band is 75 MHz wide in the United States (allocated by the US Federal Communications Commission [FCC]). The band size is slightly different in other regulatory domains. However, worldwide allocations are in the same region of the spectrum, and the same radio and antenna can be used for any of these regulatory domains' implementations.

- **ASTM Standard E2213-03:** The American Society for Testing and Materials (ASTM) developed this standard. Although the name indicates this has an American origin, ASTM is in fact a worldwide nonprofit organization that creates standards. ASTM realized that the region of the spectrum allocated by the FCC for DSRC in 1999 was also used by Wi-Fi. ASTM therefore modified 802.11 to adapt it to vehicle communications. The result of this work was published in 2006 as ASTM Standard E2213-03.

- **WAVE (802.11p):** This is an amendment to the 802.11 standard. 802.11 is defined by the IEEE, so ASTM work could not possibly be integrated directly into 802.11. In 2004, the IEEE 802.11 working group created the 802.11p task group to adapt 802.11 to vehicular communications. The group, named Wireless Access for the Vehicular Environment (WAVE), published its amendment in 2010.

- **IEEE P1556 and P1609:** This is a family of protocols related to vehicular communication. While the 802.11 group was working on WAVE, the idea of transmitting information between vehicles and infrastructure raised legitimate concerns about privacy. Another IEEE group created P1556 (Standard for Security and Privacy of Vehicle/Roadside Communication Including Smart Card Communication). This standard was renumbered IEEE 1609.2 and integrated into the larger P1609 family of protocols for WAVE listed in Table 13-1.

Table 13-1 *IEEE P1609 Family of Standards Relevant for DSRC*

Standard Number	Standard Name
IEEE P1609.0	Draft Standard for Wireless Access in Vehicular Environments (WAVE)—Architecture
IEEE P1609.1	Trial Use Standard for Wireless Access in Vehicular Environments (WAVE)—Resource Manager
IEEE P1609.2	Trial Use Standard for Wireless Access in Vehicular Environments (WAVE)—Security Services for Applications and Management Messages

Standard Number	Standard Name
IEEE P1609.3	Trial Use Standard for Wireless Access in Vehicular Environments (WAVE)—Networking Services
IEEE P1609.4	Trial Use Standard for Wireless Access in Vehicular Environments (WAVE)—Multi-Channel Operations
IEEE P1609.11	Over-the-Air Data Exchange Protocol for Intelligent Transportation Systems (ITS)

The relationship between these various standards is a bit complex. For example, WAVE is based on 802.11p, but its P1609 approach is concerned with wireless access for vehicular environments in general, not just the first two layers. Figure 13-6 summarizes the interactions between these standards and the OSI model.

OSI Model

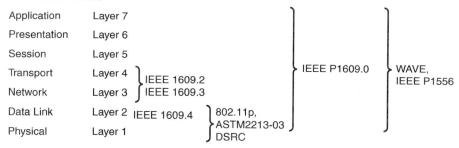

Figure 13-6   *DSRC, WAVE, 802.11p, IEEE 1609, and the OSI Model*

The Society of Automotive Engineers (SAE) also defines standards that apply to WAVE. SAE J2735 defines the messaging schema implemented over DSRC to enable V2I and V2V data exchanges, and SAE J2945 defines the minimum performance requirements for DSRC systems.

Being based on 802.11, DSRC/WAVE communications are half-duplex. 802.11 physical and data link layers are optimized for speeds up to 90 km/h. For vehicular communications, 802.11 was also modified to allow communications without the requirement for an access point. The need to rely on an access point and mandate authentication/association messages is not practical when a vehicle is moving rapidly. Therefore, communications without association are optional but allowed; the concept of a cell, or Basic Service Set (BSS), is still present, if needed. 802.11p builds on previous 802.11 amendments, integrating the concept of QoS and various statistical priorities for different frames types (defined by 802.11e in 2005).

DSRC is driven by local regulatory bodies, such as the Federal Communications Commission (FCC) in the United States; the European Telecommunications Standard Institute (ETSI) in Europe, which works in coordination with the European Committee for Standardization (CEN); and the Association of Radio Industries and Businesses (ARIB) in Japan. Each regulatory body defines the frequencies and radio output power allowed for DSRC.

For example, in the United States, the available spectrum is divided into seven 10 MHz-wide channels (channels 172, 174, 176, 178, 180, 182, and 184), allowing a data rate of 6 to 27 Mbps over a typical range of 300 meters (1000 feet) to 1000 meters (3200 feet). As described in the previous section, channel 178 sits in the middle of the band and is designated the "control channel," and some channels are reserved for specific communication requirements (for example, channel 172 for basic safety messaging).

Other regulatory bodies determine the "rules of the road." For example, in the United States, the National Highway Traffic Safety Administration (NHTSA) determines which vehicle equipment is authorized or mandated on US highways. The agency, driven by the government, is working on new rules that could mandate DSRC in all vehicles by 2020.[6]

DSRC is the primary protocol for V2I communications, but it is not the only protocol you will encounter for vehicle and roadway exchanges. Table 13-2 compares DSRC to other protocols for connected roadways.

Table 13-2   *Protocols for Connected Roadways*

Feature	DSRC/WAVE	Wi-Fi	Cellular	Mobile WiMAX
Data rate	3–27 Mbps	6–54 Mbps	<2 Mbps	1–32 Mbps
Mobility	>90 km/h	<10 km/h	>90 km/h	>90 km/h
Nominal bandwidth	10 MHz	20 MHz	<3 MHz	<10 MHz
Operating band	5.86–5.92 GHz (ITS-RS)	2.4 GHz, 5.2 GHz (ISM)	800 MHz, 1.9 GHz	2.5 GHz
IEEE standard	802.11p (WAVE)	802.11a	N/A	802.16e

Connected Roadways Network Architecture

The basis of IoT for roadways lies in two elements: vehicle equipment and roadside equipment.

The vehicle carries the OBU. The OBU does not operate independently. It needs to collect information from other sensors, such as the vehicle location unit (VLU), also called the automated vehicle location (AVL) unit. The onboard computer needs to process data about the vehicle and send it to the cloud or the other vehicles. Computer-aided dispatch (CAD) is the common name for this function. CAD was initially designed for dispatching vehicles and technicians, but was later extended to include any vehicle data and emergency management software. A ruggedized router is typically needed to connect these various elements.

The roadside features RSUs. As an RSU is also an IP forwarder, it also commonly includes a ruggedized router. The RSU may communicate with the backbone over wireless technologies. However, Ethernet and fiber are common options, as roads, streets, and roadside fixtures are more and more commonly equipped with wired communication possibilities. The RSU can also connect to streetlights. In that case, a traffic signal controller (TSC) with traffic signal priority (TSP) capability is installed either at the RSU or the street light. This functionality allows the emergency vehicles to control the streetlight through DSRC while in range of the RSU.

Several RSU routers can connect to a common ruggedized switch, still in the roadside layer. Data is then transported over the metro network. A common technology for this space is MPLS. Aggregation routers collect traffic from multiple street-level switches. Carrier-grade routers interconnect the core of the network.

Data can then be forwarded to the different actors (car manufacturers, fleet management control center, traffic authorities, emergency services, and so on), where it is processed in the respective data centers. Figure 13-7 summarizes this IoT network architecture for connected roadways.

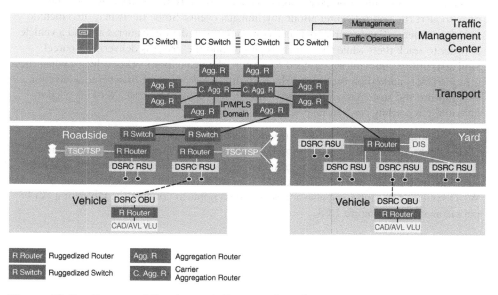

Figure 13-7   *Connected Roadways IoT Network Architecture*

Note that this OBU/RSU architecture is relevant for V2X IoT. When sensors are integrated directly into roadside objects (that is, the roadside objects are not intended to communicate with vehicles but collect their own sets of data, such as bridge vibration monitoring), the amount of data to forward is more limited. In addition, sensors may be located in places where wired connections are not practical. In this case, longer-range technologies such as LoRaWAN are more common. LoRaWAN is discussed in detail in Chapter 4.

Connected Fleet Architecture

The architecture shown in Figure 13-7 is also relevant for fleet management. Even more than for individual vehicles, the onboard CAD/AVL VLU module is a key element. The automatic vehicle location (AVL) system relies on satellite GPS signals and, sometimes, a low-frequency terrestrial radio network. The vehicle position needs to be transmitted to the operations centers. This communication often occurs using GSM. Some organizations (such as utilities and emergency services) can mandate a dual-GSM connection to make sure the vehicle information will always be sent, even in areas of low coverage from one service provider.

Communication has to happen in both directions. That is, the control center also needs to communicate with the driver about the day's mission. This part is achieved with a computer-aided dispatch (CAD) module in the vehicle that allows information exchange between the crew and the control center. This real-time exchange allows for better use of the crew schedule by incorporating events in the schedule as they occur. The CAD also reduces communication costs, and it increases operations security by allowing the crew to alert the control center about any unusual events. Some fleets may also include security cameras. For example, delivery companies may deploy cameras around a vehicle in order to track theft while the vehicle is parked and the driver is delivering a parcel. Similarly, utility companies may need to capture the behavior of other vehicles when the utility truck is parked on the side of the road. In these cases, one or several video cameras capture and store data. When the vehicle comes back to its base, Wi-Fi is used to upload the recordings to a storage server.

With this logic, the vehicle includes a switch that connects the cameras and the crew CAD system (often a tablet or a laptop that can be docked in the vehicle and undocked when the driver needs to process information outside the vehicle). A router incorporates a cellular module and a Wi-Fi client card. This card is used for connection to the yard Wi-Fi system. The router can also act as an access point to connect the tablet or a Wi-Fi phone, as shown in Figure 13-8.

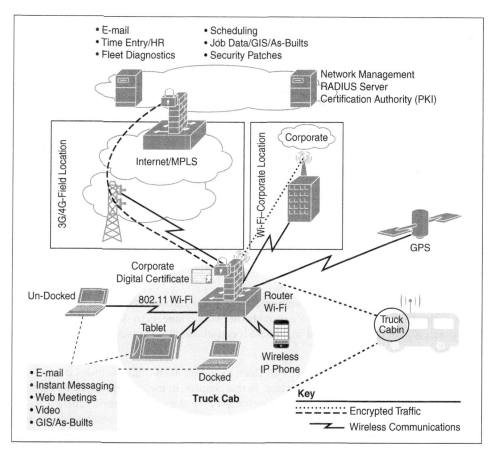

Figure 13-8   *Fleet Management Architecture*

As a result, the communication architecture is slightly different when the vehicle is on the road than when the vehicle is in the yard. The overall architecture is displayed in Figure 13-9.

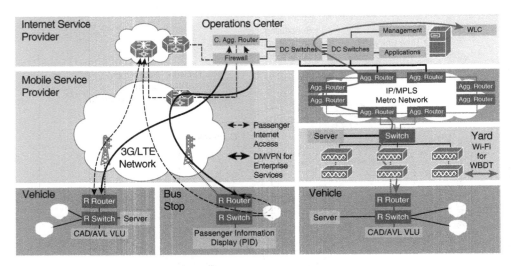

Figure 13-9 *Connected Fleet Architecture*

While the vehicle is on the road, communications occur through cellular connections most of the time. The mobile service provider network connects to the operations center, where data is stored and analyzed and where location and CAD systems interact with each vehicle.

This structure is the same for any type of fleet, including mass transit vehicles (for example, buses), as discussed further later in this chapter. In the case of buses, bus stops are also equipped with cellular connections (or Wi-Fi in dense urban environments) to provide information to the operations center (video-based automated customer count at the bus stop, for example) and return information back to the bus stop (smart panels with wait time, for example).

When the vehicle is in the yard, communication uses Wi-Fi to allow for upload of recorded data (vehicle metrics, onboard camera recordings, and so on). Each yard Wi-Fi access point communicates, typically over an IP/MPLS metro network, with the central operations center, where a central wireless LAN controller manages channels, power, and individual vehicle Wi-Fi connections (authentication, firewalling, and so on).

Management of operations in the control center is a critical element of the IoT chain. The system needs to connect securely to each vehicle's onboard system and retrieve information about the vehicle (fuel, state of various equipment, location, and so on) but also to potentially hundreds of other systems (customer interaction center, ticketing or billing, day planners, fuel or part supply chain, and specialized equipment management systems, such as truck buckets, onboard cameras, and so on). The management system is also likely to interact with smart systems that analyze specific data collected from the field to provide actionable analysis back to the system. Tire and oil pressure are obvious examples, but the system may also monitor how many meters of wire are still available on the vehicle, or monitor biometric values from a driver who is performing hazardous tasks.

While the vehicles communicate primarily with the control center, an Internet connection may also allow for communication with third parties (for example, vehicle part manufacturers or various maintenance contractors).

Fleet management also benefits from V2V communications. A growing example of leveraging these exchanges is platooning. Large 18-wheel trucks do not have a shape optimized for air penetration; rather, their shape is optimized for maximum cargo loading. Therefore, they consume a lot of energy just pushing the truck mass through the air. The air flows back in the form of turbulence a few tens of yards behind the truck, while the air just at the back of the truck moves at the speed of the truck. With platooning, a number of trucks follow one another at close range. This structure has several advantages:

- Only the first truck consumes air-penetration energy. The following trucks stay in the quiet zone and benefit from the first truck's air trail.

- The group of trucks consume less space on the road. They form a compact block instead of a long line.

- With V2V communications, a zero reaction time is implemented for the entire convoy. When the first truck brakes, all the following trucks also brake exactly the same way, immediately. This results in safer travel for the entire convoy.

- As each following truck sets its speed based on the previous one, there is no need for each driver to manually evaluate the previous truck speed, alternating between gas pedal and brake to adapt to changes and terrain. The coordinated exchanges allow the followers to simply mimic the first truck's speed pattern, resulting in lower fuel consumption.

Truck platooning is not autonomous driving, as each truck has a driver. Coordination between trucks through V2V communication optimizes the travel. At the control center, each truck is still monitored, along with individual driver action. However, the entire convoy can act as a single block.

Connected Roadways Security

When driver or personal information is transmitted, security rapidly becomes a primary concern. P1609.2 addresses the security of DSRC for communication with other vehicles and the infrastructure. Although each vehicle has an identifier, this identifier is only locally significant; vehicles around you do not associate your vehicle identifier with the car make and model or with the driver. RSUs also do not forward this identifier. At the same time, the OBU identifies the RSUs (messages on channel 178 using certificate-based authentication) to avoid the injection of malicious messages. Communication from your car to the car maker is encrypted. Inside the car itself, sensor-to-control units are increasingly protected with protocols, such as 802.1Xbx (a protocol that provides MACsec Key Agreement [MKA] protocol extensions to port-based Network Access Control), to avoid any third party connecting to the car's internal communication system from extracting data about your travels or the way you drive.

Extending the Roadways IoT Architecture to Bus Mass Transit

The solution previously described for roadways can be leveraged for mass transit as well, and this section considers buses as an example. In particular, DSRC can be used in the maintenance yard to optimize and expedite fleet maintenance. DSRC can also be used during travel to relay position and trajectory to the control center (along with operational data, such as fuel level, tire pressure, and other elements that may indicate that the bus should be serviced). This position and trajectory data can be used to evaluate traffic congestion and estimated arrival times to bus stops.

However, mass transit expands beyond buses. (The architecture for trains is discussed next.) In addition, buses need expanded capabilities beyond what is offered by DSRC.

Buses do not always travel in cities equipped with RSUs, and they are not always surrounded by other vehicles with OBUs. Therefore, leveraging IoT for buses boils down to fulfilling a need more than implementing a specific technology:

- Buses need to convey information about their location. This is basic GPS data. Technical information about the bus state is also needed.

- Buses commonly use cameras for safety and security purposes. These cameras can store recordings locally and upload via Wi-Fi their recorded content when the bus returns to its depot. However, live feed should also be accessible remotely in case of alarm or emergency.

- Users like to be connected to the Internet while on their journey.

Sending GPS coordinates or basic vehicle status information at regular intervals does not require a DSRC architecture. A simple cellular transmitter can be enough to fulfill this need. When cameras are onboard the bus, cellular can also be used to provide live access (or transmit alarm messages) to a central monitoring station. The central station can also correlate information from other buses to calculate passenger or road traffic load and suggest alternate routes around congested points, when applicable. The purpose here is not to skip stops (although the central management system can calculate that skipping stops may be valuable, as explained shortly) but to avoid roadblocks due to accidents or unusually highly loaded choke points.

A Wi-Fi access point can be installed inside a bus to provide Internet access to passengers. A cellular data connection can relay the traffic over the distances needed. In some cases, where Wi-Fi is deployed along the bus travel path, a workgroup bridge (an access point configured as a client) can be used to connect the bus to the municipality Wi-Fi infrastructure. This Wi-Fi connection can also be used when the bus is in the maintenance yard.

The bus driver may also need to be in contact with the base station. Such communication can use either dedicated radio equipment or leverage a smart phone, either connected directly to the cellular network or over the bus Wi-Fi connection. Therefore, by contrast with the vehicle onboard architecture described in Figures 13-8 and 13-9, a bus's onboard system would be as depicted in Figure 13-10.

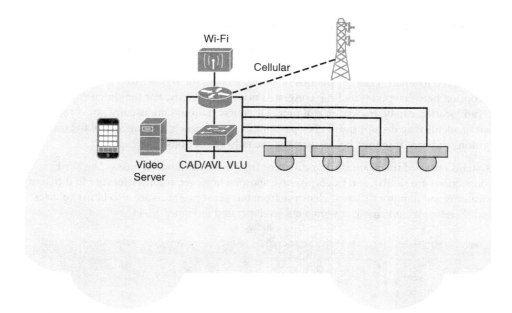

Figure 13-10 *Mass Transit: Bus Onboard System Architecture*

In the case of mass transit, IoT is not limited to the bus itself. A bus stop can be equipped with a ruggedized router to allow for Wi-Fi connection (in case of municipality Wi-Fi access) or cellular connection. A fog compute platform receives updates from the cloud, and a screen displays the calculated time before the next bus (and the one after) so that passengers can decide if they should get onboard a crowded bus or wait for the one that follows. Bus load information may also be displayed. A smart panel can also be connected to the control center system to display journey information. The panel can display a map of the town, with the current congestion points. The panel can also suggest the best route between two points to help passengers optimize their travel time.

Finally, a bus stop can also include a basic presence detector aimed at providing an approximate count of the number of people waiting for the bus. This helps the control center decide whether additional buses need to be injected along this line. When a stop is in a heavily congested area, this counter can also help the driver of an approaching bus decide whether taking a shortcut and skipping a stop may be valuable.

Mass Transit Security

Passenger Internet access typically goes directly through the cellular network. In some cases, a bus (and bus stop) can include a content firewall and filter. Data specific to the bus (video monitoring, stop and travel management, communication with the driver) is usually encrypted and travels over a VPN connection to the operations center. Chapter 15 provides a detailed architecture study for video monitoring for school buses. The same logic and architecture are valid for municipal buses.

Extending Bus IoT Architecture to Railways

The IoT communication architecture for railways is similar in many ways to that of bus mass transit systems. In both cases, vehicle location tracking processed in the cloud and relayed to smart panels in stations or stops can help the traveler find the best transit option between points and see congested points of the city. For freight customers, cargo location can be tracked in real time. Of course, railways are usually not congested, but incidents may disrupt traffic. For passengers, smart panels can suggest all the travel options (subway, tramway, buses), not just the railways options.

Systems onboard trains are slightly different from systems onboard buses. The Wi-Fi connections are similar, and trains also use sensors; however, train sensors are in different locations and monitor different elements from bus sensors. Trains are also larger vehicles and therefore include more components, as illustrated in Figure 13-11.

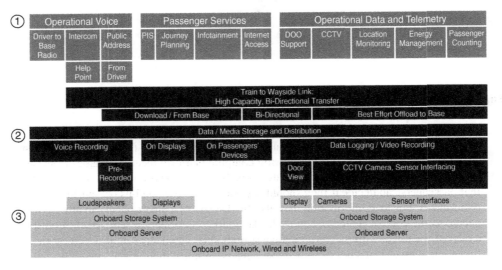

Figure 13-11   *Train IoT Technology Components*

The top layer summarizes the needs, which are similar for both trains and buses. Because train travel might be longer than bus travel, passenger services, such as infotainment, are more commonly expected in trains than on buses. Those passenger services obviously do not apply to freight.

The second layer describes the communication infrastructure used to address the needs of the train. This layer is different from the similar layer for buses. Trains run on tracks, meaning their path is controlled and predictable, allowing more deterministic connections. Dedicated communications systems can be built along the tracks and leveraged by all passing trains. CCTV recordings (full flow or triggered chunks) and sensor information can be uploaded, and prerecorded messages (matching targeted events) can be pushed to the trains when needed. Passenger Internet connection traffic also needs to transit through the railside connection system. The result is a need for high-capacity bidirectional transfers.

The third layer describes the objects involved in the connected train architecture, from sensors, cameras, and displays to onboard servers and storage systems. All of them require connectivity (and therefore an IP network).

The resulting IoT network architecture is displayed in Figure 13-12.

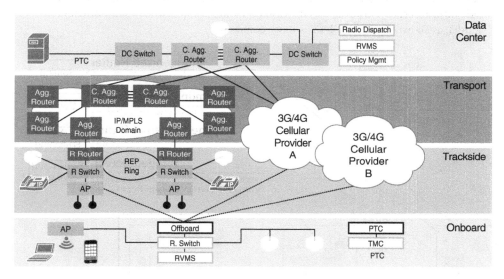

Figure 13-12   *Connected Rail IoT Architecture*

Inside the train, positive train control (PTC) and train management computer (TMC) systems integrate command, control, communications, and information networks for controlling train movements. Train vehicle management systems (TVMSs) provide detailed maintenance information and equipment status. These systems, along with other sensors, video cameras, and Wi-Fi access points, connect through an Ethernet switch, which should be ruggedized. Depending on the environment, the train communicates with the cellular network or Wi-Fi outdoor APs positioned along the tracks. Those outdoor APs connect to switches, commonly organized around robust redundant link protocols like Resilient Ethernet Protocol (REP; described in Chapter 9). Trackside cameras may also connect to the same switches, along with other equipment (specific sensors, IP phones, and so on). Ruggedized routers connect to the network transport side, the structure of which is similar in concept to that of other mass transit systems. In most cases, data is directed to the railway company data center. However, some data may be rerouted to third-party data centers (for example, cargo customers, food or parts suppliers, other contractors).

The main difference between the bus and the train mass transit architectures lies in the connection to the infrastructure network. Buses typically include a single coach. Connecting the coach and connecting the bus have the same meaning (beyond the English subtlety, where the "coach" means the passenger part of the bus). By contrast, a train consists of multiple cars. Each car includes sensors, cameras, Wi-Fi access points, and communication systems (for example, speakers, phones for staff). They need to communicate with the railside infrastructure and with one another. A completely distributed system may implement complete autonomy for each car. Each car has its own cameras, switches, sensors, APs, communication modules, rugged servers (for video surveillance, sensor data storage, and so on), and router, communicating independently with the railside infrastructure. However, this distributed model is expensive. A semi-distributed model, as shown in Figure 13-13, is more common.

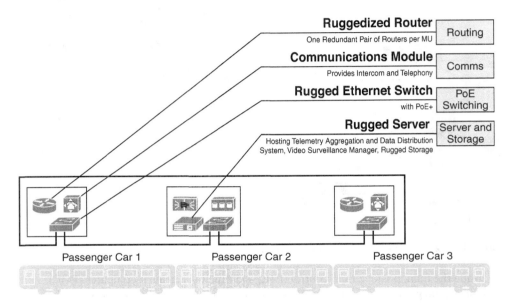

Figure 13-13 *Semi-Distributed Onboard IoT Modular Architecture for Trains*

In this semi-distributed model, each car has its own rugged switch, video cameras, sensors, and APs for its own monitoring and connectivity functions. However, cars are of different types (three in the example in Figure 13-13), and each type adds a specific component that is not present in all cars (such as rugged router, communication module, or server). Connections between cars allow the cars to share these functions. When trains are assembled, the rail operator needs to make sure to include enough cars of each type to allow for full train functionality.

The car-to-car connection can be wired. However, Wi-Fi connections are also common. In this case, a mesh Wi-Fi network is a very flexible structure. One of the APs (typically the AP associated with the car that includes the router) acts as the root access point (RAP), while the APs in the other cars are mesh access points (MAPs), as illustrated in Figure 13-14. (For a more detailed discussion on mesh Wi-Fi, refer to Chapter 14, "Mining." Refer to Chapter 2, "IoT Network Design Architecture," for more details on mesh network topologies.)

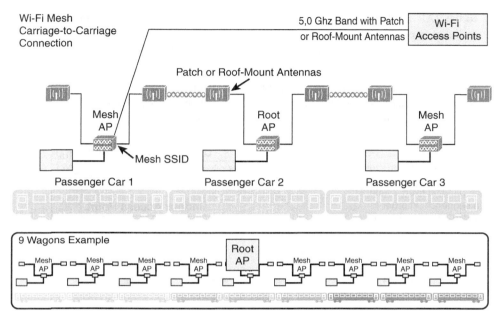

Figure 13-14 *Carriage-to-Carriage Wi-Fi for Connected Trains*

This inter-carriage Wi-Fi connection is implemented regardless of whether Wi-Fi is offered onboard. When Wi-Fi access is provided, the 2.4 GHz band is typically used for passenger access, while the 5 GHz band is used for the mesh backhaul, as shown in Figure 13-15.

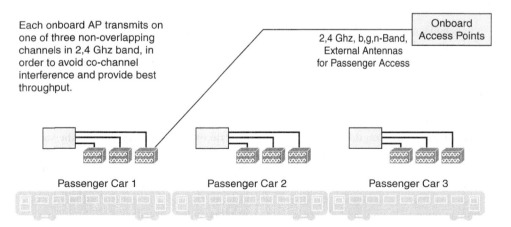

Figure 13-15 *Onboard Wi-Fi*

Each car includes one or several APs to provide consistent coverage throughout the carriage. Traffic is aggregated and passed to the mesh network and then forwarded along to the RAP. The RAP can then connect through the router to a trackside wireless system (cellular) or even to satellite connections. When Wi-Fi is available along the track, the RAP can connect to another AP configured as a wireless client (for example, workgroup bridge [WGB]).

Depending on the trackside Wi-Fi capabilities, different throughput can be offered inside the train. Higher throughputs require that more WGBs be deployed. Each WGB connects to the trackside Wi-Fi infrastructure, as shown in Figure 13-16.

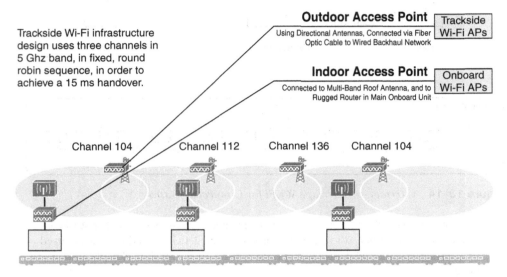

Figure 13-16 *Connection to Trackside Wi-Fi Network*

One challenge relates to the speed at which the train moves. Each WGB needs to roam from one railside AP to the next. Roaming needs to stay within 15 ms to limit communication disruptions. This requirement dictates the position of the APs on the railside, their spacing, and the type of antenna.

Connected Stations

IoT for transportation does not stop inside the train or bus; it also extends to the station or cargo terminal. Bus stops are small entities where IoT is about smart panels, Wi-Fi for waiting passengers, and cameras for safety and passenger count. A train station is much larger and needs to allow connectivity for multiple services, including smart panels and digital signage, ticketing systems (multiple machines through the station, automated or human operated), light and air-conditioning systems, video surveillance, and multiple third-party systems (ATMs, parking, stores, and so on). The station also needs to include public address systems and a rich set of sensors to monitor the trains' and station's activity. Cargo terminals also include tracing and dispatch systems for the freight.

All these systems need to communicate through a shared IP infrastructure. In addition, trains may commonly upload the core of their data once at the station. Station operations need to receive this data and process it. Therefore, the station needs to connect to the operator data center as well.

Connected Train Security

Because multiple types of data coexist on a converged IP network, security is a primary concern. Third-party terminals communicate over VPNs with their relevant DCs. Although security for sensors and ticketing systems may share the same infrastructure, physical security is coupled with traffic isolation (using protocols such as 802.1AE, for example). 802.1AE, also called MACsec, is a protocol that specifies connectionless user data confidentiality, frame data integrity, and data origin authenticity by media access–independent protocols and entities that operate transparently to MAC clients. 802.1X should also be used to control access to the network. The only exception is the onboard Wi-Fi system, which typically uses web authentication and is not encrypted. However, the use of an additional Pre-Shared Key (PSK) is more and more common, albeit somewhat difficult to manage.

Summary

The explosive growth of private and public transportation systems has been accompanied by growing challenges related to safety, travel experience, and predictability of the journey in general.

To address these challenges, vehicle manufacturers as well as transport and safety authorities have worked on several approaches. The efficiency of these approaches can be enhanced with IoT, resulting in connected vehicles, connected roadways, connected mass transit, and connected railways.

At the individual vehicle level, multiple sensors can provide a proactive view of vehicle conditions, limiting the number of surprise breakdowns. At the same time, intelligent onboard systems allow for a better travel experience by allowing the vehicle to dynamically react and adapt to surrounding conditions.

Technologies such as DSRC, which is built on 802.11, allow a vehicle to exchange information with the roadside infrastructure. This exchange is beneficial to the vehicle, which can now receive locally significant warnings. Specialized vehicles (such as emergency services) can also use this communication system to get privileged access as they pass through intersections. Private applications can leverage this system for fleet management or car monitoring.

These individual vehicle IoT enhancements also benefit mass transit vehicles (such as buses and tramways). IoT allows the transportation authority to have a global, dynamic, and adaptive view of transit conditions, anticipating maintenance needs and adapting the transport offer to the changing density of users in the network.

Travelers can directly see these benefits through more efficient transit systems and also through smart panels in bus or train stations that provide an intelligent view of the journey through the transit system. Trains also leverage these systems, with the added specifics of a vehicle moving along fixed tracks.

References

1. US Department of Transportation, Federal Highway Administration, *Roadway Safety Dashboards*, https://rspcb.safety.fhwa.dot.gov/Dashboard/Default.aspx. Accessed December 24, 2016.

2. National Highway Traffic Safety Administration, *Fatalities in the United States*, September 16, 2016, https://crashstats.nhtsa.dot.gov/Api/Public/ViewPublication/812349.

3. World Health Organization, *Global Status Report on Road Safety, 2013*, http://www.who.int/violence_injury_prevention/road_safety_status/2013/en/.

4. American Public Transportation Association, *Moving America Forward*, 2013, http://www.apta.com/resources/reportsandpublications/Documents/APTABrochure_v28%20FINAL.pdf. Accessed December 24, 2016.

5. Dr. Jean-Paul Rodrigue, *The Geography of Transport Systems*, https://people.hofstra.edu/geotrans/eng/ch3en/conc3en/usrail18402003.html. Accessed December 24, 2016.

6. S. Abuelsamid, *New Cars Could Be Required to "Talk" to Each Other as Soon as 2020*, December 13, 2016, www.forbes.com/sites/samabuelsamid/2016/12/13/nhtsa-finally-issues-draft-v2v-communications-rule-could-be-mandatory-from-2021/#2efae50f6f23.

Chapter 14

Mining

The term *mining* is often associated with old black-and-white images of hard-working men carrying pick axes and carbide lamps into dark underground tunnels and loading ore or overburden into small rail cars. While those pictures are historically accurate, technology has enabled significant progress in the mining industry, specifically around safety, production optimization, and Operational Expenses reduction.

At the most basic level, mining is the process of extracting minerals from the earth. Many types of minerals are extracted today, including copper, gold, silver, lithium, molybdenum, iron, salt, potash, coal, uranium, and precious gems. Most of these minerals, especially precious metals, are rarely just lying on the ground in large chunks, waiting for someone to pick them up. Instead, they are mixed in with other materials beneath the surface of the earth. In the case of copper ore, the average volumetric amount is less than 1%.

To separate and extract the desired minerals, you have to break up large quantities of earth and haul it to a processing facility, where it is further broken down and a variety of techniques are used to isolate the desired material. The techniques and technologies used in mining operations bear many similarities to other industries, such as manufacturing and transportation. As a result, many of the IoT principles discussed in this chapter have relevance beyond mining.

Mining can generally be classified into three major categories: surface mining, underground mining, and underwater mining. This chapter focuses on the first two categories. There are also three main types of minerals mined, in all three mining categories: coal, metal, and nonmetal.

In most countries, mining activities are regulated. For example, in the United States, mining is regulated by the US Labor Department, under the Mine Safety and Health Administration (MSHA) and is also regulated in each state. Working in a mine typically requires specialized training and certification from national regulatory agencies, such as the MSHA. In other countries, the type of mine and exploitation processes are also regulated.

The lifecycle of a mine, which goes far beyond the extraction of minerals, is shown in Figure 14-1. Much time and work is involved in the exploration, planning, construction, operations, environmental monitoring, closure, and reclamation of mine sites. However, this chapter mainly focuses on operations, which is the longest portion of a mine's lifecycle, often measured in decades.

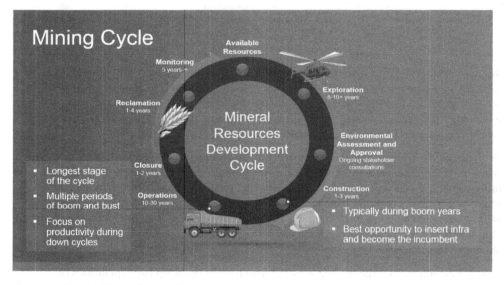

Figure 14-1   *Mining Lifecycle*

This chapter includes the following sections:

- **Mining Today and Its Challenges:** This section provides an overview of the mining industry and will help you understand the tools, scales, constraints, and challenges of this industry.

- **Challenges for IoT in Modern Mining:** This section examines the specific challenges in deploying IoT solutions in mining environments.

- **An IoT Strategy for Mining:** This section details the multiple ways IoT can improve mining operations, from increased security and efficiency to lightning and hazardous gas safety, slope and environmental monitoring, and location services.

■ **An Architecture for IoT in Mining:** This section details the architecture of an IoT network for mining, from the client side, to the access layer, to the core network, and its security. This section also discusses the application layer and provides examples of how big data changes the way mining operations are conducted.

Mining Today and Its Challenges

Over the past 50 years, the size and scale of mining operations have grown tremendously, while at the same time processes and efficiencies of extracting minerals have greatly improved. Modern mining is the safest it has ever been. However, modern mine operators still face many challenges.

Scale

For the uninitiated, one of the most difficult concepts to convey about modern mining is the unimaginably enormous size and scale of many mining operations. If you have ever had the opportunity to visit Grand Canyon National Park, you can relate to this concept. No matter how many times you read or hear about it, or how many pictures you see, you can realize the size and scale only in person. That same concept applies to mining. In mining, sites can cover hundreds of square miles and can contain pits over 2500 feet deep, with widths spanning several miles (see Figure 14-2), not unlike a large valley.

Many surface mines have several deep pits (see Figure 14-3) adjacent to each other, with long, winding haulage roads that are traversed by giant dump trucks called *haul trucks*. As shown in Figures 14-4 and 14-5, these haul trucks are machines that make full-size pickup trucks look like toy cars in comparison. Some of the larger haul trucks are capable of moving more than 350 metric tons of material at a time, with 13-foot-tall tires and powered by 4000-horsepower engines. The electric shovels used to fill these trucks (see Figure 14-6) are on the same scale.

The immense size and scale aren't unique to surface mining operations; underground mines can have hundreds of miles of tunnels, also known as *drifts*, large enough to fit two city buses next to each other, spanning great vertical distances below the surface. This large scale also means that it can take a very long time to physically get to locations within a mine. From an IoT perspective, this means it could take several hours to get a technician to equipment locations in a site.

Figure 14-2   *An Open Pit Mine in Arizona*

Figure 14-3   *An Open Pit Mine with Large Haul Trucks*

Figure 14-4   *A Typical Haul Truck Used in Copper Mining*

Figure 14-5   *Haul Truck Size Comparison*

Figure 14-6 *An Electric Shovel in an Open Pit Mine*

Mines are often in remote locations that can be difficult to reach, both physically and electronically. This means the infrastructure needed to support a large-scale mine (electricity, water, communications, rail/road/sea transport) is often not in place or not available at the scale required to facilitate mining production activities. This infrastructure must be put in place by the mine operator or a proxy. Sometimes entire towns, complete with housing, shopping, schools, medical facilities, security, and entertainment, are built and operated by mining companies to support sites that are not within reasonable commuting distances from existing towns. In addition, many mining locations are in locations where extreme environmental conditions such as altitude, humidity, and temperature must be managed and where diseases and fauna may present risks as well.

Safety

Mining is inherently dangerous, and safety is one of the most important considerations in this field. The danger of underground mines has been exposed in many movies and, unfortunately, breaking news around the world. The risk of collapse is always a concern, and monitoring the tunnel structure is always a primary priority. Explosions are also a risk. Various gases released from the ground during mining operations can reach an explosive concentration very fast. In case of collapse, the limited amount of air available in tunnels gives a very short window for relief to free trapped workers. Techniques have been developed to eliminate gas emissions and flow fresh air in all parts of mines. However, monitoring the air quality and the soundness of the tunnel structure are important everyday challenges of underground mining.

Open pit mines may look safer than underground mines. However, the forces involved in moving tons of earth and the processes required to extract minerals can be very hazardous. Landslides can be lethal, and monitoring the slopes of open mines is a key safety requirement. In addition, working around gigantic engines is hazardous. From the cabin of these very large vehicles, drivers may not be able to see pedestrians or even pickup trucks. Dust makes the problem worse, even for vehicles equipped with radar. Signaling positions and controlling locations of all workers and all vehicles is necessary.

Weather conditions can also present challenges. Many mines are located in regions of extreme weather. Sudden violent rains may quickly fill pits and holes. When thunderstorms strike, workers are exposed and may be miles away from safe, sheltered buildings.

Environment

Mining organizations have a duty to protect the environment from the effects of their operations. These effects include ground and water pollution, of course, and also noise, dust, and the effects of mining operations on flora and fauna. At the end of a mine's lifetime, the site has to be managed to avoid any pollution and to revert the site conditions to the pre-mining state.

Mine failures, such as tailing dam failures, can lay waste to vast geographies, and impacts can last for tens to even hundreds of years. Failure to be a good mining corporate citizen will result in governments not releasing new mining leases. Mining operations are concerned about the effect of the operations on the environment and need to closely monitor the weather (and its possible consequences on dust or water pollution, for example), the air, the water quality, and so on.

Security

Our modern society depends on mining to supply the minerals needed for just about everything: electrical wires in buildings, components used in every electronic device, batteries that run our gadgets, and metals that go into our buildings, cars, aircraft, ships, bridges, jewelry, and many other things. Minerals are at the very bottom of the global supply chain for almost all modern industry and a society that enjoys manufactured goods.

While general consumers do not know where minerals are located or even care how they are extracted, the people in close proximity to mineral deposits often do. Mining can be a very polarizing topic for a variety of reasons, especially geopolitical and environmental, sometimes involving local radical groups or nation-state–sponsored actors. Mining operators have a huge number of valuable assets. The obvious assets are the minerals that are mined and the equipment used to extract and refine them. However, perhaps not as obvious are assets such as exploration data and other intellectual property.

In some cases, mine operations are the target of political action groups that attempt to stop operations or use a mine as a geopolitical stage to publicize their message. In addition, some mineral deposits are located in parts of the world that are not politically stable or environmentally sensitive. When you factor in additional risks resulting from the remoteness of their operations, large-scale size, inherent safety considerations, and the use of both massive heavy equipment and explosives, physical security and cybersecurity are often top-of-mind topics for mine operators.

Volatile Markets

The output of most mines is raw materials that are sold on the commodities market. Therefore, the profitability of modern mining operators is at the mercy of market forces. Differentiation of product is typically not possible with commodities. For example, between 2011 and 2017, high-grade copper prices saw a high of $4.50 per pound and a low of $1.96 per pound. The volatility of commodities markets cannot be controlled, but having a highly efficient and adaptable supply chain can help maximize profits while prices are high and minimize losses during market lulls.

Challenges for IoT in Modern Mining

Many of the challenges in modern mining can be addressed with IoT solutions. However, deploying IoT solutions in mining environments is challenging.

The OT Roles in Mining

As with other industries, the objectives and requirements for traditional corporate IT networks in the mining industry are very different from those of OT.

(The concepts of IT and OT are introduced and discussed in Chapter 1, "What Is IoT?")
Mines typically have technical roles focused on the OT side (see Figure 14-7):

■ **Mine superintendent:** The mine superintendent is in charge of operations and,
ultimately, the profitability of the mine. He is in charge of balancing the investments
(in IoT, engines, and people) and the output expected from the mine. The superintendent is interested in any IoT solution to increase profitability and safety or
reduce costs.

■ **Engineering manager:** The superintendent works in coordination with the engineering manager. The engineering manager is in charge of the equipment of the mine.
As such, he or she is interested in any solution that can increase the reliability of the
equipment (by providing better monitoring, allowing preemptive maintenance) and
decrease the energy consumption related to mining operations.

■ **Operations IT manager:** The operations IT manager is in charge of the IT network.
Any device that will need to connect through the IT network needs to be reviewed
and approved by the IT manager's team.

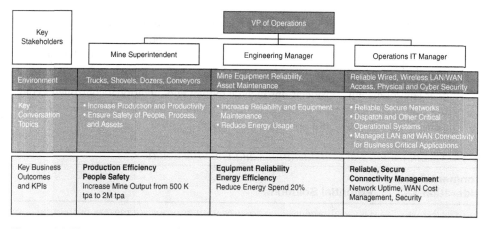

Figure 14-7 *Mining Key Roles*

Connectivity

IoT depends on connectivity, and in the world of mining, connectivity can be especially
challenging. The very nature of mining means that the physical layer is extremely dynamic, and the network can be in a constant state of change to meet the requirements of an
ever-changing mine. Overall, these challenges can typically be broken down into three
main categories.

■ **Remoteness:** In the remote areas where many mines operate, WAN connectivity can
be difficult to acquire and is often extremely expensive, relatively low bandwidth,
and often subject to high latency and high packet loss. This is especially true when
traditional terrestrial circuits are not available and satellite communications links

must be used. For many applications, these issues can be addressed with WAN acceleration and compression technologies. However, these technologies are usually not effective for real-time communications applications, such as VoIP and IP video conferencing. In addition, many mines are located in places where there isn't even cellular coverage, which means the mine operators often need to deploy their own wireless communications infrastructure and may depend on satellite communications for some data services.

■ **Extreme environmental conditions:** Mines present a wide variety of extreme conditions in which equipment must operate. Some of these conditions relate to the remoteness of the mines, while others are linked to the nature of the process. Aboveground mining operations often experience extreme humidity and temperatures, both hot and cold, as well as extreme weather, ranging from lightning and wind storms to torrential rains. Many mines, especially in South America, operate at high altitudes, often above 15,000 feet, where the air is much less dense, and equipment cooling effectiveness must be considered. Some mining processes involve corrosive chemicals or flammable and explosive atmospheres. Appropriate equipment certifications or enclosures are required to both keep the equipment safe and prevent fires and explosions. Heavy machinery, especially tracked vehicles such as dozers, create extreme vibrations that could literally shake apart nearby equipment. Such environments require creativity when mounting equipment, such as using rubber grommets to isolate vibrations and neodymium magnets to simplify installation and removal of equipment.

Other environmental considerations include regular and intentional controlled explosions during the process of blasting. Table 14-1 summarizes some of the environmental challenges in mining and possible solutions.

Table 14-1   *Environmental Considerations and Potential Solutions*

Environmental Consideration	Potential Solutions
Moisture and dust	Use equipment or enclosures with appropriate ingress protection (IP) rating, such as IP54 or IP68.
Corrosive	Use "conformal coating" equipment or an enclosure with an appropriate rating.
Lightning	Use appropriate lightning protection equipment, such as lightning arrestors, proper grounding, and electrical isolation via fiber-optic interconnects.
Extreme heat/ cold/altitude	Use equipment designed for extended temperature ranges and/or appropriate enclosures that can keep equipment within operating specifications.
Vibration	Use vibration-dampening mounts and enclosures.
Flammable or explosive atmosphere	Use equipment or enclosures rated intrinsically safe for the specific hazard(s) that received HazLoc certifications (for example, Class 1 Div 2).

■ **Scale:** Mining operations are at an entirely different size and scale than most industries. This often means that a network needs to provide connectivity to hundreds of square miles. To further complicate matters, some mining applications are not IP-based and cannot be routed. Layer 2 connectivity must sometimes be made available across a wide geography. Unlike in any other industry, the nature of mining means that the ground is constantly being moved. Physical locations that act as network distribution points today may be gone tomorrow. The topography of the mine changes daily, which often means the network's logical and physical topology must be adjusted accordingly. Due to the highly fluid nature of network topologies in a working mine, wireless connectivity is often used for the last mile at the access layer. Even this flexible last-mile access method must undergo lifecycle modifications to accommodate the mine's changing environment.

An IoT Strategy for Mining

There are a wide variety of opportunities for IoT in mining, from new operational efficiencies to life safety and environmental monitoring. Figure 14-8 provides several examples. IoT solutions provide significant benefits to mine operations, some with very short return-on-investment timeframes.

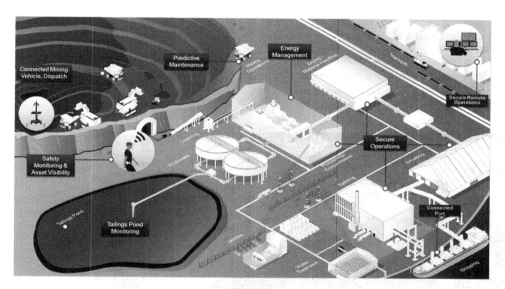

Figure 14-8 *Examples of IoT Applications to Mining Operations*

Improved Safety and Location Services

Among all the possible applications of IoT for mining operations, the first to come to mind for any mine operator is safety. Mining has long had a reputation for being dangerous because of the environment where it takes place and the vast amount of material being moved by very large vehicles. IoT provides very powerful means to improve mining safety, at multiple levels.

Driver Safety

Mines are inherently dangerous places, but IoT solutions are being deployed at mine sites around the globe to help improve the safety of miners. For example, the safety of a haul truck can be greatly compromised if the driver experiences drowsiness. A haul truck accident may cause damage to equipment and stall mining operations or, even worse, cause harm or death to the driver or workers at the mine site. To address this, IoT systems can be used to measure the level of drowsiness of a haul truck driver. These systems can operate based on three types of measures:

- **Physiological measures:** Drivers may be required to wear a wristband (analogous to a fitness tracker) that measure heart rate, breathing patterns, and other factors and generates an alert when these patterns indicate drowsiness.

- **Behavioral measures:** A camera mounted on the dashboard or the rear mirror can measure eye closure, eye blinking pattern (eyes blink slower when falling asleep), yawning, head position, and so on.

- **Vehicle track measures:** Sensors on the truck can measure movements of the steering wheel, position in the lane, pressure on the acceleration pedal, and other factors. Sudden changes reflect drowsiness.

When drowsiness is detected, an alarm can be triggered in the truck or the control center, and the truck can be stopped automatically.

In some open pit mines where terrain topology is relatively stable (that is, the travel path between the extraction zone and the treatment machines is not overturned daily), autonomous trucks are beginning to be used. Figure 14-9 shows an example of one of these autonomous guided vehicles (AGVs).

Figure 14-9   *A Komatsu AGV Haul Truck on Display*

These trucks are driverless and do not have a cabin. As a result, they do not have a front or a back, and they can offload in any direction. They are programmed with a map of the mine and configured to go to a loading site, where they are loaded with ore. When the load reaches a determined threshold, the truck drives back to a treatment area and dumps the ore into a machine. Sensors and cameras, along with the mine map, help the truck navigate on the site. The operational advantage is that a single remote operator can monitor multiple trucks, and the trucks never get drowsy. However, with the current state of the art, this solution is not practical in sites where the topology changes often because the truck control system would need to be reprogrammed often. These autonomous trucks can be extremely complex and often require multiple sensors, including computer vision, high-precision GPS location, guidance systems, and collision avoidance mechanisms. When it comes to safety, there is a serious risk associated with removing humans from behind the wheel of a 300-ton vehicle. Most autonomous haulage systems rely heavily on IP connectivity and have strict tolerances for network availability.

Weather and Lightning

In surface mining, lightning and severe weather pose a serious risk. Lightning monitoring systems and small weather stations can be deployed across a mine site and connected to the network to provide real-time weather information to mine operators. When lightning is detected less than 5 miles away, workers can receive an alert on their cell phones, instructing them to take cover until the storm has passed.

Slope Monitoring

Open pit mines are especially at risk for mine pit slope failures, which can result in massive deadly landslides. Several companies have developed systems for monitoring the integrity of pit walls, often called slope monitoring systems. These systems can use a variety of sensors.

For example, a monitoring system can be installed on a trailer and positioned on one side of an open pit. The system shoots a 3D laser beam or radar bursts over a 180-degree span, measures the signal response pattern, and compares it to the baseline. Changes in the pattern indicate a change in the slope, usually resulting from a variation in the stability of the terrain. With such a system, an alert can be sent long before an actual landslide event is likely to occur, providing hours or even days of warning. This additional level of safety also allows the mines to operate on more aggressive slopes, which can be monitored for operations safety.

Slope monitoring systems are strategically placed in an open pit mine and require network connectivity to relay the information to the mine operators.

Location Services

With the enormous scale of mining operations, it can be very difficult to locate a specific asset or worker within a mine. While there have been advances in land mobile radio (LMR; a.k.a. walkie-talkies or handie-talkies) solutions that include the ability to track a radio via an embedded GPS sensor, these solutions do not work indoors or underground, and they may not be able to provide individual miners with the ability to locate an asset.

Wireless location services have the advantage of not requiring a GPS signal and can report the position of an appropriately equipped device or worker through a mine network. Some of these solutions require the use of choke points and beacons (to detect when an asset enters or leaves a given location), and others use the signal strength or signal flight time (such as time difference of arrival [TDoA]) of the device on the network to determine the location through trilateration (the intersection of circles). While these solutions may not provide the same location accuracy as GPS (trilateration accuracy varies between 3 and 25 yards, depending on the environment and the architecture), they are helpful in locating assets or workers where GPS signals are not available. This is extremely important during an emergency, as it allows first responders to know immediately where workers are located (without a manual call and count) and concentrate their efforts where rescue efforts are most needed, based on the location of the incident and the proximity of workers to that location.

Beyond emergency cases, worker tracking may be useful to alert a truck driver when a worker is detected on the ground. (Trucks usually include sensors and radar to alert when smaller objects, such as vehicles or people, are detected in the vicinity.) A specific warning can also be displayed in the control room when workers operate in a hazardous location.

Carbon monoxide (CO) is a colorless, odorless, flavorless toxic gas produced by the incomplete combustion of carbon-containing material such as coal or wood. It is a major hazard in underground mines. For many years, workers have been carrying devices to detect CO. Today, IoT sensors can alert operators of the presence of CO anywhere in the mine, in real time, and also show CO buildup trends. An IoT system can also regulate ventilation based on the detection of CO and further modulate it, depending on the presence of trucks (which produce carbon monoxide) and humans. These location systems usually require connectivity to the network and/or actually leverage the existing Wi-Fi network.

Hazardous Gas Detection

In both underground and surface mining, there can be a wide variety of deadly or hazardous gases present, depending on the minerals being mined and how they are processed. Locations at risk for exposing workers to these gases often have both stationary gas detection systems and portable solutions for workers entering these areas. Several of these portable systems are capable of being connected to the network either directly or by leveraging a gateway capable of supporting industrial wireless protocols like ISA100.11a and WirelessHART. (Both ISA100.11a and WirelessHART are defined in Chapter 4, "Connecting Smart Objects.") The system sounds an alert when hazardous gas is detected, but connectivity also allows the system to report the hazard and its details to the control room.

Environmental Monitoring

As mentioned earlier in this chapter, mine operators are subject to strict environmental monitoring. The specific type of environmental monitoring can vary greatly, depending on the mine type, location, and regional regulations. However, it is very common for these systems to be connected to the network. They include air quality monitors, video cameras to monitor dust and particulate matter, and water quality.

One area of great environmental concern associated with mining is ensuring the integrity of tailing ponds. Tailing ponds are very large ponds that hold the waste products of mining, typically finely crushed rock, water, and any chemicals used in the mining process. Figure 14-10 shows an example.

A recent example of why monitoring the integrity of tailing ponds is important is the August 2014 Mount Polly mine disaster, in which a tailing pond failure caused approximately 6.34 billion gallons of mine waste to contaminate the lakes and rivers near the town of Likely, British Columbia, Canada. In an effort to improve the mean time to detection of a tailing pond dam failure, while simultaneously reducing the labor costs of manually inspecting the integrity of tailing pond dams, many mine operators now put IoT systems in place to monitor conditions of the tailing ponds. These systems often use strategically placed ground probe sensors along the tailings pond's earthen dams to detect signs and symptoms of failure (see Figure 14-11). The systems are often connected wirelessly to the mine's IP network to report status and potential failures.

Figure 14-10 *View of an Earthen Dam from the Outside (top) and Tailing Pond with an Earthen Dam (bottom)*

Figure 14-11   *A Tailing Pond Earthen Dam with Sensor (Left) and Close-up View of Piezo Ground Monitoring Sensors (Right)*

Improved Efficiencies

One of the most exciting use cases for IoT in mining is focused on improving efficiency. As you may recall from the beginning of this chapter, mine operations follow the commodities market. Cost is critical, and any efficiencies that can be gained directly impact the profitability of the mine.

Most mines have hundreds, or even thousands, of men and women working in various functions. When equipment fails unexpectedly, these people are often unable to perform their duties. Sometimes these failures are fairly insignificant to the overall operations of a mine (for example, failure of a light-duty truck). Other times, failures are very significant and cause major interruptions in production. This is the case in open pit copper mining when a fully loaded haul truck breaks down and interrupts the flow of ore from the shovel to the crusher. Another similar major event is when the primary crusher seizes because the tooth from an electric shovel made its way into the crusher. These types of incidents can cost a mine a significant amount of money in terms of idle labor, recovery, repair, and restart work.

Predicting equipment failures before they happen isn't exactly new, but leveraging IoT and big data analytics to accomplish it is new. Many mine operators are now installing IP-connected sensors on heavy equipment to predict and prevent failures before they occur. When this is done correctly, the return on investment can be quick, not only preventing work stoppage due to unexpected failures but optimizing the preventive maintenance costs for equipment.

A very common piece of equipment for mines is the electric rope shovel (refer to Figure 14-6). At the front, a large bucket equipped with metallic teeth digs into piles of soil or ore. There are systems available that can monitor the hardened steel teeth of the bucket and automatically detect and notify an operator when a tooth has come off and might be headed to a crusher. The mine operator can then stop the load and prevent damage to the crusher and the associated work stoppage.

Energy, in the form of electricity and fuel, is one of the biggest operational costs to mines. Nearly all equipment in a mine consumes energy. This consumption ranges from heavy-duty equipment where a single haul truck (depending on equipment type and load) can consume more than 50 gallons of diesel per hour, to the massive amounts of electricity it takes to ventilate an underground mine, run a crusher, and process ore into usable minerals.

Many IoT applications attempt to solve these energy challenges. For fuel efficiency, applications can suggest the most fuel-efficient route for a haul truck (calculating the shortest route and avoiding detected slopes and bumps) or monitor a driver's behavior and report suboptimal driving patterns. These systems can also record and report any violations of standard operating procedures, such as excessive idling. Detailed tracking of a vehicle's performance and maintenance can also ensure optimal fuel efficiency.

In underground mining, forced-air ventilation systems require significant electrical power. Through IoT monitoring and analytics, the performance can be optimized along with longevity and energy consumption. These same principles can also be applied to many systems in a mine that rely on electric motors.

Improved Collaboration

Traveling to a mine site and a specific location within the mine site can be time-consuming and costly. Access can also be difficult. The primary collaboration method in mines has traditionally been radio-based voice-only communications. While half-duplex LMR systems and voice telephony services continue to be a vital part of mine operations, modern technology and connectivity have greatly augmented these systems, allowing much richer communications methods that can shorten cycle times. For example, a technician at a mine site can use the video capabilities of his IP-connected rugged computing device to send a picture or even a live video feed of the equipment to an off-site engineer for real-time assistance with troubleshooting, potentially reducing the time to repair significantly.

Immersive video systems can also reduce the cycle times at mines. While room-based video systems are unlikely to be used in active mining areas, they are frequently used in the business offices of mines and allow remote face-to-face meetings to happen. This technology may not be an option for all meeting situations, but it is a great option for time-sensitive meetings that would otherwise require people to travel great distances.

IoT Security for Mining

As previously mentioned, security is an important topic for mining. Like many industrial and manufacturing IoT systems, the systems in mining should, and often do, follow the Purdue Model for Control Hierarchy or ISA99/IEC-62443 framework to segment plant networks into logical zones. (For more information on the Purdue Model for Control Hierarchy, refer to Chapter 2, "IoT Network Architecture and Design," where it is first introduced.) It is not unusual for individual process areas to be grouped into their own cell/area zone, but it is extremely important to separate these zones from the business or enterprise network with an appropriate DMZ, sometimes referred to as a "data diode," to protect the industrial systems from external threats.

In addition to a DMZ for the IoT systems, traditional security best practices include network authentication, role-based access controls, regular patching, control plane policing, syslog auditing, and other relevant industry best practices. While it is never possible to completely secure systems from all possible attack vectors, layering security and following industry best practices significantly improves the odds in an ever-changing threat landscape.

Beyond the cybersecurity threats to IT and OT systems, physical security is a major area of concern that must be addressed in appropriate proportion to the risk associated with the mine's physical location. Theft of assets and physical vandalism, including IoT infrastructure, is a major problem in certain parts of the world. What might initially appear to be failure of remote equipment may actually be theft.

Networking equipment theft, physical damage, or scavenging (an item being "borrowed" for a different function because borrowing is faster than waiting days while new equipment is being shipped) can also have a significant impact on the function of a mining operation. For example, it is much more difficult to recover from the theft of a wireless mesh root access point and all its associated components than it is to recover from simple remote equipment failure. To address this, it is not uncommon for mine operators to put significant physical security barriers in place to combat theft of equipment, as shown in Figure 14-12.

Figure 14-12 *Physical Security Protecting Wireless Mesh Equipment at a Mine Site*

An Architecture for IoT in Mining

Smart objects are at the entry point of the IoT network stack. In mining environments the large objects, including haul trucks and electric shovels, are now becoming smart objects. Because these large objects are often operated by a local human, sensors commonly connect to a human–machine interface (HMI) over a wired interface. The operator can directly leverage the information provided. However, in many cases, the smart object also needs to provide information to the remote operator. In this case, network connectivity is essential.

Because of their constantly changing landscape, most mines choose wireless technologies to connect people and smart objects. Many mine sites are remote and unlikely to experience interferences from nearby systems. However, because of the large scale at which wireless technologies are deployed on mining sites, powerful directional antennas are common. Due to the nature of radio frequency (RF) and the possibility of creating unintentional harmful interference with other systems, it is extremely important to coordinate all wireless communication technologies that are implemented at a particular site, regardless of wireless communications category, technology, or application. It is recommended that each mine site proactively track and manage its RF spectrum.

Again, this recommendation is not limited to a specific wireless technology. In fact, a variety of wireless technologies can be used in mining operations to enable communications for IoT. Wireless is extremely important at most mine sites as it is uniquely capable of connecting both stationary and mobile equipment and people. Most wireless networking technologies operate at frequencies in the microwave band, where line of sight is typically required for reliable communications and RF path loss is relatively high.

Wireless can be broken down into two main categories:

- **Licensed:** As the name implies, licensed wireless spectrum requires a government license to operate equipment on an assigned frequency or band. These licenses are typically tied to a physical site location or geography. In mining operations, licensed wireless is frequently used for LMR (a.k.a. walkie-talkies or handie-talkies), long-distance wireless backhaul links (a.k.a. microwave links), and traditional 3G/4G/LTE. Some sites (such as multiple remote sites in Australia) use private LTE, while others rely on agreements with cell operators to deploy a basic cellular connection to the mine site.

- **Unlicensed:** Unlicensed wireless spectrum is regulated by the same government body as the licensed wireless spectrum, but the equipment in this category does not require the owner or operator to individually seek a license to use the equipment within the rules. In the United States, the Federal Communications Commission (FCC) is the regulatory body, and unlicensed transmitters must comply with FCC Part 15 rules. This category includes technologies such as IEEE 802.11a/b/g/n/ac/ah and IEEE 802.15.4, which includes ISA100.11a, ZigBee, and WirelessHART.

Note   The concepts of licensed and unlicensed wireless spectrum are introduced in Chapter 4. Wireless technologies used in mining, such as LTE, IEEE 802.11, and IEEE 802.15.4, are also covered in Chapter 4.

Due to their relatively low cost and ease of use, unlicensed wireless technologies are very common in mining applications for data communications, including IoT. While unlicensed frequencies are convenient, care must be taken to coordinate frequency use in a mine to prevent interference. One of the most common sources of wireless communications failures in a mine is interference cause by infrastructure installed by two different teams that did not coordinate their planned frequency usage. For example, a 2.4 GHz wireless video transmitter (non–Wi-Fi) has the ability to obliterate nearby 2.4 GHz 802.11 wireless network traffic and isn't easily detected without an RF spectrum analyzer.

IEEE 802.11 as the IoT Access Layer

Providing pervasive network connectivity at mine sites can be extremely challenging. The ratio of allowed RF output power to normal path loss for unlicensed data frequencies is relatively low compared to that of licensed LMR used for voice communications. The unlicensed radio spectrum available for use in IEEE 802.11, including IEEE 802.11ah, does not penetrate earth, rock, or metal and is susceptible to multipathing. However, a properly designed and managed IEEE 802.11 network can provide high-throughput, low-latency, low-loss connectivity to assets throughout a mine, including mobile equipment. A good understanding of radio frequency (RF) and the physics of electromagnetic field (EMF) is required for success. In addition to requiring traditional IEEE 802.11 WLAN skills, designing and maintaining IEEE 802.11 wireless networks in a mine requires proficiency in path loss calculations, reading antenna principal plane diagrams, understanding of the Fresnel effect, and being familiar with regulatory considerations.

802.11 Outdoor Wireless Mesh

One of the best ways to provide reliable wireless network access for an aboveground mine where cellular connectivity is not available is with 802.11 outdoor wireless mesh. Figure 14-13 provides an example of such a deployment. Unlike traditional indoor wireless applications, where every wireless access point is connected to the network with a network cable, mesh networking allows access points without wired network connections to service clients via a wireless backhaul connection. Client devices can connect to the wireless mesh with their own 802.11 WLAN adapter or via a wired Ethernet connection into a workgroup bridge (WGB), which in turn connects to the wireless mesh. A workgroup bridge is an access point that is configured as a client. Workgroup bridges offer significant advantages over traditional WLAN client interfaces, including centralized management, high RF output, ability to connect multiple wired clients through a single WGB, options for remote mounting and external antennas, and additional Layer 2/Layer 3 features (depending on the model of WGB).

Figure 14-13   *Wi-Fi Deployment Example in an Open Pit Mine*

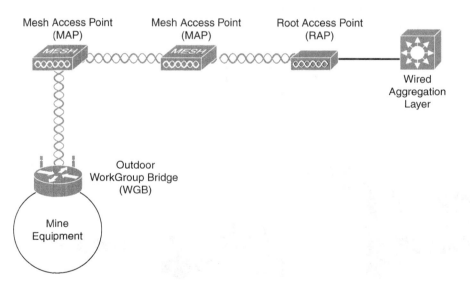

Figure 14-14   *Wi-Fi Mesh Architecture for Mining*

From an architectural standpoint, a Wi-Fi mesh network is built on the following five components, displayed in Figure 14-14:

■ **Root Access Point (RAP):** Mesh access points have wired connectivity to the network to backhaul traffic. In an underground mine, these tend to be close to switch connection points. In an open pit mine, the RAPs tend to be closer to the control center.

- **Mesh Access Point (MAP):** Mesh access points backhaul client traffic via a wireless radio interface, ideally on a different band than the client devices. Many MAPs support connecting wired clients to the network via their local Ethernet interface. All mesh access points (MAPs and RAPs) can be equipped with a GPS module so that control operators can locate them precisely on the mine map. Examples of MAPs deployed in an open mine are shown in Figure 14-15.

- **Workgroup Bridge (WGB):** A workgroup bridge is a dedicated device for bridging wired Ethernet traffic from mobile mining equipment onto the wireless mesh. Some models offer additional features such as support for multiple Ethernet devices, multiple VLANs, and Network Address Translation (NAT)/Port Address Translation (PAT). Often used as security feature and to allow multiple devices to share an IP address, NAT and PAT allow for the translation of an IP address and/or port as a packet transitions through a device.

- **Serial Backhaul:** Backhaul links traverse multiple MAPs; client traffic travels multiple Layer 2 wireless hops to reach a RAP.

- **Back-to-back or daisy-chaining:** For access points that do not contain enough dedicated radios for each function (one 2.4 GHz radio for client connectivity and two 5.8 GHz radios for backhaul), a virtual serial-backhaul MAP can be created with two access points cabled together.

Figure 14-15 *Examples of Mobile Wireless Mesh Access Points*

802.11 Wireless Mesh Backhaul Considerations

Mining environments, including underground mines, are very harsh for electronic equipment. As a consequence, all access points need to be temperature hardened, vibration resistant, and waterproof. In wireless mesh networks, a common deployment method is to dedicate the 5 GHz radio for backhaul and the 2.4 GHz radio for client connectivity. Many 802.11 wireless mesh networks can be deployed with mesh access points that support only a single radio for each band. However, deploying in this mode, without the use of serial backhaul or back-to-back daisy-chaining, has performance and throughput implications. Most mesh networks are built with a tree structure, as described in Chapter 2. A RAP connects to the wired infrastructure and uses its 5 GHz radio to connect one or several MAPs that form the first hop. Farther away, other MAPs backhaul traffic through the first-hop MAPs. All mesh APs in this scenario are on the same 5 GHz channel. A standard mesh network can include several of these hops.

Because Wi-Fi is half-duplex, a MAP cannot simultaneously communicate with the upstream RAP or MAP (the MAP that leads toward the RAP) and a downstream MAP (a MAP farther away from the RAP). The MAP spends some of its time relaying traffic upstream, some of its time relaying traffic downstream, and some of its time relaying traffic for its own 2.4 GHz–connected clients. As a consequence, each hop generates additional delay. A MAP that relays traffic from three more MAPs will proportionally spend more time relaying and less time forwarding its own client traffic than a MAP that relays traffic from a single other MAP. In a multi-hop mesh, when a single radio is used to connect to both the upstream RAP and the downstream MAPs, the available bandwidth is greatly reduced with each hop.

The single 5 GHz backhaul radio architecture also reduces range. Imagine a deployment with a RAP and two MAPs organized in a straight line (that is, a two-hop deployment scenario). The first-hop MAP must use an omnidirectional antenna to reach the RAP on one side and the second-hop MAP on the other side. An omnidirectional antenna has a lower gain than a directional antenna. Such an architecture reduces the possible inter-AP distance. An ideal configuration would include dedicated directional antennas for each direction of the link, for example, using a narrow-beam antenna for upstream connectivity to the RAP and an equally appropriate antenna to service the downstream MAPs.

When designing and deploying a mesh that requires multiple MAP hops, a more efficient architecture is to dedicate a 5 GHz radio for the uplink and another 5 GHz radio for the downlink. This can be achieved with access points that include two 5 GHz radios or by using daisy-chaining or serial backhaul. In this topology, two MAPs are connected through their wired interface, as shown in Figure 14-16.

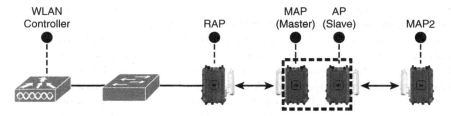

Figure 14-16 *MAP Daisy-Chaining Topology*

Upstream traffic is processed through one of the AP 5 GHz radios, called the master, and the downstream traffic is processed through the other AP 5 GHz radio, called the slave. Each AP has a directional antenna for increased range. Traffic passes from one MAP to the other via the Ethernet connection. The result is better overall throughput, over a longer range, as shown in Figure 14-17.

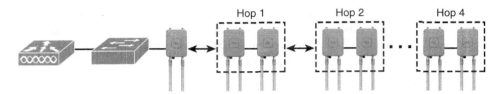

Performance Comparison	Hop 1	Hop 2	Hop 3	Hop 4
Max 20 MHz Channel Rate (802.11n, No Daisy Chaining)	83 Mbps	41 Mbps	25 Mbps	15 Mbps
Max 40 MHz Channel Rate (802.11n, No Daisy Chaining)	111 Mbps	94 Mbps	49 Mbps	35 Mbps
Max 40 MHz Channel Rate (802.11n, with Daisy Chaining)	241 Mbps	241 Mbps	241 Mbps	241 Mbps
Inside each Hop, Measured Daisy Chain Latency (ms)	2.9	6.1	8.8	13.3

Figure 14-17   *Daisy Chaining MAPs in a Wireless Mesh Deployment*

In a standard mesh tree topology, a single RAP connects a MAP tree. It is common to install a second RAP as a backup. In the case of the first RAP's failure, the MAPs automatically scan all channels in search of another RAP and can discover the backup RAP. Installing a secondary RAP increases the initial cost, but interruption of connectivity is usually costlier than a second AP. Using multiple RAPs is also common for load balancing the MAPs. Because Wi-Fi is half-duplex, each additional MAP reduces the available bandwidth of the other MAPs, regardless of the number of hops. In general, no more than 20 MAPs are connected to any given RAP. Depths of more than four hops are also uncommon.

Wi-Fi Clients

Large machines (for example, electric shovels, haul trucks, dozers, wheel loaders, borers, draglines) incorporate a multitude of sensors. For example, one popular haul truck model contains 32 engine sensors, 40 wheel sensors, and 120 load sensors. All these sensors provide a complete view of the truck's operational state and also its position in space, travel characteristics (trajectory, inclination, and location in the mine), and load information (weight, volume, and pressure on each wheel). The truck may also have up to six external cameras monitoring the surroundings (potentially sounding an alarm when specific shapes are detected close to the truck). This information is used by the driver (when there is a driver), and is also fed back to the control room. In most cases, a set of specialized sensors is connected to a module (for example, tire monitoring module, load monitoring module, position and travel monitoring module). Each module is connected to a common ruggedized router that also incorporates a wireless access point configured as a wireless client (such as a WGB). A small system and HMI is present inside the driver's cabin. The WGB relays critical data back to the mesh network.

The information gathered can be used in multiple ways. For example, dust is a critical issue in open pit mines in dry weather conditions. Sensors can help a loader get a sense of the position of a haul truck even through a dust cloud (see Figure 14-18, left side), allowing the loader driver (or the computer, in the case of a driverless loader) to get to the right range and angle before starting to load the truck. A level indicator and refined visualization (see Figure 14-18, right side) can also inform the loader about the quantity of ore loaded to the truck. The truck sensors can also provide feedback to the loader (sending a stop message when the load reaches a defined threshold). At that time, a load complete message can be sent back to the loader (and the mining operation control room) to inform the monitoring crew that the load is complete and the truck is starting to move toward the ore processing zone. This solution enables loading even in dry weather conditions, where the loader driver does not see the truck at all through the dust.

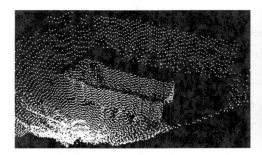 

Figure 14-18 *Sensors for Truck Loading*

Source: ri.cmu.edu

WGBs are access points configured as wireless clients. They can be mounted on vehicles equipped with a battery. Personnel typically also carry wireless devices, such as smart phones, tablets, or specialized wireless IP phones. All these devices have a Wi-Fi function, allowing their location to be tracked through trilateration. RFID tags are also common, especially in underground mines. An RFID tag includes a Wi-Fi card that is configured to emit a basic signal at a regular interval, allowing easy location tracking of each worker. More and more of these RFID tags have advanced functions, such as sensors (vibration, accelerometers, gas, or other), panic buttons, or multifunction signals.

Antenna Considerations for Wireless Mesh

With all 802.11 wireless networks, proper radio and network planning and engineering are required for optimal performance. This is especially true for outdoor wireless mesh networks in mining environments. For example, higher-gain omnidirectional antennas do not always result in better client connectivity, especially when there is a significant change in elevation.

An antenna is a passive device. The amount of energy it radiates depends on the energy inserted into the antenna. Various antennas can send energy in different directions, but the overall amount of energy sent stays the same. A classical comparison is an inflated balloon. You can press it to enlarge it in one direction, but the overall amount of air inside stays the same. Using antennas with higher gain means sending more energy in one direction and, therefore, less energy in the other directions.

A common high antenna gain changes the shape of the radiated energy from a sphere to a flat cookie, as shown in Figure 14-19. The result is a longer horizontal range but at the cost of a shorter vertical range. This is not a problem when the client and MAP antennas are at the same elevation, but it can create huge coverage gaps in open pit mines where there are often large elevation differences.

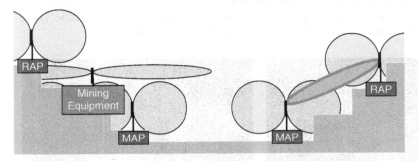

Figure 14-19 *Antennas and Coverage Limits in Three-Dimensional Spaces*

In the example shown in Figure 14-19, the haul truck's omnidirectional antenna gain is too high, and the client cannot communicate with the MAP below or the RAP above. So you can see that antenna planning is a requirement for effective connectivity. Antenna types depend on the mine topology and the device to which the Wi-Fi system is attached.

The mounting location of an antenna in also an important consideration. 802.11 antennas need clear line-of-sight to communicate, but they also need to be protected from hazards. A balance between line-of-sight and protection from rock falls and other hazards must be considered. Many installations leverage multi-antennas to achieve optimal results.

4G/LTE

Due to the remoteness of most mining operations, 4G/LTE services are typically not commercially available, and where they are available, their speed, cost, and reliability may not meet a mining operator's requirements. However, in some regulatory domains (for example, many mines of central Australia but also in several locations in Canada), there may be options for a mine operator to install and run private 4G/LTE services. Farther distances from large towns are usually also associated with cheaper spectrum costs. Where available, this solution offers impressive performance and range compared to traditional Wi-Fi solutions.

The other advantages of private LTE over commercial LTE is that it can be tailored to a mine's needs, including QoS, synchronized maintenance scheduling of radio networks, and so on. Mining has specific requirements, such as two-way real-time video or fleet autonomy management, which are very different from the requirements of traditional commercial LTE (which is more tailored to one-way video streaming, for example). However, it is important to note that private 4G/LTE solutions require significant planning and investment of resources. In many cases, the mine operator either has to purchase LTE spectrum from the government's regulatory body or must partner with another private company that owns spectrum. This solution is often used in conjunction with Wi-Fi and wireless mesh (for example, ISA100.11a, WirelessHART) services to provide the appropriate coverage for all assets in a site.

Wireless in Underground Mining

Underground mining operations bring a unique set of challenges to wireless communications. The mine geology, construction, and vehicle movements all affect underground wireless environments. The radio frequencies used for cellular or Wi-Fi communications are not capable of penetrating earth or rock. This is great for lowering the overall RF noise floor but detrimental if using traditional aboveground wireless designs. Solutions to address this range from "leaky coax" (cables that act as long antennas) and traditional distributed antenna systems to wireless mesh designs that incorporate long runs of data cable or daisy-chaining either via RF or wired Ethernet. The latter is also an effective way to provide Wi-Fi location-based services for asset and personnel tracking.

Note "Leaky coax" is the subject of many controversies. The reason is that a leaky coax acts as a very long antenna. In a standard Wi-Fi deployment (for example, an indoor office deployment), the antenna is small, and clients do not move fast. As a frame transmission lasts for at most a few milliseconds, the client and antenna are considered to be static for the duration of the transmission.

In a tunnel, with a moving client and a long antenna, the situation is very different. There can be a physical distance between the point where the beginning of the signal is received on the antenna and the point where the end of the signal is received on the antenna. This can result in the Doppler effect, in which the signal is distorted (compressed or expanded). This alteration may be sufficient for the frame to generate an error. In addition, a long cable may create scenarios where two clients, in two different parts of the tunnel, may send traffic to the same leaky cable at the same time, resulting in undetected collisions.

Therefore, leaky cables are not a good solution for all mines. The speed of the vehicles and the path of the cable must be designed carefully to provide coverage without excessive distortion or collisions, while keeping the awareness that location services will also not be available with leaky cables.

Industrial Wireless

Wireless LANs and 4G/LTE do a fantastic job moving data bidirectionally at high speed, but they do so at the cost of range and power consumption. IEEE 802.15.4 wireless networks (discussed in depth in Chapter 4) can provide better range and lower overall power consumption at the cost of data throughput. These networks are often used in mining to wirelessly connect industrial sensors, such as gas monitoring sensors. In some cases, these systems can be merged with IEEE 802.11 wireless mesh networks. Some mesh access points incorporate an IEEE 802.15.4 radio (for example, ISA100.11a, WirelessHART) to communicate with field sensors, as shown in Figure 14-20. A 5 GHz radio is used to form the mesh network and backhaul data back to the surface and the control center.

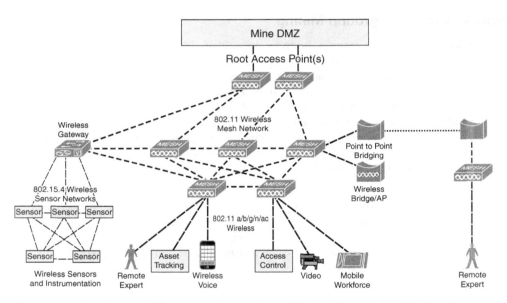

Figure 14-20 *Network Topology of a Combined IEEE 802.11 and IEEE 802.15.4 Industrial Wireless Solution*

Isolated vs. Connected Mine Networks

Figure 14-21 shows an example of a wireless network topology for a mine. MAPs use their wireless radios to connect to the RAP. The RAP connects to the wired network. In most cases, a wireless LAN controller is in charge of managing and automating AP power and channel allocation.

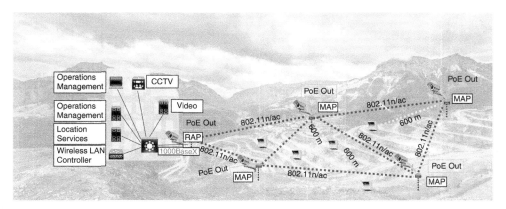

Figure 14-21   *Simple Mine Topology, with No Connections to External Networks*

This sample topology is simple but includes a few important details. The MAPs use a PoE output port. This port can be used to connect CCTV cameras that send a live video feed through the backhaul. These images can be used with human monitoring or can be fed into a compute system to analyze traffic patterns on the mine. This information can then be used to optimize operations. Any other devices (such as sensors and other protocol gateways) can also use the PoE output port.

For example, slope sensors are devices commonly connected to the mesh network, and they can be powered from the PoE output port or have their own power source. As explained earlier, slope sensors can be used to anticipate abnormal terrain movements. Analysis software can also correlate the terrain 3D view generated by these sensors with mine mapping software and monitor the mining efficiency. This information can be used to organize the daily operations based on the proximity and density of the target minerals.

In some cases, different teams take care of various aspect of the operations (for example, slope monitoring vs. RFID and personnel location tracking). As a result, several Wi-Fi systems may be deployed and may compete for RF channels. A WLAN controller helps mitigate the resulting interferences.

In the topology shown in Figure 14-21, the operations are local, and no connection to an external network is required. Larger mines may require connections to operations control centers external to the mine site. When the mine is close to an urban center, this external connection may use Wi-Fi, with a point-to-point link to the mine. Cellular connection may also be possible. Sites that are remote need a satellite connection. As shown in Figure 14-22, this type of deployment allows for a different network infrastructure. The mine site may have a limited network deployment, sufficient to ensure proper operations (location tracking and communications, for example), while more advanced compute tasks (for example, slope monitoring, 3D mapping) may be performed in the remote control center.

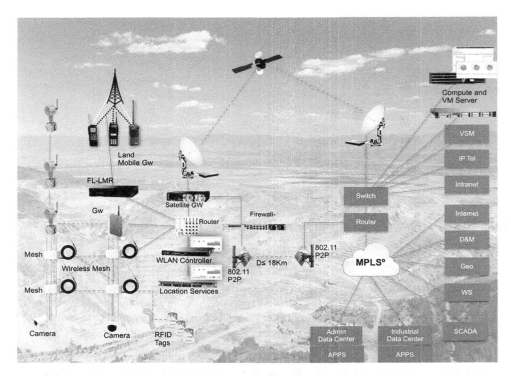

Figure 14-22 *Mine Network Topology with Connection Options to External Networks*

Core Network Connectivity

Although a mine may be a single large geographic area, different teams may be in charge of different functions of the network. It is also common to see different control towers, each in charge of specific areas, or specific operations. As a result, a common LAN topology creates a modular design, with clearly defined service blocks, managed by each relevant team. This topology allows for deterministic service delivery. The key elements at the distribution layer are redundant, as shown in Figure 14-23.

Security is also a key concern. The previous sections detail physical security, and network security is also critical. In a very competitive market, any disruption of operations and any theft of data can be very costly. When the network is modular, industrial firewalls should be installed between the modules. When the network connects to the business side of the operations, a firewall should perform perimeter security and control remote access to the mine network. Onsite, an AAA server is commonly used to control which devices and which users access the network.

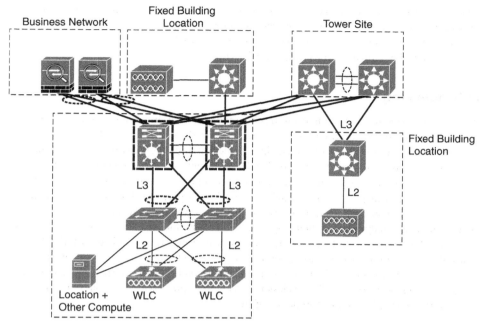

Figure 14-23 *Common Core Network Deployment for Mining*

Network Design Consideration for Mining Applications

Applications that are used to operate equipment in a mine may have specific network requirements that need to be addressed. For example, some mining dispatch systems rely on broadcast messages for communications between the server(s) and the client devices, thus requiring Layer 2 connectivity to be extended from a server room on-premises to the haul trucks and other heavy equipment throughout the mining pit(s). Other applications require the same private IP address scheme on every piece of heavy equipment, and thus require the use of NAT at a gateway device on the mining equipment. The network in a mine needs to support a wide variety of applications and use cases, and must be designed for both adaptability and reliability.

Due to the continuous operating schedule of many mines, where production happens 24 hours per day year round, resiliency and fault tolerance are also very important factors in network design. It is not uncommon for a backhaul link between intermediate distribution frames (IDFs, or intermediate wiring closets) and a main distribution frame (MDF, or central wiring closet) to be severed as a result of routine mining activity. Remember that mines are very dynamic places where the physical environment is in a constant state of change. The network needs to accommodate this constant change and allow extremely fast, if not hitless, convergence in the likely event of a physical link failure. In addition, power in a mine site can be very dynamic. Temporary power loss needs to be taken into account. Power conditioning, uninterruptable power supplies, and redundant power sources should be considered for critical infrastructure.

Data Processing

Regular 3D modeling of the mine site has become common. In open pit mines, slope monitors are complemented with drones that fly over the site and record images at various angles. These drones often use light detection and ranging (LIDAR) techniques, sending laser pulses to obtain very precise 3D representations of the environment. These representations are then fed into an operation management system, as shown in Figure 14-24. In this picture, 3D modeling is used to display the slope shape (white lines), and density estimates represent the various material types and density on a color scale. The system can analyze the current topology of the site and the size of each ore pile and compare this to the previous day's data. This information can be overlaid with the 3D map of the mineral locations and operations to better determine the best (or safest or fastest) access to minerals. The result is an optimized daily operation that also contributes to greater longevity for the mine, as less time is wasted processing material that does not contain the optimal amount of minerals of interest.

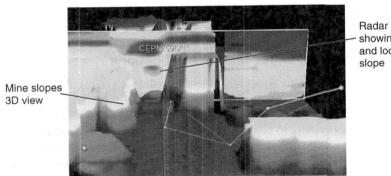

Figure 14-24   *3D Modeling of Drone-Acquired Images and Comparison to Initial Mineral Map*

Topology data can also be fed back to the vehicles on site. For example, GPS sensors located on the blades of a dozer can guide the operator to position the blades optimally, as well as measure and record the new terrain that the dozer movement just created. GPS sensors on shovels can record the exact location of each bucket. This information can be compared to the 3D model of the site to allow the operators to predict with great accuracy how much material and what type of material will be scooped. This information can be used to adapt the production and its output to the state of the market.

Summary

Mining is an extremely important part of the global supply chain, providing the minerals necessary to produce everything from metals, batteries, and electrical components to the salt we use for cooking and the coal used to create electricity and heat. The scale of the plant and equipment, mining operations, and environments where these operations are conducted create very specific operational efficiency, safety, and environmental challenges, as well as challenges for IoT deployments.

IoT is rapidly changing the way mines operate. IoT allows mines to operate more efficiently and more safely than ever before, providing tangible results to mining operators, businesses, and consumers alike. By providing critical real-time information to systems and mine operators, IoT reduces risks that were considered an unfortunate but natural consequence of the vertical activity just 10 years ago. Smart objects can automate processes and make mining easier and safer. By connecting to fog or cloud data processing applications, real-time operations can be measured with very high accuracy and can further improve the life span and efficiency of mining equipment.

While this chapter covers a wide variety of topics in IoT and mining, it is far from exhaustive and is merely an introduction to the subject, based on a snapshot in time. The relevance and value of IoT in mining continues to expand every day.

Chapter 15

Public Safety

The primary objectives of public safety organizations are to keep citizens, communities, and public spaces safe with faster response, improved operational efficiency, and reduced costs. Public safety and emergency response challenges are growing in complexity, and expectations are rising, with increasing demands for critical communications across a growing spectrum of voice, data, and video. In a crisis situation, every second counts. Potentially life-threatening situations change in a heartbeat, and decisions must be made in seconds.

Even though the Internet of Things is a fairly recent concept, it is already having a profound impact on public safety, where the demand for real-time information and situational awareness is ever present. IoT is a network of physical objects that can sense and communicate data. The technology enables users to take action based on intelligent data. In the case of public safety, there are, of course, smart objects, and this chapter provides some examples. However, the main concern of public safety is to be able to make fast use of data. IoT helps improve communications between people. IoT also helps public safety agents by preprocessing collected data, making emergency responders' actions more effective.

Public safety is a broad area that includes fire and emergency responders, law enforcement and security forces (in public places and also specific locations, such as schools), coast guard and defense, custom and border protection, and many other fields involving the general public and the need to ensure safety or protection. Covering all aspects of public safety could fill an entire book. However, most public safety organizations have similar needs and benefit from improved operations through the adoption of IoT-driven technologies in the same way. This chapter focuses on IoT's impact on typical cases of public safety needs: law enforcement, firefighting, emergency medical services (EMS), and school buses. In particular, this chapter includes the following sections:

■ **Overview of Public Safety:** This section examines the different use cases for connected public safety, including the different objects, vehicles, and services that interact to allow for an efficient emergency response.

- **An IoT Blueprint for Public Safety:** This section explains the concept of mission continuum and lists the various elements needed to ensure the public safety mission.

- **Emergency Response IoT Architecture:** This section details the IoT and communication architectures needed for various emergency response vehicles, including the command center and mobile field vehicles.

- **IoT Public Safety Information Processing:** This section provides an overview of how big data and information processing improve emergency response efficiency.

- **School Bus Safety:** This section expands public safety applications to school buses to show how connected public vehicles can improve public services and safety.

The information in this chapter can be extended to other IoT public safety use cases.

Overview of Public Safety

A common theme across public safety is the need to collect, analyze, and distribute information to enable individuals, workgroups, supervisors, and executives to carry out the missions of their respective agencies. These organizations depend on cross-agency collaboration among various groups of people, commonly referred to as the chain of command, to support public needs. This is true for both routine and emergency response events. Regardless of the event type, the safety of the public and the agency personnel themselves depend on the reliability, confidentiality, and integrity of their communications.

IoT is opening new possibilities for connecting agencies and enhancing situational awareness and response capabilities across the mission environment, helping provide the following:

- Real-time situational awareness

- Intra-agency communication and collaboration (for example, voice, data, video)

- Data analytics and information sharing

- Increased community engagement and stakeholder outreach

Public Safety Objects and Exchanges

Public safety in the twenty-first century requires real-time interactions between citizens, field personnel, law enforcement, intelligent sensors, and intelligent analytics systems. As a result, a variety of IoT solutions are applicable to public safety cases. Intelligent sensors and alarms allow agencies to capture data and create a backhaul link between sensors and data collection points. Analytics tools process data and events at the tactical edge or in the cloud and provide a visual presentation of data and events for in-depth analysis and decision making. New applications for smart objects in relation to public safety appear every day, to the point that some authors create new categories of IoT, such as the Internet of First Responder Things (IoFST), or the Internet of Live-Saving Things (IoLST).

The authors of this book believe that it is prudent to simply use the term IoT and examine the applications of IoT for public safety with the awareness that these applications broadly include three types of smart objects:

- **Objects carried by first responders:** These objects can be specialized sensors such as first responder vital sign recorders and transmitters and environmental sensors that collect information about temperature, presence of chemicals, and any other parameter likely to help the first responder assess hazards for immediate action or post-event analysis. They can also be general objects such as body cameras (recording locally or providing live feed to a central coordination and command station), or even smart phones. Data collected from these objects may also be processed locally or in the cloud (for example, gunshot-triggered alarm, image processing and analysis).

- **Objects that help the emergency services callers or victims:** This general category includes a large variety of health devices, from basic panic buttons (connected to emergency responder call-in systems) to advanced health sensors (for example, health monitors that can trigger alarms and automated calls to emergency responders through a cell phone with detailed information about the detected issue).

- **Objects present in the environment:** These are the smart objects described in the other chapters of this book that are likely to be present in public environments. (Refer to Chapter 12, "Smart and Connected Cities," for detailed examples.) These sensors improve public safety by monitoring the environment (for example, street cameras, street light controls, environmental and smoke sensors, traffic location and density). Their data can be accessed by individual emergency responders, or it can be used to feed an emergency response agency to improve situational awareness or response efficiency.

Beyond smart objects, real-time voice and video helps responders exchange information faster and more reliably within a given agency. Human to human communication does not seem to be an IoT application. However, another impact of IoT on public safety is the increasing requirement to collect, store, and process rich voice, video, and data information in real time or for post-event analysis. IoT solutions are needed to collect and process data at the edge (fog computing), while only forwarding to the cloud in real time a subset of the collected and processed data, especially in locations and situations where the amount of data exceeds the uplink capabilities. A larger or complete data set can be forwarded to a centralized storage and processing facility when emergency responders access a fast connection. Here again, merely uploading everything is not sufficient. The amount of information available is already overwhelming, and IoT is driving the need for advanced tools and analytics (for example, big data, machine learning) to ensure that events and patterns are identified for timely and accurate response. When a response is needed, IoT is an integral part of public safety's ability to coordinate resources to protect and aid the public, repel and contain threats, and recover from injury and destruction.

The success of an individual public safety agency is highly dependent on its ability to partner with other agencies and share information. The most common need for sharing information is for the coordination of field resources. This coordination can take many forms, including direct voice, video, and data communications. IoT plays a large role, with automatic sharing of real-time location, distributed and automated situation reports, and action plans. A well-known example in the United States is the ability for the public to request assistance via a 911 telephone call for police, fire, and EMS support. Many 911 answering systems use IoT technologies to allow the operator to collect information about the caller and forward it to nearby responders with the caller's real-time location and other incident information. Advanced analytics and situational awareness tools allow the operator and responders to see real-time observations and history of prior incidents.

For a police response, agencies need to exchange information such as criminal history, person-of-interest reports, and biometric data, which can generate queries across many different data sources. With one touch, field officers can also indicate whether the scene is safe or whether an officer needs immediate help. This information can be fed in real time to other agencies.

Similar examples exist for firefighter and EMS responders sharing data elements such as building and construction plans, hazardous material characteristics, medical history and prescription drug information, and consulting with remote subject matter experts and medical practitioners. For all these applications, the "things" involved are a combination of smart objects and standard data processed automatically and shared among systems.

Another example involves school buses, in which a transportation director can immediately view an altercation on a bus, assess the situation, and take appropriate action, such as providing important context or live data about the incident, including live video feed, to law enforcement officers.

Different agencies can also benefit from sharing information outside an emergency response context. For example, many agencies need access to data from departments of motor vehicles or law enforcement agencies and criminal departments, to collect information about driving or criminal history. Many agencies may also be involved in collecting or providing information about transportation, utilities, schools, or any other field of interest to the general public, such as road hazards, weather conditions, calendar events and schedules, and availability of power and water.

These examples demonstrate how IoT smart objects, intelligent analytics, and information sharing are rapidly changing the way public safety agencies operate.

Public and Private Partnership for Public Safety IoT

The partnership of information sharing extends beyond public safety to including many other government organizations. Public safety is actually built on an integral relationship between government agencies, nongovernment organizations (NGOs), and private individuals. This bond is commonly known as a public–private partnership. As the name implies, an NGO is any entity imaginable, excluding government agencies. Both NGOs and private individuals interact with and depend on public safety agencies to support the public in many different settings, from streets and highways, office building and campuses, shopping malls and local businesses, to parks and recreational areas.

The public–private partnership shown in Figure 15-1 is an ecosystem. This means that the success of the partnership depends on both sides participating. A large part of this ecosystem is the ability to be connected with each other through information sharing. In the example of 911 being called, information is shared across the public–private partnership. This kind of sharing is evolving to include rich information exchange between public safety agencies, NGOs, and private organizations. For example, banks, grocery stores, and shopping malls rely on the protection and support of law enforcement when a crime is committed and may be able to provide live access to floor plans or security camera feeds. A large campus or factory relies on fire and EMS to protect the people and property of the NGO when an event occurs such as an active shooter, fire, illness or injury, or chemical spill. During these incidents, the school or factory security team may send information about personnel location or facility equipment to emergency responders. In the case of a school bus, the ability for parents, transportation, and school administrators to know where every bus is and who is on each bus is becoming commonplace. Another growing area of information is social media, and the possibilities to collect information about current events from individuals, NGOs, and government agencies are growing without limits.

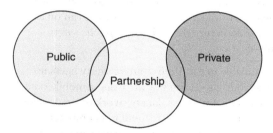

Figure 15-1   *Public–Private Partnership*

IoT is a common theme for the use cases mentioned previously. An important observation is that the "things" are not just traditional sensors, such as optical, acoustic, pressure, fluid velocity, humidity, thermal, proximity, position, chemical, and magnetic sensors. In addition, in the public–private partnership, there are many other sensor types to consider. For instance, every individual with a smart phone is a sensor. Every NGO with its various buildings and types of businesses is generating usable information from alarm systems, cameras, smoke and presence detectors, and other various sensors. Even government agencies, their vehicles, and their personnel are adding to the wealth of the IoT through things such as smart parking meters, intelligent street lighting, next-generation transportation systems, and connected vehicles. As the IoT grows, the impact of information exchange on public safety and the public–private partnership will expand exponentially. As a result of this expanding partnership, many new innovations and use cases will appear, leveraging new data sources and sensor types, and driving the need to better store, analyze, and share information.

Public Safety Adoption of Technology and the IoT

Public safety has a history of embracing technology to support its mission. In the last half of nineteenth century, inventors such as Samuel Morse, Alexander Graham Bell, Thomas Edison, and Guglielmo Marconi invented new capabilities such as Morse code, the telegraph, the telephone, the radio, and the wireless transmission and reception of information through electromagnetic waves. By 1870, US police departments were using telephones. By the 1880s, call boxes appeared in major cities to allow the public to communicate with law enforcement. Today, the use of telephony and 911 emergency dialing to reach the nearest public safety answering point (PSAP) are common in the United States and introduced to children at the elementary school level.

In addition to telephony, radio has become an integral part of public safety. In the 1920s, police departments in Detroit, Michigan, and Bayonne, New Jersey, were experimenting with the technology, shortly after its general availability. By 1934, there were 194 municipal police systems and 58 state police radio stations serving more than 5000 radio-equipped cars. As portability of these radios became practical due to the invention of the transistor, public safety continued the adoption process. By the late 1980s, it was commonplace for every police officer to have both a vehicle-mounted land mobile radio (LMR) and a handheld portable radio. These LMR devices are almost always run on a government-owned and -operated private infrastructure that is built to public safety–grade standards for mission-critical communications.

As computers and data networks became available in the 1990s, public safety agencies began to also adopt these technologies. The ability to communicate using a mobile data terminal (MDT) or notebook computer along with a wireless data network offered major improvements in efficiency and situational awareness. A vehicle-mounted computer enables applications such as computer-aided dispatch (CAD), record management systems (RMS) access, license plate recognition (LPR), in-car video recording, and automated vehicle location (AVL).

These computers were initially connected to the department's LMR data system, if available, with rates of up to 19.2 Kbps. Another option was to use commercial cellular services, with 1G or 2G cellular data. Today, 3G and 4G cellular services are commonplace and provide high-speed data connectivity between police, fire, EMS, school buses, and other vehicles. A major difference to consider between LMR voice and commercial cellular is that the LMR voice is built to mission-critical standards for availability and is private. The commercial cellular service is built on lower standards of availability and is not dedicated to public safety. However, changes are afoot, as discussed later in this chapter.

The trend for public safety to be early adopters of new technology is visible through the examples provided in this chapter. IoT will continue to accelerate this adoption trend. For example, in some countries, airport authorities already associate a person's identity (passport data) to their picture (collected through security cameras at check-in counters) and a picture of their suitcase. As a person lands in another city, this data set is combined with shape and face recognition and displayed on the customs agent's monitor as the person approaches the counter. Many law enforcement agencies use drones to monitor crowds. Onboard cameras can include data processing ability to detect crowd density and unusual movements in order to alert officers when needed, based on their relative location to the detected unusual movement.

An IoT Blueprint for Public Safety

A consequence of the rapid technology adoption and the multiplicity of data sources and processing logics is that IoT for public services cannot be limited to a strict set of use cases. Therefore, designing for IoT in the public safety space implies grouping objects and data types into actionable categories. Each use case and each environment may have a unique architecture. Above all these architectures, IoT for public safety needs a general framework. The IoT blueprint shown in Figure 15-2 provides a framework for the public safety enterprise. This framework is extensible to describe an IoT framework for almost any public safety agency, large or small. By using this blueprint as a guide, you can correlate and align new objects, applications of IoT, or requirements with the overall design.

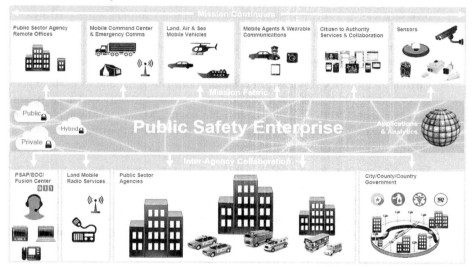

Figure 15-2   *IoT Blueprint for Public Safety*

Mission Continuum

At the top of the blueprint, six types of communication locations and devices ensure the mission continuum:

- **Remote offices and fixed sites:** These are fixed locations, such as a police precinct, a fire station, a vehicle depot, a school building, or an administrative building that supports the mission. This is where traditional networking solutions for routing, switching, unified collaboration, security, and applications are found. These networks transport IT and OT data.

- **Mobile command center and emergency communications sites:** These are temporary locations that need to be deployable, sometimes rapidly, to provide support for incident command, specialized teams, or similar functions integral to the public safety mission. IT and OT communication for these sites can be supported by kit-based or specially designed vehicle-mounted solutions for connectivity and operation. These sites may locally process data collected from the field and/or interact with the rest of the continuum to allow for a collective situational awareness.

- **Land, air, and sea mobile vehicles:** These mobile vehicle platforms require connectivity in motion. Examples are cars, trucks, buses, boats, and aircraft that support the public safety mission. These vehicles are typically equipped with multiple sensors and smart objects, such as cameras, tablets, and specialized devices. Technologies for these vehicles are designed to deal with harsh environments in which temperature, shock and vibration, and humidity can range widely. These locations also apply special attention to size, weight, and power (SWaP) requirements, which can be highly constrained.

- **Mobile agents and wearable communications:** These locations are the field agents themselves, or their immediate environment, typically forming a personal area network (PAN). Communication solutions for these locations are handheld or wearable solutions. The previously mentioned constraints for minimized SWaP requirements are increased here to avoid burdening the individual who carries the equipment.

- **Citizen-to-authority services and collaboration:** This is the interface where public safety and the public collaborate through a citizen-to-authority exchange. A common exchange is 911 emergency dialing and texting. Many other examples exist and are changing, allowing this exchange to be more robust, supporting rich media voice, video, and data in real-time interactions.

- **Sensors:** These are devices and things that collect information for the public safety mission. The possibilities in this category are expanding. The sensors can be static or mobile, located in the environment external to the public safety mission team, or integrated with the team equipment. The result is a sensor grid capable of collecting information that can be combined with applications, reporting, and analytics to drive situational awareness.

Mission Fabric

Within the public safety enterprise, the mission continuum and the various platforms are interconnected by the mission fabric. The mission fabric is a dynamic and flexible concept that enables fixed and mobile platforms to remain connected. It provides a uniform seamless method of enabling the various people, processes, and things to share a common set of security policies and to access applications and resources, and it is agnostic to the physical layer transport:

- Security policies are important and may vary depending on the physical or logical environment of each platform. For example, in a fixed site, the physical security of these locations should be well defined and should reduce the risk of unauthorized physical access and exposure. The requirements for security policies change across the mission continuum. External influences and access increase significantly from left to right across Figure 15-2. This is because the platforms operate within the community and in some cases operate completely unattended (as in the case of remote sensors).

- Access to applications and resources should also be seamless across the continuum, allowing personnel anywhere in the mission to perform their duties. This ability may change as bandwidth and network availability change, but it should not exclude or prevent a uniform and continuous ability to collaborate through voice, video, and data applications.

- Any physical layer transport should be compatible with the mission fabric to ensure that no matter where the mission must operate, connectivity is available. This means that any modern wired or wireless technology can be supported: Ethernet, serial, SONET and DWDM fiber optics, MPLS, Wi-Fi, commercial or private cellular, point-to-point and multipoint microwave, mobile ad hoc networking, and satellite.

The mission fabric is the internetworking of connectivity that ties the mission continuum together into the public safety enterprise. The mission fabric must provide a seamless integration that is independent of the location characteristics (fixed or mobile platform). The mission fabric also ensures that access to resources in the cloud is uniform and agnostic to cloud type (public, private, or hybrid). In any of these configurations, the applications should have the same level of accessibility to the end users. Similarly, tools such as data collection, reporting, and analytics tools should be extensible across the public safety enterprise. For example, a team of fire safety officials should have the ability to collaborate and share critical information to their job role, regardless of where they are—in a fixed infrastructure site, at an incident command post, in a mobile response vehicle, or on foot. Similarly, as this team is interacting with sensors or the public, the ability to communicate should be seen as a seamless interconnection of all elements, without barriers, and providing appropriate means of security and policy enforcement uniformly across the fabric.

Inter-agency Collaboration

The top half of the IoT blueprint for public safety is related to internal agency and citizen-to-authority collaboration. The lower half of the blueprint addresses inter-agency interaction. This follows the concepts mentioned earlier about the public–private partnership. Many countries have various public safety agencies, such as PSAPs (public safety answering points, where emergency calls are answered), EOCs (emergency operations centers, where representatives from one or more agencies meet to coordinate their response to emergencies), fusion centers (typically intelligence centers that collect, analyze, and disseminate information to local agencies), and LMRS (land mobile radio services, which manage mission-critical voice communications across one or more local agencies). These critical elements of the public safety infrastructure are a common point of coordination and collaboration between public and private organizations. In many cases, staffing for these organizations can be shared between public servants (police, fire, EMS) and third-party personnel with other specialized skills. Having a robust interconnect for collaboration means that timely, accurate, and meaningful information can be exchanged to more precisely and efficiently direct field resources.

A common misunderstanding exists about information sharing and collaboration among public safety agencies. In many cases, the difficulties in sharing information may be a limitation of technology, but they are often instead a limitation related to the diversity of each agency's mission and policies. For example, following the September 11, 2001 terrorist attacks, information spread that radio interoperability was a potential contributor to first responder casualties. Police units could not communicate with fire units directly by radio, ambulances could not talk with police units directly by radio, and so on. While technology could have been improved to allow first responders to communicate better, a less emphasized fact is that police, fire, and EMS personnel do not operate in the same manner and do not speak in the same operational language. Each of these organizations is trained differently, and therefore their techniques, tactics, and procedures are very different. Some post-event initial reports indicated that if these agencies could have communicated directly, lives might have been saved. In fact, later reports indicated the opposite. Connecting 100 police officers and 100 firefighters together on the same voice channel would simply have impeded their overall performance because they would not have all used the same conversational protocols. A potentially better model would be to enable a robust set of tools for voice and video collaboration, asset location tracking, and situational awareness available to middle-level supervisors and incident command staff who can speak more than one operational protocol and provide better cross-agency coordination. As IoT solutions become more pervasive in public safety, they need to be tailored to complement the agencies' missions, particularly in terms of their existing conversation protocols, methods of operation, and tactical procedures.

Another notable observation about how public safety is changing is related to the mobile vehicle. Most public safety agencies consider the vehicle an extension of the agency's office space. However, the systems and capabilities in these vehicles have been implemented disparately over time. Unlike a remote office, which has equipment that shares infrastructure and services, each of these systems operates like a remote access client, resulting in a divergence of the vehicle technology and increased security risks. For example, in most police cars today, the CAD/RMS-enabled laptop may have a cellular modem. The in-car video recorder may have a Wi-Fi radio and cellular modem, too. The LPR system may have a Wi-Fi radio. The AVL tracking system may work through the laptop or through the LMR mounted in the car, or it may be independent and have its own cellular connection. The result is a multiplicative effect on operational cost and difficulty to centrally and uniformly manage and secure these systems. This situation is not isolated to police vehicles and exists in fire, EMS, and school buses. A converged framework and architecture will allow operational cost reductions, increase availability and redundancy across all systems, and support a consistent security practice.

This IoT for public safety general blueprint can then be applied to the various agencies and their various operational models. Referring to the blueprint can help ensure that each individual solution and architecture fits into the larger model. This inclusion will facilitate inter-solution and inter-architecture communication and information sharing.

Going through each possible public safety agency and deployment model would require multiple chapters. Instead, the remainder of this chapter focuses on several key examples: police, firefighters, EMS, and schools using IoT solutions. The same logic and constructs are extensible to many other public safety agency environments and use cases.

Emergency Response IoT Architecture

Police, firefighters, and EMS are very different organizations. However, they have a common need from an IoT standpoint. IoT enables emergency responders to be more responsive in fulfilling their mission: protect and preserve life, property, and evidence. IoT also helps protect emergency response providers. Emergency responders (police officers, firefighters, and EMS personnel) operate in a very peculiar environment. Unlike workers in most other professions, emergency responders operate in unpredictable environments. It is expected that while protecting the public, they may incur personal risks. They also know that they cannot work independently. They must collaborate with other responders, their chain of command, and the public to perform their duty successfully. The emergency response solutions in this chapter look at a variety of IoT capabilities available to support public agency missions.

Most IoT architectures discussed in other chapters of this book are organized in a vertical fashion, from street level to the applications at the core. The case of the emergency response IoT architecture is slightly different because it is organized around mobile or static command or emergency centers. These centers need to establish communication downstream to field personnel and collect data from various sensors (from the sensors directly, from fog computing systems that may have partially processed the collected data, or from cloud applications that may provide data that has been further processed). Connectivity is therefore the first concern of this topology, and it drives the architecture of the various elements that interconnect with the command center.

Figure 15-3 shows the various possible emergency response mobile platforms and how they are connected to the cloud via a mobility services portal. There are three common types of mobile platforms in this environment: the mobile agent of course, but also the mobile command center and the mobile vehicle.

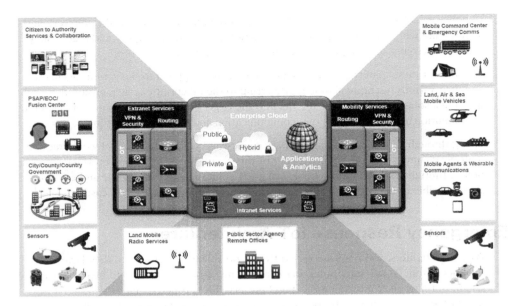

Figure 15-3   *Emergency Response Mission Fabric Architecture*

Mobile Command Center

The mobile command center is an extension of the fixed office. The mobile command center serves as a communication hub during emergency situations, such as bomb threats, demonstrations, fires, or natural disasters, and it can also be used to conduct strategy meetings and other tactical operations. It is deployed close to the location of the emergency or on the site itself to help evaluate the emergency and also facilitate physical interaction with the local stakeholders. As a result, the requirements of the mobile command center are the same as those of a static office.

Figure 15-4 shows a typical mobile command center architecture. It is designed to provide a mobile office environment similar to the environment found in the agency's fixed office locations. The primary difference is that the command center can operate completely independently of the enterprise or be a fully capable remote office. Most mobile command centers operate in two possible states. In the first state, they move to an area of interest, and their communication systems are very limited as they move. Once onsite, they run through a brief setup process that may include activating communications systems, deploying a mast with antennas and sensors, and extending compartments that create more internal work space. The command center is then in the second state, and fully operational. When the mission is completed, this process is reversed to allow the vehicle to move. This method of operation is referred to as communication "on-the-pause" because the vehicle must stop before becoming operational.

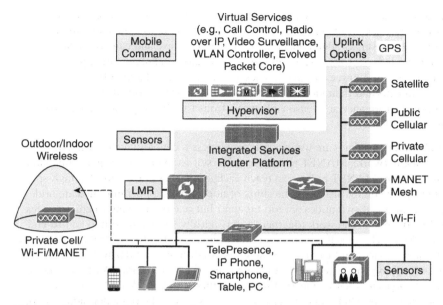

Figure 15-4 *Mobile Command Center*

Network and Security Services

The mobile command center typically has sufficient space to support traditional IT equipment, including 19-inch rack mounting space. This makes it possible to use many standard products for routing, switching, wireless control, security, and compute services. Where the command center differs from the standard remote office is that all of its connectivity to the cloud is generally wireless.

The mobile vehicle architecture is based on the concept that any uplink technology should be a useful tool in reaching the enterprise cloud. This means that almost any wired or wireless technology is acceptable. For example, a wired Ethernet connection could be provided from a local source of Internet connectivity. As Figure 15-4 shows, there are many wireless options available. These can be configured through policies to support a variety of configurations such as active/standby and active/active load sharing. The ability to automatically fail over from one link technology to another is an inherent feature of this architecture and should be mandated in the chosen solution. Tools like IP service level agreements (IP SLAs), link tracking, Bidirectional Forwarding Detection (BFD), and routing protocols that can identify conditions and change the current operating configuration in real time should be selected to guarantee an always-on uplink while optimizing and balancing bandwidth and cost based on the mission requirements. Active/active load sharing can also be accomplished in a variety of ways, such as using Policy Based Routing (PBR), Performance Routing (PfR), and Gateway Load Balancing Protocol (GLBP). The result is a flexible set of tools that can allow almost any combination of wireless or wired uplink paths to be used in a highly scalable model.

The decision to use one or more wireless uplinks is usually based on local reliability, cost, performance, and availability. Satellite and 4G cellular are the most commonly used options. However, satellite connections can be expensive and can also result in large round-trip delays of 600 ms or more. When available, cellular is often preferred to satellite, because of lower cost and latency for an equivalent bandwidth. In most urban environments and their vicinity, 4G LTE cellular service is available and can provide good performance at a reasonable price, from 1 to 30 Mbps, with round-trip delays of 30 to 80 ms.

Some public safety agencies are using a unique wireless technology called MANET (mobile ad hoc network). MANET radios provide a self-forming peer-to-peer capability. When two or more MANET radios can reach each other, they can establish a high-speed Layer 2 link. These radios also allow meshing of nodes that support intermediate node hopping. This means if two nodes are too far apart but one or more intermediate nodes are available, the nodes can work together to dynamically form a multi-hop end-to-end connection. MANETs are self-forming and self-healing. Their range is flexible, as they can change frequencies to adapt to the range and link conditions (30 MHz to 5 GHz). Some of the nodes may be connected to the Internet over a fast connection (Wi-Fi or Ethernet, for example) and share their connection with the other remote nodes. MANET radios are gaining popularity in military and government use cases, and the price per radio is coming down to a point where public safety is starting to adopt the technology. As a result, the architecture in Figure 15-4 shows MANET radios being used for both uplink and client access applications.

Private cellular service is a growing concept in public safety. Many countries are pursuing major initiatives to deploy national public safety broadband networks using 4G LTE technology. These networks operate in a dedicated band, separate from the traditional service provider systems. This system ensures that public safety agencies can communicate, regardless of the condition of public commercial cellular services. In the architecture in Figure 15-4, the mobile command center could access a private cellular system as a client and use the service as an uplink.

As a part of the public safety enterprise, a mobile command center must provide secure communications and support data privacy similar to that of the agency's remote offices. Because the mobile command center uses similar equipment to that in the remote offices, the same security policies and features can be implemented on both sides. Security in this case can be considered in two areas: physical and network security. Physical security can be addressed much as in an agency's remote office, using access control, alarm, and video surveillance systems. A variety of physical security solutions provide standard physical access readers and door actuators, as shown in Figure 15-5. Physical access control can also include a wide variety of asset control tags, identity management solutions, and alarm panels. IP video cameras are well suited to collect video streams from around a vehicle, record the content for review and playback, and distribute video to incident area personnel.

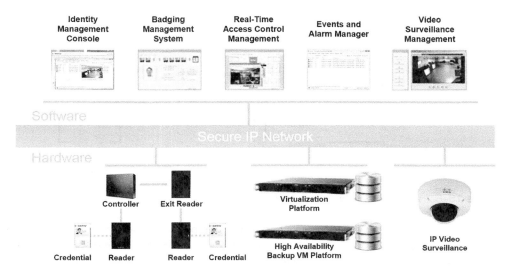

Figure 15-5 *Access Control and Video Surveillance Integration*

Network security for a mobile command center should meet or exceed the policies and procedures used in agency remote offices. In the mobile command center architecture, the router is the common integration point between the vehicle and the outside world of connectivity. The router must therefore offer advanced security services (for example, advanced encryption, firewall services, threat protection, VPN) to protect data as it traverses the wireless uplinks to the enterprise. It may also be required to protect local Internet access connectivity.

Securing open Ethernet ports and wireless access is an important consideration for a mobile command center. In a mobile platform, this is especially important because the exposure of IT infrastructure to personnel outside the public safety agency is a given. Figure 15-6 provides a sample use case. A mobile command center does not have the same physical security protections as a fixed office. Any individual in range of the command center can detect the Wi-Fi network and attempt to eavesdrop or hijack or disrupt communications. A common deployment model uses a WLAN controller-based architecture, where the AP is in the command center, but the WLAN controller stays in the static office. The AP connects to the WLAN controller over the WAN uplink. User authentication occurs through the central WLAN controller and a RADIUS server. Any port on the switch in the command center is also protected with 802.1x authentication. If an access request cannot be authenticated, policies on the local switch or Wi-Fi access point can prevent access completely or limit access until authentication can be provided. This approach ensures that access to wired and wireless connections is managed uniformly and mitigates threats based on physical access to the vehicle.

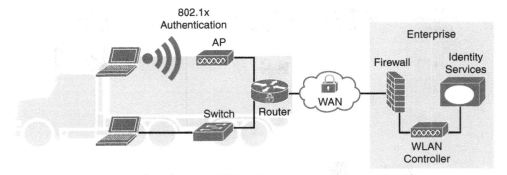

Figure 15-6 *Wi-Fi Communication Architecture*

While access points in the vehicle are configured to provide local service, the centralized management approach offers greater security and consistency (with the central team managing all deployed wireless systems and the local team focusing on the mission). This ensures that a common set of security policies and access designs are available across the public safety enterprise. It can also reduce end-user training requirements if the Wi-Fi infrastructure in the mobile command center is consistent with that of the fixed office environment.

A mobile command center can support authorized agency personnel and others at an incident. Many times when a command vehicle appears on the scene of an incident, it can provide assistance to other partnering agencies and the public, particularly for those who need Internet access. Leveraging the solution discussed previously, both wired and wireless connectivity can be provided to external agency personnel and to the public, using a guest network. These connections can be directed immediately to a local Internet connection or can be passed through the wide area uplink to the enterprise cloud for handling. Security features such as web filtering, virus scanning, and similar services can be applied in either configuration.

The WAN link is a common bottleneck in this type of deployment. Three key features are critical to successful operation, particularly if satellite services are used:

■ **Latency:** A well-known issue with using IP applications over satellite is that when network latency exceeds 500 ms roundtrip, the TCP window size in a network flow shrinks to adapt to the latency of the network. Unfortunately, even a single satellite hop introduces a minimum delay of 550 to 600 ms of roundtrip latency. Most satellite modem providers try to address this issue by implementing a performance enhancement proxy (PEP) or similar service to dynamically inspect and change the TCP window size in network flows. Without a PEP, the available bandwidth of any satellite connection goes greatly unused, and limits the end user to very poor performance. When a PEP is available, performance is greatly improved and extremely easy to notice.

■ **Encryption:** However, in order to address security requirements, the router is often configured to encrypt the network traffic before it reaches the satellite modem.

This prevents PEP services inside the modem from seeing the TCP traffic. In that case, a local service can be installed behind the router to provide PEP capability and compression over the WAN link, as shown in Figure 15-7.

■ **Appliance or Virtual Machine:** The local PEP service can be a standalone appliance, a virtual machine, or a module embedded in the router. This approach can dramatically improve performance of the WAN uplinks to allow near 100% link utilization and high compression ratios (100:1) can be achieved.

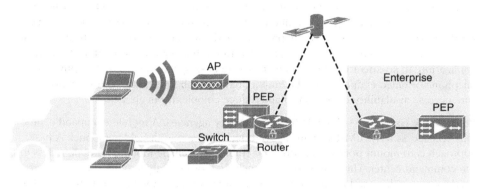

Figure 15-7   *Wi-Fi and Satellite Communication Architecture*

Compute and Applications Services

A mobile command center needs to be agile and capable of supporting the dynamic nature of the mission. The compute and application services need to work interactively and seamlessly with the enterprise and incident area resources. These services also need to be self-sufficient in times when the enterprise cloud is unavailable and the mobile command center is the only available representation of an agency's command structure in an incident. These are referred to as *dependent* and *independent* modes of operation. To support both dependent and independent operations, the mobile command center should have local compute capabilities with the ability to host virtual machines and applications. Hosting applications is possible through a dedicated server or through an embedded capability in the router, both of which are designed to support application virtualization.

The effectiveness of a mobile command center is heavily dependent on its IT and OT capabilities. Traditional IT capabilities for voice, video conferencing, and data sharing provide a foundation for the command center. OT-specific applications such as CAD, RMS, COP, fleet management, and similar tools add to this foundation and address use cases for public safety.

Local control for IT voice and video calling is at the core of collaboration. It allows a mobile command center to operate with or without a connection to the enterprise cloud. When the command center can access the enterprise cloud, services such as on-net voice and video calling can ensure security and reduce cost of operations. In independent mode, voice over IP (VoIP) services can be established between the command center and a voice service provider via an Internet connection directly. As long as at least one of the command center's uplinks can reach the Internet, voice services can be established. This approach can be the primary method of direct inward and outbound dialing, or it can be a backup approach. Using an adaptable solution provides many flexible features. For example, a staff member can take an open workspace in the command center, log into the phone on the desk, and begin making and receiving phone calls with his or her own phone number. In this case, the desk phone uses extension mobility to assume the proper personality for the end user, allowing the person to be reached wherever he or she is located. The user can log off the phone when he or she is done so that it is available for the next user. Instant messaging, presence, and voice and video dialing from computers, smart phones, and tablets is also provided through a personal communications client application. In an operational environment where desk space and access to a physical telephone or video endpoint may be limited, having such a flexible communication tool can increase availability of personnel and reduce complexity in an incident.

Push-to-talk voice is an OT staple for public safety agencies. A mobile command center relies on access to its LMR systems to effectively interact with field personnel. A basic approach is to mount portable handheld or traditional vehicle-mounted mobile radios in the command center. This can be done at each desk or in a cabinet with remote control heads with speakers and microphones. This approach is common but has issues. In a busy environment, having many speakers blaring can raise the noise floor and can be distracting, reducing the effectiveness of the operation. Also, deciding which radios to install at each desk can be challenging because the functional role of each desk position may change based on the mission. Installing too many LMR devices or the wrong kinds can be an expensive and wasteful mistake. Using an advanced radio control system, as shown in Figure 15-8, to centrally manage the radios in a command center and dynamically distribute access to users is a scalable and flexible approach. It allows any user to access any radio in the vehicle by using a mobile client installed on an Android or Apple smart phone or tablet. Such a system can also integrate with existing radio infrastructure over IP connectivity to the enterprise. This is important because it can minimize the number of radios required onboard. It can also increase accessibility of the command center, including any local public safety resources available to that agency and any other partnering agencies.

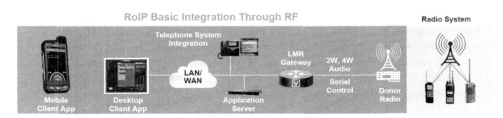

Figure 15-8   *Radio over IP Example*

IT teleconferencing, video conferencing, and web and white board collaboration are tools most people, including public safety, use to collaborate today. Software solutions providing this service are common in a mobile command center.

Public safety agency–specific OT applications can also be hosted and/or accessed via a mobile command center. These CAD, RMS, LMR dispatch, PSAP call management, and EOC management tools can be used during a deployment. Another application that is beginning to appear in these vehicles is called a common operating picture (COP), shown in Figure 15-9. Unlike a CAD tool, a COP is designed to display real-time tactical operations with various assets, such as people, vehicles, drones, and sensors. Most COP tools integrate with rich media such as video feeds and can direct other users of the COP to view something of interest. COPs can also support telestration—the ability to draw freehand or use polygons on a map, an image, or even a video display. A team leader can use a COP, for example, to direct field forces toward an objective. An important aspect of COP tools is that everyone across the mission sees a common picture; previous situational awareness tools allowed only the supervisor or commander to see the entire picture. Having this flexibility in a mobile command center can allow the platform to assume a variety of roles, based on the incident, such as a PSAP recovery solution, incident command post, joint operations and coordination center, or special task force mission.

Figure 15-9   *Common Operating Picture (COP) on a Smart Phone*

Mobile Vehicles: Land, Air, and Sea

The public safety mobile vehicle architecture, shown in Figure 15-10, describes a variety of mobile platforms used in public safety. This architecture is similar to the mobile command center from the previous section but with several important distinctions. The most important distinction is that the mobile command center architecture is based on the concept of communications on the pause, or when the vehicle is parked. A mobile command center also can operate autonomously from the enterprise network and cloud services. The land, air, and sea mobile vehicles architecture is designed for communications on the move and also acts as an extension of the public safety enterprise; therefore, it is typically dependent on enterprise services such as applications. These platforms do not use wired uplink communications. They depend on wireless uplinks and peer connections as the vehicles are in motion on land, in the air, and afloat.

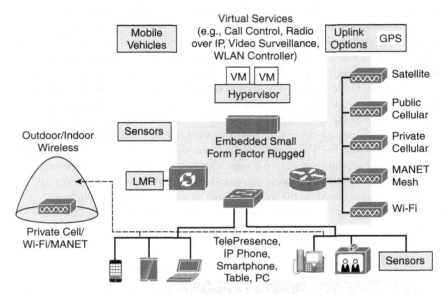

Figure 15-10   *Land, Air, and Sea Mobile Vehicles*

Another important distinction is the physical and environmental characteristics of mobile vehicles. Physically, the IoT solutions inside these vehicles are required to be self-contained, or at least provide a minimum equipment footprint. These vehicles are designed for mission objectives. For example, a fire truck or EMS vehicle has many compartments for specialized equipment. The space allocated for communications, sensors, or data processing units has to be as small as possible. Environmentally, these vehicles operate at high and low temperatures, experience shock and vibration, and are exposed to humidity, moisture, and dust. While general-purpose equipment can be used in these vehicles, the environmental conditions can greatly reduce the life of electronic equipment. Some specialized vehicles, such as aircraft or marine vessels, may mandate equipment certified for airworthiness or for use in harsh conditions. To address issues of physical and environmental requirements, public safety agencies define size, weight, and power (SWaP) specifications for onboard equipment. They also require industrial-, public safety–, or military-grade–hardening.

Network and Security Services

The land, air, and sea vehicles require routing, switching, wireless, security, and compute capabilities that can meet SWaP and hardening specifications. This network equipment needs to allow for an extended operating temperature range and many operate without internal cooling fans. The equipment must be designed to run on DC power, with wide upper and lower limits. It needs increased humidity tolerance, and some equipment is also hardened for shock and vibration. It also needs to be small and is sometimes integrated directly into the vehicle body.

The need for uplink radio flexibility and diversity in these vehicles is the same as in the mobile command center. However, the ability to carry many radios or large antennas, such as a satellite dish, may not be feasible. This limitation focuses the uplink to a more restricted set of communication media. The size, purpose, and deployment model (including the range and deployment environment) of the vehicle commonly dictates the choice of the uplink technology.

The vehicle itself may be connected to the surrounding IoT architecture through technologies like DSRC. (DSRC is covered in detail in Chapter 13, "Transportation.") This technology enables the vehicle to get privileged access through traffic and also exchange information about the travel path or other vehicles. For example, sensors are more and more often installed at rail crossing locations. As trains travel between crossings, traffic data can be fed into the OBU through LTE. Multiple IoT systems can be leveraged to achieve this goal. Trains can communicate their position in real time to a central control system (LTE, satellite, or wired networks along the track). This information can then be exported (with APIs) to an emergency response navigation database in the cloud. Relevant parts of this information can then be pushed to each emergency vehicle, based on its travel path. At the same time, trains can signal their approach to rail crossing sensors. These sensors can relay this information to approaching vehicles (DSRC or other). For an emergency services vehicle, the result is that the onboard navigation system can factor in the speed of the emergency vehicle and the rail crossing availability to dynamically reroute the vehicle if necessary, avoiding wasting time at a closed railway crossing.

Similarly, a first responder vehicle can communicate over lower ISM frequencies (for example, 433 MHz) or DSRC with smart traffic lights to make sure to always get "green" on the way to an emergency location. This control is typically decentralized (the vehicle communicates directly with the traffic lights as it approaches; the command center does not need to coordinate the lights). While the vehicle is on its way, the headquarters team may be able to connect to the data available from around the scene of the emergency, as detailed earlier in this chapter. Then, as the vehicle approaches the location of the emergency, a subset of this data is fed into the vehicle compute system. The response team can thereby access useful data relevant to the mission, such as the number of floors of a building, floorplan, number of occupants, location of nearby fire hydrants, crime history of the location or nearby locations, data from nearby environmental sensors (for example, presence of smoke, hazardous gas). During the emergency response, smart objects can facilitate the efficiency of the response. For example, when EMS vehicles are involved, tablets are used to input a basic diagnosis, helping receiving hospitals to be ready with the right equipment and the right teams.

Physical security is also challenging for these vehicles. If a vehicle or vessel is sufficiently large, it may need to use physical security solutions like those in a mobile command center. Otherwise, physical security may be limited to the trunk of a car or an equipment locker. Video surveillance in these vehicles depends on the vehicle type and its duty. For example, police vehicles are commonly equipped with dash cameras, and many have detention area cameras and microphones. In-car video recorders place a special requirement on the vehicle architecture to avoid uploading locally recorded video over metered services such as 4G cellular. Most agencies prefer that the video be uploaded when the vehicle is in close proximity to a Wi-Fi access point at a police station or similar facility. This means the vehicle router must be application-aware and permit video upload only when Wi-Fi is available.

Network security features for mobile vehicles are mostly the same as those of a mobile command center, such as robust AES 256-bit encryption, stateful firewall inspection, and VPNs. Advanced threat protection services may be limited by the performance capability of the smaller routing platforms. In cases where threat protection is a concern, adding compute resources in the vehicle may be the best approach.

Uplink compression and optimization are critical for mobile vehicles using constrained wireless uplinks, such as cellular and satellite services. However, most land vehicles do not use satellite for uplink, unless they routinely operate outside cellular coverage. Aircraft and some larger or long-distance offshore marine vessels typically have satellite requirements.

Compute and Applications Services

Land, air, and sea vehicles have different compute and application services needs than does a mobile command center. The mobile vehicles are more focused on the execution of a specific, and typically short-term, mission. A major portion of the mission is to work collaboratively with the enterprise, which means communications and applications need to be shared. There are times, though, when the focus shifts to a specific incident. In this case, it is understood that collaboration is reduced and applications are subject to availability within the incident area. The result is that most mobile vehicles carry a minimum set of applications locally—mostly client capabilities—and depend on the enterprise or the command center for hosting the applications. A good example of this logic is the push-to-talk voice service.

Vehicle-mounted mobile and handheld portable LMR devices have been a long-standing primary method of public safety communication. These devices use the communication infrastructure to talk over long distances. The infrastructure includes base stations, interconnections, and a central switching capability much like the enterprise cloud model provides. Emergency personnel also communicate locally with one another in a peer-to-peer fashion, referred to as line-of-sight, talk-around, or simplex mode. This communication is independent from the larger communication infrastructure. However, the infrastructure enables collaboration with the broader agency. In an incident, most agencies train their personnel to work in simplex mode, or at least on a tactical talk group. The primary reason for this model is efficiency. The talk-around mode eliminates any dependency on the infrastructure and limits the scope to the agents available in the immediate vicinity of the emergency scene. This model focuses communications on the incident area activities and avoids straining wide area infrastructure resources, which are always constrained in an LMR system. This model also avoids distracting the rest of the agency with local operational conversations. Communication with the agency is still possible but is limited to specific requests.

IoT has changed the push-to-talk public safety voice environment. In the 2000s, push-to-talk voice and IP were combined to provide Radio over IP (RoIP). Wireless network availability has led public safety to adopt RoIP. A key influencer is the increasing coverage and availability of commercial 4G LTE services, which now provide high-density coverage in more metro, urban, and even rural areas. Private dedicated cellular programs, such as FirstNet are also evolving to provide mission-critical–grade cellular for public safety. The applications for RoIP are also evolving, extending to soft clients and paging.

Before RoIP and networks like FirstNet can fully replace LMR, a variety of limitations must be overcome. One issue that relates to IoT is enabling both dependent and independent modes of operation for cellular communications. 3rd Generation Partnership Project (3GPP), the standards body responsible for LTE and the future cellular technologies, is working on solutions to allow cellular smart phones and similar devices to operate in an infrastructure-independent mode (that is, talk-around mode). Other issues include battery life, signaling, and application interaction.

Collaboration tools such as voice and video conferencing, instant messaging, presence, and web collaboration require access to the enterprise cloud to allow for collaboration beyond the incident area. If the applications are hosted in the enterprise cloud, collaboration is not possible without a viable uplink connection. This situation is similar to the LMR infrastructure mode for wide-area push-to-talk voice.

Public safety–specific tools like CAD, RMS, and COP are an important area of discussion for mobile vehicles, as they address mission-specific requirements of the agency. CAD and RMS, which have been around since the 1990s, help manage workflows and field personnel. They also enable field agents to run queries and reporting. These applications are client/server based, which means they have access to limited compute capability in the vehicle and depend on the uplink connection and enterprise cloud for application access and data repositories. To avoid issues with slow or intermittent connectivity, legacy CAD and RMS applications required the use of session persistence software to maintain the application connection. This software also provided VPN services to secure the applications. Next-generation CAD and RMS applications are designed for the mobile workforce; they do not suffer session persistence issues, and they support embedded security to minimize the dependency on VPN software.

A COP is a next-generation application for public safety that provides a real-time view into an incident area environment. It can function in client/server mode, where one or more servers collect multicast events from clients around the network and distribute them to all other clients. It can also operate in an incident area mode, in which case it is independent of the larger enterprise. This latter case may be a result of limited network connectivity or by design, to control the scope of collaboration and information sharing. This incident area mode maps well to the mobile vehicle architecture. Recall that a vehicle can use a variety of uplinks and peer-to-peer MANET radios. This design allows the router to dynamically manage the links and allows the COP to function in either client/server or peer-to-peer mode.

The compute resources embedded inside the vehicle platform are sized according to the application's requirements. Many of the applications already discussed for the vehicle platform are typically run on a laptop, smart phone, tablet, or similar client compute device. In some new deployment models, the client computer has limited performance and simply provides remote keyboard, video, and mouse (KVM) functions or lightweight virtual desktop capabilities. This approach limits the configuration and administrative burden of the client computer in the vehicle, and moves the processing to the enterprise cloud.

In-car video management has been available for public safety and other fleet vehicles for some time. In many cases, these solutions are independent from other equipment on the vehicle. By embedding a video management system in the in-vehicle platform, the system can be centrally managed and operated as part of the overall enterprise. Telematics is another example of this integration concept; it provides the ability to monitor and control the vehicle from the enterprise. One use case is connecting to the vehicle's onboard diagnostics (OBD) interface. An OBD interface is available in all modern vehicles. Tapping into the OBD interface allows vehicle operational characteristics to be collected and reported, including identifying maintenance needs, driving patterns, and brake status. The vehicle systems (for example, door locks) can also be controlled remotely. Emergency lights, siren, weapons locker, and other features of the vehicle can also be monitored. In the past, sensor events and events monitored via the OBD interface were streamed back to the enterprise in real time. Information could be delayed or lost in poor coverage areas. Today, the vehicle platform includes fog computing agents and lightweight microservices that run within the vehicle. The fog agents can collect, store, process, and synthesize data and then stream either the raw or synthesized data back to the enterprise. Data can also be shared with incident area peers. The fog agent is particularly useful when the vehicle is in a poor coverage area. The agent can detect the network conditions and hold the data until connectivity is restored.

IoT provides many useful and important benefits to public safety and emergency response. The mobile command center and land, air, and sea mobile vehicle platforms are built on a common reference design. The factors that influence these platforms are related to their operational, physical, and environment requirements. The operational requirements help identify the level of capability available. The capabilities change depending on whether the vehicle is connected to or disconnected from the enterprise network and depending on whether the responders are functioning in a wide area or incident area capacity. Physical requirements relate to the SWaP footprint of the equipment and to its integration into the vehicle. Environmental requirements identify the operational thresholds for hardening. As these solutions are applied to a specific public safety agency, options for network, security, compute, and application services need to be considered to meet each agency's specific needs.

IoT Public Safety Information Processing

IoT is a network of physical objects that can sense and communicate data. Processing this data is a key part of IoT, as detailed in Chapter 7, "Data and Analytics for IoT." In the case of public safety, specific smart objects facilitate the emergency response. For example, smoke detectors and fire alarms are well-known objects. With IoT, these objects can be connected to the Internet and trigger an alarm to the closest fire department. Similarly, these sensors can communicate with one another. Such communication allows a fire alarm to be triggered with a specific sound or ring pattern if a neighboring house or building is on fire, allowing proactive measures to be taken.

In schools, universities, and crime-sensitive neighborhoods, gunshot detectors are often deployed. These sensors process sounds to search for the specific pattern of a gunshot sound. If this pattern is detected, an alarm is automatically sent to the closest police station through a wired or wireless communications link. The reduction in the incident detection time in turn reduces the overall response time.

Video processing is now a common application in public safety. New machine learning algorithms increase facial recognition success rates, and processing images from crime scenes has become a common IoT application. Real-time video is also commonly used to allow for remote specialists' assistance in multiple emergency scenarios, including those involving accidents, specific hazardous materials, and automatic crowd movement pattern analysis. Video is also used for public safety cases that are not related to emergency situations to improve efficiency and reduce risks related to transportation. For example, video arraignment and remote court appearance applications have become common, limiting the cost and risk of transporting convicts. Remote language interpretation is also assisting emergency workers when interacting with citizens speaking a different language.

Big data is also being leveraged in public safety. For example, crime data can be analyzed in detail to provide a prospective view on crime potentiality. Big data systems cannot predict the future. However, these tools can analyze past crime characteristics and map criminal behavior patterns to infer the probability of future criminal activity. Figure 15-11 shows an example.

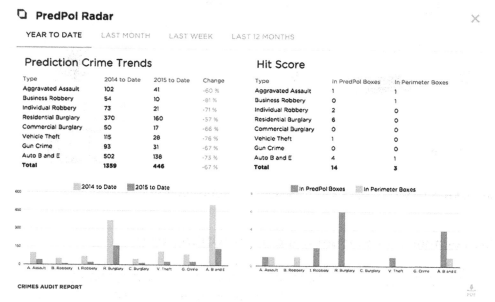

Figure 15-11   *Predictive Crime Audit Report*

Source: www.predpol.com

Police forces can use this information to deploy the right number of officers in the right locations to prevent crimes from occurring.

The same logic is used by many other public safety agencies. For example, fire department headquarters use machine learning to cross-analyze data and predict fires. Information can include obvious elements such as fire history or building material. Proactive action can then be taken to avoid fires before fire conditions arise.

School Bus Safety

Public safety spans beyond emergency services and includes any field where the general public and their safety is at stake. Today, IoT is being applied to school buses to provide new capabilities and insights to transportation directors, parents, principals, and students. A large portion of the architecture directly involves the safety of the students. In addition, buses now provide services for the onboard students to be connected and work on homework assignments. In essence, the school bus becomes an extension of the network that exists on the school campus. Figure 15-12 shows a high-level diagram of the architecture and the services offered.

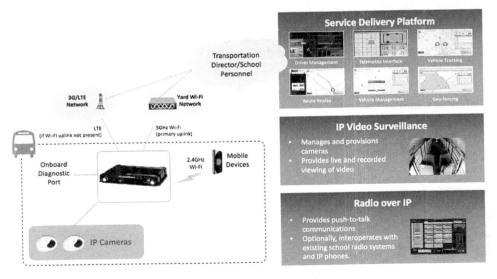

Figure 15-12   *School Bus Safety Communication Architecture*

Bus Location and Student Onboarding/Offboarding

One large problem that parents and school personnel face every day is knowing where a bus is located and whether a student is on the bus. This can become an even larger problem in school districts that are spread over large geographic areas and have a bus depot where students must change buses. A school transportation director's day is often not completed until every student is accounted for and all the buses have returned to the bus yards. In many situations, a parent, expecting his or her child to be at home, calls the transportation office looking for a student. Without the aid of IoT, transportation office personnel have to make phone or radio calls to determine whether a student is on the bus. In many cases, the bus driver may not know for sure (perhaps it is a substitute driver who doesn't know all the students). There's a good chance that the student never boarded the bus that day (maybe the student stayed at school for after-school learning or activities), or perhaps the student disembarked the bus at a friend's house. With the assistance of IoT, the transportation director can know, in real time, the exact location of a bus, which students are on the bus, and where students exited or entered the bus. Now, when a parent calls looking for his or her child, the transportation director can say, "Your child exited the bus at the corner of Smith and Jones Streets at 3:30 p.m." Or, perhaps the transportation director can say, "Your child did not get on the bus today."

Simply knowing where buses are located can be of great help to transportation directors. It is especially useful when a school activity bus has traveled a long distance from the school. In the event of a safety-related incident, the transportation director can know exactly where to direct emergency responders. The transportation director can also know approximately when to expect a bus to reach a given location (perhaps the bus yard) and can be alerted if the bus has traveled outside a previously defined boundary; this is called geo-fencing. Figure 15-13 shows an example of geo-fencing in which the area overlaid in red represents the locations where a bus might be found during a normal day. If the bus travels outside this area, school personnel are alerted.

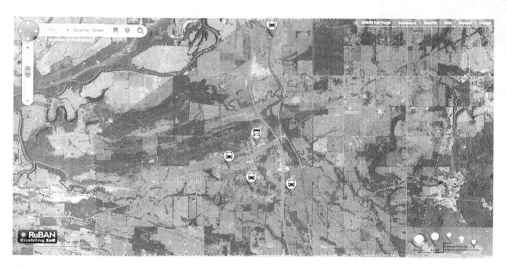

Figure 15-13 *Bus Location and Geo-Fencing*

Source: www.davranetworks.com

Driver Behavior Reporting

Another advantage of having location and telematics information is to monitor bus driver behavior. For instance, if a bus driver exceeds a safe speed, the transportation director can be alerted. This alert can occur in real time or can be recorded in a database. At one deployment, a concerned parent called the school and reported that he had been driving behind an activity bus a few days prior, and the bus had been driving at an unsafe speed. School personnel were able to review the entire history of the bus route and found that the bus was, indeed, traveling too fast. In addition, school personnel were able to review historical video footage from the bus to determine if, perhaps, there was some type of distraction on the bus that could explain the excessive speed. Figure 15-14 shows an example of the GPS replay function.

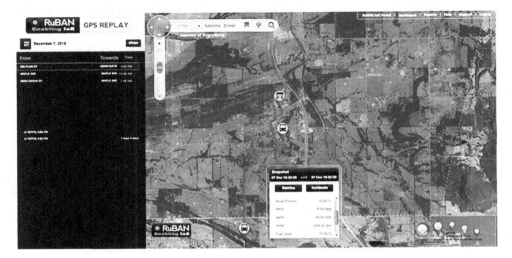

Figure 15-14   *Bus GPS Replay Feature*

Source: www.davranetworks.com

Figure 15-15 shows another example of driver behavior reporting. This type of report is useful for determining if a given driver consistently doesn't spend enough time at a bus stop for boarding students to be safely seated or if a given driver achieves unacceptable fuel mileage, perhaps due to spending an excessive amount of time idling during a route. This type of reporting can result in safer driving as well as economic savings.

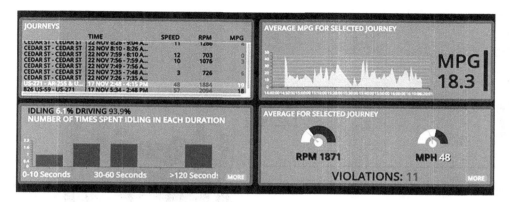

Figure 15-15 *Bus Driver Behavior Reporting*

Source: www.davranetworks.com

Diagnostic Reporting

In many cases, an issue is reported on the OBD port long before any obvious symptoms (such as low fuel mileage or a check engine light) are apparent. By harvesting this data from the bus, maintenance personnel can be alerted to potential issues, automatically, without having to physically travel to and inspect the bus.

Video Surveillance

One of the most widely used features of the school bus safety solution is video surveillance. Video surveillance can be used to monitor student safety on the bus and also to record what happens outside the bus in the event of an accident or a driver illegally passing a stopped school bus. A common case is a parent calling a school to report that her child witnessed bullying behavior, a fight, or a weapon on the bus. School personnel can watch forensic video from the day/time in question to determine what actually occurred. The video is also available for live viewing by school personnel. So, if a bus driver radios to the transportation director that students are fighting on the bus, the transportation director can view the live video and determine an appropriate course of action (for example, request emergency personnel). Figure 15-16 and Figure 15-17 show examples of live and recorded video viewing.

Figure 15-16 *Live Viewing of Bus Cameras*

Source: www.davranetworks.com

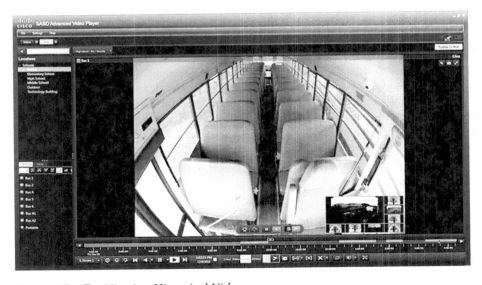

Figure 15-17 *Viewing Historical Video*

Source: www.davranetworks.com

In many countries, drivers are not allowed to pass a stopped school bus, as children may be walking around the bus or crossing the road without paying careful attention to possible traffic. For example, in 2014, the state of North Carolina found that about 3000 drivers per day passed a stopped school bus.[1] This creates an obvious safety concern for students. It is very difficult to identify and prosecute offenders, and thus it is difficult to create an effective deterrent. For instance, in 2014, even though the offense happened thousands of times per day, only 1300 cases went to court in the entire year in North Carolina, and only 29% of those drivers were found guilty. One way to improve this situation is to install an external camera (or cameras) to catch drivers that pass the stopped school bus. Video clips that capture identifying characteristics of the offending vehicle can be provided to law enforcement personnel. The speed of the bus, turn signal, and brake application data can also be overlaid on the video for accident investigation purposes. In a common deployment, due to the high bandwidth required for high-quality video capable of capturing license plate numbers, the video is stored locally on the bus camera and then uploaded over Wi-Fi when the bus is back in the bus yard.

Student Wi-Fi

Some students are on a bus for over two hours per day, which can be valuable studying time. Wi-Fi can be provided to allow students to do homework on the bus or to simply occupy them to help prevent behavioral issues. It is common for all student Wi-Fi traffic to travel back to the school network, where the school system's Internet access policy and filtering can be applied. An access point is deployed on the bus, and a small router relays the queries to a cellular data connection. In some cases, a small compute and storage system can cache frequently accessed resources, such as the school website and teacher assignment pages.

Push-to-Talk Communication

Voice communication between school personnel and bus drivers is becoming a common use case. Soft mobile clients allow a smart phone to perform push-to-talk voice communications. In the school bus application, the school can either provide smart phone or tablet devices to the bus drivers or can request that the bus drivers install an application on personal devices. In either case, the device attaches to the Wi-Fi network in the bus, thus avoiding the need to use cellular data on the smart phone device.

School Bus Safety Network Architecture

Figure 15-18 shows a high-level network diagram of the architecture for a connected school bus. This diagram maps the use cases and services discussed in the previous sections to an actual deployment.

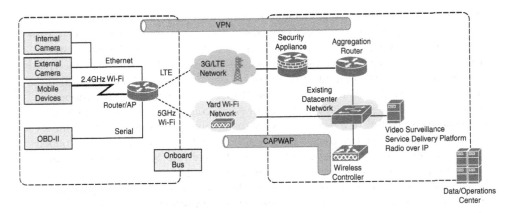

Figure 15-18 *Connected School Bus Network Architecture*

In this architecture, all services are hosted in the data/operations center. A Wi-Fi network in the bus yard is created using ruggedized, outdoor access points. The same wireless LAN controller that manages the school's traditional Wi-Fi network can manage these access points as well.

Data from the bus to the data/operations center travels over 5 GHz Wi-Fi if it is available—for example, if the bus is on campus in the bus yard. If Wi-Fi is not available, data travels, encrypted, over a commercial carrier's cellular network.

Onboard the bus, a router handles all edge network connectivity functions, as well as a fog computing function. It offers 2.4 GHz Wi-Fi onboard the bus (as an access point) and allows for connection to the bus yard's Wi-Fi as a workgroup bridge (WGB), using the 5 GHz band. The router also provides cellular connectivity and includes Ethernet ports for connecting cameras and other devices. The router also performs data encryption over cellular between the bus and the operations center.

Video cameras inside and outside the bus stream video to a media server located in the data/operations center. In some deployments, the video does not transmit over LTE all the time but is stored locally on the camera and then offloaded over Wi-Fi when the bus returns to the bus yard.

Diagnostic data from the bus is provided by the bus's onboard diagnostic port. A small software client runs inside the router to interpret the data and send relevant information to the server in the data/operations center.

Summary

While public safety covers a very broad spectrum as it relates to the IoT, a common thread forms the foundation for almost all use cases, from first responders, fire fighters, police, and school buses. In all cases, data is being gathered from sensors, transmitted over a secure network, processed and analyzed, visualized, and shared in real time (or near real time). One common requirement is the ability to process data locally and define zones where data needs to be shared among members of a field response group. At the same time, part of the data also needs to be relayed to a central command center to facilitate the overall interaction between different emergency response services. Voice and video collaboration are core tools to enable rich communication and information sharing between emergency responders. They give involved parties increased situational awareness, which helps lead to a faster, more coordinated, and safer response.

At the same time, multiple sensors are improving awareness and response efficiency. Interaction with sensors carried by emergency responders, embedded in their vehicles or integrated into the surrounding environments, extend the emergency responders' awareness and also allow response teams to respond to emergencies at a larger scale, improving their response times through traffic light control, collecting faster and better information through access to emergency area environmental sensors, and reacting faster through the support of machine-learned movement patterns identified in a crowd.

Reference

1. C. Browder, *In North Carolina, Few Drivers Found Guilty of Passing School Buses*, August 24, 2015, www.wral.com/in-nc-few-drivers-found-guilty-of-passing-school-buses/14851534/.

Index

Numbers

A

B

C

O

remote access control use case, 339

remote expert use case, 333–334

remote learning, 218

remote monitoring and scheduling management, 166

remote terminal units (RTUs), 186

REP (Resilient Ethernet Protocol), 287–289

resilient network design
in connected factories, 286–289, 298
in smart cities, 394–395
in substation automation, 362

REST (representational state transfer), 190

RFC (Request for Comments), 159

RFDs (reduced-function devices), 52

risk assessment frameworks, 262–266
FAIR, 265–266
OCTAVE, 262–265
in oil and gas industry, 335–337
reference architecture, 337–338
requirements, 337
use cases, 338–341

roaches, sensors on, 19–20

road pricing, economic impact of, 388

roadways, 414
challenges in, 9–10, 415–416
network architecture, 427–439
Bluetooth, 427–428
cellular technologies, 428
DSRC/WAVE, 428–434
security, 439
use case, 8–12

RoLL (Routing over Low-Power and Lossy Networks) working group, 156

Root Access Point (RAP), 469–470

RPL (Routing Protocol for Low Power and Lossy Networks), 167–172

RTLS (real-time location systems), 14
in connected factories, 292–293

RTUs (remote terminal units), 186

S

safety in mining, 455, 459–461

Sampled Values (SV), 253, 360

SANETs (sensor/actuator networks)
advantages/disadvantages of wireless, 88
communication protocols, 92–93
defined, 87–88
WSNs (wireless sensor networks), 88–91

SCADA (supervisory control and data acquisition), 153, 182–189
adaptation for IP, 183–185
MAP-T, 188–189
protocol translation, 187–188
in substation automation, 356–358
tunneling over IP, 185–187

scale
challenge of, 23, 29, 30
of mining operations, 451–455

scheduling in 6TiSCH, 166

school bus safety, 508
bus and student location, 508–509
diagnostic data analysis, 511
driver behavior monitoring, 510–511
network architecture, 513–514
push-to-talk communication, 513
video surveillance, 511–513
Wi-Fi availability, 513

sectorization, 132–133